THE BIG TEN

A Century of Excellence

by Dale Ratermann

Foreword by President Gerald R. Ford
Introduction by Commissioner James E. Delany
Centennial Message by Bob Hammel

Editorial Assistance from
Don Kopriva
Mark Montieth
Rick Morwick
Michael Perry
John Supinie

Officially licensed and endorsed by the Big Ten Conference.

SAGAMORE PUBLISHING
Champaign, Illinois

Interior design and layout: Michelle R. Dressen and Susan M. McKinney
Dustjacket design: Michelle R. Dressen and Deborah M. Bellaire
Factoids design: Steve Bloome, Steve Bloome Creative Services

Library of Congress Catalog Number: 96-70015
ISBN: 1-57167-037-8

Sagamore Publishing, Inc.
804 N. Neil St., Suite 100
Champaign, IL 61820

Web Site: www.sagamorepub.com

Printed in the United States.

ACKNOWLEDGMENTS

This publication, *The Big Ten: A Century of Excellence,* is the result of a combined effort of many individuals.

Providing a major assist to author Dale Ratermann were several folks at the Big Ten, headed by Commissioner Jim Delany, Associate Commissioner Kevin Weiberg, Managing Editor and Special Projects Director Mary Masters, Director of Information Services Dennis LaBissoniere, and Communication Interns Jeff Kearney and Marija Neubauer. We thank them for their perseverance in getting the project started.

Appreciation goes to former President Gerald R. Ford for writing the foreword to the book, to Bloomington (Ind.) *Herald Telephone* Sports Editor Bob Hammel for penning the Centennial Message, and to Commissioner Delany for writing the introduction.

Ratermann's staff of writers included Don Kopriva (DuPage [Ill.] *Business Ledger*), Mark Montieth (Indianapolis [Ind.] *Star-News*), Rick Morwick (Franklin [Ind.] *Daily Journal*), Michael Perry (Cincinnati [Ohio] *Enquirer*), and John Supinie (Springfield [Ill.] *State Journal Register*).

Furnishing the valuable information and photos were the sports information staffs of the University of Chicago (SID David Hilbert), the University of Illinois (Athletic Director Ron Guenther, SID Dave Johnson and Bridget Toomey), Indiana University (AD Clarence Doninger, SID Kit Klingelhoffer and Perry Mann), the University of Iowa (ADs Bob Bowlsby and Christine Grant, SID's Phil Haddy and Sherilyn Fiveash, and Eric Capper), the University of Michigan (AD Joe Roberson, SID Bruce Madej and B.J. Sohn), Michigan State University (AD Merritt Norvell, SID Ken Hoffman, Rob Kaminski and Jack Seibold), the University of Minnesota (ADs Mark Dienhart and Chris Voelz, SID's Marc Ryan and Lisa Nelson, and Brad Ruiter), Northwestern University (AD Rick Taylor, SID Brad Hurlbut and Chris Hughes), Ohio State University (AD Andy Geiger, SID Steve Snapp and Liz Cook), Penn State University (AD Tim Curley, SID Jeff Nelson), Purdue University (AD Morgan Burke, SID Mark Adams and Kevin Vicroy) and the University of Wisconsin (AD Pat Richter, SID's Steve Malchow and Tam Flarup, and Dan Meyer). Appreciation is also extended to the university News Bureaus and Archives offices of each of those outstanding institutions.

Mike Pearson, former Sports Information Director at the University of Illinois and now Director of Acquisitions and Development at Sagamore Publishing, also lended his historical expertise to the project.

A tremendous help in outlining the early sections of the book was received from the pages of *The Big Ten,* written by former commissioner Kenneth L. (Tug) Wilson and Jerry Brondfield.

Also, a thank you to Steve Bloome of Steve Bloome Creative Services, designer of the Big Ten factoids that are scattered throughout the pages of the book.

Finally, to the sponsors of the book—CompUSA, *The Columbus Dispatch,* Hostmark, the Illini Union Bookstore, JCPenney's, Prairie Gardens, Jerry's IGA, and the Radisson Suite Hotel—our appreciation for your financial support of this project.

THANK YOU

to the following sponsors for their generous support

The Columbus Dispatch

CompUSA

Hostmark Management Group

Illini Union Bookstore

JCPenney (Champaign, Illinois)

Jerry's IGA

Prairie Gardens

Radisson Suite Hotel, Champaign/Urbana

TABLE OF CONTENTS

FOREWORD

A Tradition of Excellence
By former U.S. President Gerald R. Ford

In 1994, I had the privilege of being honored by my alma mater, the University of Michigan, which felt my contributions as a collegiate football player merited the retirement of my jersey, No. 48.

Never would I have imagined, 60 years earlier lining up on the muddy fields, that one day No. 48 would be considered of any significance. But there I stood, at the center of Michigan Stadium, amidst the football teams and marching bands of Michigan and Michigan State and the spirited rivalry both institutions bring to college athletics. I was proud, thankful and deeply moved by the entire program. My recollections told me how critical my Michigan academic and athletic experiences had been in my later life in Congress and the White House.

The setting I observed on that football field illustrates so much of what makes the Big Ten a conference of remarkable stature and contribution.

Tradition. Competition. And excellence.

For 100 years, the Big Ten Conference had been a national leader in academics and athletics. As a seven-member Intercollegiate Conference of Faculty Representatives in 1896, or the 11 universities that now comprise the Conference, the Big Ten has set the standards for higher education.

Today, the Big Ten is the only conference whose members all belong to the prestigious American Association of Universities. As leading research universities, Big Ten schools have changed the course of medicine, science, business and social study. As a Conference, we account for 25 percent of federal research funding awarded nationwide.

Graduates of Big Ten schools are fiercely proud of their alma maters; a Michigan-Ohio State football game or a basketball match between Indiana and Purdue is testament to that. Yet, we alumni are equally proud of our sister schools and the knowledge we all belong to a conference that excels.

The graduates of the Big Ten have, over the years, made our world a better place in so many varied ways.

Neil Armstrong (Purdue) and Guion Bluford (Penn State) have taken our hopes and aspirations far from Earth. Georgia O'Keefe (Minnesota) has shown us beauty and perspective. Gilda Radner (Michigan) and Magic Johnson (Michgan State) have made us applaud, and have made us cry. Dr. Christian Bernard (Minnesota) has helped us live.

Jane Pauley (Indiana) and Bernard Shaw (Illinois) have informed us; Johnnetta Cole (Northwestern) has educated us. There have been the words of Joyce Carol Oates (Wisconsin), the drama of Tennessee Williams (Iowa) and the music of Bob Dylan (Minnesota). Jesse Owens (Ohio State) has unified us. I had the privilege of watching Jesse at the Big Ten track meet in Ann Arbor when he broke or tied four world records.

Equally important have been the unheralded contributions of thousands of young people who have left the campuses of the Midwest and entered the world to fill it with invention and inspiration.

Another scene at Michigan Stadium in 1995 inspired us all. A young man by the name of Juwan Howard, who thrilled fans with basketball talents so strong he left school early for the NBA, returned this past spring to Ann Arbor. He wasn't back to have a jersey retired. He returned for commencement and his diploma—an honor he worked for between games, while riding on airplanes and sitting in hotel rooms.

That's the Big Ten. Exceptional student-athletes, renowned universities and academic pursuits that know no bounds.

The 38th President of the United States, Gerald R. Ford played football at the University of Michigan from 1932 to 1934.

INTRODUCTION

Introduction by James E. Delany, Commissioner of Athletics

Established in 1896, the Big Ten Conference celebrated its centennial anniversary in 1995-96. The distinguishing characteristic which runs throughout the history of the Conference is its continuous and sustained effort to balance the academic and athletic interests of participating student-athletes. This feature has been recognized and respected by those who have attended Big Ten institutions, those who have followed Big Ten competition, and those institutions which we have competed against over many decades. The first Conference champions were named in football and baseball in 1896. Today the Conference sponsors championships in 24 sports, 12 for men and 12 for women. Almost 7,000 student-athletes participate in Big Ten sanctioned games and championships.

The values of fairness, integrity and competitiveness have also been trademarks of the Conference's history. A commitment to broad-based athletic programs for men and women, the progressive attitude the Conference has taken toward integrating women's athletics and responding to the concerns of minority student-athletes, the stand the Conference has taken on issues of academic integrity, fair play and ethical conduct speak volumes about how the Conference has embraced these principles.

On average, over three-quarters of the students that attend Big Ten universities are in the top one-quarter of their high school classes. More than 70 Nobel laureates have been faculty, students or researchers at Conference institutions. Students and faculty together create a stimulating, creative environment on each campus where new ideas are tested and knowledge is advanced everyday. The list of discoveries and inventions that have emanated from Conference universities and benefit our everyday lives in every field of endeavor is almost too numerous to mention here.

The Big Ten is unique as a conference in that its member institutions cooperate on many levels beyond athletics as well. Conference institutions collaborate in academic and research areas through two consortiums: the Committee on Institutional Cooperation (CIC) and the Midwest Universities Consortium for International Activities, Inc. (MUCIA).

The centennial year, capped off by the publication of this book, has been a wonderful opportunity to remember and celebrate the past while also preparing for the challenges of the future. The Big Ten's history is about many good people accomplishing great things in the context of higher education. It is important to recognize how people, coaches, student-athletes, faculty, and administrators, working together in an institutional and conference context, have been able to accomplish so much and contribute to the fabric of intercollegiate athletics, higher education and American society.

This book is dedicated to those who have made the Big Ten Conference what it is today and those who will contribute to its future in the next 100 years. The history of the Conference is a marvelous story. We hope you enjoy this review of the memorable people, places and events that have been a part of the Conference's first 100 years.

CENTENNIAL MESSAGE

By Bob Hammel, Sports Editor Emeritus
The Herald-Times, Bloomington, Indiana

The Big Ten, which is really 11, has completed its 100th year. Numbers, all of these: 10, 11, 100.

The Big in Big Ten is genuine because of names, not numbers. It is a century of giants, an uninterrupted stream of them from start to present.

This, after all, is the league that had Stagg and Yost and Heston; Oliphant and Nagurski; Berwanger and Harmon, Kinnick and Bruce Smith, Ameche and Archie, Horvath and Janowicz; Otto Graham, Len Dawson, Bob Griese, and Paul Brown; Alex Karras and Alex Agase.

And Red Grange.

That had Owens and Spitz, Havlicek and Magic, Robin Roberts and Frank Howard; Garvey and Winfield, Kirk Gibson and Lou Boudreau.

And Jack Nicklaus.

Bierman and Crisler, Woody and Bo; Gable and Counsilman, Taylor and Knight.

And Wooden, the player. And Gerald Ford, the MVP.

And Crazy Legs and Hopalong, and Bubba, Butkus and Buddy Young; the Whiz Kids and the Big Dog; Lucas, Bellamy and Cazzie; Isiah and McHale; Calbert, Alford and Mount.

And Jim Abbott.

It's an ancient league, but *au courant*. George Sisler played at Michigan 82 years ago. And his coach was Branch Rickey. And maybe there's never been a better college football offense than the one of Ki-Jana Carter and Kerry Collins, and Joe Paterno, in 1994. Betty Robinson was 17, not yet enrolled at Northwestern, when she won America's first women's Olympic track and field gold medal in 1928, and divers Pat McCormick (Ohio State) and Lesley Bush (Indiana) never won letters but claimed Olympic gold before collegiate competitive doors swung open. In a very short time frame, this has been the league of Suzy Favor and Judi Brown, and Tara Van DerVeer, the player and coach.

Jack McCartan, a Minnesota third baseman, was the goalie when the U.S. hockey team pulled Miracle I in the 1960 Olympics. And Herb Brooks of Minnesota was the coach and Mark Johnson of Wisconsin the leading scorer in Miracle II at the 1980 Olympics.

This is the league that has Michigan Stadium with 100,000 blues, and Assembly Hall in one bright red; Illiniwek in all that orange; the Horseshoe and the Dotted I; the lakes of Madison and The Lake at Evanston; the decibels of Mackey and the corn, yes the bridges, too, of Iowa.

In Ann Arbor, they're still running and jumping at Ferry Field, where Jesse Owens in one afternoon set or tied four world records 60 years ago, not one of those records ever beaten in a Big Ten meet.

In Champaign, they're still cutting and slashing at Memorial Stadium, 71 years after Red Grange dedicated the place with what would be the biggest thing that ever happened in a Big Ten stadium if they hadn't split the atom under the University of Chicago's.

The dynasties that began with Stagg and Yost and Williams and continued with Meanwell and Lambert were never more dominant than Indiana swimming through the '60s and '70s under Doc Counsilman (20 straight Big Ten championships, a record six straight NCAA titles) or Iowa wrestling under Dan Gable in the '80s and '90s (20 straight Big Ten championships, a record 14 NCAA titles through '96).

The Big Ten, which is really 11, is 100 years old and golden as ever.

BIG TEN

SINCE 1896

CENTENNIAL ™

1895-1904

THE BIG EVENT

Founding of the Big Ten Conference

James Smart

James Smart may have been the ultimate visionary. The Purdue University president took a hard look at intercollegiate athletics in the late 1800s and didn't like what he saw. The emphasis to win was prompting unethical actions throughout the country: athletes not enrolled in school were competing on the field; high school students were being used at the collegiate level; professionals were used; students in their sixth, seventh, even eighth years of school were competing; and so-called "tramp athletes" were playing for different schools in different sports in the same year.

There was no National Collegiate Athletic Association, no individual conferences, no governing body to watch over college sports, to monitor and police them. Therefore, there were no penalties or ramifications for the abuses that were taking place.

Through a great deal of this, university faculty and administration had paid little attention and showed little to no concern about what was going on in the athletic programs.

Enter President Smart. In November 1894, Smart wrote to his counterpart at the University of Minnesota, President Cyrus Northrup: "Is it not about time for college officials to gather to relieve interstate collegiate athletics of some of their more objectionable features?" This much was clear to Smart: The abuses would not come to a halt without faculty control. And that was precisely his goal when he set out to form what would be later known as the Big Ten Conference.

The Palmer House, birthplace of the Big Ten.

Palmer House Restaurant

Chicago wins first Big Ten baseball title

1896 Chicago Baseball Team

Amos Alonzo Stagg

Chicago won the first Big Ten championship in any sport—and the first of three straight Big Ten baseball titles—with a 6-2 record. The Maroons won three of five from Michigan to take the title by a game over the 6-3 Wolverines. Illinois (2-4) and Wisconsin (0-5) also fielded teams. Leading Coach Amos Alonzo Stagg's team was pitcher Frederick Nichols, who hit .406 with seven home runs, 49 runs scored and 28 stolen bases in 30 games. Catcher Hayden Jones was the team's top fielder with a .956 percentage with nine errors in 197 chances. He also hit .308 and scored 28 runs.

JAMES SMART
President, Purdue

If there is a singular founding father of the Big Ten Conference, James Smart must be that person. The president of Purdue University thought there was a need for some control of intercollegiate athletics. Guidelines needed to be set, rules needed to be followed. There were actions taking place he thought were detrimental, and he decided that collectively the heads of universities could help establish institutional control. Smart wrote letters to presidents of seven other universities—Chicago, Illinois, Michigan, Minnesota, Northwestern, Wisconsin, and Lake Forest College. He proposed a meeting in Chicago with this goal: to establish faculty control of college sports. The gathering took place Jan. 11, 1895 (Michigan's president could not attend), and the presidents voted on 12 rules that would be the seeds of the Western Conference, later to be known as the Big Ten. Smart was Purdue's president from 1883-1900.

WILLIAM RAINEY HARPER
President, Chicago

Considered one of the foremost educators of his day, William Rainey Harper has influenced higher education in the almost hundred years since his death. Born in 1856, the 5-foot-7, bespectacled Harper matriculated at Muskingham College (Ohio) at age 10 and received a Ph.D. from Yale before his 19th birthday. After serving on the faculty at Denison University, Harper was named president of the University of Chicago in 1890. Forever affecting intercollegiate athletics and football, Harper hired Amos Alonzo Stagg to establish a physical education department. Harper's friendship with John D. Rockefeller resulted in a $35 million contribution to the university. An optimist and enthusiast, Harper had a conservative attitude toward athletics, saying "Sports will be conducted for the students, not for the spectacular entertainment of enormous crowds of people." He died of cancer in 1906 at the age of 50. Harper Junior College in northwest suburban Chicago is named after him.

HENRY WADE ROGERS
President, Northwestern

Henry Wade Rogers, Northwestern's president as the 19th century closed, impacted the careers of university athletes for years to come. As participation in sports grew late in the century, it became necesssary for colleges to establish guidelines and organizations to control them. The matter of eligibility was a major issue, as some colleges recruited non-students to aid their cause, and growing violence in football threatened the very existence of that sport. At a meeting on Dec. 8, 1894, President Rogers requested that Northwestern's faculty make recommendations to the Board of Trustees on some of the issues confronting the school's athletic teams. The following month the presidents of seven midwestern universities met in Chicago to discuss their problems and establish a means of addressing them. The following winter faculty representatives from each of those schools met in Chicago to form what would become the Big Ten Conference.

JAMES BURRILL ANGELL
President, Michigan

James Burrill Angell, president at Michigan since 1871, was one of the Big Ten's founders and most influential leaders in its formative years. In 1893, he formed the Board in Control of Athletics at Michigan to supervise the athletics program. After a carnage-filled 1905 football season, Northwestern announced that,it was withdrawing from football competition. Although President Theodore Roosevelt even intervened to save the sport, ordering colleges to clean up the game, greater efforts to save intercollegiate athletics were clearly needed. To that end, Angell, a firm believer in presidential control, called a meeting—subsequently called the "Angell Conference"—for March 9, 1906, which offered a platform of reforms to reduce the excesses of a burgeoning big-time sport. Ironically, some of the items that Angell championed went even further in final form than he expected, ultimately leading to Michigan's nine-year withdrawal from the Big Ten in protest.

LEADING THE WAY

THE THOMPSON/WILSON/PETERSON FAMILY
Illinois

The only known four-generation family in the Big Ten began in 1895 when Fred Thompson earned a baseball letter at Illinois. His son, David Wilson, was captain of the Illini football team in 1922. Fred's grandson, Waldo Peterson lettered in track for the Illini in 1954, and Fred's great-grandson, David Peterson earned a varsity "I" in gymnastics in 1981.

Fred Thompson   *David Peterson*

· BIG TEN PIONEERS ·

First intercollegiate basketball game

H.F. Callenberg, a physical education professor at Iowa, noticed that basketball games with seven-to-nine players for each team competing at the same time made for a crowded court. So when Iowa and Chicago met on Jan. 18, 1896 at the Iowa Armory, he decided to make a change, limiting the teams to five players on the court at once. This marked the first 5-on-5 college basketball game, and it came just one month before the Intercollegiate Conference of Faculty Representatives—which would come to be known as the Big Ten Conference—was founded. A crowd of about 400 watched Chicago beat the Hawkeyes, 13-12.

Academic Achievements

Big Ten universities employ more than 30,000 full-time faculty members and enroll nearly one half million undergraduate, graduate and professional students on their principle campuses, conferring nearly 10 percent of all master's and professional degrees, and 15 percent of all Ph.D. degrees awarded in the U.S.

The BIG TEN's First 100 Years
The Most Big Ten Championships Won By Conference Schools In Any Sport

THE BIG EVENT

The presidents meet in Chicago

By November 1895, Purdue president James Smart decided it was time to stop talking and take action. He wrote to six other Midwest university presidents and proposed a meeting in Chicago. On Jan. 11, 1896, they gathered at what was then known as the Auditorium. Presidents from Chicago, Illinois, Minnesota, Northwestern, Purdue, Lake Forest College and Wisconsin were present; Michigan's president could not attend.

The university administrators approved 12 rules that would be debated and revised over time. The purpose, however, was quite clear: the faculty would establish control over intercollegiate athletics at their schools.

On Feb. 8, 1896, at the Palmer House in Chicago, faculty representatives from the universities got together and officially became the Intercollegiate Conference of Faculty Representatives. The organization would later become the Western Conference, then the Big Ten. The faculty reps decided to meet twice annually to discuss, rewrite, add or delete rules that would continue to ensure a balance between athletics and academics. They would uphold the rules and eventually serve as a means for scheduling games between schools and to consider expansion.

While it was vital to establish that the faculty representative from each school would not be a member of the physical education department, it should be noted that there was one exception: Amos Alonzo Stagg. The University of Chicago proved to be one step ahead of the rest of the country when it awarded Stagg, its athletic director and coach, faculty status.

Football Conference championship goes to Wisconsin

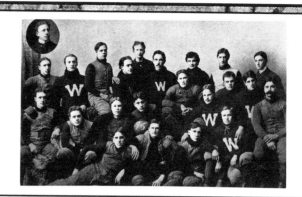

Wisconsin made history in 1896 by winning the inaugural Big Ten football championship. The Badgers did so again in 1897 by repeating as champions. Wisconsin's 1896 squad plowed through the season in dominating fashion. The Badgers, under the direction of coach Phil King, opened the season with seven straight victories. Northwestern, a charter league member along with Chicago, Illinois, Minnesota, Michigan and Purdue, halted the win streak by playing the Badgers to a 6-6 tie. Wisconsin lost its next game—the season finale and the first night game in school history—against Carlisle. The game was played indoors at the Chicago Coliseum. Despite their late-season skid, the Badgers collected enough victories to claim the first Conference title. Defense was the primary reason why, as six of Wisconsin's seven victories were shutouts. The following year, the Badgers were equally dominating and, as a result, successfully defended their championship. The Badgers posted a 9-1 record and registered eight shutouts along the way. Their only loss was a 6-0 setback against the UW Alumni. The Badgers were led that year by famed Australian kicker Pat O'Dea, otherwise known as "The Kangaroo Kicker." O'Dea fueled Wisconsin's offense with 14 field goals. The Badgers would win one more league crown under Coach King, who posted a career 65-11-1 record at Wisconsin.

FIRST CONFERENCE RULES

Adopted Jan. 11, 1895 by presidents of Chicago, Illinois, Michigan, Minnesota, Northwestern, Purdue and Wisconsin

1. Each college and university which has not already done so shall appoint a committee on college athletics which shall take general supervision of all athletic matters in the respective college or university, and which shall have all responsibility of enforcing the college or university rules regarding athletics and all intercollegiate sports.

2. No one shall participate in any game or athletic sport unless he be a bona fide student doing full work in a regular or special course as defined in the curriculum of his college; and no person who has participated in any match game as a member of any college team shall be permitted to participate in any game as a member of another college team, until he has been a matriculate in said college under the above conditions for a period of six months. This rule shall not apply to students who, having graduated at one college, shall enter another college for professional or graduate study.

3. No person shall be admitted to any intercollegiate contest who receives any gift, remuneration or pay for his services on the college team.

4. Any student of any institution who shall be pursuing a regularly prescribed resident graduate course within such institution, whether for an advanced degree or in one of its professional schools, may be permitted to play for the period of the minimum number of years required for securing the graduate or professional degree for which he is a candidate.

5. No person who has been employed in training a college team for intercollegiate contests shall be allowed to participate in any intercollegiate contest as a member of any team which he has trained, and no professional athlete or person who has ever been a member of a professional team shall play at any intercollegiate contest.

6. No student shall play in any game under an assumed name.

7. No student shall be permitted to participate in any intercollegiate contest who is found by the faculty to be delinquent in his studies.

8. All games shall be played on grounds either owned by or under the immediate control of one or both of the colleges participating in the contest, and all games shall be played under student management and not under the patronage or control of any other corporation, association or private individual.

9. The election of managers and captains of teams in each college shall be subject to the approval of its committee on athletics.

10. College teams shall not engage in games with professional teams nor with those representing so-called athletic clubs.

11. Before every intercollegiate contest a list of men proposing to play shall be presented by each team or teams to the other or others, certifying that all members are entitled to play under conditions of the rules adopted, such certificate to be signed by the registrar or the secretary of the college or university. It shall be the duty of the captain to enforce this rule.

12. We call upon the expert managers of football teams to so revise the rules as to reduce the liability to injury to a minimum.

ANDREW DRAPER
President, Illinois

At the time when Illinois joined the Conference, Illinois was awarding about 40 letters a year, had a football team for six years and Andrew Draper was the school's president. Under Draper, the University's athletic department grew, just as the school did. In 1895-96, the University had nine buildings, 84 faculty members and 855 students, about 80 percent of the enrollment being male. In 1896-97, Illinois played its first Conference football game, going against rival Chicago and its legendary coach, Amos Alonzo Stagg. Illinois' student newspaper charged that Chicago used a professional player to lead the Maroons to a 12-0 win over Illinois. Later in the school year, three Illinois baseball players were named All-Conference by *Harper's Weekly* magazine.

CYRUS NORTHROP
President, Minnesota

Cyrus Northrop's education and early vocations probably gave no one the foresight to predict the contributions he would make in the formation of the Big Ten Conference. Born in Connecticut in 1834, he was an honor student at Yale, graduating in 1857. He entered the Yale law school and received his degree in 1859. After a short stint as an attorney (working as a clerk in the Connecticut House of Representatives and later the state Senate) he became editor of the *New Haven Palladium*. He was Professor of Rhetoric and English Literature at Yale from 1863-84 and made an unsuccessful attempt at being elected to the U.S. Congress in 1867. In 1884 he began his work as president of the University of Minnesota. When he began, there were but three buildings on campus. By the time he left in 1911, there were 30. The student body increased from 300 to 5,000 and the faculty from 30 to 212. An administrator who never lost touch with the students, he died suddenly from heart trouble in his home in Minneapolis, Apr. 3, 1922.

CHARLES KENDALL ADAMS
President, Wisconsin

Charles Kendall Adams was born in Vermont in 1835. He moved to Iowa with his family in 1856, and, a year later, he enrolled at the University of Michigan and graduated in 1861. He continued at Michigan as a graduate student and soon was named a professor of history. Adams was named president of Cornell University in 1885 and remained there for seven years, resigning to concentrate on writing and editing. Two months later, he accepted the post of president of the University of Wisconsin. Under Adams' leadership, Wisconsin's status grew. He not only attended the games and cheered the team on, but sometimes took a hand to help the team, wooing unmotivated student-athletes out for the team and getting Camp Randall for the University as a playing field. During the initial meetings in the creation of the Big Ten Conference, Adams was as emotionally attached to sports as anyone. Ill health caused by age forced Adams to offer his resignation from the presidency in 1901. He died in July, 1902.

YEARS OF MEMBERSHIP

BIG TEN LIST

Seven schools made up the original "Intercollegiate Conference of Faculty Representatives." In all, 12 teams have been members at some point in the "Big Ten" Conference. Here are the years of membership:

University of Chicago:	1896-1946
University of Illinois:	1896-present
Indiana University:	1899-present
University of Iowa:	1899-present
University of Michigan:	1896-1908; 1917-present
Michigan State University:	1949-present
University of Minnesota:	1896-present
Northwestern University:	1896-present
Ohio State University:	1912-present
Penn State University:	1990-present
Purdue University:	1896-present
University of Wisconsin:	1896-present

(Note: Some schools did not compete in every sport in their first year of membership.)

LEADING THE WAY

HENRY EVERETT
Illinois

Illinois' third athletic director and first faculty representative was Henry Houghton Everett. A native of Chicago, Everett was an all-star athlete for Chicago, participating in football, track and wrestling. He left UC to become assistant superintendent of the Chicago YMCA, but after only a year, he quit to enroll at Northwestern's medical school. Medicine soon took a back seat to Everett's intense interest in athletics, and he was on the move again, this time to Wisconsin as an instructor in UW's gymnasium. In 1895, Illinois hired the 31-year-old Everett as its director of athletics, faculty representative and track coach. Perhaps his greatest contribution was as Illinois' representative at the Jan. 11, 1895 meeting in Chicago, which formed the Big Ten Conference. Everett gave way to George Huff after one year as AD, but coached Illini track teams for the next three years. He returned to his career in medicine, serving at both Rush Medical College and at Chicago's Presbyterian Hospital. Everett died in 1928 at the age of 61.

· BIG TEN PIONEERS ·

Chicago beats Michigan in first indoor football game

Chicago beat Michigan, 7-6, before 8,000 spectators indoors on Thanksgiving Day in 1896 at the old Chicago Coliseum to deny the Wolverines the first championship of the Intercollegiate Conference of Faculty Representatives. The closing-game loss for Michigan in the first year of competition in the new Midwest conference gave the first-ever Conference title to Wisconsin.

Academic Achievements

In the 1990s, Big Ten universities collectively engage in more than $2.8 billion of funded scientific and engineering research annually, amounting to 14 percent of the total funds expended on research by the nation's universities. Approximately $1.5 billion of this research is derived from federal sources.

THE BIG EVENT

Steamroller used to drag infield of baseball diamond.

Big Ten Conference serves as model for intercollegiate athletics

During its early years, the Big Ten conference made it clear that each member was supposed to be its own watchdog, though members could bring charges against each other if they were aware of a rule being violated. While there were no real means for investigating such charges or imposing penalties, it provided a starting point for de-emphasizing a winning-at-all-costs attitude.

When the Big Ten boasts of being a leader nationally, the roots of those claims can be traced back to its beginning. The principles on which the Big Ten was founded would serve as the foundation for every new conference to follow. Within its first three years of existence, the Intercollegiate Conference of Faculty Representatives adopted rules: requiring students who failed in school or were dropped to be ineligible to compete athletically until they were back in school and in good standing academically; limiting athletic participation to four years; making graduate students ineligible to compete; and prohibiting schools to compete against professional teams or clubs using professional players.

One area in which they compromised was in naming Conference champions. The faculty did not want to crown a league champion to further undermine the emphasis on winning, but college sports had developed such a public following and demand was so great that in 1896 the league declared Wisconsin as the first champion in football. Chicago was the first baseball champion. The faculty did, however, refuse to award team trophies.

The actions taken by the Midwestern universities did not go unnoticed. The public and media had become very aware of what was taking place and the impact it might have across the country. In *Harper's Weekly,* prominent sports writer Caspar Whitney, from New York wrote: "The most notable clearing of the atmosphere is to be seen in the West. Football—indeed all Midwestern college sports—was very near total extinction because of a rampant professional spirit that had raged throughout nearly all the universities, leaving corruption in its wake. The meeting last winter in Chicago marked the beginning of a new and clarified era in Western collegiate sport!"

It couldn't have been said better.

Chicago wins third straight Big Ten baseball title

Chicago won its third straight Big Ten baseball championship with an 8-3 record to Michigan's 7-3 and Illinois' 4-6 marks. The Chicago yearbook noted that each had "an equally poor claim to the honor," since Chicago won all four of its games with Illinois, but lost three of five to Michigan. The Wolverines, in turn, were twice shut out by the Illini.

Other Big Ten Champs:

- **FOOTBALL: Wisconsin, coached by Phil King**

OTHER NEWS...

George Ade, an 1887 Purdue graduate, was a newspaper reporter for the *Chicago Record* when he had opportunity for a "scoop." Purdue President James Smart offered to provide the remarks he prepared for a meeting with presidents of other Midwest universities as an exclusive. Smart, of course, was pushing for faculty control of intercollegiate athletics and the meeting on Jan. 11, 1895 marked the beginnings of what would later be the Big Ten Conference.

Smart wrote to Ade: "No doubt the reporters want to know something of my views in regard to the subject to be considered. If you choose to use it, you can have the preference. I shall want it to go in as an interview and not as a communication. If you do not care to use it, throw it in the wastebasket."

Ade, who became a famous humorist, writer and major benefactor for Purdue's Ross-Ade Stadium, didn't use the story, though the *Record* did send a reporter to cover the meeting. That report was published in the Lafayette (Ind.) *Daily Courier* on Jan. 12, 1895.

J.K. HOAGLAND
Track, Illinois

It wasn't until 1901 that the Conference honored an official outdoor track champion, but all the league schools got together for annual open meets in the years preceding that. And it was J.K. Hoagland that captured the Illini's first "unofficial" individual title in 1898. He won the 880-yard walk in the first Indoor Western Intercollegiate meet held in Chicago. The Illini didn't fare as well as a team. Illinois was fifth among the five teams entered.

PAT O'DEA
Football, Wisconsin

Pat O'Dea, the "Kangaroo Kicker," played for the Badgers from 1896 to 1899 and was renowned for his amazing ability—many regarded as ahead of his time—to drop-kick and punt a football. A native of Melbourne, Australia, he first honed his football skills as a rugby player. In addition to kicking, he also played fullback for the Badgers from 1897-99 and was a two-time Walter Camp All-American. His punts routinely sailed 80 to 100 yards downfield, and he is regarded as one of the greatest drop-kickers of all-time. O'Dea averaged 50 yards a punt during his remarkable four years with career-long punts of 110 yards (1897 against Minnesota) and 100 yards (1899 against Yale) when fields were 110 yards long. His first college punt in 1896 soared 86 yards. He successfully converted 31 drop-kick field goals in his career, including 13 in 1899. He booted four in a single game in 1899 and kicked a career-long 65-yarder in 1898 against Northwestern.

BIG TEN LIST

CHRONOLOGY OF MEMBERSHIP

1896- Chicago, Illinois, Michigan, Minnesota, Northwestern, Purdue and Wisconsin.

1899 - Iowa and Indiana join.

1912 - Ohio State joins; name "Big Ten" coined.

1946 - Chicago withdraws.

1949 - Michigan State joins.

1990 - Penn State joins, becoming 11th team; league name remains the same.

BIG TEN LIST

NCAA CHAMPIONSHIPS

Big Ten Conference teams have accounted for numerous official NCAA team championships and several individual titles through the years.

	Team Titles	Individual Titles
Chicago	1	16
Illinois	16	114
Indiana	19	125
Iowa	17	99
Michigan	27	224
Michigan State	17	100
Minnesota	7	50
Northwestern	1	46
Ohio State	18	188
Penn State	21	96
Purdue	1	12
Wisconsin	19	112

(Note: Totals include men's and women's championships and all years in the school's athletic history.)

LEADING THE WAY

ANDREW O'DEA
Wisconsin

Andrew O'Dea spent his formidable years working with livestock on his father's ranch in Melbourne, Australia. But his claims to fame in adult life came on the athletic venues at Wisconsin, where the Aussie-born athlete was a three-sport star and later a celebrated coach in the sport of rowing. O'Dea, older brother of legendary Badgers' kicker Pat "The Kangaroo Kicker" O'Dea, ventured to the United States in the early 1890s and soon earned fame athletically as a rowing oarsman, a football player and a boxer. He soon found success as a rowing coach at the Lurlines, an amateur rowing club in Minneapolis. He wound up at Wisconsin in 1895 as a varsity crew coach, where he was soon joined by his brother, Pat, who came to the U.S. in 1896. Although Pat went on to carve a reputation for himself as one of the greatest athletes in Wisconsin history, Andrew's contributions to Wisconsin's rowing success were no less significant. He was also an outstanding football player in his own right, having honed his skills on the rugby fields of his native Australia. He was equally tough in the boxing ring, where he fought under the name Frank "Paddy" Slavin upon his arrival in the U.S.

· BIG TEN PIONEERS ·

Gertrude Dudley
Chicago

Women's sports competition wasn't a popular notion at the turn of the 20th century, but that wasn't going to stop Gertrude Dudley, who adopted the motto: "A sport for every girl and a girl in every sport." Dudley, who played tennis, basketball and baseball at Mount Holyoke College, came to Chicago in 1898 as the director of women's gymnasium. Founder of the Women's Athletic Association (1904) and the Middle West Society of Physical Education (1917), Dudley headed Chicago's Department of Physical Education for 37 years before retiring in 1935. She died at 75 in 1945. Dudley Field was named in her honor in 1925 and the Dudley Scholarships for scholar-athletes were established in 1973.

Academic Achievements

Big Ten universities' libraries hold in excess of 58 million volumes and maintain more than 550,000 serials subscriptions. Eight of the nation's twenty largest academic libraries reside on Big Ten campuses.

Gertrude Dudley

BIG TEN
SINCE 1896
CENTENNIAL

BIG TEN
SINCE
1896
CENTENNIAL

1898-99

Two of Northwestern's first football stars, Jesse Van Doozer (left) and Al Potter.

THE BIG EVENT

The original rules of football

Football in the 1890s displayed some startling differences from today's game. The field was 110 yards long without end zones of any kind. There were two 50-yard lines, 10 yards apart. The halves were 45 minutes long and nobody wore helmets. Touchdowns and field goals were worth five points each. (The field goal was cut to four points in 1904 and three in 1909. The touchdown went up to six points.) With no forward pass, it was strictly a ground offense and the defense played it accordingly to stop the running game. Therefore, only five yards were needed for a first down, but there were only three downs instead of four to make it. There was no rule requiring seven men on the offensive line and bulky linemen frequently were called back to lead a formation on momentum plays.

OTHER MEMORABLE EVENTS

- The two selectors of the All-America football teams named their first Midwesterners: Michigan center William Cunningham by Caspar Whitney and Chicago fullback Clarence Herschberger by Walter Camp.

- Northwestern's administration raised $100 to start its first band.

- Wisconsin became the first "Western" school to receive national recognition in sports: Its crew team finished third in the famed Poughkeepsie Regatta.

- Ohio State, though not a Conference member yet, was not allowed by the school faculty to field a baseball team because the Student Athletic Association had debts of $14 and cash on hand of two cents.

- A Conference committee devised and printed a set of football rules to contrast with the "Eastern Rules." Later, the Conference returned to the Eastern Rules.

Michigan sweeps football and baseball

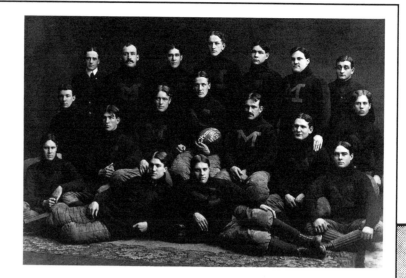

The 1898-99 school year was a very good one for Michigan, which with Chicago was asserting itself as a power in the youthful Big Ten. Although the Conference sponsored championships in just football and baseball, a sweep is still a sweep. In the fall of '98, under coach Gustave Ferbert, the Wolverine football team won 10 games without a loss, including six shutouts while outscoring its opponents, 205-26. Key to its 3-0 mark that won the Big Ten was a 12-11 road victory over defending champion Chicago which had an even more profound effect on UM than its first Big Ten title. The victory inspired Louis Elbel to write "The Victors," one of the great college marching songs. Center William Cunningham, who had a great performance in that Chicago game, was Michigan's first All-American. Graduate manager for that team was Charles Baird, who would soon become Michigan's first director of athletics. Baseball, the era's other major sport, also brought Michigan its second Big Ten title that school year. Coach C.F. Watkins' team posted a 14-5 overall mark and 5-2 Big Ten slate.

CLARENCE HERSCHBERGER
Football, Baseball and Track, Chicago

Clarence Herschberger was a man for all seasons for the Maroons from 1895-99, starring in football, baseball, and track and field. Chicago's first representative on Walter Camp's All-America team, and the first player west of the Alleghenies to be so recognized, "Herschie's" power as a runner came from his cleverness. Weighing only 158 pounds, Herschberger could pivot off either foot with the same skill and could squirm loose from tackles. But he was also a great drop kicker and could kick field goals from nearly any angle or distance. Herschberger also won four letters as a center fielder, batting .432 in 1899. As a track man, he held Chicago records in the pole vault, hammer, shot put and 220-yard low hurdles. Also an excellent student, Herschberger earned Phi Beta Kappa honors. He later became a real estate agent.

WILLIAM CUNNINGHAM
Football, Michigan

Of the more than 100 football players who've won All-America honors at the University of Michigan, William Cunningham holds a very special distinction. Among such great names as Tom Harmon, Anthony Carter and Desmond Howard, Cunningham was the very first Wolverine All-American in 1898. A four-year letter winner from 1896-99, Cunningham's Michigan squads won the '98 title and combined for a cumulative record of 33-4-1. His all-star selection by Caspar Whitney may have been cemented by a recommendation from Chicago coach Amos Alonzo Stagg whose team was defeated by Cunningham and his Michigan teammates. In fact, it was that contest that inspired songwriter Louis Elbel to write The Victors, one of the greatest college fight songs.

FOOTBALL HALL OF FAMERS

BIG TEN LIST

A total of 74 football players in Big Ten history are members of the College Football Hall of Fame. Here are the totals from each school and the oldest member from the school in the Hall of Fame:

Chicago (5):	Clarence Herschberger, FB, 1898
Illinois (8):	Bart Macomber, HB, 1915
Indiana (1):	John Tavener, C, 1944
Iowa (5):	Aubrey Devine, QB, 1921
Michigan (16):	Neil Snow, E, 1901
Michigan State (3):	Don Coleman, T, 1951
Minnesota (13):	John McGovern, QB, 1909
Northwestern (5):	Ralph Baker, HB, 1926
Ohio State (12):	Charles Harley, FB, 1919
Penn State(8):	(0 in Big Ten, but 8 in its history)
	Glenn Killinger, B, 1921
Purdue (3):	Alex Agase, T, 1943
Wisconsin (5):	Robert Butler, T, 1912

LEADING THE WAY

GEORGE HUFF
Illinois

When he entered Illinois as a student in 1887, there was no way that George Huff knew he would someday be referred to as "The Father of the Fighting Illini." Huff began his Illinois career as an athlete, a member of the school's first football team in 1890, lettering twice in football as the team's center and three times in baseball as a multi-positional player, including one time as the catcher. His greatest contribution at Illinois, however, came as a coach and athletic director. He coached the football team for four years, compiling a modest 21-16-3 record before giving up the position in 1899. As the school's baseball coach, Huff led Illinois to a winning percentage of nearly 70 percent, directing the Illini to 11 Conference championships. He served the school as athletic director from 1901-36, and had a knack for hiring outstanding coaches. His coaching hires included Illinois legends Bob Zuppke, Craig Ruby and Harry Gill. Huff's direction led to the construction of Memorial Stadium and Huff Gymnasium, the basketball arena that housed the Illini until 1963. Huff died in 1936 at the age of 64.

· BIG TEN PIONEERS ·

Dr. Jacob Shell
Illinois

Dr. Jacob Kinzer Shell's tenure as athletic director at Illinois from 1898-1901 was generally accented by achievement. Though football and track success in his era was minimal, the Illinois baseball team won the Conference championship in 1899-1900, the school's first title in the newly formed league. Shell played a role in welcoming Indiana and Iowa to the Conference, and he established the Illinois campus as the training headquarters for the Chicago Cubs. During his undergraduate days at Pennsylvania, Shell starred in six sports, winning the American middleweight wrestling championship, and he was one of the founders of the Amateur Athletic Union. He died in 1940 at the age of 78.

Academic Achievements

Among the most famous alumni from the University of Chicago are: astronomer Edwin Powell Hubble; former senator, Charles Percy; actor Ed Asner; writer Kurt Vonnegut, Jr.; former Green Bay Packer, Willie Davis; crime fighter, Eliot Ness; theatrical director Mike Nichols; Cosmos host Carl Sagan; author Philip Roth; and former Secretary of Health, Education and Welfare, Patricia Roberts Harris.

The BIG TEN's First 100 Years
Big Ten Football Trophies

Big Ten schools have 15 football trophy games. Here are the five oldest:

TROPHY	TEAMS	YEAR BEGAN	SERIES
Little Brown Jug	Michigan-Minnesota	1909	MICH 55-21-2
Old Oaken Bucket	Purdue-Indiana	1925	PUR 45-22-3
Illibuck (wooden turtle)	Ohio State-Illinois	1925	OSU 49-20-2
Floyd of Rosedale (bronze pig)	Minnesota-Iowa	1935	MINN 35-24-2
Purdue Cannon	Purdue-Illinois	1943	tied 23-23-2

The Little Brown Jug, Old Oaken Bucket and Floyd of Rosedale are the three oldest trophies in college football.

BIG TEN
CENTENNIAL
SINCE 1896

THE BIG EVENT

Indiana and Iowa join Conference

The Big Ten wasn't yet big, nor was it ten, when Indiana and Iowa were admitted to the Conference on Dec. 1, 1899. Seven schools had formed the Intercollegiate Conference of Faculty Representatives in 1896, so the first "expansion" brought the membership to nine. (The addition of Ohio State in 1912 made it ten.) The Hoosiers and Hawkeyes have played integral roles in the development of the Conference throughout the century, producing nationally prominent teams, athletes and coaches. Indiana swimming coach James "Doc" Counsilman has won more Big Ten titles (23) than any other Conference coach, 20 of them consecutively. Iowa wrestling coach Dan Gable ranks second with 20 Conference championships, all of them in a row. Indiana has won more NCAA basketball titles (5) than any other Conference school, but Iowa has a unique roundball distinction of its own. It hosted the nation's first intercollegiate basketball game on Jan. 16, 1896, losing to Chicago, 15-12, before 400 fans.

OTHER MEMORABLE EVENTS

- Wisconsin's Pat O'Dea drop kicked a 62-yard field goal, a Conference record that stood until 1981.

- Chicago's football team won its first of six Conference championships.

- Illinois lost nearly all of its historical athletic records as well as championship banners and trophies on June 9, 1900, when fire destroyed the UI woodshops.

- Robert "Red" Matthews of Illinois became the nation's first acrobatic cheerleader.

Illinois baseball wins its first-ever Conference crown

During the 1899-1900 school year, William McKinley became the first U.S. president to ride in an automobile and Theodore Roosevelt accepted the nomination for vice president, replacing the deceased Garret Hobart. The Conference celebrated its fourth anniversary, and Illinois had reason to rejoice with its first title in the Conference when the baseball team placed first under coach George Huff. The squad returned the nucleus of its members from the 1898-99 team that finished as the Conference runner-up, and Illinois began its preseason preparation with an exhibition series against the Chicago White Sox. After winning three and tying one game against the White Sox, Huff knew he had the makings of a championship club. The team was led by pitcher Carl Lundgren, who later pitched for seven seasons with the Chicago Cubs and guided Illinois to four Conference titles and tied for a fifth as head coach in 12 years. Other standouts were pitcher Harvey McCollum, second baseman Billy Fulton, third baseman Carl Steinwedell and center fielder Jimmy Cook. The Illini won seven of their first eight games, winding up with an 11-2 record.

Other Big Ten Champs:

- **FOOTBALL: Chicago, coached by A.A. Stagg**

JUSTA LINDGREN
Football, Illinois

For more than 40 years, the name of Justa Lindgren was a part of football at Illinois. Lindgren first joined Illinois as a freshman lineman from Moline, Ill., in 1898-99. He earned four letters, then left to serve as football coach at Cornell College in Iowa. Just two seasons later, he returned to Illinois as one of four graduates in coach George Huff's alumni coaching system. Lindgren served one season as head coach (1906), but the conservative and detail-minded Lindgren felt more comfortable as an assistant, working as line coach under Arthur Hall, Bob Zuppke and Ray Eliot through 1943. Lindgren developed seven All-America players at Illinois, and played a key role himself in eight Conference championship teams. He died in 1951 at the age of 72.

RAY EWRY
Track, Purdue

He set a standard that would be upheld through decades of international competition. Ray Ewry, a Lafayette, Ind., native and 1894 Purdue graduate, won a record eight track and field gold medals at the Olympic Games in 1900 (three in Paris), 1904 (three in St. Louis), and 1908 (two in London). He set Olympic and world records in the standing high jump, the standing broad jump and three standing jumps. Ewry's story was all the more remarkable considering he was orphaned at age 5 and struck by polio at age 7. He was told he'd probably be confined to a wheel chair for the rest of his life. Ewry received an electrical engineering degree from Purdue. He died in 1937.

BASKETBALL HALL OF FAMERS

There are 31 men with Big Ten ties in the Naismith Memorial Basketball Hall of Fame in Springfield, Mass. They are:

- Justin Barry (Iowa)
- Walt Bellamy (Indiana)
- Everett Case, (Wisconsin)
- Everett Dean (Indiana)
- James Enright (Conference referee)
- Harold Foster (Wisconsin)
- John Havlicek (Ohio State)
- Connie Hawkins (Iowa)
- Paul "Tony" Hinkle (Chicago)
- Neil Johnston (Ohio State)
- George Kiogan, (Minnesota)
- Bob Knight (Ohio State/Indiana)
- John Kundla (Minnesota)
- Ward Lambert (Purdue)
- Arthur Lonborg (Northwestern)
- Jerry Lucas (Ohio State)
- Branch McCracken (Indiana)
- Walter Meanwell (Wisconsin)
- Ralph Miller (Iowa)
- Charles Murphy (Purdue)
- Peter Newell (Michigan State)
- Harold Olsen (Ohio State/Northwestern/Wisconsin))
- Harlan "Pat" Page (Chicago)
- Andy Phillip (Illinois)
- Abe Sapperstein (Illinois)
- John Schommer (Chicago)
- Amos Alonzo Stagg (Chicago)
- Christian Steinmetz (Wisconsin)
- Lynn St. John (Ohio State)
- Fred Taylor (Ohio State)
- John Wooden (Purdue)

BIG TEN LIST

LEADING THE WAY

AMOS ALONZO STAGG
Chicago

Football and Amos Alonzo Stagg. The names are inextricably entwined, as the NCAA recognized when it designated its Division III championship game the Stagg Bowl. Ironically, Stagg came late to the sport; as a Yale undergraduate, he was one of the best pitchers in the country and six National League teams were interested in him. He went out for football as a Yale senior in 1887 as a reserve and the following year, as an end, was named to the first recognized All-America team. After coaching a YMCA and seminary team, Stagg was enticed to Chicago in 1892 at age 30 and fielded a team of 13 players, including himself. Stagg would coach the Maroons for 40 years, winning Conference football titles in 1899, 1905, 1907, 1908, 1913 and 1924. After turning 70 and being forced to retire at Chicago, Stagg coached at the College of the Pacific for 14 years, upping his then-record college win total to 314 before, at age 84, joining his son as "co-coach" at Pennsylvania's Susquehanna University for five more years. Stagg coached until he was 98, retiring in 1960, saying "I've coached for 70 years. It is a good time to stop." The only man elected to the National Football Foundation College Football Hall of Fame as a player and as a coach, Stagg died in Stockton, Cal., in 1965 at 102.

· BIG TEN PIONEERS ·

Arthur Hall, Illinois

The story goes that Arthur Hall was 99 percent grit. As a captain for the Illinois football team in 1900, he was carried from the field near exhaustion. Hearing someone else call the signals, he broke free, stormed onto the field, ordered his replacement off, and carried the ball on the game-winning score against Purdue. Hall's legend at Illinois wasn't yet complete, as he coached the Illini in 1910 to an undefeated season, the school's first Conference football title and a season when Illinois didn't allow a single point. In six seasons as coach at Illinois, Hall led the Illini to a 27-10-3 record, although it wasn't his only profession. By day, he practiced law in nearby Danville, Ill., and he retired from coaching in 1912. Hall served as a county probate judge until his retirement in 1954, playing a key role in developing Illinois' hard road system. He died in 1955.

Academic Achievements

The current Indiana University president, Myles Brand, has continued to set a good example for the IU students, just like his predecessors. They must be making their job as a university leader look rewarding and fun. How else can you explain the 209 IU alumni who went on to head institutions of higher learning? There have been so many that IU has been dubbed, "The Mother of College Presidents."

The BIG TEN's First 100 Years
Big Ten Football Series Highlights

Oldest 104	(most games) Minnesota-Wisconsin (began in 1890) the most played rivalry in NCAA Division I-A
Closest tied one	(20 games played minimum) Minnesota 25 games won, Illinois 25, 3 tied Iowa 35 games won, Wisconsin 34, 2 tied Iowa 15 games won, Michigan State 14, 2 tied Illinois 16 games won, Michigan State 15, 2 tied
Lopsided 43	Ohio State 54, Indiana 12, 5 tied

BIG TEN
SINCE 1896
CENTENNIAL

THE BIG EVENT

First outdoor track championship

Michigan staked its claim as the dominant force in Big Ten outdoor track and field from the beginning. The Wolverines won the first-ever Conference championship at the inaugural Conference meet, conducted in 1901 at Chicago's Marshall Field. The meet was open to teams outside of the Conference between its inception and 1926. But unlike other early Conference championships, like golf and cross country, in which teams outside the Conference won the debut title, Big Ten teams owned the outdoor track crown from the beginning. Michigan out-pointed runner-up Wisconsin in the first meet, 38-28, to win its first of four straight league championships. The Wolverines own the most titles with 30. Illinois, which has also been an irresistible force with 28 championships, won its first title in 1907. Purdue, Penn State, and Northwestern—which discontinued the sport in 1988—are the only teams to have never won the event.

OTHER MEMORABLE EVENTS

- Purdue's Ray Ewry became the first Conference athlete to win a gold medal at the Olympics. He won eight golds in three Olympiads.

- Ohio State increased the size of its football stadium and used money collected by the faculty, not the students, in a radical departure from the day's norm.

- The "White Resolution" (named for Northwestern's H.S. White) was adopted: Any university may object to new legislation if the objection is made within 30 days, otherwise the new legislation is binding on all members.

- Purdue's E.C. Robertson booted seven field goals in one game vs. Rose Poly, a Conference record that still stands.

Iowa football machine rolls over competition

Iowa quarterback Clyde Williams.

This was said of the 1900 Iowa football team: "The greatest 11 that ever played in the Hawkeye state, if not the greatest the West has ever seen," and "From the standpoint of attack, brilliancy and rapidity of execution and general efficiency, Iowa's game is unsurpassed by that of any college in the country." Thus were the accolades for a team that went 7-0-1, 2-0-1 in league play, and tied Minnesota (8-0-1, 3-0-1) for its first Conference title. It was Iowa's second consecutive undefeated season, and during that 17-game span the Hawkeyes did not allow a touchdown. Most of their games weren't even close: they beat Upper Iowa, 57-0; State College of Iowa, 68-0; Simpson, 47-0; Drake, 26-0; Chicago, 17-0; Michigan, 28-5; and Grinnell, 63-2. And so it went. Right up until the final game of the season against Northwestern. That contest ended 5-5, prompting at least one former Hawkeye to speculate that the food at the hotel in Rock Island was intentionally tainted by the chef because he had a bet that Iowa would not win, 40-0. Almost everyone on the team was sick the night before the game with stomach cramps. That would be Iowa's last game in Rock Island. Iowa quarterback Clyde Williams, halfbacks Ray Morton and Billy Edson and tackle Joe Warner were selected first-team all-league by the *Chicago Post*. Williams was also third-team All-America.

OTHER BIG TEN CHAMPIONS

- **BASEBALL:** Michigan, coached by C.F. Watkins

- **OUTDOOR TRACK:** Michigan (no coach)

NEIL SNOW
Football, Baseball and Track, Michigan

Neil Snow captained Fielding Yost's first Michigan team, the famous "Point-A-Minute" eleven that rolled to an unbeaten season and 49-0 victory over Stanford on Jan. 1, 1902, in the first Rose Bowl. Snow was picked an All-Big Ten Conference end for four seasons although he also played fullback and was picked by Caspar Whitney as Michigan's second All-American. In that inaugural Rose Bowl game, Snow scored five touchdowns—a mark not since equalled. He earned 12 letters at Michigan in football, baseball and track. Snow went on to become a successful businessman before dying at age 34 in 1914. He was named to the National Football Foundation Hall of Fame in 1960.

JOE HUNTER
Football, Northwestern

The name Joe Hunter doesn't roll off the tongue of most Northwestern football fans with ease, but he surely ranks as one of the most colorful Wildcats in school history. Shortly after being elected the team's captain in 1898, the quarterback left school to enlist in the Spanish-American War. He returned to campus the following autumn weak from malaria and typhoid, and again was elected captain. He was injured early in practice, however, and turned over his title to Harry Little. Hunter was named captain again in 1900, but he still had not returned from a summer tour of Europe when the season began. He did return in time to lead the Wildcats to a 5-0 victory over Chicago, however. The school's newspaper reported: "Hunter's generalship stood out like the North Star guiding a sailor home." He later married the daughter of Georges Clemenceau, premier of France during World War I.

BASEBALL COACHES' HALL OF FAME

These former Big Ten coaches are members of the American Association of Collegiate Baseball Coaches' Hall of Fame:

- Lee Eilbracht, Illinois (1952-78)
- Ray Fisher, Michigan (1921-58)
- George Huff, Illinois (1896-1919)
- Martin Karow, Ohio State (1950-75)
- John Kobs, Michigan State (1925-63)
- Danny Litwhiler, Michigan State (1964-82)
- Arthur Mansfield, Wisconsin (1940-70)
- Frank McCormick, Minnesota (1931-41)
- Richard Siebert, Minnesota (1947-78)
- Otto Vogel, Iowa (1925-46, 1946-66)

BIG TEN LIST

LEADING THE WAY

DR. HENRY WILLIAMS
Minnesota

Dr. Henry Williams — "The Grand Old Man of Football" at Minnesota — became the Gophers' football coach following a successful stint at West Point, where his innovative offensive schemes helped the Cadets earn their first-ever victory against archrival Navy, 32-16, in 1892. A former football and track star at Yale, he was a teammate of gridiron legends Amos Alonzo Stagg and "Pudge" Heffelfinger and a former world record hurdler. A physician by profession, Williams was a football coach at heart. During his 21 years at Minnesota, the first eight of which he co-served as track coach, he built the football program into a dynasty that reigned supreme in the Big Ten in the first two decades of the 20th century. The Gophers, who were undefeated his first season, won outright league titles five times and shared two more with Michigan. Williams is credited for developing an offensive scheme called "The Minnesota Shift," which was later adopted and reworked by Knute Rockne at Notre Dame. The play was ground-breaking in its day and revolutionized the offensive phase of the game. Williams' career record at Minnesota was 140-33-11, for a career winning percentage of .791. He died in 1931 at age 62.

· BIG TEN PIONEERS ·

1900-01 Indiana basketball team

Indiana's magnificent tradition as a Big Ten basketball power began Feb. 8, 1901. Though that first game against Butler ended in a defeat, 20-17, the Hoosiers would eventually become a powerhouse on the hard wood, winning five national championships.

Academic Achievements

Michigan was the first university in America to be governed by the people of a state (rather than state government or a church) and to include the entire statewide public education system in its charter, established in 1817. Its first class (of one) graduated in 1858.

The BIG TEN's First 100 Years
Highest Scoring Big Ten Men's Basketball Teams
(per game; Conference games only)

Avg. Pts. Per Game	School	Year	
102.9	Iowa	1970	
97.1	Purdue	1969	
95.4	Michigan	1966	
92.9	Michigan	1965	
92.4	Illinois	1965	

BIG TEN
SINCE 1896
CENTENNIAL

THE BIG EVENT

Michigan wins first Rose Bowl game

The first Rose Bowl game on Jan. 1, 1902, almost was a polo match. Organizers of the Tournament of Roses Parade had originally scheduled polo in conjunction with the parade, but decided that something more dramatic was needed. So they turned to unbeaten Michigan—"the best team in the West"—to play against Stanford—champion of the "Pacific Coast universities." After a slow start, with no scoring for 23 minutes, Michigan built a 17-0 halftime lead and then turned it on in the second half, scoring on nearly every possession and running up 527 yards on the ground to win, 49-0. Fielding Yost's team had outscored its opponents, 555-0, in winning 11 games. But the tournament association thought the disparity between the teams would make an annual game unappealing to spectators. A chariot race replaced football as the 1903 companion to the parade. Football did not return to the Rose Bowl until 1916.

OTHER MEMORABLE EVENTS

- The faculty representatives voted to limit football training camp to two weeks prior to the season opener.

- Minnesota's Mueller was declared ineligible for future athletic competition because he accepted a $5 prize for winning a "Fat Man's Race."

- Bicycling was dropped from the Conference track meet.

- Northwestern's Alton Johnson formed the first football huddle. Unable to remember the next play after a bump on the head, he gathered his teammates around to get the signals straight. (Illinois Coach Bob Zuppke is credited with making the huddle a strategic, regular occurrence.)

First gymnastics championship

Although a Big Ten men's gymnastics team champion was crowned in 1902, the Conference didn't officially begin recognizing "official" championships until 1926, when Chicago edged host Purdue, 1,234.80 to 1,214.50, to claim the "first" title. However, the first "unofficial" team champion was Wisconsin, which hosted the inaugural league event—which was open to teams outside the Conference—in 1902. The Badgers won again in 1904 and '05, with Minnesota winning in '03. The Gophers' J.W. Dye became the Big Ten's first all-around champion that season. The meet took hiatus in 1906 and was resumed in '07 in Chicago, where Minnesota beat Wisconsin, 25.00 to 19.50, to claim the championship. It was 1907 when the Big Ten began keeping official records of all the individual events. Wisconsin's Felix Zeidlhack was the dominant individual that year, as he won championships in the horizontal bar, pommel horse and parallel bars events and was the all-around champion. Zeidlhack duplicated his all-around championship in 1908, winning the horizontal bar and parallel bars titles to lead Wisconsin to its fourth team crown. Illinois has won the most team championships with 22, followed by Minnesota with 21. Indiana, Purdue, Wisconsin and Northwestern have since discontinued the sport.

OTHER BIG TEN CHAMPIONS

- **FOOTBALL:** Michigan, coached by Fielding Yost, and Wisconsin, coached by Phil King

- **BASEBALL:** Wisconsin, coached by Oscar Bandelin

- **OUTDOOR TRACK:** Michigan (no coach)

ALTON JOHNSON
Football, Northwestern

Quarterback Alton Johnson was honored as Northwestern's first All-American, as selected by *Collier's* magazine, for his play in 1901 when he led the Wildcats to an 8-2-1 record. Described as a "will-o'-the-wisp" athlete, his speed and daring made him a renown figure on campus. He ran 50 yards for a touchdown and kicked the extra point that gave his team a 6-5 victory over crosstown rival Chicago in 1901. He also inadvertently invented the huddle during a game in which he was hit on the side of the head and couldn't remember the numbers of the team's plays, so he gathered his teammates around him to describe the play he wanted to run. Johnson was elected to the All-Big Ten team — or as it was called then, the All-Western team.

CARL LUNDGREN
Baseball, Illinois

It's difficult to determine where Carl Lundgren made the greatest contribution to Illinois baseball. As a player or a coach? As a pitcher from 1898-1902, Lundgren led Illinois to Conference titles in his sophomore and senior seasons and a runner-up finish as a freshman, posting a 22-10 record. He pitched for the Chicago Cubs for seven seasons, and was part of two Cubs World Series championships. He accounted for 92 wins as a pro pitcher before beginning a coaching career with the freshmen at Princeton. He won four Conference championships while coaching at Michigan, then returned to Illinois for the 1920-21 season to lead the Illini to Conference titles in 1921 and 1922 and a runner-up finish the following season. Overall, his Illinois teams won four titles and shared another before his death in 1934.

WILLIAM "WILLIE" HESTON
Football, Michigan

Prohibition hadn't yet come to the United States, but Michigan halfback Willie Heston ran the first bootleg play. In the first Rose Bowl game, on Jan. 1, 1902, coach Fielding Yost had 10 men line up to the right of center. The quarterback handed off to Heston, who scampered 40 yards up the left side for college football's first bootleg play. He scored 71 career touchdowns as the mainstay of Fielding Yost's "Point-A-Minute" teams of 1901-04. The greatest halfback of football's early days, Heston could spot the slimmest opening in a line and would hurdle anyone who wasn't upright. Michigan's third All-American, and the first selected by Walter Camp, Heston was also selected to several all-time All-America teams. He was named to both the Michigan and National Football Foundation halls of fame. Heston died at 85 in 1963.

GYMNASTICS EVENTS

BIG TEN LIST

Today, gymnasts compete in seven events:

- All-Around
- Floor Exercise
- Pommel Horse
- Still Rings
- Vault
- Parallel Bars
- Horizontal Bar

But through the years, there have been championships awarded in a number of other gymnastics events:

- Long Horse
- Trampoline
- Tumbling
- Rope Climb
- Flying Rings
- Indian Clubs

LEADING THE WAY

FIELDING YOST
Michigan

No coach could have had a better debut than Michigan's Fielding Yost, and it was one that lasted five years. Hired by athletic director Charles Baird in 1901 to continue Michigan's astounding football success, West Virginia native Yost did just that. Through his first five seasons at Michigan, from 1901-05, Michigan's record was 55-1-1 as the famous "Point-A-Minute" Wolverines scored 2,821 points to just 42 for the opposition. In four of those years, his teams were called the nation's best. Yost coached 25 Michigan teams from 1901-26—retiring temporarily in 1924—to 164 victories against 28 losses and 10 ties. Ten times his teams won Big Ten titles, despite Michigan's withdrawal from the Conference for 10 of those seasons. Fourteen of Yost's players earned All-America status, from halfback William Heston in 1903 to end Bennie Oosterbaan in 1926. Yost became Michigan's athletic director in 1921 and, in 20 years in that post, became a great builder of a multi-million dollar athletic plant, espousing a philosophy of "athletics for all." Such facilities as Yost Field House, Michigan Stadium, the nation's first intramural sports building, an ice rink and golf course were constructed under his direction. Yost died in 1946.

· BIG TEN PIONEERS ·

John Sigrist, Ohio State

The 1901-02 school year included a 5-3-1 football season for Ohio State, but the season was remembered for another low point. It was the only season in the history of Ohio State football when a player was killed. Center John Sigrist died when his neck was dislocated when he tried to buck the line with his head. Ohio State won the game against Case Western, 6-5, on Oct. 26, and Sigrist died two days later. The incident stirred the campus, and some advocated the abolition of football. A debate ensued, and the football team and members of the Athletic Association voted to continue the season's schedule after the game with Ohio Wesleyan was abandoned. Eventually, the faculty voted to continue the season, and Ohio State fell to Michigan, 21-0, when play resumed.

Academic Achievements

At the turn of the century most major cities had several daily newspapers. After all, it was the only way of getting the news at the time. But not every college had a newspaper. In 1901 The Daily Iowan became the first daily student newspaper west of the Mississippi River, and it's been published ever since.

The BIG TEN's First 100 Years

Big Ten Football Winning Streaks

All Games
29 Michigan 1901-03

Conference Games Only
19 Michigan 1990-92

Home
50 Michigan 1901-07

Unbeaten (tied but not beaten)
56 Michigan 1900-05

THE BIG EVENT

Huff's baseball juggernaut

CONFERENCE CHAMPIONS 1903
MGR. SCHACHT   PITTS   ENGLE   PARKER   ZANGERLE   HILL   COACH HUFF
BEEBE   ASHMORE MILLER CAPT. J.F.COOK   STAHL   L.P.COOK
                        STEINWEDELL   ROBERTS

Under coach George Huff, the Illinois baseball program was a powerhouse at the turn of the century. Illinois won its first Conference title in any sport in 1900, as the Illini compiled an 11-2 record. Illinois finished second in the next two seasons before the 1903 campaign, when Illinois completed the season 17-1 overall, 13-1 as Conference champions. It was the second of 11 Conference titles for Illinois before Huff retired as coach in 1919, and Illinois needed a win over rival Michigan to claim the championship. On May 9, before a crowd of 2,000 at Illinois Field, Illini fans saw Illinois score an 8-2 victory when catcher Jake Stahl ripped a grand slam, a towering shot that cleared two outfielders and bounded to a tree 400 feet from home plate. The tree stood for years, a monument to Stahl's smash. Meanwhile, he played eight years in the majors, a part of two World Series championships.

OTHER MEMORABLE EVENTS

- Minnesota's J.W. Dye was the first individual all-around champion crowned in gymnastics.

- Michigan scored 107 points vs. Iowa, the most points ever scored in a Conference football game.

- The Wolverines went 11-0 in football, outscoring their opponents, 644-12.

- Michigan State (then called Michigan Agriculture & Mechanical College and still 50 years from joining the Big Ten) installed electric lights on its football practice field.

The "Point-a-Minute" machine

Michigan's All-America running back Willie Heston.

Michigan's football team continued its domination in 1902, rolling to an 11-0 overall record and 5-0 Conference mark. Offensively, it was the most potent of coach Fielding Yost's "Point-a-Minute Machine." The Wolverines scored 644 points in the 11 games, an average of 58.5 points per game. Defensively, UM allowed only 12 points all year—six to Case and six to Minnesota. In between, Michigan beat Michigan State, 119-0, Iowa, 107-0, Ohio State, 86-0, and Indiana, 60-0. The closest game was a 6-0 victory over Wisconsin. Other wins came over Albion (88-0), Case (48-6), Notre Dame (23-0), Chicago (21-0), Oberlin (63-0) and Minnesota (23-6). Chicago wound up second in the league race with a 5-1 record (11-1 overall); Minnesota was 3-1 (7-2 overall).

OTHER BIG TEN CHAMPIONS

- **BASEBALL:** Illinois, coached by George Huff

- **GYMNASTICS:** Minnesota, coached by Dr. L.J. Cooke

- **OUTDOOR TRACK:** Michigan (no coach)

GARLAND "JAKE' STAHL
Football and Baseball, Illinois

To Illinois baseball fans, there stood a constant reminder for many years of Garland "Jake" Stahl, an All-America tackle who led Illinois to 25 victories in three seasons on the gridiron. But as a baseball player, Stahl ripped a grand slam into the giant tree in right-center field at Illinois Field, a shot that led Illinois to a win over Michigan. The debate continues whether the mammoth shot reached the tree on the fly. Stahl's .444 batting average in his senior season at Illinois stood as the school record for 23 years, and he wound up hitting over .400 during his three-year varsity career. He enjoyed a magnificent pro career, playing eight years in the major leagues. Stahl won World Series championships with the Boston Red Sox in 1903 and '12, the last one as a manager. In 1910, the catcher led the American League with 10 home runs. Stahl died on Sept. 18, 1922, at the age of 43.

CHARLIE WARD
Football, Northwestern

Charlie Ward was one of the most versatile, durable players in Northwestern's football history. He played every minute of every Conference game his first three seasons, and missed only the second half of the Chicago game as a senior in 1902, when he served as the team's captain. He also played every position but quarterback. Ward's talents also extended beyond the football field. En route to a game at Minnesota in 1899, Ward made national news by impersonating the famous politician and orator William Jennings Bryan from the rear platform of the train when it stopped in Elroy, Wisc. Ward was introduced by teammate Ed Dietz, and he performed so eloquently that the assembled crowd did not realize a hoax had been perpetrated until after the train pulled away. Northwestern won the game, by the way, 11-5. Ward remained with the University in administrative capacities for many years.

BIG TEN LIST

HOME RUN LEADERS

Garland "Jake" Stahl was one of the nation's first power hitters. But the Big Ten has had several sluggers since it began keeping home run statistics. Since 1948, here are the season champs with the most home runs in Conference games:

14	Shane Gunderson, Minn., 1994
14	Mike Smith, Ind., 1992
11	Jamie Taylor, OSU, 1991
10	Scott Ayotte, MSU, 1995
9	Dan Ruff, Mich., 1990
9	Bubba Smith, Ill., 1989
9	Scott Makarewicz, MSU, 1988
9	Tom Steinbach, Minn., 1983
8	Matt Huff, NU, 1993
8	Sloan Smith, NU, 1993
8	Jim Sepanek, MSU, 1985
8	Mike Eddington, MSU, 1984

LEADING THE WAY

EDGAR HOLT
Illinois

Before the turn of the century, it was Harvard and Princeton that were two of the kingpins of college football. So, thought Illinois athletic director George Huff, why not hire an Eastern coach to turn the sluggish Illini football program into a winner? Huff's choice was Edgar Garrison Holt, a product of both the Harvard and Princeton systems. Holt had toiled as a lineman during his playing days, so he spent the bulk of his time tutoring Illinois' front-line players such as "Jake" Stahl, Fred Lowenthal and Justa Lindgren. In two seasons, 1901 and '02, Holt guided Illinois to its first two winning records in Big Ten play and a cumulative record of 18-4-1. Holt died Apr. 19, 1924, at the age of 49.

· BIG TEN PIONEERS ·

Andrew Wyant
Chicago

Today, Andrew Wyant would be on the cover of *Sports Illustrated* for his iron-man abilities. He'd also be on the inside for breaking today's eligibility rules. With Northwestern's Charlie Ward getting the local "pub" for playing all but one-half in his four-year career (as well as playing every position, but quarterback), Wyant was quietly going about his business. Wyant played four years at Bucknell, then three more at Chicago under A.A. Stagg and never missed a minute of play in seven years and 98 games. Wyant became a Baptist minister and lived to the age of 97.

Academic Achievements

Among the most famous alumni from Illinois are: film critic Roger Ebert; former Secretary of Labor, Lynn Martin; Philippine President, General Fidel Ramos; inventor of nylon, Wallace Carothers; Motorola president, George Fisher; actor Ben Murphy; Nobel Prize winner in medicine, Rosalyn Yalow; former Walt Disney Studio president, Richard Frank; and the founder of Playboy, Hugh Hefner.

Andrew Wyant

BIG TEN
SINCE 1896
CENTENNIAL
™

THE BIG EVENT

Thirteen Boilermakers die in train crash

A special 14-car train was carrying the Purdue football team, band and fans—more than 950 people total—to Indianapolis for a game against Indiana. It was Oct. 31, 1903, around 9:45 a.m., when the train crashed into a 10-car section of a coal train, which was being backed down the same track. Sixteen people—including 13 players—were killed and 40 injured. In the collision, the train's first car was halved. Riding in the second car of the train, band members escaped serious injuries when the car left the track and went down an embankment. Purdue's Memorial Gymnasium is named in memory of those who died in the accident: players Thomas Bailer, Joseph Coates, Gabriel Drollinger, Charles Furr, Charles Grube, Jay Hamilton, Walter Hamilton, Russell Powell, Wilburt Price, Walter Roush, George Shaw, Samuel Squibb and Samuel Truitt, assistant coach Edward Robertson, trainer Patrick McClaire, and fan Newton Howard, a Lafayette businessman.

OTHER MEMORABLE EVENTS

- Wisconsin's president, Charles Van Hise, showed his enthusiasm for sports by riding his horse to watch football practice every night.

- More than 30,000 fans watched the Michigan at Minnesota football game, a record for the Midwest.

- Michigan won its fourth straight outdoor track title, a streak for track championships that has been matched, but never surpassed by any school.

- Grinnell's Walleser won the all-around championship at the Conference's open gymnastics meet, but Wisconsin won its second title in three years.

- The Conference had 10 athletes at the 1904 Summer Olympics in St. Louis, more than any league in the nation.

6-6 tie sends shockwaves through college football

1903 Minnesota football team.

Ordinarily, a 6-6 tie in a college football game would be regarded as a monumental bore. But for college football fans at the turn of the century, Minnesota's 6-6 tie against mighty Big Ten rival Michigan was a monumental spectator's delight that sent shockwaves through the nation. A then-record breaking crowd of 30,000-plus showed up at Minnesota's old Northrup Field to watch the undefeated Gophers duel the unbeaten Wolverines in a game billed —at the time—as the biggest clash in college football history. The game lived up to its billing, as it also marked the beginning of the annual battle for the Little Brown Jug, the nation's oldest intercollegiate trophy. Michigan, which had gained nation-wide fame with coach Fielding "Hurry Up" Yost's "Point-a-Minute" offense, averaged 50 points a game and sported a league-record 29-game undefeated streak. Minnesota boasted an equally strong team bent on breaking the Wolverines' stranglehold on the Conference championship. The Gophers' defense was brilliant in slowing Michigan's powerful offense, fueled by All-American Willie Heston, who was regarded as the nation's best halfback. Likewise, the Wolverines handcuffed Minnesota's offense as the teams settled for a 6-6 tie. They finished with identical 11-0-1 records and shared the Big Ten championship.

OTHER BIG TEN CHAMPIONS

- **BASEBALL: Illinois, coached by George Huff**

- **GYMNASTICS: Wisconsin, coached by J.C. Elsom**

- **OUTDOOR TRACK: Michigan (no coach)**

JAMES LIGHTBODY
Cross Country and Track, Chicago

One of the first Big Ten stars in track and field was the University of Chicago's James Lightbody. The 1904 Olympian was the premier middle distance runner of his day. Lightbody's victories at the 1905 Big Ten Outdoor Track and Field Championship in the 880-yard run (1:57.4) and the mile (4:25) helped lead the Maroons to their first Conference title in that sport. The Maroons had been runner-up to Michigan outdoors the previous three seasons. Also an accomplished cross country runner, Lightbody won the Henry Trophy Cup in 1903— presented by "Pat" Henry, the "father" of cross country at Chicago—for his victory in a long distance race on the campus among cross country club members.

ARCHIE HAHN
Track, Michigan

Diminutive 5-foot-5, 138 pound Archie Hahn was one of Michigan's, and America's, first great track stars. He won Big Ten sprint titles from 1901- 03, but saved his spectacular efforts for the 1904 St. Louis Olympics and the unofficial 1906 Games in Athens. In the former, he won all three sprint events, the 60, 100 and 200 meter dashes, setting a world record of 7.2 in the 60. Hahn repeated at 100 meters in the 1906 Olympics. He also won three Amateur Athletic Union sprint titles. After his amateur career, Hahn ran professionally, including a victory at 55 yards in a county fair race against a horse. Hahn then coached Michigan's freshman track team and later assisted his old Michigan coach, Keene Fitzpatrick, at Princeton. Hahn became coach at Virginia in 1929 and remained there until retiring in 1951. He died at 74 in 1955.

RALPH ROSE
Track, Michigan

Ralph Rose, the 1904 Big Ten shotput and discus champion who won six medals in four events over three Olympic Games, is best remembered for something he didn't do. Flagbearer for the U.S. contingent in the 1908 London Games, Rose refused to dip the American flag in submission to King Edward VII, saying, "This flag dips to no earthly king." That action began a tradition, later enshrined in the U.S. Statutes, that the flag would not be dipped to any person or thing. The six-foot-six Rose then won his second shot put gold, nearly duplicating his 1904 achievement at St. Louis when he set a world record of 48-feet-7-inches. At Stockholm in 1912, Rose was second in the shot, but won the combined left and right-handed shot. Rose attended Michigan law school from 1905-08, but returned to his California home without graduating. He died at age 28 in 1913, a typhoid fever victim.

BIG TEN LIST

FOOTBALL ALL-AMERICANS

The Big Ten and Ivy League dominated the All-America football teams prior to World War I. The Big Ten had 34 selections before 1918. Here are the players who received mention at least twice:

- William Heston, Michigan, HB 1903-04
- Walter Eckersall, Chicago, QB 1904-05-06
- Albert Benbrook, Michigan, G 1909-10
- Charles Harley, Ohio State, FB 1916-17-19

LEADING THE WAY

J.C. ELSOM
Wisconsin

Before Walter "Doc" Meanwell established his reputation as a Big Ten and Wisconsin coaching legend, before Emmett Angell did likewise as a player/coach, and before the Big Ten recognized formal team champions, J.C. Elsom laid the first foundation from which future Badger basketball teams would build success around. Elsom was Wisconsin's first head basketball coach, a position he held for six seasons spanning 1899 to 1904. In an era when schedules were light and record-keeping virtually non-existent, Elsom set a precedent for winning that Angell and Meanwell would later expand. Elsom's first team in 1899 went 0-3. But that would be the Badgers' last losing season until 1918. Wisconsin's best campaign under Elsom proved to be his last, as the Badgers went 11-4 in 1904. Two years later, Angell — serving as player and coach — guided Wisconsin to the first of consecutive Big Ten championships. The Badgers would, in fact, collect 12 Conference championships from 1906-29, earning bragging rights as the league's first true basketball dynasty. And the way was paved by Elsom, whose career record was 26-11.

· BIG TEN PIONEERS ·

Hiram Hanibal Wheeler, Illinois

One of the first African-American athletic stars at Illinois, Hiram Wheeler was a varsity quarterback and star sprinter on the Illinois track team that finished tied for fifth place in the Conference championships. Born in Chicago, he developed an early love for agriculture. He graduated from the Tuskegee Institute, where his father was a trustee, then enrolled at Illinois and played football and performed as a track sprinter for three years. He later taught at the Tuskegee Institute and other southern schools before returning to Illinois, where he was in charge of the mail office at the College of Agriculture. Wheeler also worked for the YMCA before he died in 1918 from pneumonia which developed from influenza.

Academic Achievements

When Anton J. Carlson joined the faculty at Chicago in 1904, no one knew the young scholar would soon make major scientific discoveries. He ended a century-old controversy by proving that the heartbeat begins in the nerve, not the muscle. For his other research, he often used himself as a subject. He also was the first person to label alcoholism as a disease.

The BIG TEN's First 100 Years
Top Three All-Time Big Ten Men's Basketball Scorers

2000-Point Club (all games)

2,613 Calbert Cheaney, Indiana, 1989-93
2,531 Shawn Respert, Michigan State, 1991-95
2,442 Glen Rice, Michigan, 1985-89

1000-Point Club (Conference games only)

1,544 Shawn Respert, Michigan State, 1992-95
1,503 Mike McGee, Michigan, 1978-81
1,477 Mychal Thompson, Minnesota, 1975-78

THE BIG EVENT

Chicago wins its first Big Ten track title

Chicago, with perhaps its best team ever, won the first of its three Big Ten outdoor track titles by scoring 56 points to easily outdistance Michigan (38), which had won the first four Conference championships. Chicago won eight of the 15 events, paced by James Lightbody, who won the 880-yard run in 1:57.4 and the mile in 4:25 as the Maroons rolled to the title on their own Marshall Field track. Other Chicago winners on the track included: Clyde Blair in the 100-yard dash; William Hogenson in the 220; Mark Catlin in the 120-yard high hurdles; and the mile relay team of Charles Groman, Norman Barker, Raymond Quigley and Blair. Triumphing in the field for the Maroons were broad jumper Hugo Friend and hammer thrower Edwin Parry. Although losing twice to arch-rival Illinois by close scores in indoor duals, the Maroons beat their downstate opponents, 79-47, a month before the Conference meet.

OTHER MEMORABLE EVENTS

- Minnesota football coach Dr. Henry Williams first advocated legalization of the forward pass. (The rule "passed" two years later.)

- The faculty representatives voted that an athlete to be eligible first had to complete a full semester of academic work.

- Chicago became the first Conference school with two players on the football all-America team: quarterback Walter Eckersall and end Fred Speik.

- Ohio State president William Oxley Thompson stated that athletics were "an inescapable part of the college scene...faculties must recognize not only their right, but their duty to lead in all forms of college athletics." Ohio State was admitted to the Conference in 1912.

- In the highest scoring non-Conference football games in Big Ten history, Minnesota beat Grinnell, 146-0, and Michigan defeated West Virginia, 130-0.

Michigan and Minnesota tie for Conference football title

1904 Minnesota football team.

Michigan and Minnesota tied for the Conference football title in 1904, demonstrating that the two Midwestern powers may have possessed the best two teams in the nation. Which was better? No one will ever know. The two teams didn't face each other that season. Minnesota (which tied Michigan, 6-6, in 1903), coached by Dr. Henry Williams, wound up 3-0 in the Conference and 11-0 overall. Michigan, coached by Fielding Yost, was 2-0 in league play and 10-0 overall. Minnesota outscored its foes, 618-12; Michigan was better than its opponents, 567-22. Chicago wasn't far behind. It finished 5-1-1 in the Conference—8-1-1 overall—and became the first league team to place two men on the All-America squad: quarterback Walter Eckersall and end Fred Speik.

OTHER BIG TEN CHAMPIONS

- **GYMNASTICS:** Wisconsin, coached by J.C. Elsom

- **OUTDOOR TRACK:** Chicago (coach not known)

- **BASEBALL:** Michigan, coached by L. W. McAllister

CHRIS STEINMETZ
Basketball, Wisconsin

Chris Steinmetz is called the "Father of Wisconsin Baketball." He was a scorer extraordinaire who is regarded as the player who put Badger basketball on the map. He was instrumental in establishing the program—which had no coach in 1903—at the turn of the century. He was a prolific scorer decades before prolific scorers began to flourish. As team captain in 1905, he led the Badgers to an undefeated regular season and a berth in the national championship game, where they lost to Columbia. His career highlights include: 50 points in a game, 20 field goals in a game, 26 free throws in a game, 233 free throws in a season (in those days, one player could shoot all of a team's free throws), and 462 total points in a season. For years, all of the aforementioned feats were team, Conference and, in some cases, national records. He was inducted into the Wisconsin Athletic Hall of Fame in 1954.

FRANK SPEIK
Football, Chicago

Left end Frank Speik captained the 1904 University of Chicago football team that finished with an 8-1-1 record, shutting out six opponents. Only a 6-6 tie with Illinois and a 22-12 loss at Michigan marred the Maroons' season. In its eight victories, Chicago outscored its opponents by an average score of 38-2. Speik, a four-time letter winner for Chicago, won varsity monograms from 1901-04 for coach Amos Alonzo Stagg.

BASKETBALL SCORING LEADERS

Wisconsin's Chris Steinmetz was the first great scorer among Big Ten teams, registering 50 points in one game when 20 by a whole team was the norm. Since then, there have been many great scorers. Here are the Big Ten's career scoring leaders for all games:

2,613	Calbert Cheaney, Ind., 1990-93	2,157	Michael Finley, Wis., 1992-95
2,531	Shawn Respert, MSU, 1992-95	2,145	Scott Skiles, MSU, 1983-86
2,442	Glen Rice, Mich., 1986-89	2,129	Deon Thomas, Ill., 1991-94
2,439	Mike McGee, Mich., 1978-81	2,116	Roy Marble, Iowa, 1986-89
2,438	Steve Alford, Ind., 1984-87	2,103	Voshon Lenard, Minn., 1992-95
2,323	Rick Mount, Pur., 1968-70	2,096	Dennis Hopson, OSU, 1984-87
2,263	Steve Smith, MSU, 1988-91	2,074	Dave Schellhase, Pur., 1964-66
2,222	Gary Grant, Mich., 1985-88	2,061	Mike Woodson, Ind., 1977-80
2,192	Don Schlundt, Ind., 1952-55	2,028	Troy Lewis, Pur., 1985-88
2,175	Joe Barry Carroll, Pur., 1977-80	2,014	Gregory Kelser, MSU, 1976-79
2,164	Cazzie Russell, Mich., 1964-66	2,011	Herb Williams, OSU, 1976-79

BIG TEN LIST

LEADING THE WAY

THOMAS MORAN
Purdue

The Big Ten, then known as the Western Conference, was governed largely by faculty representatives from each university in the early years of existence. Thomas Moran, a Michigan alum, served as Purdue's faculty rep from 1900 to 1928, when he died. He was a professor of history and economics who emerged as a leader among the faculty representatives. In March, 1906, Michigan President James Angell called a meeting where revised eligibility rules were established, including one that permitted no more than three years of eligibility for an athlete. The rule was retroactive, meaning seniors would be ineligible the next fall. When Angell realized this, he wanted to revise that rule to allow seniors to compete in 1906-07. Moran led the opposition, and a vote taken kept the rule as it was written. Angell protested, saying Michigan would not follow the rule, and Moran drafted the resolution that essentially barred Michigan from the Conference. Michigan did not rejoin the league until 1917.

· BIG TEN PIONEERS ·

Big Ten residency rule

This was the kind of forward thinking that would make the Conference a national trend-setter throughout the years. In 1904, the Conference faculty representatives were the catalysts for a new rule that would require student-athletes to complete a full semester of work at that university before becoming eligible to compete on the intercollegiate athletics level. Freshmen would no longer be able to compete on varsity teams, and athletes would be discouraged from transferring to another school. These kinds of regulations were thought necessary because, throughout the nation, coaches were bringing in ringers, known then as "tramp athletes," to compete even though they may not have been a true student at that school.

Academic Achievements

Universities always have taught a wide range of subjects and classes. Or have they? Programs had to start somewhere, sometime. And Michigan can lay claim to being the first school to offer classes in a number of subjects: journalism, speech, American literature, pharmacy and data processing, to name a few.

The BIG TEN's First 100 Years
Most Big Ten Men's Team Championships Won By School, All-Time

248	MICHIGAN
192	ILLINOIS
116	INDIANA
113	OHIO STATE
108	WISCONSIN
105	MINNESOTA

BIG TEN
SINCE 1896
CENTENNIAL

1905-1914

1905-06

THE BIG EVENT

President Angell calls for reform

President James Burrill Angell of Michigan called a meeting—subsequently called the "Angell Conference"—for Jan. 20-22, 1906, to discuss what would be regarded as far-sighted regulations for participation in and control of intercollegiate athletics. Agreed upon and adopted the next day were the following: one year of residence would be necessary for eligibility as would the meeting of all entrance requirements and completion of a full year's work; only three years of competition would be allowed, with no graduate students having eligibility; the football season would be limited to five games; no training table or training quarters would be permitted; and prices of student and faculty tickets would not exceed 50 cents.

OTHER MEMORABLE EVENTS

- Michigan's 56-game football unbeaten streak was snapped by Chicago, 2-0, in front of a crowd of 25,791.

- Chicago's football team finished 7-0 in Conference play and 11-0 overall to win the unofficial national championship.

- Wisconsin won its first football game in three years, 16-12, over Minnesota, behind A.R. Findley's two 85-yard touchdown runs.

- Michigan's Archie Hahn, Chicago's James Lightbody and Purdue's Ray Ewry all repeated as Olympic champions.

Minnesota earns first basketball championship

Minnesota had won a plethora of basketball games—including back-to-back undefeated seasons—under legendary coach L.J. Cooke during his first eight years at the helm. But it wasn't until the 1905-06 campaign that the Gophers won the first of five Big Ten championships they collected under Cooke. The 1905-06 season marked the first that the league recognized a champion. The Gophers posted a 6-1 Conference slate, were 13-2 overall and nudged out second-place Wisconsin for the title. The Badgers had an overall record identical to Minnesota's, but played and lost one more Conference game. The Gophers were led that year by center George Tuck, their first-ever first-team All-American. The 1905-06 season paved the way for a successful Big Ten title defense in 1907, when first team All-America guard Garfield Brown led the way. Minnesota, which was 6-2 in the Conference and 10-2 overall, shared the 1907 crown with Wisconsin and Chicago. The Gophers went on to win Big Ten titles in 1911, '17, and '19 under Cooke, who coached from 1897 until 1924. His career record at Minnesota was 238-122.

OTHER BIG TEN CHAMPIONS

- **FOOTBALL:** Chicago, coached by A.A. Stagg

- **BASEBALL:** Illinois, coached by George Huff

- **GYMNASTICS:** No record

- **OUTDOOR TRACK:** Michigan (no coach)

HUGO BEZDEK
Football, Chicago

Hugo Bezdek, a native of Prague, Czechoslovakia who grew up on the tough South Side of Chicago, was an All-America fullback for Amos Alonzo Stagg's 1905 squad that won Chicago's first Big Ten football championship. He also played second base in baseball for the Maroons. Bezdek went on to an illustrious coaching career and garnered a reputation as a stern taskmaster at Oregon, Arkansas and Penn State. His Oregon team won the 1917 Rose Bowl over Penn. From 1917-19, Bezdek then managed the National League's Pittsburgh Pirates for three years. He then moved to Penn State from 1918-36, Bezdek posted a 65-30-11 record in 12 years as head coach and also served as athletic director. He had consecutive undefeated seasons in 1920 and 1921 and was named to the National Football Foundation Hall of Fame in 1954 and the Helms Hall in 1960. Bezdek died in 1952.

WALTER "BABE" MEIGS
Football, Basketball and Swimming, Chicago

Walter C. "Babe" Meigs certainly is one of the few former football players to have an airfield named after him—Meigs Field on Chicago's lakefront. The Iowa-born Meigs, who became a Chicago newspaper publisher and aviation pioneer, began his athletic career under the tutelage of Amos Alonzo Stagg. A tough, brilliant lineman on Stagg's 1905 Maroon squad which won Chicago's first Big Ten title, Meigs was called "a perfect specimen of the young college athlete" by Stagg. Meigs, who acquired the lifelong nickname "Babe" at the university, also swam and starred on the great Chicago basketball teams of that early era. In 1954, he served on the panel that selected the site for the U.S. Air Force Academy. Meigs remained an active flyer after age 80, taking up a co-pilot with him as a concession to age. He died in 1968 at age 84.

BIG TEN LIST

BASKETBALL TITLES

Purdue has won a record 21 Big Ten men's basketball championships. Here's how many titles each school has won:

	Total Championships	Shared Titles
Chicago	6	3
Illinois	12	6
Indiana	19	8
Iowa	8	4
Michigan	12	5
Michigan State	6	3
Minnesota	8	4
Northwestern	2	1
Ohio State	15	5
Penn State	0	0
Purdue	21	10
Wisconsin	14	8

LEADING THE WAY

Charles Baird

Charles Baird served as Michigan's first athletic director from 1898-1908, during which time Michigan established itself as one of the premier programs in the fledgling intercollegiate athletics movement. Baird had captained the 1897 Michigan team that went 6-1-1 and placed third in the Big Ten. His most notable move may have been the hiring in 1901 of Fielding Yost, who would guide Michigan football to 10 Big Ten titles in 25 years as coach.

· BIG TEN PIONEERS ·

Emmett Angell
Wisconsin

Emmett Angell was a Big Ten basketball pioneer—and legendary figure—in more ways than one. A gifted student of the game as well as an insightful teacher of it, Angell was the Big Ten's first scoring champion in 1906, the same year the league began recognizing team champions. Angell scored 96 points that season, leading Wisconsin to a 12-2 overall record, a 6-2 Big Ten mark and a runner-up finish in the Conference standings. Angell averaged 6.9 points per game in immortalizing himself as the league's first in a long line of distinguished scoring champions. He also served as Wisconsin's coach that same season, immortalizing himself as the first and only basketball player in Big Ten history to star concurrently as a player and as a coach, doing so between 1905 and 1908. He guided the Badgers to consecutive Big Ten championships in 1907 and '08.

Academic Achievements

"We is, very excited I goes to the grocery store." If that sentence doesn't seem quite write—er, right—it's because Chicago has done an excellent job of getting you to right—er, write—it right. It was 1906 when The Chicago Manual of Style premiered. Just 21 pages long, the Style Book contained 169 rules of grammar and is the basis of every grammar book on the market today.

Emmett Angell

BIG TEN
SINCE 1896
CENTENNIAL
™

THE BIG EVENT

Chicago wins first of four straight basketball titles

Chicago shared its first Big Ten basketball title with Minnesota and Wisconsin in 1906-07 as all three teams posted 6-2 Big Ten records, although the Maroons' 22-2 overall mark was clearly superior to the Gophers' 13-2 and the Badgers' 11-3 records. Beginning with the 1907-08 season, basketball entered a golden era on the Midway as Chicago posted a 7-1 Conference mark and then beat Wisconsin for the right to meet Eastern champion Penn for the "national" championship, which Chicago earned by beating the Quakers. The Maroons finished 21-2. The next two seasons were also glorious for UC basketball, which had been upgraded from minor to major sport status after the 1907-08 season. The Maroons responded with a 12-0 Conference and overall mark in 1908 for their only unbeaten season and then carved out a 9-3 record in 1909-10 for their fourth straight Big Ten championship.

OTHER MEMORABLE EVENTS

- Northwestern discontinued its football program for two years because of the state of the game on a national level.

- Chicago quarterback Walter Eckersall—named for the third straight year—was the Conference's lone football All-American.

- Wisconsin (3-0-0), Minnesota (2-0-0) and Michigan (1-0-0) all went undefeated and untied in Conference play to share the championship. It was the only time three teams had perfect league records.

- With the forward pass now legal, Chicago's A.A. Stagg claimed to have 64 different pass formations; however, the Maroons didn't throw a single pass all season.

- Illinois' Pomeroy Sinnock was the nation's first noted passer. He connected on more than a dozen that year.

Gill's Illinois track begins its dynasty

The Illinois track and field program had traveled a less than spectacular road during the first three seasons under coach Harry Gill. Illinois had finished no higher than fifth in the Conference track championship meet. Therefore, on a cold first day in June, the Illini could only be cautiously optimistic about what would ultimately turn out to be the greatest day of what was still a growing sport at Illinois. The Illini won the Conference title, the first Conference championship in track for a program that would later win 31 Conference titles and five NCAA championships. Already an Illinois football star, Wilbur Burroughs was the star of the championships in track, placing first in the shot put and hammer throw to account for nearly one-third of Illinois' team points. Billy May finished first in the 100-yard dash and placed second in the 220. Illinois was able to edge host Chicago, 31-29, in team scoring. During his 29-year career as Illinois track coach, Gill would lead Illinois to 19 Conference championships and two NCAA titles.

OTHER BIG TEN CHAMPIONS

- **FOOTBALL:** Michigan, coached by Fielding Yost, Minnesota, coached by Dr. Henry Williams, and Wisconsin, coached by C.P. Hutchins

- **BASEBALL:** Illinois, coached by George Huff

- **GYMNASTICS:** Minnesota, coached by Dr. W.K. Foster

- **BASKETBALL:** Chicago, Minnesota, coached by Dr. L.J. Cooke, and Wisconsin, coached by Emmett Angell

POMEROY SINNOCK
Football, Illinois

A three-year member of the Illini football team, Pomeroy Sinnock was the quarterback on a team that continued to improve under his leadership. The Illini were 1-3-1 overall and tied for fifth place in the Conference in his first season as a sophomore quarterback, then jumped to third in the Conference standings with a 3-2 record. In his senior year in 1908-09, Sinnock spearheaded an Illinois season during a campaign where the Illini finished 5-1-1 overall and 4-1 in the Conference. Illinois' second-place finish in the Conference standings was the best since the league was formed. A contractor, Sinnock died at age 76 on Oct. 10, 1962.

WALTER ECKERSALL
Football, Chicago

Chicago quarterback Walter Eckersall, a three-time member of Walter Camp's All-America team from 1904-06, was a great kicker, strategist and open-field runner who once ran for a 105-yard touchdown to beat Wisconsin. In 1905, against Michigan's "Point-a-Minute" wonders, with the ball on his own two-yard line, "Eckie" signaled for a punt but instead ran the ball to the 50. Halted again, Eckersall punted into the Michigan end zone, where the Wolverine halfback was caught for a safety, giving Chicago a 2-0 win and the Conference title. He twice kicked five field goals in a game. Weighing only 140 pounds, Eckersall drove Chicago teams at a furious pace, running more than 100 plays in a 45-minute half in the days when teams tried to wear down opponents. Eckersall became a football official and covered sports for the *Chicago Tribune*, where he worked until his death.

ROBERT K. "BOBBY" MARSHALL
Football, Minnesota

Bobby Marshall was a football pioneer at Minnesota in more ways than one. For not only was he one of the Gophers' first legitimate gridiron stars, he was also their first—and the Big Ten's first—African-American football player. He was also a standout on the Gopher's baseball, boxing, track, and hockey teams between 1904 and 1906. On the football field, however, is where his star shined brightest. He was a starting end and kicker for three years, leading Minnesota to the Conference championship in 1904 with a perfect 11-0 record. Minnesota, in fact, lost only two games during Marshall's career. He kicked a 60-yard field goal in 1906 to beat Chicago 4-2, as field goals were worth four points in those days. He later enjoyed a long career in professional football, playing for several teams until his retirement at age 44. He died Aug. 27, 1968 and was inducted posthumously into the College Football Hall of Fame.

BIG TEN LIST

INDIAN CLUBS CHAMPIONS

Labitt of Minnesota helped lead Minnesota to the Big Ten title in gymnastics by winning the Indian Clubs competition. The Indian Clubs, similar to weighted bowling pins and tossed in the air, was an event off and on from 1907 to 1931. Here are the yearly winners:

1907—Labbitt, Minnesota
1908—Nelson, Minnesota
1914—Replinger, Wisconsin
1922—Kessler, Chicago
1924—Van Meter, Purdue
1926—Van Meter, Purdue
1927—McRoy, Chicago
1928—McRoy, Chicago
1929—Bromund, Chicago
1930—Bromund, Chicago
1931—Bromund, Chicago

LEADING THE WAY

HARRY GILL
Illinois

A Canadian brought Illinois to prominence as a national track and field power. During Harry Gill's 29-year coaching career from 1904-29 and 1931-33, Illinois steamrolled the Big Ten, winning 19 team titles—11 outdoors and another eight indoors. In the 25-year span that began in 1904, Gill's teams compiled 914 points in Conference championships, more than 320 points ahead of its closest competitor. His third team at Illinois won the school's first track championship, edging Chicago by two points. The Illini won two NCAA titles—1921 and 1927—plus three Spalding Cups, an annual invitational meet that attracted the nation's top teams. The height of Gill's coaching career came in the 1924 Paris Olympics, when three Illinois athletes scored more points than any other nation in track and field. Gill also was the collegiate coach for Avery Brundage, longtime president of the International Olympic Federation, and Tug Wilson, former Olympic performer and Big Ten commissioner. Gill died in 1956 at the age of 80. The Harry Gill Company, a sporting goods manufacturer specializing in track equipment, remains in Urbana.

· BIG TEN PIONEERS ·

Wisconsin football team banned from "big games"

Perhaps no sport suffered as excruciatingly under the turn-of-the-century growing pains of intercollegiate athletics as did the Wisconsin football team. Personality clashes, ego-sparring and gross differences of opinion threatened the very existence of the Badgers' football program in 1906, when Wisconsin faculty members—awed and dismayed by the "proselytizing" and "subsidizing" of athletes—voted to abolish football. A storm of protest from fans and alumni convinced the faculty to change their minds—somewhat. Football was allowed to continue, but the Badgers were limited to a five-game schedule and barred from their "big games" against arch-rivals Chicago, Minnesota and Michigan—the only games that produced significant revenue. The Badgers won all five games in 1906 but brought in only $3,400 compared to $35,000 the previous year. Reluctantly, the faculty allowed the Badgers to add their traditional Big Ten rivals back on the schedule—but one at a time.

Academic Achievements

Iowa has always had a grand tradition in education. It was the first University in the U.S. to have a college-level department of education in the 1870s. Then in 1907, it became the first school to offer a professorship in education and today remains one of the top universities for studying education.

The BIG TEN's First 100 Years
Big Ten - Jesse Owens Men's Athlete Of The Year Award Winners By School

5 MICHIGAN
4 INDIANA
3 IOWA
1 MINNESOTA
1 OHIO STATE
1 PURDUE

BIG TEN
SINCE 1896
CENTENNIAL

THE BIG EVENT

Michigan withdraws from Big Ten

One of seven charter members of the Big Ten, Michigan withdrew from Conference membership on Jan. 14, 1908, because of a disagreement over a rules change. In meetings following the 1905 season, a rule was proposed, and passed, that would allow only three years of varsity play for all athletes. Michigan objected to the rule's retroactive application to include those student-athletes already registered.

Michigan's All-America lineman, Al Benbrook, a letterman from 1908-10, never competed as an official Big Ten player.

OTHER MEMORABLE EVENTS

- Minnesota's Dr. Henry Williams was credited with using the first "flanker" in connection with the forward pass.

- The limit on football games per season was raised from five to seven.

- Michigan lost a home football game to Penn, 6-0, snapping a 50-game home winning streak, still the third longest in NCAA history.

- Illinois became the first school to win three straight baseball titles.

- Wisconsin's Felix Zeidelhack won his second straight Conference all-around gymnastics championship.

Chicago wins Big Ten, "national" basketball titles

Chicago's 1907-08 basketball season made basketball a major sport at the University. Not only did Chicago win what was acknowledged to be its first undisputed Conference crown, but it also went on to beat Penn twice in five days by 21-18 and 16-15 scores for what was then deemed the national championship. The Maroons finished 21-2 overall and 7-1 in the Big Ten, with their only Conference loss to Wisconsin in Madison by a 29-17 count. Later victories over the Badgers by 24-19 in Bartlett, Ill., and by an 18-16 score, again in Madison, gave the Maroons the right to meet Penn, the Eastern champion. John Schommer, the team's captain and the leading scorer for the Maroons with an 11.4 average, was lauded as an All-America center. He would become the Big Ten's first three-time scoring champion.

OTHER BIG TEN CHAMPIONS

- **FOOTBALL:** Chicago, coached by A.A. Stagg
- **BASEBALL:** Illinois, coached by George Huff
- **GYMNASTICS:** Wisconsin, coached by J.C. Elsom
- **OUTDOOR TRACK:** Chicago

WALTER STEFFEN
Football, Chicago

Walter "Wally" Steffen, another great quarterback for Amos Alonzo Stagg's championship football teams at the start of the 20th century, was the first man to use the forward pass as a feint. The wiley Stagg was quick to take advantage of the new rule allowing the pass and the swift, versatile Steffen—who could run equally well to his right or his left—was the perfect man to fake out his opponents. With strong hands and adept ball control, Steffen would fake to a receiver and then streak wide when the defense backed off. Selected an All-American in 1908, Steffen ran wild against Minnesota in a 29-0 win that was key to the Maroons' second consecutive Conference championship. Steffen later became a highly respected federal judge who left the bench each fall to coach Carnegie Tech.

HARLAN "PAT" PAGE
Football, Basketball and Baseball, Chicago

The first nine-time letter winner in Conference history, Harlan "Pat" Page distinguished himself on three different Big Ten championship teams at the University of Chicago. In football, Page starred at end on the Maroons' Big Ten title teams of 1907 and 1908 and quarterbacked the 1909 eleven that lost only to Minnesota. He was the starting guard on Chicago's 1908-10 basketball champs. As a pitcher with the 1909 UC baseball champs, Page was good enough to get big league offers which he spurned to stay on the Midway as baseball coach. Within three years, he had his team atop the Conference and by 1920, as basketball coach, had won the Big Ten crown. He later became football coach at Butler and at Indiana.

ADOLPH "GERMANY" SCHULTZ
Football, Michigan

Adolph "Germany" Schultz, the first of the roving centers or "linebackers", dropped back to plug holes anywhere in the line for Fielding Yost's great Michigan teams of the 20th century's first decade. Reporting to Yost fresh from Fort Wayne, Ind., in 1904, the 6-foot-2, 240 pound Schultz was immediately installed at center. His feats were such that he became the first lineman to achieve a measure of notoriety, with his play mentioned in the same breath as that of halfbacks. Although chosen All-America in 1907, Schultz was praised to the hilt by Yost in 1908 for his play against Pennsylvania, when he almost singlehandedly limited the great Quaker team to a touchdown before injuries forced him from the game. He was eventually named by Walter Camp as college football's greatest pivotman. Schultz was named to the all-time All-America team in 1955.

BIG TEN LIST

CHICAGO'S GYM CHAMPS

Chicago had 10 all-around champions at the Big Ten gymnastics championships.

1913—Parkinson
1922—Schneidenbach
1927—Floyd Davidson
1928—Floyd Davidson
1929—John Menzies
1930—John Menzies
1931—Everett Olson
1932—Everett Olson
1933—George Wrighte
1934—George Wrighte

LEADING THE WAY

DR. LOUIS J. COOKE
Minnesota

When Dr. Louis J. Cooke arrived at Minnesota in 1897 as a part-time gymnasium director, organized athletics were virtually unknown at the school. That changed abruptly when his position became full-time a year later, organizing and coaching basketball, baseball, wrestling, boxing, handball and gymnastics teams at the university. A former pitching star during his playing days at the University of Vermont, Cooke's first love was basketball. He coached the Gophers for 28 years (1897-1925) and guided them to five Big Ten championships. He coached them to back-to-back undefeated seasons in 1902 and '03, as they earned the unofficial national champion title in 1903. Cooke was nationally renowned for helping create the Little Brown Jug tradition in football in 1903. The Little Brown Jug is presented to the winner of each Minnesota-Michigan football game. Cooke retired in 1936 and died in 1943.

· BIG TEN PIONEERS ·

Avery Brundage
Illinois

He was best known for his 20-year reign as the controversial president of the International Olympic Committee, but few know that Avery Brundage's athletic career took a giant leap at Illinois. He was a member of the 1907-08 Illinois basketball team that was 20-6, and he was the discus champion in the Conference track meet in 1908-09. An Olympic decathlon competitor in 1912, Brundage won the national decathlon championship in 1916 and '18. He was president of the Amateur Athletic Union for seven years and the U.S. Olympic Committee for four years, but he's best known as an IOC administrator who fought for the Olympic ideals of amateurism. An imposing figure well into his 80s, Brundage died at 87 in 1975.

Academic Achievements

The Wisconsin Union was founded in 1907 as one of the first student unions in the nation (second only to Harvard). Among its firsts: established the first craft shop housed in a union, the first outing club (1931), as well as the controversial first public university union to serve beer (1933). And finally, it was the first union to house a theater.

Avery Brundage

THE BIG EVENT

Chicago's Walter Comstock.

First cross country championship

Although the first Big Ten cross country championship was conducted in 1908 at Chicago, the Conference would have to wait another year before one of its own won the team title. That's because outsider Nebraska won the first event, outdistancing runner-up Purdue by a score of 41-51 (as in golf, the lowest score in cross country signifies the winner). Chicago's Walter Comstock, however, was the first Big Ten individual champion in that first meet, run on a five-mile course. Minnesota became the league's first team champion in 1909, outpacing Nebraska, 40-50, on the same Chicago course. Purdue's H.B. Wasson won the individual title with a time of 27:08, just more than a minute faster than Comstock's time the previous year. Minnesota's F.O. Watson was the first runner to win more than one individual championship, earning three between 1913 and 1915. He led the Gophers to the team title in 1914. Wisconsin has easily won the most team championships with 31 and boasts the most individual champions with 19.

OTHER MEMORABLE EVENTS

- **Chicago's basketball team became the first to go undefeated in the Conference (12-0) and was considered the No. 1 team in the nation.**

- **Chicago's football team also went undefeated (for the second straight year) to win the league title.**

- **Chicago quarterback Wally Steffen was credited with being the first player to use a fake pass in a game.**

- **Northwestern restored its football team after a two-year hiatus.**

- **Chicago's John Schommer was the Conference's leading basketball scorer for the third straight season.**

Purdue baseball team captures first title

This was to be the first of many shining moments for Purdue in the Big Ten. The Boilermakers baseball team captured the first league championship for the school in any sport, going 11-2 overall and 7-2 in league play. It was a team that started strong, winning its first 11 games before finally losing to Illinois (5-0) and Chicago (7-2) in its last two games. Along the way, the Boilermakers got past Rose Poly (8-3), Wisconsin (7-6), Indiana (7-2), DePauw (6-4), Northwestern (12-1), Earlham (3-0), DePauw (4-1), Northwestern (8-3), Illinois (4-3), Wisconsin (3-2) and Chicago (2-1). Walt Tragesser, a first baseman and catcher, was the team captain. Other members of the championship squad: W.G. Hier (first base), Lou Geupel (second base), H.P. Binder (shortstop), Bert Westover (third base), Fred Boltz (outfield), P.R. Brown (outfield), Carl Dalton (outfield), DeCamp Myers (outfield), P.F. Sargent (outfield), Ray Rosenbaum (catcher), Dave Charters (pitcher) and Raleigh Shade (pitcher). Unofficially, Myers (.354) and Shade (.323) led the team in hitting, and Shade was also the top pitcher at 10-2.

OTHER BIG TEN CHAMPIONS

- FOOTBALL: Chicago, coached by A.A. Stagg

- GYMNASTICS: Chicago (coach not known)

- OUTDOOR TRACK: Illinois, coached by Harry Gill

- BASKETBALL: Chicago (coach not known)

- +CROSS COUNTRY: Nebraska
+open meet

FOREST VAN HOOK
Football, Illinois

Forest Van Hook, captain of the 1908 Illinois football team, was the first Illini to earn All-Western honors each of the three seasons he lettered. An outstanding guard for coach Arthur Hall, Van Hook and his teammates had their best performance in 1908 during his senior season. The 5-1-1 Illini lost their only game, 11-6, at Chicago and eventually placed second in the Conference standings to the undefeated Maroons. Van Hook was a burly, dark-haired man, weighing around 230 pounds, a huge person in those days. Walter Eckersall, long-time sports editor of the *Chicago Tribune* and college football's most noted critic, said that despite his size "Van" could have starred at any position on the field. Van Hook was a medical general practicioner in his hometown of Mt. Pulaski, Ill., until his death in 1937 from diabetes at the age of 52.

JOHN SCHOMMER
Basketball, Chicago

Center John Schommer was player of the year as a senior in the 1908-09 season as the Chicago Maroons won their third of four consecutive Big Ten titles. "Long John," as he was known, led the Conference in scoring with 95, 105 and 104 points, respectively, from 1907-09 as the Maroons went 55-4 overall and 25-3 in Conference play. Not until Indiana's Don Schlundt accomplished the feat from 1953-55 would the Big Ten again have a three-time scoring leader. Schommer would later become one of the Conference's leading football and basketball referees.

WALTER "PHIL" COMSTOCK
Cross Country, Chicago

Walter "Phil" Comstock outsprinted Purdue's Bob Kinkhead to become the Big Ten's first individual champ in cross country on Nov. 14, 1908, running a five-mile course at Chicago in 28:12. Nebraska won the team title with 41 points to Purdue's 51, Wisconsin's 59, Chicago's 69 and Drake's 105. Though Chicago never won a Big Ten cross country team championship during its half century as a member of the Big Ten Conference, Comstock was one of three Maroon runners who claimed individual titles.

BASKETBALL SCORING CHAMPS

Chicago's John Schommer won three consecutive Conference basketball scoring titles from 1907-09. A total of 15 men have won scoring titles in consecutive years:

John Schommer, Chicago, 1907-08-09
Jewell Young, Purdue, 1937-38
Max Morris, Northwestern, 1945-46
Don Rehfeldt, Wisconsin, 1949-50
Don Schlundt, Indiana, 1953-54-55
Archie Dees, Indiana, 1957-58
Terry Dischinger, Purdue, 1960-61-62
Gary Bradds, Ohio State, 1963-64
Rick Mount, Purdue, 1968-69-70
Mike Robinson, Michigan State, 1972-73
Terry Furlow, Michigan State, 1975-76
Mychal Thompson, Minnesota, 1977-78
Jay Vincent, Michigan State, 1980-81
Glen Rice, Michigan, 1988-89
Glenn Robinson, Purdue, 1993-94

LEADING THE WAY

HUGH NICOL
Purdue

Before becoming Purdue's baseball coach and athletic director in 1906, Hugh Nicol had established himself as a professional baseball standout for 10 years. As a player with the Chicago Whitestockings, St. Louis Browns and Cincinnati Reds, Nicol had a career batting average of .254. He stole 138 bases while playing for Cincinnati in 1887 and stole 103 the next season. He also scored 122 and 112 runs during those two seasons. In addition to his primary position in the outfield, he also played second base, shortstop and third base during his career. He was later manager of the Browns (1897-1900). As Purdue's athletic director, Nicol was known as a good businessman and an efficient, congenial person with whom to work. He resigned from Purdue in 1914 for health-related reasons. He died in 1921 at age 63. A native of Campsie, Scotland, Nicol came to the United States with his family when he was a child and settled in Rockford, Ill. He coached the Rockford Red Sox of the Three I League in 1901-02 and won the pennant in '02.

· BIG TEN PIONEERS ·

Chicago and Minnesota join NCAA

From its inception in 1906, the National Collegiate Athletic Association has had strong support from Big Ten universities, with Chicago and Minnesota among the early members that helped establish the NCAA. Its formation came with the decidedly strong encouragement of U.S. President Theodore Roosevelt, who decried the increasing violence in college football and called upon the nation's universities to police their own programs or face their elimination. One of the first meetings of Big Ten Conference presidents to discuss necessary reform was the "Angell Conference," called by Michigan president James B. Angell at the behest of professors at various colleges. Measures were adopted at that Jan. 20-22, 1906 meeting and eventually became the forerunners to NCAA regulation.

Academic Achievements

Among the most famous alumni from Indiana University are: NBC newscaster, Jane Pauley; former Supreme Court Justice, Sherman Minton; World War II correspondent and Pulitzer Prize winner, Ernie Pyle; CEO and chairman of the board of Ford Motor Co., Harold "Red" Poling; actress Patricia Kalember; actor Kevin Kline; and women's rights activist, Jill Strickland Ruckelshaus.

The BIG TEN's First 100 Years
Big Ten Baseball
Season Average Records

PITCHING (ERA)
0.99 MINNESOTA, 1966

BATTING AVERAGE
.398 OHIO STATE, 1994

FIELDING PERCENTAGE
.986 ILLINOIS, 1981

THE BIG EVENT

First Conference tennis championship

Paul Gardner

The first Big Ten tennis championship was hosted by Chicago, which shared the team title with Minnesota. Chicago and Minnesota, in fact, dominated the first several years, as Chicago won or shared five championships from 1910-18. Minnesota won or shared the title four times during the same span, including three straight wins from 1910-12. Chicago's Paul Gardner was the first singles champion, while Minnesota's Adams and Sischo were the first champion doubles tandem. Minnesota's J.J. Armstrong was the first player in league history to win back-to-back singles championships (1911-12) and was also the first to win singles and doubles titles in the same year, which he did twice (1911 and '12). Between 1910 and '33, team champions were determined by this method: if players from one team swept singles and doubles, that team was the champion. If the singles and doubles split, co-champions were named.

OTHER MEMORABLE EVENTS

- Conference teams went 21-2 in non-league basketball games, the best record ever.

- Michigan guard Al Benbrook was named a football All-American; he became the first Conference lineman to earn that honor two years in a row in 1910.

- Chicago's baseball team toured Japan and went 10-0.

- Chicago won its fourth straight Conference basketball championship.

- Illinois' E.B. Styles won the first of three straight Conference all-around gymnastics championships.

Illinois baseball team wins marathon versus Chicago

John Buzick pitched all 17 innings in Illinois' baseball marathon vs. Chicago.

The date was May 20, 1910, and the baseball matchup between Illinois and Chicago was described by the Illinois student newspaper as "the most brilliant game ever played on Illinois Field." The game lasted three hours and 20 minutes, and when it ended Illinois had won its 10th consecutive game under coach George Huff. The win streak lasted until Illinois had won 14 straight games, the result a Conference championship for Illinois. John Buzick and his Chicago counterpart, Pat Page, each pitched in the marathon game's 17 innings. With the score tied at one apiece, Illinois scored the decisive run in the 17th inning when Ray Thomas led off with a double, moved to third on a sacrifice by E.B. Righter, and scored when Page uncorked a wild pitch. The Illini went on to win their final four games and finished as the first school to capture the Conference baseball title with an undefeated record. The Conference title was one of 11 won by Illinois under Huff, who had spent 13 days in the 1906-07 school year with the Boston Americans professional club before he was given his release that allowed his return to Illinois.

OTHER BIG TEN CHAMPIONS

- **FOOTBALL:** Minnesota, coached by Dr. Henry Williams

- **GYMNASTICS:** Minnesota, coached by Dr. W.K. Foster

- **+OUTDOOR TRACK:** Notre Dame

- **BASKETBALL:** Chicago (coach not known)

- **CROSS COUNTRY:** Minnesota (no coach)

- **TENNIS:** Chicago (coach not known) and Minnesota (no coach)

+open meet

DAVID "BABE" CHARTERS
Basketball, Purdue

There was a reason Purdue couldn't wait to get its first "big man" on the court: in his first game, David "Babe" Charters scored 33 points in a 63-6 victory over Indiana State. At 6-foot-5, Charters was a dominating center in the era of the center jump. After each scoring play, the ball returned to the center of the court for a jump ball, and Charters would often outleap the opponent, giving Purdue the ball back. As a sophomore in 1908-09, he finished fifth in the Big Ten in scoring, but he took over as a junior, becoming the first Boilermaker to become the league's scoring leader (11.2 points per game). Charters was the school's first basketball All-American, an honor he received two straight years. The Peru, Ind., native also was first-team All-Big Ten two years in a row. He helped Purdue win a share of its first Big Ten championship in 1911, his senior year.

PAUL GARDNER
Tennis, Chicago

Before future Big Ten tennis stars Marty Riessen, Victor Amaya and Todd Martin were even born, it was a man named Paul Gardner who ruled the courts. In the spring of 1910 on the clay courts of the University of Chicago, Gardner became the Conference's very first Big Ten singles titlist, defeating Illinois' Dale Wiley by scores of 6-1 and 6-2 in the finals. Fourteen other Maroon players would eventually follow in Gardner's footsteps as the Big Ten singles champion. The Maroons won the team championship over Minnesota, the first of 20 tennis titles that Chicago teams would win or share over the next 30 years.

JOHN McGOVERN
Football, Minnesota

Few football players were made as durably—or as multi-talented and versatile—as John McGovern, a standout quarterback and defensive player for Minnesota from 1908-10. He was a two-time All-Big Ten selection in 1909 and '10 and was a consensus first team All-American in 1909. McGovern was also an outstanding defensive player, as he routinely played both sides of the ball for the Gophers. Incredibly, he missed only one game during his three seasons because of injury — a powerful testimony to his toughness during an era when players wore little padding and typically played both offense and defense. McGovern was inducted into the College Football Hall of Fame in 1966. He was inducted into Minnesota's 'M' Club Hall of Fame in 1995.

FOOTBALL RIVALRIES

BIG TEN LIST

- Little Brown Jug (Michigan-Minnesota, started in 1909)
- Old Oaken Bucket (Purdue-Indiana, 1925)
- Illibuck (Illinois-Ohio State, 1925)
- Floyd of Rosedale (Minnesota-Iowa, 1935)
- Purdue Cannon (Purdue-Illinois, 1943)
- Sweet Sioux Tomahawk (Illinois-Northwestern, 1945)
- Paul Bunyan Axe (Wisconsin-Minnesota, 1948)
- Old Brass Spittoon (Michigan State-Indiana, 1950)
- Governor of Michigan (Michigan-Michigan State, 1953)
- Governors' Victory Bell (Penn State-Minnesota, 1993)
- Land Grant Trophy (Penn State-Michigan State, 1993)

LEADING THE WAY

W.K. FOSTER
Minnesota

The second of only seven men who've served as head coaches of Minnesota's men's gymnastics team was W.K. Foster, who led the Golden Gophers from 1908 through 1929. One of Foster's two Big Ten team titles as UM's coach came in 1910. That squad was led by high bar and rings champion Roy Calloway, high bar titlist Russell Baker, and parallel bars specialist Elmer Haeberle. Foster's 1925 team also won the Conference championship. The '25 squad starred seven-time individual champ Julius Pearlt, who later gained additional fame as the long-time Gophers' basketball public address voice. Foster's Gopher gym teams were runners-up in the Conference standings twice, and place third on six other occasions.

· BIG TEN PIONEERS ·

James Patten,
Northwestern

Northwestern's Patten Gymnasium was one of the finest athletic facilities of its day, housing the school's basketball, swimming and track teams, with room left over for other sports to conduct practice. It was the gift of James A. Patten, a wealthy Chicago grain broker and a member of the University's board of trustees, who in 1909 donated what he called "pocket money" — $330,000 — to build the facility. He also set aside a fund for maintenance. The gymnasium, which had a capacity of 6,000 for basketball, an impressive size in its day, also was used for commencement exercises and music festivals.

Academic Achievements

I f you want to be an art teacher, the top place to learn is Ohio State University. As early as 1874, OSU students could study Mechanical and Freehand Drawing. A short time later a Department of Art was started and in 1910, a four-year degree program was instituted in the College of Education emphasizing the teaching of art, as opposed to creating art.

James A. Patten

THE BIG EVENT

Big Ten holds inaugural indoor track and swimming championships

Northwestern's Patten Gymnasium hosted the first Big Ten indoor track championships.

The 1911 campaign marked the introduction of Big Ten championship competition in what would become two staple sports: swimming and indoor track. Illinois was the dominant team in both sports in the early years. The Illini won the first three Conference swimming championships and won four of the first six indoor track titles. The other two were won by coach Amos Alonzo Stagg's Chicago Maroons, including the inaugural event at Northwestern's Patten Gymnasium, where the first 12 meets were held. Patten Gym was the first indoor facility of its kind in the Midwest and featured a spacious in-field and a 10-lane track. Chicago edged Illinois, 36-33, to win the first meet. As for swimming, the first 11 swimming championships were also held at Northwestern, where the Illini won the first meet ahead of Northwestern, Chicago and Wisconsin, which finished in a three-way tie for second place. Illinois, led by W.R. Vosburgh, won four of the seven events in that first meet, with Vosburgh picking up blue ribbons in the 40-yard freestyle and 100-yard freestyle races.

OTHER MEMORABLE EVENTS

- Illinois' football team went 4-0 in the Conference and 7-0 overall for its first unde-feated season.

- Ohio State's 3-3 tie with Michigan marked the first time the Buckeyes scored against the Wolverines since the football series began in 1897 and spurred OSU to seek Conference membership.

- The faculty representatives voted to prohibit games against any university that had ceased to be a Conference member, forcing schools to drop Michigan from their schedules.

Illinois' perfect football season

Illinois' football team's unbeaten, unscored upon season of 1910 is a feat that's been duplicated only 19 times in the history of college football. Despite those successes, Illinois only tied for the Conference title with Minnesota, which also went undefeated in league play. Though coach Arthur Hall's squad wasn't an offensive juggernaut, averaging just 13 points a game, it was an immovable force when it came to playing defense. In fact, their opponents rarely crossed Illinois' 50-yard line the entire season. The Illini opened their campaign with easy non-Conference victories over Millikin and Drake before the school's historic first Homecoming game on Oct. 15, a 3-0 win over Chicago. Two weeks later, Illinois shut out Purdue, then blanked Indiana and Northwestern on consecutive Saturdays to wrap up the school's very first Conference football title. Otto Seiler kicked his third game-winning field goal of the year in the season finale at home against Syracuse to give the Illini a perfect 7-0 record.

OTHER BIG TEN CHAMPIONS

- **CROSS COUNTRY:** Wisconsin, coached by Charles Wilson

- **FOOTBALL:** Illinois, coached by Arthur Hall, and Minnesota, coached by Dr. Henry Williams

- **BASEBALL:** Illinois, coached by George Huff

- **GYMNASTICS:** Illinois, coached by Leo Hana

- **+OUTDOOR TRACK:** Missouri

- **INDOOR TRACK:** Chicago (coach not known)

- **BASKETBALL:** Purdue, coached by R.R. Jones

- **TENNIS:** Minnesota (no coach)

- **SWIMMING:** Illinois, coached by George Norris

+open meet

E.B. STYLES
Gymnastics, Illinois

The headlines, almost assuredly, during the 1910-11 school year centered on Illinois' football team, a squad that posted an undefeated record while scoring shutouts in all seven games it played. During the same season, Illinois became the first school to hold Homecoming for its alumni, and the school also fielded a championship baseball team. Unheralded went the accomplishment of E.B. Styles, who helped lead Illinois to its first Conference title in gymnastics. Styles, R.J. Roarke, Edward Hollman and Harry Geist combined to sweep all the individual events to place the Illini ahead of runner-up and host Chicago. The following season, Styles won his second consecutive all-around championship to lead Illinois to its second straight team title, this time ahead of runner-up Wisconsin.

NORMAN PAINE
Football, Chicago

Norman Paine followed Walter Eckersall and Walter Steffen in a series of great Chicago quarterbacks who coach Amos Alonzo Stagg used artfully as rules changed to favor quarterback options. In 1910, for the first time, a quarterback could run anywhere with the ball instead of at least five yards left or right of the center. Paine learned to fake to the fullback or halfback, then whirl around and into the line over center or guard. It was the first offensive spinner and allowed an offense to do all sorts of things to confound a defense. That Stagg suffered through a rare losing season, with the Maroons posting only two wins against five shutout losses, may have made the crafty Stagg more amenable to new rules which helped his offense move the ball.

JIM WALKER
Football, Minnesota

An All-America lineman named Jim Walker was the man around whom the Minnesota football team built its championship squads in 1909 and 1910. The burly tackle helped the Gophers to a cumulative 12-2 overall record and a 5-0 mark in Conference play. Walker played a key role in Minnesota's defensive effort of 1910 which saw it team post six shutouts and allow only six total points to its opponents. In its lone defeat that year, a 6-0 thriller at the hands of Michigan, Walker blocked a Wolverine punt which was scooped up by a teammate and run into the endzone for an apparent touchdown. However, one of the officials nullified the Gopher score. Walker earned All-Big Ten and All-America honors both his junior and senior seasons.

MULTIPLE TENNIS WINNERS

BIG TEN LIST

Minnesota's J.J. Armstrong won back-to-back Conference tennis singles titles in 1911 and '12. There have been a total of 11 men with multiple singles crowns:

J.J. Armstrong, Minnesota, 1911-12
Walter Westbrook, Michigan, 1919-20
Thomas O'Connell, Illinois, 1926-27-28
Scott Rexinger, Chicago, 1930-31
Seymour Greenberg, Northwestern, 1940-41
Ted Peterson, Northwestern, 1947-49
Barry MacKay, Michigan, 1956-57
Marty Riessen, Northwestern, 1962-63-64
Victor Amaya, Michigan, 1973-74
Francis Gonzalez, Ohio State, 1975-76
Ernie Fernandez, Ohio State, 1979-81-82

LEADING THE WAY

BRANCH RICKEY
Michigan

Branch Rickey (right), who would change baseball forever by bringing Jackie Robinson to the major leagues as the first African-American player, served as Michigan's head baseball coach from 1910-13 while attending law school. Rickey guided the Wolverines to a 69-31-4 mark in his four seasons, including a 21-4-1 mark in his last year, but never could win a Big Ten title since Michigan had withdrawn from the Conference. Rickey always had a great eye for talent, and as Michigan's coach spotted the ability of future hall of famer George Sisler, who not only became an all-time Michigan great but eventually joined the St. Louis Browns when Rickey managed them. Rickey also steered major league pitcher Ray Fisher (left) toward Michigan when the baseball job opened. Rickey invented baseball's farm system in 1919 while president of the St. Louis Cardinals and also instituted Ladies' Day, the batting cage and the sliding pit. But Rickey is best remembered for signing Robinson to a major league contract with the Brooklyn Dodgers in 1947, breaking baseball's unwritten color barrier. Rickey was named to the baseball Hall of Fame in 1963.

· BIG TEN PIONEERS ·

The First Homecoming

Clarence Williams and Elmer Ekblaw aren't familiar names in the world of college athletics, but the two former Illinois students are credited as the inventors of Homecoming weekend, a regular event on each college campus every fall. Williams and Ekblaw, the editor of the *Daily Illini* newspaper, conceived the idea in the fall of 1909. They brought the idea before a student panel, then called upon President Edmund James and Dean Thomas Arkle Clark. A year later, during the first Homecoming weekend — Oct. 14-16— officials and students welcomed back to campus more than 1,500 alumni, nearly one-third of the school's graduates. The culmination of the weekend was a 3-0 win over Chicago, a football game decided on a field goal by Otto Seiler.

Academic Achievements

The Land Grant Act was passed by the U.S. Congress in 1862 and provided for public land sale to benefit agricultural education. Today there is one university in each state designated as the Land-Grant Institution. Michigan State was the inaugural school. Other Big Ten schools with Land Grant status are: Illinois, Minnesota, Ohio State, Penn State, Purdue and Wisconsin.

The first Homecoming game.

THE BIG EVENT

Ohio State joins Conference

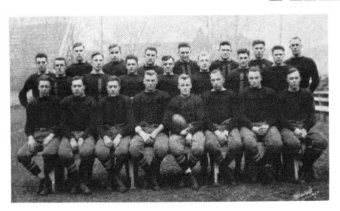

The Ohio State-Michigan football rivalry began in 1897 and eventually was a catalyst for the Buckeyes joining what was then the Western Conference. The schools met every year starting in 1900 in an annual showdown, and that gave Ohio State cause to think twice about joining the league. Michigan had left the Conference in 1908, and there was a rule prohibiting a league member from competing against a team that had left the league. So, Ohio State's membership would mean an end to its rivalry with the Wol-

The 1916 Buckeye football team won Ohio State's first Big Ten championship in that sport since it became a member four years earlier.

verines. Still, Ohio State applied for membership on Jan. 26, 1912, and was admitted on April 12, 1912. Ohio State made it clear that it wanted Michigan back in the fold. Michigan was invited to return to the league in June 1917 and accepted five months later, setting the stage for one of college football's most intense and storied football rivalries to continue.

OTHER MEMORABLE EVENTS

- The Conference voted that the faculty representative at each university must be a person who receives no pay connected with athletics or the department of physical culture.

- Michigan's Ralph Craig won the 100 and 200-meter dashes at the Olympics in Stockholm.

- No Conference players were named to the All-America football team, the last time that's happened.

- Wisconsin basketball star Otto Stangel scored 177 points, the first time anyone had exceeded the magic plateau of 150.

Boilermakers and Badgers share basketball crown

Purdue's 1911-12 team went 12-0 and captured a share of the Big Ten title.

It was unfortunate that Purdue and Wisconsin never faced each other during this season. Both went unbeaten in the league (10-0) and shared the Big Ten Conference championship. They defeated some of the same opponents. Officials tried but failed to get a postseason showdown arranged. The Boilermakers, who finished 12-0 overall, were never really challenged all season. No opponent scored more than 23 points, and only one opponent came within 10 points. The Boilermakers outscored their opponents 462-179. Chicago twice gave Purdue a game, losing 33-23 in West Lafayette and 31-22 in Chicago. Purdue's victories included such lopsided scores as: 51-12 over Butler, 67-8 over Earlham, 54-18 over Indiana and 45-11 over the Hoosiers. Purdue had four regulars returning from its 1910-11 co-Big Ten championship team, including leading scorer and team captain Ed McVaugh and defensive star Karp Stockton, who was named first-team All-Big Ten. The other starters on the team were leading scorer J.J. Malarkey (13.4 ppg), C.R. "Crow" Barr and G.W. Johnson. Coach Ralph Jones, who liked his teams to push the ball up the court, left after this season—his third at Purdue—to coach at Illinois.

OTHER BIG TEN CHAMPIONS

- **FOOTBALL:** Minnesota, coached by Dr. Henry Williams

- **BASEBALL:** Wisconsin, coached by Gordon "Slim" Lewis

- **GYMNASTICS:** Illinois, coached by Leo Hana

- **+OUTDOOR TRACK:** California

- **INDOOR TRACK:** Illinois, coached by Harry Gill

- **+CROSS COUNTRY:** Iowa State

- **TENNIS:** Minnesota (no coach)

- **SWIMMING:** Illinois, coached by E.J. Manley

+open meet

WILLIS "FAT" O'BRIEN
Football, Iowa

Willis "Fat" O'Brien, who lettered from 1909-11 for the Iowa Hawkeyes, was a rarity in his day. An outstanding center, he also was a star field goal kicker. As an athlete for UI head coaches John Griffith and Jess Hawley, he had a 52-yard drop kick against Minnesota in 1911, the longest field goal in the nation that year.

RALPH CRAIG
Track, Michigan

Michigan's Ralph Craig was the Olympic sprint champion in the 100- and 200-meters in 1912. He also became an Olympian as a yachtsman. Craig's brother, James, was an All-America halfback for the Wolverine football team, serving as a ball carrier and as a defensive back.

OTTO STANGEL
Basketball, Wisconsin

Otto Stangel played only one season for Wisconsin, but made the most of it. He led the undefeated Badgers to the 1911-12 Big Ten basketball championship by leading the Conference in scoring with 177 points—a league record that stood until 1920. Wisconsin was designated the 1912 national champion by Helms Athletic Foundation. Stangel's career highlight came in a 38-12 win against Iowa, when he scored a then-record 13 field goals. At 5-feet-6 and 145 pounds, he was regarded as one of the quickest, most athletic players of his time. A native of Tisch Mills, Wisc., he was the second player in Badgers' history to lead the Conference in scoring. He was inducted into the Wisconsin Athletic Hall of Fame in 1995.

■ BASKETBALL COACHING WINS

BIG TEN LIST

Here are the top 15 coaches with the most victories in Big Ten Conference basketball games:

316, Bob Knight, Indiana (1972-)
228, Ward Lambert, Purdue (1917, 1919-45)
214, Lou Henson, Illinois (1976-96)
210, Branch McCracken, Indiana (1935-43, 1947-65)
191, Gene Keady, Purdue (1981-)
182, Jud Heathcote, MSU (1976-95)
174, Harry Combes, Illinois (1948-67)
158, Fred Taylor, OSU (1959-76)
158, Walter Meanwell, Wisconsin (1912-17, 1921-34)
154, Harold Olsen, OSU (1923-46)
143, Harold Foster, Wisconsin (1935-59)
138, Arthur Lonborg, NU (1928-50)
120, John Orr, Michigan (1969-80)
112, L.J. Cooke, Minnesota (1897-1924)
103, Dave MacMillan, Minnesota (1927-42, 1945-48)

LEADING THE WAY

WALTER MEANWELL
Wisconsin

Walter Meanwell, known as "The Little Doctor" by his players, was the man responsible for propelling the Wisconsin basketball team into national prominence. A native of Leeds, England, who was raised in Rochester, N.Y., Meanwell came to Wisconsin in 1911 to serve as gymnasium director and coach of the wrestling and basketball teams. Although he did not play college basketball, Meanwell—a practicing physician who received a medical degree from Maryland in 1909—was regarded as one of the sport's first geniuses. At Wisconsin, he employed a revolutionary complex system that involved short passes, pivots, criss-cross passes, dribbling and short shots. A perfectionist and stickler for details, Meanwell was sometimes known as "The Little Giant" because of his frequent outbursts when execution didn't meet his standards. His methods were remarkably successful, however, as the Badgers posted a 256-99 record—including the postseason—during his 20-year tenure. Wisconsin won eight Big Ten championships under Meanwell, including a pair of undefeated campaigns in 1912 and '14. The Badgers had only five losing seasons under Meanwell, who gave up coaching at the end of the 1934 season and served as Wisconsin's athletic director until 1936. He died after complications from surgery at the age of 69, Dec. 2, 1953.

· BIG TEN PIONEERS ·

Buckeye Cheerleaders

Sis-boom-bah. Give me an O. Give me an H. Give me a I-I-I. Hit 'em again, hit 'em again, harder, harder. Whether it was the yelling or the inevitable, the 1911 football season was significant in that it was the first time a school paid the expenses of a cheerleader to go on the road to follow a team. Ohio State's athletic board sent Hub Atkinson on the road to cheer on the Buckeyes. Atkinson, selected in a student election, was eternally grateful. He later became a member of the school's board of trustees. Rah.

Academic Achievements

If it hadn't been for Orville and Wilbur Wright, there might have been one less department at Michigan. But then again, if it hadn't been for Michigan, there might be a lot less flying going on. Shortly after the Wrights made their historic flight, Michigan began the first program in the nation in aeronautical engineering and it's been instrumental in the field ever since.

1911 Buckeye Cheerleaders

BIG TEN
SINCE 1896
CENTENNIAL
™

1912-13

THE BIG EVENT

Badger All-Stars

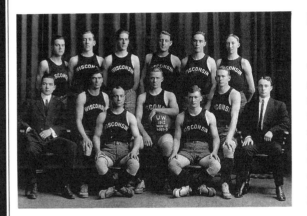

The 1912-13 season marked a banner year for Wisconsin's football and basketball teams, both in terms of wins and losses and in terms of All-Big Ten recognition. In football, the Badgers emerged — for the first time — as a national power. Under the direction of coach Bill Juneau, Wisconsin won the league championship with an undefeated season. The Badgers outscored their opponents, 246-29, and were led by tackle Robert "Butts" Butler, their first All-America performer. But Butler wasn't the only star. He was one of nine Badgers — a league record for a single team — named to the All-Big Ten first team. The others were Ed Samp, Ed Hoeffel, Hod Ofstie, Max Gelein, Ray Keeler, Eddie Gillette, John Van Riper, and Al Tanberg. In basketball, the Badgers — led by coach Walter "Doc" Meanwell — also enjoyed an undefeated regular season and placed an unprecedented four players on the All-Big Ten first team. They were Gene Van Gent; Allan Johnson; Carl Harper; and Van Riper (who also was on the all-league football squad).

OTHER MEMORABLE EVENTS

- The limit on basketball games was set at 12 Conference games and five non-Conference contests.

- Illinois won the indoor and outdoor track championships, the first time any school swept the two titles.

- Purdue's Elmer Oliphant scored 43 points (5 TD, 13 1XP) in a football game against Rose Poly, a Conference record that remained unbroken until 1990.

- The sport of water polo was dropped as an unofficial championship sport in the Conference after only three seasons. Illinois won all three titles.

The Big Ten's first wrestling championship

Wrestling made its debut as a Big Ten championship sport in 1913 but, as with many of the Conference's tournaments during their first several years of existence, competition for the title was open to teams outside of the league. However, Illinois and Minnesota shared the first Conference championship, which was hosted by Purdue. The 1912-13 season proved to be a year of "firsts" for Big Ten sports, as men's fencing and gymnastics also held their first league championship competitions at Purdue. As for wrestling, Indiana — in 1914 — was the first team to win sole possession of the Conference crown, edging Wisconsin 15.67 to 13. The championship would be one of 12 the Hoosiers would win or share between then and 1943, when they won their last one. In 1921, the Conference meet was open only to Big Ten teams, with Indiana winning that year. Iowa won the first of its league-record 26 championships in 1916. The Hawkeyes won 23 straight titles between 1974 and 1996. Illinois has the second most championships with 16. The last team to win the crown other than Iowa was Michigan State, which did so in 1973. Wisconsin, Northwestern, and Penn State have never won the team title.

OTHER BIG TEN CHAMPIONS

- **FOOTBALL:** Wisconsin, coached by W.J. Juneau

- **BASEBALL:** Chicago (coach not known)

- **GYMNASTICS:** Wisconsin, coached by H.D. MacChesney

- **OUTDOOR TRACK:** Illinois, coached by Harry Gill

- **INDOOR TRACK:** Illinois, coached by Harry Gill

- **BASKETBALL:** Wisconsin, coached by Dr. Walter Meanwell

- **CROSS COUNTRY:** Wisconsin, coached by Clarence Cleveland

- **TENNIS:** Chicago (coach not known)

ROBERT BUTLER
Football, Wisconsin

Robert "Butts" Butler, a native of Glen Ridge, N.J., was a standout tackle for the Wisconsin football team from 1910-14. He won the prestigious "W" Award in 1911, 1912 and 1913. He was a key figure on the Badgers' undefeated Big Ten championship team of 1912. He was a Walter Camp All-American that same season, named to the same team that included the legendary Jim Thorpe of Carlisle. Butler was also a first-team All-Big Ten selection in 1912 and 1913. Between 1911 and '13, the Badgers posted a 15-4-2 record. In 1912, he played in a game against Minnesota in which all 11 Wisconsin starters played the entire game. He was inducted into the National Football Foundation Hall of Fame in 1972 and was inducted into the Wisconsin Athletic Hall of Fame in 1992. He briefly played professional football for the Canton Bulldogs.

CLARK SHAUGHNESSY
Football, Basketball and Track, Minnesota

Clark Shaughnessy was one of the most versatile athletes in Minnesota's history. In 1912-13, he played end, tackle and fullback and won All-Big Ten football honors; starred as a guard on Minnesota's basketball team; and ran the 440, 880 and competed in field events, in track. Later, after coaching at Tulane and Chicago, he went to Stanford to become the father of the modern T-formation. It was 1940 and Shaughnessy was in his first season at Stanford when the football world got a revolutionary style of football that would forever change the game. The "T"—with the quarterback taking the snap from directly behind the center—proved to be an offense filled with innovative tricks that left fans astonished and opponents flat-footed. Stanford was 9-0 in Shaughnessey's first regular season, then beat Nebraska, 21-13, in the 1941 Rose Bowl. That win convinced football purists that the "T" was the offense of the future.

GEORGE SISLER
Baseball, Michigan

Hall of Famer George Sisler, who had a .340 career batting average in the major leagues, first impressed Branch Rickey with his pitching prowess as a freshman, throwing a one-hitter at Rickey's Michigan varsity in 1912. Sisler won three letters for the Wolverines from 1913-15 but never played a Big Ten game since U-M was out of the Conference then. Sisler hit .404 for his U-M career while compiling a 13-3 mark on the mound with 200+ strikeouts. Sisler hit .338 for Rickey's St. Louis Browns during the 1916-19 dead ball era and then hit .407, .371 and .420 with the addition of the lively ball. Sisler played 15 seasons with St. Louis, Washington and Boston and managed the Browns from 1924-27. He was elected to the Hall of Fame in 1939.

BIG TEN LIST

WINNINGEST FOOTBALL COACHES

Here are the top 15 football coaches with the most overall victories while coaching in the Big Ten Conference:

243, Amos Alonzo Stagg, Chi. (1892-1932)
205, Woody Hayes, OSU (1951-78)
194, Bo Schembechler, Mich. (1969-89)
165, Fielding Yost, Mich. (1901-23, '25-26)
140, Henry Williams, Minn. (1900-21)
131, Bob Zuppke, Ill. (1913-41)
124, Hayden Fry, Iowa (1979-)
109, Duffy Daugherty, MSU (1954-72)
98, John Pont, Ind.-NU (1965-77)
93, Bernie Bierman, Minn. (1932-41, '45-50)
86, Murray Warmath, Minn. (1954-71)
84, Jack Mollenkopf, Pur. (1956-69)
83, Ray Eliot, Ill. (1942-59)
81, Fritz Crisler, Mich. (1930-31, 1938-47)
78, John Wilce, OSU (1913-28)

LEADING THE WAY

ED MANLEY
Illinois

For 41 years, the name Ed Manley was synonymous with Illinois swimming. He was lured to Champaign-Urbana by Illini athletic director George Huff in 1912 from Springfield, Mo., where he served as an aquatic instructor. Manley's Illini swimming teams captured Conference titles his first two years at Illinois, and placed among the top five in the league 24 times. He also developed 20 Conference champions in the sports of water polo and water basketball, and directed those teams to dual-meet victories nearly 75 percent of the time. Manley called 1930s performer Chuck Flachmann his greatest single performer. The veteran coach was honored posthumously in 1975 when the University named the historic Huff Gymnasium natatorium the Edwin Manley Memorial Pool. Manley died in 1962 at the age of 75.

· BIG TEN PIONEERS ·

Mickey Erehart's
98-yard Run

When Indiana's Mickey Erehart took off on a 98-yard touchdown run from scrimmage in a game at Iowa on Nov. 9, 1912, he surely had no idea he was making history that would last through most of the century. Erehart's gallop wasn't matched until Minnesota's Darrell Thompson did so when the Gophers played Michigan on Nov. 7, 1987. Erehart's effort wasn't enough to bring victory, however, as the Hoosiers lost to Iowa, 13-6.

Academic Achievements

Among the most famous alumni from the University of Iowa are: former executive director of the NCAA, Dick Schultz; playwright Tennessee Williams; jazz singer Al Jarreau; NBC correspondent, John Cochran; Goodhousekeeping publisher, Alan Waxenberg; pioneer of public opinion polling, George Gallup; president and CEO of Amana, Charles Peters; and actress Mary Beth Hurt.

Mickey Erehart

BIG TEN
SINCE 1896
CENTENNIAL
TM

THE BIG EVENT

Ohio State's first Big Ten football team.

Maroons claim football title

Chicago won the Conference football title in 1913 and laid claims to national honors after going 7-0. Amos Alonzo Stagg's squad was led by halfback Nels Norgren and center Paul Des Jardiens. Three other teams lost just once in the Conference season, making it one of the closest finishes ever. Iowa tallied a then-record 310 points in seven games and missed out on the title by losing to the Maroon, 6-0. Illinois saw the college debut of coach Bob Zuppke and finished 2-2-1. Ohio State competed in the league football race for the first time and went 1-2 (4-2-1 overall) under coach John W. Wilce, a 25-year-old medical student and former star at Wisconsin. There were 76 loyal rooters who made the Buckeyes' first road trip to Wisconsin, including four who shipped themselves as "blind baggage" at a cost of 80 cents each.

OTHER MEMORABLE EVENTS

- Wisconsin beat Parsons College, 50-0, to record the only shutout in Conference basketball history; UW was considered the No. 1 team in the nation after going 15-0.

- Northwestern's Harold Whittle led the Conference in basketball scoring, the first of four NU players to do it.

- Michigan State, still not a member of the Conference, had its first undefeated football season, led by Gideon Smith.

- At the advice of the medical staff at Wisconsin, crew was dropped as a varsity sport because the four-mile races were deemed injurious to health.

Gill's Illini trackmen sweep indoor and outdoor titles

The track team at Illinois had become a dominant force under coach Harry Gill by the time the Illini reached the 1913-14 season, having won five outdoor Conference championships in the first 10 seasons under Gill. It was a rare occasion when the Illini lost a dual meet, and they entered the 1913-14 season as the two-time defending Conference champ. During that year, the Illini cruised to the indoor and outdoor Conference team titles, a superbly balanced outfit that scored points in nearly every event. At the Conference indoor meet at Northwestern, Illinois won the championship by nine points, outdistancing runner-up Wisconsin. At the outdoor championships later that school year, the disparity between Illinois and the rest of the Conference was even greater, as the Illini won the team title, 22 points ahead of their nearest competitor. The star for Illinois was Fred Henderson, who scored first-place finishes in the 440- and 880-yard runs. The Conference title was the fifth in six years under Gill, who formed a dynasty that also won four of five Conference titles during a span in the 1920s.

OTHER BIG TEN CHAMPIONS

- **FOOTBALL:** Chicago, coached by Amos Alonzo Stagg

- **BASEBALL:** Illinois, coached by George Huff

- **GYMNASTICS:** Chicago (coach not known)

- **BASKETBALL:** Wisconsin, coached by Dr. Walter Meanwell

- **CROSS COUNTRY:** Wisconsin, coached by Thomas Jones

- **TENNIS:** Chicago (coach not known) and Illinois, coached by W.A. Oldfather

- **SWIMMING:** Northwestern, coached by Tom Robinson

- **WRESTLING:** Indiana, coached by Elmer Jones

ELMER OLIPHANT
Football and Basketball, Purdue

In just one game, Elmer Oliphant established his legacy at Purdue. Against Rose Poly in 1912, he scored 43 points in a 91-0 Boilermaker victory—a record that still stands. Oliphant went on to score 135 career points at Purdue before transferring to Army, where he scored 300 career points and was a two-time All-American at West Point. The 5-foot-7 halfback was a seven-time letter winner at Purdue but was most regarded for his football accomplishments; he was twice first-team All-Big Ten. He later became Army's first four-sport athlete—he also competed in football, basketball, baseball and track in high school and once scored 60 points in a football game—and was eventually named to the Indiana Hall of Fame and the Football Hall of Fame. He played one year in the pros with the Buffalo All-Americans, and he coached at Union College in New York for two years. Oliphant died at age 82 in 1975.

PAUL DES JARDIEN
Football, Basketball, Baseball and Track, Chicago

One of only two Chicago men— teammate Nels Norgren was the other—to win 12 letters in three years of varsity competition, 6-foot-6 Paul Des Jardien was a mainstay of teams in four sports. Nicknamed "Shorty," Des Jardien was a center on the football team, a center in basketball, a pitcher in baseball, and a weightman on the track team. As a roving center who made devastating tackles, he was the bulwark of the great line that helped the Maroons win the Conference football title in 1913 and was selected to Walter Camp's All-America team. His pitching helped Chicago win the Big Ten baseball championship in 1913, its first in 15 years.

NELS NORGREN
Football, Basketball and Track, Chicago

Nels Norgren, with teammate Paul Des Jardien, was one of two 12-time letter winners at Chicago in a glory era for sports on the Midway. Norgren never missed a game in three years as a punter and halfback for Amos Alonzo Stagg's undefeated 1913 Big Ten champs, who also claimed national honors. Norgren was named a second-team Walter Camp All-American as a punter. He was an All-Conference forward in basketball, played on the Big Ten championship baseball team, and threw the discus and put the shot in track. At 22, upon graduation, Norgren became athletic director at the University of Utah. He returned to Chicago in 1921 as head basketball and baseball coach, but his teams' fortunes began to decline in the mid-1920s as Chicago's de-emphasis of athletics began and the Maroons became non-competitive with the other Big Ten schools.

BIG TEN LIST

BASKETBALL ARENA NAMES

Illinois: Assembly Hall (1963, 16,450)
Indiana: Assembly Hall (1971, 17,357)
Iowa: Carver-Hawkeye Arena (1983, 15,500) (benefactor, Roy Carver)
Michigan: Crisler Arena (1967, 13,562)(football coach/athletic director, H.O. Crisler)
Michigan State: Jack Breslin Student Events Center (1989, 15,138) (university administrator)
Minnesota: Williams Arena (1928, 14,300) (football coach, Dr. Henry Williams)
Northwestern: Welsh-Ryan Arena (1951, 8,117) (parents of benefactor, Patrick G. Ryan)
Ohio State: St. John Arena (1957, 13,276) (athletic director, L.W. St. John)
Penn State: Bryce Jordan Center (1995, 15,000) (president emeritus)
Purdue: Mackey Arena (1967, 14,123) (athletic director, Guy Mackey)
Wisconsin: UW Field House (1930, 11,500)

LEADING THE WAY

LYNN ST. JOHN
Ohio State

The single greatest force in building Ohio State's athletic program and the school's athletic facilities was Lynn St. John, the athletic director at Ohio State from 1913 until his retirement in 1946. While administration occupied most of his time, he never lost his love for coaching. St. John would contribute his time as line coach in football when the need arose, and he also led the Buckeyes to a 79-69 record in an eight-year run as basketball coach. His greatest coaching achievement at Ohio State came in baseball, where he led the Buckeyes to a 191-99 record and two Conference titles. A great believer in fundamentals, his teams were known for sound execution. However, St. John is remembered for leading a dramatic growth at the school. He was the force behind building Ohio Stadium. He planned and made possible the three-pool Ohio Natatorium, and he planned and financed the 36-hole University Golf Course. He also played a major role in the building of the basketball arena, known now as St. John Arena. He was a graduate of the College of Wooster.

· BIG TEN PIONEERS ·

Fair catch results in touchdown

One of the most bizarre plays in the history of Big Ten football occurred during a game between Indiana and Iowa in 1913. Indiana's defense had made a goalline stand against the Hawkeyes, but the offense failed to advance the ball. The Hoosiers' punter was then forced to kick from his own end zone, but a strong gust of wind sent his high-arching kick floating backward into the end zone. Iowa safety Leo Dick, who had been standing on the 25-yard line when the play began, ran in and caught the ball for an instant touchdown.

Academic Achievements

In 1891, Northwestern's Greene Vardiman Black was honored by the American Dental Association as the "Father of American Dentistry." Black, founder and dean of NU's dental school, invented the first cord-driven, foot-powered dental machine.

The BIG TEN's First 100 Years
Big Ten Baseball Season Batting Records

BATTING AVERAGE
.585 Bill Freehan, MICH, 1961

HOME RUNS
14 Mike Smith, IND, 1993
14 Shane Gunderson, MINN, 1994

RUNS BATTED IN
42 Josh Klimek, IL, 1996

325ft

THE BIG EVENT

Big Ten Medal of Honor

December 5, 1914 marked the birth of the most prestigious award the Big Ten bestows upon its elite scholastic/athletic achievers — the Big Ten Medal of Honor. The award was created to emphasize — and celebrate -- academic success on an equal par with stellar athletic accomplishments. The medal is given to a senior male and female athlete from each school who, as its founders noted, "attained greatest proficiency in athletics and scholastic work." The medal was embraced by the NCAA as a brilliant concept, and other conferences later created similar awards for their athletes. The Big Ten medal, designed by R. Tait McKenzie, is presented annually to student/athletes of each respective university's own choosing. Women recipients were first chosen in 1982. The inaugural winners in 1915 were: F.T. Ward (Chicago), Edward A. Williford (Illinois), Matthew Winters (Indiana), Herman L. Von Lackun (Iowa), Boles A. Rosenthal (Minnesota), Harold G. Osborn (Northwestern), Arthur S. Kieger (Ohio State), Harry B. Routh (Purdue), and Martin Thomas Kennedy (Wisconsin).

OTHER MEMORABLE EVENTS

- Illinois won the Conference basketball title via a one-point win over second-place Chicago when Ernie Wilford tapped the ball through the basket on a jump ball.

- Wisconsin edged Chicago for the Conference outdoor track title, 38-37, the first of five one-point decisions in league track history.

- Illinois became the first school to win three straight Conference swimming titles.

- Football teams were limited to two "secret practices" a week.

- Ohio State's baseball team featured the battery of pitcher Red Trautman (who became commissioner of baseball's minor leagues) and catcher John Bricker (who became a U.S. Senator).

Undefeated Illini roll to basketball champion- ship

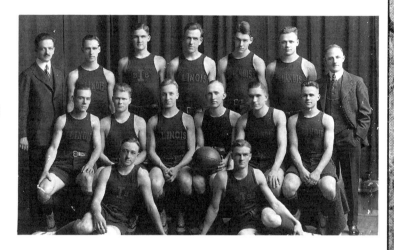

What a year to be a fan of football and basketball at Illinois. During the fall, Illinois posted a 7-0 record and finished tied with Army for the football national championship. Months later, the basketball team rolled through the schedule, finishing with a 16-0 overall record, the school's only undefeated season in basketball, to earn Illinois' first Conference basketball title. Under coach Ralph Jones, the 16-0 season put Illinois well on its way to a 25-game win streak, thanks to a hot start the following season. The big game in 1914-15 came against rival Chicago, a team that would eventually finish as the Conference runner-up to Illinois. The Illini trailed Chicago 11-9 at halftime, and the teams traded baskets and the lead much of the second half. Only a minute remained when Chicago's George Stevenson threw in a field goal, and Maroons fans sensed an upset. But Illinois' Frank Bane weaved through the Chicago defense to score a field goal, giving Illinois a 19-18 win and an 11-0 Conference record.

OTHER BIG TEN CHAMPIONS

- **FOOTBALL: Illinois, coached by Robert Zuppke**
- **BASEBALL: Illinois, coached by George Huff**
- **GYMNASTICS: Wisconsin, coached by H.D. MacChesney**
- **OUTDOOR TRACK: Wisconsin, coached by Thomas Jones**
- **INDOOR TRACK: Chicago (coach not known)**
- **CROSS COUNTRY: Minnesota, coached by Dick Grant**
- **TENNIS: Chicago (coach not known) and Ohio State (no coach)**
- **SWIMMING: Northwestern, coached by Tom Robinson**
- **+WRESTLING: Nebraska**

JOHN BRICKER
Baseball, Ohio State

John W. Bricker was a star catcher for the Ohio State baseball team in 1915 and '16. That's a big enough accomplishment for most people's lifetime. But the Pleasant Township, Ohio, native went on to even greater heights: He was the class president, then spent two years in the Army before he received his law degree from OSU in 1920. He began a law practice in Columbus in 1920 and was the attorney general of Ohio from 1933-37. He was governor of Ohio from 1939-45 and a candidate for vice president of the U.S. in 1944 on the Republican ticket with Thomas Dewey. He served as a U.S. senator from Ohio from 1947-59 and was a University trustee for many years after that. In 1983 the University Administration Building was named in his honor. Bricker received honorary degrees from more than a dozen colleges. He died Mar. 22, 1986, at the age of 93.

CHARLES CARRAN
Tennis, Ohio State

Before there was Hopalong Cassady, Woody Hayes, Jerry Lucas or any other sports star at Ohio State, there was Charles Carran. He starred on two tennis teams that combined for 13 match wins over a two-year period, capped by a championship season in 1914-15. That year, Carran won the Conference singles championship, the first of nine Big Ten singles champions at Ohio State, although the Buckeyes wouldn't win another singles title until 1937. Carran's success led the Buckeyes to the Conference team title as well, one of three Conference tennis champiosnhips for Ohio State — the Buckeyes also won the title in 1942-43 and 1990-91. Behind Carran, the Buckeyes posted an 8-2 record in the 1913-14 season. Carran was the team's captain for two seasons.

GEORGE "POTSY" CLARK
Football, Illinois

Illinois enjoyed a perfect football season in 1914-15, winning the Conference championship in coach Bob Zuppke's second year with the program and finished in a tie for the national title with Army. It was the first of four national championships for the Illini, and the team was led by quarterback George "Potsy" Clark. It was an era when quarterbacks didn't pile up fancy statistics passing the ball, and the bruising game was basically ground oriented, but Clark set himself apart with leadership and determination. While Clark's head coach was Zuppke, he also played under assistant coach Justa Lindgren, who played at Illinois before the turn of the century and served as an assistant until 1943. Upon his retirement, Lindgren formed his own all-time Illinois football team, and he chose Clark as the team's quarterback.

ILLINI ALL-AMERICANS

BIG TEN LIST

Illinois has had 18 consensus football All-Americans. They are:

Ralph Chapman, G, 1914
Perry Graves, E, 1914
Bart Macomber, HB, 1915
John Depler, C, 1918
Charles Carney, E, 1920
James McMillen, G, 1923
Harold "Red" Grange, HB, 1923-24-25
Bernie Shively, G, 1926
Alex Agase, G, 1946
John Karras, HB, 1951
J.C. Caroline, HB, 1953
Bill Burrell, G, 1959
Dick Butkus, C, 1963-64
Jim Grabowski, FB, 1965
David Williams, WR, 1984-85
Moe Gardner, NT, 1989-90
Dana Howard, LB, 1994
Kevin Hardy, LB, 1995

LEADING THE WAY

THOMAS E. JONES
Wisconsin

Few coaches associated with Wisconsin athletics—before or since—have been as revered and beloved by the University as Thomas Jones, the Badgers' track and cross country coach from 1913-48. Renowned as a visionary who was more concerned about the development of men than in victories, Jones was himself a former track star before enjoying a legendary coaching career that spanned nearly half a century. His teams won 20 Big Ten championships, and 137 of his athletes won league titles. Five more won NCAA championships. He mentored world class runners like Charles Fenske, Walter Mehl, Don Gehrmann, Loyd LaBeach and Charles McGinnis. Jones' other career highlights included being co-coach of the 1948 U.S. Olympic track team and being inducted into the State of Wisconsin Hall of Fame in 1954. He was also inducted into the Drake Relays Hall of Fame in 1977, the U.S. Track and Field Hall of Fame in 1977, the Helms Foundation Hall of Fame in 1950, and into the Madison Pen and Mike Club-Bowman Sports Foundation Hall of Fame in 1963. Five of his former athletes went on to be major college track coaches themselves, including John Nicholson of Notre Dame, George Bresnahan of Iowa and Guy Sundt of Wisconsin. Jones died on April 30, 1969.

· BIG TEN PIONEERS ·

Edward Williford
Illinois

Edward Williford, (below) the leading scorer of the 1914-15 Illinois basketball team, was the school's first Big Ten Conference Medal of Honor recipient. A letter winner from 1913-15, the Nokomis, Ill. native led the Fighting Illini in scoring his junior and senior seasons, averaging nearly 10 points per game. During his three seasons, the Illini compiled a record of 35-10, including a perfect 16-0 mark (12-0 in Conference play) in 1914-15. Following his graduation from Illinois, Williford became the head coach at Indiana University, serving in that role during the 1915-16 season. After serving in World War I, Williford eventually joined Link Aviation, where he was President and Chief Executive Officer. He then became a management and engineering consultant in Corpus Christi, Texas. Williford died in 1981.

Edward Williford

 ## Academic Achievements

Harvard is recognized as having the most famous law school in the nation. But did you know that Minnesota is credited with offering the first course in the practice of law at an American university? Or that Iowa had the first law school west of the Mississippi River?

1914-15 Conference MEDAL OF HONOR Winners

CHICAGO	F.T. Ward
ILLINOIS	Edward A. Williford
INDIANA	Matthew Winters
IOWA	Herman L. Von Lackun
MICHIGAN	No award
MINNESOTA	Boles A. Rosenthal
NORTHWESTERN	Harold G. Osborn
OHIO STATE	Arthur S. Kiefer
PURDUE	Harry B. Routh
WISCONSIN	Martin Kennedy

BIG TEN
SINCE 1896
CENTENNIAL ™

1915-1924

THE BIG EVENT

Wildcats continue swim dominance

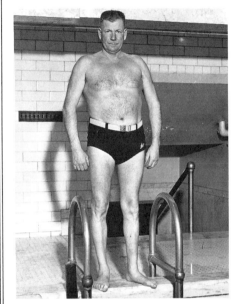

Northwestern swimming coach Tom Robinson.

Northwestern's first swimming team was formed in 1911, and it didn't take long for the Wildcats to emerge as the Big Ten's power under coach Tom Robinson. They finished 4-2 in 1912, went undefeated in 1913 (but didn't win the league title because their best swimmer was ineligible) and then won five consecutive championships from 1914-18. The 1914 title came by a single point over Illinois. The 1915 championship featured four league records, three of them from sophomore Vincent Johnson who competed in the 40-, 100- and 220-yard events. Johnson returned the following season to score 44 points in the Big Ten meet, setting records in the 100- and 220-yard swims. Johnson was ineligible for the 1917 meet, but the Wildcats won anyway. No dual meets were held in 1918 because of World War I, but Northwestern won its fifth straight Conference meet, easily outscoring Chicago.

OTHER MEMORABLE EVENTS

- Minnesota's F.O. Watson won his third consecutive Conference cross country title.

- Illinois and Minnesota battled to a 6-6 tie in football. It was the only blemish on Minnesota's record; Illinois added another tie with Ohio State.

- Minnesota claimed the best passing combination in the nation prior to World War I: Arnold "Pudge" Wyman to Bert Baston.

- Wisconsin's basketball team, at 18-1, was considered the best in the nation.

- The Conference had two football All-Americans: Illinois halfback Bart Macomber and Wisconsin tackle Howard Buck.

Badger basketball team honored as national champs

Coach Walter Meanwell guided Wisconsin to the first of its eight Big Ten basketball championships under his 21-year direction in 1912. But of all of the great team's of Meanwell's dynasty, arguably none was more dominating than the league championship squad of 1916. The Badgers cruised to the title with a 20-1 overall record and an 11-1 Big Ten slate. They were undefeated in 10 home games and were named Helms Athletic Foundation National Champions, the second team under Meanwell to be honored as such. The other was the undefeated 15-0 squad of 1912. However, the 1916 Badgers were the first Wisconsin as well as Big Ten team to win 20 games in a season. They would be the only one of Meanwell's teams to do so. It would be 24 years before another conference team won 20 games, that squad being Indiana in 1940 under coach Branch McCracken, the same year the Hoosiers became the league's first NCAA national champions. Ironically, Indiana was runner-up to Purdue in the conference standings. As for Meanwell's 1916 team, it was led by All-American and two-time All-Big Ten performer George Levis and standouts William Chandler, Mel Haas, Paul Meyers, and Harold Olsen. The Badgers' only loss was a 27-20 setback at Illinois. Their most lopsided win was a 51-12 victory at the University of Wisconsin-Milwaukee.

OTHER BIG TEN CHAMPIONS

- **FOOTBALL:** Illinois, coached by Robert Zuppke, and Minnesota, coached by Dr. Henry Williams
- **BASEBALL:** Illinois, coached by George Huff
- **GYMNASTICS:** Wisconsin, coached by H.D. MacChesney
- **OUTDOOR TRACK:** Wisconsin, coached by Thomas Jones
- **INDOOR TRACK:** Illinois, coached by Harry Gill
- **CROSS COUNTRY:** Wisconsin, coached by Fred Lee
- **TENNIS:** Chicago (Coach not known)
- **SWIMMING:** Chicago (coach not known) and Northwestern, coached by Tom Robinson
- **WRESTLING:** Iowa, coached by Pat Wright

ALBERT "BERT" BASTON
Football, Minnesota

Bert Baston, a sure-handed receiver with a propensity for making the spectacular catch, was one of the first all-time great football players in Minnesota history. He starred with the Gophers from 1914-16, leading them to a stellar 18-2-1 record during that span—including a 6-0-1 campaign in 1915. Baston was the favorite target of celebrated quarterback Arnold "Pudge" Wyman—a lethal combination that kept the Gophers cruising through the air while star running back Bernie Bierman powered them on the ground. Baston was a two-time All-American as well as a two-time member of the All-Big Ten first team. He was the first player in Minnesota history to repeat as an All-American, as he was honored in 1915 and '16. He was the Gophers' leading scorer in 1916 after collecting six touchdowns and booting five extra points. He later served 18 years as an assistant football coach at Minnesota under Bierman.

CEDRIC SMITH
Football, Michigan

Cedric "Pat" Smith was captain of Michigan's 1917 team, the same year he was named fullback on the All-America team named by Walter Camp. Wolverine teammates Ernest Allmendinger and Frank Culver, both guards, were also All-Americans that season for Michigan and key blockers for Smith. Joining the Navy in 1917 for World War I service, Smith later transferred to the Army Air Force and played for Selfridge Field. He returned to Michigan following his service career and graduated in 1919. Smith later played professional football for the Massilon, O., and Buffalo, N.Y., teams against the famous Jim Thorpe and the Canton Bulldogs.

FRED WATSON
Cross Country, Minnesota

Long before Craig Virgin, Bob Kennedy and Gary Bjorklund ruled Big Ten cross country courses, the king of Conference harriers was a wiry Minnesotan named Fred Watson. Watson's three consecutive titles in 1913, '14 and '15 stood as a Conference record for 56 years, tied in 1971 by Bjorklund, then surpassed in 1976 by Virgin when the Illinois standout won his fourth title in a row. Watson's individual success only translated into success for the team once (1914) when coach Dick Grant's Minnesota squad claimed the Big Ten title by 36 points over runner-up Iowa State. Since 1967, Watson's name has been connected to an annual Minnesota award that goes to the most valuable Gopher cross country runner.

MULTIPLE CROSS COUNTRY WINNERS

BIG TEN LIST

There have been 16 men win multiple Conference cross country titles, beginning with Minnesota's F.O. Watson in 1913-14-15.

Fred Watson, Minn., 1913-14-15
H.R. Phelps, Iowa, 1923-24
Earl Mitchell, Ind., 1942-46
Don Gehrmann, Wis., 1947-48
Don McEwen, Mich., 1949-50
Rich Ferguson, Iowa, 1952-53
Henry Kennedy, MSU, 1955-56
Allen Carius, Ill., 1962-63
Lee Assenheimer, NU, 1964-65
Larry Wieczorek, Iowa, 1966-67
Garry Bjorklund, Minn., 1969-70-71
Craig Virgin, Ill., 1973-74-75-76
Jim Spivey, Ind., 1980-82
Tim Hacker, Wis., 1981-84-85
Bob Kennedy, Ind., 1988-89-90-92
Kevin Sullivan, Mich., 1993-94-95

LEADING THE WAY

BOB ZUPPKE
Illinois

Bob Zuppke was born 10 years before the first collegiate football game, but the native of Germany established Illinois as a national powerhouse. He was hired in 1913-14 for the salary of $1,500, and he would quickly build upon earlier efforts by coach Arthur Hall. In the fall of 1914, Zuppke showed he was worth his salary, leading Illinois to the national championship. His teams in 1919, 1923 and 1927 would also win national championships. Before Zuppke retired in 1941, his Illinois teams recorded seven Big Ten championships. Zuppke was known as one of the most innovative coaches in the young game, being credited with such ideas as the huddle, the screen pass and the flea flicker. Among the stars Zuppke coached were consensus All-Americans Chuck Carney, Bernie Shively and Harold "Red' Grange (as well as Ernest Hemingway as a prep in suburban Chicago). Zuppke was the coach when Grange scored touchdowns the first four times he touched the ball in a win over Michigan in 1924. Zuppke was a charter member of the College Football Hall of Fame in 1951, and he died in 1957 at the age of 78. In 1966, the playing field at Memorial Stadium was named in his honor.

· BIG TEN PIONEERS ·

Baseball dropped for six months

In the end, it didn't really matter. Even though the Conference decided to drop baseball as an intercollegiate sport in December 1915 (by a 7-2 vote), there never was a noticeable interruption. Because so many players were involved in professional summer programs and the league couldn't quite keep track, it decided to simply end the sport. It wasn't quite that simple, however. Only six months later, by a 7-1 vote, the league lifted the ban. Because it was decided that the sport would not be discontinued until after the 1916 season, no games were ever lost as a result of the temporary ban. The issue had been brewing since 1912, when the league first voted to allow members to compete on semi-pro teams in the summer, then rescinded three months later. In an ongoing battle, the Conference's goal was to prohibit members from playing for pay in the off-season, even though other schools allowed students to do just that.

Academic Achievements

Vitamins have been around as long as mankind has been eating. But it wasn't until 1915 when Wisconsin professor E.V. McCollum "discovered" Vitamins A and B. Before he was through, McCollum and his team of researchers identified 13 different vitamins.

The BIG TEN's First 100 Years

Top Five Big Ten Baseball Seasons
by percentage, Conference games only, 10 games min.

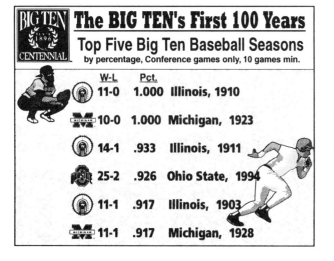

	W-L	Pct.	
	11-0	1.000	Illinois, 1910
	10-0	1.000	Michigan, 1923
	14-1	.933	Illinois, 1911
	25-2	.926	Ohio State, 1994
	11-1	.917	Illinois, 1903
	11-1	.917	Michigan, 1928

1915-16 Conference MEDAL OF HONOR Winners

CHICAGO	Paul S. Russell
ILLINOIS	Elmo Hohman
INDIANA	George J. Shively
IOWA	Forrest W. Deardorff
MICHIGAN	No award
MINNESOTA	Bernard W. Bierman
NORTHWESTERN	John H. Ellis
OHIO STATE	Charles A. Carran
PURDUE	Paul L. Walter
WISCONSIN	William Dow Harvey

THE BIG EVENT

Illini gridders upset Minnesota

The sports writers and editors for the Sunday *Chicago Herald* newspaper didn't exactly know quite what to think, other than utter surprise, when producing copy for Nov. 5, 1916 editions. So the best advice to its readers came with headlines: "Hold on tight when you read this," and "Don't faint." The big fuss came when Illinois played a Minnesota football team that was called a "perfect" team. This wasn't an Illini team that compared to its national championship team in 1914 or the 1920s, but coach Bob Zuppke's team scored a 14-9 win over Minnesota, the Gophers' only loss that season. Minnesota was so dominant in its other six games—outscoring opponents 339-14—that it made this loss just that much harder to comprehend. The Illini led, 14-0, at halftime on first-quarter touchdowns by Bart Macomber and Ren Kraft. Minnesota narrowed the gap with a touchdown and safety in the third quarter, but couldn't complete the rally.

OTHER MEMORABLE EVENTS

- The javelin throw was added to the outdoor track championships.

- Michigan State's Lyman Frimodig graduated as the school's only 10-letter winner in history; he earned four letters in baseball and three each in football and basketball.

- The date for the start of fall football practice was moved up to Sept. 15.

- Illinois' Ralf Woods and Minnesota's Harold Gillen both scored 126 points in Conference basketball games, the only time in league history the scoring title was shared.

- Chicago, led by Binga Desmond, won the indoor and outdoor track team titles, the last track titles won by the Maroons.

Ohio State takes first Big Ten baseball title

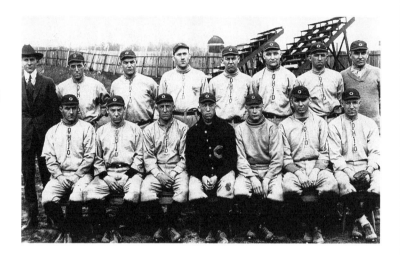

During the previous season, Ohio State finished second in the Conference standings with a 4-2 record in the league and 13-2 overall. So the Buckeyes were determined to take another step forward the following season, and Ohio State did just that under coach L.W. St. John. Ohio State compiled a 15-1 record overall and a 6-1 mark to finish first in the Conference, the school's first league title in the sport. The Buckeyes were overpowering, winning only one game by one run and taking 12 wins by five runs or more and four victories by 10 runs or more. It was the first of two titles won by the Buckeyes under St. John, who compiled a 191-99-8 record as baseball coach before resigning those duties to become the school's athletic director. Before he stepped down, the Buckeyes also won the Conference championship in 1924, tying for first place with an 8-2-1 Conference mark in a 15-7-2 season. Those were two of the three championships won through the first 65 years of baseball at Ohio State.

OTHER BIG TEN CHAMPIONS

- **FOOTBALL:** Ohio State, coached by Dr. J.W. Wilce
- **GYMNASTICS:** Chicago (coach not known)
- **OUTDOOR TRACK:** Chicago (coach not known)
- **INDOOR TRACK:** Chicago (coach not known)
- **BASKETBALL:** Illinois, coached by Ralph Jones, and Minnesota, coached by Dr. L.J. Cooke
- **CROSS COUNTRY:** Purdue, coached by Eddie O'Connor
- **TENNIS:** Illinois (no coach)
- **SWIMMING:** Northwestern, coached by Tom Robinson

PADDY DRISCOLL
Football, Northwestern

John Leo "Paddy" Driscoll played just two years of football for Northwestern, but he made his mark as one of the school's all-time great quarterbacks. Weighing just 145 pounds, the Evanston native was an exceptional open-field runner, kicker and leader. After starting as a sophomore, he was named captain for the 1916 season and directed a 6-1 record that was the school's best since the turn of the century. The victories included a 10-0 decision over Chicago that was the first in 15 years. The only defeat came in the final game of the season, at Ohio State. Driscoll was named to the first All-Conference team for his performance. He later was drafted by the professional Decatur Staleys and became an NFL hall of famer.

RAY WOODS
Basketball, Illinois

Ray Woods' name isn't mentioned in the same breath as George Mikan, Bill Russell or Oscar Robertson, but he's got one thing in common. He was college basketball's player of the year, winning the award as an Illinois senior following the 1916-17 season. He was the Illini's first basketball All-American. Though he never did lead his team in scoring—that fell to his half brother, Ralf—no one was a better all-around ballhandler, defender or leader than Ray Woods. The crafty guard led Illinois to a record of 42 victories against six losses over a three-year span. The 1915-16 team was a part of a 25-game win streak, still a record at Illinois. Woods' teams won Conference titles in his sophomore and senior seasons, and finished as runner-up in his junior campaign. Woods died in Berwyn, Ill., in 1965 at the age of 70.

BINGA DISMOND
Track, Chicago

Binga Dismond became the first African-American athlete to win a Big Ten track title as he was clocked in :47.4 in the 400-yard dash at the 1916 outdoor championships at Evanston. He also anchored the Maroons' second-place mile relay quarter. Dismond repeated in the quarter-mile at the indoor meet the following year in Evanston and again anchored Chicago's winning mile relay unit. Coach Amos Alonzo Stagg's trackmen won both the indoor and outdoor championships that year, the last that Chicago would win.

BIG TEN LIST

TOP SCORING FOOTBALL TEAMS

49.7, Minnesota, 1916
48.1, Penn State, 1994
41.0, Michigan State, 1978
40.0, Ohio State, 1969
39.5, Michigan, 1991
38.4, Ohio State, 1973
37.4, Ohio State, 1974
37.4, Ohio State, 1980
36.8, Ohio State, 1995
36.6, Iowa, 1968
36.3, Ohio State, 1983
35.5, Ohio State, 1975
35.1, Ohio State, 1979
35.0, Michigan, 1992
34.5, Michigan, 1943

LEADING THE WAY

TOM ROBINSON
Northwestern

Tom Robinson coached Northwestern's swimming team for 35 years, directing a program that won six national championships, 10 Big Ten titles and produced numerous individual champions. He also coached 12 Big Ten water polo champions and invented a game of water basketball that was played in the Big Ten from 1907-25. He even served as the Wildcats' basketball coach during World War II. A pioneer in the development of the crawl stroke, his greatest contribution might have been to the general student population. When he was hired by the University to be its first swimming coach in 1910, he immediately established a rule that every student must learn to swim before graduation. It is estimated that he taught more than 50,000 people during his career. His decree no doubt grew from something he experienced as a 19-year-old in 1901, when he jumped into a lake to save a four-year-old boy who had loosened the brake of the family car. The boy's grateful parents arranged for him to enroll at Evanston Academy and set him up with part-time employment. That put Robinson in the right place at the right time when Northwestern built its first swimming pool and University officials went looking for a coach. They couldn't have found a better one.

· BIG TEN PIONEERS ·

Gopher football powerhouse

Although Minnesota wound up third in the Big Ten standings, the 1916 Gophers did one thing exponentially better than any other Conference rival: score points. Under the direction of coach Dr. Henry Williams, the Gophers compiled a league-record 348 points — a standard that stood until 1994, when Conference newcomer Penn State racked up 385. The 1916 Gophers were powered offensively by All-Big Ten and All-America end Bert Baston, who was among the nation's most prolific pass-catchers. On the ground, they were led by fullback Arnold "Pudge" Wyman, who motored liberally behind All-Conference linemen Frank Mayer and Conrad L. Eklund. The Gophers finished the year with a 6-1 overall record and a 3-1 Conference slate, losing a 14-9 defensive struggle against Illinois. Minnesota's biggest output was an 81-0 shellacking of South Dakota. The Gophers also humbled Iowa, 67-0, and Wisconsin, 54-0.

Academic Achievements

*D*ance marathons were popular in the teens and '20s. So popular, in fact, that laws had to be passed to regulate them. Offers of lucrative prizes tempted couples to stay on their feet for weeks, risking their health. But today, Penn State uses a dance marathon to help the unhealthy. PSU's Interfraternity Council Dance Marathon is the largest student-run fund-raiser in the nation. Its proceeds benefit children with cancer.

1916-17 Conference MEDAL OF HONOR Winners

CHICAGO	Daniel J. Fisher
ILLINOIS	Clyde Alwood
INDIANA	DeWitt T. Mullett
IOWA	Wayne J. Foster
MICHIGAN	No award
MINNESOTA	Joseph M. Spafka
NORTHWESTERN	Edgar Williams
OHIO STATE	Allen R. Rankin
PURDUE	Melvin Proud
WISCONSIN	Meade Burke

The BIG TEN's First 100 Years
An Early Swimming Power

Between 1937 and 1973, Big Ten teams won 27 of the first 37 (73%) NCAA Men's Swimming and Diving Championships. Here is the national team championships count during that time.

- 11 Ohio State
- 10 Michigan
- 6 Indiana
- 5 Southern California
- 4 Yale
- 1 Stanford

THE BIG EVENT

Coach Fielding Yost's Michigan Wolverines rejoined Big Ten action in 1917, but played only one game, losing to Northwestern in the season finale, 21-12.

Michigan returns to Big Ten

After almost 10 years out of the Big Ten, Michigan resumed its membership in the Conference on Nov. 20, 1917, following a June 9 invitation to return. Students and alumni had initially supported Michigan's withdrawal and independent status following a disagreement over a Conference eligibility rule, but by 1913 sentiment began to change, leading to Michigan's return.

OTHER MEMORABLE EVENTS

- Wisconsin's basketball team went 18-1 and once again was considered the No. 1 team in the nation.

- Northwestern won its fifth straight Conference swiming title, its longest streak of championships in school history.

- Ohio State didn't give up a touchdown all season in rolling to a 9-0-1 record and won its second straight football crown.

- Northwestern's Floyd Smart finished first in six events in a dual track meet with Indiana and had five firsts against Ohio State.

- Northwestern's basketball team was coached by Dr. Norman Elliott. He became the father of two boys, Bump and Pete, who both went on to become head football coaches in the Conference.

Michigan wins three titles on return to Big Ten

Michigan's Carl Johnson.

Conference opponents may have wished that Michigan had waited another year to return after the way the Wolverines performed in the 1917-18 school year. On its return to Big Ten membership and competition after an 11-year absence, Michigan ran amok on its league foes, winning titles in indoor track, outdoor track and baseball in the winter and spring of 1918. Competing in its first Big Ten indoor track meet (the indoor championship had begun in 1911), coach Steve Farrell's team upended defending champion Chicago by a 42-22 count at Evanston. Carl Johnson won the first of three straight 60-yard dash and 60-yard high hurdle titles to pace Michigan. In outdoor track, the Wolverines continued their mastery and regained the outdoor track title they had last won in 1906, scoring 37.5 points to beat Illinois by 11 points in the outdoor meet at Chicago in which 16 teams competed. Johnson won the high hurdles and long jump. And Michigan's baseball team posted a 9-4 Big Ten mark to beat Illinois by two games for the Conference championship. Playing on that squad was infielder Mike Knode, who would play in the big leagues two years later with the St. Louis Cardinals.

OTHER BIG TEN CHAMPIONS

- **FOOTBALL:** Ohio State, coached by Dr. J.W. Wilce

- **GYMNASTICS:** No meet

- **BASKETBALL:** Wisconsin, coached by Guy Lowman

- **CROSS COUNTRY:** No meet

- **TENNIS:** Chicago (coach not known) and Minnesota (no coach)

- **SWIMMING:** Northwestern, coached by Tom Robinson

- **WRESTLING:** No meet

GEORGE HALAS
Football, Basketball and Baseball, Illinois

Better known as Papa Bear, George Halas first enjoyed days as a three-sport letterman at Illinois from 1916-18. Playing at end, a broken jaw and a fractured leg kept him from more playing time on the gridiron, though he still lettered in basketball and baseball. Halas graduated from Illinois, then earned a starting spot in right field for the New York Yankees. He injured his leg, giving his position to a player named Babe Ruth. A founding member of the NFL, Halas led the Chicago Bears to 326 wins in four separate tenures as coach, a victory total that stood as an NFL record until 1993. He coached the Bears to six of their nine NFL championships, his last coming in 1963. He oversaw a franchise that cost him $100 in 1920 and grew to $40 million when he died in 1983.

ARTHUR C. "A.C." NIELSEN, SR.
Tennis, Wisconsin

Arthur Nielsen was as renowned for his philanthropic activities as he was for his tennis playing exploits at Wisconsin. His financial gift of nearly $1.2 million helped fund the University's $1.4 million Nielson Tennis Stadium indoor facility in 1968. He spent 50 years in the marketing research business and founded the A.C. Nielsen Co., the nation's largest marketing and television research firm. His other philanthropic interests included support for educational institutions, hospitals, medical research, the elderly and the blind. As a player, he captained the Badgers' tennis team in 1916, 1917 and 1918. His career was interrupted by a tour of military service in World I, and upon his return to Wisconsin, he was Big Ten doubles runner-up in 1918 with partner Edwin Hammen. Later, he had the distinction of winning three U.S. father-son doubles championships with his son A.C. Nielsen, Jr., who was captain of Wisconsin's 1941 team. Nielsen, Sr. was inducted into the National Lawn Tennis Hall of Fame in 1971 and into the Wisconsin Athletic Hall of Fame in 1992.

FLOYD SMART
Track, Northwestern

World War I limited Floyd Smart's track career to just one season, but he made the most of it. The versatile runner set school records in 1917 in the 220-yard dash, the 220-yard low hurdles and the broad jump. He captured first place in six events in a dual meet with Indiana, and won five events in a meet with Ohio State. Smart placed second to Chicago's Binga Dismond in the quarter-mile in the indoor Conference championships, losing a photo finish. Dismond set a league record in the process. Smart ran on a relay team that won the half-mile and placed fourth in the mile in the Drake Relays later in the year. The following week Smart won the 440-yard low hurdles in the Penn Relays in 55.2 seconds and placed third in the 120-yard high hurdles.

BIG TEN FOOTBALL STADIUMS

B I G   T E N   L I S T

Illinois: Memorial Stadium (1923, 70,904)
Indiana: Memorial Stadium (1960, 52,354)
Iowa: Kinnick Stadium (1929, 70,397) (named after Heisman Trophy winner, Nile Kinnick)
Michigan: Michigan Stadium (1927, 102,501)
Michigan State: Spartan Stadium (1923, 72,027)
Minnesota: HHH Metrodome (1982, 63,669) (named after politician, Hubert H. Humphrey)
Northwestern: Dyche Stadium (1926, 49,256) (named after NU VP and business manager, William A. Dyche)
Ohio State: Ohio Stadium (1922, 89,841)
Penn State: Beaver Stadium (1960, 93,967) (named after University pioneer James A. Beaver)
Purdue: Ross-Ade Stadium (1924, 67,861) (named after former Board of Trustees president David E. Ross and PU alumnus George Ade)
Wisconsin: Camp Randall Stadium (1917, 76,027) (named after Civil War-time governor Alexander Randall)

LEADING THE WAY

RALPH JONES
Illinois

After arriving at Illinois from Purdue, Ralph Jones left an impressive legacy in Champaign. Besides coaching freshman football and baseball during his tenure at Illinois, he posted the highest winning percentage as the school's basketball coach. The 85-34 record (71.4 percent) was boosted by his undefeated team in 1914-15, a squad that recorded a 16-0 mark and won the school's first Conference title in the sport. Jones was credited with originating the fast break, and his teams from 1913-14 to 1915-16 combined to win 25 consecutive games and 17 straight games in the Conference, both school records that still stand. Jones produced the school's first basketball All-American, Ray Woods, the sport's national player of the year in 1916-17. Jones' team in 1916-17 also won the Conference championship before he left the school following the 1919-20 season. Jones coached at Wabash College in Indiana and eventually Lake Forest Academy, north of Chicago. Jones coached the Chicago Bears from 1930-33, where he revived the T-formation offense and created the use of a man in motion.

· BIG TEN PIONEERS ·

Opening of Camp Randall Stadium

Built in 1917, Camp Randall Stadium (below) is the oldest football stadium in the Big Ten. The 76,027-seat facility rests on a site once used as a training site for Union Civil War soldiers; as a prison for Confederate troops; and later as a state fair grounds. When the state legislature donated the land to the University of Wisconsin, veterans groups persuaded the school to call the stadium Camp Randall instead of Randall Field to honor fallen veterans who are buried at a nearby cemetery. Built at an initial cost of $15,000 from a legislative grant, the facility initially seated 10,000. It has been expanded nearly a dozen times since. The first game was played there in 1917, when Wisconsin won its Homecoming game against Minnesota, 10-7.

Academic Achievements

Drive through the rural Midwest any day during the summer and you'll see rows and rows of soybeans. They weren't always there. It was research at Illinois that helped introduce soybeans as a major U.S. crop. Today, the research continues: to make each soybean crop richer and more plentiful, as well as finding more uses for the product.

1917-18
Conference MEDAL OF HONOR
Winners

CHICAGO	Walter C. Earl
ILLINOIS	John Kleine
INDIANA	Wilbur J. Dalzell
IOWA	John K. Von Lackum
MICHIGAN	Alan W. Boyd
MINNESOTA	George W. Hauser
NORTHWESTERN	No award
OHIO STATE	Howard F. Yerges
PURDUE	Herbert L. Hart
WISCONSIN	Ebert Simpson, Jr.

SINCE 1896

1918-19

THE BIG EVENT

Big Ten suspends competition because of war

So many of the Big Ten Conference's stars were active in the military because of World War I that schools were unable to field top-quality teams. That was true in many instances throughout the country. The league suspended play before the football season started and offered to the War Department "it's services in carrying on athletic activities, both intramural and intercollegiate, in and among its members." Illinois went 5-0—though it lost to military teams Great Lakes Naval Training and Municipal Pier—and was the unofficial Big Ten champion in football. Chicago finished 0-5—the first time coach Amos Stagg would go a season without a victory. There was a basketball season, in which Wisconsin went on to win the league title, but there were no championships for cross country and gymnastics. Northwestern won the swimming title, and Michigan won Conference championships in baseball, indoor and outdoor track. The most notable graduate at the end of the year was George Halas, a three-sport star at Illinois (football, basketball and baseball), who eventually enlisted for military service. He, of course, would go on to be the legendary coach of the Chicago Bears.

OTHER MEMORABLE EVENTS

- Minnesota, 10-0 in Conference games and 13-0 overall, was considered the top basketball team in the nation.

- Michigan's baseball team won its second of three straight baseball titles, going undefeated in Conference play.

- Michigan fullback Frank Steketee was the Conference's lone football All-American.

- Illinois' George Huff coached his final baseball season to devote full-time duties as athletic director.

- Illinois went undefeated in Conference football play, but lost twice to service teams.

Minnesota wins Big Ten basketball championship

Although L.J. Cooke would enjoy five more successful campaigns as legendary coach of the Minnesota basketball team, the Gophers won the last of their five Big Ten championships under Cooke in 1919. And the Gophers were perfect every step of the way during the title march. First team All-America guard Erling Platou led the way, as Minnesota posted an undefeated 13-0 record and 10-0 Conference slate. The Gophers finished two full games ahead of second-place Chicago, which finished 10-2 in the Conference. The league championship would be Minnesota's last until 1937. The Gophers, in fact, have won only three league basketball crowns since 1919, including 1937. The 1919 team was one of three Gophers' squads to enjoy an undefeated season under Cooke, but it was the first to claim the Big Ten championship. Cooke's 1902 and '03 teams were also undefeated with respective records of 15-0 and 13-0. But the Conference didn't begin recognizing team champions until 1906. Incidentally, the Gophers won that title, as well. Minnesota also won — or shared — championships in 1907, '11, and '16. The Gophers' last championship was in 1982.

OTHER BIG TEN CHAMPIONS

- **FOOTBALL:** Illinois, coached by Robert Zuppke, Michigan, coached by Fielding Yost, and Purdue, coached by A.G. "Butch" Scanlon

- **BASEBALL:** Michigan, coached by Carl Lundgren

- **GYMNASTICS:** No meet

- **OUTDOOR TRACK:** Michigan, coached by Stephen Farrell

- **INDOOR TRACK:** Michigan, coached by Stephen Farrell

- **CROSS COUNTRY:** No meet

- **TENNIS:** Michigan (no coach)

- **SWIMMING:** Chicago (coach not known)

ARNIE OSS
Basketball, Minnesota

Long before the likes of Kevin McHale, Mychal Thompson, and "Sweet" Lou Hudson carved reputations for themselves as being among the best basketball players in Minnesota history, Arnie Oss set a precedent that not all of the aforementioned three would even accomplish. In 1921, Oss became the first player in Gophers' history to be named a two-time first team All-American. He did the trick on non-consecutive occasions, the first being in 1919. He led Minnesota to the Helms Athletic Association national championship as well as the Big Ten title that same season. He was named team captain for the 1920 and 1921 seasons. In 1921, he guided the Gophers to a 10-5 overall record and a second-place finish in the Big Ten standings. He was named All-Conference in 1919, '20, and '21 and was regarded as Minnesota's greatest player for the first half of the century. In 1921, he averaged 3.67 baskets per game — a superb average for the era — and finished the season with 90 points.

BURT INGWERSEN
Football and Basketball, Illinois

More than a three-sport star, Burt Ingwersen was an All-American in football, a three-year starter in basketball, and a member of the original Chicago Bears before a lengthy college coaching career. Before graduating in 1920, he was named a second-team All-American as a tackle and was a starter in basketball and baseball. A member of the Bears in 1920, he also worked on a highway crew before returning to Illinois as an assistant football coach. Ingwersen was named head football coach at Iowa in 1924, then moved to Louisiana State as assistant coach and head of the physical education department. He later coached baseball at Northwestern and served as assistant football coach at Illinois for 20 years, helping develop four Big Ten championship teams. He died in 1969 at age 70.

FRANK STEKETEE
Football, Michigan

Michigan's football program has been blessed with some terrific fullbacks over the years, but none better than consensus All-American Frank Steketee. Following fellow Wolverine great Cedric "Pat" Smith as an all-star fullback, "Stek's" performance in 1918 was legendary. That 1918 "M" squad, coached by Fielding Yost, was undefeated and out-scored its opponents by a count of 96-6. Steketee also was a tremendous punter and place kicker, and his field goals were the difference in games against Syracuse and Illinois. Following his service in World War I in 1919, Steketee returned to Michigan in 1920 and '21, defeating Minnesota the latter year with three place kicks and a touchdown. Cumulatively, Steketee and his teammates put together an overall record of 15-3-1 during those three seasons.

MICHIGAN'S TENNIS CHAMPS

BIG TEN LIST

Michigan has crowned 15 Conference men's singles champions in tennis, beginning with Walter Westbrook in 1919.

1919—Walter Westbrook
1920—Walter Westbrook
1923—Charles Merkel
1948—Andy Paton
1956—Barry MacKay
1957—Barry MacKay
1959—Jon Erickson
1961—Raymond Senkowski
1969—Dick Dell
1970—Mark Conti
1971—Joel Ross
1973—Victor Amaya
1974—Victor Amaya
1977—Bill Rennie
1978—Jeff Etterbeek
1980—Michael Leach

LEADING THE WAY

WARD 'PIGGY' LAMBERT
Purdue

As Purdue's basketball coach, Ward 'Piggy' Lambert's teams established the Boilermakers as a national power and set a standard for the program for years to come. He coached Purdue to 11 Big Ten championships, including six outright titles, and his teams were 371-152 (70.9%) in 28 1/2 seasons with 228 league victories. He was still the school's all-time winningest basketball coach at the end of the 1995-96 season, with Gene Keady closing in. Lambert coached 10 consensus All-Americans and nine Big Ten scoring champions, including John Wooden. When Lambert became Purdue's head coach in 1916, the program had just suffered through three straight losing seasons, including 4-10 in 1915-16. Lambert immediately turned the Boilermakers into a winner, going 11-3 his first season. Lambert had to leave Purdue in 1918 when called to serve in the military. Replaced briefly by J.J. Maloney, he returned for the 1918-19 season. Spurned as being too short as a high school player, Lambert later relied on smaller players as a coach. Lambert's only losing seasons were 1918-19 (6-8), 1942-43 (9-11) and 1944-45 (9-11). He was nicknamed 'Piggy' when he was young and tassels that resembled pigtails hung from his stocking cap. Lambert, born in Deadwood, S.D., was reared in Crawfordsville, Ind., just down the road from Purdue.

· BIG TEN PIONEERS ·

Walter Westbrook wins Michigan's first tennis title

Walter Westbrook (below) won Michigan's first singles title in tennis in the 1919 meet at Chicago as the Wolverines won the first of their 36 Conference championships in the sport. It was the culmination of a spectacular season for the Detroit native, who went through the entire season without losing a single game, let alone a match.

Walter Westbrook

Academic Achievements

Among the most famous alumni from Michigan are: General Motors Corp. CEO, Roger Smith; "Cathy" cartoonist, Cathy Guisewiete; host of "60 Minutes," Mike Wallace; author Arthur Miller; attorney Clarence Darrow; founder of Mayo Clinic, Dr. William J. Mayo; actor James Earl Jones; former U.S. President Gerald Ford; race car driver, Janet Guthrie; and Forbes magazine editor, Ann Catherine Brown

1918-19 Conference MEDAL OF HONOR Winners

CHICAGO	William C. Gorgas
ILLINOIS	G.C. Gucheit
INDIANA	William M. Zeller
IOWA	Homer W. Scott
MICHIGAN	No award
MINNESOTA	Erling S. Platou
NORTHWESTERN	Ruben A. Marquardt
OHIO STATE	Sheldon J. Mann
PURDUE	Robert E. Markley
WISCONSIN	Charles H. Carpenter

THE BIG EVENT

Big Ten hosts first golf championship

Chicago's Rudolph Knepper.

The inaugural Big Ten team golf championship tournament was held at Olympia Fields in Chicago. The 72-hole meet was won by Drake, which breezed by runner-up Chicago by nine strokes. Chicago's Rudolf Knepper, however, took low-medalist honors and was the Conference's first individual champion. Drake also won the second tournament and Chicago finished in second place. But Chicago won the third meet in 1922, and the title would belong exclusively to Big Ten teams from that point on. In 1926, Chicago's K.E. Hisert became the first player in league history to win back-to-back individual championships. He led Chicago to the team title that same year. Minnesota's Leo Bolstad was the first player to win non-consecutive individual championships. He won in 1927 and again in '29. Michigan's John Fischer was the first player to win three titles, doing so in 1932, '33 and '35. Michigan won four straight team championships during that span, becoming the first team to win more than three.

OTHER MEMORABLE EVENTS

- Illinois upset Ohio State, 9-7, in football when Bobby Fletcher connected on the first field goal attempt of his career.

- Northwestern lost to Notre Dame, 33-7, in the final game of the season. The star for the Irish was an ill halfback by the name of George Gipp. The Gipper died two weeks later.

- Illinois' Chuck Carney set a Conference record with 188 points in the basketball season.

- Michigan's Walter Westbrook won his second straight Conference tennis singles title.

Illini football team beats Ohio State, wins national championship

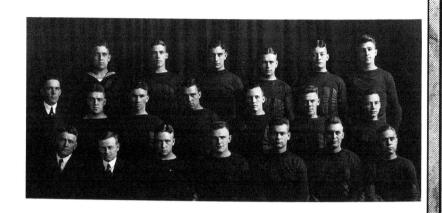

Illinois traveled to Ohio State for the 1919 season finale with both the Big Ten championship and the national title on the line. Coach Bob Zuppke's men trailed the Buckeyes, 7-6, with just five minutes left in the game. Quarterback Lawrence Walquist and end Chuck Carney connected for three pass completions, putting the Illini deep into Ohio State territory. With only 12 seconds remaining in the game and Illinois placekicker Ralph Fletcher out of the game with an ankle injury, Coach Zuppke called upon Ralph's younger brother, Bob, to kick a game-winning 25-yard field goal—the first field goal he'd ever attempted in a game! The 9-7 victory gave Illinois its second national championship.

OTHER BIG TEN CHAMPIONS

- BASEBALL: Michigan, coached by Carl Lundgren
- OUTDOOR TRACK: Illinois, coached by Harry Gill
- INDOOR TRACK: Illinois, coached by Harry Gill
- BASKETBALL: Chicago (coach not known)
- +CROSS COUNTRY: Iowa State
- TENNIS: Chicago (coach not known) and Michigan (no coach)
- SWIMMING: Northwestern, coached by Tom Robinson
- WRESTLING: Illinois (no coach)
- +GOLF: Drake
- GYMNASTICS: Chicago (coach not known)

+open meet

CHIC HARLEY
Football, Ohio State

One of the original Buckeye greats, Charles "Chic' Harley was Ohio State's first All-American and four-sport letterman. Harley scored 23 touchdowns during a three-year career when he led Ohio State to Conference football titles in 1916 and '17, then a runner-up finish in the '19 season after he spent a year in military service. Ohio State compiled a 21-1-1 record in his three varsity seasons, the only loss a 9-7 defeat at Illinois in 1919. A three-time All-American who helped create much of the early mania behind Buckeyes football, he was a talented kicker (who prefered the drop kick) and a staunch defender. The Buckeyes played at old Ohio Field during the Harley years. Largely because of his play and the crowds he attracted, Ohio Stadium was built and nicknamed the "House that Harley built."

AUBREY DEVINE
Football, Iowa

Without question the greatest Iowa football player of his era, quarterback Aubrey Devine ran for more than 2,000 yards and scored 161 points during his career. He set single-season school records with 895 yards rushing and 1,316 total yards in 1921. When Devine's name is mentioned, it's hard not to bring up THE game. HIS game. In 1921, Devine had 464 total yards (162 rushing, 122 passing, 180 returning punts and kickoffs) and scored on four TDs and five extra points against Minnesota. He was captain of the Hawkeyes' Big Ten championship team in '21. The Des Moines, Iowa, native was All-Big Ten three years and a consensus All-American as a senior. His coach, Howard Jones, once said: "I have never known any backfield man whose accomplishments in running, punting, dropkicking and passing combined equal those of Aubrey Devine. Devine was selected to the National Football Foundation's College Football Hall of Fame in 1973 as a pioneer player. He died in 1981 at the age of 84.

GAYLORD STINCHCOMB
Football, Basketball and Track, Ohio State

A halfback and quarterback on Ohio State football teams in 1917, '19 and '20, Pete Stinchcomb led Ohio State to two Big Ten titles and a three year record of 21-2-1. He was an All-America selection following the 1920 season, the second player from Ohio State chosen for the prestigious team. Ohio State won the Conference title in 1917 when Stinchcomb was a sophomore, and the Buckeyes were Conference runners-up with a 6-1 record in 1919 before the Buckeyes won the title again in '20 with a 7-0 regular season record. Ohio State made its first trip to the Rose Bowl, where they met the California Bears. Ohio State lost the game, 28-0, in what was considered a big upset, even though Stinchcomb carried the ball 11 times for 82 yards. He also lettered in basketball and track, setting the school record with a leap of 23 feet, 2 inches in the long jump. Stinchcomb was heralded as Ohio State's first two-sport All-American.

BIG TEN LIST

INAUGURAL CHAMPIONSHIPS

The Big Ten has awarded team championships in 14 men's sports. Here are the initial years of team titles:

Baseball—1895-96
Football—1896-97
Outdoor Track—1900-01
Gymnastics—1901-02
Basketball—1905-06
Cross Country—1908-09
Tennis—1909-10
Indoor Track—1910-11
Swimming—1910-11
Wrestling—1912-13
Golf—1919-20
Fencing—1925-26 (discontinued after 1985-86)
Hockey—1958-59 (discontinued after 1980-81)
Soccer—1991-92

LEADING THE WAY

JOHN WILCE
Ohio State

When Ohio State hired John W. Wilce as head football coach prior to the 1913-14 school year, the Buckeyes had three coaches over the three previous seasons in football. In his 16 years as coach, Ohio State saw an enormous growth in fan interest, and much of it was because of Wilce and the success of the program. Wilce led the Buckeyes to a 78-33-9 record overall, and Ohio State won three Conference football championships. The best run in his tenure came in back-to-back seasons that began in the fall of 1916, when Ohio State posted the school's second undefeated season, winning all seven games and outscoring the opposition 258-29. The Conference championship the Buckeyes won was the school's first in the sport. The following season, only a 0-0 tie with Auburn kept Ohio State from another unblemished season as the Buckeyes were 8-0-1 and Conference champions after outscoring their opponents, 292-6. In 1920, the Buckeyes won the Conference with a 7-0 record and made the school's first appearance in the Rose Bowl. Support grew so much that the team moved from Ohio Field to magnificent Ohio Stadium.

· BIG TEN PIONEERS ·

Rudolf Knepper
Chicago

Rudolf Knepper, recruited to a hastily formed University of Chicago golf team by Coach Amos Alonzo Stagg, became the first Big Ten golf champion in 1920. Seven teams, six from the fledgling Big Ten, competed in the Conference's first team tournament at Olympia Fields Golf Course in south suburban Chicago. Knepper fired a 7 over-par 303 for the 72-hole match play tournament, beating Drake's McKee by six strokes to become the first of four Big Ten medalists for Chicago in the 1920s. Drake, the only non-Conference school in the two-day tourney, won the team title by eight strokes over Chicago.

Academic Achievements

One of only two Conference universities to not bear the state name in its title, Purdue University is named after a local entrepreneur who contributed funds to start the university in 1869. John Purdue's donation, along with 100 acres of land donated by local citizens, made the founding of the university in West Lafayette possible. In appreciation of Purdue's gift, Indiana legislators named the institution in his honor.

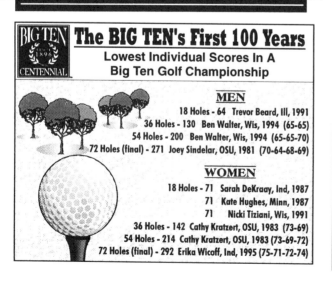

The BIG TEN's First 100 Years
Lowest Individual Scores In A Big Ten Golf Championship

MEN
18 Holes - 64 Trevor Beard, Ill, 1991
36 Holes - 130 Ben Walter, Wis, 1994 (65-65)
54 Holes - 200 Ben Walter, Wis, 1994 (65-65-70)
72 Holes (final) - 271 Joey Sindelar, OSU, 1981 (70-64-68-69)

WOMEN
18 Holes - 71 Sarah DeKraay, Ind, 1987
71 Kate Hughes, Minn, 1987
71 Nicki Tiziani, Wis, 1991
36 Holes - 142 Cathy Kratzert, OSU, 1983 (73-69)
54 Holes - 214 Cathy Kratzert, OSU, 1983 (73-69-72)
72 Holes (final) - 292 Erika Wicoff, Ind, 1995 (75-71-72-74)

1919-20 Conference MEDAL OF HONOR Winners

CHICAGO	Charles G. Higgins
ILLINOIS	John B. Felmley
INDIANA	Willard Rauschenback
IOWA	Charles Mockmore
MICHIGAN	Carl E. Johnson
MINNESOTA	Norman W. Kingsley
NORTHWESTERN	Bruce DeSwarte
OHIO STATE	Harold Kime
PURDUE	Paul B. Church
WISCONSIN	Anthony G. Zulfer

THE BIG EVENT

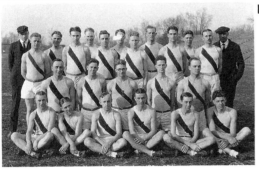

NCAA outdoor track title
won by Illinois

The first NCAA track and field championship meet was held in Chicago, and midwestern schools quickly established themselves as track powerhouses. In that first meet, an Illinois team that already won the Conference championship used four second-place performances to win the NCAA title. Despite not recording a first place, Illinois scored 20.5 points to win the meet, finishing ahead of runner-up Notre Dame, which ended up with 16.5 points. The NCAA title was the first of two championships won by Illinois under coach Harry Gill. Thanks to some balanced scoring, the Illini were able to hold off the Irish. Illinois' Dewey Alberts placed second in the high jump, while teammate Gordon McGinnis was second in the mile run. Russell Wharton was second in the two-mile run, and Harold Osborn placed second in the long jump.

OTHER MEMORABLE EVENTS

- The first basketball game broadcast on radio was a Michigan State game on station WKAR.

- Minnesota's Ernest Carlson won his second straight Conference all-around gymnastics title.

- Iowa State won the Conference cross country title, prompting league officials to ban non-members from competing in future championships.

- Chicago's B.E. Ford became the first Conference golfer to win the individual crown of the league's invitational championship.

Ohio State football team makes its first Rose Bowl appearance

Ohio State was the most sensational team in college football during the 1920 season, winning the Conference title and appearing in what would become the Rose Bowl for the first time in school history in 1921. The Rose Bowl stadium wasn't built and ready for the bowl game until 1923, but Ohio State brought a brilliant team westward nevertheless. The Buckeyes had rolled to an impressive 7-0 record during the regular season, finishing with four shutouts. Ohio State scored 109 points while keeping its opponents scoreless in the first three games of the season — wins over Ohio Wesleyan, Oberlin and Purdue — before grinding out wins over Wisconsin, Chicago, Michigan and Illinois. Only the 7-6 victory over Chicago was won by less than a touchdown. Coach John "Doc" Wilce produced a winner that used the talents of quarterback Harry Workman and all-America left halfback Pete Stinchcomb. Though Ohio State was the favorite, California stunned the Buckeyes for a 28-0 bowl game victory, the first significant win by a college football team from the west. The victory produced instant notoriety for football in California.

OTHER BIG TEN CHAMPIONS

- **BASEBALL:** Illinois, coached by Carl Lundgren
- **GYMNASTICS:** Chicago (coach not known)
- **OUTDOOR TRACK:** Illinois, coached by Harry Gill
- **INDOOR TRACK:** Illinois, coached by Harry Gill
- **BASKETBALL:** Michigan, coached by E.J. Mather, Purdue, coached by Ward Lambert, and Wisconsin, coached by Dr. Walter Meanwell
- **+CROSS COUNTRY:** Iowa State
- **TENNIS:** Chicago (coach not known) and Indiana (no coach)
- **SWIMMING:** Chicago (coach not known)
- **WRESTLING:** Indiana, coached by James Kase
- **+GOLF:** Drake

+open meet

CHUCK CARNEY
Football and Basketball, Illinois

Earning letters in two sports is one thing. Attaining All-Conference honors is the next step. Reaching All-America in two sports is rare, but that's the accomplishments of Chuck Carney: Illinois' only two-sport All-American. He was as handy at shooting baskets as he was snaring passes as an end. A three year-starter from 1918-19 to 1921-22 in basketball and football, Carney was named All-America following his junior season in football. In basketball, Carney set a Conference record with 188 points in 12 games, a mark that stood for 22 years. Returning from a leg injury that slowed him in his junior season, Carney earned national college player of the year honors. He finished with 404 points in his career, a school record that wasn't broken for 22 years. He coached football at three schools before turning his attention to a career as an investment banker. He died in 1984.

EVERETT DEAN
Basketball, Indiana

Everett Dean was Indiana's first All-American basketball player, in 1921, and went on to become a highly successful coach in basketball and baseball. Dean, who won letters in both sports from 1919-21, served as head coach in both from 1925-38. His teams won Big Ten co-championships in basketball in 1926, '28 and '36 and baseball titles in 1925, '32, and '38. He is the only person who has coached a team to the NCAA basketball title (Stanford, 1942) and into the baseball College World Series (Stanford, 1953). Dean also is the only person elected to the halls of fame for both sports as a coach. His roots remained deepest in the Big Ten; at one time three of his former basketball players, Branch McCracken, Ozzie Cowles and Forddy Anderson were all coaching in the Conference. Dean died in 1992 at the age of 95.

HENRY "ERNIE" VICK
Football and Baseball, Michigan

Following in the footsteps of such giant gridiron immortals as William Cunningham and Germany Schulz, Henry "Ernie" Vick became one of Michigan's greatest centers, despite his comparatively small stature. His terrific tackling and blocking earned him nationwide attention. Walter Camp wrote: "Ernie is the most accurate passer ever to put a ball into play. Dependable under great pressure, a wonderful tackler." During his four seasons with the Wolverines from 1918-21, Michigan compiled a cumulative won-loss record of 18-7-1 and posted 16 shutouts. Vick also starred in baseball for the Wolverines.

BIG TEN LIST

TRACK NATIONAL CHAMPIONS

Big Ten schools have won the NCAA men's outdoor track championship nine times, beginning with the inaugural meet in 1921. Here are the champions:

1921—Illinois
1923—Michigan
1927—Illinois
1929—Ohio State
1932—Indiana
1944—Illinois
1946—Illinois
1947—Illinois
1948—Minnesota

LEADING THE WAY

RAY FISHER
Michigan

In 38 years as baseball coach at Michigan, Ray Fisher guided Wolverine teams to a 637-294-8 record, good for a .687 winning percentage. Fourteen of his teams captured Big Ten championships, with the 1953 club winning Michigan's first NCAA baseball championship by beating Texas, 7-5, in the title game of the College World Series. A native of Middlebury, Vermont, Fisher was born in 1887 and played professional baseball from 1910-20, compiling a lifetime record of 102-98 and an ERA of 2.38. He pitched for the New York Highlanders (to become the Yankees) and for the Cincinnati Reds, losing a game to Dickie Kerr and the White Sox in the tainted "Black Sox" World Series of 1919. Fifteen of his players made it to the majors, including Don Lund, who would succeed him as Michigan's coach. Ray Fisher Stadium—a site on which Wolverine teams have played since 1923—was dedicated in his honor in 1967. Fisher also was inducted into halls of fame by the state of Michigan and by the University. Michigan's most valuable player award is named for him. Fisher died in Ann Arbor at age 95 in 1982 and prior to his death was the oldest living former player for both the Yankees and Reds.

· BIG TEN PIONEERS ·

Lloyd Wilder
Wisconsin

The Big Ten made the biggest splash possible at the inaugural NCAA outdoor track and field championships. And individually, no Conference athlete made bigger waves than Wisconsin star Lloyd Wilder. Although Illinois won the team title, Wilder earned the distinction of being the Big Ten's first NCAA individual pole vault champion. He finished in a three-way tie for the pole vault championship, setting a precedent for success in an event that would be dominated by Big Ten vaulters. Wilder shared the first crown with Longino Welch of Georgia Tech and Eldon Jenne of Washington State. All three cleared 12-feet. Michigan's John Landowski was NCAA co-champion the following year, becoming the second of 25 Big Ten vaulters who would win outright or co-championships from 1921 to 1993, when Indiana's Mark Buse won with a vault 18-feet, 4-1/2-inches.

Academic Achievements

In 1921, Wisconsin professor Edgar Gordon started the nation's first course ever broadcast over radio, "Music Appreciation." It was heard on WHA, the first radio station in America which began in Wisconsin's Sterling Hall. Today, WHA reaches some 275,000 listeners in Wisconsin and its syndicated programs reach tens of thousands more around the world.

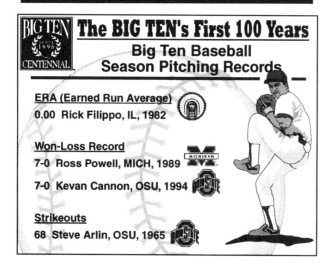

The BIG TEN's First 100 Years
Big Ten Baseball
Season Pitching Records

ERA (Earned Run Average)
0.00 Rick Filippo, IL, 1982

Won-Loss Record
7-0 Ross Powell, MICH, 1989
7-0 Kevan Cannon, OSU, 1994

Strikeouts
68 Steve Arlin, OSU, 1965

1920-21 Conference MEDAL OF HONOR Winners

CHICAGO	Harold L. Hanisch
ILLINOIS	John S. Prescott
INDIANA	Everett S. Dean
IOWA	Robert J. Kaufman
MICHIGAN	Elton E. Wieman
MINNESOTA	Neal A. Amston
NORTHWESTERN	Robert W. Townley
OHIO STATE	Andrew J. Nemecek
PURDUE	Cecil Cooley
WISCONSIN	Allan C. Davey

THE BIG EVENT

Major John L. Griffith becomes Big Ten's first commissioner

Major John L. Griffith — the Big Ten's first commissioner was appointed in 1922 — was also the Conference's first true visionary and activist. An Army veteran of World War I, Griffith laid the groundwork for solving problems and dealing with issues that still crop up today. A 1902 graduate of Beloit College in Wisconsin, Griffith spearheaded such drives as: stemming the tide of illegal recruiting, making clear definitions between amateur and professional athletes, and carving an agreement with professional baseball to prevent scouts from raiding college campuses. Griffith heightened levels of awareness for his crusades as president of the NCAA, a post he held concurrently as Big Ten Commissioner, from 1933 to 1937. He was also a member of the American Olympic Committee. Before joining the Big Ten, Griffith served as athletic director at Yankton College and later had the same positions at Morningside College and Drake, where he founded what would later become the famous Drake Relays. He died Dec. 7, 1944 in his Chicago office shortly after receiving a five-year renewal on his commissioner's contract.

OTHER MEMORABLE EVENTS

- Iowa went undefeated in football and was considered the top team in the nation.

- Michigan's Howard Hoffman became the first person to throw the javelin more than 200 feet.

- Iowa's Charles Brookins won the first of two straight NCAA titles in the 220-yard low hurdles.

- Illinois' Chuck Carney won his second Conference basketball scoring title.

- Chicago won the Conference golf team title, the first league school to actually win the open tournament.

Defense-minded Hawkeyes win school's first outright Big Ten football title

This Iowa football season, which concluded with the school's first outright Big Ten title, was marked by spectacular team and individual performances. The Hawkeyes (7-0, 5-0 Big Ten) allowed just 36 points all season and surrendered a total of only three touchdowns after a season-opening 52-14 victory over Knox. But the greatest team accomplishment came in its second game against Notre Dame, which entered with a 20-game winning streak. The Hawkeyes won 10-7, handing legendary coach Knute Rockne's squad its first defeat since 1918. As for the individual superlatives? How about quarterback Aubrey Devine scoring four touchdowns, throwing for two others and kicking five extra points in a 41-7 victory over Minnesota. In that game, Devine ran for 162 yards, threw for 122 and returned punts and kickoffs for 180, giving him 464 toal yards for the day. Devine scored a combined 57 points in eight days, including the game against Minnesota and a game against Indiana. Looking for another star? Fullback Gordon Locke rushed 37 times for 202 yards and two touchdowns in a 14-2 victory over Illinois. After the season, Iowa was invited to play in the Rose Bowl, but it had to be turned down because Iowa's athletic board and the Big Ten opposed postseason play. Devine, Locke and Fred "Duke" Slater were first-team All-Big Ten picks, and those three and Les Belding were honored by numerous All-America teams.

OTHER BIG TEN CHAMPIONS

- BASEBALL: Illinois, coached by Carl Lundgren
- GYMNASTICS: Chicago (coach not known)
- OUTDOOR TRACK: Illinois, coached by Harry Gill
- INDOOR TRACK: Illinois, coached by Harry Gill
- BASKETBALL: Purdue, coached by Ward Lambert
- CROSS COUNTRY: Illinois (no coach)
- TENNIS: Chicago (coach not known) and Illinois, coached by E.E. Bearg
- SWIMMING: Minnesota, coached by Niels Thorpe
- WRESTLING: Illinois (no coach)
- GOLF: Chicago (coach not known)

IOLAS HUFFMAN
Football, Ohio State

Ohio State was already building it-self into a football power in the early 1920s behind talented runners such as Pete Stinchcomb and Chic Harley, the first players to earn All-America honors in more than one season while playing for the Buckeyes. The leader of Buck-eye football teams in 1920 and '21 was a lineman named Iolas Huffman. Chosen All-America at guard during the 1920 season, Huffman changed positions to tackle the following season, where he nonetheless was named an All-American. He was a four-time letterman who was the captain of the 1920 team that won the Conference title with a 7-0 record and made the school's first appearance in the Rose Bowl. A talented student, Huffman was awarded the Conference's medal of honor in 1922.

FRED "DUKE" SLATER
Football and Track, Iowa

His name will always be some-what linked with Iowa's great 1921 Big Ten championship foot-ball team, quarterback Aubrey Devine and fullback Gordon Locke. But Fred "Duke" Slater's ac-complishments do quite well standing on their own. Because of a war-time rule, Slater was able to play as a freshman in 1918 and he was a standout lineman for four years. He was first-team All-Big Ten three times and was on various All-America teams. Slater was often double-teamed, and he preferred playing without headgear in an era when it was not mandatory. He also lettered two years on Iowa's track team. Slater went on to play nine years professionally with the Rock Island Independents and Chicago Cardinals, earning All-Pro honors from 1926-31. He was elected to the National Football Foundation's College Football Hall of Fame in 1956. Slater, a Normal, Ill., native who was raised in Chicago, earned a law degree from Iowa in 1928 and eventually became a superior court judge in Chicago's Cook County. He died in 1966 at the age of 67.

HAROLD OSBORN
Track, Illinois

Legally blind in one eye from a teenage accident, Harold Osborn nevertheless overcame the ob-stacle to become one of 26 ath-letes selected as charter members to the National Track and Field Hall of Fame. Osborn was a world record holder and a double winner at the Paris Olympics in 1924, the only Olympic athlete to win the decathlon and another indi-vidual event in the same Olympiad. He set an Olympic record in the high jump and a world record in the de-cathlon. Osborn had already set the world record in the high jump, clearing 6 feet, 8 1/2 inches in the Olympic Trials. In his career, Osborn set world records in six events and also earned a bronze medal in the high jump at the 1928 Amsterdam Olympics. As a collegian, he led Illinois to three straight Conference titles. He died in 1975.

CONFERENCE LOCALES

BIG TEN LIST

When the Big Ten announced its first commissioner in 1922, it also estab-lished its first office. Through the years, the office has remained in the Chicago area, but has been at five locations.

1922-50—Hotel Sherman (downtown Chicago)
1950-62—LaSalle Hotel (downtown Chicago)
1962-74—Sheraton-Chicago Hotel (downtown Chicago)
1974-91—1111 Plaza Drive Schaumburg, Ill. (suburban Chicago)
1991-present—1500 W. Higgins Road Park Ridge, Ill. (suburban Chicago)

LEADING THE WAY

PAUL PREHN
Illinois

The most prosperous coach in Illinois history is Paul Prehn, who led the Illini to wrestling dominance. Prehn was the Illini wrestling coach from 1919-20 to 1927-28, a span of nine seasons when Illinois won Big Ten titles seven times. During the nine-year stretch, Illinois compiled an impressive 42-5 dual-meet record. Among Prehn's stars at Illinois were Hek Kenney and Allie Morrison, who had an undefeated career at Illinois and won the gold medal at the 1928 Amsterdam Olympics. Prehn quickly put the Illini on top of the podium, developing two Big Ten individual champs—heavyweight H.A. Whitson and 175-pounder H.L. Hoffman—on his 1919-20 Illinois team that won the Big Ten title. When he left the Illini, Prehn began a highly successful restaurant business in Champaign-Urbana. He also served as chairman of the Illinois Athletic Commission for four years, a period that included the Jack Dempsey-Gene Tunney "Battle of the Century" boxing match in Chicago. Prehn was the state director of the Illinois Republican party for 10 years, and he died in 1973 at the age of 80.

· BIG TEN PIONEERS ·

Les Belding
Iowa

Lester Belding was Iowa's initial consensus football first-team All-American, a feat he accomplished as a sophomore. He was third-team as a freshman and senior and second-team after his junior year. Considered one of the top receivers in the nation during his era, he was three times named first-team All-Big Ten. Belding helped lead Iowa to its first outright league title in 1921 when he was the No. 4 scorer in the Conference. Belding received special mention by fans in 1989 when Iowa's all-time team was selected in conjunction with the school's first 100 years of football. He also was a star on Iowa's track team and was captain in 1921.

Lester Belding

Academic Achievements

*W*ithout research and development at the University of Illinois, there never would have been a movie like "Gone with the Wind" or "The Wizard of Oz." Of course, there wouldn't have been 27 sequels to "Friday the 13th," either. The invention of "talkies" took place at UI in 1922 with the development of adding a sound recording to film.

1921-22
Conference MEDAL OF HONOR
Winners

CHICAGO	Herbert O. Crisler
ILLINOIS	Clarence Crossley
INDIANA	William G. McCaw
IOWA	Aubrey Devine
MICHIGAN	Robert J. Dunne
MINNESOTA	Arnold Oss
NORTHWESTERN	Graham Penfield
OHIO STATE	Iolas M. Huffman
PURDUE	Clifford C. Furnas
WISCONSIN	George Bunge

1922-23

THE BIG EVENT

Michigan baseball goes unbeaten in Big Ten

Michigan's 1923 baseball team posted a 22-4 overall record and was 10-0 in the Big Ten, one of only seven teams to go unbeaten in the Conference since baseball play began in 1896. The Wolverines regained the Big Ten's top spot after a two-year hiatus on May 28 with a 5-2 win over Ohio State at Columbus. Howard Liverance threw a five-hitter at the Bucks and twice hit safely to pace Ray Fisher's team to its eighth Big Ten win, good enough to assure Michigan the title. Michigan started the season slowly with a 4-3 record after seven games, but then won 18 of its last 19, including a 17-game winning streak, to finish 22-4. The Wolverines' .846 winning percentage was the second best in Fisher's 37-year coaching career, trailing only the 20-1 mark (.952) posted by his 1945 team.

OTHER MEMORABLE EVENTS

- Michigan won the NCAA outdoor track championship.

- Iowa's Eric Wilson won his second 220-yard dash title at the NCAA championship.

- The Conference called a meeting to discuss "fan control" at basketball games.

- Chicago (one tie), Iowa and Michigan all were undefeated in Conference football games, the last time three schools finished the season unbeaten.

- The league enacted rules that any athlete who "flunked out" of school had to be in residence for two years to regain eligibility, and raised the limit on football games per season from seven to eight.

Barry leads Hawkeyes to Conference cage crown

Iowa had never finished better than fifth place in conference basketball play. Until 1923, that is. Under first-year coach Sam Barry, the Hawkeyes rolled to 11 consecutive Big Ten victories to clinch their first league title, which they ended up sharing with Wisconsin after losing their season finale to Indiana. The Badgers and Hawkeyes did not play during the season. Iowa finished 13-2 overall, including an 8-1 mark at home. It was a 20-18 victory over Michigan on March 8 that secured a piece of the championship. But the Hoosiers then beat Iowa, 23-21. Iowa's only other loss came against Notre Dame (24-23) in the third game of the season. The Hawkeyes' starting five was Hector Janse, James Laude, Robert Burgitt, Jack Funk and Wayland Hicks. Janse was named to the All-Big Ten team. That entire starting lineup was gone three years later when Barry coached Iowa to another share of the league championship (8-4). But the Hawkeyes would not match the 11-1 league record of the 1923 team for 22 years. Barry coached seven years at Iowa, with his teams going 62-54 overall and 43-41 in league play.

OTHER BIG TEN CHAMPIONS

- **FOOTBALL:** Iowa coached by Howard Jones, and Michigan, coached by Fielding Yost
- **BASEBALL:** Michigan, coached by Ray Fisher
- **GYMNASTICS:** Wisconsin, coached by Frank Leitz
- **OUTDOOR TRACK:** Michigan, coached by Stephen Farrell
- **INDOOR TRACK:** Michigan, coached by Stephen Farrell
- **CROSS COUNTRY:** Michigan, coached by Stephen Farrell
- **TENNIS:** Chicago (coach not known) and Michigan, coached by Paul Leidy
- **SWIMMING:** Northwestern, coached by Tom Robinson
- **+WRESTLING:** Iowa State and Ohio State, coached by Al Haft
- **GOLF:** Illinois, coached by George Davis
- **+open meet**

EDWARD H. "KILLER" TEMPLIN
Wrestling, Wisconsin

Ed "Killer" Templin was among the nation's best collegiate wrestlers from 1921-24 and is one of the greatest grapplers in Wisconsin history. He was a three-time major "W" award recipient and was the first of only four wrestlers in Badgers' history to win three Big Ten championships (1922, '23 and '24). Don Ryan (1950, '51 and '56), Bob Konovsky (1954, '55 and '56), and Lee Kemp (1976, '77 and '78) were the only others. Templin competed in middleweight divisions, ranging from 158- to 175-pounds. He wrestled for the first-ever full-time coach of Wisconsin's program, George Hitchcock. He was captain of the Badgers' 1923 team. He majored in agriculture and was inducted into the University of Wisconsin Athletic Hall of Fame in 1995.

GORDON LOCKE
Football, Iowa

Gordon Locke was among the stars of Iowa's Big Ten championship teams of 1921 (outright) and '22 (shared), playing fullback for three seasons and also playing quarterback as a senior. As a junior, he was named to several All-America teams after rushing for more than 700 yards. He was first-team All-Big Ten two straight years and a consensus All-American in '22. As a senior captain, he scored 72 points in five Big Ten games, a record that lasted until 1943. He had four TDs against Northwestern and three against Minnesota that season. Locke also was a three-time letterman as a first baseman on the Iowa baseball team. The Denison, Iowa, native won the Conference Medal of Honor. Locke remained at Iowa as an assistant football coach (1923-26). He then coached and was athletic director at Case Western Reserve in Cleveland and was an Iowa assistant again in 1931. Locke was selected to the National Football Foundation's College Football Hall of Fame in 1960 and the Helms Athletic Foundation Hall of Fame in 1961. He died at the age of 71.

HARRY KIPKE
Football, Basketball and Baseball, Michigan

A nine-letter winner in football, basketball and baseball, Harry Kipke was an all-time Michigan great as a punter, booting kicks with amazing accuracy and renowned for kicking the ball out of bounds. As a halfback for Fielding Yost, Kipke was a solid runner, but his precision kicks made Yost consider him an integral part of the offense. He was a starter for three seasons and was named All-America in 1922. In 1923, he captained the undefeated squad that won the Big Ten title. Kipke coached the football Wolverines from 1928-37, with his 1930-33 squads going 31-1-3 and capturing four outright Conference championships and national titles in 1932 and 1933. He quit coaching in 1937 after posting a nine-season mark of 46-24-4 and became a University regent. Kipke died in 1972 at age 73.

BIG TEN LIST

NCAA TRACK TITLES

Big Ten men have won 200 individual titles at the NCAA outdoor track championships. By school:

- 7, Chicago
- 38, Illinois
- 21, Indiana
- 12, Iowa
- 31, Michigan
- 11, Michigan State
- 8, Minnesota
- 12, Northwestern
- 43, Ohio State
- 1, Penn State (15 prior to joining Big Ten)
- 4, Purdue
- 13, Wisconsin

LEADING THE WAY

PAUL GOEBEL
Michigan

Paul Goebel was an excellent example of a man who carried gridiron success into later life. A brilliant student, later an engineer and businessman, he also became a Big Ten official, a University Regent, and a member of Michigan's Athletic Board. During World War II, he served as Lieutenant Commander on an aircraft carrier. The Grand Rapids, Mich., native entered Michigan in 1919, started at end and played in every game. He continued through 1922 as an outstanding all-around wingman. Symbolically, Goebel was the first All-American to wear jersey No. 1 for the Wolverines, leading the way for two other future No. 1's, Anthony Carter and Derrick Alexander.

· BIG TEN PIONEERS ·

President Walter Dill Scott
Northwestern

Northwestern President Walter Dill Scott had played football for the Wildcats, showing so much tenacity that when, as a 170-pound guard in 1892, he broke his hand in a game early in the season, but came back two weeks later wearing a boxing glove to finish the year. So it wasn't all that surprising when President Scott jumped out of the stands to lead cheers during a game against heavily favored Minnesota. The fans went wild, and moments later Chuck Palmer recovered a fumble in the end zone and ran 105 yards—still a Big Ten record—for a touchdown that enabled the Wildcats to finish in a 7-7 tie.

 ## Academic Achievements

Northwestern's famous School of Speech was the first of its type to be established in 1878. Today, it is home to the largest student-run college radio station in the nation, WNUR-FM, among many other programs.

The BIG TEN's First 100 Years
Big Ten Football Three-Time Consensus First-Team All-American Selections

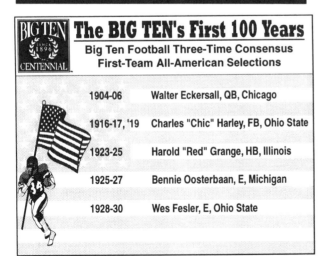

1904-06	Walter Eckersall, QB, Chicago
1916-17, '19	Charles "Chic" Harley, FB, Ohio State
1923-25	Harold "Red" Grange, HB, Illinois
1925-27	Bennie Oosterbaan, E, Michigan
1928-30	Wes Fesler, E, Ohio State

1922-23
Conference MEDAL OF HONOR
Winners

CHICAGO	**Harold A. Fletcher**
ILLINOIS	**Otto H. Vogel**
INDIANA	**Omar Held**
IOWA	**Gordon C. Locke**
MICHIGAN	**Paul C. Goebel**
MINNESOTA	**Rudolph Hultkrans**
NORTHWESTERN	**James J. Peterson**
OHIO STATE	**Charles H. Workman**
PURDUE	**William R. Swank**
WISCONSIN	**Gustave K. Tebell**

THE BIG EVENT

Illinois athletes star at Paris Olympics

Harold Osborn (left) was an osteopathic physician who worked out on his own for two years in near seclusion heading to the 1924 Paris Olympics. "I don't think anybody knew he was there," said his wife, Margaret. Osborn and a group of three other track athletes from Illinois made sure they were seen during the Olympic Games, combining to score 35 points—a total higher than any other country entered in track and field competition. Osborn was the star from Illinois, scoring wins in the high jump and decathlon to become the only athlete ever to win the decathlon and another individual event in the same Olympics. In the process, Osborn set an Olympic record in the high jump at 6-feet-6 inches and set an Olympic and world record in the decathlon with 7,710 points, marks that stood 12 years. Meanwhile, Dan Kinsey won the 110-meter high hurdles and H.M. Fitch was second in the 400-meter run to complete scoring from Illinois competitors.

OTHER MEMORABLE EVENTS

- Wisconsin's Ed "Killer" Templin, at 145 pounds, was the first man to win three straight Conference wrestling titles.

- Iowa's H.R. Phelps won the first of two straight Conference cross country championships.

- "Wildcats" was chosen as Northwestern's official school nickname, replacing "Purple."

- Ohio State's Harry Steel won the Olympic heavyweight wrestling title.

- Wisconsin's Schmidt won the first of two consecutive Conference all-around gymnastics championships.

Northwestern swimming team dunks competition at Big Ten meet

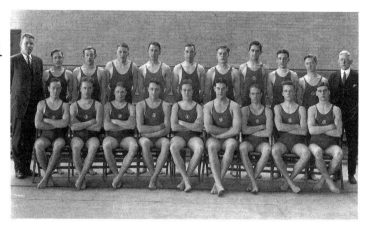

Northwestern won 10 Big Ten championships under swimming coach Tom Robinson, and three of them came consecutively from 1923-25. The Wildcats won all eight of their dual meets in 1923, then edged Minnesota in the Conference finals, 32-30. They came back even stronger the following season, rolling over second-place Michigan in the league championship, 32-14, to complete another undefeated season. The 1924 team also won the national championship, as Ralph Breyer and Dick Howell swept the freestyle events—Breyer in the 100 and 200 meters and Howell in the 400 and 1,500 meters. Those two also broke the Big Ten and NCAA records in their events, and qualified for the 1924 U.S. Olympic team. Breyer and Howell returned to captain the 1925 team that completed the three-year run of championships, scoring 36 points in the Big Ten meet. The team was so successful that four of the members, Breyer, Howell, Paul Corbett and Paul Manovitz, accompanied the school's glee club on a tour of the West and defeated college and AAU teams along the way. The four set a national collegiate record in the 160-yard relay in one of the meets.

OTHER BIG TEN CHAMPIONS

- FOOTBALL: Illinois, coached by Robert Zuppke, and Michigan, coached by Fielding Yost
- BASEBALL: Michigan, coached by Ray Fisher, and Ohio State, coached by L.W. St. John
- GYMNASTICS: Chicago (coach not known)
- OUTDOOR TRACK: Illinois, coached by Harry Gill
- INDOOR TRACK: Illinois, coached by Harry Gill
- BASKETBALL: Chicago, (coach not known), Illinois, coached by J. Craig Ruby, and Wisconsin, coached by Dr. Walter Meanwell
- CROSS COUNTRY: Ohio State, coached by Frank Castleman
- TENNIS: Chicago (coach not known), and Illinois, coached by E.E. Bearg
- WRESTLING: Illinois, coached by Paul Prehn, and Indiana, coached by Jack Reynolds
- GOLF: Chicago (coach not known)

RALPH BREYER
Swimming, Northwestern

Northwestern's swim program boasted many outstanding athletes early in the century, but freestyler Ralph Breyer was among the very best. It was no coincidence that during Breyer's three years of competition the Wildcats won all of their dual meets and all three Big Ten championships. Breyer, a sophomore in 1923, won the national collegiate title in the 440-yard freestyle in a record 5:29.4. He returned in 1924 to win the 100- and 200-meter events in the NCAA meet, breaking the Big Ten and national collegiate records along the way. After competing on the 1924 U.S. Olympic team, Breyer returned to lead the Wildcats to another Big Ten title. He later gave credit to his coach, Tom Robinson: "It was generally felt that if a swimmer put his complete confidence in Tom, and did what he asked, that swimmer would attain the very utmost of his capabilities," he said.

HARRY STEELE
Football and Wrestling, Ohio State

Playing more than one sport is an unusual phenomenon in today's college athletic scene. Specialization keeps players locked into one sport. Years ago, athletes would play whatever sport was in season, and Harry Steele was one of those athletes who was a standout in more than one arena. A two-time wrestling letterman who captured the Conference title as a heavyweight in the 1923-24 season, he also won the gold medal at the 1924 Olympics held in Paris. Steele also lettered twice on football teams at Ohio State. More than an athlete, he was also an excellent student, earning the Conference Medal of Honor at the conclusion of the 1923-24 school year. He was inducted into the Ohio State Sports Hall of Fame in 1980.

HARRY FRIEDA
Track, Chicago

Harry Frieda starred on Chicago track teams of the mid-1920s, winning the 1923 NCAA javelin title at 191-feet-6 inches in the third national collegiate championships hosted by Chicago, after taking only fifth in the event at the Big Ten meet. Frieda was the Maroons' top scorer in three dual meets, with his three firsts against both Northwestern and Purdue providing Chicago's margin of victory. He also made the 1924 U.S. Olympic team in the javelin. Frieda was Chicago's Conference Medal of Honor winner in 1925.

BIG TEN LIST

NORTHWESTERN SWIMMING CHAMPS

A total of 14 Northwestern male swimmers and divers have been multiple winners of the same event at the Conference championships:

V. Johnson, 100-yd. freestyle, 1915-16
V. Johnson, 220-yd. freestyle, 1915-16
Simonsen, 440-yd. freestyle, 1916-18
McDonald, fancy diving, 1917-18
Raymond, 150-yd. backstroke, 1917-18
A. Crawley, fancy diving, 1920-21
Ralph Breyer, 40-yd. freestyle, 1923-24-25
Ralph Breyer, 440-yd. freestyle, 1923-24
Richard Howell, 220-yd. freestyle, 1924-25
Albert Swartz, 220-yd. freestyle, 1928-29-30
Albert Swartz, 100-yd. freestyle, 1929-30
Dick Hinch, 150-yd. backstroke, 1929-30
Donald Horn, 200-yd. breaststroke, 1933-34
William Heusner, 1500-meter freestyle,
    1947-49

LEADING THE WAY

HAROLD OLSEN
Ohio State

He was hired as the basketball coach prior to the 1923-24 season, and Ohio State hadn't won a Conference title in the sport. That would change under Harold Olsen, who guided the Buckeyes to five Conference championships in his 24 years as coach. Ohio State won 255 games under Olsen, a mark only surpassed by Fred Taylor. The Buckeyes were 4-11 the year before Olsen arrived, and two seasons later Ohio State won its first Conference title with an 11-1 record and a 14-2 mark overall. The Buckeyes won the title again in 1938-39 and played in the first NCAA tournament, finishing as the runner-up. In a three-year run that ended with his final Big Ten title in 1945-46, the Buckeyes won two Conference championships and finished as runner-up the other season. In all three years, the Buckeyes reached the NCAA semifinals, losing twice in the semifinals and finishing as runner-up in 1945-46. Olsen produced Johnny Miner, the school's first All-America basketball player in 1924-25. Ohio State has had 14 players win All-America honors a total of 19 times, including Olsen's other All-American, Jimmy Hull in 1938-39.

· BIG TEN PIONEERS ·

Jim McMillen
Illinois

Behind every superstar is the unsung hero. The superstar during the early 1920s at Illinois was a halfback they called the Galloping Ghost. Red Grange led Illinois to an undefeated Conference title in the 1923 season, as Illinois posted an 8-0 record overall and 5-0 mark in the league. The Illini also won the national championship that season, and such feats weren't possible without the contribution of Jim McMillen, (below) voted as an All-America guard. McMillen was one of six Illinois linemen to earn All-America selection under coach Bob Zuppke. A three-year letterman in football from 1921-23, McMillen was also honored by Illinois as an honorable mention pick for the school's all-century team in 1990.

Jim McMillen

Academic Achievements

A wind tunnel aids engineers in a variety of tasks. Auto designers use it to build more efficient-moving vehicles. Bicycle racers use it to find a position on the bike that offers the least wind resistance. And aeronautical engineers use it to create aircraft that is easier to handle. Michigan has been a leader in wind tunnel development and in 1924 was the first school to own one.

1923-24
Conference MEDAL OF HONOR
Winners

CHICAGO	Chapbell Dickson
ILLINOIS	Walter Roettger
INDIANA	John Nay
IOWA	Wayland Hicks
MICHIGAN	Franklin C. Cappon
MINNESOTA	Earl Martineau
NORTHWESTERN	Guy Davis
OHIO STATE	Harry D. Steele
PURDUE	Edward R. Dye
WISCONSIN	Harold J. Bentson

THE BIG EVENT

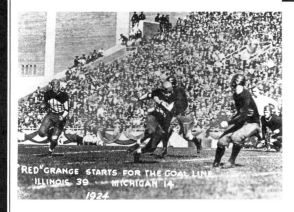

RED"GRANGE STARTS FOR THE GOAL LINE
ILLINOIS 39 - MICHIGAN 14
1924

Grange "gallops" past Michigan

It was a warm, sunny October afternoon in 1924, a crowd of 66,609 making its way to Memorial Stadium in Champaign, thanks to 24 regular and 20 special passenger trains. The game between Michigan and Illinois was a showdown between the West's top two teams, Michigan and Illinois, the day the stadium was officially dedicated and the day one of America's greatest football legends—the Galloping Ghost, Red Grange—was christened. Grange was the league's star the previous season, when Michigan and Illinois didn't meet, but he would never be forgotten after this day. He returned the opening kickoff 95 yards for a touchdown, then scored on runs of 67, 56 and 44 yards the next three times he touched the ball. The scored was 27-0 just 12 minutes into the game, the crowd reaching a frenzy. When the day was complete, Grange had scored 30 points on runs, carrying it for 212 yards, while also passing for another touchdown in the 39-14 victory.

OTHER MEMORABLE EVENTS

- Northwestern halfback Chuck Palmer went 102 yards with a fumble recovery, the second-longest run in Conference history.

- Chicago's football team went undefeated to win the Conference title.

- Ohio State's Johnny Miner won the Conference basketball scoring title, despite standing just 5-foot-8.

- Michigan's DeHart Hubbard was the first Conference athlete to win two NCAA track titles in one year—the 100-yard dash and broad jump.

- Minnesota's John Faricy became the first Gopher to win a national crown, winning the 200-yard breaststroke.

Indiana claims school's first baseball title

1925 SOUTHERN TEAM TRIP

Indiana's baseball team won the school's first Big Ten championship in 1925 under a first-year coach, Everett Dean. The Hoosiers had never finished higher than third since beginning Conference play in 1906 and had been mired in the bottom half of the league standings the previous three seasons, but they put together an 11-6 overall record and 9-2 Conference mark — although they never did get the hang of beating the smaller colleges. Indiana lost its opener to Ohio State, 6-5, and followed with an 8-4 defeat to Transylvania. It rebounded with victories over Chicago, Northwestern and Minnesota, then lost to the Gophers in the second game of a doubleheader. It beat Iowa and Purdue, lost to non-Conference opponents DePauw and Wabash, beat Northwestern, lost to Wabash again, and beat Chicago and Purdue to wrap up the championship. Dean, who doubled as IU's basketball coach, also won league baseball titles in 1932 and '38 before taking over as Stanford's basketball and baseball coach. Indiana won its next league baseball championship in 1949, then didn't win another until the '96 team captured the postseason tournament title.

OTHER BIG TEN CHAMPIONS

- **FOOTBALL:** Chicago, coached by Amos Alonzo Stagg
- **GYMNASTICS:** Minnesota, coached by Dr. W.K. Foster
- **OUTDOOR TRACK:** Michigan, coached by Stephen Farrell
- **INDOOR TRACK:** Michigan, coached by Stephen Farrell
- **BASKETBALL:** Ohio State, coached by Harold Olsen
- **CROSS COUNTRY:** Wisconsin, coached by Meade Burke
- **+TENNIS:** Butler
- **SWIMMING:** Northwestern, coached by Tom Robinson
- **WRESTLING:** Illinois, coached by Paul Prehn, and Indiana, coached by Jack Reynolds
- **GOLF:** Northwestern, coached by Leon Kranz

+open meet

HAROLD CUNNINGHAM
Football and Basketball, Ohio State

It was hard to figure out where Harold "Cookie" Cunningham was best suited — on the football field or the basketball court when he lettered three times in both sports. As an end, Cuningham was chosen as an All-American following the 1924 football season. He served as captain the following year in football, when the Buckeyes finished with a 4-3-1 record. As a 6-foot-4 center, Cunningham was named to the first All-Conference team in the 1924-25 season when he was a junior. He was a three-year starter, including his final season with the Buckeyes in the 1925-26 season. Teammate Johnny Miner was also named as an All-Conference player that season. After his graduation from Ohio State, Cunningham played professional basketball and professional football in 1929 with the Chicago Bears.

EDLIFF R. SLAUGHTER
Football, Michigan

Edliff R. Slaughter was a standout on both offense and defense for the Wolverine football squads of 1922, '23 and '24. In his three seasons, Michigan was 20-2-1 with the only losses coming in his senior season (to Illinois and Iowa). The Wolverines were Big Ten champions in 1922 (4-0) and '23 (4-0). A Walter Camp All-American, Slaughter was described by Camp as: "A veteran guard who has always towered in the line. A big man, but extremely active, he provides the pivotal spot upon which a line-plunging attack may rest." Slaughter, who made his jersey No. 32 famous in his day, played in the first East-West Shrine all-star football game in 1925.

AUSTIN "FIVE YARDS" McCARTY
Football, Chicago

Rampaging fullback Austin "Five Yards" McCarty was one of the stars of Coach Amos Alonzo Stagg's last great Chicago football team, which posted an undefeated Conference season, marred only by three ties. One of those came by a 21-21 count against a Red Grange-led Illinois team at Stagg Field in perhaps the greatest game ever at that site. And it was McCarty, crashing through the line, and Grange, running around end, who dueled through the afternoon, each scoring a touchdown. McCarty was edged for All-America honors by Elmer Layden of Notre Dame "Four Horsemen" fame.

BIG TEN LIST

MULTIPLE GOLF WINNERS

Chicago's K.E. Hisert became the Big Ten's first back-to-back winner of the Conference golf tournament in 1925 and '26. Since then, 10 other golfers have won multiple titles.

K.E. Hisert, Chicago, 1925-26
Les Bolstad, Minnesota, 1927-29
Richard Martin, Illinois, 1930-31
John Fischer, Michigan, 1932-33-34
Sid Richardson, Northwestern, 1937-38
Ed Schalon, Michigan, 1947(co)-1949
Fred Wampler, Purdue, 1948-49(co)-50
Joe Campbell, Purdue, 1956-57
John Konsek, Purdue, 1958-59-60
John Cook, Ohio State, 1978-79(co)
Steve Stricker, Illinois, 1986-88-89

LEADING THE WAY

RALPH AIGLER
Michigan

Ralph Aigler had as much influence on the Big Ten Conference for a longer period of time than anyone in the league's history. The veteran law professor at Michigan was the school's faculty representative for nearly 40 years. Born in Bellevue, Ohio, in 1885, Aigler graduated from Michigan with a degree in law in 1907. After three years of private practice, he returned to Ann Arbor as a member of the law faculty. He got involved with the school's athletic board in 1913 and was named the faculty representative in 1917, a position he held until 1955. He was instrumental in Michigan returning to the Conference in 1917 (after a 10-year hiatus). His perspective of college athletics changed little over the years: a stern insistence that athletes are playing games, instead of working for wages...there is a proper place for athletics, but team members must be primarily students.

· BIG TEN PIONEERS ·

Final year of swimming's 60-yard plunge

The year 1925 marked the final time one of men's swimming's most unique—and challenging—events was included in Big Ten competition: the 60-yard plunge for distance. Competitors were required to dive in and swim as fast as they could for 60 yards—under water. The event had a short life span. It was a Big Ten championship event only from 1911 to 1925. Yet the race was one in which its athletes improved exponentially from the first race for the Big Ten title in 1911—when Chicago's F. Rundell won it in a time of 52 seconds flat—to the last in 1925, when L.E. Eldredge of Illinois took the blue ribbon with a time of :16.4 seconds. Illinois' A.P. McDonald was the only swimmer to win the event twice, doing so in 1914 and '15.

Academic Achievements

Northwestern's School of Law was not only the first law school opened in the Midwest in 1859, but was also the first to introduce the case study method in 1879. It was also the birthplace of the lie detector, an invention of the NU Law School's Scientific Crime Lab Detection Laboratory.

1924-25
Conference MEDAL OF HONOR
Winners

CHICAGO	Harry G. Frieda
ILLINOIS	Gilbert J. Roberts
INDIANA	Harlan Logan
IOWA	John Hancock
MICHIGAN	William B. Giles
MINNESOTA	Louis Gross
NORTHWESTERN	Ralph T. Breyer
OHIO STATE	Lawrence H. Snyder
PURDUE	Ferdinand J. Wellman
WISCONSIN	Lloyd Vallely

1925-1934

As much a part of the University of Illinois as the Galloping Ghost

ILLINI UNION BOOKSTORE
The Official University Bookstore

on the corner of Wright and Daniel Streets

THE BIG EVENT

Big Ten hosts first fencing championship

Fencing's 61-year life span as a Big Ten championship event began in 1926, when Ohio State won the first team title. Ohio State also had the distinction of hosting the first NCAA fencing championship in 1941, won by Conference rival Northwestern. Although Ohio State won the first Big Ten team championship, the first two individual titles, however, belonged to Ed McNamara of Northwestern and G.H. Borland of Illinois. McNamara was the first foil champion. Borland was the first epee victor. As for team competition, Illinois dominated the sport throughout its existence. The Illini won 30 Conference championships, including the final league crown in 1986, when the sport was discontinued for men and women. Illinois' 30 titles are the third most by any Conference school in any sport. The Illini won eight championships in the 1950s, highlighted by Art Schankin's NCAA sabre championship in 1958. He was the only fencer in history to win Conference championships in two different weapons — foil in 1957 and sabre in '58.

OTHER MEMORABLE EVENTS

- Chicago's Amos Alonzo Stagg was elected president of the NCAA.

- Iowa and Wisconsin combined for 34 fumbles—18 in the first quarter—while playing in a snowstorm.

- Chicago's K.E. Hisert won the Conference golf championship, the first tournament decided by medal play.

- Illinois' Tim O'Connell won the first of three straight Conference tennis titles.

- Michigan's Harry Hawkins was an All-America football guard, as well as the NCAA hammer champion.

Chicago wins seventh of its 14 gymnastics titles

Chicago won its sixth gymnastics title in eight Conference meets, scoring 1,234.80 points to defeat host Purdue by 20 points at West Lafayette, Ind. It would be the seventh of 14 Big Ten gymnastics titles that the Maroons would win and avenged an earlier 20-point loss to the Boilermakers before a full house at the same site. Chicago coach Dan Hoffer had only three experienced gymnasts at the start of the season, but by the time of the Conference meet the others had improved significantly. Despite the absence of team captain Jeremiah Quin because of a dislocated arm suffered on the parallel bars, Burton McRoy ably subbed for him and barely missed a tie in the club swinging event. Chicago ended its season by defeating Eastern champion Pennsylvania, 25-20, in Philadelphia.

OTHER BIG TEN CHAMPIONS

- **FOOTBALL:** Michigan, coached by Fielding Yost
- **BASEBALL:** Michigan, coached by Ray Fisher
- **OUTDOOR TRACK:** Michigan, coached by Stephen Farrell
- **INDOOR TRACK:** Iowa, coached by George Bresnahan
- **BASKETBALL:** Indiana, coached by Everett Dean, Iowa, coached by Sam Barry, Michigan, coached by E.J. Mather, and Purdue, coached by Ward Lambert
- **CROSS COUNTRY:** Wisconsin, coached by Meade Burke
- **TENNIS:** Illinois, coached by A.R. Cohn
- **SWIMMING:** Minnesota, coached by Niels Thorpe
- **WRESTLING:** Illinois, coached by Paul Prehn
- **GOLF:** Chicago (coach not known)
- **FENCING:** Ohio State, coached by F.A. Riebel

RED GRANGE
Football, Illinois

In a three-year career from 1923-25, Grange led Illinois to a national championship, finished as a three-time All-American, the Conference MVP, and became known as the Galloping Ghost. His legend was complete in 1924 when he scored four touchdowns the first four times he touched the ball in a win over Michigan—runs of 95, 67, 56 and 44 yards—in the game's first 12 minutes, inspiring a poem from legendary sportswriter Grantland Rice. Grange's No. 77 was retired following his final game at Illinois, and he immediately began a pro career with the Chicago Bears. Football's answer to Babe Ruth, Grange drew crowds to pro football, handing it instant credibility. He led the Bears to two NFL titles and was a charter member of the college and pro football halls of fame. He died in 1991.

KEN HISERT
Golf, Chicago

Chicago's Ken Hisert became the first of 11 men in Big Ten golf history to win consecutive individual titles. His first victory in 1925 was in match play, defeating defending Conference champion M.J. Holdsworth of Michigan, 3 and 2, in a 36-hole match at Sunset Ridge Country Club. Hisert defended his title the following spring at Lake Forest, shooting 316 for 72 holes. He and the 1926 Maroon squad also claimed the team title, the last of its three team championships in that sport.

NICHOLAS KUTSCH
Football, Iowa

Nicholas Kutch was really from the West...that is, western Iowa. As a result, he was nicknamed "Cowboy" upon his transfer to the state's big university from Sioux City's little Trinity College. Kutsch was a 178-pounder who became a triple threat in his first varsity game in 1925, running with a free-wheeling motion and hitting with power. He scored 50 points in his first three games for the Hawkeyes, with that third game against a Red Grange-led Illinois team bringing him notice. The Cowboy rushed for 144 yards, kicked two 25-yard field goals and bulled his way across the goal line in the final minute to upset the Illini, 12-10. In 1926, he was as good, if not better, rushing for 781 yards. An All-Conference choice, Kutsch was passed over for All-America, likely because of Iowa's mediocre record.

B I G   T E N   L I S T

SPORTS INFORMATION DIRECTORS

Michigan State's Jim Hasselman was considered one of the first (if not the first) sports information directors in the country when he began his duties in 1917. The Big Ten is considered the birthplace of the profession with an all-star line-up of SIDs in the 1920s. Here were the first sports publicists (and year) of each school's first:

Illinois: L.M. "Mike" Tobin (1922)
Indiana: George Gardner (1935)
Iowa: Eric Wilson (1923)
Michigan: Phil Pack (1925)
Michigan State: Jim Hasselman (1917)
Minnesota: Les Etter (1930)
Northwestern: Walt Paulison (1926)
Ohio State: William Griffith (1923)
Penn State: George (Pat) Sullivan (1922)
Purdue: Robert McMahon (1925)
Wisconsin: Les Gage (1923)

LEADING THE WAY

ERIC WILSON
Iowa

During an era when most sports information directors were part-time employees, Iowa made Eric Wilson one of the first full-time SIDs in the country in 1924. He held the position for 44 years before retiring in 1968, when he was honored with the Arch Ward Memorial Award as the nation's outstanding sports information director. Wilson's SID career spanned periods when schools provided little but scores of games to a time when more information about athletes and teams was documented and dispersed. Before becoming a pioneer in the sports information field, Wilson was a track standout at Iowa. He won NCAA and Big Ten Conference championships in the 220-yard dash in 1921 and '23 and was a sprinter on the 1924 U.S. Olympic team in Paris. Wilson set world records in the 200- and 400-meter races during the Olympic trials and was one of four Americans to run the 400 at the Olympic Games. After retiring, Wilson lived during the winters in Sarasota, Fla., but still spent the summers in Iowa City. He died in July, 1985, at the age of 85.

· BIG TEN PIONEERS ·

Four-way tie for basketball title

In 1926, an anomaly occurred in the race for the Big Ten basketball championship that has never been repeated: Four teams earned a share of the title. Indiana, Michigan, Purdue, and Iowa all laid a claim to the championship with identical league records. Indiana was the only team of the four not to have won — or shared — the title previously. The Hoosiers (below) were led by captain Julius Kreuger and Art Beckner. Kreuger was the league scoring champion that season. Michigan was powered by star Dick Doyle. Purdue was fueled by George Spradling. And Charley McConnell was the leading force behind Iowa. Doyle, Spradling, and McConnell were all first-team All-Americans.

Academic Achievements

It's a fact. More school children called in sick the day that the Iowa Basic Skills Tests were administered than any other day of the year. Despite its less than glorious following, the Skills Test was the best measure available to compare a student's abilities to others across the nation. It was developed at the University of Iowa in 1925 by education professor E.F. Lindquist.

1925-26
Conference MEDAL OF HONOR Winners

CHICAGO	Graham A. Kernwein
ILLINOIS	John W. Mauer
INDIANA	Daniel G. Bernoske
IOWA	D.M. Graham
MICHIGAN	Harold Freyberg
MINNESOTA	Raymond F. Rasey
NORTHWESTERN	Walter Seidel
OHIO STATE	Ralph E. Seiffer
PURDUE	Donald S. Cunningham
WISCONSIN	Stephen H. Pulaski

THE BIG EVENT

Oosterbaan an All-American in football and basketball

While multi-sport stars were common in the 1920s and '30s, multi-sport All-Americans certainly were not, but then, nine-time letterwinner Bennie Oosterbaan was anything but common. The Muskegon, Mich., native became one of the most honored athletes in collegiate history, earning All-America honors in football and basketball in 1927-28. He was a three-time All-American at end, the only Michigan player to be so honored. In basketball, Oosterbaan was the Big Ten's leading scorer in 1928. To top it off, in baseball, he led the Conference in hitting as a senior. Oosterbaan served as an assistant football coach for 20 years before taking charge in 1948 and guiding the Wolverines to the Big Ten and national championships. In 11 seasons, his teams went 63-33-4 and won three Conference titles and the 1951 Rose Bowl. He was Michigan's director of athletic alumni relations until 1972.

OTHER MEMORABLE EVENTS

- **Northwestern's Tiny Lewis, known more for his football skills, scored in six events in a dual track meet vs. Indiana.**

- **Michigan and Minnesota faced each other twice in football, in 1926 the only time teams have done that on the gridiron.**

- **Illinois won the NCAA outdoor track title.**

- **Northwestern had its first undefeated Conference football season.**

- **Athletes were banned from using their names in advertising or athletic writing.**

- **Illinois and Iowa tied for the Conference baseball title, literally. Both teams finished with 7-3 records, plus a tie game—against each other.**

Sittig leads Illinois to NCAA track and field title

The star of the 1927 NCAA track and field championships for Illinois was Johnny Sittig, one of four athletes who broke NCAA records as the Illini won their second NCAA title in a meet held in Soldier Field. Sittig ran the best half-mile race in his career in his last race wearing Illinois colors, setting a meet record with a 1:54.2 that also broke a 13-year-old school record. Ten athletes from Illinois placed, as the Illini compiled 35.4 points to finish ahead of runner-up Texas, which scored 29.5 points. Illinois' Joe Simon managed to finish second in the long jump while teammate Dan Lyon was second in the shot put. Dan McKeever, a third-place finisher in the Conference meet, placed fourth in the 120-yard high hurdles. It was the second NCAA title won by Illinois under coach Harry Gill. Earlier that year, Illinois claimed one of 11 outdoor Conference championships under Gill after the Illini edged Michigan by less than two points. The high jump was the final event of the day, the event having been moved indoors because of poor weather conditions, and Illinois' Ted Wachowski cleared 6-feet-3 inches—his best mark of the year—to win the event and hand the Illini the team title.

OTHER BIG TEN CHAMPIONS

- **FOOTBALL:** Michigan, coached by Fielding Yost, and Northwestern, coached by Glenn Thistlethwaite
- **BASEBALL:** Illinois, coached by Carl Lundgren, and Iowa, coached by Otto Vogel
- **GYMNASTICS:** Chicago (coach not known)
- **INDOOR TRACK:** Wisconsin, coached by Thomas Jones
- **BASKETBALL:** Michigan, coached by E.J. Mather
- **CROSS COUNTRY:** Wisconsin, coached by Thomas Jones
- **TENNIS:** Illinois, coached by A.R. Cohn, and Michigan (no coach)
- **SWIMMING:** Michigan, coached by Matt Mann
- **WRESTLING:** Illinois, coached by Paul Prehn
- **GOLF:** Illinois, coached by D.L. Swank
- **FENCING:** Ohio State, coached by Ted Lorber

WALLY COLBATH
Diving, Northwestern

Wally Colbath is perhaps the finest diver in Northwestern's history, winning NCAA championships all three years of his career that spanned from 1927-29. Colbath enjoyed a great rivalry with Illinois' Harold Groh, finishing second to him in the 1927 Big Ten meet, then beating Groh for the national championship. Colbath came back the following year to win the Conference and NCAA meets, and earned a place on the U.S. Olympic team that competed in Amsterdam. He returned for the 1929 season as the team's captain. The Wildcats were defeated by Michigan—and Colbath was beaten by Groh—in the Conference meet, but those setbacks were avenged in the NCAA meet in St. Louis, as Northwestern won the title over Michigan and Colbath nosed out Groh by a fraction of a point.

BERNIE SHIVELY
Football, Wrestling and Track, Illinois

When a list of Illinois' finest all-around athletes is compiled, the name Bernie Shively always appears. Perhaps most famous as a guard running interference for the immortal Red Grange, Shively was selected as the Fighting Illini's eighth consensus All-America football player following the 1926 season. He was inducted into the College Football Hall of Fame in 1982. The former prep star from Paris, Ill., also excelled on the wrestling mat, grappling to a draw with his heavyweight opponent from Indiana in the 1926 Big Ten championship match, but losing on a coin toss. Shively also was a three-time letter winner for the UI track and field squad, placing twice in Conference championship competition as a hammer thrower. Altogether, he won eight varsity letters at Illinois. Following his graduation in 1927, Shively began a distinguished career at the University of Kentucky, culminating in a 30-year career as director of athletics. He died in 1967 at the age of 64.

BENNY FRIEDMAN
Football, Michigan

Benny Friedman, an All-America quarterback in 1925 and 1926 for Fielding Yost's last two Michigan teams, was the first of the great college passers, teaming with receiver Bennie Oosterbaan for six scoring passes in 1925. Originally a bench-warmer, Friedman came off the bench for five minutes in 1924 against a Red Grange-led Illinois team, but played 60 minutes in every game from then on, becoming one of college football's immortals as Michigan went 14-2 and won Big Ten titles behind his signal-calling. He also was a placekicker and defensive back. Friedman was an all-pro quarterback for five years in the National Football League's infancy and starred for Cleveland, Detroit, New York and Brooklyn. He later entered coaching and became athletic director at Brandeis University. Friedman was selected to both the Michigan and College Football Hall of Fame. He died in 1982.

BIG TEN LIST

NORTHWESTERN'S BIG TEN FOOTBALL CHAMPIONSHIPS

1. 1903 (1-0-2 record) (tied with Michigan and Minnesota)
2. 1926 (5-0-0 record) (tied with Michigan)
3. 1930 (5-0-0 record)(tied with Michigan)
4. 1931 (5-1-0 record)(tied with Michigan and Purdue)
5. 1936 (6-0-0 record)
6. 1995 (8-0-0 record)

L.W. LABREE
Purdue

He represented continuity and stability for the Purdue tennis program, having guided the Boilermakers through parts of five decades. L.W. LaBree was coach from 1925-64, leading Purdue to a record of 150-210-9 in dual meets and 68-155-3 in invitationals. LaBree was coaching with limited resources in terms of equipment, facilities and scholarships. Before LaBree, Purdue had four different coaches from 1914-24. LaBree's emphasis was not on winning. His teams almost never fared well at state or Conference tournaments, and sometimes didn't even enter those competitions. His 1932 team did win the state singles title, and Purdue won the state meet in 1947. The Boilermakers best finish in the Big Ten championship under LaBree was third place in 1945.

· BIG TEN PIONEERS ·

Les Bolstad, Minnesota

Les Bolstad's Big Ten golf legacy is three-pronged. As a player, the former Minnesota great was a two-time Conference medalist. As a long-time coach, the Gophers were a perennial competitive force. As a highly re-spected Conference figure in the sport, his name was im-mortalized when it was attached to the annual Big Ten award presented to the player with the lowest seasonal average score — the Les Bolstad Award. During his play-ing days, Bolstad was among the nation's top players. He was the Big Ten's low medalist on non-consecutive occa-sions in 1927 and 1929, leading the Gophers to their first league championship the latter year. Bolstad fired a 72-hole round 313 during each of his victories. As a coach, he led Minnesota to the Conference crowns in 1938 and 1963.

Academic Achievements

Religion has been taught at our nation's colleges since the pilgrims landed. But those classes were taught at private schools, mostly run by religious denominations. It wasn't until 1927 that Iowa established a school of religion to become the first state uni-versity to do so.

The BIG TEN's First 100 Years
Big Ten Men's Tennis Championship Records

Most Individual Titles, 6
Marty Riessen, Northwestern
(singles 1962-64, doubles 1962-64)

Most Singles Titles, 3
Thomas O'Connell, Illinois (1926-28)
Marty Riessen, Northwestern (1962-64)
Ernie Fernandez, Ohio State (1979, '81-'82)

Most Doubles Titles, 3
(For a team) Michigan
Barry McKay - Dick Potter (1955-57)

1926-27
Conference MEDAL OF HONOR
Winners

CHICAGO	Anton B. Burg
ILLINOIS	Doran T. Rue
INDIANA	Charles F. Benzel
IOWA	Carl D. Voltmer
MICHIGAN	Paul C. Samson
MINNESOTA	Roger Wheeler
NORTHWESTERN	Robert W. Johnson
OHIO STATE	Harold W. Kennedy
PURDUE	J.E. Little
WISCONSIN	Jefferson Burrus

1927-28

THE BIG EVENT

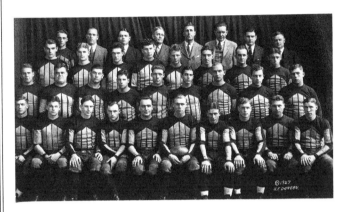

Illinois football team reigns as national champs

A strong-willed defense was the hallmark of the 1927 football team at Illinois. The Illini were unbeaten in eight games, scoring five shutouts on the way to winning the school's fourth—and final—national championship. It was also the fourth national title for coach Bob Zuppke, whose team also held two other opponents to one touchdown or less. A 12-12 tie with Iowa State was Illinois' only flaw. The stars of Zuppke's team were All-America linemen Bob Reitsch, Russ Crane and Butch Nowack. Among the key performers on a steady, but unspectacular, offense were end Jud Timm and backs Frank Walker, Fred Humbert and Doug Mills, who later coached Illinois basketball teams to three Big Ten titles. Illinois was 5-0 in the Big Ten, winning the Conference title. Perhaps the biggest win of the season came at Northwestern, where the Illini scored a 7-6 win to snap a seven-game Northwestern win streak.

OTHER MEMORABLE EVENTS

- In the first NCAA wrestling meet, Conference wrestlers won two titles—Northwestern's Ralph Lupton (125) and Iowa's Les Beers (158). Michigan's Ed Don George won the Olympic heavyweight championship.

- Also at the Olympics, Iowa's George Baird ran a leg on the winning 1,600-meter relay team and Michigan's Paul Samson swam a leg on the winning 800-meter freestyle swimming team.

- Five Conference teams finished in the top 10 of the NCAA outdoor track championships.

- Michigan's Carl Darnall won his second straight NCAA 100-yard freestyle title, and Chicago's Floyd Davidson won his second consecutive Conference all-around gymnastics championship.

Buckeyes earn first Big Ten golf championship

Names such as Jack Nicklaus, Tom Weiskopf, John Cook and even Meg Mallon are mentioned when Ohio State golf is the topic. But before there was the Golden Bear or NCAA championships, there was the 1928 season. The Buckeyes finished with a score of 1,332 strokes to win the school's first Conference title in golf under coach George Sargent. Ohio State has won a total of 20 Big Ten championships in golf, including a streak of eight titles in 10 years under Jim Brown, a span that concluded in 1989-90. Ohio State has two NCAA team titles while Buckeyes have earned NCAA individual titles five times. After a two-year varsity career at Ohio State where he finished as the NCAA champion in 1961, Nicklaus would win 20 major championships during his PGA tour career before embarking on a Senior tour campaign. Weiskopf won the 1973 British Open, and Mallon won two major championships on the LPGA tour in 1990.

OTHER BIG TEN CHAMPIONS

- **FOOTBALL:** Illinois, coached by Robert Zuppke
- **BASEBALL:** Michigan, coached by Ray Fisher
- **GYMNASTICS:** Chicago (coach not known)
- **OUTDOOR TRACK:** Illinois, coached by Harry Gill
- **INDOOR TRACK:** Illinois, coached by Harry Gill
- **BASKETBALL:** Indiana, coached by Everett Dean, and Purdue, coached by Ward Lambert
- **CROSS COUNTRY:** Wisconsin, coached by Thomas Jones
- **TENNIS:** Illinois, coached by A.R. Cohn
- **SWIMMING:** Michigan, coached by Matt Mann
- **WRESTLING:** Illinois, coached by Paul Prehn
- **FENCING:** Chicago (coach not known)

THOMAS "TIM" O'CONNELL
Tennis, Illinois

Mention Tommy O'Connell to Illinois fans, and they may recall a record-setting quarterback. The original record-setting Tommy O'Connell at Illinois was a guy his friends called Tim. He was the first player to win Big Ten tennis titles three consecutive seasons, from 1926-28 His singles championships led the Illini to three straight team titles, and O'Connell also won two doubles championships. His total of five crowns wasn't surpassed until 1964 by Northwestern star Marty Riessen, who finished with six titles overall. Riessen's three singles titles left him as the only Big Ten player to match O'Connell's feat. Since O'Connell's three-year run, Illinois has recorded one singles title and one team championship in Big Ten play. Following school, O'Connell won state amateur doubles titles in Illinois, Indiana, Ohio and Michigan while working in the chemical industry. He died in 1987.

RALPH WELCH
Football, Purdue

He wasn't exactly a secret weapon, but he was a surprise. Purdue coach Jim Phelan unveiled Ralph "Pest" Welch in the second game of his sophomore season against Ivy League power Harvard. It was Oct. 8, 1927, and Welch made his debut in grand style. He scored on a 3-yard touchdown run, then threw a 40-yard touchdown pass to Leon Hutton, and added a 13-yard TD run in a 19-0 victory. Welch was twice first-team All-Big Ten and was one of Purdue's first consensus All-Americans in 1929. Phelan thought so highly of Welch that he later hired him as an assistant coach at the University of Washington, where Welch became head coach in 1942. His teams were 27-20-3 in six years and played in the 1944 Rose Bowl. Welch got his nickname when he was growing up in Sherman, Texas, north of Dallas. He was 14 and always playing with older kids, and they told him, "... you're the darnedest pest we've ever seen." The name stayed with him.

HERBERT JOESTING
Football, Minnesota

Known as the "Owatonna Thunderbolt," Herb Joesting was the focal point of the Minnesota football team's powerful running attack from 1925-27. A punishing runner with blazing speed, Joesting was college football's premier fullback of the era for coach Clarence "Doc" Spears. Famed Notre Dame coach Knute Rockne made this challenge to his vaunted defense prior to the 1927 season: "I'll buy a new suit for the guy who can throw Joesting for a loss." Rockne never had to pay off, as Joesting helped the Gophers play the Irish to a 7-7 tie. Minnesota finished the year 6-0-2, as Joesting became only the second Gopher gridder to earn consecutive first-team All-America recognition. In 1926, he accomplished the once-unthinkable feat of duplicating Illinois star "Red" Grange's Big Ten record of 13 touchdowns in a season. He was also only 55 yards shy of breaking Grange's record for total offense with 1,017 yards. Joesting was inducted into the Helms College Football Hall of Fame in 1961.

BIG TEN LIST

NCAA WRESTLING CHAMPS

1932—Indiana
1967—Michigan State
1975—Iowa
1976—Iowa
1978—Iowa
1979—Iowa
1980—Iowa
1981—Iowa
1982—Iowa
1983—Iowa
1984—Iowa
1985—Iowa
1986—Iowa
1991—Iowa
1992—Iowa
1993—Iowa
1995—Iowa
1996—Iowa

LEADING THE WAY

ARTHUR "DUTCH" LONBORG
Northwestern

Dutch Lonborg gained athletic fame as a player, coach and administrator. An outstanding three-sport star at Kansas, where he earned all-conference honors in football as a receiver and quarterback and All-America honors as a basketball guard, Lonborg went on to graduate from law school. He chose a career in coaching, however, first at McPherson College and then at Washburn College in Kansas. His Washburn team won the national AAU title in 1925, the only college team ever to do so. Lonborg took over as Northwestern's basketball coach in 1928 and enjoyed immediate success. His first team became the first in school history to win at least 10 games in a season (it won 12), and his 1931 and '33 teams won the Big Ten championship — still the school's only league cage titles. He finished with a career record of 234-205 and gained election to the Naismith Hall of Fame. Lonborg returned to Kansas in 1950 to become athletic director, a position he held for 14 years. The respect he earned was evident by his position as chairman of the NCAA tournament committee for 13 years and as chairman of the U.S. basketball committee for the 1959 Pan American Games and the 1960 Olympics.

· BIG TEN PIONEERS ·

Dave Abbott
Illinois

When Illinois won the NCAA track title in 1926-27, Dave Abbott was an engineering student at Purdue, the first year he ran competitively. A year later, he transferred to Illinois because of a landscape architectural course, and he eventually became an NCAA champion. Abbott never ran in high school, but he was the two-mile NCAA champion in 1928 and '29, winning both titles in meets held in his hometown of Chicago. Behind Abbott, the Illini won the Conference outdoor title and placed third in the NCAA meet during his individual championship seasons. He ran in the 5,000 meters at the 1928 Amsterdam Olympics, but he was unable to qualify for the finals. After graduation, Abbott oversaw the improvement at Abraham Lincoln's tomb in Springfield, Ill.

The BIG TEN's First 100 Years
Facts About Big Ten Universities

More than 70 Nobel laureates have been faculty, students or researchers at Big Ten universities.

Source:
Data provided by universities

Academic Achievements

Long before there was Jacques Cousteau, the University of Illinois established the field of marine biology in the 1920s. Even more amazing is that the Champaign-Urbana campus is land-locked without even a river nearby.

1927-28
Conference MEDAL OF HONOR
Winners

CHICAGO	Kenneth A. Rouse
ILLINOIS	Richard G. Finn
INDIANA	Arthur J. Beckner
IOWA	Lawrence Harrison
MICHIGAN	Norman Gabel
MINNESOTA	Malvin J. Nydahl
NORTHWESTERN	William H. Droegemueller
OHIO STATE	Cornelius Ackermann
PURDUE	Harry A. Kemmer
WISCONSIN	Louis Behr

Iowa athletic director Paul Belding, successor to Edward Laurer.

THE BIG EVENT

Iowa suspended by Big Ten

When the presidents of the Big Ten said they wanted control over intercollegiate athletics, this is what they had in mind. The league's faculty committee voted to suspend Iowa because of its practice of recruiting and subsidizing athletes against the rules of the Conference. Iowa was accused of using a fund that provided loans to athletes. Iowa's athletic board voted to accept the Big Ten's penalty and declared 22 athletes ineligible. Previous to the December, 1928, vote, Iowa's athletic director Edward Laurer and faculty representative C.C. Williams had argued that the fund was not against the rules and steadfastly held that the athletes should not be penalized. In June, 1929, Iowa President Walter A. Jessup applied for reinstatement to the Conference, saying that the alumni, and not the University, were responsible for the rules violations and that Iowa would "live up to all rules in letter and spirit." He said University officials did not know of the fund until the Big Ten faculty committee discovered it. Iowa did return to league competition the following year.

OTHER MEMORABLE EVENTS

- Ohio State, led by sprinter George Simpson, won the NCAA outdoor track championship.

- Northwestern's Wally Colbath won his third straight NCAA diving title to become the first Conference athlete to win three consecutive national championships in any sport.

- Michigan won the first Conference wrestling team tournament; previous Conference champions were determined by dual meet records.

- Minnesota's Les Bolstad won his second straight Conference golf title.

- Wisconsin football announcer called the Badger-Minnesota game in five different languages—Norwegian, Swedish, German, Yiddish and Chinese.

- Indiana won the first of six straight cross country Conference championships.

Illini edge Wolverines for fencing title

Coaches often toil for years before they can build a championship program. In his first year as fencing coach, Herb Craig led his Illini unit to a Conference championship in a meet held at the Old Gym on the Illinois campus. The Illini scored 13 points to finish ahead of runner-up Michigan. The Wolverines finished the meet with seven points. Otto Haier of Illinois was first in the individual foil competition, and teammate P.F. Schlicher won the individual sabre title. Meanwhile, Illinois' Wilbur Menke was second in the individual epee finals. The following season, Illinois again won the title, this time sweeping the competition by winning first places in all three weapons. Haier again won the foil while Fred Seibert was first in the epee and Chalmer Gross champion in the sabre as the Illini were the first team to finish with a perfect score of 15 points. These two team titles were the first two of five consecutive Conference championships Illinois garnered in fencing.

OTHER BIG TEN CHAMPIONS

- **FOOTBALL:** Illinois, coached by Robert Zuppke
- **BASEBALL:** Michigan, coached by Ray Fisher
- **GYMNASTICS:** Illinois, coached by R.C. Heidloff
- **OUTDOOR TRACK:** Illinois, coached by Harry Gill
- **INDOOR TRACK:** Iowa, coached by George Bresnahan
- **BASKETBALL:** Michigan, coached by George Veenker, and Wisconsin, coached by Dr. Walter Meanwell
- **CROSS COUNTRY:** Indiana, coached by Earle "Billy" Hayes
- **TENNIS:** Chicago (coach not known)
- **SWIMMING:** Michigan, coached by Matt Mann
- **WRESTLING:** Michigan, coached by Clifford Keen
- **GOLF:** Minnesota, coached by Leon Kranz

CHUCK BENNETT
Football, Indiana

Halfback Chuck Bennett was the first Indiana football player to be named the Big Ten's Most Valuable Player. He won the award in 1928, when as a co-captain he led the Hoosiers to a 4-4 record despite missing some games because of injury. He also earned All-America honors that season and played for the winning East team in the East-West Shrine game in San Francisco. Bennett scored two of the East's four touchdowns, threw the key block for another, and earned game MVP honors. Bennett played two years of professional football, with the Portsmouth Spartans in 1930 and the Chicago Cardinals in 1933. Said Indiana athletic director Zora Clevenger: "His modesty and his personalilty make him an inspiring player."

EDWARD GORDON
Track, Iowa

When Edward Gordon arrived from Gary, Ind., in the fall of 1927, Iowa track coach George Bresnahan took a hurdling specialist and converted him to a broad jumper. It turned out to be a pretty good move. Gordon won NCAA championships three straight years and made the 1928 U.S. Olympic team after his freshman year. Despite competing with a bad heel, he finished seventh at the Olympic Games in Amsterdam. As it so happened, that was just a warm up. After a college career in which he also won three Conference championships, Gordon returned to the Olympics and won a gold medal at the 1932 Games in Los Angeles with a broad jump of 25-feet, 3/4-inch. Among the field of competitors was the world record holder and the winner of the U.S. trials. His all-time best jump was a meet-record 25-4 3/8 at the 1931 Kansas Relays. While at Iowa, Gordon also won two Amateur Athletic Union senior titles and three Drake Relays championships.

GEORGE LOTT
Tennis, Chicago

George Lott, who won the Big Ten singles and doubles titles in 1929, went on to become an international star in the sport, making the Davis Cup team and pairing with Lester Stoeffer to twice win the U.S. doubles title. Chicago—beginning a run of nine Conference titles in 11 years—went undefeated during the 1929 season en route to its first of three straight Big Ten titles. Lott teamed with William Calohan to win the Conference doubles crown.

NCAA DIVING CHAMPIONS

BIG TEN LIST

One-Meter: Walter Colbath, NU (1927-28-29), Al Patnik, OSU (1938-39-40), Frank Dempsey, OSU (1942-43), Miller Anderson, OSU (1946-47), Bruce Harlan, OSU (1948-49-50), Fletcher Gilders, OSU (1954-55), Lou Vitucci, OSU (1962-63), Rick Gilbert, Ind. (1964) Ken Sitzberger, Ind. (1965-66-67), Jim Henry, Ind. (1968-69-70), Tim Moore, OSU (1973-74-75) Rob Bolinger, Ind. (1982) and Mark Lenzi, Ind. (1989-90).

Three-Meter: Richard Degener, Mich. (1933-34), Frank Fehsenfeld, Mich. (1935-36), Al Patnik, OSU (1938-39), Earl Clark, OSU (1940-41), Frank Dempsey, OSU (1942-43), Miller Anderson, OSU (1946-47-48), Bruce Harlan, OSU (1949-50), Donald Harper, OSU (1956-58), Sam Hall, OSU (1959-60), Lou Vitucci, OSU (1961-62-63), Jim Henry, Ind. (1969-70), Tim Moore, OSU (1973-75) and Brian Bungum, Ind. (1976-77).

LEADING THE WAY

ZORA CLEVENGER
Indiana

Zora Clevenger was a man of great athletic stature despite his small physical stature. Clevenger, a native of Muncie, Ind. who enrolled at Indiana in 1900, won letters in football, basketball and baseball despite standing just 5-foot-7 and weighing 150 pounds. A center for the football team, his 75-yard punt return for a touchdown led to a 17-0 upset of Illinois in 1903. He was the team captain that season and was named an All-American, the first player in IU's football history to achieve that honor. In baseball, he once hit a ninth-inning game-winning home run against Minnesota, a feat which so excited the local fans they immediately took up a collection and marched downtown to buy him a watch. Clevenger went on to achieve great fame as the football coach at Tennessee, Kansas State and Missouri, and as athletic director at Indiana from 1923-46. He was elected to the College Football Hall of Fame in 1968. He died in 1970 at the age of 89.

· BIG TEN PIONEERS ·

Betty Robinson,
Northwestern

Betty Robinson became one of the most famous sprinters in the world for her accomplishments and courage. Robinson (below) set a world record of 12 seconds for the 100-yard dash as a 16-year-old in 1928 in just the second meet of her career, and shortly thereafter won a gold medal in the 100 meters in the Olympic games at Amsterdam — the first to include women. She was seriously injured in an airplane crash three years later. But with the help of Northwestern track coach Frank Hill and trainer Carl Erickson, she rehabilitated herself and earned a spot on the 1936 Olympic team, running on the winning 400-meter relay team.

Betty Robinson

Academic Achievements

If the students of 1929 did what today's students at Ohio State University do, there might never have been the stock market crash of 1929. OSU students enrolled in a finance course called "The Stock Market," manage a $5 million portfolio from a University endowment fund. In the first year (1988), students generated a $1 million return, outperforming Standard and Poor's.

1928-29
Conference MEDAL OF HONOR
Winners

CHICAGO	Rudolph P. Leyers
ILLINOIS	Robert B. Orlovich
INDIANA	Wilmer T. Rinehart
IOWA	Forest Twogood
MICHIGAN	Ernest B. McCoy
MINNESOTA	George E. MacKinnon
NORTHWESTERN	Bertrand Fox
OHIO STATE	William P. Tooley
PURDUE	C.S. Lyle
WISCONSIN	Theodore A. Thelander

THE BIG EVENT

Al Schwartz dominates Big Ten swimming

Few Big Ten athletes have dominated their sport as thoroughly as Al Schwartz, Northwestern's freestyle swimmer. Schwartz set a world record in the 40-yard dash (17.8 seconds) as a junior in 1929 and was part of a 300-yard medley relay team that set world records for the 60- and 75-foot pools. He also won the 100- and 220-yard titles that year in the Big Ten meet, captured the 100-yard swim in the national championship meet, and was a member of the 300 medley relay team that set a world record in the national finals. Schwartz led Northwestern to the Big Ten title in 1930, winning the 40-, 100- and 220-yard events. The 'Cats went on win their second consecutive national championship, as he won the 50-, 100- and 220-yard swims — the first time in the history of the NCAA meet that one swimmer had won three events.

OTHER MEMORABLE EVENTS

- Purdue's Ralph "Pest" Welch was the Conference's first "five-way" football threat. It was claimed he could beat you with his running, kicking, passing, defending and inspirational leadership.

- Three centers—Purdue's Stretch Murphy, Wisconsin's Bud Foster and Indiana's Branch McCracken—were chosen to the first-team All-Conference basketball squad.

- Chicago's John Menzies won his second straight Conference all-around gymnastics title.

- The Conference had three tackles named to the All-America football squad: Minnesota's Bronko Nagurski, Purdue's Elmer Sleight and Illinois' Lou Gordon.

- Illinois' Joe Sapora won his second straight NCAA 115-pound wrestling title.

Unbeaten Boilermakers claim Big Ten crown

This was the Boilermakers' first undefeated football season since 1892. Purdue finished 8-0, winning the Big Ten championship at 5-0 and surrendering a total of just 44 points all season. It shut out four opponents, and held two others to just seven points. Only Kansas State and Michigan, in the first two games, scored in double digits against coach James Phelan's squad. Notre Dame was selected as the national champion with Purdue second and Pittsburgh third. The Boilermakers clinched a share of the Conference title with a 7-0 victory over Iowa before what was then the biggest crowd ever at Ross-Ade Stadium (27,000). Purdue scored on a second-quarter touchdown pass from Glen Harmeson to Bill Woerner. The following week, the Boilermakers hammered Indiana 32-0 in their final game to wrap up the league championship. Tackle Elmer Sleight and halfback Ralph Welch were Purdue's first consensus All-Americans. Those two, along with quarterback Harmeson, were named first-team All-Big Ten. Harmeson also was a forward on the Purdue basketball team and competed on the track team. Phelan was inducted into the College Football Hall of Fame in 1973.

OTHER BIG TEN CHAMPIONS

- **BASEBALL:** Wisconsin, coached by Guy Lowman
- **GYMNASTICS:** Chicago (coach not known)
- **OUTDOOR TRACK:** Michigan, coached by Charles Hoyt
- **INDOOR TRACK:** Wisconsin, coached by Thomas Jones
- **BASKETBALL:** Purdue, coached by Ward Lambert
- **CROSS COUNTRY:** Indiana, coached by Earle "Billy" Hayes
- **TENNIS:** Chicago (coach not known)
- **SWIMMING:** Northwestern, coached by Tom Robinson
- **WRESTLING:** Illinois, coached by H.E. Kenney
- **GOLF:** Illinois, coached by J.H. Utley
- **FENCING:** Illinois, coached by Herbert Craig

JOHN WOODEN
Basketball, Purdue

The nation will always think first of John Wooden the coach, who led UCLA to a record 10 national championships. Purdue, however, recalls that first Wooden was a standout player, a three-time All-American and national player of the year as a senior who led the Boilermakers to a mythical national championship in 1932. The Martinsville, Ind., native was named first-team All-Big Ten three straight years. He set a Big Ten scoring record his final season with 154 points and led Purdue to league titles in 1930 and '32. Wooden's immediate impact was obvious: During the 1929-30 season he suffered a leg injury; and without its star, Purdue lost to Butler, then after a victory over Vanderbilt, it lost again to Montana State when Wooden was unable to play more than the first half. The Boilermakers didn't lose again. Wooden is a member of the Naismith Hall of Fame and Purdue's Hall of Fame. He graduated in the top one percent of his class and in 1994 was inducted into the GTE/CoSIDA Academic Hall of Fame.

BRONKO A. NAGURSKI
Football, Minnesota

Bronko Nagurski was one of the most celebrated athletes ever to play at Minnesota and was its brightest football star in the first half of the century. Born in 1908 in Ontario, Canada, Nagurski grew up in International Falls, Minn. and played for the Gophers from 1927-30. He was an All-America fullback and tackle in 1929 and '30 and was, physically, one of the most massive players of his era (6-foot-2, 217 pounds, size 19 neck and 19-1/2 ring finger). He was also among the quickest and most agile. Professionally, he starred for coach George Halas' Chicago Bears from 1930-37, leading them to the NFL championship in 1933. He rejoined the Bears after retirement for one season in 1943 and led them to another championship. A charter member of the pro football hall of fame, he later became a professional wrestling champion. He died in 1990 at age 81.

BRANCH McCRACKEN
Basketball, Indiana

Branch McCracken achieved his greatest notoriety as a coach, leading Indiana to NCAA basketball championships in 1940 and '53, but was an equally accomplished athlete. He is the only undefeated coach in Final Four games (4-0) among those who have made at least two trips to the finals, was 9-2 overall in NCAA play, and received national coach of the year honors in 1940 and '53. But he was an outstanding basketball player before he ever donned a whistle, achieving first team All-Big Ten and All-America status as a senior in 1930 for the Hoosiers. He finished his career as the Big Ten's all-time leading scorer and dabbled in professional basketball in the pioneering days of that game. He was inducted into the Naismith Hall of Fame as a player in 1960.

BIG TEN LIST

NCAA SWIMMING CHAMPIONS

Northwestern's Al Schwartz won three NCAA swimming titles in the 1930 meet. Only five other Big Ten men have matched that feat:

Al Schwartz, Northwestern, 1930
(50 free, 100 free, 220 free)
Charlie Hickcox, Indiana, 1968
(100 back, 200 back, 200 IM)
Mark Spitz, Indiana, 1969
(200 free, 500 free, 100 fly)
Gary Hall, Indiana, 1971
(200 back, 200 IM, 400 IM)
Artur Wojdat, Iowa, 1991
(200 free, 500 free, 1,650 free)
Tom Dolan, Michigan, 1995
(500 free, 1,650 free, 400 IM; also swam on one winning relay team)

LEADING THE WAY

OTTO VOGEL
Iowa

Otto Vogel was what you would call a "mainstay" at Iowa during parts of five decades. As baseball coach from 1925-66 (not including three years spent in the Navy in the mid-'40s), Vogel led the Hawkeyes to one outright Big Ten title (1939), four shared championships, four second-place finishes and three third places. His teams finished 505-431-14, 218-216-2 in Conference play. Vogel took over at Iowa after arm trouble ended his brief pro career; he played outfield and third base for the Chicago Cubs in 1924. Vogel was a three-time All-American baseball player at Illinois, where he also lettered in football and basketball. Vogel suffered a stroke in 1962 and never fully recovered, and he spent his last four seasons as Iowa's coach mostly as an adviser. He authored the baseball textbook, "The Ins and Outs of Baseball" in 1951. In '52, he was the first U.S. college baseball coach invited to participate in an overseas baseball clinic, and he spent a month in Germany working with the armed forces recreation program. The Mendota, Ill., native served as president of the American Association of College Baseball Coaches and was a member of the Helms Athletic Hall of Fame. He died in 1969 at age 71.

· BIG TEN PIONEERS ·

Glen Harmeson
Purdue

"Versatile" is kind of an understatement. Glen Harmeson (below) won nine letters at Purdue as a standout contributor to the football, basketball and baseball teams. The Indianapolis native helped lead the football team to a three-year record of 19-4-1, including an 8-0 season and a Big Ten title in 1929 when he was a first-team All-Big Ten quarterback. He was a basketball teammate of John Wooden and "Stretch" Murphy during a time in which Purdue went 41-8 and won the 1930 league title. Wooden once said of Harmeson: "Glen was one of the most talented and graceful athletes I ever saw." Harmeson also was a center fielder on the baseball team. He coached Purdue's freshman football and basketball teams from 1930-34, and after two head coaching stints at Lehigh University (1934-42) and Wabash College (1946-51), he returned to Purdue as backfield coach in '51. He died in 1983 at age 75.

Academic Achievements

Athletic facilities on college campuses have been commonplace since the turn of the century. Schools spent hundreds of thousands of dollars to build huge football stadiums and large basketball arenas. But it wasn't until 1929 that a university constructed a building to house athletic facilities for the whole student body and not just the athletes. That facility was the Intramural Sports Building at Michigan.

1929-30 Conference MEDAL OF HONOR Winners

CHICAGO	Harold E. Haydon
ILLINOIS	Richard C. Oeler
INDIANA	W.E. Clapham
IOWA	Willis A. Glassgow
MICHIGAN	Edwin B. Poorman
MINNESOTA	Robert Tanner
NORTHWESTERN	Richard L. Hinch
OHIO STATE	Joseph A. Ujhelyi
PURDUE	Elmer N. Sleight
WISCONSIN	Donald W. Mieklejohn

1930-31

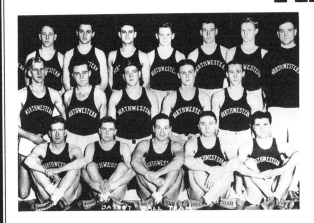

THE BIG EVENT

Northwestern captures its first Big Ten basketball title

Northwestern won its first Big Ten basketball championship in impressive fashion, breezing to an 11-1 Conference record and a 16-1 overall mark. With three lettermen returning from the 1930 team that had won half of its games, the Wildcats added three sophomores, the most prominent being forward Joe Reiff, who won the league scoring championship with 122 points and earned All-America honors. The only mishap was a homecourt loss to Illinois, 35-28, a team it had defeated at Illinois earlier in the year. The most dramatic win came with three games left in the season at Minnesota, which was still in title contention. The Wildcats jumped to a 43-15 lead, then let the reserves play out the 45-23 victory. The team survived an injury to starting guard Bob Lockhart in the second game of the season, thanks to the contributions of reserve Arthur "Bus" Smith.

OTHER MEMORABLE EVENTS

- Northwestern almost recorded two national titles in the same school year, but lost to Notre Dame in the football season finale for its only loss.

- Conference teams finished 2nd through 7th at the NCAA outdoor track championships.

- Chicago's Dale Letts set an NCAA record in the 880-yard run.

- Iowa's Edward Gordon won his third consecutive NCAA outdoor long jump championship, and Northwestern's Tom Warne won his third consecutive NCAA pole vault title.

- Illinois' Richard Martin won the Conference golf title for the second straight year, and Chicago's Scott Rexinger won the Conference tennis singles championship for the second straight year.

Indiana continues cross country dominance

BIG TEN CROSS COUNTRY CHAMPIONS
APP, MGR., ABROMSON, STEELE, SEARS, CAINE, CAPT. FIELDS, C.A. BANKS, SCHAEFFER, COACH H

The rolling hills of Bloomington must have been the perfect training ground for runners throughout the 1930s, given the way Indiana's cross country team dominated the competition. The Hoosiers won the Big Ten title in 1928, initiating a run of six consecutive Conference championships. The only thing that prevented them from continuing their streak was the fact the Big Ten discontinued its championship meet from 1934-37, but they won the alternative Central Intercollegiate AAU meet all three of those years. IU also won the national AAU title in 1936 with a perfect score of 15 by placing each of the top five finishers, including winner Don Lash. It placed second in the meet the following year. The Hoosiers won the Big Ten meet again when it resumed in 1938, and also won titles in '40 and '42. The 1930 league championship came at Illinois, where the Hoosiers had the top two individual finishers.

OTHER BIG TEN CHAMPIONS

- **FOOTBALL:** Michigan, coached by Harry Kipke, and Northwestern, coached by Dick Hanley
- **BASEBALL:** Illinois, coached by Carl Lundgren
- **GYMNASTICS:** Chicago (coach not known)
- **OUTDOOR TRACK:** Wisconsin, coached by Thomas Jones
- **INDOOR TRACK:** Michigan, coached by Charles Hoyt
- **BASKETBALL:** Northwestern, coached by Arthur Lonborg
- **TENNIS:** Chicago (coach not known)
- **SWIMMING:** Michigan, coached by Matt Mann

WES FESSLER
Football, Ohio State

Wes Fessler was a valuable contributor as a player and a coach at Ohio State. He was the school's second three-time football All-American, earning the award for the third straight time following his senior season in 1930 as an end, when he was named the team's MVP. He also was the team's captain in 1930. As a basketball player, he was a two-year starter and a team captain during his junior year, helping the Buckeyes to 14 wins over the two seasons, finishing his career as an All-Conference pick in his senior year. He also won three letters in baseball. Fessler returned to serve as head football coach at Ohio State beginning with the 1947 season, and the Buckeyes compiled a 21-13-3 record in his four years, the high point a 7-1-2 record in the 1949 season when Ohio State finished as Big Ten champs with the school's first Rose Bowl win.

TOM WARNE
Track, Northwestern

Tom Warne raised the standard of Northwestern's outstanding pole vaulting tradition. Warne tied for first in the Big Ten outdoor meet as a sophomore in 1929 with a record vault of 13 feet, 7 inches and later tied for the NCAA outdoor championship at a record height of 13 feet, 8 7/8 inches. He won the Big Ten indoor title and the NCAA outdoor title as a junior, vaulting 13 feet, 9 7/8 inches to establish a meet record in the latter. Earlier in the season he had set a school record with a vault of 14 feet at the Ohio State Relays. Despite undergoing surgery for a chipped bone in his foot over the Christmas holidays his senior year, he won the outdoor Conference meet and then tied for first in the NCAA meet at a record 13 feet-10 5/16-inches.

EDDIE TOLAN
Track, Michigan

When Eddie Tolan won the 100- and 200-meter dashes at the 1932 Olympic Games in Los Angeles, it made Michigan the only university to have three double sprint gold medalists. (Archie Hahn had a triple sprint win in the 1904 St. Louis Games and Ralph Craig had won the 100 and 200 at Stockholm in 1912.) The 5-foot-4 Tolan set Olympic records of 10.3 in the 100 and 21.2 in the 200 and got a third gold medal on the winning 400-meter relay. His 100 record in the Games held up until 1960. Tolan, a Detroit native, who won the NCAA 220-yard dash title in 1931, also won the Big Ten 100-yard crown twice, in 1929 and 1931, and the Conference 220 in 1931; he also claimed a Big Ten 60-yard dash title indoors that year. Tolan later taught physical education in Detroit public schools.

BIG TEN LIST

NCAA HEAVYWEIGHT WRESTLING CHAMPIONS

Jack Riley, Northwestern, 1931-32
Charles McDaniel, Indiana, 1935, 38
George Downes, Ohio State, 1940
Leonard Levy, Minnesota, 1941
George Bollas, Ohio State, 1946
Verne Gagne, Minnesota, 1949
William Oberly, Penn State, 1955
   (prior to joining Big Ten)
Robert Norman, Illinois, 1957-58
Sherwyn Thorson, Iowa, 1962
Dave Porter, Michigan, 1966, 68
Lou Banach, Iowa, 1981, 83
Kirk Trost, Michigan, 1986
Jon Llewellyn, Illinois, 1991
Kerry McCoy, Penn State, 1994
Jeff Walter, Wisconsin, 1996

LEADING THE WAY

MATT MANN
Michigan

Matt Mann of Michigan. The words were inseparable, as if "of Michigan" were part of his name. And maybe it was. After all, Michigan for 29 years was a big part of his life and he an integral part of its athletic program. Born in 1884 in Yorkshire, England, Mann was a national schoolboy champion and later won the British Empire free style title. He came to the United States in 1905 and quickly developed champion swimmers at the high school level, at Syracuse, Harvard and Navy and at the New York and Detroit athletic clubs. Within two years of his arrival at Michigan in 1925, the Wolverines were Big Ten champions and unofficial national titlists. From then until his retirement in 1954, Mann guided Michigan to 201 dual meet victories, 16 Conference titles and 13 NCAA championships. Michigan swimmers competed in every Olympic Games held during Mann's tenure and he was himself coach of the U.S. team in the 1952 Games. More than 40 college coaches learned from him, including successor Gus Stager, a member of Mann's 1948 NCAA championship squad. Michigan's pool was named in Mann's honor upon his retirement, and although the Don Canham Natatorium has replaced it, the pool is still the Matt Mann Pool. Mann died in 1962.

· BIG TEN PIONEERS ·

Jack Riley
Northwestern

Jack Riley (below) was the first Big Ten wrestler to win an NCAA championship and was Northwestern's first two-sport All-American. Riley, a standout tackle on the football team, had never wrestled before joining the school's team as a junior in 1931, but won the Big Ten and NCAA meets in the heavyweight division. He lost his Big Ten title in an overtime match the following year, but went on to win the NCAA title again. He also won a silver medal in the 1932 Olympic Games in Los Angeles, losing a controversial match for the gold. He was elected to the Football Foundation Hall of Fame in 1988, and died in '93 at the age of 83.

Jack Riley

Academic Achievements

Among the most famous alumni from Michigan State are: General Motors Corp. president, Robert C. Stempel; USA Network president, Kay Koplovitz; CBS News correspondent, Susan Spencer; actor James Caan; Julliard's violin instructor, Dorothy Delay; scriptwriter Jim Cash; chairman of magazine group for Time, Inc., Jack Meyers; Nobel prize winner, Alfred Hershey; and Michigan governor, John M. Engler.

1930-31
Conference MEDAL OF HONOR
Winners

CHICAGO	Dale Letts
ILLINOIS	Lee Sentman
INDIANA	J.E. Hatfield
IOWA	No award
MICHIGAN	J. Perry Austin
MINNESOTA	Lowell Marsh
NORTHWESTERN	Laurence E. Oliphant
OHIO STATE	Richard C. Larkins
PURDUE	George VanBibber
WISCONSIN	Louis E. Oberdeck

1931-32

Indiana wrestling team.

THE BIG EVENT

Indiana wins NCAA wrestling and track meets

Indiana enjoyed one of the greatest seasons in its athletic history during the 1931-32 school year by winning NCAA championships in both wrestling and track. The wrestlers won the Big Ten regular season and tournament titles with ease, then hosted the NCAA championship. They captured that handily as well, as 134-pounder Eddie Belshaw won the national title and Dale Goings placed second. Belshaw's brother, George, was favored to win a national title as well, but was struck with a flu virus a few days before the meet and lost his first match in overtime. The track team edged Ohio State for the NCAA title in Chicago, winning in dramatic fashion. The two teams were tied heading into the final event, the pole vault, but Indiana's Bryce Beecher clinched the championship with a winning vault of 13-feet-10-inches. OSU's John Wonsowitz, who had won the Big Ten championship, tied for second.

OTHER MEMORABLE EVENTS

- Northwestern had three players—Pug Rentner, Jack Riley and Dallas Marvil—named to the football All-America team.

- With an extra football game added to the end of the schedule to raise money for the needy during the Great Depression, Northwestern saw its undefeated record disappear and wound up in a three-way tie for the title.

- Michigan's Taylor Drysdale won the first of three NCAA 150-yard backstroke titles, in addition to swimming a leg on the winning 300-yard medley relay.

- Michigan's John Fischer won the NCAA golf championship.

- Northwestern's Jack Riley won his second straight NCAA heavyweight wrestling title, and Chicago's Everett Olson won his second straight Conference all-around gymnastics championship.

- Conference athletes won four gold medals at the Olympics in Los Angeles, led by Eddie Tolan's double win in the 100- and 200-meter dashes.

Wooden wins national championship — as player!

With a guard by the name of John Wooden leading the way, Purdue rolled to a 17-1 record, winning the Big Ten at 11-1 and being named national champion by the country's sportswriters after defeating Chicago, 53-18, in the last game. Wooden scored 21 points in the finale. This was the sixth of Ward 'Piggy' Lambert's 11 Big Ten championships, and third of six outright titles. Wooden, who averaged a team-high 12.2 points per game, was the national player of the year. His team co-captain for the second straight year, forward Harry Kellar, averaged 6.9 ppg, and both were named first-team All-Big Ten. Wooden, who set a Big Ten scoring record with 154 points, was named All-America for the third time. The Boilermakers' only loss was against Illinois, 28-21, in the seventh game of the season. Lambert was in a car accident on the way to the game, with his car overturning. He was at the game, but the players appeared shaken by the incident. Purdue's 11-game unbeaten streak dating back to the previous season ended. Ray Eddy was the team's No. 2 scorer at 7.9 ppg. The other starters were center Charles Stewart and guard Ralph Parmenter.

OTHER BIG TEN CHAMPIONS

- **FOOTBALL:** Michigan, coached by Harry Kipke, Northwestern, coached by Dick Hanley, and Purdue, coached by Noble Kizer
- **BASEBALL:** Indiana, coached by Everett Dean
- **GYMNASTICS:** Chicago (coach not known)
- **OUTDOOR TRACK:** Michigan, coached by Charles Hoyt
- **INDOOR TRACK:** Indiana, coached by Earle "Billy" Hayes
- **CROSS COUNTRY:** Indiana, coached by Earle "Billy" Hayes
- **TENNIS:** Illinois, coached by C.W. Gelwick, and Minnesota, coached by Phil Brain
- **SWIMMING:** Michigan, coached by Matt Mann
- **WRESTLING:** Illinois, coached by H.E. Kenney, and Indiana, coached by W.H. Thorn
- **GOLF:** Michigan, coached by Thomas Trueblood
- **FENCING:** Illinois, coached by Herbert Craig

JOE REIFF
Basketball, Northwestern

Joe Reiff wasted no time getting acclimated to Big Ten basketball when he joined Northwestern's team as a sophomore in 1931. He immediately went out and won the league scoring title with 122 points and led the Wildcats to their first Conference championship in the sport with an 11-1 record. Reiff, a 6-foot-3 forward, had tremendous speed that was belied by a calm demeanor that allowed him to maintain command of every situation he faced. The Wildcats finished 9-3 in league play to finish second in Reiff's junior season, but they rebounded to win the title again in 1933. Reiff, who had given up the league scoring title to Purdue's John Wooden in 1932, took it back in '33 with 167 points He was named an All-American all three of his seasons in Evanston.

IVAN FUQUA
Track, Indiana

Ivan Fuqua was an integral member of Indiana's 1932 NCAA champion track squad, then went on to win a gold medal in the '32 Olympics in Los Angeles. Fuqua, who also played football at IU, became the school's first gold medalist as a member of the 1,600-meter relay team that set a world's record. He went on to win Big Ten indoor and outdoor championships in both the 440-yard dash and the mile relay in 1933 and '34. Fuqua, who was captain of Indiana's track team as a senior in 1934, later served as Brown University's track coach for 27 years. He is a member of Indiana's athletic hall of fame, the state of Indiana's track hall of fame, and the Helms Athletic Hall of Fame.

JOHN FISCHER
Golf, Michigan

John Fischer arguably was the best golfer in Michigan history, winning three Big Ten golf tournaments and an NCAA championship as the Wolverines won Big Ten titles from 1932-36 and NCAA crowns in 1934 and 1936. Fischer himself was medalist in the 1932 Big Ten and NCAA as a sophomore—the first Conference golfer to win the NCAA. He repeated his Big Ten title in 1933 but missed the 1934 season to play in the Walker Cup. In 1935, Fischer won Conference honors for the third time. He and teammate Jack Lenfesty once played Walter Hagen and Argentine champ Jose Jurado in a best-ball match, which the Michigan pair won one-up; Fischer said he actually beat Hagen on the scorecard. Fischer later won the 1936 U.S. Amateur title in a sudden-death playoff. Inducted into the Michigan Hall of Honor in 1980, Fischer died in 1984 at age 72.

NCAA GOLF CHAMPIONS

J.W. Fischer, Michigan, 1932

Charles Kocsis, Michigan, 1936

Louis Lick, Minnesota, 1944

John Lorms, Ohio State, 1945

Dave Barclay, Michigan, 1947

Fred Wampler, Purdue, 1950

Tom Nieporte, Ohio State, 1951

Joe Campbell, Purdue, 1955

Rick Jones, Ohio State, 1956

Jack Nicklaus, Ohio State, 1961

Clark Burroughs, Ohio State, 1985

LEADING THE WAY

CLIFF KEAN
Michigan

Based on longevity alone, Cliff Kean would be one of the giants of collegiate wrestling. But add a coaching record that showed a 268-91-9 dual meet record, eight Big Ten titles and three NCAA runner-up slots, and you get some idea why Kean is remembered as one of the greats in his sport. His 45 years as head wrestling coach at Michigan, which took him from the post-World War I era to the dawn of the space age, are the most at one school in NCAA annals. Kean coached 68 All-Americans and 81 Big Ten champions during his tenure and his teams finished among the top three in the Conference in 40 of 45 seasons. Kean also was a member of Michigan's football staff for 33 years and guided UM's 150-pound team to two titles in as many years. Kean himself was an outstanding athlete at Oklahoma A&M in the early 1920s, earning All-America honors in football, winning a national wrestling title and sprinting on the track team. He was the head coach of the 1948 U.S. Olympic team and a member of the U.S. Olympic Wrestling Committee for 12 years. Kean was a charter inductee into the U.S. Wrestling Hall of Fame.

· BIG TEN PIONEERS ·

James "Scotty" Reston
Illinois

James "Scotty" Reston (below) , a 1932 Illinois graduate, was one of the school's most influential alumni. The native of Scotland worked as a student assistant in Illinois' sports information office and competed in varsity golf and soccer. Reston moved to *The New York Times* in 1939 following a stint in Ohio State's athletic publicity office and an assignment with the Associated Press. He became one of America's most noted journalists. *Time* magazine said in a 1960 edition, "Politicians and other newsmen watch Reston's tone and are influenced by it." Reston won two Pulitzer prizes for national reporting. He retired as vice president of the *Times* in December of 1974, and died in 1995.

James "Scotty" Reston

Academic Achievements

In 1932, the University of Iowa opened the world's first educational television station, the original PBS station. It was W9XK and the picture was transmitted via closed circuit, separately from the sound. The sound was transmitted over the campus radio station.

1931-32
Conference MEDAL OF HONOR
Winners

CHICAGO	Everett C. Olson
ILLINOIS	Edward F. Gbur
INDIANA	Henry A. Brocksmith
IOWA	Stuart W. Skowbo
MICHIGAN	Edwin F. Russell
MINNESOTA	Earl W. Loose
NORTHWESTERN	Volney C. Wilson
OHIO STATE	James R. Bachman
PURDUE	John R. Wooden
WISCONSIN	Harvey H. Schneider

1932-33

THE BIG EVENT

"M" wins Big Ten, national football titles in '32, '33

That the 1932 and 1933 Michigan football teams claimed national championships is not surprising. The Wolverines' 8-0 (6-0 Big Ten) and 7-0-1 (5-0-1 Big Ten) records in those two seasons should have been reason enough for coach Harry Kipke's teams to grab national honors. Indicative of Michigan's domination was the 31 points it allowed opponents over that 16-game span. In 1932, Michigan yielded Northwestern six points and Princeton seven. In 1933, Michigan allowed only 18 points in eight games and none, ironically, in the only game it didn't win, a scoreless tie with Minnesota. Pacing Michigan in 1932 was All-America quarterback Harry Newman, who passed, ran and place-kicked his way to 57 points. Key to both title teams were two-way center Charles Bernard, labeled the nation's best by some pro coaches, and two-time All-America end Ted Petoskey.

OTHER MEMORABLE EVENTS

- **Chicago's Amos Alonzo Stagg retired at the age of 70.**

- **Michigan's J.W. Fischer won his second straight Conference golf title.**

- **Northwestern's Joe Reiff won his second consecutive Conference basketball scoring championship.**

- **Chicago's George Wrighte won the first of two straight Conference all-around gymnastics titles.**

- **Ohio State's All-Conference center Bill Hosket led the Buckeyes to a basketball co-championship. A generation later, Bill, Jr., would do likewise.**

Gophers claim first-ever baseball title

The year was 1933. Franklin Roosevelt was in his first term as President of the United States, Jimmie Foxx was tearing up American League pitching with a .356 batting average and 48 home runs, the Chicago Bears were the "Monsters of the Midway," and Minnesota's baseball team was claiming its first of 17 Big Ten titles. Coach Frank McCormick's Gophers had struggled to just a .500 record in 1932, but during the spring of '33 Minnesota raced to a nearly perfect 6-1 mark in Conference play and a 12-2 overall record. UM started horribly, losing 15-3 at Wisconsin, but then rebounded to win its last half dozen league games, including a 20-3 clincher at home versus Iowa. Among the Gopher diamond standouts was a youngster named Milt Bruhn, who also starred for Minnesota's football team. Bruhn went on to a brilliant coaching career on the gridiron, leading Big Ten rival Wisconsin to a berth in the 1960 Rose Bowl.

OTHER BIG TEN CHAMPIONS

- FOOTBALL: Michigan, coached by Harry Kipke
- GYMNASTICS: Chicago (coach not known)
- OUTDOOR TRACK: Michigan, coached by Charles Hoyt
- INDOOR TRACK: Indiana, coached by Earle "Billy" Hayes
- BASKETBALL: Northwestern, coached by Arthur Lonborg, and Ohio State, coached by Harold Olsen
- CROSS COUNTRY: Indiana, coached by Earle "Billy" Hayes
- TENNIS: Chicago (coach not known) and Minnesota, coached by Phil Brain
- SWIMMING: Michigan, coached by Matt Mann
- WRESTLING: Indiana, coached by W.H. Thorn
- GOLF: Michigan, coached by Thomas Trueblood
- FENCING: Illinois, coached by Herbert Craig

WES BROWN
Wrestling, Northwestern

Wes Brown won the 175-pound weight classification in the Big Ten wrestling championships all three of his seasons at Northwestern. As a sophomore in 1931, his victory helped the Wildcats—who had lost five dual meets and were without their captain—to a stunning Big Ten victory, their first wrestling title in school history. Brown won the title again as a junior, when the Wildcats won three of five dual meets. He served as team captain that season. His third Conference championship, in 1933, climaxed a brilliant season in which he won all seven of his matches in dual meet competition. His dream of winning a national championship ended when a knee injury forced him to default in the semifinals of the NCAA meet.

CHARLES BERNARD
Football, Michigan

Famed journalist Grantland Rice called football lineman Charles Bernard "another of Michigan's great pivotmen." Bernard had understudied behind Maynard Morrison in 1931 and was well prepared to be a brilliant center on two Big Ten championship teams. Called the greatest college player in the country by the pro coaches his senior season, Bernard was equally effective on offense and defense from 1931-33. "Without Bernard," said Associated Press sports editor Alan Gould, "the Wolverines could hardly have topped the toughest league in the country." During Bernard's three letter-winning seasons in Ann Arbor, coach Harry Kipke's troops won a nearly perfect 94 percent of their games, compiling a cumulative record of 23-1-1.

HARRY NEWMAN
Football, Michigan

Analyzing his 1932 All-America team selections, legendary sportswriter Grantland Rice said that Michigan quarterback Harry Newman "stood well above the mass." Newman's heroics during the Wolverines' 1932 national championship season included those as not only a signal-caller, but also as a runner and a place kicker. An effective triple-threat back, Newman was personally responsible for scoring 57 of Michigan's 83 points during its string of six consecutive Conference victories that season. From 1930-32, he paced Michigan to an amazing overall record of 24-1-2 and three consecutive Big Ten titles. Newman later played pro football with the New York Giants and the old Brooklyn Dodgers. His son, Harry Jr., also was a gridiron letter winner at Michigan in the late 1950s.

MISSING IN ACTION

B I G   T E N   L I S T

Not every Big Ten team title has been presented every year. There have been numerous lay-offs, mostly for wars. Here are the gaps in the Conference titles and the reasons why:

• **Men's Gymnastics:** No meets in 1917-18 and 1918-19 school years, because of World War I; no meets in 1942-43, 1943-44, 1944-45 and 1945-46 school years, because of World War II.

• **Men's Cross Country:** No meets in 1917-18 and 1918-19 school years, because of World War I; no meets in 1933-34, 1934-35, 1935-36, 1936-37 and 1937-38 school years, because of the Great Depression.

• **Wrestling:** No meets in 1917-18 and 1918-19 school years, because of World War I.

• **Men's Fencing:** No meets in 1943-44, 1944-45 and 1945-46 school years, because of World War II. Championships suspended following 1985-86 school year, because not enough schools fielded a team.

• **Ice Hockey:** Championships suspended following 1980-81 school year, because not enough schools fielded a team.

• **Women's Fencing:** Championships suspended following 1986-87 school year, because not enough schools fielded a team.

• **Field Hockey:** Championships suspended following 1988-89 school year, because not enough schools fielded a team; championships resumed in 1992-93 with the addition of Penn State to the Conference.

LEADING THE WAY

RALPH PIPER
Minnesota

Ralph Piper arrived at Minnesota in 1929 as a physical education instructor and gymnastics coach. Although he was supremely efficient at both tasks, it was the latter that brought him the most acclaim during his years with the Gophers' athletic program. As gymnastics coach, Piper guided Minnesota to five Big Ten championships (1936, '38, '40, '47, '48). He coached eight league all-around champions; 32 individual conference champions, one all-around NCAA champion, and six individual NCAA champions. On the topic of physical education, Piper wrote several books and served, from 1944-46, as head of physical education reconditioning for the U.S. Army Medical Department. He was head of Minnesota's teacher training program for physical education majors. He was also an expert in folk, square, and ballroom dancing and co-authored a number of books on dancing with his wife, Zora.

· BIG TEN PIONEERS ·

Wisconsin boxing tradition

A dominating tradition was born in 1933 when Wisconsin formed its first boxing team, thanks to the school's Athletic Publicity Director George F. Downer and coach John J. Walsh, the team's co-founders. The Badgers dueled St. Thomas College to 4-4 draw in their debut, but seldom found themselves anything but winners after that. Walsh's teams made 20 NCAA Tournament team appearances and won a remarkable eight team championships (1939, '42, '43, '47, '48, '52, '54, '56). Badger boxers won 35 NCAA individual titles under Walsh and three under coach Vern Woodward, who coached in 1959 and '60. Intercollegiate boxing ended at Wisconsin in 1960 following a fatal injury to Charley Mohr. Legendary pugilists Gene Rankin and Cliff Lutz were three-time NCAA champions for the Badgers, who posted a remarkable 105-8-10 all-time home record.

Academic Achievements

In 1889, Northwestern University was the first Midwest university to be admitted to Phi Beta Kappa.

The BIG TEN's First 100 Years

Facts About Big Ten Universities

Over 6,000 employers conducted recruitment visits on Big Ten campuses in 1993.

Source: Peterson's Guide to Colleges

1932-33 Conference MEDAL OF HONOR Winners

CHICAGO	Keith I. Parsons
ILLINOIS	R. Dean Woolsey
INDIANA	Noble L. Biddinger
IOWA	William A. McCloy
MICHIGAN	Ivan B. Williamson
MINNESOTA	Kenneth Gay
NORTHWESTERN	Kenneth A. Willard
OHIO STATE	John A.C. Keller
PURDUE	Roy J. Horstman
WISCONSIN	Nello Pacetti

1933-34

THE BIG EVENT

"Short" Boilermakers win Big Ten crown

The 1933 Boilermakers won the Big Ten Championship. Head Coach Ward Lambert instructs (left to right) Emmett Lowery, Ed Shaver, Ray Edy, Norman Cottom and Dutch Fehring.

Purdue coach Ward "Piggy" Lambert wasn't concerned with what his team *didn't* have: height. Instead, he focused on his players' speed, quickness and courage, their defensive abilities and passing skills, and a balanced scoring attack. The shortest team in the league with no player taller than 6-feet, the Boilermakers went 17-3, and won the Big Ten with a 10-2 mark. It was the school's third outright league title in five years. Purdue set school and Conference records for team scoring, and forward Norman Cottom led the Big Ten with 120 points. His 9.0 scoring average led the team. Ray Eddy was the team's floor leader, and William 'Dutch' Fehring (4.8 ppg) Emmett Lowery (7.2 ppg) and Ed Shaver (5.3 ppg) shared the ball unselfishly. Robert Kessler was the top reserve. Cottom and Lowery were All-Americans and first-team All-Big Ten. The Boilermakers' only losses were to Notre Dame, Iowa and Illinois.

OTHER MEMORABLE EVENTS

- Michigan went unbeaten in football and was crowned the mythical national champion.

- Michigan, led by John Kocsis, won the NCAA golf championship.

- The Conference cross country meet was cancelled because of the Great Depression.

- Indiana's Charles Hornbostel won his third straight NCAA 880-yard run title.

- Chicago's Bill Haarlow, who later became the Conference's chief of referees, was an All-Big Ten basketball selection.

Michigan wins five straight Big Ten, two NCAA golf titles

Michigan's John Fischer missed the 1934 season to play in the Walker Cup, but was the Conference's medalist for the third time in 1935.

It was a golden era for coach Tom Trueblood's fledgling Michigan golf program in the early and mid-1930s as the Wolverines claimed five straight Big Ten titles from 1932-36 and NCAA crowns in 1934 and 1935, the latter among only five won by Conference members. John Fischer and Chuck Kocsis led the team in those years, with Fischer taking the Big Ten and NCAA titles as a sophomore in 1932 and then repeating the Conference win the next year. Fischer missed the '34 season to play in the Walker Cup but Kocsis took his place in good fashion, medaling in the Big Ten and taking runner-up honors nationally as Michigan—only 12 years after starting varsity golf—won the team crown. Fischer returned in 1935 to win Conference medalist honors for the third time. He and Kocsis were the foundation of what may have been UM's best team ever as it successfully defended its Conference and national titles. Kocsis closed the era with his second Big Ten win and his first NCAA title in '36.

OTHER BIG TEN CHAMPIONS

- **FOOTBALL:** Michigan, coached by Harry Kipke
- **BASEBALL:** Illinois, coached by Carl Lundgren
- **GYMNASTICS:** Chicago (coach not known)
- **OUTDOOR TRACK:** Illinois, coached by Don Cash Seaton
- **INDOOR TRACK:** Michigan, coached by Charles Hoyt
- **BASKETBALL:** Purdue, coached by Ward Lambert
- **CROSS COUNTRY:** No meet
- **TENNIS:** Chicago (coach not known)
- **SWIMMING:** Michigan, coached by Matt Mann
- **WRESTLING:** Indiana, coached by W.H. Thorn
- **FENCING:** Chicago (coach not known)

NORMAN COTTOM
Basketball, Purdue

Though Norm Cottom was somewhat known for his ball-handling skills, Purdue coach Ward 'Piggy' Lambert used him on the frontline to play forward on an under-sized squad. Cottom went on to shoot 72 percent from the field and lead the Big Ten in scoring (9.0 ppg). As a junior, he was first-team All-Big Ten and a consensus All-American. He helped Purdue (17-3 overall) win the league championship with a 10-2 record. During his senior season, with opponents keying on him, Cottom helped the Boilermakers to a share of the Conference title (17-3, 9-3). He was second-team All-Big Ten. In a game against Temple University in Philadelphia, Cottom connected on a last-second shot from halfcourt to win the game, 35-34. During his three seasons, Purdue went a combined 45-13.

RALPH EPSTEIN
Fencing, Illinois

The only fencer to win three consecutive Big Ten individual championships is Ralph Epstein. The foil specialist from Chicago won championships in 1932, '33 and '34, a streak unmatched (although another Illini fencer won three individual titles and 11 other fencers from Illinois have won two titles). His individual titles led Illinois to the Big Ten team championship his sophomore and senior seasons. Also a standout in the classroom, Epstein became the school's 20th winner of the Big Ten Conference Medal of Honor. As a serviceman in World War II, he helped the U.S. Air Corps develop this nation's first jet airplane. After the war, Epstein returned to his hometown and joined the Chicago architectural firm of Epstein & Sons International, where he retired as president. He died in 1986 at the age of 72.

CHARLES HORNBOSTEL
Track, Indiana

Charles Hornbostel was a versatile runner who won 10 Big Ten championships for Indiana from 1932-34. His specialty was the 880-yard run, in which he won Big Ten indoor and outdoor titles in 1932, '33 and '34. He also was the mile indoor and outdoor champion in '34 and ran a leg on two winning mile relay teams. Hornbostel won cross country letters from 1931-33, serving as honorary captain the final season. He participated on two Big Ten championship cross country teams and placed 11th when the Hoosiers won the 1931 national AAU title. He also won the NCAA outdoor 880-yard track titles from 1932-34, and ran the 800 meters for the U.S. Olympic teams in 1932 (finishing sixth) and 1936 (fifth).

BIG TEN LIST

FIT TO BE TIED

With a tie-breaker now in place for all football games, here's one record that will not be broken—or tied. Minnesota finished the 1933 Big Ten football season with two wins, no losses and a record four ties. The Gophers were 4-0-4 overall. Here are the Conference football teams who had more than two ties in a season:

1900—Northwestern, 6-2-3 overall (2-1-2 in Conference)
1903—Northwestern, 5-1-3 (1-0-2)
1924—Chicago, 4-1-3 (3-0-3)
1924—Ohio State, 2-3-3 (1-3-2)
1924—Wisconsin, 2-3-3 (0-2-2)
1932—Ohio State, 4-1-3 (2-1-2)
1933—Minnesota, 4-0-4 (2-0-4)
1956—Wisconsin, 1-5-3 (0-4-3)
1988—Iowa, 6-4-3 (4-1-3)
1992—Michigan, 8-0-3 (6-0-2)

LEADING THE WAY

DAVID ARMBRUSTER
Iowa

The contributions of long-time Iowa swimming coach David Armbruster affected not just those in Iowa City, but throughout the world. Armbruster is credited with inventing the butterfly stroke and flip turn. He was Iowa's first swim coach and remained in that position from 1917-58. He coached 75 swimmers to All-America honors, and had 14 NCAA individual champions. His team won the Big Ten title in 1936, finished second in the nation in 1949 and were in the top 10 at the NCAA meet 18 of 23 years. He also coached two Olympians: Wally Ris, 100-meter freestyle gold-medalist in 1948; and Bowen Stassforth, 200-meter breaststroke silver-medalist in 1952. Armbruster was inducted into the International Swimming Hall of Fame in 1966. He died at age 94 in 1985.

· BIG TEN PIONEERS ·

Gophers "tie up" Championship

Coach Bernie Bierman's first Big Ten championship team was arguably his strangest, in terms of how Minnesota won the title. The 1933 Gophers (below) won their first of three straight crowns under Bierman by going undefeated — sort of. They compiled a bizarre 4-0-4 record, including a 2-0 Conference slate, to win the championship. The Gophers earned victories against South Dakota State, Pittsburgh, Iowa and Wisconsin but played Indiana, Purdue, Northwestern and Michigan to stalemates. Minnesota was led by All-Big Ten selections Frank "Butch" Larson and Francis "Pug" Land. The Gophers shared the 1933 championship with Michigan. No other team in league history has won or shared the title with four ties.

Academic Achievements

Among the most famous alumni from Minnesota are: actress Loni Anderson; author Harvey Mackey; CBS News correspondent, Harry Reasoner; radio host, Garrison Keillor; artist Georgia O'Keefe; former Supreme Court justice, Warren Burger; first heart transplant doctor, Dr. Christiaan Barnard; singer/ songwriter, Bob Dylan; actor Peter Graves; former U.S. Vice President, Hubert H. Humphrey; and Nobel prize winners, Norman Borlaug and Melvin Calvin.

1933-34 Conference MEDAL OF HONOR Winners

CHICAGO	George H. Wrighte
ILLINOIS	Ralph J. Epstein
INDIANA	Raymond F. Dauer
IOWA	Tom W. Moore
MICHIGAN	James C. Cristy, Jr.
MINNESOTA	Marshall Wells
NORTHWESTERN	Donald Brewer
OHIO STATE	R. Bartlett Ewell
PURDUE	W.P. Fehring
WISCONSIN	Robert A. Schiller

1934-35

THE BIG EVENT

Owens enjoys "record" day

It's hard to believe that Jesse Owens could hardly move with a sore back, the result of wrestling with fraternity brothers, within one day of the Conference track championships near the end of the 1934-35 season. Though he tied the world record in the 100-yard dash as a high school senior and won four gold medals to embarrass Adolph Hilter and his Aryan thinking, it's quite possible that Owens' finest moments came at the Conference meet when he set three world records and tied another within a 70-minute span. In his only jump of the day, he broke the long jump record by 6 inches just 10 minutes after tying the 100 in 9.4 seconds. Twenty minutes after his jump, he ran the 220-yard dash in :20.3, breaking the record by three-tenths of a second. Fifteen minutes later, he set the world record in the 220-yard low hurdles.

OTHER MEMORABLE EVENTS

- Michigan won its second straight NCAA golf championship; the Wolverines' John Fischer won his third consecutive Conference title.

- Minnesota went undefeated in football and was crowned the mythical national champion.

- Michigan won the NCAA swimming championship. Jack Kelsey won the first ever butterfly title, his first of three straight.

- Indiana's Charles McDaniel won the first of two NCAA heavyweight wrestling championships.

- The first regulations were adopted governing broadcasting rights to home football games.

1934 Gophers lay claim as one of college football's greatest teams

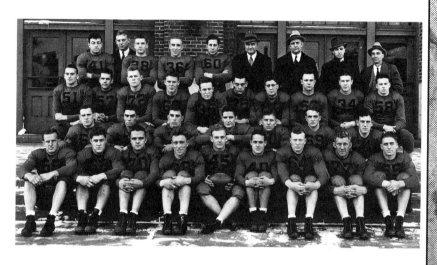

There was little or no national debate as to whether or not Minnesota was the cream of college football's plentiful crop. What was at issue was whether or not the 1934 Gophers, under legendary coach Bernie Bierman, were the greatest of all time to that point. Famed sportswriter Grantland Rice was convinced they were, as he wrote after the '34 campaign from Minneapolis: "Football fans here are no longer discussing whether Minnesota's team is the best in the country. They are taking it for granted. What they want to know is: shouldn't it be rated the greatest of all time?" The Big Ten and national champion Gophers were so powerful and stacked with talent that it was common knowledge that their reserve unit was more than a formidable match for anybody else's starters. Led by stars Ed Widseth, Butch Larson, Bill Bevan, Dick Smith, Pug Lund, Sheldon Beise, Babe Levoir and Bud Wilkinson, Minnesota won its first of three straight national titles and had the second of three straight unbeaten seasons in 1934. The Gophers reigned as Big Ten champions in 1934 and '35 and as national champs from 1934-36. In 1934, Bierman correctly boasted the Gophers were two-deep at every position and three-deep in most. The season was marked by impressive victories against powerhouses Nebraska, Pittsburgh and Wisconsin and was highlighted by a 34-0 thrashing of archrival Michigan in the battle for the Little Brown Jug trophy. The win was Minnesota's first home victory against Michigan since 1900.

OTHER BIG TEN CHAMPIONS

- **BASEBALL:** Minnesota, coached by Frank McCormick
- **GYMNASTICS:** Illinois, coached by H.D. Price
- **OUTDOOR TRACK:** Michigan, coached by Charles Hoyt
- **INDOOR TRACK:** Michigan, coached by Charles Hoyt
- **BASKETBALL:** Illinois, coached by J. Craig Ruby, Purdue, coached by Ward Lambert, and Wisconsin, coached by Harold Foster
- **CROSS COUNTRY:** No meet
- **TENNIS:** Chicago (coach not known)
- **SWIMMING:** Michigan, coached by Matt Mann
- **WRESTLING:** Illinois, coached by H.E. Kenney
- **GOLF:** Michigan, coached by Thomas Trueblood
- **FENCING:** Illinois, coached by Herbert Craig

JESSE OWENS
Track, Ohio State

A grandson of a slave, born the 10th of 11 children and whose family moved from the southern cotton fields to Cleveland when he was 9, Jesse Owens was an Olympic track hero. He won four gold medals before a crowd of 110,000 people at the 1936 Berlin Olympics, Adolph Hitler himself among those in attendance. No exaggeration was necessary to convey the importance of Owens' performance to the world, and his athletic talents were equally impressive. Owens won the long jump, and his times in the 100 meters (10.3), 200 meters (20.7) and 400-meter relay would have been good for Olympic medals as late as 1960. He had tied the world record in the 100 as a high school senior and set three world records and tied another in the 1935 Big Ten championships. He died in 1980 at age 66.

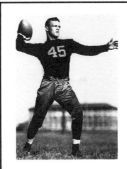

DUANE PURVIS
Football and Track, Purdue

At the time, he was probably the greatest athlete at Purdue. The Boilermakers' Duane Purvis and legendary Jim Thorpe shared this distinction: they were two of an elite group of athletes named All-America in two sports the same year. Purvis was a star halfback for the Purdue football team who rushed for 1,802 career yards, which was then a school record. He also passed the ball, played linebacker and defensive back. Purvis was twice first-team All-Big Ten and twice an All-American. He was most valuable player of the football team in 1934. Purvis also excelled in track and field. He was a national champion in the javelin in 1932, and set a Big Ten record in the event in 1933 (216-feet-6 1/4-inches). Unfortunately, his football career ended after he suffered a leg injury that didn't heal correctly during practice for the 1935 East-West Shrine all-star college football game. He later served more than three years in the U.S. Army. Purvis died at age 76 in 1989.

GERALD FORD
Football, Michigan

Jerry Ford would have been a noteworthy name in Michigan football annals even had he not become president of the United States. Ford lettered three years as a consistent snapper at second-string center from 1932-33 and played on two national championship teams, receiving the team's MVP award as a senior starter. That team won only one game and Ford later ruefully admitted he would rather have been "the least valuable player on a winning team." He later played in the College All-Star Game and the East-West Shrine Game and was named to the 1959 Sports Illustrated Silver Anniversary All-America roster. Ford assisted in football at Yale while pursuing his law degree. He later represented his hometown of Grand Rapids in Congress from 1949 until becoming vice president in 1973. Ford assumed the presidency in 1974.

BIG TEN LIST

WHAT'S IN A NAME?

Here are some of the more colorful and recognizable nicknames in Big Ten football history:

"Woody" Hayes, "Bo" Schembechler, "Red" "The Galloping Ghost" Grange, "Hopalong" Cassady, "The Horse" Ameche, "Moose" Wistert, "Pest" Welch, "Bubba" Smith, "Moon" Baker, "Germany" Schulz, "Shorty" DesJardien, "Nels" Norgren, "Fritz" Crisler, "Five Yards" McCarty, "Heavy" Twist, "Slooie" Chapman, "Potsy" Clark, "Bart" Macomber, "Butch" Nowack, "Buddy" Young, "Cotton" Berndt, "Chick" Kirk, "Bunt" Kirk, "Duke" Dunne, "Pudge" Wyman, "Shorty" Almquist, "Pug" Lund, "Butch" Larson, "Bud" Wilkinson, "Babe" LeVoir, "Paddy" Driscoll, "Tiny" Lewis, "Red" Woodworth, "Pug" Rentner, "Reb" Russell, "Chic" Harley, "Shifty" Bolen, "Hap" Courtney, "Truck" Myers, "Hoge" Workman, "Jumbo" Stiehm, "Hod" Ofstie, "Keckie" Moll, "Tubby" Keeler, "Butts" Butler, "Cub" Buck, "Rowdy" Elliott, "Toad" Crofoot, "Duffy" Daugherty, "Bo" McMillan, "Bump" Elliott, "Pappy" Waldorf, "Fat" O'Brien, "Hurry-Up" Yost, "Hard-Luck" Bruder, "Lefty" Leach, "Biggie" Munn, "Eggs" Manske, "Close-the-Gates-of-Mercy" Schmidt, "Sonny" Franck, "Crazy Legs" Hirsch, "Hunchy" Hoernschemeyer, "Jug" Girard, "Dike" Eddleman, "Sonny" Grandelius and "Moose" Skowron.

LEADING THE WAY

BERNIE BIERMAN
Minnesota

As a football player, Bernie Bierman was a winner. As a football coach, he routinely built Minnesota teams into one. Bierman starred for the Gophers as a halfback between 1913-15 under coach Dr. Henry L. Williams, captaining the undefeated league co-champion team of 1915. Despite his success as a player, his greatest fame came as a coach, first at the University of Montana, but ultimately at Minnesota, where he arrived in 1932. He guided the Gophers to five national championships (1934, '35, '36, '40, '41), six Big Ten titles and five undefeated seasons. His teams won 21 straight games between 1933-36 and 17 straight between 1939-41. A proponent of the single-wing offense, he coached such legendary performers as All-American and NFL Hall of Famer Ed Widseth; All-America lineman/quarterback Bud Wilkinson, who later gained remarkable fame as a college coach at Oklahoma; and All-Conference standout Butch Larson. Bierman left Minnesota during the war from 1942-44, but returned in 1945. His career college coaching record is 162-51-10. He died in 1977 at age 82.

· BIG TEN PIONEERS ·

Francis Schmidt
Ohio State

When he arrived at Ohio State in 1934 from Texas Christian, Francis Schmidt (below) brought with him the razzle-dazzle offense prevalent in the Southwest. Colorful in more ways than one, Schmidt had been a bayonet instructor during World War I, and his vocabulary was in keeping with his calling. He wore a bow tie and looked more like a businessman than a coach. During his seven years at Ohio State, his teams were 39-16-1, winning the Conference title in his second and sixth seasons. He favored plays with passes, then a lateral, and his offense was a leader in wide open play. His teams were also strong on defense, posting 25 shutouts in his 56 games as Ohio State coach. He was relieved of his duties in 1940.

Francis Schmidt

Academic Achievements

The famed Chicago School of Economics began in the 1930s. It has grown to the point where since 1970 seven alumni have received the Nobel Prize in Economic Science. The idea most strongly associated with the school is its belief in the ability of the free market to allocate resources and distribute income.

1934-35 Conference MEDAL OF HONOR Winners

CHICAGO	E.C. Patterson, Jr.
ILLINOIS	Irving Seeley
INDIANA	Don A. Veiler
IOWA	James P. McClintock
MICHIGAN	Harvey Smith
MINNESOTA	Robert Tanner
NORTHWESTERN	Chester H. Taylor
OHIO STATE	No award
PURDUE	Carl Heldt
WISCONSIN	Rolf Poser

BIG TEN

SINCE 1896

CENTENNIAL ™

1935-1944

THE BIG EVENT

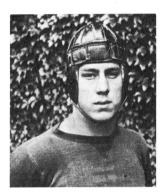

Chicago's Berwanger wins first Heisman Trophy

The once-mighty football program at Chicago was already being de-emphasized in 1935, but you would never have known it to see Jay Berwanger play. That the Downtown Athletic Club in New York gave its first award—called the Heisman Trophy in honor of coach John Heisman of Georgia Tech—drew no criticism, because the 6-foot, 200-pound halfback may just have been college football's best player since Jim Thorpe. Berwanger had that rare ability to swiftly photograph downfield situations while cutting back, changing speed and dealing with immediate tacklers. "That faraway look," Red Grange called it. Whatever, in 23 games over three years Berwanger racked up some remarkable stats—like 22 touchdowns and a 4.2 yards-per-carry average—while playing for a team that never had a winning season. On defense, Berwanger was a deadly tackler, but he was more remembered for his runs, with an 85-yard scamper from scrimmage against Ohio State his most famous and perhaps the play that cemented his victory in the New Yorkers' vote for the first Heisman.

OTHER MEMORABLE EVENTS

- For the second straight year, Ohio State's Jesse Owens won four individual titles at the NCAA outdoor track championship.

- Michigan's Charles Kocsis won the NCAA golf title and his second Conference championship.

- Michigan's Dick Degener won a gold medal in the three-meter dive at the Olympic Games.

- Ohio State's Bruce Laybourne scored a rare feat: the basketball and tennis star received a Conference Medal of Honor, along with being elected senior class president.

- Minnesota had the nation's top football team for the second year in a row, but tied Ohio State for the Conference title.

Hoosiers out-score Owens to win Big Ten track crown

Indiana won the 1936 Big Ten outdoor track championship despite the individual brilliance of Ohio State's Jesse Owens. The Hoosiers, coached by Billy Hayes, scored 47 points in the meet, held in Columbus, Ohio, while Michigan and the Buckeyes tied for second with 39 points. It was the Hoosiers' first outdoor crown. Ohio State was so strong, it won six individual events at the NCAA meet a short time later, but Indiana's depth proved insurmountable in the Conference meet. Indiana's Don Lash was Indiana's lone champion. He set Conference records in winning the mile (4:10.8) and two-mile (9:19.0), then went on to win the 5,000-meter run at the NCAA meet. OSU's NCAA titles came from Owens (in the 100, 200, broad jump and 220 low hurdles), Charles Beetham (in the 800) and David Albritton and Melvin Walker (who tied in the high jump). The Hoosiers wound up third nationally.

OTHER BIG TEN CHAMPIONS

- **FOOTBALL:** Minnesota, coached by Bernie Bierman, and Ohio State, coached by Francis Schmidt
- **BASEBALL:** Michigan, coached by Ray Fisher
- **GYMNASTICS:** Minnesota, coached by Dr. Ralph Piper
- **INDOOR TRACK:** Michigan, coached by Charles Hoyt
- **BASKETBALL:** Indiana, coached by Everett Dean, and Purdue, coached by Ward Lambert
- **CROSS COUNTRY:** No meet
- **TENNIS:** Northwestern, coached by Paul Bennett
- **SWIMMING:** Iowa, coached by David Armbruster
- **WRESTLING:** Indiana, coached by W.H. Thorn
- **GOLF:** Michigan, coached by Ray Courtright
- **FENCING:** Chicago (coach not known)

CHARLES FENSKE
Track, Wisconsin

Charles "Chuck" Fenske was known as "The Monarch of the Mile," prior to World War II. He was one of the best track athletes in the history of the Big Ten and certainly one of its greatest distance runners. Fenske set a number of world records, one of which he still holds in the three-quarter mile (2:59.7), set in 1940 at the Armour Relays. A 1938 graduate, he was the Big Ten indoor mile champion in 1936, '37 and '38 and was the Mile of the Century winner at the 1939 outdoor Princeton Invitational. He lettered in track and cross country, was captain of both teams and was named "Miler of the Year" in 1940. Fenske ran mile times of 4:11 or better 19 times in his career, and once held the world record in the 1,000-yard run at 2:09.3. He twice ran the mile in 4:07.4. Fenske served in the military from 1941 until 1946.

BUD WILKINSON
Football and Hockey, Minnesota

Bud Wilkinson achieved nationwide acclaim as a legendary college football coach at Oklahoma. He was equally successful as a college player at Minnesota, although his athletic exploits aren't as nationally celebrated as his dazzling coaching accomplishments. Wilkinson was a standout guard and later a quarterback for the Gophers. Wilkinson was an All-American who helped lead the Gophers to three straight national championships (1934-36). He also played goalie for the Gophers' hockey team. As coach, he was a renowned innovator who developed the split-T formation and the no-huddle offense. A member of the National Football Coaches Hall of Fame, Wilkinson compiled a 145-29-4 record in 17 seasons as head coach at Oklahoma, where he guided the Sooners to three national championships, five undefeated seasons and an NCAA record 47-game winning streak. He coached briefly in the NFL with the St. Louis Cardinals and took a respite from coaching in the 1960s to pursue a career in politics. He died in 1994 at age 77.

CHARLES KOCSIS
Golf, Michigan

Charles, "Chuck" Kocsis was one of the heroes of a golden era in Michigan golf, when the fledgling program leaped to prominence in the Big Ten and national collegiate ranks. Kocsis won the Conference individual crown in 1934 and placed second in the NCAA individual standings while Michigan won both titles. In 1935, he and John Fischer led the Wolverines to their second straight NCAA win. As a senior, Kocsis regained his Big Ten championship and finally won the elusive NCAA title. After graduation, Kocsis continued in the amateur ranks, winning the Michigan Amateur an unprecedented six times between 1930 and 1951. He also won three Michigan Open championships, the first in 1930 when he beat the great Tommy Armour by a stroke. A great tee-to-green player, Kocsis was runner-up in the 1956 U.S. Amateur.

BIG TEN LIST

HEISMAN TROPHY WINNERS

1935—Jay Berwanger, Chicago
1939—Nile Kinnick, Iowa
1940—Tom Harmon, Michigan
1941—Bruce Smith, Minnesota
1944—Les Horvath, Ohio State
1950—Vic Janowicz, Ohio State
1954—Alan Ameche, Wisconsin
1955—Howard Cassady, Ohio State
1974—Archie Griffin, Ohio State
1975—Archie Griffin, Ohio State
1991—Desmond Howard, Michigan
1995—Eddie George, Ohio State

LEADING THE WAY

LYNN "PAPPY" WALDORF
Northwestern

Pappy Waldorf, who coached at Northwestern from 1935-46, still ranks as the school's all-time winningest football coach with a record of 49-45-7. An All-American player at Syracuse, his first Wildcat team became the first to upset Notre Dame in 35 years. He received Big Ten coach of the year honors that season, and then came back to direct a league championship team in 1936, when the Wildcats finished 6-0 in league play and 7-1 overall. That team remained the most recent Northwestern team to win the league title until 1995. Waldorf's 1943 team, led by quarterback Otto Graham, nearly won another Big Ten championship, finishing 5-1 in league play. Waldorf took over at the University of California in 1947. His 1948 team there reached the Rose Bowl, but lost to Northwestern, 20-14. He later worked as personnel director for the National Football League's San Francisco 49ers before retiring in 1972. He was elected to the National Football Foundation Hall of Fame as a coach in 1966. He died in 1978, a coach long remembered for his philosophy that "the players should enjoy the game."

· BIG TEN PIONEERS ·

Ozzie Simmons
Iowa

One of Iowa's initial African-American football players, Ozzie Simmons (below) was named first-team All-America by *The Sporting News* in '35, and was second-team by other organizations in 1934 and '35. He was twice first-team All-Big Ten. The Hawkeyes finished 4-2-2 in 1935, and Simmons played a key role throughout the season. His grandest performance came during a 19-0 victory over Illinois in the fourth game of the year. Simmons had 87 yards in punt and kickoff returns, intercepted one pass, scored one touchdown and ran for 192 yards. Simmons was voted by fans to Iowa's all-time team (on offense) in 1989 when the school celebrated its first 100 years of football.

Ozzie Simmons

 ## Academic Achievements

The University of Iowa was among the first universities in the nation to award graduate credit for creative work in the arts. Then in 1936 it became home of the acclaimed Iowa Writers' Workshop. Later it began the Iowa Playwrights Workshop and the International Writing Program, the only one of its kind in the world. Among the attendees was playwright Tennessee Williams.

1935-36
Conference MEDAL OF HONOR
Winners

CHICAGO	Gordon C. Peterson
ILLINOIS	Arthur Fisher
INDIANA	Reed H. Kelso
IOWA	Francis X. Cretzmeyer
MICHIGAN	Harvey W. Patton
MINNESOTA	Glenn Seidel
NORTHWESTERN	Curtis M. Shananahn
OHIO STATE	Bruce B. Laybourne
PURDUE	Robert L. Kessler
WISCONSIN	Howard Heun

THE BIG EVENT

Michigan swims to first NCAA title

Michigan won the first of its record 11 NCAA swimming titles in the inaugural meet at Minnesota in 1938, scoring 75 points to runner-up Ohio State's 39. Under the direction of legendary coach Matt Mann, four Michigan swimmers won six individual events at that first official national collegiate meet and two relay quartets took NCAA titles. Double winners for Mann's men were freestylers Ed Kirar in the 50 and 100 and Tom Haynie in the 200 and 440. The Wolverines, who won seven unofficial collegiate titles prior to the start of NCAA competition, would continue to dominate, winning the first five NCAA meets and taking second place in the next six before winning again in 1948. Until Southern Cal's win in 1960, no team other than Michigan, Ohio State or Yale had won an NCAA swim title.

OTHER MEMORABLE EVENTS

- Iowa, led by Conference all-around champion Gene Wettstone, won the NCAA gymnastics championship.

- Minnesota had its 28-game unbeaten streak in football snapped by Northwestern, 6-0.

- Three Conference athletes won NCAA track titles: Michigan's Sam Stoller (100), Ohio State's Dave Albritton (high jump) and Wisconsin's Chuck Fenske (mile).

- Northwestern's Sid Richardson won the first of two straight Conference golf titles.

- Michigan's Johnny Gee not only was the captain of the Wolverines' basketball team, but at 6-foot-9, went on to be one of the tallest big league pitchers in history.

Wildcats nab first outright Big Ten football crown

Northwestern won its first outright Big Ten football championship in 1936, and nearly picked up a national title in the process. The Wildcats had shared Conference championships in 1903, '26, '30 and '31, but had never won the title outright until Lynn "Pappy" Waldorf directed his second team to a 7-1 overall record, 6-0 in league play. Only three opponents managed to score in double figures, two were shut out and another scored just two points. The Wildcats' biggest victory of the season came against Minnesota in a Homecoming game on a rainy Halloween afternoon in Dyche Stadium. Fullback Steve Toth scored the game's only touchdown in the 6-0 victory against the defending national champions. It turned out to be the season's only loss for the Gophers, who were again voted national champs by the Associated Press despite the defeat. Northwestern's bid for the national title was lost when it fell to Notre Dame in the final game of the season, 26-6, in South Bend. The Wildcats were known as a "starless" squad that succeeded through teamwork and effort. Three of the most prominent players were sophomores: tackle Bob Voigts, who later coached the 1948 team that won the Rose Bowl, halfback Bernie Jefferson and end Cleo Diehl. Toth and fellow seniors Steve Reid, the team's MVP, and Don Geyer also stood out. The 1936 Big Ten title was the school's last in football until the 1995 team ended the drought.

OTHER BIG TEN CHAMPIONS

- **BASEBALL:** Illinois, coached by Walter Roettger
- **GYMNASTICS:** Iowa, coached by Albert Baumgartner
- **OUTDOOR TRACK:** Michigan, coached by Charles Hoyt
- **INDOOR TRACK:** Michigan, coached by Charles Hoyt
- **BASKETBALL:** Illinois, coached by Doug Mills, and Minnesota, coached by Dave MacMillan
- **CROSS COUNTRY:** No meet
- **TENNIS:** Chicago, coached by Wally Hebert
- **SWIMMING:** Michigan, coached by Matt Mann
- **WRESTLING:** Illinois, coached by H.E. Kenney
- **GOLF:** Northwestern, coached by Ted Payseur
- **FENCING:** Chicago (coach not known)

LOU BOUDREAU
Basketball and Baseball, Illinois

He came to Illinois as a star basketball player, eventually earning All-America honors on the hardcourt following his junior year at Illinois. But Lou Boudreau ended up in the baseball Hall of Fame following a successful career as a player, manager and broadcaster. Major-league scouts took notice after Boudreau's junior year at Illinois in 1937, when he hit .347 to lead Illinois to the Big Ten title. He joined the Cleveland Indians the next spring, was promoted to player-manager by the Indians four years later and guided Cleveland to the World Series title in 1948. He hit .295 in a 15-year playing career and was a manager for four different franchises. He served as a television and radio broadcaster for the Chicago Cubs for more than two decades. Now retired, he lives in the Chicago suburb of Dolton.

ED WIDSETH
Football, Minnesota

Ed Widseth anchored a Minnesota offensive line that was one of college football's elite in the mid-1930s. He was the primary reason why. A three-time All-Big Ten tackle and a two-time All-American, Widseth was the cornerstone of a powerful unit that helped power the Gophers to three straight national championships in 1934, '35, and '36. Minnesota was a combined 23-1 during the time Widseth played. He was co-captain of the 1936 team and was voted its MVP. He played 410 of a possible 430 minutes and was named the most valuable lineman of the 1937 East-West Shrine Game. Widseth joined the NFL's New York Giants the same year and played five spectacular seasons before an injury ended his career in 1941. He was a first team pro bowler in 1938 and '39, and he was voted league MVP — a rarity for a lineman — in 1938 after helping the Giants win the NFL championship. Widseth was inducted into the pro football hall of fame in 1954.

JEWELL YOUNG
Basketball, Purdue

Jewell Young, a homegrown Purdue star from Lafayette, Ind., was part of the "Three Musketeers," which included Pat Malaska (Crawfordsville, Ind.) and Johnny Sines (Lafayette). The left-handed Young led the league in scoring in 1937 and '38, and was named first-team All-Conference and consensus All-America both years. He was the school's first two-time All-American since John Wooden (1930-32). Young helped lead the Boilermakers to a share of the Big Ten championship as a sophomore and an outright league title as a senior. Jewell set a single-game league mark when he scored 29 points against Illinois on Feb. 15, 1937. His 172 points during the 1936-37 season set a Big Ten record, a mark he would break the next season when he scored 184. His three-year career total of 465 points also set a league record.

BIG TEN LIST

SPRINT CHAMPIONS

Big Ten men have won the NCAA 100-yard/meter dash championship 11 times.

1925—DeHart Hubbard, Michigan, 9.8 seconds*
1929—George Simpson, Ohio State, 9.4*
1935—Jesse Owens, Ohio State, 9.8*
1936—Jesse Owens, Ohio State, 10.2
1937—Sam Stoller, Michigan, 9.7*
1944—Buddy Young, Illinois, 9.7*
1946—William Mathis, Illinois, 9.6*
1952—Jim Golliday, Northwestern, 10.4
1953—Willie Williams, Illinois, 9.7*
1954—Willie Williams, Illinois, 9.5*
1955—Jim Golliday, Northwestern, 9.6*
*100 yards

LEADING THE WAY

HAROLD "BUD" FOSTER
Wisconsin

Bud Foster knew how to win on the basketball court. As a player, he was a two-time All-Big Ten center and an All-American at Wisconsin. As a coach, he guided the Badgers to their only NCAA championship in 1941 — a feat they performed as underdogs. Foster's storied career at Wisconsin began in 1928, when he joined the Badgers' basketball team. He earned All-Big Ten honors in 1929 and '30 and was an All-American in 1930. After a short stint playing professionally with the Oshkosh All-Stars, he began his lengthy tenure as Badgers' head coach in 1935, where he served until 1959. He guided Wisconsin to Big Ten titles in 1935, '41 and '47 and posted a career record of 265-267. His crowning achievement, however, was leading the Badgers to a 39-34 upset victory against the taller, more athletic Washington State team in the 1941 NCAA championship game. The Badgers had a propensity for winning close games and were a team that liked to pass and work painstakingly for shots. The Cougars were the opposite, preferring an uptempo style predicated on taking quick shots. But the Badgers' approach proved more effective, as All-America sophomore guard John Kotz, the game's MVP, and All-America senior center and Big Ten MVP Gene Englund proved too much for Washington State. Kotz scored 12 points while Englund scored 13 points and performed a stellar defensive job on the Cougars' star player. Foster's teams were centered around pressure defense and offensive patience. He was inducted in the Helms Basketball Hall of Fame, the National Basketball Hall of Fame, the Wisconsin State Athletic Hall of Fame, and the University of Wisconsin Athletic Hall of Fame. Foster died on July 16, 1996 at the age of 90.

· BIG TEN PIONEERS ·

First AP national football poll

It was only fitting that in 1936, college football's undisputed top program — Minnesota — was the first team to earn the No. 1-ranking in the inaugural Associated Press national poll, created by Alan Gould. Coach Bernie Bierman's Gophers were the nation's premier dynasty, as the 1936 national title was their third straight. Ironically, Minnesota lost the Big Ten championship that year after a 6-0 defeat against eventual league champion Northwestern, which ascended to No. 1 for three weeks before losing its season-finale against Notre Dame. That allowed Minnesota to regain the top spot and become the nation's first poll-anointed national champion. Northwestern was No. 7 in the final poll. As testimony to the Gophers' worthiness of being the AP's first champions, between 1934 and 1941 they posted a 58-9-5 record and won seven Conference championships and five national titles.

Academic Achievements

Northwestern's McCormick School of Engineering and Applied Science pioneered creation of the field of materials science and established one of the first centers in biomedical engineering research.

The BIG TEN's First 100 Years
Big Ten Men's Basketball
Scoring Records

Game
61 Rick Mount, Purdue vs. Iowa Feb. 28, 1970

Season
1,030 Glenn Robinson Purdue 1993-94

Career
2,613 Calbert Cheaney Indiana 1989-93

1936-37
Conference MEDAL OF HONOR
Winners

CHICAGO	Floyd R. Sauffer
ILLINOIS	Harry Coombes
INDIANA	Vernon R. Huffman
IOWA	Cornelius J. Walker
MICHIGAN	John A. Gee
MINNESOTA	Charles B. Wilkinson
NORTHWESTERN	Albert Adelman
OHIO STATE	Inwood Smith
PURDUE	Glynn M. Downey
WISCONSIN	Leonard L. Lovshin

1937-38

THE BIG EVENT

Chicago wins first NCAA gymnastics title

Despite a third place Big Ten finish behind Minnesota and Illinois, Chicago's gymnasts excelled at home and came away with the first NCAA gymnastics championship in 1938. Coach Dan Hoffer's team scored 22 points to arch-rival Illinois' 18, gaining more than a measure of revenge for mid-season dual meet losses suffered at the hands of the Illini and the Gophers. Minnesota, the Conference champ, was third. Chicago's Erwin Beyer became a three-time national champion in that first meet, winning the side horse, parallel bars and long horse. Albert Guy took a second and a fourth in the NCAA meet for the Maroons while George Hays grabbed a fourth.

OTHER MEMORABLE EVENTS

- The Conference lifted a ban to compete against the U.S. Military Academy.

- Purdue's Jewell Young led the Conference in basketball scoring for the second straight year.

- Ohio State's David Albritton won his third straight NCAA outdoor high jump title.

- Michigan won the NCAA swimming championship.

- Ohio State's Al Patnik won the first of five NCAA diving championships.

- Indiana's Corbett Davis was the first selection in the NFL college draft.

Buckeye swimmers claim national AAU title

The Buckeyes lost the NCAA title by one point and one foot, but Ohio State came back a month later and won the school's first national championship by scoring a first-place finish in the national AAU meet in Columbus, Ohio, under coach Mike Peppe. The NCAA meet came down to a wild finish in the 400-yard relay. Michigan's Edward Kirar finished six inches ahead of Harvard's Charles Gutter, who was second just ahead of Ohio State's Bill Neunzig. The thrilling finish allowed Michigan to score its fifth straight collegiate title by a 46-45 score, rallying past an Ohio State team that led nearly the entire meet. The Buckeyes were led by Al Patnik, who won both the low-board and high-board diving championships. The results were different when Ohio State won both the Big Ten team title (62-54 over Michigan) and the AAU nationals. At the AAU meet Patnik again won both diving events and Neunzig anchored the Buckeyes' victorious 400 freestyle relay team. Ohio State won the team title with 41 points ahead of Michigan's 19.5. Princeton was third with 17 points.

OTHER BIG TEN CHAMPIONS

- **FOOTBALL:** Minnesota, coached by Bernie Bierman
- **BASEBALL:** Indiana, coached by Everett Dean, and Iowa, coached by Otto Vogel
- **GYMNASTICS:** Minnesota, coached by Dr. Ralph Piper
- **OUTDOOR TRACK:** Michigan, coached by Charles Hoyt
- **INDOOR TRACK:** Michigan, coached by Charles Hoyt
- **BASKETBALL:** Purdue, coached by Ward Lambert
- **CROSS COUNTRY:** No meet
- **TENNIS:** Chicago, coached by Wally Hebert
- **WRESTLING:** Michigan, coached by Clifford Keen
- **GOLF:** Minnesota, coached by W.R. Smith
- **FENCING:** Chicago (coach not known)

DAVE ALBRITTON
Track, Ohio State

It might have been hard for Dave Albritton to endure living in the shadows of teammate Jesse Owens if the two hadn't been good friends since the age of five when both of their parents were sharecroppers in Alabama. Albritton was a track phenom himself, a three-year letterman and three-time All-American at Ohio State as a high jumper. He won three NCAA titles in the event, also taking home a silver medal in the 1936 Berlin Olympics when Owens was busy shattering world records. Albritton cleared the same height as teammate Cornelius Johnson, who did it on fewer attempts. Albritton was also known as Owens' closest friend, the man who drove the car across state lines when Owens and his fiancee, Ruth, were looking to get married. Albritton is a member of the Ohio State Sports Hall of Fame.

JOE GIALLOMBARDO
Gymnastics, Illinois

In high school, Joe Giallombardo served on the cheerleading squad that cheered for classmate Jesse Owens, soon to become an Olympic sprint star. Giallombardo made his own headlines when he arrived at Illinois. He won all-around and tumbling individual NCAA championships in 1938, '39 and '40, also grabbing the NCAA title in the rings in 1938. The seven individual titles set an NCAA record that wasn't matched until the early 1980s. Giallombardo was a three-time all-around individual Big Ten champ, leading Illinois to the 1939 team title in the Big Ten. His success also helped Illinois begin a string of four straight NCAA championships, beginning in 1938. He coached at New Trier and New Trier West high schools in suburban Chicago until his retirement in 1975. Giallombardo now resides in southern Illinois.

ERWIN BEYER
Gymnastics, Chicago

Erwin Beyer, one of only three men in Chicago history to win an NCAA gymnastics title, set some standards for years to come when he won three events in the inaugural NCAA gymnastics meet in 1938 at Chicago. Beyer won the side horse, parallel bars and long horse titles as coach Don Hoffer's Maroons edged Illinois, 22-18. Beyer repeated as side horse champ in 1939.

BIG TEN LIST

INDIANA'S WRESTLING CHAMPS

Indiana has had eight NCAA wrestling champions, including six in the 1930s:

1932—Edwin Belshaw, 134 pounds
1933—Patrick Devine, 135 pounds
1934—Richard Voliva, 175 pounds
1935—Charles McDaniel, heavyweight
1938—Charles McDaniel, heavyweight
1939—Chris Traicoff, 175 pounds
1940—Robert Antonacci, 121 pounds
1990—Brian Dolph, 150 pounds

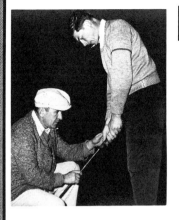

LEADING THE WAY

ROBERT KEPLER
Ohio State

He lettered three times in golf and missed winning the NCAA title by two strokes, but his name is more associated with coaching rather than playing. Robert Kepler (left) coached golf from 1938 to 1965, leading the Buckeyes to one NCAA crown, one second-place finish and four Big Ten titles. The NCAA title came in 1945, and he coached Ohio State to Conference titles in 1945, 1951, 1954 and 1961. A college golf coaches hall of fame selection, Kepler coached four NCAA medalists, including John Lorms (1945), Tom Nieporte (1951), Rick Jones (1956), and Jack Nicklaus (1961). His star golfer was Nicklaus, a recruit from nearby Upper Arlington who won the U.S. Amateur as an Ohio State freshman. When he could finally compete on the varsity, Nicklaus won a Big Ten title and an NCAA championship before a career when he won 20 major titles. Kepler was a charter member of the Ohio State Sports Hall of Fame and a golf tournament at Ohio State is named in his honor.

· BIG TEN PIONEERS ·

Don Lash
Indiana

Don Lash (below) became the first Big Ten athlete to win the Sullivan Award as America's outstanding amateur athlete after a standout career at Indiana in cross country and track. Lash won three consecutive national AAU championships in cross country from 1934-36, and won Big Ten indoor championships in the two-mile run (1935, '37) and outdoor titles in the mile and two-mile runs from 1935-37. He also was the NCAA champion in the 5,000 meter outdoor run and was a member of the 1936 U.S. Olympic team, placing eighth in the 10,000 meters and 14th in the 5,000 meters. In 1937 he was a member of relay teams that set world records in the four-mile and distance medley runs.

Don Lash

Academic Achievements

This academic achievement is for adults only: Without Indiana University, there would be a lot less knowledge about sex. The internationally known Kinsey Institute for Research on Sex, Gender and Reproduction is located on the Bloomington campus.

1937-38
Conference MEDAL OF HONOR
Winners

CHICAGO	George C. Halcrow
ILLINOIS	Allen Sapora
INDIANA	Charles E. McDaniel
IOWA	Robert G. Lannon
MICHIGAN	John Townsend
MINNESOTA	Dominick Krezowski
NORTHWESTERN	Daniel Zehr
OHIO STATE	Ralph C. Wolf
PURDUE	Martin A. Schreyer
WISCONSIN	Charles H. Fenske

THE BIG EVENT

Indiana wins NCAA cross country title

Indiana was proud possessor of the Big Ten's dominant cross country program throughout the 1930s, and the team in the fall of 1938 only added to the reputation. The Hoosiers defeated Purdue, Butler, Michigan State and Ohio State to go undefeated in dual meet competition, then easily won a state championship meet. They went on to win the Big Ten meet at Purdue with 30 points, ahead of second-place Wisconsin's 49. They capped off the season by winning the NCAA championship in Milwaukee with 51 points, 10 points ahead of second-place Notre Dame. Mel Trutt, who had won the Conference meet, placed third overall, highest among IU's finishers. Indiana dropped to second in the Big Ten meet in 1939, but came back in '40 to win the Big Ten and NCAA championships again.

OTHER MEMORABLE EVENTS

- Illinois won the NCAA gymnastics championship with Joe Giallombardo winning the all-around title.

- Michigan won the NCAA swimming title.

- Northwestern's Sid Richardson won the NCAA golf medalist championship.

- Chicago brothers Chet and Bill Murphy combined to win the Conference tennis doubles title for the second time.

- Minnesota's Dale Hanson was named the most outstanding wrestler at the NCAA championship.

Coach Hartley Price

Illinois Gymnasts enjoy perfect season

If there ever was a perfect season, Illinois enjoyed one in the 1938-39 school year in gymnastics. The Illini were undefeated during the dual meet season, then played host to the Conference championships. Illinois didn't disappoint its hometown fans, scoring 22 points more than runner-up Minnesota. At the NCAA championships a month later, Illinois won its first title. Joe Giallombardo led the Illini to the team titles, winning the individual all-around championship in the Conference and NCAA meets, and he finished his career with three straight NCAA all-around titles, three more NCAA championships in tumbling and another title in the rings. Pommel horse specialist Harry Koehnemann won the first of three straight titles. The Illini would follow the 1938-39 season by winning a total of four striaght NCAA championships through the 1941-42 season under coach Hartley Price. Illinois teams would win 14 Conference titles from 1938-39 through the 1959-60 season, including an astonishing 11 straight through the 1959-60 season. Since that season, Illinois has won four Conference titles, the last one coming in 1988-89.

OTHER BIG TEN CHAMPIONS

- **FOOTBALL:** Minnesota, coached by Bernie Bierman
- **BASEBALL:** Iowa, coached by Otto Vogel
- **OUTDOOR TRACK:** Michigan, coached by Charles Hoyt
- **INDOOR TRACK:** Michigan, coached by Charles Hoyt
- **BASKETBALL:** Ohio State, coached by Harold Olsen
- **CROSS COUNTRY:** Indiana, coached by Earle "Billy" Hayes
- **TENNIS:** Chicago, coached by Wally Hebert
- **SWIMMING:** Michigan, coached by Matt Mann
- **WRESTLING:** Indiana, coached by W.H. Thorn
- **GOLF:** Northwestern, coached by Ted Payseur
- **FENCING:** Chicago (coach not known)

JOHN KUNDLA
Basketball, Minnesota

Success followed John Kundla on the basketball court at each one of his stops as a player and as a coach. It began during his playing days at Minnesota, which spanned 1935-39. In 1937, he was a sophomore starter on the last Gophers' squad to win the Big Ten championship until 1972. In 1939, as captain, he broke his own school single-season scoring record with 201 points. However, Kundla earned his greatest fame as coach — and founder of — the Minneapolis Lakers' dynasty between 1948 and 1959. Armed with legendary players George Mikan, Elgin Baylor, and former Minnesota Vikings' coach Bud Grant, Kundla led the Lakers to four NBA championships, one NBL title, and one BAA championship. He departed the Lakers after the 1959 season to take over the coaching reins at Minnesota, where he built a long-struggling program into a contender until his retirement in 1968. His career record with the Gophers was 110-105. His career record with the Lakers was 423-302.

CHET MURPHY
Tennis, Chicago

Chet Murphy won the singles title in the 1939 Big Ten tennis tournament and paired with twin brother Bill to repeat as double champs. The Murphys were ranked 10th nationally in doubles. Chicago won its third consecutive Conference title for Coach Wally Hebert as it defeated Northwestern, 25-16, taking a perfect 27 of 27 matches in the Big Ten tournament. The Maroons won all nine of their dual meets in 1939, and only once in 106 individual matches was a Chicago player defeated. It was the last of Chicago's 20 Big Ten championships in tennis, most by the school in any sport. In fact, during a particularly strong run from 1929 through 1942, Chicago placed its team either first or second in the Conference standings 13 of 14 times.

DALE HANSON
Wrestling, Minnesota

Individual Big Ten wrestlers have frequently claimed the Outstanding Wrestler Award at the national collegiate tournament over the years, but the very first man to be so honored was Minnesota's Dale Hanson in 1939. The 128-pounder was the second of only nine Gopher grapplers who was able to earn the top spot in any weight classification at the NCAA level. Hanson joined fellow Gopher John Whitaker as the only Minnesota wrestlers who won All-America honors. Though his team claimed no better than fourth-place finishes in the Big Ten standings in 1939 and 1940, Hanson breezed to individual titles both seasons, becoming the first Gopher ever to win back-to-back Conference crowns.

TOP HITTERS

The Big Ten began keeping hitting statistics in 1939. Here are the top batting averages for the league leaders:

.585, Bill Freehan, Michigan, 1961
.514, Randy Wolfe, Michigan, 1985
.500, Scott Weaver, Michigan, 1995
.500, Fred Erdmannn, Michigan, 1983
.500, Bill Skowron, Purdue, 1950
.485, George Smith, Michigan State, 1955
.484, Lee Eilbracht, Illinois, 1946
.477, Mike Fitzenberger, Minnesota, 1974
.476, Mike Smith, Indiana, 1991
.475, John Hoyman, Iowa, 1980
.475, Ron Causton, Minnesota, 1959
.473, Rick Leach, Michigan, 1978

LEADING THE WAY

WALT PAULISON
Northwestern

Walter Paulison was one of the pioneers of the profession of people who publicize collegiate athletics. A 1924 graduate of Northwestern, he was hired as the Big Ten's second sports information director — a job then known as a "press agent" — in 1926, one year after Illinois hired Mike Tobin to handle the attention received by football star Red Grange. Paulison began his duties the same year Dyche Stadium was built and continued until 1969, when he retired. The press box at the stadium is named in his honor. He was among a charter group of SIDs voted into the Helms Foundation Athletic Hall of Fame. He also wrote a history book of Northwestern athletics, "Tale of the Wildcats." Paulison, who died at age 88 in 1990, was known for his soft-spoken, dignified approach. Speaking once at a testimonial dinner in his honor, he revealed the identity of the greatest Northwestern athlete he ever witnessed: "Every time I see a boy walking across campus wearing that N jacket or meet a fellow with an N Man's button in his lapel, that's the greatest athlete I've ever seen at Northwestern, because I know how hard it was for him to make it."

· BIG TEN PIONEERS ·

First NCAA basketball tourney at Northwestern

The NCAA basketball tournament wasn't always the money-spewing machine it is today. It had a humble beginning in Northwestern's Patten Gymnasium (below), where Oregon defeated Big Ten champ Ohio State for the first NCAA title, 46-33. The eight-team tournament was the brainchild of Ohio State coach Harold Olsen, who wanted to compete with the NIT in New York City, which was a huge success in its debut in 1938. The National Association of Basketball Coaches sponsored the first NCAA tourney, but no more than 1,500 fans attended the final game and it lost $2,531. The NCAA took over sponsorship the following year.

 # Academic Achievements

The first U.S. college program in wildlife management was established in 1938 by famous conservationist and UW wildlife ecologist Aldo Leopold.

1938-39 Conference MEDAL OF HONOR Winners

CHICAGO	Robert E. Cassels
ILLINOIS	Archie Deuschman
INDIANA	Christopher Traicoff
IOWA	Wilbur V. Nead
MICHIGAN	Leo C. Beebe
MINNESOTA	John A. Kundla
NORTHWESTERN	Marvin Wachman
OHIO STATE	James A. Whittaker
PURDUE	Joseph Mihal
WISCONSIN	Walter I. Bietila

1939-40

THE BIG EVENT

Maroons suffer through final football season

A proud Big Ten tradition ended on a sour note for the University of Chicago football team in 1939, as coach Clark Shaughnessy's Maroons played their final Conference gridiron season. Though UC's 2-6 overall record was disappointing, it didn't come close to matching its pitiful 0-3 record in league games in which they were cumulatively outscored by Michigan, Ohio State and Illinois by a count of 192 to nothing. During Chicago's first 13 seasons in the Big Ten from 1896 through 1908, the Maroons won four Conference championships. Only Michigan with its four titles during that span was competitive with Amos Alonzo Stagg's football machine. Over its first 29 years as a league member, Chicago accumulated 107 victories against only 45 losses and 12 ties. However, over its last 15 years in the Big Ten from 1925 to 1939, UC football dipped from a winning percentage of .689 to one of a paltry .204. Former UC president Robert Hutchins reasoned that the size of the student body, the requirements of their course of study, and the standards of University were the major factors in discontinuing the sport. "I greatly fear," said Hutchins, "that my administration will be remembered solely because it was the one in which intercollegiate football was abolished."

OTHER MEMORABLE EVENTS

- Iowa's Nile Kinnick won the Heisman Trophy.

- Indiana won the NCAA basketball tournament with Marvin Huffman named the most outstanding player.

- Michigan won the NCAA swimming championship.

- Wisconsin's Walter Mehl won the NCAA cross country title.

- Northwestern tied for the Conference baseball title, led by 23-year old coach Stan Klores.

- Michigan's Don Nichols was named the most outstanding wrestler at the NCAA championship; Ohio State's George Downes won the heavyweight crown.

- Illinois' Joe Giallombardo won his third straight NCAA all-around gymnastics title.

Purdue captures Big Ten title, but Indiana goes on to win NCAA tourney

Indiana's 1940 NCAA champs

Purdue finished 16-4, captured its seventh outright Big Ten title at 10-2, set school a scoring record (514 points) and won its final game in dramatic fashion—outscoring Illinois 15-2 in the final nine minutes. What the Boilermakers did not do was represent the Conference in the two-year-old NCAA tournament. Purdue officials decided the team's 20-game schedule was enough and declined an invitation to the tourney, opening the door for rival Indiana to be asked. From the hard to believe department: Purdue's coach Ward "Piggy" Lambert and Athletic Director Noble Kizer recommended the Hoosiers—who finished with a better overall record at 20-3—for the invitation. Must've been a kinder, gentler era. Two of Purdue's losses were to Indiana; the others were against DePaul and Southern California early in the season. The Hoosiers went on to win the national championship, defeating Kansas in the final game. There were reports that the Hoosiers were the first choice of the NCAA to be in the tournament despite their finishing second in the Big Ten. Donald Blanken was the leading scorer for the Boilermakers (9.2 points per game), and seven players averaged four points or better. Fred Beretta (5 ppg) was a Helms Foundation All-American.

OTHER BIG TEN CHAMPIONS

- **FOOTBALL:** Ohio State, coached by Francis Schmidt
- **BASEBALL:** Illinois, coached by Walter Roettger, and Northwestern, coached by Stanley Klores
- **GYMNASTICS:** Minnesota, coached by Dr. Ralph Piper
- **OUTDOOR TRACK:** Michigan, coached by Kenneth Doherty
- **INDOOR TRACK:** Michigan, coached by Kenneth Doherty
- **CROSS COUNTRY:** Wisconsin, coached by Thomas Jones
- **TENNIS:** Northwestern, coached by Paul Bennett
- **SWIMMING:** Michigan, coached by Matt Mann
- **WRESTLING:** Indiana, coached by W.H. Thorn
- **GOLF:** Illinois, coached by W.W. Brown
- **FENCING:** Chicago (coach not known)

SEYMOUR GREENBERG
Tennis, Northwestern

Seymour Greenberg, a Chicago native, enjoyed one of the most successful tennis careers in Big Ten history. In his debut as a sophomore in 1940, the former Illinois state high school champion gained the No. 1 position on the team, won the Conference singles title and teamed with doubles partner Jerry Clifford to win the doubles title as the Wildcats won the team title. Greenberg won the single championship again as a junior and teamed with Gene Richards to win the doubles. Greenberg's quest for a third straight title was denied by Calvin Sawyier of Chicago, but he teamed with Bobby Jake to win the doubles title. Greenberg attained national acclaim by winning the U.S. Clay Courts championship in 1942 and '43, and was ranked among the nation's top 10 players from 1942-45 and in 1947.

NILE KINNICK
Football, Iowa

Ex-teammates later would talk of the "aura" about Nile Kinnick, the way a humble, student-athlete in the truest sense would dominate on the football field. Kinnick's spot in Iowa history is secure. He was a first-team All-Big Ten halfback in 1939 who rushed for 374 yards, passed for 638 and totaled 16 touchdowns. He finished the year with eight interceptions, a 39.9-yard punting average, 604 yards in punt and kickoff returns and 41 points kicking. He was a consensus All-American and winner of the Maxwell Award, Walter Camp Trophy and Heisman Trophy as the nation's top college football player. He set numerous season and career Iowa records on the field, and was a Phi Beta Kappa in the classroom. The Philadelphia Eagles made him their No. 1 draft choice. Tragically, the Omaha, Neb., native was killed when a Navy fighter plane he was piloting went down in the Atlantic Ocean, off the coast of Venezuela in June 1943. He was presumed drowned. Kinnick had enlisted in the Navy after one year of law school and was called to active duty three days before Pearl Harbor.

WALTER J. "WALLY" MEHL
Track, Wisconsin

Regarded as one of America's greatest distance runners in the first half of the century, Wally Mehl is also among the greatest cross country and track athletes in Wisconsin history during a brilliant career spanning 1935-39. A member of the Drake Relays Hall of Fame and a former world record holder in the indoor 2-mile, Mehl was cross country team captain in 1938 and '39 and captained the track team in '39. In track in 1938, he won Big Ten championships in the outdoor and indoor 2-mile and was NCAA champion in the 2-mile. In cross country, he was runner-up for the NCAA championship. In 1939, he was the Big Ten indoor and outdoor mile champion and, in cross country, won the NCAA title. After college, he won the AAU indoor mile championship in 1940, the AAU 1,500-meter title in 1940, and was the Wanamaker mile champion in '41. He was a lieutenant in the U.S. Army during World War II and became a Presbyterian minister in 1958.

SERVICE BUREAU CHIEFS

William R. Reed began the Big Ten Service Bureau in 1939, handling all of the Conference's public relations.

Service Bureau Directors

1939-42	William R. Reed
1942-43	James T. Maher
1946-47	William R. Reed
1947-51	Walter Byers
1951-61	William R. Reed
1961-70	Kay Fred Schultz
1970-73	Michael D. McClure
1974-86	Jeff Elliott
1986-90	Mark D. Rudner

Managing Editor & Special Projects Director

1990-	Mary Masters

Information Services Director

1992-	Dennis LaBissoniere

LEADING THE WAY

LEO JOHNSON
Illinois

If the measure of success for a coach is the number of championships won, then Leo Johnson was a giant in his era as a track and field coach. From the time he was hired in 1938 until he retired in 1965 at the age of 70, Johnson guided Illinois teams to 18 Big Ten titles and three national championships. Since 1944, when Johnson's Illini won the NCAA title, he is one of only four coaches outside the Sun Belt states to win a national championship. Illinois also won back-to-back national titles in 1946 and 1947, outdistancing runner-up Southern California each year. Under Johnson, Illinois track athletes captured 27 NCAA titles and 158 Big Ten championships. Another highlight to Johnson's career came at the 1952 Olympics when two former Illinois pole vaulters—Bob Richards and Don Laz—finished one-two in their event. A member of numerous track and field halls of fame, Johnson was also a valuable member of the Illinois football coaching staff, serving as a scout. Johnson played briefly with George Halas' Decatur Staleys. He died in 1982 at the age of 87.

· BIG TEN PIONEERS ·

Patty Berg
Minnesota

Few, if any, women golfers enjoyed a more distinguished career than Minnesotan Patty Berg (below) . Playing in an era before organized women's sports, she went on to become a charter member of the LPGA Hall of Fame. She won the Minneapolis City Tournament in 1934 at age 16 — the first of 85 professional and amateur wins she collected worldwide in a dazzling 40-year career. Berg won 15 LPGA major championships, was selected the Associated Press Woman Athlete of the Year three times; and was the first president of the LPGA in 1948. In 1992, she was voted by the PGA of America as one of 15 of Golf's Legendary Teachers — the only woman to ever receive the honor. Berg was a charter member of the World Golf Hall of Fame in 1974.

Patty Berg

 # Academic Achievements

Elizur Wright, "the father of insurance," used mathematical formulas to lend certainty to a risky business. His great-grandson, Chicago's Sewall Wright, became the "father of population genetics" by using abstract mathematical models to outline the shifting balances of evolution. By breeding guinea pigs, he proved that natural selection—not chance or mutation—is the major force that controls and guides evolution.

1939-40 Conference MEDAL OF HONOR Winners

CHICAGO	Martin Levit
ILLINOIS	Frank E. Richart, Jr.
INDIANA	Robert I. Hokey
IOWA	Andrew J. Kantor
MICHIGAN	James R. Rae
MINNESOTA	Harold Van Every
NORTHWESTERN	John Ryan
OHIO STATE	Esco Sarkkinen
PURDUE	Richard C. Potter
WISCONSIN	Ralph H. Moeller

THE BIG EVENT

Illinois gymnasts reign again

A 6-0 season in Conference duals led everyone to believe that Illinois was again the team to beat in gymnastics, and the Illini backed that up by rolling through the postseason to win the Conference title and the third of four straight NCAA titles under coach Hartley Price. In the Conference meet, Illinois took five of the six individual titles. Sophomore Caton Cobb (bottom), won the high bar, tied for first in the parallel bars and finished second in the pommel horse, one-half point behind teammate Harry Koehnemann, who was winning his third Big Ten title in the event. Illinois' Louis Fina (top) also finished first in the rings and Jack Adkins was first in tumbling. Illinois won the Conference team title with 105.5 points ahead of runner-up Minnesota's 96.5

OTHER MEMORABLE EVENTS

- Wisconsin won the NCAA basketball tournament with John Kotz named the most outstanding player.

- Michigan's Tom Harmon won the Heisman Trophy.

- Minnesota won the mythical national football championship.

- Indiana won the NCAA cross country title, Michigan the NCAA swimming championship and Northwestern the first NCAA fencing team title.

- Northwestern's Seymour Greenberg won the Conference tennis singles title for the second straight season.

- Minnesota's Leonard Levy won the NCAA heavyweight wrestling championship.

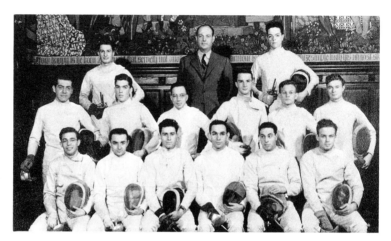

Chicago's last team title comes in fencing

Chicago won the last of its 72 Big Ten team championships by taking its sixth consecutive fencing crown in 1940-41. Joe Molkup won the last sabre bout of the championship over his Northwestern foe to assure Coach Alvar Hermanson's Maroons their eighth Conference title in the sport. Co-captain Herb Ruben won the foil championship while co-captain Paul Siever was runner-up in sabre. In a prophecy that would not come to pass, the 1941 Chicago yearbook predicted that "Chicago's tenure as king of Big Ten schools in this sport seems reasonably secure."

OTHER BIG TEN CHAMPIONS

- **FOOTBALL:** Minnesota, coached by Bernie Bierman
- **BASEBALL:** Michigan, coached by Ray Fisher
- **GYMNASTICS:** Illinois, coached by H.D. Price
- **OUTDOOR TRACK:** Indiana, coached by Earle "Billy" Hayes
- **INDOOR TRACK:** Indiana, coached by Earle "Billy" Hayes
- **BASKETBALL:** Wisconsin, coached by Harold Foster
- **CROSS COUNTRY:** Indiana, coached by Earle "Billy" Hayes
- **TENNIS:** Michigan, coached by LeRoy Weir
- **SWIMMING:** Michigan, coached by Matt Mann
- **WRESTLING:** Minnesota, coached by Dave Bartelma
- **GOLF:** Illinois, coached by W.W. Brown

EDWARD MCNAMARA
Fencing, Northwestern

Edward McNamara captained one of the most unusual team success stories in Big Ten history. Northwestern's 1941 fencing team had a most unimpressive dual meet season, finishing with a 3-9 record. But it went on to place second in the Conference meet, falling just one-half point short of Chicago for the title, and then won the inaugural national collegiate title. McNamara led the well-balanced squad by placing third in the foil in the Conference meet, and then won the competition in the NCAA meet. Dave Melbye (third in sabre) and Art Hutchinson (fourth in epee) also scored in the meet. The Wildcats had gone 8-7-1 the previous year, placing second in the Conference meet, one point behind Chicago. McNamara was a letter winner on that team, which was captained by Cliff Groh, who won the league foil title.

JOHN KOTZ
Basketball, Wisconsin

John "Johnny" Kotz was one of the greatest basketball players in Wisconsin history. A native of Rhinelander, Wisc., he was one of the state's most highly recruited players before joining the Badgers in 1940, where he played between 1941-43. He helped lead the Badgers to the 1941 Big Ten and NCAA championships his sophomore season and was All-Conference that same year. He was voted MVP of the national championship game and was the Conference scoring leader in 1942. That same season, he set a then-school single-game scoring standard of 31 points in a game against Iowa. He was Wisconsin and Big Ten MVP in 1942 and earned All-America honors. He captained the Badgers in 1942 and 1943 and was again made All-America in 1943. He scored 841 points during his career, which was a school record at the time.

TOM HARMON
Michigan, Football

Tom Harmon, "Old 98," is recognized as one of the greatest players in college football history. A two-time All-America halfback, Harmon twice led the nation in scoring. Michigan's first Heisman Trophy winner, Harmon started from 1938-40, rushing for 2,134 yards and completing 101 passes for 1,396 yards. His last game against Ohio State was perhaps his greatest: a virtual one-man team, Harmon ran for 139 yards, completed 11 of 12 passes for 151 yards and two touchdowns, scored three TDs and four extra points, intercepted three passes and averaged 50 yards per punt as Michigan won 40-0. His number was retired upon his graduation. Harmon signed with the pros but World War II interrupted his football career and injuries kept him from matching his collegiate success. He became a nationally known sportscaster. Harmon died in 1990 at age 70 in California.

BIG TEN LIST

WISCONSIN'S SCORING CHAMPS

The first basketball scoring leader—Emmett Angell—played for Wisconsin. Through the years, seven Conference scoring champions were from Wisconsin:

1906—Emmett Angell, 96 points
1912—Otto Stangel, 177 points
1915—George Levis, 140 points
1942—John Kotz, 242 points,
    17.3 avg.
1947—Bob Cook, 187 points,
    15.6 avg.
1949—Don Rehfeldt, 229 points,
    19.1 avg.
1950—Don Rehfeldt, 265 points,
    22.1 avg.

LEADING THE WAY

CLAUDE REECK
Purdue

Purdue's wrestling program had been discontinued for years, and Claude Reeck was brought in to get it rolling again. It needed organization and leadership, and he provided just that. He didn't need too much time to build a successful program, either. Reeck coached the Boilermakers to a Big Ten championship as soon as 1942, with four individual champs. Under Reeck, Purdue went on to win the league in 1945, '48, '49, '50 and '54 and finish second in 1944 and '47. He also coached numerous Big Ten and NCAA champions. At Cornell College in Iowa, Reeck was a standout football player and also competed in wrestling, basketball and baseball. He actually gave up wrestling as a college sophomore because his parents did not like the sport. A native of Grafton, Iowa, he received All-Conference recognition in 1924 and '25 and was named to the all-state team in '25 in football. Reeck would later coach the United States wrestling team in the Pan American Games and was named to the Wrestling Hall of Fame.

· BIG TEN PIONEERS ·

Northwestern fencing team wins first NCAA meet

The first official NCAA fencing championship, in 1941, could easily have been mistaken for a Big Ten meet, as Northwestern (below) edged Illinois for the team title, 28 1/2 to 27, in the finals held at Ohio State. The championship was a stunning accomplishment for the Wildcats, coached by Henry Zettleman. They had won just three of nine dual meets that season, but showed signs of life by placing second to Chicago in the Big Ten meet. Ed McNamara won the foil championship in the NCAA meet, after finishing third in the Big Ten finals, while G.H. Boland of Illinois won the epee title.

1941 Northwestern fencing team

 # Academic Achievements

P urdue has more undergraduates studying chemistry than at any other university in the nation.

1940-41
Conference MEDAL OF HONOR
Winners

CHICAGO	James Ray
ILLINOIS	Park Brown
INDIANA	Harold L. Zimmer
IOWA	James R. Murphy, Jr.
MICHIGAN	Forest Evashevski
MINNESOTA	George Franck
NORTHWESTERN	Glenn E. Thistlewaite
OHIO STATE	Clifford P. Morgan
PURDUE	William J. Neff
WISCONSIN	Kenneth E. Bixby

THE BIG EVENT

Gophers record second perfect season

Like most of legendary coach Bernie Bierman's Minnesota football teams, the 1941 Gophers knew how to run, knew how to hit — and knew how to win. Minnesota capped its second straight perfect 8-0 season and Big Ten championship with its second consecutive national title — the last of five Minnesota won under Bierman. The Gophers' powerful ground attack was fueled by Heisman Trophy-winning halfback Bruce Smith, bruising fullback Bob Sweiger, and swift scatback Herman Frickey. The trio had the luxury of running behind a mountainous offensive line anchored by stalwarts Urban Odson, Dick Wildung, Len Levy, Helge Pukema and Bill Fitch. The Gophers, who had won five of the previous seven Big Ten crowns, earned successive season-ending victories against Nebraska, Iowa, and Wisconsin to seal their status as college football's No. 1-ranked football team and national championship. Bierman insisted the team compared favorably to his 1934 championship squad, which was widely regarded at the time as the best college football team ever assembled.

OTHER MEMORABLE EVENTS

- Minnesota's Bruce Smith won the Heisman Trophy.

- Indiana's Fred Wilt won the NCAA cross country title.

- Illinois won the NCAA gymnastics championship.

- Ohio State won the NCAA fencing championship; OSU's Ben Burtt was the epee winner.

- Northwestern's Dick Haskell was the NCAA golf medalist.

- Minnesota's Newton Loken won the NCAA all-around gymnastics title and Chicago's Earl Shanken won his third straight national long horse championship.

Buckeyes dominate Conference track meets

No disputes can be lodged over the best track team in the Conference during the 1941-42 season. The Buckeyes from Ohio State, coached by Larry Snyder, won the indoor title before sweeping to the outdoor track championship. Described as a piston-legged runner, Bob Wright was the team's star, winning both hurdles events—including a record time in the 70-yard low hurdles—as Ohio State won the indoor title by scoring 37 points, well ahead of second-place Illinois' 28 points and Indiana's 27. Ohio State crushed its opponents in the dual meet season, and the Buckeyes rolled into the Drake Relays, where Ohio State's Ralph Hammond was a member of three relay teams that registered three first place finishes. George Hoeflinger also tied for first in the high jump at the Drake Relays. Later in the season at the Conference outdoor championships, the Buckeyes' power was on display as Ohio State scored 66.5 points to win the title. Illinois placed second with 31 points while Indiana was third with 30.

OTHER BIG TEN CHAMPIONS

- **FOOTBALL:** Minnesota, coached by Bernie Bierman
- **BASEBALL:** Iowa coached by Otto Vogel, and Michigan, coached by Ray Fisher
- **GYMNASTICS:** Illinois, coached by H.D. Price
- **BASKETBALL:** Illinois, coached by Doug Mills
- **CROSS COUNTRY:** Purdue, coached by Herman Phillips
- **TENNIS:** Northwestern, coached by Paul Bennett
- **SWIMMING:** Michigan, coached by Matt Mann
- **WRESTLING:** Purdue, coached by C.C. Reeck
- **GOLF:** Michigan, coached by Ray Courtright

ELROY "CRAZY LEGS" HIRSCH
Football,
Wisconsin/Michigan

Elroy "Crazy Legs" Hirsch is among the most famous athletes in Wisconsin history and is certainly one of its most prolific. Although he played only two seasons with the Badgers before war-time circumstances caused him to play his final two years at Michigan, "Crazy Legs" was an All-American at Wisconsin in 1942, which marked the beginning of a storied athletic and administrative career. As a sophomore halfback in 1942, he led the Badgers to an 8-1-1 record and a No. 3 national ranking. Renowned for his speedy zig-zag running style, he was given the nickname "Crazy Legs" by former Chicago Daily News sportswriter Francis Powers, who wrote after a game: "Hirsch ran like a demented duck. His legs were gyrating in six different directions ...." Hirsch joined the U.S. Marines and was sent to Officers' Training School at Michigan, where he resumed his career. He was again an All-American in 1943 and '44.

BRUCE "BOO" SMITH
Football, Minnesota

Of the many football stars responsible for Minnesota's storied gridiron tradition, Bruce Smith is arguably the brightest of them all. A multi-gifted halfback, Smith was the Gophers' first and only Heisman Trophy winner in 1941, the same year Minnesota won one of its six national championships. Former coach Bernie Bierman called Smith, "the most complete football player I ever saw." A three-year starter between 1939-41, Smith led the Gophers to consecutive 8-0 records in 1940-41. He rushed for 1,203 yards and 14 touchdowns during his career. He also completed 20 of 55 passes for 475 yards and four touchdowns. An outstanding special teams player, Smith was the Gophers' top punt returner and top punter in 1941, earning All-Big Ten and consensus All-America honors in addition to the Heisman Trophy. After serving in the military during World War II, he had a brief professional career with the Green Bay Packers. He starred in a Hollywood film about his life — "Smith of Minnesota" — in 1942. He died in 1967 in Minneapolis.

FRED WILT
Cross Country, Indiana

Fred Wilt was Indiana's first NCAA cross country champion, capturing the individual title in 1941. Wilt, who also won the Big Ten title that year, was a standout track performer as well, winning the Big Ten indoor and NCAA outdoor championships in the two-mile run. He was a member of the 1948 U.S. Olympic team (placing 11th in the 10,000 meters) as well as the '52 team (placing 21st in the same event). Wilt worked for the FBI for many years after college, then coached at Indiana's in-state rival, Purdue, from 1978-89 as the women's cross country and track coach. He coached Purdue's 1980 cross country team to its first ever Big Ten title and the '87 track team to its first-ever outdoor title. He coached 17 All-Americans in all. Wilt died in 1995.

ALL-TIME NO-HITTERS

B I G   T E N   L I S T

Illinois' Chuck Schiller threw the first complete-game no-hitter in a Big Ten Conference game, Apr. 25, 1942. Since then, there have been 14 more.

Chuck Schiller, Illinois, 1942
Don Zitek, Northwestern, 1954
Albion Hayes, Indiana, 1957
Doug Mills, Illinois, 1961
Joe Sparma, Ohio State, 1963
Bob Shutts, Northwestern, 1968
Gene Rogers, Ohio State, 1969
Jim Burton, Michigan, 1971
Kirk Maas, Michigan State, 1971
Lary Rosin, Indiana, 1976
Dave Mumaw, Ohio State, 1989
Aaron Puffer, Purdue, 1990
Sherard Clinkscales, Purdue, 1992
Dan Garman, Michigan State, 1993
Joe Westfall, Minnesota, 1993

LEADING THE WAY

MAX GARRET
Illinois

He came to Illinois as a part-time assistant coach, and he left the school as a giant in his profession. Max Garret led Illinois to a 243-71-1 dual-meet record in 27 years as the school's head fencing coach, taking over the program in 1944-45, building Illinois into a national power by the 1950s, when Illinois claimed seven Big Ten team championships. Under Garret, Illinois won 17 Conference titles and placed in the top 10 in NCAA competition 19 times. The Illini won NCAA titles in 1955-56 and 1957-58. Illinois rolled to three straight Big Ten titles with undefeated records, the last one in the 1952-53 season. Garret produced 14 first-team All-Americans, including 1971-72 NCAA foil runner-up Dave Littell in his final year at Illinois. His top athlete was Art Schankin, who became the first undefeated collegiate fencer to win the NCAA title when he swept to the NCAA sabre title in the 1957-58 season. The 1960 U.S. Olympic coach, two-time president of the National Fencing Coaches Association and the 1970 coach of the Israeli national team in the World University Games, Garret left Illinois in 1972 to coach at Penn State.

· BIG TEN PIONEERS ·

Chuck Schiller
Illinois

Lanky Chuck Schiller filed his name in the athletic annals as the third pitcher in Illinois history to throw a no-hit, no-run game as the Illini defeated Chicago 6-0. It was the first no-hitter in a Conference game. Schiller permitted only three Chicago batters to reach base to become the first Illinois pitcher to throw a no-hitter in 21 years and the third since Harvey McCollum threw the initial no-hitter. The 6-foot-3 senior from Oak Park, Illinois, mixed a sharp-breaking curve with a fastball to baffle Chicago all afternoon. Schiller permitted only four batters to hit the ball out of the infield all day, pleasing a crowd of 662 at Illinois Field. Schiller retired the first nine batters before hitting a Chicago batter on the elbow with a pitch.

Academic Achievements

Among the most famous alumni from Northwestern are: Chicago Bulls and White Sox owner, Jerry Reinsdorf; sportscaster Brent Musburger; mystery writer Edith Skern; astronaut Joseph Kerwin; creator of "All My Children," Agnes Nixon; Supreme Court Associate Justice, John Paul Stephens; Nobel prize winner for literature, Saul Bellow; L.A. Times syndicated columnist, Georgie Anne Geyer; and humorist Edgar Bergen.

The BIG TEN's First 100 Years
Facts About Big Ten Universities

Ten percent of the nation's Fulbright Fellowships were awarded to Big Ten faculty and students in 1994. Indiana and Penn State led the nation with the most number of faculty recipients, 14 each.

Source: Penn State fellowship office

1941-42
Conference MEDAL OF HONOR
Winners

CHICAGO	Calvin C. Sawyier
ILLINOIS	William Hocking
INDIANA	Hugh B. McAdams
IOWA	Richard E. Hein
MICHIGAN	David M. Nelson
MINNESOTA	Eugene Flick
NORTHWESTERN	Richard Erdlitz
OHIO STATE	Benjamin P. Burtt
PURDUE	Paul B. Anthony
WISCONSIN	Burleigh E. Jacobs

THE BIG EVENT

Indiana ties Penn State for NCAA cross country title

Indiana's run of cross country dominance was winding down in the early 1940s, but the 1942 team added another Big Ten title and an NCAA co-championship. The Hoosiers defeated Purdue and Michigan State in dual meets to open the season, then won the state championship meet by placing five of their runners among the top nine finishers. They went on to claim the Big Ten championship in Chicago on Nov. 14 with 34 points, well ahead of second-place Illinois' 69 points. IU's Earl Mitchell was the individual winner, marking the third consecutive championship for a Hoosier runner. Charles Labotka placed second, Paul Kendall sixth and Tom Judge seventh. Indiana went on to tie Penn State for the NCAA championship in East Lansing, Mich., as both teams finished with 57 points. Mitchell finished second overall in that meet, while Labotka placed eighth, Judge 10th and Kendall 13th.

OTHER MEMORABLE EVENTS

- Ohio State won its first Big Ten baseball title in 19 years.

- Certain eligibility rules were waived for the duration of the war to permit the use of freshmen on varsity teams. All eligibility rules were waived for students in the armed forces, receiving major instruction at a member institution.

- NCAA competition was cancelled in gymnastics, fencing and wrestling because of World War II.

- Ohio State was named the national football champion.

- Ohio State won the NCAA swimming championships.

- Summer football practice was allowed.

Illinois' "Whiz Kids" roll to basketball title

Doug Mills, coach of Illinois' most famous basketball team, placed his Whiz Kids in a class of their own. Of all the players Mills coached, only Lou Boudreau could have played with the all-star quartet of Andy Phillip, Jack Smiley, Gene Vance and Ken Menke, along with two-year Whiz Kid Art Mathisen. The group of 6-foot-3 athletes compiled a cumulative Big Ten record of 33-6, including overall marks of 18-5 in 1941-42 as sophomores and 17-1 the following season as juniors, when wartime travel restrictions kept them from competing in the NCAA championship or NIT. The Whiz Kids won Conference titles both seasons, including a 12-0 mark in 1942-43. World War II broke up the team, but it was reunited for the 1946-47 season when the Whiz Kids led Illinois to a second-place finish in the Conference race. The Whiz Kids were led by Phillip, who enjoyed an 11-year pro career, the highlight to it an NBA championship while playing for the Boston Celtics. Mills coached Illinois for 11 seasons, winning three Conference titles before retiring as coach to serve as athletic director.

OTHER BIG TEN CHAMPIONS

- **FOOTBALL:** Ohio State, coached by Paul Brown
- **BASEBALL:** Ohio State, coached by Fred Mackey
- **GYMNASTICS:** No meet
- **OUTDOOR TRACK:** Michigan, coached by Kenneth Doherty
- **INDOOR TRACK:** Michigan, coached by Kenneth Doherty
- **CROSS COUNTRY:** Indiana, coached by Earle "Billy" Hayes
- **TENNIS:** Ohio State, coached by Herman Wirthwein
- **SWIMMING:** Ohio State, coached by Michael Peppe
- **WRESTLING:** Indiana, coached by W.H. Thorn
- **GOLF:** Michigan, coached by Ray Courtright
- **FENCING:** Illinois, coached by Maxwell Garret

OTTO GRAHAM
Football, Northwestern

Otto Graham is one of the greatest athletes in Big Ten history, a genuine star in football, basketball and baseball. Before becoming an NFL hall of fame quarterback with the Cleveland Browns, Graham, who played football at Northwestern from 1941-43, was named the Big Ten's Most Valuable Player and earned All-America honors. His 27 points against Wisconsin in 1943 remains the school's single-game scoring record, and his 93-yard punt return against Kansas State in '41 has yet to be surpassed. In basketball, Graham set a school scoring record with 196 points during his sophomore season in 1941-42. He earned All-America honors the following year and placed second in the league scoring race. His senior season was cut short by military duty.

BILLY HILLENBRAND
Football, Indiana

He played just two seasons of college football, but Billy Hillenbrand left his mark on the Big Ten. The sturdy running back earned All-Big Ten honors in 1941 and '42, and was a consensus All-American in '42. He was all-purpose, to say the least. He led Indiana in passing (412 yards) and scoring (7 touchdowns) as a sophomore, and in rushing (498 yards) and passing (901 yards) as a junior. He remains by far Indiana's career leader in punt return yardage, with 1,042 on 65 returns. Hillenbrand, who was featured in a 1942 Look magazine article, had his career interrupted by World War II. He passed up his senior year of eligibility after the war to turn professional. He played with the Chicago Rockets of the All-American Football League and the Baltimore Colts of the NFL.

ANDY PHILLIP
Basketball, Illinois

The wizard of Illinois' famed Whiz Kids, Andy Phillip led a group that won back-to-back Big Ten titles in basketball in 1942 and '43, compiling a 25-2 record in the league. World War II broke up the Whiz Kids, but they reunited for a second-place finish in the Big Ten in 1947. Phillip was an All-American, and he set Big Ten records with a 21.3-point scoring average and a single-game mark of 40 points. Following a four-year career in the St. Louis Cardinals baseball organization, Phillip returned his attention to basketball and enjoyed an 11-year pro career, the last nine in the newly organized NBA. Phillip was an extraordinary ball-handler, the first NBA player to reach 500 assists. He finished his career with the Boston Celtics, winning a championship ring in 1957. Phillip is a retired probation officer living in California and a member of the Naismith Basketball Hall of Fame.

BIG TEN LIST

MINNESOTA'S TRACK CHAMPS

Minnesota has had eight champions at the NCAA Outdoor Track & Field Championships:

1942— Jack DeField, pole vault
1942— Bob Fitch, discus throw
1943— Jack DeField, pole vault
1946— Fortune Gordien, discus throw
1947— Fortune Gordien, discus throw
1948— Fortune Gordien, discus throw
1948— Lloyd Lamois, triple jump
1971— Garry Bjorklund, 10,000-meter run

LEADING THE WAY

PAUL BROWN
Ohio State

When Ohio State named Paul Brown as coach of the Buckeyes' football team prior to the 1941 season, it was the first time the school hired a head football coach directly from the high school ranks. He showed right away that it wasn't a mistake, leading the Buckeyes to a 6-1-1 record and second-place finish in the Conference. A year later, the Buckeyes were 9-1, finishing the season as Big Ten champs and winning the school's first national championship. Brown finished his three-year career with an 18-8-1 record, accepting a commission in the U.S. Navy during World War II. When he returned, he resigned his position as head coach with the Buckeyes and quickly turned the Cleveland Browns into a pro football powerhouse. After leading the Browns to four All-America Football Conference titles, the team joined the NFL, and he guided Cleveland to three NFL championships and a berth in the NFL title game seven times in the next 13 years. He founded the Cincinnati Bengals in 1968, coaching the team through the 1975 season. A perfectionist, he was attributed with sending the plays in from the sidelines. He died in 1991.

· BIG TEN PIONEERS ·

10 All-American football players

The 1943 all-America football team read like a "Who's Who" of Big Ten Conference stars. In all, seven players from Big Ten teams were named to the first-team honor squad — the most representatives ever on the team from one Conference. Highlighting the list was consensus pick and Big Ten MVP Otto Graham, Northwestern's standout halfback and future NFL Hall of Fame quarterback. Indiana wide receiver Pete Pihos, another future Hall of Famer, was also a consensus pick. The Conference's other representatives were Northwestern's Herb Hein; Michigan's Bill Daley and Merv Pregulman; and Purdue's Alex Agase and Tony Butkovich.

Academic Achievements

More than 70 Nobel laureates have been faculty, students or researchers at Big Ten universities. And 10 percent of the nation's Fulbright Fellowships are awarded to Big Ten faculty and students.

1942-43 Conference MEDAL OF HONOR Winners

CHICAGO	Raymond Siever
ILLINOIS	Edwin S. Parker
INDIANA	Fred Huff
IOWA	Thomas Farmer
MICHIGAN	George F. Ceithaml
MINNESOTA	Christie Geankoplis
NORTHWESTERN	Russell Wendland
OHIO STATE	Esten W. Vickroy, Jr.
PURDUE	Allen Carl Menke
WISCONSIN	Frederick R. Rehm

THE BIG EVENT

War-time Illini track team keeps winning

Illinois athletic director Doug Mills decided that "athletics in wartime should be carried on in as nearly pre-war fashion as possible." With that in mind, Illinois continued its tradition of strong track teams, and coach Leo Johnson put together an outstanding unit in 1943-44, when Illinois placed second in the Big Ten indoor and outdoor championships. Later that season, Illinois won four individual events to blow the competition away at the NCAA championships. Illinois scored 79 points, well ahead of runner-up Notre Dame's 43. Before he became a pro football star with the Baltimore Colts, Buddy Young won the 100-yard dash in the NCAA championships. Teammate Robert Kelley won the 880-yard run, while Dave Nichols took home first in the 120-yard high hurdles and Robert Phelps won the first of his back-to-back NCAA titles in the pole vault.

OTHER MEMORABLE EVENTS

- War-time regulations limited athletic teams to 18-year olds, upperclassmen excused on physical grounds and on-campus Naval trainees.

- Chicago announced its withdrawal from championship competition for the 1944-45 school year.

- Michigan gave up an average of 131 yards of total offense per game, the fewest allowed in Conference football history.

- Minnesota's Louis Lick won the NCAA golf championship.

- Ohio State's Neo Nakama won the NCAA 440 and 1,500 freestyle swimming events for the second straight year.

- Indiana's Bob Hoernschemeyer set a national record for freshmen with 458 yards of total offense and six touchdowns in a game vs. Nebraska.

Boilermakers breeze to Big Ten football title

The Purdue football season was special for several reasons. Not only was it the last time the Boilermakers would go unbeaten (they finished 9-0), it came following a 1-8 record in 1942. It was a most remarkable turnaround in the second and last season for coach Elmer Burnham, who led the Boilermakers to a share of the Big Ten title with Michigan at 6-0. Not only did Purdue go undefeated, but most of the games weren't close. It won by an average of 17.7 points, and only twice (Minnesota and Indiana in the last two games) did an opponent come within seven points. Tony Butkovich rushed for 626 yards and led the Big Ten in scoring with a league-record 78 points, topping players like Michigan's Elroy Hirsch and Northwestern's Otto Graham. Butkovich only played in four league games before leaving for Marine training for World War II. Against Illinois, Butkovich scored four TDs on runs of 80, 2, 7 and 25 yards. The Boilermakers finished No. 5 in the country. Guard Dick Barwegen was named team MVP. Butkovich, Barwegen and guard Alex Agase were first-team All-Big Ten, and Butkovich and Agase were consensus All-Americans.

OTHER BIG TEN CHAMPIONS

- **BASEBALL:** Michigan, coached by Ray Fisher

- **GYMNASTICS:** No meet

- **OUTDOOR TRACK:** Michigan, coached by Kenneth Doherty

- **INDOOR TRACK:** Michigan, coached by Kenneth Doherty

- **BASKETBALL:** Ohio State, coached by Harold Olsen

- **CROSS COUNTRY:** Purdue, coached by Homer Allen

- **TENNIS:** Michigan, coached by LeRoy Weir

- **SWIMMING:** Michigan, coached by Matt Mann

- **WRESTLING:** Michigan, coached by Clifford Keen

DON GRATE
Basketball, Ohio State

Ohio State had plenty of experience playing in the NCAA tournament finals before the Buckeyes reached the NCAA title three straight years, beginning with the championship team in 1960. Ohio State was the NCAA runner-up in the first tournament in 1938-39, and the Buckeyes reached the NCAA finals three straight years, including the 1943-44 and 1944-45 seasons behind star Don Grate. A two-time All-Conference forward who led the Buckeyes to the Conference championship in 1943-44 and a runner-up finish in the league standings the following season, Grate averaged 13 points a game as a junior as Ohio State finished 14-7 overall. The Buckeyes lost in the NCAA tournament semifinals after Grate scored 17 points in a win over Temple in a first-round game. As a senior, Grate led the Buckeyes to the semifinals again.

CLAUDE "BUDDY" YOUNG
Football and Track, Illinois

His reputations as a track sprinter and football player were much larger than Claude "Buddy" Young's 5-foot-5 frame. His speed revolutionized pro football. Young set an indoor world record and won NCAA titles in the 100 and 220 as a freshman at Illinois in 1943-44, but his legend grew largest on the gridiron. He tied Red Grange's school record with 13 touchdowns the following year, served in the U.S. Navy one year and returned to lead Illinois to the Big Ten title and a win in the 1947 Rose Bowl, becoming the first African-American to score a touchdown in the bowl game. Young gained 9,419 yards in a 10-year NFL career with the New York Yankees, Dallas Texans and Baltimore Colts; his No. 22 jersey was the first retired by the Colts. He died in 1983 while working as an assistant to the NFL commissioner.

LOUIS LICK
Golf, Minnesota

From 1932 to 1961, Big Ten golfers won more NCAA individual championships (10) than any other conference. And lodged in the middle of that list is Minnesota's Louis Lick. His accomplishment in 1944 at Inverness makes him the northern-most golfer ever to be the national collegiate medalist. Lick led his Golden Gopher teammates to a second-place finish in the NCAA team standings that year, just one stroke behind Notre Dame, 311 to 312. A Big Ten championship wasn't held in 1944 due to World War II. Lick was the first of a dozen Minnesota golfers who've earned All-America honors.

■ CROSS COUNTRY RECORDS

BIG TEN LIST

Purdue's cross country team set a record in 1943 (later broken) by scoring 26 points at the Conference championship. It's runners finished 1st, 2nd, 6th, 8th and 9th. Here are the 10 best winning scores of all-time (a "perfect" score is 15):

17, Michigan State, 1959 (1-2-3-5-6)
19, Wisconsin, 1983 (1-2-3-5-8)
21, Michigan State, 1956 (1-2-5-6-7)
24, Wisconsin, 1978 (1-3-4-5-11)
25, Wisconsin, 1991 (1-2-3-9-10)
26, Purdue, 1943 (1-2-6-8-9)
26, Wisconsin, 1985 (1-2-6-8-9)
27, Minnesota, 1964 (1-3-6-8-9)
27, Wisconsin, 1982 (2-5-6-7-9)
28, Wisconsin, 1939 (1-3-4-7-13)
28, Michigan State, 1952 (2-5-6-7-8)

LEADING THE WAY

DOUG MILLS
Illinois

The 40-year association between Illinois and Doug Mills has separate chapters, since Mills was a celebrated athlete, coach and administrator. During his playing career from 1927-30, Mills was a two-time All-Big Ten basketball player and three-year letterwinner in football. He coached high school basketball in Joliet (Ill.), then returned to Illinois in 1935 and accepted the role of head basketball coach a year later, compiling a 151-66 record and three Big Ten titles in 11 years as head coach. Mills led his first team to a share of the Big Ten championship in the 1936-37 season, but Illini basketball reached its peak shortly before World War II when four players—Gene Vance, Ken Menke, Andy Phillip and Jack Smiley—enrolled to form the nucleus of the Whiz Kids. They were 13-2 as sophomores and the top-rated team in the country the following year with a 17-1 record. Mills became athletic director in 1941, and the extra responsibilities led him to retire as a coach following the 1946-47 season. He remained as athletic director until his retirement in 1966. He died in 1983 at the age of 75.

· BIG TEN PIONEERS ·

Twin milers Ross and Bob Hume tie for NCAA title

Michigan's "Dead Heat Twins," Ross and Bob Hume, really outdid themselves in the 1944 NCAA track and field championships at Milwaukee, tying for the mile run title after twice tying for Big Ten honors in the event. The Cannonsburg, Pa., brothers dead-heated 11 times in the mile in their careers, but probably no so dramatic as in the national collegiate meet. Together they ran the mile six times under 4:17 and held the Michigan school record of 4:14.6. "They just couldn't run AGAINST each other in a competitive mood," said famed Michigan coach Ken Doherty, who tried to run the twins in separate events. But the coach learned, he said, that "they just couldn't run WITHOUT each other."

Ross and Bob Hume

 # Academic Achievements

It was Dec. 2, 1943, under the west stands of Stagg Field at Chicago when professor Enrico Fermi ordered a shutdown of the world's first self-sustaining nuclear chain reaction. That led to the Manhattan Project—development of the first atomic bomb. A year-and-a-half later, despite protests from several Chicago scientists, the U.S. released atomic bombs on Hiroshima and Nagasaki.

1943-44
Conference MEDAL OF HONOR Winners

CHICAGO	Edward A. Cooperrider
ILLINOIS	Warren F. Goodell
INDIANA	No award
IOWA	No award
MICHIGAN	Paul G. White
MINNESOTA	Stuart A. Olson
NORTHWESTERN	Arthur Nethercot, Jr.
OHIO STATE	George R. Hoeflinger
PURDUE	No award
WISCONSIN	Edward M. Dzirbik

THE BIG EVENT

"Tug" Wilson succeeds Griffith as Big Ten commissioner

Following—and expounding—on a successful path mapped by his predecessor, Kenneth L. "Tug" Wilson steered the Big Ten in a prosperous direction during his tenure as the Conference's second commissioner from 1945 until 1961. Succeeding the late Major John L. Griffith, Wilson continued to build on the rich tradition established before him. Renowned as a strict disciplinarian with zero tolerance for rules violations, Wilson routinely punished member schools — in the form of probation and scholarship suspensions — for any and all infractions that hurt the integrity of the Conference or its glittering image, setting a precedent for adhering to rules that is vigorously enforced today. Wilson also entered the Big Ten into its agreement with what is today the Pac 10 in 1946, which states that the football winner of their respective conference meet annually in college football's biggest event, the Rose Bowl. Wilson also was the first commissioner to permit Conference games to be televised. Like Griffith, Wilson served as Drake's athletic director for a number of years prior to joining the Big Ten. He also held the same post at Northwestern for 20 years. He retired as commissioner on July 1, 1961 and died Feb. 4, 1979.

OTHER MEMORABLE EVENTS

- Major John L. Griffith, the Conference's first commissioner (1922-44) died Dec. 7, 1944.

- Ohio State won the NCAA swimming championship.

- Ohio State's Les Horvath won the Heisman Trophy.

- Ohio State won the NCAA golf championship. Howard Baker won medalist honors while teammate John Lorms took the match play title.

- Purdue's Ward "Piggy" Lambert retired after 28 years as head basketball coach.

Buckeye golfers undaunted by lightning

There could be no greater handicap than lightning on the golf course, but Ohio State overcame a bolt of lightning to shock the field in winning the school's first NCAA golf championship during the 1944-45 season. The Buckeyes managed to score a victory by 19 strokes over Michigan and Northwestern thanks to the play of Howard Baker, who had already helped lead Ohio State to the Big Ten team championship by finishing as individual co-champ with John Lorms. Baker was hurled to the ground by a bolt of lightning midway through the final round of team competition, but he nevertheless slashed his way through two thunderstorms on the second 18-hole round to card a 68 that paced Ohio State's win under coach Robert Kepler. One under par through the first five holes, Baker was part of a foursome that was dropped by a bolt of lightning on No. 6. He said "it was like being hit on the head by a baseball bat." He calmly stepped up to birdie No. 6 and complete a 36-hole round that saw him shoot a 74-68—142. Meanwhile, Lorms worked his way through the 16-man match-play tournament to win the NCAA individual honors.

OTHER BIG TEN CHAMPIONS

- FOOTBALL: Ohio State, coached by Carroll Widdoes
- BASEBALL: Michigan, coached by Ray Fisher
- GYMNASTICS: No meet
- OUTDOOR TRACK: Illinois, coached by Leo Johnson
- INDOOR TRACK: Michigan, coached by Kenneth Doherty
- BASKETBALL: Iowa, coached by Lawrence Harrison
- CROSS COUNTRY: Wisconsin, coached by Thomas Jones
- TENNIS: Michigan, coached by LeRoy Weir
- SWIMMING: Michigan, coached by Matt Mann
- WRESTLING: Purdue, coached by C.C. Reeck
- FENCING: No meet

LES HORVATH
Football, Ohio State

Ohio State players have won the Heisman Trophy six times in the Buckeyes' storied football tradition, and the first player to win the award from Ohio State was Les Horvath, who earned the trophy in 1944. By leading the Buckeyes to a perfect 9-0 record, he was a consensus all-America pick as a senior. He played quarterback, halfback and defensive back, leading the Conference in rushing (669) and total yards (953) as a senior when he won the Conference MVP award. He finished his career with 1,546 yards rushing and 509 yards passing, and he played on two Conference championship teams. The team in his junior year in 1942 won the national championship. During his three-year career, he averaged 5.3 yards per carry, and he is a member of the College Football Hall of Fame.

JOHN LORMS
Golf, Ohio State

He entered the NCAA golf championships as a senior in 1944-45 as the co-favorite from the Conference — and the Ohio State golf team. John Lorms and teammate Howard Baker were co-champions in individual competition at the Big Ten championships, and their chances at winning an NCAA title were strong considering the duo was playing on Ohio State's University Golf Course. After Baker and Lorms helped the Buckeyes win the NCAA team title by 19 strokes over Michigan and Northwestern, Lorms and Baker were entered in the 16-man individual match play championship. Lorms won individual honors to earn the first NCAA golf title in Ohio State's rich golf tradition. Earlier in the season, Ohio State won the Big Ten team title. After his collegiate golf career, Lorms continued to find the holes — as a dentist.

WALTON KIRK
Basketball, Illinois

It was a star-studded cast of nominees for the Daily Illini's annual "Illini Athlete of the Year" award in 1944-45, but a junior basketball guard nicknamed "Junior" ran away from his competition. Unanimous All-Big Ten selection Walton Kirk was his classmates' first choice, out-distancing two-sport standout Howie Judson by a two-to-one margin. A native of Mt. Vernon, Ill., Kirk was the MVP of Doug Mills' Illinois cagers, averaging nearly 11 points per game. His best effort of the year came at Michigan in a 55-37 victory when he scored a season-high 21 points. Kirk went into the service in June of 1945, then returned to Illinois for the 1946-47 season. He then signed a $10,000 NBA contract with the Ft. Wayne Pistons, joining former Illini teammates Jack Smiley and Ken Menke. Kirk scored 907 points during his 163-game NBA career with Ft. Wayne, Tri-Cities and Milwaukee. In 1952, he began a long high school coaching career, with stops at Harvard and Salem, Ill., and at Dubuque, Ia. Now retired, he and his wife reside in Dubuque.

BIG TEN LIST

LEADING THE WAY

GUY MACKEY
Purdue

Purdue continues to benefit from the era in which Guy "Red" Mackey was its athletic director. Mackey became A.D. in 1942 and would become instrumental in improving the athletic department's facilities and business affairs. It was under his leadership that a $6 million, 14,123-seat arena was built, mainly for the basketball team. Completed in 1967, Mackey Arena was named for the athletic director. Also during Mackey's tenure, Ross-Ade Stadium was enlarged five times, without the use of state money. Mackey came to Purdue in 1925 as a freshman student. He was an honorable mention All-America end on the football team. But it was after his graduation in 1929 that Mackey would really distinguish himself. He was inducted into Purdue's Athletic Hall of Fame in 1994.

· BIG TEN PIONEERS ·

Back-to-back Buckeyes

Harold Olsen coached at Ohio State for 24 years, winning 255 games and five Conference titles. He put together outstanding teams late in his tenure as the Buckeyes coach, reaching the NCAA tournament championship game in 1939 before finishing as runner-up. In 1943-44 and 1944-45, Ohio State became the first Conference school to appear in the NCAA tournament in back-to-back seasons, finishing the tournament in third place each time. The Buckeyes were led by two-time All-Conference forward Don Grate, and center Arnold Risen was a two-year starter who also was named to the All-Conference squad. Each year, the Buckeyes posted 10-2 records in Conference play.

Academic Achievements

One of Northwestern's strongest areas is neuroscience. Significant brain research in this country began at NU, where the nature of the nervous system's process of recovery was first explored.

1944-45
Conference MEDAL OF HONOR
Winners

ILLINOIS	Donald Delaney
INDIANA	No award
IOWA	No award
MICHIGAN	Robert L. Wiese
MINNESOTA	Arnold Lehrman
NORTHWESTERN	Ben Schadler
OHIO STATE	Jack R. Dugger
PURDUE	Joseph Collings
WISCONSIN	Ken Chandler

BIG TEN
SINCE 1896
CENTENNIAL
™

1945-1954

THE BIG EVENT

Chicago withdraws as a member of the Big Ten Conference

Chicago's last Big Ten baseball team

On March 8, 1946, the Big Ten became the Big Nine. That's the fateful day University of Chicago president Robert M. Hutchins announced that his university was withdrawing its membership in the Conference it helped to establish some 50 years earlier. Chicago had abandoned its football program in Conference play following the 1939 season, but continued to compete in the so-called "minor" sports. In his State of the University report of 1949, Hutchins criticized the American public for the viewpoint it displayed toward intercollegiate athletics. "The questions were asked," Hutchins said, "whether it was possible to have a great university without a football team; what the moral consequences of such a drastic action would be, and how the university could be expected to have any "spirit" without the rallying point provided by a football team. I regard our action as the most rudimentary application of common sense and think it has importance only because it has demonstrated the proposition, which should be self-evident, that a university can flourish without a football team and that it is, in fact, likely to be a better university without one."

OTHER MEMORABLE EVENTS

- Conference officials approved a nine-game football schedule, the first game of the season not played before the last Saturday in September and the last game not played after the last Saturday before Thanksgiving.

- Illinois won the NCAA outdoor track championship.

- Ohio State won the NCAA swimming title.

- A Conference record 22,822 fans watched Ohio State and Northwestern battle in basketball at Chicago Stadium.

- Ohio State's George Bollas won the NCAA heavyweight wrestling title.

BIG TEN BOWLING

Big Ten teams have played in 21 different bowl games since Michigan appeared in the first Rose Bowl in 1901. Here are all the different bowls that have featured a Conference team:

Rose (Pasadena), Orange (Miami), Sugar (New Orleans), Hall of Fame/Outback (Birmingham, Ala./Tampa), Peach (Atlanta), Gator (Jacksonville), Bluebonnet (Houston), Holiday (San Diego), Fiesta (Tempe, Ariz.), Liberty (Memphis), Garden State (E. Rutherford, N.J.), Independence (Shreveport), Freedom (Anaheim), Cherry (Pontiac, Mich.), Florida Citrus (Orlando), All-American (Birmingham, Ala.), Cotton (Dallas), Aloha (Honolulu), Sun/John Hancock (El Paso), Copper (Tucson) and Alamo (San Antonio).

Hoosier gridders of 1945 the best in school history

Pete Pihos

The only football team in Indiana's history to win an outright Big Ten championship was the one that finished 9-0-1 in 1945. The Hoosiers, coached by Bo McMillin, had finished 7-3 the previous season, and received a major boost from a few new faces. George Taliaferro, who would later earn induction into the College Football Hall of Fame, joined the team as a freshman back, and led the team to a season-opening victory at Michigan. The next week Pete Pihos, another future hall of famer, and guard Howard Brown returned from military service. Indiana had to scramble to tie Northwestern in the second game, but never looked back after that. It defeated Purdue 26-0 in the final game to clinch the league title and finish the only unbeaten season in school history. Other crucial team members included All-America receiver Bob Ravensberg, tackle Russ Deal, the team captain, and receiver Ted Kluszewski, who went on to a standout baseball career. The Hoosiers were ranked fourth nationally at the end of the season, but had no opportunity to play in a postseason bowl game to prove themselves against the best. They'll have to settle for being the best in school history.

OTHER BIG TEN CHAMPIONS

- **BASEBALL:** Wisconsin, coached by Arthur Mansfield
- **GYMNASTICS:** No meet
- **OUTDOOR TRACK:** Illinois, coached by Leo Johnson
- **INDOOR TRACK:** Illinois, coached by Leo Johnson
- **BASKETBALL:** Ohio State, coached by Harold Olsen
- **CROSS COUNTRY:** Wisconsin, coached by Thomas Jones
- **TENNIS:** Illinois, coached by Ralph Johnson
- **SWIMMING:** Ohio State, coached by Michael Peppe
- **GOLF:** Michigan, coached by William Barclay

Big Ten Office Headquarters

The Big Ten Conference

When presidents of the universities that ultimately formed the Big Ten Conference established an office of the commissioner with the hiring of Major John L. Griffith in 1922, it's unlikely they could have imagined how that office would grow. Today the home of the Big Ten, once just a room in a downtown Chicago hotel, is now a 25,000-square-foot, two-story headquarters with office and meeting room space near Chicago's O'Hare International Airport.

While the Big Ten Conference Office Headquarters and Meetings Center in suburban Park Ridge is the league's first privately owned facility, it is also just the fifth home of the Conference since the Big Ten established an Office of the Commissioner in 1922. After a 28-year stay at the Hotel Sherman, the Conference office headquarters was moved to the LaSalle Hotel in downtown Chicago. Then, 12 years later in 1962, the Sheraton-Chicago Hotel became the official site of the headquarters until 1971, when the league moved to an office building in northwest suburban Schaumburg. After two decades there, the Big Ten moved in 1991 to its current home in Park Ridge.

The facility in Park Ridge not only serves the needs of the more

than 140 athletic and academic groups that meet in the building each year, but it also efficiently and comfortably houses the entire Conference office staff. Besides office space and six conference rooms, the building features two workrooms with state-of-the-art computers and equipment, a library and video room, a fully-equipped kitchen and dining room, and a wellness room complete with locker rooms and exercise equipment.

The Conference office is comprised of a 28-member staff, including three supervisors of officials who work outside the office. Acting as the chief executive officer of the Conference, Commissioner Jim Delany oversees the operation of all office activities, and works with the Big Ten presidents and chancellors, and all Conference governance groups to develop and administer policies that ensure the welfare of student-athletes on and off the playing fields. He also takes an active leadership role in national governance affairs.

A variety of administrative services provided "behind the scenes" help promote quality experiences for the close to 7,000 student-athletes competing in 250 varsity sports at Conference universities. Services rendered by the Conference office

include championship and sport management; compliance and legislative services; staffing the numerous policy-making and advisory groups that meet annually; liaison with bowl game representatives, the NCAA and other outside entities; officiating management; business services; and communications, which includes everything from administration of television contracts to production of publications and press releases, media relations, and community outreach.

Big Ten Commissioner James Delany

COMP USA IS A PROUD MEMBER OF THE BIG TEN TEAM.

To be on the CompUSA team, you've got to be good. You've got to know your game, understand the equipment and be able to pass your knowledge on to beginners and experts alike. You've got to be a pro.

The CompUSA Florida Citrus Bowl is just one example of our commitment to excellence. As America's Favorite Computer Superstore℠,

we're proud to support some of the country's most valuable players... no matter what field they're in. Plus, we score extra points with added services such as hands-on training classes and expert technical support. Of course, great service is just one reason why CompUSA is America's Favorite Computer Superstore℠. We carry more than 5,000 name brand products from hardware to

software to accessories. And everything is at CompPrices℠, where it's the Low Price. Period℠*. So, no matter what your computer needs are, choosing CompUSA is always a winning strategy.

CompUSA salutes 100 years of excellence in the Big Ten and we're looking forward to being a part of the next 100.

1 • 800 • COMP USA

www.compusa.com

THE COMPUTER SUPERSTORE.

The Florida Citrus Bowl Stadium has been the site of games involving Big Ten football teams since 1985. (Photo: Florida Citrus Sports Association)

CompUSA-Florida Citrus Bowl

Big Ten football's runner-up team is rewarded each December with a trip to Orlando, Florida, and a berth in the highly popular CompUSA-Florida Citrus Bowl.

The CompUSA-Florida Citrus Bowl and Big Ten football teams have been tied together for a January 1 game since 1992, with the current contract continuing through the 2000 season. The Big Ten representative is matched against the runnerup from the Southeastern Conference.

The game's average attendance over the past three seasons has been 71,482.

Formerly known as the Tangerine Bowl, the Florida Citrus Bowl is orchestrated by Executive Director Charles "Chuck" Rohe. The game is televised by ABC Sports.

A Buckeye runner breaks through the line in action during the 1992 Florida Citrus Bowl. (Photo: Florida Citrus Sports Association)

Quarterback Kerry Collins and his Penn State teammates beat Tennessee in 1993 by a score of 31-13. (Photo: Florida Citrus Sports Association)

CompUSA-Florida Citrus Bowl results (attendance)

1985	OHIO STATE 10, Brigham Young 7	(50,920)
1990	ILLINOIS 31, Virginia 21	(60,016)
1993	Georgia 21, OHIO STATE 14	(65,861)
1994	PENN STATE 31, Tennessee 13	(72,456)
1995	Alabama 24, OHIO STATE 17	(71,195)
1996	Tennessee 20, OHIO STATE 14	(70,797)

The Columbus Dispatch

An independent newspaper
serving Ohio
since July 1, 1871

During the 125 years *The Dispatch* has been a
part of Columbus and the state of Ohio,
many milestones have made news.

The Ohio State University joining the Big Ten
Conference in 1912 is certainly one of significance.

The achievements of OSU student athletes have made
The Dispatch Sports pages "must" reading for thousands.

The Columbus Dispatch is proud to have reported
the past one hundred years of Big Ten history
and looks forward to the next.

The Columbus Dispatch

34 South Third Street
Columbus, Ohio 43215

For great OSU sports coverage in *The Dispatch*,
call 461-5100 for home delivery.

For online coverage of OSU sports, visit us on
the World Wide Web at http://www.dispatch.com.

OHIO STATE HEISMAN TROPHY WINNERS

Les Horvath made Ohio State history in 1944 by becoming the school's first Heisman Trophy winner. (Photo: Courtesy of Downtown Athletic Club of New York City, Inc.)

Though only a junior, Ohio State's Vic Janowicz won the 1950 Heisman Trophy. (Photo: Courtesy of Downtown Athletic Club of New York City, Inc.)

Archie Griffin is the only collegiate player to win two Heisman Trophies (1974 and 1975). (Photo: Courtesy of Downtown Athletic Club of New York City, Inc.)

Howard "Hopalong" Cassady was the first of Woody Hayes' Buckeyes to win the Heisman Trophy (1955). (Photo: Courtesy of Downtown Athletic Club of New York City, Inc.)

Eddie George won the 1995 Heisman Trophy, the fifth Buckeye player to be so honored. (Gaines Du Vall Sports Portraits)

BIG TEN HEISMAN TROPHY WINNERS

Chicago's Jay Berwanger won the first Heisman Trophy in 1935. (Photo: Courtesy of Downtown Athletic Club of New York City, Inc.)

Iowa's only Heisman Trophy winner, Nile Kinnick (1939) died in military service during World War II. (Photo: Courtesy of Downtown Athletic Club of New York City, Inc.)

Tom Harmon was the first Michigan football player to win the Heisman Trophy (1940). (Photo: Courtesy of Downtown Athletic Club of New York City, Inc.)

Minnesota's Bruce Smith, the Heisman Trophy winner in 1941, continued a Big Ten streak of three consecutive awards. (Photo: Courtesy of Downtown Athletic Club of New York City, Inc.)

Alan "The Horse" Ameche of Wisconsin is the only Badger player who's been awarded the Heisman Trophy. (Photo: Courtesy of Downtown Athletic Club of New York City, Inc.)

Michigan's Desmond Howard was the 10th Big Ten player to be awarded the Heisman Trophy (1991). (Photo: Courtesy of Downtown Athletic Club of New York City, Inc.)

Jesse Owens, shown here in cap and gown, is the namesake of the Big Ten Male Athlete of the Year. (Photo: Ohio State Archives)

JESSE OWENS

The date was May 25, 1935. The site was Ferry Field in Ann Arbor. The performance was legendary. In a span of just 45 minutes at the Big Ten Outdoor Track and Field Championships, Jesse Owens may have put forth the greatest individual one-day performance in the history of intercollegiate athletics. The Ohio State sophomore re-wrote the track and field record book by setting world marks in the long jump, the 220-yard dash and the 220-yard low hurdles, and tying the 100-yard dash record.

Owens also became an Olympic track hero, winning four gold medals at the 1936 Berlin Olympics. He died in 1980 at age 66. Two years after Owens' death, Big Ten Directors of Athletics approved a recommendation of the sports information directors to establish a Big Ten Athlete of the Year, and named it in Owens' honor.

BIG TEN - JESSE OWENS MALE ATHLETE OF THE YEAR

1982 Jim Spivey, Indiana, track and field/cross country
1983 Ed Banach, Iowa, wrestling
1984 Sunder Nix, Indiana, track and field
1985 Barry Davis, Iowa, wrestling
1986 Chuck Long, Iowa, football
1987 Steve Alford, Indiana, basketball
1988 Jim Abbott, Michigan, baseball
1989 Glen Rice, Michigan, basketball
1990 Anthony Thompson, Indiana, football
1991 Mike Barrowman, Michigan, swimming
1992 Desmond Howard, Michigan, football
1993 John Roethlisberger, Minnesota, gymnastics
1994 Glenn Robinson, Purdue, basketball
1995 Tom Dolan, Michigan, swimming
1996 Eddie George, Ohio State, football

Wisconsin superstar Suzy Favor earned the Big Ten Jesse Owens Athlete of the Year Award for an unprecedented third time in 1990. No other athlete, male or female, has been a multiple winner. (Photo: Univ. Wisconsin Sports Information)

SUZY FAVOR HAMILTON

Suzy Favor Hamilton was paid the ultimate compliment in 1992 when the Big Ten Directors of Athletics named the Conference's Female Athlete of the Year Award in her honor. Is she the greatest female athlete? It's difficult *not* to choose her when one studies the multitude of individual track championships she won. From 1987 to 1990, the Wisconsin standout won nine national titles, including an unprecedented four consecutive championships in the 1,500-meter run. Counting Favor's 23 Big Ten titles, more than any other Conference athlete at the time, she boasted a streak of 40 consecutive track victories.

In celebration of the 10th anniversary of women's athletics in the Conference, she was named Female Athlete of the Decade. Selecting someone other than the three-time Big Ten Female Athlete of the Year for that honor would clearly have been an injustice. Additionally, Favor won the 1989-90 Honda-Broderick Cup, an award presented annually to the top collegiate female athlete.

BIG TEN - SUZY FAVOR FEMALE ATHLETE OF THE YEAR

1983 Judi Brown, Michigan State, track and field
1984 Lisa Ishikawa, Northwestern, softball
1985 Cathy Branta, Wisconsin, cross country/track and field
1986 Stephanie Herbst, Wisconsin, cross country/track and field
1987 Jennifer Averill, Northwestern, field hockey/lacrosse
1988 Suzy Favor, Wisconsin, track and field/cross country
1989 Suzy Favor, Wisconsin, track and field/cross country
1990 Suzy Favor, Wisconsin, track and field/cross country
1991 Julie Farrell-Ovenhouse, Michigan State, diving
      Joy Holmes, Purdue, basketball (tie)
1992 MaChelle Joseph, Purdue, basketball
1993 Lara Hooiveld, Michigan, swimming
1994 Kristy Gleason, Iowa, field hockey
1995 Laura Davis, Ohio State, volleyball
1996 Olga Kalinovskaya, Penn State, fencing

TED KLUSZEWSKI
Football and Baseball, Indiana

Ted Kluszewski gained his greatest fame as a power hitter for the Cincinnati Reds, but he was a standout football player for Indiana, as well. Kluszewski was a receiver on IU's 1945 team that finished 9-0-1 and won the Big Ten title. He caught 10 passes, carried the ball once for a 5-yard gain, completed two passes, punted once for 56 yards and scored three touchdowns. He showed just as much promise in baseball, however, and gave up his final two seasons of collegiate eligibility to sign with the Reds, where he became one of the most popular players in team history. "Big Klu" played 10 years at first base (1948-57) and led the National League in home runs (49) and RBI (141) in 1954. He also hit three home runs for the Chicago White Sox in a World Series game in 1959. He died in 1988, at age 63.

HERB McKENLEY
Track, Illinois

Once compared to a golf ball bouncing down a highway, Herb McKenley came to Illinois from his native Jamaica, a transfer from Boston College, and quickly began setting records. Excluding relays, he ran 34 races in his final two seasons of college track, 1946 and '47. McKinley won 31, setting records in 18 races with three of those marks world records. He broke the world record in the 440-yard dash, an event that he swept in Big Ten and NCAA competition for six titles overall. He repeated his world-record time of 46.2 seconds in the 440 to win the 1947 NCAA title, the same season he set the world indoor 440 record. McKenley competed in the 1948 and '52 Olympics, winning two gold medals. He later became coach and director of Jamaica's Olympic track squad. Now retired, McKenley still resides in Jamaica.

MAX MORRIS
Football and Basketball, Northwestern

Two-sport star Max Morris won the Big Ten basketball scoring championship in 1945 and '46, scoring 189 points his first season and 198 the following year. He was voted the first recipient of the *Chicago Tribune's* Most Valuable Player award after his final season and was a unanimous choice for All-America honors. Morris, whose athletic career got off to a late start because of World War II, also was named an All-American as a football receiver in his second season of play, in 1945, when he was the team captain. He played in the College All-Star Game in Chicago in 1946, and played both football and basketball professionally for a brief time. He was described by teammates as a "grand guy whose success never went to his head."

OLLIE CLINE
Football, Ohio State

Ollie Cline helped lead Ohio State to a perfect record (9-0) as a freshman fullback in 1944. The Buckeyes, who had their first undefeated and untied season since 1920, wound up the year as the nation's No. 2 ranked team, behind Army. OSU didn't lock up the title until the final game of the season, an 18-14 Homecoming victory over runner-up Michigan. Then in 1945 Cline, a native of Fredericktown, Ohio, led the Big Ten in rushing (606 yards) and scoring (36 points). The sophomore was named the league's MVP. The 5-foot-11, 202-pounder sat out the 1946 season, then returned in '47 to lead OSU in total offense, rushing and scoring. "No. 33" was a unanimous all-league selection in 1945.

LEADING THE WAY

MICHAEL PEPPE
Ohio State

The first swimming and diving coach at Ohio State was also the most successful. Michael Peppe set a precedent that might never be matched at Ohio State, where his teams won a total of 33 major titles. During his career, the Buckeyes won 11 NCAA team titles, 10 national AAU titles and 12 Conference championships. Under Peppe, Ohio State swimmers and divers captured 312 individual championships, including 94 NCAA titles and 94 Conference championships. His specialty was in diving, where 137 divers accounted for major championships. In 1946-47 and 1955-56, Ohio State divers swept the top four positions on the NCAA championships boards. From 1937 until his retirement following the 1962-63 season, Peppe's divers accounted for 101 of the possible 113 NCAA champions. He produced five individual Olympic gold medal winners — Bill Smith, Ford Konno, Yoshi Oyakawa, Bob Clotworthy and Bruce Harlan — and nine Buckeyes who were members of the 25-man U.S. Olympic team for the 1952 Helsinki Games. He was inducted into the International Swimming Hall of Fame in 1966.

· BIG TEN PIONEERS ·

Big Ten signs Rose Bowl pack with PCC

It was 1946 when the Big Ten joined the Pacific Coast Conference (now the Pacific-10) and the Pasadena Tournament of Roses Association in an exclusive Rose Bowl Game contract. Though the contract was often referred to as a "shotgun marriage," officials had been in negotiation with the Tournament for eight years. The contract was effective immediately, voted on by the faculty representatives from the two conferences. Both sides agreed that each conference could designate its own representative, regardless of season records. Prior to the 1947 game (Illinois vs. UCLA), the Rose Bowl Game (which began in 1902) drew five sellouts. Every game since then has been a sellout.

Academic Achievements

Among the most famous alumni from Ohio State are: Metropolitan Opera Co. soloist, Diane Kesling; The Limited president, Leslie Wexner; Ohio senator, Howard Metzenbaum; Nobel prize winners, Paul Flory and William Fowler; actress Eileen Heckert; artist Roy Lichtenstein; USA Today columnist, Barbara Reynolds; Washington Post executive editor, Leonard Downie; and former president of the N.Y. Stock Exchange, William M. Batten.

1945-46 Conference MEDAL OF HONOR Winners

ILLINOIS	**Robert Phelps**
INDIANA	**No award**
IOWA	**Arthur Johnson**
MICHIGAN	**Bliss Bowman, Jr.**
MINNESOTA	**John Adams**
NORTHWESTERN	**Andrew Ivy**
OHIO STATE	**Donald Steinberg**
PURDUE	**Thomas P. Hughes**
WISCONSIN	**Jerry Thompson**

The BIG TEN's First 100 Years
Most Decorated Big Ten Women's Swimming and Diving Champions

Top Five Swimmers
Number of Individual Championships Won

10 Janelle Bosse, OSU, 1985-88
8 Alecia Humphrey, MICH, 1992-95
7 Marcie Ballard, OSU, 1982-85
7 Martha Jahn, MSU-NU, 1982-84
6 Mindy Gehrs, MICH, 1991-93

Top Two Divers
Number of Individual Championships Won
(Springboard Only)

4 Kelly McCormick OSU, 1982-83
4 Julie Farrell-Ovenhouse MSU, 1989-91

THE BIG EVENT

Illinois wins first Big Ten-PCC Rose Bowl

World War II was over, the GIs returned from across the globe and they enrolled in universities on the GI Bill. Depleted teams were suddenly overwhelmed with football players, and coach Ray Eliot saw 300 men try out for the Illinois football team in the 1946-47 season. By the end of the year, Illinois smelled the roses, scoring the school's first victory in its first appearance in the Rose Bowl. The Illini split their first four games, then won the final five games to finish with a 6-1 Conference record. The West Coast media didn't respect the 11-point underdogs from Illinois, and Eliot let the team read the clippings in the pregame huddle. UCLA led 7-6 after the first quarter, but Illinois rallied to score a one-sided 45-14 win. The game's MVP, Illinois running back Buddy Young, rushed for 103 yards, matching teammate Julius Rykovich's effort, and the Illini had seven players score touchdowns.

OTHER MEMORABLE EVENTS

- Illinois won the NCAA outdoor track championships.

- Ohio State won the NCAA swimming championships.

- Michigan's Dave Barclay won the NCAA golf title.

- Indiana's Earl Mitchell won his second straight Conference cross country championship.

- The Wisconsin-Purdue basketball game took two weeks to complete. After a bleacher collapsed at halftime in West Lafayette, the game was resumed at Northwestern. Wisconsin won, 72-60, to win the title.

- Illinois pitcher Marv Rotblatt went 6-0, for the best record in league history in 42 years.

Badgers go from last to first in basketball race

Bob Cook

It was the prototypical rags-to-riches story. In 1946, the only thing the Wisconsin men's basketball team was in contention for was the Big Ten cellar — which is where it finished 4-17 overall and 1-11 in league play. In 1947, however, coach Bud Foster's Badgers were front-runners all the way for the Conference championship, which they won easily — along with an invitation to the NCAA tournament — with a 15-5 overall record and a 9-3 league record. The Conference title was their first since 1941, when Foster guided the Badgers to their first and only NCAA championship. Led by team scoring leader Bob Cook, a forward, Wisconsin was never out of first place at any time during the season and was the league's highest-scoring team with 677 points, including 248 field goals and a then-Conference-record 181 free throws. The Badgers also led the Conference in field goal percentage at 29.8 percent. Again, Cook led the way with 70 field goals and 47 free throws while shooting 34.7 percent from the field. However, guard Glen Selbo was voted team MVP and made first team All-Conference. Cook and guard Walt Lautenbach were also first team All-Conference picks.

OTHER BIG TEN CHAMPIONS

- FOOTBALL: Illinois, coached by Ray Eliot
- BASEBALL: Illinois, coached by Walter Roettger
- GYMNASTICS: Minnesota, coached by Dr. Ralph Piper
- OUTDOOR TRACK: Illinois, coached by Leo Johnson
- INDOOR TRACK: Illinois, coached by Leo Johnson
- CROSS COUNTRY: Indiana coached by Gordon Fisher, and Wisconsin, coached by Thomas Jones
- TENNIS: Northwestern, coached by Paul Bennett
- SWIMMING: Ohio State, coached by Michael Peppe
- WRESTLING: Illinois, coached by H.E. Kenney
- GOLF: Michigan, coached by William Barclay
- FENCING: Northwestern, coached by Tully Friedman

BOB RICHARDS
Track, Illinois

Before Michael Jordan, Mary Lou Retton and Bruce Jenner, there was Illinois' Bob Richards, the first athlete to be featured on the front of a Wheaties cereal box. Known as the parson pole vaulter, Richards won the Sullivan Award that goes to the nation's top amateur athlete in 1951, just when he was dominating the pole vault worldwide. The Big Ten and NCAA champion in 1947, Richards earned the bronze medal in the 1948 Olympics before wining the gold in 1952 and '56. He was an ordained minister when he won the Sullivan Award, and he was chosen from a group of 500 athletes by General Mills to be the first to appear on a Wheaties box, serving as a company spokesman for 14 years. The second man to clear 15 feet, Richards won 26 national indoor and outdoor championships. His post-athletic career came as a motivational speaker.

VERNE GAGNE
Wrestling, Minnesota

Verne Gagne enjoyed a glowing reputation as a star football player at Minnesota. But his reputation — and success — as a wrestler outshined everything he accomplished on the gridiron, which was quite a bit. As a halfback and end for the Gophers, Gagne earned some All-America recognition and had a brief professional career with the Green Bay Packers. As a grappler on the Gophers' wrestling team, he was the first four-time Big Ten champion, won two NCAA titles and was a member of the 1948 U.S. Olympic team. He later enjoyed a career as one of the nation's best-known professional wrestlers. At Minnesota, Gagne won league championships in 1944, '47, '48 and '49. His career was interrupted between 1944 and '46 when he served in the Marines during World War II. Upon his return, he won NCAA titles in 1948 and '49 at 191 pounds and won an AAU National Championship in 1949. Professionally, he reigned as the World's Heavyweight Champion in the late 1950s, and into the 1970s.

ALEX AGASE
Football, Purdue/Illinois

Alex Agase made his mark at two Big Ten universities as a player, and later as a coach at two schools. One of the more aggressive guards in his day—if not THE most aggressive— Agase was an All-American in 1942 at Illinois, in '43 at Purdue, then again at Illinois in 1946 when he also was the league's most valuable player. He competed at Purdue while in Marine training, and his college career was interrupted by active duty in 1944-45 (he was in battles of Iwo Jima and Okinawa). Agase played on three championship teams as a member of the Cleveland Browns during his six-year pro career. He was coach at Northwestern (1964-72) and Purdue (1973-76) and was national coach of the year in '70. Agase later was athletic director at Eastern Michigan (1977-81) and a volunteer assistant for Bo Schembechler at Michigan. He was inducted into the College Football Hall of Fame in 1963.

DAVE BARCLAY
Golf, Michigan

Michigan golf coach Bill Barclay was very proud of his 1947 squad. Not only did his linksmen win the Big Ten title by five strokes over Ohio State and have among its roster the Conference co-medalist, Ed Schalon, Barclay's son, Dave, was a member of the team. However, the elder Barclay's greatest source of pride was the fact that his son won the 1947 NCAA individual championship on the University of Michigan's home course. A native of Rockford, Illinois, the 26-year-old Wolverine captain shot near par golf in defeating Louisiana State freshman ace Jack Coyle. Barclay withstood Coyle's late rally by posting a birdie on the 36th and final hole. Dave Barclay was the third and final Wolverine golfer to earn NCAA medalist honors, joining J.W. Fischer (1932) and Charles Kocsis (1936).

LEADING THE WAY

PAUL BENNETT
Northwestern

Paul Bennett not only guided Northwestern's tennis program for 27 years, he changed the face of collegiate tennis. Bennett, a native of Waterloo, Iowa, grew up in Winnipeg, Canada. He won the Canadian singles title (1920) and played on the Canadian Davis Cup team (1921) before moving back to the U.S. He attended the University of Chicago, where he played basketball and tennis, and was runner-up for the Big Ten singles title his senior year. He took over as Northwestern's coach in 1931 and received his Master's degree from the school a year later. He coached the Wildcats to seven Big Ten championships, including four straight from 1947-50. Six of his players won Conference singles championships and five of his doubles teams captured titles. Outside of coaching, he founded the College Tennis Coaches' Association and chaired the NCAA Tennis Committee. He also was responsible for moving the NCAA championships from a private club to college campuses. The Bennett Bowl, awarded annually to the senior tennis player in the NCAA finals who exhibits the best all-around sportsmanship, is named in his honor. Bennett was elected an honorary N Club member in 1950, retired in '58, and died in '59.

POST-SEASON BASEBALL

The College World Series NCAA baseball championships began in 1947. A total of 19 Big Ten teams have advanced to the CWS since then:

7— Michigan (champions in 1953, '62)
5— Minnesota (champions in 1956, '60, '64)
4— Ohio State (champions in 1966)
1— Iowa
1— Michigan State
1— Wisconsin

BIG TEN
SINCE 1896
CENTENNIAL ™

 Academic Achievements

In 1947, Michigan became the first university in the nation to maintain a commercial airport—Willow Run Airport in Ypsilanti.

1946-47
Conference MEDAL OF HONOR
Winners

ILLINOIS	Robert Richards
INDIANA	Ralph Hamilton
IOWA	John Kenneth Hunter
MICHIGAN	Paul G. White
MINNESOTA	Robert Sandberg
NORTHWESTERN	John Hennerich
OHIO STATE	Warren E. Amling
PURDUE	Myrwin Anderson
WISCONSIN	Exner Menzel

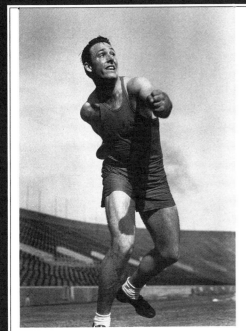

Fortune Gordien

THE BIG EVENT

Minnesota track "fortunes" rest on Gordien

Minnesota's track "fortunes" rested on the powerful right arm of renowned discus thrower Fortune Gordien, whose long throws powered the Gophers to their first and only NCAA national men's championship in 1948, under the direction of coach Jim Kelly. Gordien, who had helped lead Minnesota to a third place finish at the 1947 NCAA meet, won his third straight NCAA discus title in 1948 with a throw of 164-feet, 6$\frac{1}{2}$-inches. Gordien would later gain fame as an Olympian and as a former world record holder. But Gordien wasn't the only standout on the Gophers' NCAA championship team. Lloyd LaMois was among the nation's premier long jumpers of his era. Dick Kilty was among the nation's top distance runners. And Lee Hofacre was a brilliant hurdler and a valuable component of relay teams. Other key team members were Clark Rice, Charles Lindekugel, Jim Nielsen, Fred Brass, Bill Ewing, Bob Comer, Tom Mason and Paul Neff.

OTHER MEMORABLE EVENTS

- Michigan won the NCAA swimming championships.

- Ohio State's Miller Anderson won his third straight NCAA diving title.

- Michigan won the first NCAA hockey championships.

- Michigan's Bob Chappuis set a Rose Bowl record (later broken) with 279 yards of total offense in leading the Wolverines to a 49-0 win over Southern California.

- Wisconsin's Don Gehrmann won the first of two straight Conference cross country titles.

- Four schools—Illinois, Michigan, Ohio State and Wisconsin—began 150-pound intercollegiate football.

Purdue escapes with title in closest wrestling championship ever

1948 Big Ten Champion Arnold Plaza

Led by four-year standout Arnold Plaza, Purdue claimed the 1948 Big Ten wrestling championship in the closest meet in Conference history. The Boilermakers boasted only one individual champion — Plaza — but had seven of its wrestlers place in the top five of the 11 weight classes to win the meet by one point, 24-23, ahead of three teams that tied for second. They were Illinois, Iowa and Michigan. For Plaza, a 114$\frac{1}{2}$-pound competitor, the meet marked his fourth individual championship — a feat accomplished by only nine wrestlers in league history. Minnesota's Verne Gagne, who would join the list of nine, won the second of his four titles during the 1948 meet as would Joe Scarpello, 175-pounder from Iowa. Purdue's other top five finishers in that meet were Joe Patascil (121 pounds), William Bayles (136), Warren Gregory (155), William Detert (165), Waldemar Van Cott (175), and Ray Gunkel (heavyweight).

OTHER BIG TEN CHAMPIONS

- **FOOTBALL:** Michigan, coached by H.O. Crisler
- **BASEBALL:** Illinois coached by Walter Roettger, and Michigan, coached by Ray Fisher
- **GYMNASTICS:** Minnesota, coached by Dr. Ralph Piper
- **OUTDOOR TRACK:** Ohio State, coached by Larry Snyder
- **INDOOR TRACK:** Ohio State, coached by Larry Snyder
- **BASKETBALL:** Michigan, coached by Osborne Cowles
- **CROSS COUNTRY:** Illinois, coached by Leo Johnson
- **TENNIS:** Northwestern, coached by Paul Bennett
- **SWIMMING:** Michigan, coached by Matt Mann
- **GOLF:** Northwestern, coached by Sid Richardson
- **FENCING:** Northwestern, coached by Tully Friedman

BILL HEUSNER
Swimming, Northwestern

Bill Heusner was one of the greatest performers in Northwestern's proud swimming history. After a standout freshman season he missed the following year because of military duty. He returned for the 1947 season and won the Big Ten 1,500-meter championship. He won the 440-yard Big Ten title in 1948 in a record time of 4:56.7, and placed second in the 1,500 meters, then won the 1,500 meters in the NCAA finals. Heusner went on to earn a place on the 1948 U.S. Olympic team, qualifying in both the 400 and 1,500 meter events, but became ill from ptomaine poisoning. He rounded out his college career in 1949 by going undefeated in dual meet competition in the 220- and 440-yard swims and won the 1,500 meters in the Big Ten meet in a record 19:20.6. He bettered that in the NCAA meet, winning in 19:04.8. Today Huesner is a professor at MSU and has served as a referee for several Conference men's swimming and diving championships.

MURRAY WIER
Basketball, Iowa

Being 5-foot-8 didn't stop Murray Wier from rising to the top on the basketball court. Competing for Iowa from 1945-48, Wier set a single-season school record with 399 points, and a Big Ten scoring record with a 22.6-point average. He also held the league's three-year scoring record with 515 points and four-year mark with 584. Named Iowa's most valuable player in 1947 and '48, Wier was first-team All-Big Ten, league MVP and a consensus All-American as a senior. The Muscatine, Iowa, native scored a career-high 34 points against Illinois in 1948, setting another Conference standard. He was noted for his outside shooting, especially while off-balance. Wier went on to a professional career with Moline (Ill.) and Waterloo (Iowa) of the NBA. He later became a successful basketball coach at East Waterloo (Iowa) High School, where he coached for 24 seasons before becoming boys tennis coach and athletic director. His basketball teams were 372-140. He retired as A.D.

MAL WHITFIELD
Track, Ohio State

Prior to World War II, the track star at Ohio State was Jesse Owens. Following the war's conclusion, Ohio State enjoyed the successes of another track phenom, Malvin Whitfield. He lettered in track for the Buckeyes for four straight seasons, the last one in his senior year in 1948-49, and Whitfield finished his college track career as a two-time NCAA champion and two-time All-America selection. But his career was just taking off. After his junior season, Whitfield competed in the 1948 London Olympics, winning the gold medal in the 800-meter run and the 1,600-meter relay. His time in the 800 — 1:49.2 — set an Olympic record. Four years later, he successfully defended his gold medal in the Helsinki Olympics. In 1954, he was the winner of the Sullivan Award, honoring the nation's top amateur athlete.

FORTUNE GORDIEN
Track, Minnesota

Fortune Gordien once said, "I don't consider myself as anybody great, I just remember myself as an athlete who had some good days and some bad ones." Suffice it to say, Gordien's good days as a standout discus thrower for the Minnesota track team far outweighed his bad. A Minneapolis native, Gordien was a three-time Big Ten champion; a six-time AAU national champion; a three-time Olympian; and a former world record holder. He attended Minnesota from 1942-48, with two years of interrupted U.S. Naval service during World War II. Upon resuming his athletic career, Gordien was a member of the 1948, '52 and '56 U.S. Olympic teams. He won a bronze medal in 1948; barely missed a medal in '52 after placing fourth; and won the silver in '56. In 1953, he established a world record throw of 194-feet, 6-inches that stood for 10 years. He retired from competition in the early 1960s and was one of 17 charter members of the Minnesota Sports Hall Fame in 1958. He later coached track and field at a California high school until shortly before his death in 1990.

LEADING THE WAY

FRITZ CRISLER
Michigan

In 30 years in Ann Arbor, H.O. "Fritz" Crisler built an amazing record as a coach and athletic director, but the 1947 football season is one which old Maize and Blue loyalists remember. That year, Crisler's 10th and last as head coach, was his best, as the Wolverines stormed to an unbeaten season, climaxed by a 49-0 win over Southern Cal in the Rose Bowl for the national championship. Crisler was named national coach of the year for that season, but he was hardly a one-season wonder. His teams were 71-16-3 and also won the Big Ten title in 1943. A native of Earlville, Ill., Crisler had learned his football from the master, Amos Alonzo Stagg, for whom he played at Chicago before graduating in 1922. Crisler is credited with the founding of the "two platoon" system in 1945 and he created the unique winged helmet design still worn by the Wolverines today. Athletic director as well since 1941, Crisler devoted his full attention to that job until his 1968 retirement, twice enlarging Michigan Stadium, developing the overall plant and forging plans for the basketball arena that now bears his name. Crisler died in 1982 at age 83 in Ann Arbor.

· BIG TEN PIONEERS ·

Marv Rotblatt, Illinois

A small left-hander from Illinois named Marv Rotblatt left a big imprint on Big Ten baseball during the 1947 and 1948 baseball seasons. The Chicago native appeared in six Big Ten games for the Illini in 1947, compiling a 6-0 record with 49 strikeouts in 54 innings, thanks in part to a wicked curve ball. A year later, Rotblatt registered his finest game, striking out 18 batters in a victory over Purdue, a strikeout record that lasted until 1988. During his three-year career, he was 25-4 with a school-record 286 strikeouts. He pitched for three seasons with the Chicago White Sox and is a retired insurance salesman living in Chicago.

 ## Academic Achievements

Often times, the only way to discern why an aircraft has crashed is from information gathered on the plane's flight recorder. The "black box" airplane flight recorder was invented at Minnesota in 1948 and has been required on all U.S. flights since 1959.

1947-48 Conference MEDAL OF HONOR *Winners*

ILLINOIS	**George Fischer**
INDIANA	**LeRoy Deal**
IOWA	**Herbert W. Wilkinson**
MICHIGAN	**John E. Weisenburger**
MINNESOTA	**Steve Silianoff**
NORTHWESTERN	**Charles Tourek**
OHIO STATE	**Robert O. Jabbusch**
PURDUE	**Hank Stram**
WISCONSIN	**Carlyle Fay, Jr.**

THE BIG EVENT

Michigan State joins the Big Ten

The genesis of Michigan State College's admission to the Big Ten probably began in 1941, five years before the University of Chicago would formally resign from Conference membership, when athletic-minded, 39-year-old John Hannah was named president. Hannah, athletic director Ralph Young and football coach Charley Bachman had to scramble every year to fill the football schedule, often ending up with meaningless games that had little attraction to fans. Hannah knew his growing school had to end its scheduling problems and move into an elite athletic conference. When Chicago quit, the door was open, and although MSC's immediate application for membership was tabled, Hannah asked that State be considered whenever expansion was again discussed. Spartan leaders always credited Notre Dame's willingness to agree on home-and-home play as instrumental. Hannah also enlisted the valuable support of Minnesota president J. Louis Morrill, another important step that eventually resulted in Michigan State College being admitted to membership on Dec. 12, 1948.

OTHER MEMORABLE EVENTS

- Minnesota's Verne Gagne won his fourth Conference wrestling title (at three different weights) and added the NCAA heavyweight crown.

- Michigan won the national football title.

- Northwestern's Ted Peterson won his second Conference tennis singles championship, while Minnesota's Jim Peterson (no relation) won his third straight Conference all-around gymnastics title.

- Ohio State won the NCAA swimming championships, led by Bill Smith's fourth national title in the 220 freestyle.

- Northwestern beat California in the Rose Bowl.

- Big Ten adopted new Eligibility Rule No. 6, providing that the awarding of scholarships to athletes must conform to academic standards set by the Conference.

Indiana, Iowa and Michigan battle to three-way tie in baseball

*Jack Bruner,
University of Iowa
pitcher*

Only once in Big Ten history have three teams shared the Conference baseball championship. In 1949, that distinction belonged to Indiana, Iowa, Michigan — the latter having won the most titles in league history with 30. For Indiana, 1949 marked the last time the Hoosiers would own any piece of the championship. Of the four they have won in their history, two were shared — including the last two. Indiana was led in 1949 by Big Ten batting champion Don Ritter. The first baseman hit a sparkling .439. For Iowa, its strength in 1949 eminated from the pitcher's mound, where Jack Bruner led all Conference pitchers with a 5-1 record. He was also named a first team All-American. Second baseman Jack Dittmer joined Bruner and Ritter on the All-Big Ten team. Michigan's star player that year was slugger Jack McDonald, who belted a league-high four home runs. That total stood as the Big Ten record for six years, until Illinois' Vic Petreshne blasted six. Wolverines' third baseman Ted Kobrin was named to the All-Big Ten team.

OTHER BIG TEN CHAMPIONS

- **FOOTBALL:** Michigan, coached by Bennie Oosterbaan
- **GYMNASTICS:** Minnesota, coached by Dr. Ralph Piper
- **OUTDOOR TRACK:** Minnesota, coached by James Kelly
- **INDOOR TRACK:** Ohio State, coached by Larry Snyder, and Wisconsin, coached by Guy Sundt
- **BASKETBALL:** Illinois, coached by Harry Combes
- **CROSS COUNTRY:** Wisconsin, coached by Guy Sundt
- **TENNIS:** Northwestern, coached by Paul Bennett
- **SWIMMING:** Ohio State, coached by Michael Peppe
- **WRESTLING:** Purdue, coached by C.C. Reeck
- **GOLF:** Michigan, coached by Bert Katzenmeyer
- **FENCING:** Ohio State, coached by Robert Kaplan

DIKE EDDLEMAN
Football, Basketball and Track, Illinois

An all-stater in football, the state's all-time scorer when he led his hometown Centralia, Ill., to a state title in basketball and a two-time high jump champion as a schoolboy star, Dike Eddleman has always been Illinois' favorite son. The governor even helped recruit Eddleman to the Illinois campus, and Eddleman completed his Illinois career—interrupted by World War II—with a record 11 varsity letters. He was a member of the 1946 Big Ten football champs and the first Illinois team to play in the Rose Bowl, a school record holder with an 88-yard punt in 1948. In 1948-49, he was the Big Ten's MVP in basketball and led Illinois to the Big Ten title. As a high jumper, Eddleman won four Big Ten championships and tied for third in the 1948 Olympics. He played in the fledgling NBA for five years and was named an all-star twice. He retired as a fundraiser for Illinois' athletic department in 1991.

BILL SMITH
Swimming, Ohio State

There are few winning streaks that are as amazing, either individual or as a team. Ohio State swimming saw one of those miracle runs in varsity swimming when Bill Smith went undefeated during a four-year Buckeyes career that was postponed by World War II. Smith competed at Ohio State in 1942-43, then returned to school following the war in 1946-47, finishing his career in 1948-49. A freestyler, Smith was a four-time All-American. He set seven world records and won 15 Amateur Athletic Union championships. He also captured seven NCAA titles and two Olympic gold medals during his career. He was inducted into the Ohio State Sports Hall of Fame in 1977.

GEORGE TALIAFERRO
Football, Indiana

George Taliaferro made an immediate impact on Big Ten football. Joining an Indiana team in 1945 that would become the only one in the school's history to win an outright league title, he played his first game before 80,000 fans at Michigan. Although stunned by the surroundings, he rushed for 95 yards on 20 carries to lead the Hoosiers to a 13-7 victory. His career was interrupted by military service the following year, but he returned to lead the Hoosiers in scoring and punting in 1947 and '48, and in rushing and passing in '48. Taliaferro, a member of the College Football Hall of Fame, played seven years of professional football, for five teams. He later worked as a university administrator. Retired, he still lives in Bloomington.

PETE ELLIOTT
Football, Basketball and Golf, Michigan

Besides quarterbacking Michigan's 1948 national football champions, Pete Elliott became the only Michigan athlete to earn 12 letters. He earned letters in football, basketball and golf. He played on four Conference championship teams—two in football and one each in basketball and golf. He went to Michigan in 1945 as a Navy trainee, and wound up starring as a runner and passer. Shifted to quarterback, his blocking and defensive strength became invaluable. Later he served as head football coach at Nebraska, California and Illinois, leading the Illini to a 1964 Rose Bowl title, and later enjoyed success in the building business and as a sports commentator. He currently serves as the director of the Pro Football Hall of Fame.

LEADING THE WAY

RAY ELIOT
Illinois

He played football at Illinois as Ray Nusspickle. By the time he returned to the Illini after five years as a coach at Illinois College, he answered to Ray Eliot. No matter the name, the folks in Champaign called him "Mr. Illini." Eliot took over a once-proud Illinois football program in 1942 that hadn't produced a winning season since 1930 and had failed to win a Big Ten game in the previous two seasons. In his first year, Illinois posted a 6-4 record, including a win over defending national champion Minnesota. It was a prelude of things to come. During his 18-year career, Eliot led Illinois to an 83-73-1 record. The Illini won Big Ten championships in 1946, 1951 and 1953, representing the Big Ten in the 1947 and 1952 Rose Bowls. Illinois won both Rose Bowl appearances, and he retired as coach following the 1960-61 school year to assume a position in the school's administration. Eliot served as assistant athletic director for 13 years, coming out of retirement as interim athletic director when he was 74 years old. Months after that assignment ended, he died in 1980 and was buried across the street from Memorial Stadium.

· BIG TEN PIONEERS ·

Wistert and Elliott brothers

Brotherly talent paid off big for Michigan football teams in the 1930s and 1940s. Three Wistert brothers—each a tackle wearing No. 11, now retired—starred, with the eldest, Francis ("Whitey"), earning All-America honors as a senior. Second brother Albert, nicknamed "The Ox" because of his size and determination, was an All-American in 1942 and twice led Michigan to once-beaten seasons. Youngest brother Alvin ("Moose") outdid his brothers by twice earning All-America status. The Elliotts were another legendary brother tandem, with Bump an All-America halfback and Big Ten MVP for Fritz Crisler's last team, the 1947 national champs, and Pete—the only Wolverine ever to win 12 letters—the All-America quarterback for Bennie Oosterbaan's undefeated champs of '48.

Academic Achievements

Following the development of the atomic bomb on one Big Ten campus (Chicago), another school—Michigan—became the first to sponsor a project designed to study and develop the use of atomic energy for purposes other than war-related uses. The "Phoenix Project" began in 1948.

1948-49 Conference MEDAL OF HONOR Winners

ILLINOIS	T. Dwight Eddleman
INDIANA	Joseph Lawecki
IOWA	Evan Hultman
MICHIGAN	Peter R. Elliott
MINNESOTA	James B. Peterson
NORTHWESTERN	William Heusner
OHIO STATE	Lloyd T. Duff
PURDUE	Keith E. Carter
WISCONSIN	Donald R. Peterson

THE BIG EVENT

Purdue golf team catapults its ways to a championship

This was a breakthrough year for Purdue as far as Big Ten golf competition was concerned. Going into the 1950 season, the Boilermakers were 78-102 in league play. But they would go on to finish 10-1 in dual meets, 9-0 in invitationals and No. 1 at the Big Ten meet. Purdue's only loss in the Conference was to Ohio State, and it finished second at the NCAA championships. Fred Wampler won the NCAA individual championship and his third consecutive Big Ten title; four years later he would win the Los Angeles Open on the PGA Tour. Wampler, the team captain, was All-America. John Hare finished third at the Big Ten meet, and Gene Coulter was fourth. Other members of the school's first league championship team: Bob Buchanon, Norm Dunlap, Dave Laflin, Dwight Marsee and George Thomas. Coulter was the Big Ten individual champion in 1951.

OTHER MEMORABLE EVENTS

- Illinois won the NCAA gymnastics championship.

- Led by Bruce Harlan's third straight NCAA crown, Ohio State won the national swimming championship.

- Purdue's Fred Wampler (who won the NCAA title) had a record 64 in the final round of the Conference championships on his way to three Big Ten titles.

- Wisconsin's Don Gehrmann won his third straight NCAA outdoor mile championship.

- Michigan's Gil Buford scored a record five goals in the NCAA hockey third-place game.

- Purdue's Arnold Plaza and Iowa's Joe Scarpello both won their fourth straight Conference wrestling title.

- The Big Ten approved a 14-game Conference basketball schedule and set a limit of 22 games overall.

Northwestern continues tennis dominance

Northwestern's tennis team dominated the Conference as the midway point of the century approached, winning four straight uncontested championships from 1947-50 — the first time a league team had put together a streak that long. Ted Petersen was a key performer on the first three title teams, winning the league singles championship in 1947 and '49. He became the second Northwestern athlete to win two singles titles, following Seymour Greenberg, who won in 1940 and '41. The 1947 championship was a surprise, a 22.5 to 21 upset of Illinois. The 1948 and '49 titles came over Michigan, while the final title in 1950 was the most difficult. Three of the team's key members had graduated, but the Wildcats still edged Illinois, 19.5 to 17, in the Conference meet. Grant Golden won the singles title that year, while Bill Landin won the No. 2 singles title. The two then teamed to win the doubles championship. Landin, who had become eligible as a freshman because of wartime rules, played on all four title teams. The four league titles were the nucleus of seven directed by legendary coach Paul Bennett, whose teams also won in 1936, '40 and '42.

OTHER BIG TEN CHAMPIONS

- **FOOTBALL:** Michigan, coached by Bennie Oosterbaan, and Ohio State, coached by Wesley Fesler
- **BASEBALL:** Michigan, coached by Ray Fisher, and Wisconsin, coached by Arthur Mansfield
- **GYMNASTICS:** Illinois, coached by Charles Pond
- **OUTDOOR TRACK:** Indiana, coached by Gordon Fisher
- **INDOOR TRACK:** Ohio State, coached by Larry Snyder
- **BASKETBALL:** Ohio State, coached by W.H.H. "Tippy" Dye
- **CROSS COUNTRY:** Wisconsin, coached by Guy Sundt
- **SWIMMING:** Ohio State, coached by Michael Peppe
- **WRESTLING:** Purdue, coached by C.C. Reeck
- **GOLF:** Purdue, coached by Loomis Heston
- **FENCING:** Illinois, coached by Maxwell Garret

ARNOLD PLAZA
Wrestling, Purdue

Arnold Plaza's Purdue wrestling resume sounds like it reads from a University of Iowa media guide. Plaza, a Chicago native, was a four-time national champion, four-time All-American and four-time Big Ten Conference champion. He was named the league's Wrestler of the Year as a senior, and he led the Boilermakers to Big Ten championships in 1948, '49 and '50. Two of his national titles were from the NCAA and two from the Amateur Athletic Union. He was selected to the Amateur Wrestling Hall of Fame and was among the athletes in the first class elected to Purdue's Hall of Fame in 1994. Plaza was a teacher in Chicago and El Paso, Texas, before retiring to live in Anthony, N.M.

DON GERHMANN
Track, Wisconsin

Don Gerhmann, who competed from 1947 until 1950, was not only one of Wisconsin's greatest distance runners ever, but one of the Big Ten's, as well. He was named the Conference's "Greatest Miler" for its first 50 years of existence. During his dazzling career, Gehrmann won 87 of 99 races between 880 yards and two miles. He was a four-time Big Ten indoor mile champion and was the Conference's indoor two-mile champion in 1947; its 880-yard champion in 1949 and 1950; its outdoor 880 champion in 1950; and its indoor mile champion in 1949 and 1950. He was the NCAA mile champion in 1948, '49 and '50 and won the heralded Drake Relays Outstanding Performer Award three times. He finished seventh in the 1,500-meter run in the 1948 Olympics in London. Gehrmann was also an outstanding cross country athlete, leading the Badgers to Conference titles in 1948, '49 and '50. He is a member of the State of Wisconsin Hall of Fame and a member of the Drake Relays Hall of Fame.

JOE SCARPELLO
Wrestling, Iowa

Iowa's storied wrestling tradition had to begin somewhere, and Joe Scarpello can lay claim to a piece of that history. He was Iowa's first four-time Big Ten champion, winning league titles from 1947-50 while going unbeaten in 21 dual matches during his career (10 by falls). Scarpello was a four-time All-American at 175 pounds and won national championships in 1947 and '50. In 1948, he finished third at the NCAA Championships and second at the Olympic trials. He was NCAA runner-up in 1949. He earned a spot on the 1948 U.S. Olympic team in London as an alternate—the second Hawkeye to be named to an Olympic squad. Scarpello won the national Amateur Athletic Union title in 1942, and he finished second in 1950 as a senior. He was inducted into the National Iowa Letterman's Club Athletic Hall of Fame in 1991.

BILL "MOOSE" SKOWRON
Football and Baseball, Purdue

Bill "Moose" Skowron will be more remembered for his Major League Baseball career than his collegiate accomplishments. Skowron played just one season at Purdue before leaving after his sophomore year to sign with the New York Yankees. As a member of the Boilermakers, he led the Conference in hitting with a .500 average. He was All-Big Ten and team MVP. Skowron also was a reserve halfback and kicker on the Purdue football team in 1948 and '49. During a 14-year professional baseball career, Skowron batted .282 with 211 home runs. He played in eight World Series games, hitting .293. He played for the Yankees, Los Angeles Dodgers, Washington Senators, Chicago White Sox and California Angels. He was inducted into Purdue's Athletic Hall of Fame in 1996.

LEADING THE WAY

HANK STRAM
Purdue

Hank Stram is mostly known for having coached the NFL's Kansas City Chiefs and winning Super Bowl IV against Minnesota. But during a lengthy tenure at Purdue as a player, then a coach, he was important to the football and baseball programs. The Gary, Ind., native played baseball at Purdue in 1943, '46-'48, and football in 1942, '46 and '47. His playing career was interrupted when he was called to duty in the U.S. Army during World War II in the spring 1943— two months before he was to play in the college football all-star game. When Stram returned to Purdue a year after being discharged in 1945, he went on to play halfback and kicker for the football team. He also was an infielder on the baseball team, and won the Big Ten Conference's Medal of Honor as a senior for his athletic and academic accomplishments. After graduating in 1948, Stram remained at Purdue as an assistant football coach. During a seven-year stint, he also was the Boilermakers' baseball coach (1949-55). Stram was an assistant football coach at Southern Methodist, Notre Dame and the University of Miami before becoming head coach and vice president of the Dallas Texans of the American Football League in 1959. He finished with a 124-76-10 career coaching record in the NFL. His team lost Super Bowl I to Green Bay. Stram became a color commentator for CBS in 1975. He was inducted into Purdue's Athletic Hall of Fame in 1996.

BIG TEN ENLIST

THREE-PEAT TRACK CHAMPIONS

A total of six Big Ten outdoor track and field performers have won their event three consecutive years at the NCAA Championships. They are:

David Albritton, Ohio State
(high jump 1936-37-38)
Don Gehrmann, Wisconsin
(mile run 1948-49-50)
Fortune Gordien, Minnesota
(discus throw 1946-47-48)
Edward Gordon, Iowa
(long jump 1929-30-31)
Charles Hornbostel, Indiana
(880-yard run 1932-33-34)
Tom Warne, Northwestern
(pole vault 1929-30-31)

Academic Achievements

Among the most famous alumni from Penn State are: first African-American astronaut, Guion S. Bluford; **Vogue** magazine's international executive editor, Barbara Culley McKibbin; Merrill Lynch & Co. chairman, William A. Schreyer; CNN correspondent Charles Bierbauer; author Vance Packard; heart surgeon James W. Giacobine; "Casablanca" author, Julius Epstein; and U.S. Secretary of Commerce, Barbara Hackman Franklin.

1949-50 Conference MEDAL OF HONOR Winners

ILLINOIS	Russell W. Steger
INDIANA	Walter C. Bartkiewicz
IOWA	Donald C. Hays
MICHIGAN	Thomas R. Peterson
MINNESOTA	Richard S. Kilty
NORTHWESTERN	Donald M. Burson
OHIO STATE	Bruce Harlan
PURDUE	Norbert H. Adams
WISCONSIN	Robert J. Wilson

1950 Purdue football squad

THE BIG EVENT

The Purdue "Spoilermakers"

The nation was stunned. Mighty Notre Dame had won 39 consecutive football games, and had not lost to Purdue since 1933. Notre Dame Stadium was packed (56,746). Legendary coach Frank Leahy was on the "other" sideline. But none of that mattered to the Boilermakers. They took a 21-0 lead in the first half and went on to register a shocking 28-14 upset victory over Notre Dame. Purdue's sophomore quarterback Dale Samuels—who outplayed Notre Dame All-America quarterback Bob Williams—made sure Purdue held on. When Notre Dame closed to within 21-14 in the fourth quarter, Samuels connected with Mike Macciolo for a 56-yard touchdown to ensure the victory. Samuels finished 9-of-21 for 151 yards, and he added four extra points. "Yes sir, it was the best ballgame I ever saw, or hope to see," Boilermakers coach Stu Holcomb said afterward. It was Notre Dame's first defeat since Dec. 1, 1945. Purdue lost its next six games and finished 2-7. Its only other victory was in the season finale against Indiana, 13-0.

OTHER MEMORABLE EVENTS

- Northwestern's Ray Ragelis set a Conference basketball scoring record, as did the championship team, Illinois.

- Ohio State's Tom Nieporte won the NCAA golf championship.

- Illinois swept the Conference fencing titles: Allen Mills (foil), Leonard Atkin (epee) and Jorge Quiros (sabre).

- Michigan State's Mel Stout won the gymnastics all-around title for the Spartans' first Conference championship in any sport.

- Michigan's Edsel Buchanan won his third straight NCAA trampoline championship, while fellow Wolverine Don McEwen won the Conference cross country title for the second straight year.

- Ohio State won Big Ten team titles in baseball, swimming, wrestling, and golf.

Michigan wins Big Ten, Rose Bowl

Michigan won its third Rose Bowl in as many tries in 1951 with a 14-6 upset victory over an unbeaten and once-tied California team that was making its third straight appearance in Pasadena. It was an improbable ending to a 4-1-1 Big Ten season that saw the Wolverines take the Conference title with a 9-3 win over Ohio State in the regular season closer. Coach Bennie Oosterbaan's team was 2-3-1 after six games but closed with wins over Indiana, Northwestern and Ohio State. In the Rose Bowl, California led 6-0 at the half, off a 192-65 edge in offensive yardage and a 10-2 first down advantage, but a new defensive formation for U-M kept the Golden Bears off the board thereafter. Michigan turned the first half stats around, with a 15-2 first down margin and a 226-52 edge over Cal in total yardage. MVP Don Dufek ran four straight identical plays from the 4-yard line, finally scoring on fourth-and-one in the fourth quarter. Dufek again scored on a 7-yard run later in the period to ice the victory.

OTHER BIG TEN CHAMPIONS

- **BASEBALL:** Ohio State, coached by Martin Karow
- **GYMNASTICS:** Illinois, coached by Charles Pond
- **OUTDOOR TRACK:** Illinois, coached by Leo Johnson
- **INDOOR TRACK:** Illinois, coached by Leo Johnson
- **BASKETBALL:** Illinois, coached by Harry Combes
- **CROSS COUNTRY:** Wisconsin, coached by J. Riley Best
- **TENNIS:** Michigan, coached by William Murphy
- **SWIMMING:** Ohio State, coached by Michael Peppe
- **WRESTLING:** Ohio State, coached by Casey Fredericks
- **GOLF:** Ohio State, coached by Robert Kepler
- **FENCING:** Illinois, coached by Maxwell Garret

TOM NIEPORTE
Golf, Ohio State

He was a member of the Ohio State team that won the Big Ten championship by 12 strokes over Purdue, but Tom Nieporte wasn't the medalist at the Conference golf championships hosted by Northwestern. Nevertheless, Nieporte finished the season in 1950-51 by winning the NCAA individual golf title, the second golfer from Ohio State to win the NCAA championship. The previous season, Nieporte helped Ohio State finish second in the Big Ten tournament. Nieporte was one of three NCAA champions from Ohio State during an 11-year span, since Rick Jones (1955-56) and Jack Nicklaus (1960-61) also won NCAA championships for the Buckeyes.

BILL GARRETT
Basketball, Indiana

Bill Garrett would be a notable figure in Big Ten history even if he hadn't been a great athlete. After leading his high school team to the Indiana state championship, he became one of the first African-American basketball player in Conference history when he enrolled at Indiana in the fall of 1947. He went on to become a dominant center—despite standing just 6-foot-2—leading the Hoosiers in scoring and rebounding all three of his seasons (1949-51). He earned All-America honors as a senior when he led the Hoosiers to a 19-3 record while averaging 13.1 points and 9.8 rebounds. He went on to a successful career as a high school coach, leading Crispus Attucks to the championship of the Indiana state tournament in 1959. He died in 1974.

VIC JANOWICZ
Football, Ohio State

In the by-gone era when a player performed more than one duty, tailback Vic Janowicz was a multi-talented player who was the second player from Ohio State to win the Heisman Trophy, winning the award as a junior in 1950. That year, he led the Buckeyes in rushing and passing while also handling the punting and placekicking. Janowicz was a consensus All-America pick as a junior when he also earned the Big Ten's MVP award after leading the league in total offense with 703 yards. As a junior, he established records with 10 extra-point kicks against Iowa, and he set marks of 21 punts and 685 punting yards in the Snow Bowl against Michigan. An Ohio State MVP in his final two seasons, Janowicz had 450 yards of total offense as a senior. He's a member of the National Football Hall of Fame.

ALBERT (AB) NICHOLAS
Basketball, Wisconsin

One of the best guards in Wisconsin basketball history, Ab Nicholas was an outstanding all-around player during his four-year career. A feisty defender and a productive scorer, Nicholas scored 982 points in 66 games during a career spanning 1948-52. Once cut from his high school team in Rockford, Ill., because he was "too small," Nicholas earned all-state recognition as a high school senior before joining Wisconsin, where he graduated as the highest scoring guard in Badgers' history. Renowned for an uncanny knack to avoid fouls, he was a first team All-Big Ten selection in 1951 and '52. He was also a second team member of *Look* magazine's All-America team in 1952. He averaged 11.6 points a game as sophomore; 16.6 as a junior; and 16.0 his senior year, when he won "W" Club Athlete of the Year. He was inducted into the Wisconsin Athletic Hall of Fame in 1994.

LEADING THE WAY

JOHN KOBS
Michigan State

Current Big Ten baseball players probably have never heard of John Kobs, but they have played ball on his field. It's only fitting that the baseball park at Michigan State be named for the legendary Spartan coach, who in 39 years in East Lansing compiled a 574-377-16 record for a spectacular .656 winning percentage. From 1924-63, Kobs had only four losing teams. His 1954 squad won the Conference title and advanced to the College World Series, where it finished third, still the best Spartan effort ever. He developed 11 All-Americans and a host of major leaguers, most notably Hall of Fame pitcher Robin Roberts. Kobs came to State in 1924 from Hamline University, where he was a four-sport star. One of three men in Spartan history to be head coach of three different teams, Kobs served as basketball coach for the 1925-26 season and as hockey coach from 1925-30. Active in promoting his sport, Kobs was one of the first presidents of the American Association of Baseball Coaches and a charter member of its hall of fame. He was head coach of the U.S. team in the 1955 and '59 Pan American Games. Kobs died in East Lansing in 1968 at age 69.

B I G T E N L I S T

UPSETS GALORE!

Big Ten football teams have beaten or tied the nation's then-No. 1 ranked team 27 times since the polls were introduced in 1936:

1936— Northwestern 6, No. 1 Minnesota 0;
1942— Wisconsin 17, No. 1 Ohio State 7;
1950— Purdue 28, No. 1 Notre Dame 14;
1950— Illinois 14, No. 1 Ohio State 7;
1952— Ohio State 23, No. 1 Wisconsin 14;
1953— (tie) Iowa 14, No. 1 Notre Dame 14;
1954— Purdue 27, No. 1 Notre Dame 14;
1956— Illinois 20, No. 1 Michigan State 13;
1957— Purdue 20, No. 1 Michigan State 13;
1960— Minnesota 27, No. 1 Iowa 10;
1960— Purdue 23, No. 1 Minnesota 14;
1961— Minnesota 13, No. 1 Michigan State 0;
1962— Wisconsin 37, No. 1 Northwestern 6;
1965— Purdue 25, No. 1 Notre Dame 21;
1966— (tie) Michigan State 10, No. 1 Notre Dame 10;
1967— Purdue 28, No. 1 Notre Dame 21;
1968— Ohio State 13, No. 1 Purdue 0;
1969— Michigan 24, No. 1 Ohio State 12;
1973— (tie) Michigan 10, No. 1 Ohio State 10;
1974— Michigan State 16, No. 1 Ohio State 13;
1976— Purdue 16, No. 1 Michigan 14;
1977— Minnesota 16, No. 1 Michigan 0;
1981— Wisconsin 21, No. 1 Michigan 14;
1981— Michigan 25, No. 1 Notre Dame 7;
1984— Michigan 22, No. 1 Miami (Fla.) 14;
1985— Ohio State 22, No. 1 Iowa 13;
1990— Michigan State 28, No. 1 Michigan 27.

 ## Academic Achievements

The Little 500 Bicycle Race began at Indiana University in 1951 as a fund-raising event to raise scholarship money for working students. Now a month-long series of events culminating with a 25-mile women's race and a 50-mile men's race, the Little 500 has raised approximately $600,000 for scholarships. It was the subject of the acclaimed motion picture, "Breaking Away."

1950-51
Conference MEDAL OF HONOR
Winners

———◆———

ILLINOIS	Don Laz
INDIANA	John H. Phillips
IOWA	Ralph W. Thomas
MICHIGAN	Leo R. Koceski
MICHIGAN STATE	Everett Grandelius
MINNESOTA	Myer U. Skoog
NORTHWESTERN	Donald C. Blasius
OHIO STATE	Richard D. Widdoes
PURDUE	Neil Schmidt
WISCONSIN	David Staiger

THE BIG EVENT

1952 Illinois baseball team

Illini win eight of 12 Conference titles

The national television audience caught a glimpse of Illinois' dream season, as the Illini's Rose Bowl win over Stanford was the first college football game broadcast nationally. It was a piece of history, since the Illinois football team was one of eight Illini squads to win Big Ten titles that season. The total matched Michigan's eight championships won during the 1943-44 season. Illinois captured Conference titles in baseball, basketball, fencing, gymastics, indoor track, outdoor track, wrestling and football. The Illini basketball team reached the Final Four. The era was a high point of prosperity for Illinois. From 1950-51 through the 1953-54 season, the Illini claimed titles in 23 of the 48 Conference team championships. The eight titles surpassed Illinois' record of six, set in 1921-22 and 1923-24. Illinois won five championships in six different seasons.

OTHER MEMORABLE EVENTS

- Ohio State won the NCAA swimming championships.

- Indiana was whistled for 29.3 personal fouls per game, still an NCAA basketball record.

- Ohio State swimmer Ford Konno set three Conference records in one meet.

- A total of 37 Conference athletes competed in the Olympics in Helsinki, including 13 swimmers from Ohio State.

- Iowa's Charles Darling recorded the Conference's first 30-rebound game.

BIG TEN LIST

BIG TEN RBI LEADERS

Wisconsin's Harvey Kuenn had 16 runs batted in during the 1952 Big Ten season. Even though that led the Conference, that's far from the season record of 42 set by Illinois' Josh Klimek in 1996. Here are the top seasons by the league RBI leaders:

42, Josh Klimek, Illinois, 1996
39, Jamie Taylor, Ohio State, 1991
39, Shane Gunderson, Minnesota, 1995
36, Mark Dalesandro, Illinois, 1990
36, Mike Smith, Indiana, 1992
35, Shane Gunderson, Minnesota, 1994

Ohio State wins NCAA swimming championship

1951 Ohio State swim team

The team title came down to two squads who also featured two stars at the NCAA swimming championships at Princeton University's Dillon Gym pool. Defending NCAA champion Yale was led by John Marshall, the defending champion in the 1,500 meter freestyle. Ohio State's star was a 19-year-old from Hawaii, Ford Konno. Konno won two final events, including the 1,500, to lead Ohio State to the team championship ahead of Yale. When the final scoring announcement was made, Ohio State threw its coach, Mike Peppe, into the pool to celebrate the school's first NCAA team title. Konno showed his prowess in the first event, the 1,500 meters. Trailing Marshall in the marathon event, Konno closed fast to clock an 18:11.5, a meet record but well off the pace Konno set at the Big Ten championships. Konno also won the 440-yard freestyle ahead of Marshall. Ohio State teammate Dick Cleveland scored a first-place finish in the 50-yard freestyle sprint, and the Buckeyes' Yoshi Oyakawa tied teammate Jack Taylor's American and intercollegiate record with a 2:07.2 in the 200-yard backstroke. OSU won the Big Ten over second-place Michigan State, 125-66.

OTHER BIG TEN CHAMPIONS

- **FOOTBALL:** Illinois, coached by Ray Eliot
- **BASEBALL:** Illinois, coached by Lee Eilbracht, and Michigan, coached by Ray Fisher
- **GYMNASTICS:** Illinois, coached by Charles Pond
- **OUTDOOR TRACK:** Illinois, coached by Leo Johnson
- **INDOOR TRACK:** Illinois, coached by Leo Johnson
- **BASKETBALL:** Illinois, coached by Harry Combes
- **CROSS COUNTRY:** Michigan, coached by Don Canham
- **TENNIS:** Indiana, coached by Dale Lewis
- **WRESTLING:** Illinois, coached by B.R. Patterson
- **GOLF:** Michigan, coached by Bert Katzenmeyer
- **FENCING:** Illinois, coached by Maxwell Garret

HARVEY KUENN
Baseball, Wisconsin

One of the most popular baseball figures in Wisconsin history, Harvey Kuenn enjoyed unbridled success as a college and Major League player and — later — as a big league manager. Kuenn was one of the greatest hitters in Badgers' history and was a gifted defensive shortstop, playing from 1951-52 before signing a big league contract with the Detroit Tigers after his junior season. In 1952, he hit a team-high .436 and belted a school-record nine triples. He was an All-American that season after leading shortstops in fielding percentage at .972, committing only two errors in 71 chances. A letterwinner in baseball and basketball, he later played with five big league teams. He was the American League Rookie of the Year in 1953 and was the AL batting champion in 1959. He later managed the Milwaukee Brewers — despite poor health and an amputated right leg — to the 1982 AL championship and a berth in the World Series. Kuenn died at his home in Chandler, Ariz. in 1988 at age 57.

CHUCK DARLING
Basketball, Iowa

When they spoke of Chuck Darling's versatility, they were referring to his work in and out of the classroom. Darling was an All-American center on the basketball team who set 11 Big Ten and Iowa scoring records. He was the Big Ten's MVP as a senior after averaging a school-record 25.5 ppg (26 ppg in league play). Darling also excelled on the academic side. He was senior class president in the college of liberal arts and had a 3.2 GPA while majoring in petroleum geology. He was Phi Beta Kappa and received the Big Ten Medal of Honor for excellence in athletics and academics. Darling also was a weight man on the Iowa track team in 1950 and '51. He competed on the Phillips 66 Oilers AAU basketball team, which defeated a college all-star team to win the Olympic trials in 1956. That college team included Bill Russell and K.C. Jones. Darling was a member of the U.S. Olympic squad which included Russell and Jones and won a gold medal in Melbourne, Australia.

CHUCK BOERIO
Football, Illinois

Linebacker Chuck Boerio typified the group of players who made up Illinois' 1952 Rose Bowl team. At 5-foot-11 and 190 pounds, Boerio was Coach Ray Eliot's star linebacker, earning first-team All-Big Ten honors. As the Illini's defensive signal caller, the Kincaid, Ill., walk-on was the leader of a unit that allowed its six Big Ten foes an average of only five points per game during the 1951 campaign. Boerio, named Illini Athlete of the Year for 1951-52, was selected defensive captain of the 1952 College All-Stars in their game against the NFL champion Los Angeles Rams. His pro football career lasted only half a season with the Green Bay Packers, primarily due to his lack of size and speed. Boerio returned to UI in 1956 and coached under Eliot for three seasons. He served as an assistant coach at Colorado from 1959-61, helping guide the Buffaloes to the school's first Big Eight title. Boerio was a teacher and coach in the Boulder, Colo., school district for 28 years, retiring in 1990.

CLARKE SCHOLES
Swimming, Michigan State

Three-time All-American Clarke Scholes' exploits will long be remembered at Michigan State. In a Conference that has produced many great swimmers, Scholes ranked among the best of his era. In three years at East Lansing, Scholes, a native of Detroit, earned seven NCAA and National AAU titles and three Big Ten crowns. He capped his senior season of 1951-52 with a gold medal and world record in the 100 freestyle at the 1952 Helsinki Olympics. Scholes became State's first Big Ten swim champ in 1951 by winning the 50- and 100-yard freestyles and then repeated those victories in the NCAA. Scholes came back at age 25 to win a 100-meter freestyle gold and swim on the winning 4x100 relay team in the 1955 Pan American Games. He was inducted into the International Swimming Hall of Fame in 1980. Scholes lives in Grosse Pointe, Mich.

LEADING THE WAY

NEWT LOKEN
Michigan

Newt Loken was another one of those legendary Michigan coaches for whom longevity beget success which in turn beget tradition and even greater success. In 36 seasons as head gymnastics coach, from 1947 to 1983, Loken guided the Wolverines to a 250-72-1 record along with 12 Big Ten championships, two NCAA gymnastics titles (1963, 1970) and two NCAA trampoline crowns. Twice the national coach of the year, Loken saw his gymnasts win 71 individual Conference titles and 21 NCAA championships. Also a teacher in Michigan's Department of Physical Education, Loken was in charge of the football cheerleading squad and emceed pep rallies. Loken, who received his bachelor's degree from Minnesota in 1942, later added master's and doctoral degrees at Michigan. An outstanding athlete himself, Loken was an NCAA high bar and all-around champion for the Gophers and also was an all-American cheerleader. He was named to the Minnesota Hall of Fame, the Michigan Amateur Sports Hall of Fame and the Michigan Hall of Honor. An endowed scholarship at Michigan is named in Loken's honor.

· BIG TEN PIONEERS ·

Willie Williams, Illinois

Growing up in Gary, Ind., young Willie Williams idolized former Ohio State and Olympic track champion Jesse Owens. Though Williams' aspirations were probably unrealistic, the future Illinois track star not only matched many of Owens' records, he surpassed them. No, even with nine Big Ten titles and two NCAA individual championships during his Illini career from 1952-54, Williams didn't come close to Owens' legendary Olympic accomplishments, but on August 3, 1956 in Berlin, Germany, Willie lived out his dream. In just 10.1 seconds, Williams made history, breaking his hero's world's 100-meter dash record on the *same* soil, in the *same* stadium and in the very *same* lane that Owens had run 20 years earlier at the 1936 Olympic Games. Since 1982, he's coached Illini sprinters in Urbana-Champaign.

Academic Achievements

Today surgeons almost routinely cut open a patient's chest and work on their heart. But it wasn't until 1952 that the first open-heart surgery was performed. And it took place at Minnesota.

The BIG TEN's First 100 Years

Big Ten Volleyball Milestones

The Career Leaders in Big Ten Volleyball Statistical Categories

2000 KILLS

2,140 Kills
Andrea Gonzales, Minnesota (1985-88)

2,108 Kills
Debbie McDonald, Purdue (1986-89)

6000 ASSISTS

6,024 Assists
Sharon Oesterling, Minnesota (1986-89)

600 BLOCKS

618 Blocks
Arlisa Hagen, Wisconsin (1989-92)

1951-52
Conference MEDAL OF HONOR
Winners

ILLINOIS	Richard Calisch
INDIANA	Robert Masters
IOWA	Charles F. Darling
MICHIGAN	Donald S. McEwen
MICHIGAN STATE	Ottis H. Bender
MINNESOTA	Richard K. Means
NORTHWESTERN	Richard H. Alban
OHIO STATE	Stewart Hein
PURDUE	John G. Durham
WISCONSIN	Walter E. Deike

1952-53

Don Schlundt, Indiana

THE BIG EVENT

"Slick" Hoosiers win
NCAA basketball title

Indiana's 69-68 victory over Kansas for the NCAA championship was a repeat of its 1940 title. Both games were played in Kansas City, where the Hoosiers overcame the Jayhawks' homecourt edge. The 1940 championship came relatively easily, 60-42. But this time they had to survive an emotional, breathtaking game that wasn't decided until Kansas' Jerry Alberts missed a forced jumper at the final buzzer. Indiana's margin of victory was a free throw by junior guard Bob Leonard with 12 seconds left. Leonard, who was fouled with 27 seconds remaining, missed the first attempt and Kansas coach Phog Allen called a timeout to let him think about the second. But Leonard, who would earn the nickname "Slick" in later years, nailed the second one. "I was scared to death; scared to death," he recalled. "When you're that age ... boy, that was a heckuva ballgame. That was a heckuva ballgame."

OTHER MEMORABLE EVENTS

- **Michigan won the NCAA baseball championship.**

- **Michigan and Minnesota squared off in the title game of the NCAA hockey championships with Michigan winning its third straight national crown.**

- **Michigan State, in its final season as a football independent, went 9-0 and was ranked No. 1 in the final polls.**

- **Michigan State won the NCAA cross country championship.**

- **Ohio State's Bob Grimes caught four touchdown passes in a game, a Big Ten record that remained unbroken until 1993.**

- **Howie Williams of Purdue was the first Conference athlete on the U.S. Olympic basketball team (1952 Summer Games).**

Illini trackmen sweep Big Ten meets

1953 Illinois track squad

Illinois had swept to the Big Ten track double in the previous season, winning the indoor and outdoor championships on the way to a sixth-place finish in the NCAA championships, so there was plenty of reason to anticipate big things in 1952-53. Illinois kept its role as a track powerhouse, winning the indoor and outdoor championships again, pushing the total to seven outdoor titles in a 10-year period. Illinois completed the year by finishing second in the NCAA championships, falling short of the school's sixth national title. Speedster Willie WIlliams was the star, winning two events in the indoor championship, two more outdoors and the 100 at the NCAA championships. Stacey Siders won the 880 both indoors and outdoors, while Joe McNulty was an indoor hurdles champion who won two hurdles titles outdoors. Illinois also received Conference titles from Jim Wright (pole vault), Thomas Floyd (long jump) and Richard Wham (high jump). Williams' NCAA title was the first of two he would win in the 100. Coach Leo Johnson led Illinois to 17 Big Ten titles and three NCAA championships.

OTHER BIG TEN CHAMPIONS

- **FOOTBALL:** Purdue, coached by Stu Holcomb, and Wisconsin, coached by Ivan Williamson
- **BASEBALL:** Illinois, coached by Lee Eilbracht, and Michigan, coached by Ray Fisher
- **GYMNASTICS:** Illinois, coached by Charles Pond
- **BASKETBALL:** Indiana, coached by Branch McCracken
- **CROSS COUNTRY:** Michigan, coached by Don Canham
- **TENNIS:** Indiana, coached by Dale Lewis
- **SWIMMING:** Ohio State, coached by Michael Peppe
- **WRESTLING:** Michigan, coached by Clifford Keen
- **GOLF:** Purdue, coached by Sam Voinoff
- **FENCING:** Illinois, coached by Maxwell Garret

AL BROSKY
Football, Illinois

Imagine the all-time streaks recorded in sport: Joe DiMaggio's 56-game hitting streak or UCLA's record of seven straight NCAA basketball championships. Let's not forget the record of 15 consecutive games with an interception for Illinois' Al Brosky, a first-team all-America safety in 1951 and two-time all-Big Ten pick. His 15-game streak and 29 career interceptions still stand in NCAA record books, although neither total takes into account an interception as Illinois defeated Stanford in the 1952 Rose Bowl—a theft that actually pushes his totals to 16 straight games with an interception and 30 interceptions in 28 college games. Brosky intercepted 11 passes in each of his first two years at Illinois, not bad for a guy who played on the freshman team at St. Louis University. A back injury kept him from pursuing a pro career.

FRANK KUSH
Football, Michigan State

Frank Kush combined explosive speed and quick reactions to become an All-American defensive lineman on Michigan State's 1952 undefeated national champions. The 5-foot-9, 185-pound Pennsylvania native's toughness was legendary. Called State's "hardest physical specimen" by the Spartans' team doctor, Kush lived up to that image as head coach at Arizona State from 1958-79, where he compiled a 176-54-1 record, including an 11-0 mark in 1970 and a 12-0 slate in 1975. He believed discipline was a key not only to winning, but also to steering players in the right direction in life. Kush was inducted into the National Football Foundation's College Hall of Fame in December, 1995. Since retiring from coaching in the NFL and USFL, Kush has worked as an administrator for Arizona Boys Ranch, a Phoenix-area home for wayward youngsters.

YOSHI OYAKAWA
Swimming, Ohio State

It's easy to say that Yoshi Oyakawa made a big splash during his four-year career as a swimmer at Ohio State. A specialist in the backstroke, Oyakawa won 22 major championships during his Buckeye career, the second highest total in Ohio State history when he graduated. He lettered all four years at Ohio State, including his senior season in 1954-55 when he served as Buckeye captain. He competed on three NCAA championship teams and four squads that won Big Ten titles. A participant in the 1952 Helsinki Olympics and the 1956 Melbourne Olympics, Oyakawa won seven NCAA titles, including four consecutive championships in the 200-yard backstroke. In 1953, he broke the American record in the event and set the world record in the 100-yard backstroke in '54. He was a three-time All-American.

DON SCHLUNDT
Basketball, Indiana

Don Schlundt was a player ahead of his time. He stood 6-foot-9, four or five inches taller than many of the centers he played against, and he had rare agility for a man his size. Able to play at Indiana as a freshman because of the Korean War, he was so dominant that he became the Big Ten's career scoring leader during his sophomore season in 1953, when he was named the Big Ten's MVP and led the Hoosiers to the NCAA championship, scoring 30 points in the final game against Kansas. He was voted college basketball's Player of the Year in 1955, but wasn't impressed by a $5,500 offer from the NBA's Syracuse Nationals. He became a highly successful insurance salesman instead. Schlundt died of a rare form of cancer in 1983 at the age of 52.

LEADING THE WAY

DICK SIEBERT
Minnesota

Dick Siebert could have enjoyed a lengthy, fulfilling career as a Major League Baseball first baseman or as a Lutheran minister. But he found his true calling as coach of the Minnesota baseball team, which he guided to unprecedented success during a remarkable 31-year tenure. A former big league player who once considered joining the clergy, Siebert took the Gopher reins in 1947 after playing stints with the Brooklyn Dodgers, St. Louis Cardinals and Philadelphia Athletics. He was a career .290 hitter and worked briefly as a sports radio announcer and a Minnesota assistant coach prior to taking over as head coach. Nicknamed "The Chief," Siebert led the Gophers to 11 Big Ten championships and three NCAA titles (1956, '60 and '64). His teams won a combined 754 games and endured only three losing seasons. He was named college baseball's coach of the year twice; is a member of the College Baseball Hall of Fame; and is a former recipient of college baseball's highest award, the Lefty Gomez Trophy. His former players include ex-big league stars Dave Winfield, Paul Molitor, Steve Comer, Mike Sadek, and Paul Giel, who later served as Minnesota's athletic director. Siebert retired in 1981 at age 56 and died 10 years later at 66.

· BIG TEN PIONEERS ·

Wisconsin's First Rose Bowl Appearance

Led by legendary running back Alan Ameche and a powerful defense, Wisconsin made its first Rose Bowl appearance in 1953. The Badgers were one-touchdown underdogs against USC and indeed found themselves on the losing end of a 7-0 score. The defeat broke a seven-year Rose Bowl winning streak for the Big Ten against Pac 10 opponents. But the game was still a moral victory of sorts for Wisconsin, which played one of its best — if not its best — games of the season in the losing effort. The Badgers surrendered the game's only touchdown in the third quarter when Al Carmichael caught a touchdown pass from quarterback Rudy Bukich, capping a nine-play, 73-yard drive. Wisconsin was unable to answer offensively despite the exceptional running of Ameche, who rushed for a game-high 138 yards on 26 attempts.

Academic Achievements

Want to know how the vote will turn out for a presidential race? Need to know how the public feels about race relations? Or maybe you're curious about how workers like their employers? All those questions and more are routinely asked by the Gallup Poll, founded at The University of Iowa by George Gallup.

The BIG TEN's First 100 Years

Big Ten Football Scoring Records
(Conference Games Only)

Most Points

Game	107	Michigan 107, Iowa 0, 1902
Game (by both teams)	115	Minnesota 59, Purdue 56, 1993
Season Average	48.1	Penn State, 1994
Season (by opponents)	64.0	Chicago, 1939

Fewest Points

Season Average	0	Chicago, 1939
Season (by opponent)	3.8	Illinois, 1951

1952-53 Conference MEDAL OF HONOR Winners

ILLINOIS	Clive Follmer
INDIANA	George E. Branam
IOWA	J. Burton Britzmann
MICHIGAN	David J. Tinkham
MICHIGAN STATE	John D. Wilson
MINNESOTA	Robert D. Gelle
NORTHWESTERN	Raymond W. Huizinga
OHIO STATE	Jerry F. Wellbourn
PURDUE	Walter R. Viellien
WISCONSIN	James T. Moran

THE BIG EVENT

Michigan State goes to Rose Bowl in first football season

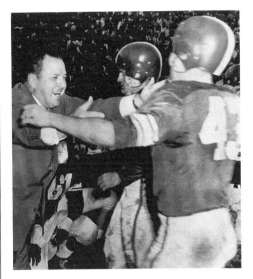

After three straight undefeated seasons that included the 1952 national championship, Coach Biggie Munn's '53 Michigan State team was primed for its first Big Ten season. The Spartans won their first four games, extending their win streak to 28, before being stunned 6-0 by previously winless Purdue. Although State won its last four games to finish 8-1 overall, 5-1 in the Conference, MSU's drive to the Rose Bowl came down to a vote in the proverbial smoke-filled room. State and Illinois, which didn't play one another, had tied for the Conference crown and although Illinois was 7-1-1 overall, a telephone vote by athletic directors to determine the Rose Bowl representative was needed. When a 5-5 tie was clearly firm, Commissioner Tug Wilson summoned the directors to Chicago, where, after more discussion, State got the nod. (It proved to be a good choice: the Spartans beat UCLA 28-20.)

OTHER MEMORABLE EVENTS

- **Ohio State won the NCAA swimming championships.**

- **Ohio State's Paul Ebert gained All-America honors in baseball (as a pitcher) and basketball.**

- **Michigan State's Tom Yewcic was named the most outstanding player at the College World Series.**

- **Michigan's Norvard Nalon won his second straight NCAA wrestling title, and Illinois' Willie Williams won his second straight NCAA 100-yard dash championship.**

- **Iowa's Rich Ferguson won his second straight Conference cross country title.**

- **Purdue's Don Albert shot a record 136 to win the NCAA golf medalist honors.**

Illinois continues fencing domination

1953-54 fencing squad

The fencing program at Illinois could be called a dynasty in the 1950s. In that decade, the Illini won two NCAA titles and earned the Big Ten championship in seven of those years. As a sophomore, Herman "Pete" Velasco sparked Illinois to its fifth straight Big Ten championship after Illinois was 8-2 in the dual meet season. Illinois later placed eighth in the NCAA championship when Velasco finished second, earning him All-America honors and most valuable Illini. In the dual meet season, Illinois had a string of 36 consecutive wins ended by a 15-12 loss to Notre Dame, but the Illini came back to win the Big Ten title by scoring 40 points, well ahead of second-place Wisconsin's 31 points and third-place Ohio State's 30 points. Illinois' success was built under coach Max Garret, who guided the Illini to seven Big Ten championsips, two NCAA titles and a dual meet record of 243-71-1 in 27 years as coach.

OTHER BIG TEN CHAMPIONS

- **FOOTBALL:** Illinois, coached by Ray Eliot, and Michigan State, coached by Clarence "Biggie" Munn
- **BASEBALL:** Michigan State, coached by John Kobs
- **GYMNASTICS:** Illinois, coached by Charles Pond
- **OUTDOOR TRACK:** Illinois, coached by Leo Johnson
- **INDOOR TRACK:** Illinois, coached by Leo Johnson
- **BASKETBALL:** Indiana, coached by Branch McCracken
- **CROSS COUNTRY:** Michigan, coached by Don Canham
- **TENNIS:** Indiana, coached by Dale Lewis
- **SWIMMING:** Ohio State, coached by Michael Peppe
- **WRESTLING:** Purdue, coached by C.C. Reeck

PAUL EBERT
Basketball and Baseball, Ohio State

As a baseball pitcher, Paul Ebert won 21 of 28 games during his career as a three-year starter at Ohio State. He was 13-4 in Big Ten play, and his best year was a spotless 7-0 mark in his sophomore season in 1952. On the basketball court, Ebert was a three-year starter, the Buckeyes' team captain in his senior year and was a three-time All-Big Ten pick. The 6-foot-4, 188-pounder from Columbus averaged 23.4 points a game, leading Ohio State to an 11-11 record. As a junior the previous season, Ebert averaged 21.7 points for a team that finished 10-12. In his first season with the varsity, Ebert averaged 20.1 points, and the Buckeyes ended the regular season with an 8-14 mark. Ebert played for coach Floyd Stahl.

DICK GARMAKER
Basketball, Minnesota

A prolific scorer with a golden shooting touch and a knack for scoring under the basket, Dick Garmaker was widely regarded as one of college basketball's best jump-shot artists in the mid-1950s after transferring from a junior college to Minnesota. He was among the nation's top scorers his junior and senior seasons in 1954 and '55 and was formerly the Gophers' all-time scoring leader. He earned All-Big Ten and All-America honors his junior year after finishing third in the Conference in scoring and leading the Gophers in field goal percentage. He was All-Conference and a first team All-American as a senior after averaging 24.6 points a game. He was the only Big Ten player to be recognized as a first team All-American that year, as Indiana star Don Schlundt and Ohio State standout Robin Freeman were named to the second team. Garmaker was also an outstanding defender, as he was part of a Gophers squad that led the Big Ten in defense in 1955.

J.C. CAROLINE
Football, Illinois

Though he played for only two seasons, J.C. Caroline made a tremendous impact on the college football scene, ultimately being named as a hall of famer. The personable South Carolinian made headlines as a sophomore, rushing for a Big Ten record 1,256 yards in 1953, shattering Red Grange's Illini single-season mark. Of the myriad of stars Ray Eliot coached during his 18 years at Illinois, the veteran mentor rated Caroline at the very top. Having averaged six yards per carry from scrimmage—1,696 yards on 287 attempts—who can argue with Eliot's choice? In 1956, coach George Halas of the Chicago Bears inked Caroline after only one year in the Canadian Football League, converting him into a defensive back. He retired as a player in 1965 after 10 seasons with the Bears, earning all-pro honors and being a member of three NFL championship teams. Caroline served as an assistant coach at Illinois from 1967-76, then coached at Urbana (Ill.) High School. He continues to live in Urbana and works as a teacher in that city's school system.

TOM YEWCIC
Football and Baseball, Michigan State

Tom Yewcic was a man for nearly all seasons at Michigan State in the early 1950s as the Spartans entered the Big Ten and promptly ascended to its top ranks. His stellar play at quarterback led State to the 1952 national title and its first Big Ten crown and Rose Bowl appearance in 1953. And Yewcic's three-year stats showed 78 completions in 182 attempts for 1,480 yards and 18 touchdowns. Despite those credentials, Yewcic opted for the glamor of a potential professional baseball career rather than the still growing NFL. A power-hitting catcher with a good arm, Yewcic mixed his sports for a long time, earning 10 high school letters at Conemaugh, Pa., in football, basketball and baseball.

LEADING THE WAY

RALPH YOUNG
Michigan State

One of the original big men on campus, Ralph Young, Michigan State's longest-serving athletic director, was a major player in the development of intercollegiate athletics at State, in the Midwest and nationally. At 12 pounds reputedly the biggest baby ever born in Crown Point, Ind., Young grew over the years to Orwellian proportions and would admit to being at least 300 pounds. His girth—and stories about his appetite—notwithstanding, Young's accomplishments in 31 years as State's athletic director took the school from its Aggie days to membership in the Big Ten and official designation as a university. Perhaps Mr. Young (as he was addressed by virtually all) saw his school's admission to the Big Ten in 1949 as his proudest moment. But he also made a big imprint as State's track coach from 1924-40, producing 27 All-Americans and four Olympians and, in 1926, joining with Notre Dame's Knute Rockne and Marquette's Conrad Jennings to form the Central Collegiate Conference, a midwest track and field association still in existence. In 1938, he started the NCAA cross country championship meet which would be held at State for the next 26 years. After retiring, Young served three terms in the Michigan legislature. He died in 1962 at age 72. The outdoor track at MSU is named in his honor.

BIG TEN E LIST

OHIO STATE SWIM CHAMPS

Ohio State swimmers won a record nine titles at the 1954 NCAA championships:

Richard Cleveland:
　　50-yard freestyle
　　100-yard freestyle
Ford Konno:
　　440-yard freestyle
　　1,500-meter freestyle
Yoshi Oyakawa:
　　100-yard backstroke
　　200-yard backstroke
Fletcher Gilder:
　　one-meter diving
Morley Shapiro:
　　three-meter diving
Relay Team:
　　300-yard medley

Academic Achievements

O ne of the things that makes the Big Ten unique as a conference is that its member institutions also collaborate on academic and research initiatives. Much of this collaboration is facilitated through two consortia, the Committee on Institutional Cooperation (CIC) and the Midwest Universities Consortium for International Activities (MUCIA).

1953-54
Conference MEDAL OF HONOR
Winners

ILLINOIS	Robert Lenzini
INDIANA	E. Duane Gomer
IOWA	William Fenton
MICHIGAN	Richard E. Balzhiser
MICHIGAN STATE	Bob Hoke
MINNESOTA	Paul R. Giel
NORTHWESTERN	Lawrence E. Kurka
OHIO STATE	Paul Allen Ebert
PURDUE	Gene R. Matthews
WISCONSIN	Norbert J. Esser

THE BIG EVENT

1954 Ohio State football squad

Buckeyes win "Quagmire Bowl"

Rainy conditions turned the Rose Bowl into what one report described as the Quagmire Bowl, but there was little that was going to slow down the Ohio State Buckeyes that season under coach Woody Hayes. Already the Big Ten champions, Ohio State finished the season with a 10-0 record and the national championship, winning the Rose Bowl for the second time in three appearances and ninth for the Big Ten since it joined with the Pacific Coast Conference in the Rose Bowl agreement. The muddy conditions didn't slow the Buckeyes against Southern California, who gained 304 yards — just 16 short of the record — behind the running of Hopalong Cassady's 92 yards. Ohio State marched 77 yards for a fourth-quarter touchdown to put the game away, and Hayes was left with the first of three national championships.

OTHER MEMORABLE EVENTS

- Iowa wins its first Big Ten basketball title since 1945.

- Illinois won the NCAA gymnastics championships, but Michigan State's Carlton Rintz won three NCAA titles.

- Ohio State won the NCAA swimming title, led by Yoshi Oyakawa's fourth straight title in the 200 backstroke.

- Minnesota and Purdue played six overtimes, the longest basketball game in Conference history.

- Michigan won the NCAA hockey title.

- Purdue's Joe Campbell won the NCAA golf championship.

- Illinois' Herman Velasco won the NCAA foil fencing title.

- Wisconsin's Alan Ameche won the Heisman Trophy.

- Michigan breaks Illinois' Big Ten track grip by sweeping the indoor and outdoor chmpionships.

Illini gymnastics team creates dynasty

The gymnastics team at Illinois was the sport's dynasty in the 1950s, as Illinois strung together 11 consecutive Big Ten championships, a run that concluded with the 1959-60 season. The success has been unmatched in Big Ten gymnastics, but the pinnacle to Illinois gymnastics came under coach Charlie Pond in 1954-55 and 1955-56, when the Illini won back-to-back NCAA titles. In 1955, the Illini earned the title even though Illinois didn't record one single individual title. The Illini offset the lack of individual championship points with depth, at least two athletes scored in every event except the rings. Illinois' Jeff Austin finished as the runner-up in the trampoline. Illinois captain Tom Gardner was fifth in the all-around, followed by teammates Tony Hlinka (sixth) and Dick Jirus (seventh). The depth allowed Illinois to amass 82.5 points, enough to earn first ahead of runner-up Penn State's 69. A year later, Pond's outfit nearly doubled runner-up Penn State's score, finishing with a 123.5-67.5 advantage to capture a second straight NCAA crown. The margin of victory is the second greatest in the history of the NCAA championships.

OTHER BIG TEN CHAMPIONS

- **FOOTBALL:** Ohio State, coached by Woody Hayes
- **BASEBALL:** Ohio State, coached by Martin Karow
- **OUTDOOR TRACK:** Michigan, coached by Don Canham
- **INDOOR TRACK:** Michigan, coached by Don Canham
- **BASKETBALL:** Iowa, coached by Frank O'Connor
- **CROSS COUNTRY:** Michigan, coached by Don Canham
- **TENNIS:** Michigan, coached by William Murphy
- **SWIMMING:** Ohio State, coached by Michael Peppe
- **WRESTLING:** Michigan, coached by Clifford Keen
- **GOLF:** Purdue, coached by Sam Voinoff
- **FENCING:** Wisconsin, coached by Archie Simonson

ALAN AMECHE
Football, Wisconsin

Regarded as one of the greatest football players in Wisconsin history, Alan Ameche was known as "The Horse" during his stellar four-year career from 1951-54. A standout since his freshman season, he led the Badgers in rushing all four seasons and was named All-Big Ten three times (1952, '53, '54). Ameche was a three-time first team All-American and led Wisconsin to the 1952 Rose Bowl against USC. He was the 1954 Heisman Trophy winner and won the Walter Camp Trophy, awarded to the top collegiate player of the year. His four-year career rushing total of 3,212 yards was an NCAA record, which has since been broken. Ameche rushed for 824 yards as a freshman; 946 as a sophomore; 801 as a junior; and 641 as a senior. His career-best game was a 200-yard outing his freshman year in the season-finale against Minnesota. He later enjoyed a fine career in the NFL.

CARLTON RINTZ
Gymnastics, Michigan State

Superman masquerading as Carlton Rintz? Carlton Rintz as Michigan State's top athlete? Perhaps and perhaps. The scholarly looking, bespectacled engineering major from Quarryville, Pa., didn't look like gymnastics' version of the caped crusader nor, for that matter, like your "typical" athlete. But looks were deceiving. Rintz, possibly the finest gymnast ever to wear Spartan green, climaxed his senior year in 1955 by winning three NCAA individual titles and scoring what was believed to be a record number of points. That performance came on the heels of a senior campaign in which he captured 23 first places and four seconds in 31 performances, including all-around, rings and sidehorse titles in the Big Ten. His sophomore and junior seasons had been no less exceptional, with six previous Big Ten crowns and an NCAA win. Rintz is a member of Michigan State's athletic hall of fame.

LEN DAWSON
Football, Purdue

He couldn't have gotten off to a better start. In Len Dawson's first game as Purdue's quarterback in 1954, he threw four TD passes in a 31-0 victory over Missouri. In his second game, he threw four TD passes in a 27-14 victory over Notre Dame. Dawson hooked up with receiver Erich Barnes for a 95-yard touchdown pass in 1955, setting a Big Ten record for longest pass play. He was first-team All-Big Ten in 1954 and became Purdue's first academic All-American in 1956. The Alliance, Ohio, native threw for 3,325 yards and 29 touchdown passes in his college career. Dawson was a first-round draft pick of the Pittsburgh Steelers in 1957 and played in the NFL through 1975. He led the Kansas City Chiefs to three American Football League titles and a victory over Minnesota in the 1970 Super Bowl. Dawson was inducted to the Pro Football Hall of Fame in 1987. In 1973, he was voted the NFL's Man of the Year for his charity work. He was inductrd into Purdue's Hall of Fame in 1996.

JOE CAMPBELL
Golf, Purdue

He wasn't allowed to compete on the varsity level as a freshman, but when Purdue's Joe Campbell hit the golf course as a sophomore, he made up for lost time. He finished second in the Big Ten Conference championship, then went on to win the NCAA Individual Medalist title. That would be his only national championship, though he won Big Ten titles his last two years. Campbell also played three years on Purdue's basketball team, lettering twice and being named captain as a senior. He was the team's No. 3 scorer in 1956-57. After a successful stint on the PGA Tour, which included five Tennessee State PGA titles, Campbell returned to Purdue as the golf coach in 1973. Through his retirement in 1993, his teams went 1,485-1,226-25 in invitationals and championship meets. Purdue won the 1981 Big Ten title under Campbell and finished second in 1985. He was named Rookie of the Year by Golf Digest in 1961 when he won the Beaumont Open—his first PGA event. He was PGA Player of the Year in Tennessee in 1969. Campbell is a member of the Indiana Golf Hall of Fame.

LEADING THE WAY

CHARLES POND
Illinois

He was a boxer, football player and gymnast during his college days, but Charles Pond is best known for his work as gymnastics coach at Illinois. He led the Illini to four NCAA titles, including back-to-back NCAA championships in the 1954-55 and 1955-56 seasons. The final NCAA title came in the 1957-58 season — when Illinois and Michigan State actually shared the NCAA championship — as Illinois finished a run of three national titles in four years. His Illinois teams dominated the Big Ten, winning 11 straight Conferences titles, a streak that ended in the 1959-60 season, a mark that stood unmatched in any Big Ten sport until Indiana swimmers won their 12th straight title in the 1972-73 season. The inventor of the sunken tumbling pit, Pond coached 11 Olympic performers, 19 American AAU champions, 23 NCAA champions and 47 Big Ten champions. Pond retired in 1973. Illini teams won 70.9 percent of their dual matches, posting a 142-66-1 record in 24 years under Pond. Among his most proiminent Illini were 1952 Olympic gold medalist David "Skip' Browning and 1952 NCAA champ Frank Bare, a former USGF director.

BIG TEN ENLISTS

SPARTAN BASEBALL STARS

Michigan State tied a modern-day record with 11 wins in the 1954 Big Ten baseball season, then added 10 more victories in 1955. Among the Spartan stars in the 1950s were these All-Conference selections:

Darrell Lindley, OF, 1951
Charles Matthews, 1B, 1954-55
Jack Risch, CF, 1954
Tom Yewcic, C, 1954
Bob Powell, LF, 1955
Dick Idzkowski, P, 1955
Jim Sack, LF, 1956
Roscoe Davis, 1B, 1957
Alan Luce, C, 1957
Frank Palamara, 2B, 1958
Dean Look, CF, 1958
Ron Perranoski, P, 1958
John Fleser, LF, 1959
Dick Radatz, P, 1959

Academic Achievements

Among the most famous alumni from Purdue are: astronaut Neil Armstrong, Eli Lilly & Co. president, Richard D. Wood; C-SPAN founder, Brian Lamb; author Booth Tarkington; popcorn king, Orville Redenbacher; actor George Peppard; Nobel Laureate, Ben Roy Mottelson; Zurich Opera tenor, Robert Gambill; Bechtel Corp. chairman, Stephen D. Bechtel, Jr.; and Campbell Soup Co. V.P., Zoe E. Coulson.

1954-55 Conference MEDAL OF HONOR Winners

ILLINOIS	Edwin G. Jackson, Jr.
INDIANA	Arthur Michael Cusick
IOWA	LeRoy Anton Ebert
MICHIGAN	J. Daniel Cline
MICHIGAN STATE	R. Kevan Gosper
MINNESOTA	Charles J. Mencel
NORTHWESTERN	Sigmund Niepokoj
OHIO STATE	Richard Allen Young
PURDUE	Dennis C. Blind
WISCONSIN	Richard W. Cable

1955-1964

Jerry's IGA

is
HOMETOWN PROUD
of Illinois' Linebacker Tradition

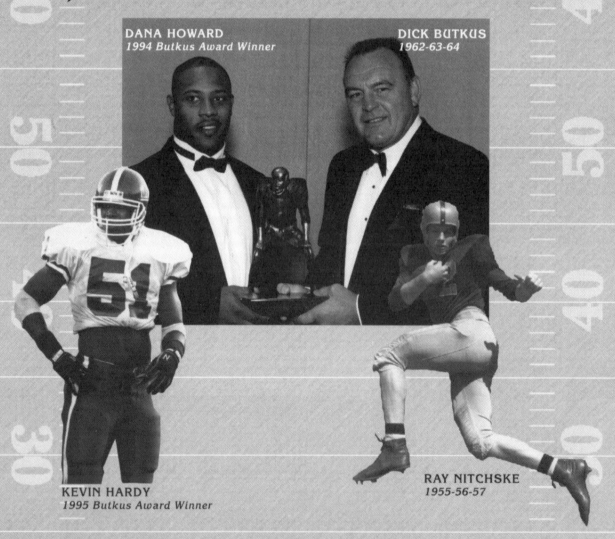

DANA HOWARD
1994 Butkus Award Winner

DICK BUTKUS
1962-63-64

KEVIN HARDY
1995 Butkus Award Winner

RAY NITCHSKE
1955-56-57

Serving Illini fans with locations throughout
Champaign-Urbana

THE BIG EVENT

Minnesota wins College World Series

1956 Minnesota baseball team

Heading into the 1956 campaign, coach Dick Siebert's Minnesota baseball team had reason to be optimistic. The Gophers were coming off a 19-9 season the previous spring and were confident of making a legitimate bid for the Big Ten Conference championship. The Gophers met that stated objective and another less-calculated one—the NCAA championship. The Gophers featured a superb blend of dominating pitching, intimidating hitting and smooth fielding. Led on the mound by star pitcher Jerry Thomas, who was 5-0 in Conference games, the Gophers won the first of what would be 11 Big Ten championships and three NCAA titles under Siebert. Leading the way offensively were sluggers Jerry Kindall, the league batting champion shortstop, and third baseman John McCartan. The Gophers hit .320 as a team and boasted a .976 fielding percentage. Besides winning the team's first NCAA title, the Conference championship ended an 18-year drought for Gopher baseball teams, which were typically disadvantaged geographically against southern teams which have the luxury of lengthier periods of temperate practicing weather.

OTHER MEMORABLE EVENTS

- Purdue claimed its second straight golf title and its third in the last four years.

- Ohio State's Howard Cassady won the Heisman Trophy.

- Illinois won the NCAA fencing and gymnastics championships, while Ohio State won the NCAA swimming title and Michigan State the national cross country championship.

- Iowa's Calvin Jones won the Outland Trophy, given to the nation's top lineman.

- Ohio State's Rick Jones won the NCAA golf championship, Iowa's Charles Jones the NCAA cross country championship, and Illinois' Don Tonry the NCAA gymnastics all-around title.

- Ohio State's Robin Freeman finished second in the nation in basketball scoring with 32.9 points per game.

- Iowa repeated as basketball champ, the first time that had happened in school history.

Michigan State wins 1955 NCAA cross country title

The proud history of Michigan State cross country teams became just a bit prouder on a snowy, windy 12-degree November day at Old College Field in East Lansing. Placing five runners among the top 30 team finishers—and four among the top six—the Spartans climaxed a brilliant season in the 17th NCAA championship, held every year at East Lansing. It was the fourth of five titles that venerable coach Karl Schlademan would win and the first of a string of four in five years for State. Pacing MSU in the closest NCAA individual finish ever was previously unbeaten sophomore Henry Kennedy, who battled furiously with Iowa's Deacon Jones over the last 300 yards before losing by one-tenth second over the four-mile route. MSU's 46-point total was the third-lowest in meet history at that time and still is among the all-time 10 best scores, Despite winning their fourth Big Ten title in their five years in the Conference, the Spartans were underdogs to Big Seven titlist Kansas, even on their home course. But up-front running early in the race by Kennedy, Gaylord Denslow, Selwyn Jones and Terry Block made MSU a convincing winner by 22 points.

OTHER BIG TEN CHAMPIONS

- **FOOTBALL:** Ohio State, coached by Woody Hayes
- **BASEBALL:** Minnesota, coached by Dick Siebert
- **GYMNASTICS:** Illinois, coached by Charles Pond
- **OUTDOOR TRACK:** Michigan, coached by Don Canham
- **INDOOR TRACK:** Michigan, coached by Don Canham
- **BASKETBALL:** Iowa, coached by Frank O'Connor
- **TENNIS:** Michigan, coached by William Murphy
- **SWIMMING:** Ohio State, coached by Michael Peppe
- **WRESTLING:** Michigan, coached by Clifford Keen
- **GOLF:** Purdue, coached by Sam Voinoff
- **FENCING:** Illinois, coached by Maxwell Garret

HOPALONG CASSADY
Football, Ohio State

He entered the season opener as a freshman named Howard Cassady. By the end of the game, he already scored three touchdowns in a victory over Indiana, and Hopalong Cassady was on his way to becoming a household name. Cassady played in 36 of 37 games during his four-year career, when Ohio State compiled a 29-8 record. As a junior, he was named All-America after gaining 701 yards on a Buckeye team that finished 10-0 and won the first of five national championships for coach Woody Hayes. He gained 964 yards as a senior, when he was named All-America and the Heisman Trophy winner. Also a three-year starter at shortstop, Cassady played for three NFL teams during his pro football career. Cassady lives in Tampa, Fla., but spends his summers as a coach for the Class AAA Columbus Clippers in the New York Yankees organization.

MILT CAMPBELL
Football and Track, Indiana

Milt Campbell gained athletic fame before he arrived at Indiana by winning the national decathlon championship and finishing second in the 1952 Olympics while still a high school student in New Jersey. He competed in football at Indiana, but track remained his primary sport. He won three events in the 1955 Big Ten meet — the low and high hurdles and the discus — as the Hoosiers won the team title. He later won the 120-yard high hurdles in the NCAA meet in Los Angeles, breaking a record that had stood since 1939 and becoming the Hoosiers' first NCAA track champion since 1941. Campbell's greatest achievement came in the 1956 Olympics, when he won the gold medal in the decathlon with an Olympic record 7,937 points.

RICK JONES
Golf, Ohio State

Failing to win the Big Ten individual championship doesn't mean that the NCAA title is out of the question. Ohio State's Tom Nieporte proved that was the case when he didn't win the Big Ten but claimed the NCAA individual title in 1950-51. Rick Jones copied that formula for his own success, winning the NCAA title in the 1955-56 season. It was the third individual title overall for Ohio State and the second of three individual NCAA championships during an 11-year span. During Jones' career, Ohio State won one Big Ten team championship and finished second one year and third in another season.

CHARLES JONES
Cross Country and Track, Iowa

He would eventually become one of the top collegiate long-distance runners in the country, but in 1956 Charles "Deacon" Jones was competing on a much larger stage. He was the only American to qualify for the 3,000-meter steeplechase final at the 1956 Olympic Games in Melbourne, Australia, where he finished ninth overall. During the 1955 cross country season, Jones became the first sophomore to win the national collegiate title. Jones set an NCAA meet record in the 2-mile run in 1957, and set American and meet records at the Amateur Athletic Union championships in the 2-mile steeplechase that same year. Jones set another National AAU meet record in 1958 in the 3,000-meter steeplechase. He was the Big Ten indoor mile, 2-mile and outdoor mile champion in 1957 and '58, and he won the outdoor 2-mile in '57. He also won the 1958 Conference cross country championship.

LEADING THE WAY

DUFFY DAUGHERTY
Michigan State

Sporting a name like "Duffy," a pixie-like grin and a witty tongue that must have kissed the blarney stone, Hugh Duffy Daugherty, it was sometimes said, should have been coaching the Fighting Irish of Notre Dame instead of the Spartans of Michigan State. But a Spartan Daugherty was, to the core, through a 19-year tenure that produced a 109-65-5 record and some of State's greatest teams, including the famous 1966 squad that was tied 10-10 by Notre Dame. That game ended a two-year span during which State went 19-1-1 and earned recognition as national champ in 1965 by UPI and as co-champ with Notre Dame in 1966 by the National Football Foundation and Hall of Fame. The football writers named him national coach of the year for that 1965 season. Daugherty's first MSU team went 3-6 in 1954, but stormed back in '55 to an 8-1 record and Rose Bowl win that garnered him coach of the year honors. All told, Duffy's teams won two Big Ten titles, finished second four times and ranked among the nation's top 10 on seven occasions. State's indoor practice facility was named after Duffy in 1980. Daughtery died at 72 in California in 1987.

BIG TEN LIST

KEEPING UP WITH THE JONESES

The 1955-56 school year was a good one for athletes named Jones. There was Iowa's Charles Jones who won the NCAA cross country title, Ohio State's Rick Jones who won the NCAA golf championship, Michigan State's Selwyn Jones who won the NCAA 10,000-meter run and Iowa's Calvin Jones who won the Outland Trophy as the most outstanding lineman in the nation. Here are some other successful Joneses in Big Ten history:

Willie, Northwestern (basketball team MVP '59 and '60); Gerry, Iowa (basketball team MVP '67; Bill, Iowa (basketball team MVP '88); Tony, Purdue (basketball team MVP '80); Danny, Wisconsin (basketball team MVP '80); Burwell, Michigan (swimming champ '53); Clint, Michigan State (football All-American '66); Gomer, Ohio State (football All-American '35); Howard Harding, Iowa (football coach 1916-23); Thomas, Wisconsin (track coach 1913-48); Richard "Itch", Illinois (baseball coach 1990-); Fred, Minnesota (faculty rep. 1897-1906); James, Ohio State (athletic director 1988-94); Dr. Ruth, Purdue (women's basketball coach 1976-86); Tom, Wisconsin (athletic director 1920-24); Donithy, Ohio State (track champ '82); Elaine, Iowa (track champ '84); Bob, Indiana (wrestling champ '33); Warren, Ohio State (wrestling champ '48); Chris, Iowa (wrestling champ '74); Anthony, Illinois (track champ '94); Bumpy, Michigan (swimming champ '54); Terry, Indiana (baseball All-Conference '76); Dan, Northwestern (baseball All-Conference '91); Robert, Indiana (football team MVP '33); Keith, Illinois (football team MVP '86); and Ernie, Indiana (football team MVP '87).

Academic Achievements

The University of Illinois maintains the oldest agricultural test field in the nation. The Morrow Plots, now surrounded by the central campus, have been an experimental corn field since 1876 and have been designated a National Historic Landmark.

1955-56 Conference MEDAL OF HONOR Winners

ILLINOIS	**Daniel E. Dudas**
INDIANA	**Sam Reed**
IOWA	**Andrew Marc Houg**
MICHIGAN	**James M. Kruthers**
MICHIGAN STATE	**Carl Nystrom**
MINNESOTA	**Darrell R. Cochran**
NORTHWESTERN	**Alfred John Kuhn**
OHIO STATE	**Arthur Charles Borror**
PURDUE	**Joe W. Sexson**
WISCONSIN	**Robert E. Konovsky**

THE BIG EVENT

Michigan takes NCAA net title

Barry MacKay

Second-seeded Barry MacKay's five-set victory over Texas's Sammy Giammalva gave coach William Murphy's Michigan team its first NCAA tennis title at Salt Lake City in 1957. It's the only NCAA championship in the sport by a Big Ten school. Two-time Big Ten singles champ MacKay, playing at top form with deadly placements, outlasted top-seeded Giammalva 6-4, 3-6, 6-2, 3-6, 6-3 to take the singles title and give Michigan 10 points to Tulane's 9, Texas's 7 and Iowa's 5. MacKay and partner Dick Potter, three-time Big Ten doubles champs, lost in the doubles finals.

OTHER MEMORABLE EVENTS

- Michigan State won the NCAA cross country championship; Spartan Henry Kennedy won his second straight Conference title.

- Purdue's Joe Campbell won his second straight Conference golf title, while Wisconsin's Roger Rubendall tied for NCAA golf medalist.

- Illinois' Robert Norman won the first of two NCAA heavyweight wrestling championships.

- Michigan won the NCAA swimming title.

- Lamar Lundy was a basketball and football player at Purdue, then went on to become a member of the Los Angeles Rams' "Fearsome Foursome" defensive line.

Michigan State wins its only Big Ten swimming title

The 1957 Big Ten meet at Minneapolis may have been Coach Charles McCaffree's finest hour in his 27 years as swimming coach at Michigan State. The Spartans won their only Big Ten swimming title with 87 points to 79 for runner-up Michigan and 71 for eight-time defending champ Ohio State, avenging earlier dual meet losses to the two powers. It was the first time since 1936 that a team other than Michigan or OSU had won the Conference crown. State did it with depth, with 12 men scoring in 13 events. The Spartans' only wins came from Paul Reinke in the 100-yard breaststroke and from the freestyle and medley relays. With State leading Michigan by only two points heading into the final event, the medley, it got a much-needed win to cement the title. In that race, Don Nichols matched strokes with his Michigan opponent in the opening backstroke while Reinke moved to the lead in the breaststroke, with butterflyer Rog Harmon and freestyler Frank Parrish maintaining the edge en route to a 3:50 victory. The Spartans went on to finish third in the NCAA championships, with the medley relay also taking the national title.

OTHER BIG TEN CHAMPIONS

- **FOOTBALL:** Iowa, coached by Forest Evashevski
- **BASEBALL:** Northwestern, coached by Freddie Lindstrom
- **GYMNASTICS:** Illinois, coached by Charles Pond
- **OUTDOOR TRACK:** Indiana, coached by Gordon Fisher
- **INDOOR TRACK:** Indiana, coached by Gordon Fisher
- **BASKETBALL:** Indiana, coached by Branch McCracken, and Michigan State, coached by Forrest Anderson
- **CROSS COUNTRY:** Michigan State, coached by Karl Schlademan
- **TENNIS:** Michigan, coached by William Murphy
- **WRESTLING:** Minnesota, coached by Wallace Johnson
- **GOLF:** Wisconsin, coached by John Jamieson
- **FENCING:** Wisconsin, coached by Archie Simonson

TOM HALLER
Football, Illinois

He was a man for all seasons, until major league baseball took Tom Haller away from Illinois with a lucrative signing bonus. An honorable mention All-Big Ten quarterback and a reserve in basketball, Haller's ticket to professional sports came in baseball, where he accepted an offer from the San Francisco Giants. Haller led Illinois to the College World Series in 1957, and he left school just before his junior season in baseball. A portion of his deal with the Giants paid Illinois $2,500, the approximate worth of his scholarship. Haller's ability to bargain paid off during and after his career as a catcher. He played for four teams over a 12-year span, batting .257 with one World Series appearance. A union representative for the Major League Players Association during his playing career, Haller eventually served as general manager for the Chicago White Sox.

FRANK HOWARD
Basketball, Ohio State

A two-time All-Big Ten pick as a forward and an All-American during his junior season when he averaged 20.1 points and set a single-game holiday tournament record with 32 rebounds, Frank Howard eventually made a bigger name for himself on the baseball diamond. He enjoyed a 16-year career in the major leagues, hitting .273 with 382 homers and 1,119 RBIs. He still holds records for most homers in a week (10), most homers in five consecutive games (eight) and most homers in six consecutive games (10). The National League's rookie of the year when he hit .268 with 23 homers and 77 RBIs with the Los Angeles Dodgers, Howard's best years were a seven-year period with the Washington Senators when he averaged 34 homers and 96 RBIs per season. A former manager of the San Diego Padres, Howard coaches third base for the New York Mets.

KEN KRAFT
Wrestling, Northwestern

Ken Kraft achieved notoriety as both a wrestler and wrestling coach at Northwestern, and the two careers fit together seamlessly. As a senior in 1957, Kraft won the Big Ten 167-pound title by going undefeated and winning 10 of 15 matches by falls. The Wildcats' coach, Jack Riley, retired after that season, and Kraft was asked to stay on as interim coach while working on his Master's degree. He took the position on a full-time basis the following year, continuing a 22-year career that brought 128 victories, 105 defeats and six draws. His older brother, Art, who had taken time out for military duty, won the NCAA 157-pound title in 1960 and helped lead the team to a 6-2-2 dual meet record. Kraft also was an active participant on Olympic and NCAA committees and founded the Midlands Wrestling Championships. He's now senior associate athletic director at Northwestern.

JIM PARKER
Football, Ohio State

Jim Parker was the yardstick by which coach Woody Hayes used to measure all the linemen at Ohio State. A guard, Parker was Ohio State's first winner of the Outland Award, given to the nation's top interior collegiate lineman. Parker was a three-year starter and two-time All-American for the Buckeyes who could pull and run block. He won the Outland in his senior season in the 1956-57 school year, and Parker played on Ohio State teams that won 23 of 28 games, finishing as the Buckeyes' MVP as a senior. Parker played on two Big Ten championship teams, including the 1954 national champion. A first-round pick by the Baltimore Colts, Parker was a perennial all-pro pick who is a member of the College Football Hall of Fame, Pro Football Hall of Fame and a charter member of the Ohio State Sports Hall of Fame.

LEADING THE WAY

ROBERT RAY
Iowa

While he joined the faculty at Iowa in 1949, it was in 1956 that Robert Ray became faculty representative, a title he would hold for 27 years—longer than anyone in school history. Ray was NCAA president from 1963-65 and a member of the NCAA's executive committee from 1965-71. He served as dean of Iowa's division of continuing education until September 1982, when he died at age 60. Ray was Iowa's faculty representative to the Big Ten from 1956 until his death. An undergraduate of Coe College, he earned master's and doctorate degrees from Iowa, where he became director of the Institute of Public Affairs when hired in '49. He was dean of the University's Division of Special Services from 1961-63, and in 1981 served as president of the North Central Association of Colleges and Schools. Ray was a member of the third class inducted into the National Iowa Letterman's Club Athletic Hall of Fame in 1991.

HITTING THE BOARDS

The 1950s were a decade for rebounders. Iowa's Charles Darling grabbed 30 in a 1952 game, then was matched the following season by Wisconsin's Paul Morrow. But Indiana's Walt Bellamy topped them both with a record 33 boards. Here are the top rebounding performances in Conference history:

33, Walt Bellamy, Indiana, 1961
30, Charles Darling, Iowa, 1952
30, Paul Morrow, Wisconsin, 1953
30, Jerry Lucas, Ohio State, 1962
29, Jim Pitts, Northwestern, 1965
28, Horace Walker, Michigan State, 1960
28, Walt Bellamy, Indiana, 1961
28, Larry Mikan, Minnesota, 1970

Academic Achievements

In 1956, Michigan State was the first American university to appoint a Dean of International Programs. MSU has formal ties with more than 50 universities worldwide and has an on-campus enrollment of more than 2,200 international students from 108 countries.

1956-57 Conference MEDAL OF HONOR Winners

ILLINOIS	Robert Dintelmann
INDIANA	Harold R. Neal
IOWA	Frank O. Sebolt
MICHIGAN	Terry A. Barr
MICHIGAN STATE	Selwyn Jones
MINNESOTA	Robert D. Hobert
NORTHWESTERN	John Smith
OHIO STATE	Albert M. Wiggins
PURDUE	Joe Campbell
WISCONSIN	Patrick J. Levenhagen

THE BIG EVENT

Illinois ties Michigan State for NCAA gymnastics title

1957-58 Illinois gymnastics team

Illinois won the Big Ten title in 1957-58, but the NCAA title went through Michigan State, the meet's host. Illinois had already won a fencing championship a month earlier, and sought their third national gymnastics championship in the past four years under coach Charlie Pond. Illinois got predicted championships from Abie Grossfeld in the horizontal bars and free exercise events, but it was a junior tumbler named Allan Harvey who gave Illinois its biggest surprise. For the first time in his career, he executed the double back somersault, a performance that netted him second place in tumbling. Michigan State's Ted Muzyczko won a championship on the parallel bars, and the two teams each scored 79 points to finish in a tie for the national championship.

OTHER MEMORABLE EVENTS

- Michigan's Barry MacKay and Dick Potter won their fourth straight Big Ten tennis doubles title.

- Michigan won the NCAA swimming championships.

- Illinois' Art Schankin won the NCAA sabre championship to lead the Illini to the NCAA fencing title.

- Iowa quarterback Randy Duncan led the nation in passing yards, completion percentage and touchdown passes.

- Ohio State earns third football title in four years.

- Indiana repeats as Big Ten basketball champ.

- Iowa wins first and only Big Ten tennis crown.

- Hawkeyes capture first Conference wrestling title in 42 years.

Illinois captures NCAA fencing crown

1958 fencing champions

National titles were nothing unusual at Illinois during the 1957-58 school year. The Illini won two NCAA championships, tying Michigan State for the NCAA gymnastics title. About a month earlier in Lubbock, Tex., the Illini fencers probably weren't in the mood to share, and Illinois won the NCAA fencing title ahead of challengers Columbia, Yale and Navy. Illinois scored 47 points, 21 coming in the sabre from individual champion Art Schankin, 14 in the foil from Abbey Silverstone and 12 from Lee Sentman in the epee. Schankin became the first collegiate fencer to win the NCAA title following an undefeated season, the cap to a career that already saw him place fifth nationally as a sophomore and third as a junior. The Illini also won the Big Ten title on their way to winning seven Conference titles in the 1950s under coach Max Garret. Illinois posted a 243-71-1 mark in the 27 seasons under Garret, also winning the NCAA national championship in the 1955-56 season. Schankin later took over the Illinois program when Garret retired, leading the Illini to a 391-51 record in 21 years, including seven Big Ten titles.

OTHER BIG TEN CHAMPIONS

- **FOOTBALL:** Ohio State, coached by Woody Hayes
- **BASEBALL:** Minnesota, coached by Dick Siebert
- **GYMNASTICS:** Illinois, coached by Charles Pond
- **OUTDOOR TRACK:** Illinois, coached by Leo Johnson
- **INDOOR TRACK:** Illinois, coached by Leo Johnson
- **BASKETBALL:** Indiana, coached by Branch McCracken
- **CROSS COUNTRY:** Michigan State, coached by Karl Schlademan
- **TENNIS:** Iowa, coached by Donald Klotz
- **SWIMMING:** Michigan, coached by Augustus Stager, Jr.
- **WRESTLING:** Iowa, coached by David McCuskey
- **GOLF:** Purdue, coached by Sam Voinoff

GLENN DAVIS
Track, Ohio State

When the talk concerns medals and Ohio State track, the first thought is Jesse Owens. But Ohio State has another runner who won more than a handful of awards. Glenn Davis won 300 medals during his four-year track career that finished in the 1958-59 season. He lettered in all four seasons with Ohio State, and he won the gold medal in the 1956 Olympics in the 400-meter hurdles, setting an Olympic record at 50.1. He established a world record in the 440-yard dash at the Big Ten championships in 1958. In the summer of '58, he competed on a U.S. team that toured Europe and Russia, and Davis won nine of 10 races held in a 14-day span, setting a world record at 49.2 in the 400-meter low hurdles. Before the tour, Davis won NCAA championships in the 440 and the hurdles.

ALEX KARRAS
Football, Iowa

Yes, Alex Karras is the guy who punched the horse in "Blazing Saddles." He's also the defensive tackle who helped lead Iowa to a 35-19 victory over Oregon State in the 1957 Rose Bowl, who was twice named All-America, and who won the Outland Trophy award as the nation's top lineman his senior year. Karras was All-Big Ten two straight years and was chosen by fans to Iowa's all-time football team in 1970. The Gary, Ind., native was a first-round draft pick of the Detroit Lions, with whom he played 12 seasons, building a reputation as a relentless nightmare to opposing quarterbacks. Karras, a four-time NFL Pro Bowler, was later selected to Iowa's Sports Hall of Fame and the College Football Hall of Fame. His acting career started with "Paper Lion" in 1968. He also was on the Monday Night Football broadcast team with Howard Cosell and Frank Gifford.

ABIE GROSSFELD
Gymnastics, Illinois

Abie Grossfeld was a Big Ten gymnastics champion, national champion and two-time Olympian who was Illinois' Athlete of the Year in 1958-59, his senior season. In his three years at Illinois, Grossfeld won seven Big Ten titles and was a member of three Big Ten championship teams, earning the Big Ten's Medal of Honor as Illinois' top scholar-athlete. Grossfeld entered the coaching world in 1963, taking over the head coaching position at Southern Connecticut State. He's led the school to three national titles and coached 27 individuals to national titles, including Olympic bronze medal winner Peter Kormann. Grossfeld was head coach of the U.S. Olympic team in 1972, '84 and '88, after serving as assistant coach for the team in 1964 and '68. The gymnastics Hall of Fame selection resides in Woodbridge, Conn.

BARRY MACKAY
Tennis, Michigan

Barry MacKay, one of the Big Ten's all-time tennis greats, had a hand in five Big Ten tennis titles during a stellar career with Wolverine teams that won three Conference titles in as many years. More notably, he won the NCAA singles crown as a senior in 1957 to pace Michigan to a 10-9 win over Tulane for the national collegiate championship, the only tennis title won by a Big Ten school. MacKay and teammate Dick Potter are still the only doubles team to win three Conference championships. MacKay himself won Big Ten singles titles twice, one of 11 men in Conference history to do so. MacKay went on to become a nationally ranked star.

LEADING THE WAY

HARRY COMBES
Illinois

Earning success as a player and coach at Illinois, Harry Combes played a role in 24 seasons of Illini basketball. A guard and forward at Illinois, Combes was a two-time All-Big Ten pick while playing from 1934-37, twice leading Illinois to Big Ten titles. He also excelled in the classroom, receiving the Big Ten Medal of Honor for academics and athletics. Following a nine-year high school head coaching career, Combes took over the Illinois program prior to the 1947-48 season, and the Illini won three Big Ten titles in his first five years as coach. In 1948-49, 1950-51 and 1951-52, Illinois teams reached the NCAA tournament semifinals and placed third each of those seasons. Combes' 20-year coaching record at Illinois was 316-150, a school record for wins that stood until broken by Lou Henson. Combes' teams loved the fast break, even though he was once chided for losing 102-101 to Indiana. Combes replied: "We made just one mistake. We failed to get possession of the ball for the final shot." He died in 1977 at age 62.

BIG TEN FINALIST

FENCING CHAMPIONSHIPS

Big Ten teams have won five NCAA team championships and 14 individual men's and women's titles.

    1941—Northwestern
    1942—Ohio State
    1956—Illinois
    1958—Illinois
    1995—Penn State
    1996—Penn State

Foil: 1941—Edward McNamara, Northwestern; 1955—Herman Velasco, Illinois; 1992—Olga Chernyak, Penn State; 1993—Olga Kalinovskaya, Penn State; 1994—Olga Kalinovskaya, Penn State; 1995—Olga Kalinovskaya, Penn State; 1996—Olga Kalinovskaya, Penn State..

Sabre: 1958—Art Schankin, Illinois; 1964—Craig Bell, Illinois; 1992—Thomas Strzalkowski, Penn State; 1993—Thomas Strzalkowski, Penn State; 1994—Thomas Strzalkowski, Penn State.

Epee: 1941—G.H. Boland, Illinois; 1942—Ben Burtt, Ohio State; 1966—Bernhardt Hermann, Iowa.

Academic Achievements

Ohio State likes to take its research to the extremes—the extremes of the Earth, that is. OSU's Byrd Polar Research Center studies the Antarctic and the Arctic.

1957-58 Conference MEDAL OF HONOR *Winners*

ILLINOIS	Lee Sentman
INDIANA	Gregory Bell
IOWA	Gary E. Meyer
MICHIGAN	James B. Orwig
MICHIGAN STATE	Robert W. Jasson
MINNESOTA	John W. McCartan
NORTHWESTERN	Tom Scheuerman
OHIO STATE	Donald D. Harper
PURDUE	William R. Stroud
WISCONSIN	Walter V. Holt

THE BIG EVENT

Spartans capture inaugural Big Ten hockey title

Goaltender Joe Selinger earned All-America honors for the Big Ten champion Spartans.

In 1959, Michigan State won the inaugural Big Ten ice hockey championship. In 1981, Minnesota won the last. Although Big Ten hockey has been around, in one form another, since 1895, the league ceased recognizing a champion at the end of the 1981 campaign because of a splintering of its members joining other conferences. Five Big Ten schools sport hockey teams, those being Minnesota, Wisconsin, Michigan, Michigan State, and Ohio State. In 1959, four of those schools belonged to the Western Collegiate Hockey Association. Ohio State never joined and was included in the equivalent of Big Ten standings only three times. In 1982, Michigan and Michigan State joined Ohio State in the Central Collegiate Hockey Association, marking the end of the Big Ten championships. Minnesota, the league's dominant team throughout its history, captured the most titles with 10. Wisconsin, Michigan and Michigan State each won five. Ohio State was shutout. Minnesota's 22 trips to the NCAA tournament is the most by any school in the nation, although Michigan has won more national championships than any team in the country with seven.

OTHER MEMORABLE EVENTS

- Michigan State's Crawford Kennedy won the NCAA cross country championship and led the Spartans to the team title.

- Iowa's Randy Duncan was the first pick in the NFL draft.

- Michigan won the NCAA swimming championship.

- Indiana scored 122 points in a Conference basketball game to set a record that has been topped just twice since then.

- Illinois' Abie Grossfeld won his third consecutive Conference all-around gymnastics title.

- Michigan State averaged 63.7 rebounds a game, still a Conference best.

Michigan State wins its first Big Ten basketball crown

It was a record-breaking 1958-59 season for Coach Forddy Anderson's Michigan State team, which won its first undisputed Big Ten title in its nine years of Conference competition. Its 12-2 Big Ten mark gave State a four-game margin on runner-up Indiana, the largest edge for a Conference champ since 1914. The Spartans, fittingly, nailed down the championship with an 86-82 win over Indiana, the team with which it had shared the 1956-57 title and to which it had finished second in the previous campaign. Pacing the Spartans was "Jumpin' Johnny" Green, an All-America selection whose 16.6 rebounds per game led State. Top scorer for MSU was Bob Anderegg at 19.5 ppg, just ahead of Green's 18.5. Horace Walker and Lance Olson also averaged in double figures. Record-breaking stats for the Big Ten champs showed more wins—19—than any previous MSU squad; a then all-time single game high of 103 points; an 82 point-per-game average; and record home attendance of 103,504 for 11 games. The Spartans went on to beat Marquette, 74-69, in the NCAA Mid East Regional before falling to Louisville, 88-81. Green was named regional MVP.

OTHER BIG TEN CHAMPIONS

- **FOOTBALL:** Iowa, coached by Forest Evashevski
- **BASEBALL:** Minnesota, coached by Dick Siebert
- **GYMNASTICS:** Illinois, coached by Charles Pond
- **OUTDOOR TRACK:** Illinois, coached by Leo Johnson
- **INDOOR TRACK:** Michigan, coached by Don Canham
- **CROSS COUNTRY:** Michigan State, coached by Fran Dittrich
- **TENNIS:** Michigan, coached by William Murphy
- **SWIMMING:** Michigan, coached by Augustus Stager, Jr.
- **WRESTLING:** Minnesota, coached by Wallace Johnson
- **GOLF:** Purdue, coached by Sam Voinoff
- **FENCING:** Wisconsin, coached by Archie Simonson
- **HOCKEY:** Michigan State, coached by Amo Bessone

JOHN GREEN
Basketball, Michigan State

That John Green's nickname was "Jumpin' Johnny" said much about the Michigan State All-American's rebounding ability, which proved integral to MSU's two Conference titles and berths in two NCAA tournaments during his three seasons. At 6-foot-5, Green was not a great scorer, averaging 18.5 points as a senior, but he pulled down 16.6 rebounds a game as State won its first undisputed Conference crown. Green closed his collegiate career with a 29-point, 23-rebound effort in the Spartans' loss to Louisville in the NCAA regional. In State's run to the Final Four in Green's sophomore season, he averaged 19.25 rebounds and 13.5 points a game. Three times All-Big Ten and twice a third-team All-American, Green was the first-team All-America center in 1959 and the Big Ten's MVP. Green, who now lives in Dix Hills, N.Y., has owned a McDonald's restaurant since 1975.

BERNIE ALLEN
Football and Baseball, Purdue

Bernie Allen made his mark at Purdue on the football and baseball fields. He was the Boilermakers' shortstop for three years before going on to a 12-year Major League Baseball career. He decided to attend Purdue only after football coach Jack Mollenkopf agreed to let him miss spring practices so he could play baseball. After being told by Ohio State coach Woody Hayes that he was too small to play Division I football, Allen played three years at Purdue. He was a defensive back as a sophomore and became the quarterback in 1959 when Ross Fichtner was injured in the second game of the season. Allen got his chance to play and defeat Hayes' Buckeyes, 24-21, in a shocking upset during the 1960 season. Allen also led Purdue to an upset of top-ranked Minnesota. The East Liverpool, Ohio, native was Purdue's MVP in 1960. Allen had been offered a free-agent baseball contract with the New York Yankees out of high school but chose to attend Purdue instead. He batted .372 with seven home runs in 1959 and .323 with three homers in 1960. He signed with the Minnesota Twins.

HENRY AND CRAWFORD KENNEDY
Cross country, Michigan State

The Kennedy brothers were famous at Michigan State before another set of Kennedys rose to national prominence. Natives of Glasgow, Scotland, Henry (left) and Crawford (Forddy) (below) Kennedy had a hand in four Big Ten and four NCAA cross country titles for the Spartans in the mid-to-late 1950s. Henry, the elder, was State's first Big Ten cross country champion in 1955 and then repeated the feat in '56 as State totaled 21 points, still the third best score ever in the Conference meet. He also won the 1956 NCAA steeplechase title in track. Forddy, three years younger,  won State's only NCAA individual harrier title in 1958. He won his only Big Ten crown a year later. Both gained advanced degrees, taught in college and coached soccer or cross country teams. They were inducted into the MSU Athletics Hall of Fame in 1992.

GEORGE KERR
Track, Illinois

The most famous Kerr to attend Illinois was Johnny "Red" Kerr, an All-America basketball player in the early 1950s. Later that decade, Illinois found another Kerr, this one with the first name of George. He became the second valuable sprinter to compete for the Illini in track, and before he was through, Kerr won seven Big Ten track championships while competing from 1958-60. Of those seven titles, two were in relay events. Kerr has been compared to Herb McKenley, another Jamaican runner who led Illinois to two NCAA track championships in the 1940s. Kerr set a Big Ten record while winning one title in the 880-yard run, and he also won a gold medal in the Pan American Games. Kerr was an accomplished relay runner, leading Illinois to titles by constantly rallying his team on the final lap of the mile relay.

LEADING THE WAY

FRED TAYLOR
Ohio State

One of his former players is known as the General and has led Indiana to three NCAA titles, but Fred Taylor and his Ohio State teams were generally the team to beat in the Big Ten race in the 1960s. Taylor took over Ohio State prior to the 1958-59 season, putting together an 11-11 season. The following year, the Buckeyes used a group of sophomores — one of them Bob Knight, the legendary Indiana coach — as Ohio State won the NCAA title, defeating defending champ California to complete the season with a 25-3 record. The Buckeyes returned to the title game in each of the next two seasons, finishing as the runner-up both years. The three-year run started the Buckeyes on a streak of six Big Ten championships in the first 10 seasons under Taylor, and he finished his coaching career with a 297-158 record and seven Big Ten championships. A member of the Naismith Basketball Hall of Fame, Taylor coached five All-Americans at Ohio State, where he was the center on the Buckeyes' team that won the Big Ten title in 1949-50. A standout first baseman, he played briefly with the Washington Senators.

CROSS COUNTRY CHAMPIONS

Big Ten runners have captured eight men's NCAA cross country championships and four women's titles.

Men
1939—Walter Mehl, Wisconsin
1941—Fred Wilt, Indiana
1955—Charles Jones, Iowa
1958—Crawford Kennedy, Michigan State
1975—Craig Virgin, Illinois
1985—Timothy Hacker, Wisconsin
1988—Bob Kennedy, Indiana
1992—Bob Kennedy, Indiana

Women
1984—Cathy Branta, Wisconsin
1987—Kimberly Betz, Indiana
1988—Michelle Dekkers, Indiana
1996—Kathy Butler, Wisconsin

Academic Achievements

Purdue has awarded more doctorates in pharmacy than any other university in the nation.

1958-59 Conference MEDAL OF HONOR Winners

ILLINOIS	**Abraham Grossfeld**
INDIANA	**Ronald Walden**
IOWA	**James Van Young**
MICHIGAN	**Walter N. Johnson**
MICHIGAN STATE	**Robert Anderegg**
MINNESOTA	**Leroy J. Gehring**
NORTHWESTERN	**Andy Cvercko**
OHIO STATE	**Larry Pahl Huston**
PURDUE	**Walter Eversman**
WISCONSIN	**Jon R. Hobbs**

THE BIG EVENT

Buckeyes begin championship string

Buckeye basketball fans knew something special was coming during the 1958-59 season, despite an 11-11 record by Ohio State under first-year coach Fred Taylor. A talented group of freshmen scrimmaged against the varsity six times, winning two. A year later as sophomores, the group led Ohio State to the NCAA championship and a 25-3 record. The team's Big Ten championship was the first of an unprecedented five straight Conference titles by the Buckeyes, and the league title was the first for Ohio State since Taylor was a center on the 1949-50 team. The Buckeyes were led by sophomore center Jerry Lucas, who averaged 26.3 points and 16.3 rebounds. Ohio State defeated New York University in the NCAA semifinals, and the Buckeyes pulled away for a convincing 75-55 win over defending champion California in the title game.

OTHER MEMORABLE EVENTS

- Minnesota won the NCAA baseball championship with second baseman John Erickson chosen the tourney's most outstanding player.

- Michigan State won the NCAA cross country title for the fifth time in eight years.

- Purdue's Gene Francis was the NCAA golf medalist, while teammate John Konsek won his third consecutive Conference golf title.

- Ohio State's Jerry Lucas became the first Conference basketball player to record more than 400 rebounds (442) in an entire season, but Michigan State's Horace Walker had a record 256 (18.3 per game) in Conference games only.

- A total of 28 Conference athletes competed in the summer Olympics.

- Boxing had its final national collegiate tournament with Wisconsin winning two crowns (Brown McGhee and Jerry Turner) and Michigan State one (John Horne).

Michigan State wins NCAA cross country . . . again

Ho-hum. Another cross country season, another Michigan State juggernaut. The Spartans' formula for hill-and-dale success under second year mentor Fran Dittrich didn't change from whatever potion had been used by previous NCAA championship team coaches Lauren Brown and Karl Schlademan, who had guided State to six NCAA titles. In 1959, however, MSU's domination took on even larger dimension, with wins by ridiculously easy margins and only a 28-29 dual meet loss to Western Michigan marring its record. For instance, the Spartans' 17 points in the Conference meet, off a 1-2-3-5-6 finish, still stands as the record. Paced by Conference champ Forddy Kennedy, State then won by 50 over Army in the IC4A meet. The Spartans' 44-120 edge over Houston in the NCAA meet on their home course reflected their supremacy and gave State its eighth NCAA championship, a mark that would stand until 1995. Kennedy, trying for a third straight major title, finished third behind a pair of Houston runners. Dittrich, who would coach State's harriers for 10 years, had in his first two seasons guided the talented Spartans to a harrier's "double triple," winning the Big Ten, IC4A and NCAA titles.

OTHER BIG TEN CHAMPIONS

- **FOOTBALL:** Wisconsin, coached by Milt Bruhn
- **BASEBALL:** Minnesota, coached by Dick Siebert
- **GYMNASTICS:** Illinois, coached by Charles Pond
- **OUTDOOR TRACK:** Illinois, coached by Leo Johnson
- **INDOOR TRACK:** Michigan, coached by Don Canham
- **BASKETBALL:** Ohio State, coached by Fred Taylor
- **TENNIS:** Michigan, coached by William Murphy
- **SWIMMING:** Michigan, coached by Augustus Stager, Jr.
- **WRESTLING:** Michigan, coached by Clifford Keen
- **GOLF:** Purdue, coached by Sam Voinoff
- **FENCING:** Illinois, coached by Maxwell Garret
- **HOCKEY:** Minnesota, coached by John Mariucci

MANNIE JACKSON
Basketball, Illinois

He remembers his first basketball game at Illinois because Mannie Jackson and two of his teammates from his hometown all started for the Illini. But Jackson is remembered at Illinois as the first African-American to serve as team captain as a senior in the 1959-60 season. When his Illini career was completed, Jackson was the school's fifth leading all-time scorer. He played in the NBA one year, but most of Jackson's pro career came with the Harlem Globetrotters. He played with the Globetrotters for a total of three seasons. Jackson began a business career as a contract administrator. Named a senior vice president and corporate officer at Honeywell, Jackson was named one of the 40 most influential African-American executives by one magazine. Jackson remained interested in basketball, and he purchased the Harlem Globetrotters in 1993.

JERRY LUCAS
Basketball, Ohio State

Wilt Chamberlain called him the toughest player he ever faced in the NBA, so just imagine how talented Jerry Lucas was at Ohio State, where he played before knee injuries hindered his game. Lucas won two NBA titles with the New York Knicks and was a seven-time selection for the NBA All-Star Game, but his legend is built around his play at Ohio State, where he became the Big Ten's only three-time MVP in basketball. He led Ohio State to the NCAA title as a sophomore in 1959-60, averaging 26.3 points and 16.3 rebounds. He led the Buckeyes to the NCAA title game in his junior and senior seasons, when he was named the nation's Player of the Year. Lucas shot 62.4 percent — still a school record — and held Ohio State's scoring mark with 1,990 points when he graduated. Ohio State was 78-6 during the Lucas era.

JOHN KONSEK
Golf, Purdue

John Konsek will always have this: he once defeated Jack Nicklaus. Konsek led Purdue to three straight Big Ten Conference golf titles and was medalist all three times, the last time defeating Ohio State's Nicklaus by two strokes. Konsek, a Buffalo N.Y., native was first-team All-America three times. He averaged 73.8, 74.4 and 72 during three years of Conference competition, and he won the league's individual championship three times by shooting 293 (1958), 301 (1959) and 282 (1960). While Nicklaus became a golfing legend, Konsek went on to be a doctor specializing in internal medicine. Konsek was 12 years old when he and Nicklaus squared off for the first time. Nicklaus ended up finishing first and Konsek second in the U.S. Golf Association's National Juniors Tournament when Konsek - who had a two-stroke lead going into the final hole - triple-bogeyed to lose it.

DAN LANPHEAR
Wisconsin, Football

The 1959 football season was a memorable one for Madison, Wis. native Dan Lanphear. Not only did he and his Badger teammates win the Big Ten championship and play in the 1960 Rose Bowl, Lanphear also earned All-America and All-Big Ten honors. In rebounding from an injury-plagued junior season, he will forever be remembered for his 1959 performance against Ohio State, a game in which he recovered a fumble, blocked a punt for a safety, and knocked two Buckeye runners out of the game with bone-jarring hits. Lanphear went on to play defensive end for the American Football League's Houston Oilers and was a member of their league championship teams in 1960 and '61. During his Badger athletic career, he also served as captain of the Wisconsin track and field team.

LEADING THE WAY

BIGGIE MUNN
Michigan State/Minnesota

Biggie Munn's personal motto said it all: "The difference between good and great is a little extra effort." That Clarence L. Munn, "The Big Man," succeeded as much in his 18 years as State's athletic director as in seven years as football coach attested to the extra effort he always put forth. Munn led State to a position of Big Ten prominence in facilities and programs, vying with arch-rival Michigan each year for Conference all-sports supremacy. A native of Grow Township, Minn., Munn played fullback, tackle and guard at Minnesota, winning the Big Ten's MVP award and earning unanimous Big Ten and All-America honors as a senior in 1926. After coaching stops at his alma mater, Albright, Michigan and Syracuse, Munn led his first Spartan squad to a 7-2 mark in 1947 and went on to compile a 54-9-2 mark as State's grid boss. Most notable were the mythical national title in 1952, "Coach of the Year" selection, a share of the Big Ten title and Rose Bowl win in 1953 and the 28-game winning streak from the fourth game of the 1950 season through the fourth game in 1953. Munn died in 1975 at age 66. The ice arena at MSU is named in his honor.

· BIG TEN PIONEERS ·

Jack McCartan
Minnesota

Jack McCartan enjoyed a doubly outstanding career at Minnesota. As a baseball player, he was a standout third baseman for the Gophers and a three-year starter. As a hockey player, he was a three-year star goalie who later led the U.S. Olympic Team to a gold medal. He was awarded the coveted Big Ten Medal of Honor in 1959 and won the Outstanding Alumni Player awards in baseball and hockey that same year. He was a two-time all-American in hockey and was regarded as the Big Ten's top goalie during his playing days. He was also considered to be the Gophers' fastest skater. McCartan was also awarded the E.B. Pierce Memorial Award in 1959, presented to the top athletes in all Big Ten sports.

Academic Achievements

I n 1983, Purdue became one of the first universities in the world to acquire a supercomputer.

The BIG TEN's First 100 Years
Big Ten Women's Soccer As A Varsity Sport

First Year Of Varsity Status		
1981	W	WISCONSIN
1986	S	MICHIGAN STATE
1993		INDIANA
1993		MINNESOTA
1993		OHIO STATE
1994		MICHIGAN
1994	N	NORTHWESTERN
1994		PENN STATE

First Big Ten Championship held November, 1994

1959-60 Conference MEDAL OF HONOR Winners

ILLINOIS	Robert J. Madix
INDIANA	Donald G. Noone
IOWA	William Lloyd Voxman
MICHIGAN	Terry O. Miller
MICHIGAN STATE	Stanley Tarshis
MINNESOTA	Orville Peterson
NORTHWESTERN	Arthur Kraft
OHIO STATE	Richard Lee Rurry
PURDUE	John P. Konsek
WISCONSIN	Dale L. Hackbart

THE BIG EVENT

William Reed becomes
Big Ten's third commissioner

Of the Big Ten's five chief executives, none had more on-the-job training — or credentials — prior to his appointment in 1961 than William R. Reed, who succeeded "Tug" Wilson to become the Conference's third commissioner. Reed had worked for the Big Ten since 1939, when he served as its Service Bureau Director after being hired by the first commissioner, Major John Griffith. As bureau director, Reed created the Big Ten Records Book which is still in use today. He was promoted to assistant commissioner in 1951 and held that post until his promotion to commissioner. He is best remembered for establishing the grants-in-aid regulations that prevent athletes from receiving gifts from alumni to stem illegal recruiting. He also raised the academic requirements for athletes and founded the Big Ten all-academic teams. He died in office May 20, 1971, at age 55 after fighting a long bout with rheumatoid arthritis.

OTHER MEMORABLE EVENTS

- Ohio State's Jerry Lucas was named the national basketball player of the year.

- Minnesota won the national football championship; the Gophers' Tom Brown won the Outland Trophy as the nation's top lineman.

- Purdue, even though it didn't win the Conference title, won the NCAA golf championship. Ohio State's Jack Nicklaus was the NCAA champ.

- Michigan's Bill Freehan batted a record .585 for the Conference baseball season.

- Michigan won the NCAA swimming title.

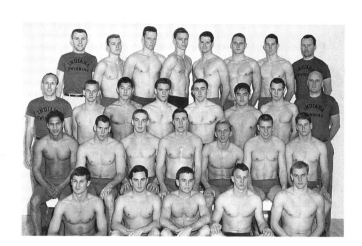

Indiana wins first of 20 swimming titles

Doc Counsilman wasn't quite an overnight sensation when he took over Indiana's swimming program in 1958, but he was close. Once diving coach Hobie Billingsley arrived the following year, the two combined to lead the Hoosiers to a sudden and lasting ride atop the Big Ten. The Hoosiers finished second in the Big Ten in both 1959 and '60, and were third in the NCAA meet both years. They broke through with the first of their 20 consecutive Big Ten titles in 1961 by a mere 3 1/2 points over Michigan, which went on to win the NCAA championship. Indiana's outstanding competitors in the Big Ten meet included Frank McKinney, who set an American, NCAA and Big Ten record in the 200-meter breaststroke with a time of 1:59.8. McKinney also set a Big Ten record in the 100 backstroke. Other winners included Alan Somers, who set a Big Ten record in the 1,500-meter freestyle and broke the Big Ten and NCAA records in the 440-yard freestyle; John Roethke, who set a Big Ten record in the 200 individual medley; Mike Troy, who set a Big Ten record in the 200 butterfly; and Pete Sintz, who won the 220 freestyle.

OTHER BIG TEN CHAMPIONS

- **FOOTBALL:** Iowa, coached by Forest Evashevski, and Minnesota, coached by Murray Warmath
- **BASEBALL:** Michigan, coached by Don Lund
- **GYMNASTICS:** Michigan, coached by Newton Loken
- **OUTDOOR TRACK:** Michigan, coached by Don Canham
- **INDOOR TRACK:** Michigan, coached by Don Canham
- **BASKETBALL:** Ohio State, coached by Fred Taylor
- **CROSS COUNTRY:** Michigan State, coached by Fran Dittrich
- **TENNIS:** Michigan, coached by William Murphy
- **WRESTLING:** Michigan State, coached by Fendley Collins
- **GOLF:** Ohio State, coached by Robert Kepler
- **FENCING:** Illinois, coached by Maxwell Garret
- **HOCKEY:** Michigan, coached by Allen Renfrew

WALT BELLAMY
Basketball, Indiana

Walt Bellamy cut a wide swath through the Big Ten during his career from 1959-61. He led the Hoosiers in scoring, rebounding and field goal percentage all three seasons, and was named the team's MVP each time. He achieved All-Big Ten and All-America status his final two seasons. Nicknamed "Bells," the 6-foot-11, 245-pound center finished his career with averages of 20.6 points and 15.5 rebounds. He was a member of the 1960 gold medal-winning U.S. Olympic basketball team, and was the first player chosen in the 1961 NBA draft, by the Chicago Zephyrs. He was the NBA Rookie of the Year in 1962 when he averaged 31.6 points, and played 14 seasons in the league. He was elected to the Naismith Hall of Fame in 1993.

DON NELSON
Basketball, Iowa

The roots of Don Nelson's brilliant NBA playing and coaching career can be found in Iowa's history books. Nelson was the Hawkeyes' MVP for three straight seasons during which, as a forward and center, he set school records for career points, single-season points, career rebounds, single-season rebounds, most free throws in a game, most free throws in a season and field goal percentage for a season. During the 1960-61 season, Nelson averaged 23.7 ppg and 10.7 rebounds and led the team in scoring 20 of 24 games. He was first-team All-Big Ten as a junior and senior, and was third-team All-America in 1962. A third-round draft pick of the NBA's Chicago Zephyrs in 1962, Nelson went on to score 10,898 career points during 14 pro seasons with Chicago, the Los Angeles Lakers and Boston Celtics. He played on five world championship teams with Boston before retiring in '76. Nelson was an NBA head coach for Milwaukee (1976-87), Golden State (1988-95) and New York (1995-96, 59 games).

JACK NICKLAUS
Golf, Ohio State

When he enrolled at Ohio State in the fall of 1958, Jack Nicklaus was already on his way to becoming the world's greatest golfer of all time. His first major title came before he played a varsity match, winning the U.S. Amateur following his freshman season. Nicklaus won the Big Ten title and the NCAA championship in his junior year in 1960-61, turning pro before he began his senior year. With two U.S. Amateur titles and 18 major titles as a professional, Nicklaus' count of 20 majors is unprecedented. He won his first pro tournament in 1962, taking a playoff over Arnold Palmer to win the U.S. Open. From 1971-73, he finished in the top 10 in 45 of 55 tour events. The six-time Masters winner also won five PGA Championships, four U.S. Open titles and three British Open championships while earning $5.4 million on the PGA tour. He still wins on the Senior Tour.

BILL FREEHAN
Baseball, Michigan

Bill Freehan left a great legacy as a player, both at Michigan and with his hometown Detroit Tigers, for whom he starred for 15 seasons. As a sophomore for the Wolverines in 1961, Freehan batted .446, .585 in Big Ten play, both still single season records, in leading Don Lund's team to the Big Ten title. *Baseball America* selected him as the all-time collegiate catcher for the 1947-64 period. Freehan was an 11-time American League all-star and won five Gold Glove Awards while setting several Tiger records, including best fielding percentage by a catcher in a season (.997) and career fielding chances, putouts and fielding percentage. Freehan returned to his alma mater as head baseball coach in 1990, remaining for six seasons until resigning in 1995. He coached two All-Americans and eight first team All-Conference players. Twenty-six of his players signed professional contracts.

LEADING THE WAY

JAMES "DOC" COUNSILMAN
Indiana

Indiana swimming coach James Counsilman, known around the world as "Doc," was the primary architect behind one of the greatest dynasties in the history of college athletics. He won the Big Ten breaststroke title for Ohio State, then worked as a graduate assistant coach at Illinois and Iowa before taking over as head coach at Indiana in 1958. The Hoosiers won their first Big Ten title in 1961 and proceeded to win 20 in a row. Their run was interrupted for two years by Iowa, but they added three more beginning in 1983. Their streak of NCAA titles was delayed by a four-year probation leveled on the school's athletic program for football recruiting violations, but finally, after three near misses from 1964-66 and a third-place finish in 1967, they broke through with an NCAA title in 1968 and went on to win six in a row. Counsilman coached Indiana for 33 years. His swimmers won more than 200 individual NCAA titles and captured 288 dual meet victories, including 140 in a row from 1966-79. Counsilman, the U.S. Olympic coach in 1964 and '76, was recognized around the world for his research and development of swim strokes. He put his preachings to impressive practice in 1979, when he became the oldest man to swim the English Channel.

B I G T E N L I S T

BASKETBALL SCORERS

Purdue's Terry Dischinger became the first Big Ten player to score 50 or more points in a Conference basketball game in 1961. Here are the top performances:

61— Rick Mount, Purdue, 1970

57— Dave Schellhase, Purdue, 1966

56— Jimmy Rayl, Indiana, 1962

56— Jimmy Rayl, Indiana, 1963

53— Dave Downey, Illinois, 1963

53— Rick Mount, Purdue, 1970 (twice)

52— Terry Dischinger, Purdue, 1961

50— Terry Dischinger, Purdue, 1962

50— Terry Furlow, Michigan State, 1976

 Academic Achievements

The Peace Corps is thankful for the Big Ten. It was on the steps of the Michigan Union in 1960 that the Peace Corps was first announced in a speech by President John F. Kennedy. Today, Wisconsin provides the Corps with more volunteers than any other school in the nation.

1960-61 Conference MEDAL OF HONOR Winners

ILLINOIS	Charles Campbell
INDIANA	Gary V. Long
IOWA	William Buck
MICHIGAN	John D. Gallanders
MICHIGAN STATE	William Reynolds
MINNESOTA	Robert J. Schwarzkopf
NORTHWESTERN	Michael Stock
OHIO STATE	Richard Hoyt
PURDUE	Robert T. Orrill
WISCONSIN	Gerald L. Kulcinski

1961-62

THE BIG EVENT

Michigan claims NCAA baseball crown

As an at-large selection to the 1962 NCAA baseball tournament, Coach Don Lund's Michigan team had nothing to lose. It turned out that they didn't...lose, that is. The Wolverines, behind reliever Jim Bobel's two wins in the College World Series at Omaha, clipped Santa Clara, 5-4, in 15 innings to win their second NCAA baseball title. Bobel was not only a hero on the mound, but also drove in a run in the climactic 15th with a triple and eventually scored the winning run. Michigan had not advanced to Omaha in easy fashion; it took a 5-1 win over Conference champ Illinois and a 3-2 victory over Mid-American champ Western Michigan in an NCAA regional doubleheader at Kalamazoo to keep its tournament hopes alive. Highlighting Series play was a 3-1 win over Texas in which Ron Tate tried to execute a two-out hit-and-run play with Dick Honig, but homered instead.

OTHER MEMORABLE EVENTS

- The Big Ten and Pac-8 entered into a new Rose Bowl agreement.

- Ohio State won the NCAA swimming championship.

- Iowa's Sherwyn Thorson won the NCAA heavyweight wrestling title.

- Illinois' Ray Hadley won the Conference all-around gymnastics title for the second straight year.

- Ohio State's Jerry Lucas was named the national basketball player of the year for the second straight season; the Buckeyes had a 47-game overall and 27-game Big Ten winning streaks snapped.

- Michigan's hockey team went 4-0 for the first undefeated season in league play.

- Ohio State's Bob Ferguson won the Maxwell Award as the top collegiate football player.

Michigan icers win Big Ten, WCHA titles

Michigan won Big Ten and Western Collegiate Hockey Association titles in 1961-62, posting a 22-5 overall mark (4-0 Big Ten, 15-3 WCHA) en route to a third place finish in the NCAA tournament under Coach Al Renfrew. Michigan had winning streaks of nine, five and six games and notched four important regular season wins over Michigan State that were crucial to its championship drive. Leading the charge for the Wolverines was senior Gordon "Red" Berenson, who would become the Wolverines' coach 22 years later after a stellar 17-year NHL career. Vital, too, were the contributions of goalie Bob Gray—who had 15 saves in the NCAA consolation game—and defenseman Don Rodgers. Berenson, the WCHA's MVP, paced that league in scoring with 41 points (24 goals, 17 assists) in 18 games. Eventual national runner-up Clarkson beat Michigan, 5-4, in the NCAA semi-finals but Michigan rallied in the third place game to beat St. Lawrence, 5-1. After the game, Berenson boarded a train for Boston, where he played for the Montreal Canadiens that night against the Bruins, becoming the first collegiate player to move directly into the NHL.

OTHER BIG TEN CHAMPIONS

- **FOOTBALL:** Ohio State, coached by Woody Hayes
- **BASEBALL:** Illinois, coached by Lee Eilbracht
- **GYMNASTICS:** Michigan, coached by Newton Loken
- **OUTDOOR TRACK:** Michigan, coached by Don Canham
- **INDOOR TRACK:** Wisconsin, coached by Charles Walter
- **BASKETBALL:** Ohio State, coached by Fred Taylor
- **CROSS COUNTRY:** Iowa, coached by Francis Cretzmeyer
- **TENNIS:** Michigan, coached by William Murphy
- **SWIMMING:** Indiana, coached by James Counsilman
- **WRESTLING:** Iowa, coached by David McCuskey
- **GOLF:** Indiana, coached by Robert Fitch

BOB FERGUSON
Football, Ohio State

The offense at Ohio State was described as three yards and a cloud of dust under coach Woody Hayes. One of his favorite fullbacks was Bob Ferguson, a three-year starter who finished his career as a two-time all-America pick for the Buckeyes. Virtually unstoppable in short-yardage situations, Ferguson simply bowled over defenders. Once through the line, he had breakaway speed, evidenced by his four runs of 50 yards or more in his junior year. Ferguson led Ohio State in rushing in each of his three seasons on the varsity, compiling 2,162 yards and 26 touchdowns, and he lost yardage on just one carry. As a senior in 1961, he rushed for 938 yards and finished as the runner-up in the balloting for the Heisman Trophy. The Buckeyes were 15-2-1 in his three years, winning the title his senior season.

TERRY DISCHINGER
Basketball, Purdue

Terry Dischinger and Indiana's Jimmy Rayl were battling for the Big Ten scoring title in 1962, and before IU's last game against Ohio State, Dischinger received a telegram from Buckeye stars John Havlicek and Jerry Lucas saying: "You are going to win the scoring race." Dischinger scored 30 that day, and Rayl was held to 10. Dischinger led the Conference in scoring three straight years. The Terre Haute, Ind., native is Purdue's No. 2 all-time rebounder (958) and No. 5 all-time scorer (1,979 points) and has the school's third-highest career scoring average (28.3) and best career rebounding average (13.6). He was a three-time All-American, three-time first-team All-Big Ten pick and three-time Purdue MVP. A sophomore when selected, Dischinger was a starter on the gold-medal winning 1960 U.S. Olympic men's basketball team, along with Lucas, Oscar Robertson, Walt Bellamy, and Jerry West. During a nine-year NBA career, he was a three-time all-star. He was inducted into Purdue's Athletic Hall of Fame in 1996.

TOM WEISKOPF
Golf, Ohio State

Tom Weiskopf didn't stay long at Ohio State. A native of Massillon, Ohio, he played just one year with the Buckeyes, finishing third in the Big Ten championships to cap the 1961-62 season, but not before earning a share of the OSU Scarlet Course record with an 8-under-par 64. Weiskopf spent 19 years on the PGA tour, winning 15 events before temporarily retiring in 1984. The highlight of his career was winning the 1973 British Open, undoubtedly his best season when he scored six tournament victories. At one point in that year, he won five tournaments in a span of eight weeks. A top 60 moneywinner for 17 straight seasons, Weiskopf earned $2.2 million on the PGA tour, and he resurfaced in PGA Senior tour play by winning the U.S. Senior Open in 1995.

GORDON "RED" BERENSON
Hockey, Michigan

Two-time All-American Gordon "Red" Berenson was one of the top players in Michigan history. As a senior, Berenson led the Wolverines to second in the Western Collegiate Hockey Association and third in the NCAA. He was the WCHA's top scorer and MVP. He set a Michigan record with 70 points in just 28 games, and his 43 goals and nine hat tricks remain UM records. After his final game in Michigan's 1962 consolation win over St. Lawrence, Berenson traveled to Boston, where that night he played for the Montreal Canadiens, becoming the first collegiate player to step immediately into the league. In a 17-year NHL career, Berenson scored 261 goals, including four over a 9-minute span, and six overall, in a game against Philadelphia. Berenson guided Michigan to the 1996 NCAA title in his 12th season as coach.

LEADING THE WAY

ARA PARSEGHIAN
Northwestern

Ara Parseghian gained his greatest fame as a football coach at Notre Dame, but prior to that he had tremendous success at Northwestern. Parseghian came to the Wildcats after a successful playing and coaching career at Miami of Ohio, where he compiled a 39-6-1 record. He was hired by Northwestern in 1956 and directed his first team to a 4-4-1 record. His second team failed to win a game — despite having future head coaches Bo Schembechler and Alex Agase on hand as assistant coaches — but he built the program into one of the nation's best. Northwestern achieved the No. 1 ranking in the country for four weeks in 1962, when the Wildcats finished 7-2 and defeated Illinois (45-0), Notre Dame (35-6) and Ohio State (18-14). Parseghian's success over the Irish, whom his teams defeated four consecutive years from 1959-62, induced Notre Dame to hire him away in 1963. He quickly returned the Irish to national prominence and retired in 1974 with a 95-17-4 record. The hall of fame member went on to become a network television commentator, and is widely respected as one of the game's true sportsmen. He lives in South Bend, Ind.

· BIG TEN PIONEERS ·

John Havlicek, Ohio State

Although known as the premier "sixth man" in the NBA while playing for the Boston Celtics, where he was a member of 13 NBA championship teams, Havlicek was a three-year starter for Ohio State, beginning with the NCAA champion team in 1959-60. A two-time All-Big Ten pick, he was a first-team All-American as a senior. A two-time selection on the All-tournament team at the NCAA's Final Four, Havlicek scored 1,223 points as a player at Ohio State. He was also a valuable rebounder, averaging 8.6 boards and ranking 11th all-time at Ohio State. After leaving Ohio State, he was the last player cut after being drafted by the NFL's Cleveland Browns. With the Celtics, he played in 13 NBA all-star games and scored 26,395 points in his career.

Academic Achievements

Everyone who's used a suntan lotion knows about SPF (Sun Protection Factor) levels. There's SPF-4 when you want a fast tan and SPF-32 when you want major protection. But did you know that the SPF rating was developed at Wisconsin's medical school? It was professor Derek Cripps who devised the method to measure protection levels of sunscreen and cosmetic products against ultraviolet light.

The BIG TEN's First 100 Years
The Big Ten In The NCAA Field Hockey Championship

School	APP	W-L	PCT	1ST	2ND	3RD	4TH	
Iowa	14	22-15	.595	1	3	1	2	
Northwestern	12	10-14	.417	0	0	2	2	
Penn Sate	4	4-4	.500	0	0	1	0	
Ohio State	1	0-1	.000	0	0	0	0	
Purdue	1	0-1	.000	0	0	0	0	
Total	32	36-35	.507	1	3	4	4	

1961-62 Conference MEDAL OF HONOR Winners

ILLINOIS	Stuart R. Cohn
INDIANA	William D. Elyea
IOWA	Joen D. Novak
MICHIGAN	Thomas N. Osterland
MICHIGAN STATE	Edward J. Ryan
MINNESOTA	James A. Fischer
NORTHWESTERN	Boyd C. Melvin
OHIO STATE	Roger K. Beck
PURDUE	John D. Vogel
WISCONSIN	Thomas M. Hughbanks

1962-63

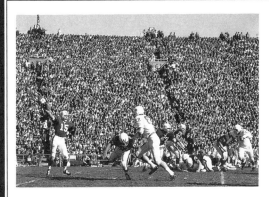

THE BIG EVENT

Badgers lose Rose Bowl's most exciting game

The 1963 Rose Bowl went into the record book as a defeat for Wisconsin. But from virtually every other perspective, coach Milt Bruhn's Badgers were winners despite being on the short end of a 42-37 score against No. 1 USC. A phenom-enal Wisconsin fourth quarter-rally that came up short turned the game into one of the most exciting and memo-rable in storied bowl history. Badger quarterback Ron VanderKelen was the reason why. Trailing 42-14 heading into the fourth quarter, VanderKelen led a furious comeback attempt as Wisconsin scored 23 points and held USC scoreless the rest of the way. But coach John McKay's Trojans with-stood the charge — barely — and were crowned national champions with an 11-0 record. Wisconsin's 37 points were the most ever scored by the losing team, and the teams combined to break or tie 19 Rose Bowl records. VanderKelen passed for a record 401 yards and was voted game MVP. USC quarterback Pete Beathard also enjoyed a spectacular day with a record-tying four touch-down passes, including two to wide receiver Hal Bledsoe.

OTHER MEMORABLE EVENTS

- Michigan won the NCAA gymnastics championship with Gil Larose taking three individual titles.

- Michigan's Richard Nelson (100 breaststroke) and Ohio State's Lou Vitucci (dive) won their third straight NCAA swimming and diving championships.

- Minnesota's Bobby Bell was named the Outland Trophy winner as the nation's top lineman.

- Indiana became the first Conference team to connect on better than 75 percent (75.8) of their free throws over an entire season.

- Northwestern's Marty Riessen won the second of three straight Conference tennis singles titles.

- Conference officials agreed to honor the "Letter of Intent" signed by high school athletes who commit-ted to attend a university.

Michigan gymnasts take Big Ten, NCAA titles

Michigan won the first of its two NCAA gymnastics titles in 1963, scoring 129 points to 73 for Southern Illinois behind champions in six events. Gil Larose had three wins, in the all-around, the horizontal bar and long horse. Mike Henderson tied for the floor exercise championship, Arno Lascari won the parallel bars and Gary Erwin took the first of his two straight trampoline wins. Coach Newt Loken's squad had stormed through a 6-0 dual meet season before decimating its Big Ten competition, scoring 210½ points in the Conference meet for a huge margin over runner-up Iowa (83½). LaRose, Lascari and Jim Hynds were 1-2-3 in the all-around while Lascari took three apparatus titles and Larose two. In a convincing show of dominance, Michigan took 19 of a possible 27 top three places in the Big Ten meet.

OTHER BIG TEN CHAMPIONS

- **FOOTBALL:** Wisconsin, coached by Milt Bruhn
- **BASEBALL:** Illinois, coached by Lee Eilbracht
- **OUTDOOR TRACK:** Iowa, coached by Francis Cretzmeyer
- **INDOOR TRACK:** Iowa, coached by Francis Cretzmeyer, and Michigan, coached by Don Canham
- **BASKETBALL:** Illinois, coached by Harry Combes, and Ohio State, coached by Fred Taylor
- **CROSS COUNTRY:** Michigan State, coached by Fran Dittrich
- **TENNIS:** Northwestern, coached by Clare Riessen
- **SWIMMING:** Indiana, coached by James Counsilman
- **WRESTLING:** Michigan, coached by Clifford Keen
- **GOLF:** Minnesota, coached by Les Bolstad
- **FENCING:** Michigan State, coached by Charles Schmitter
- **HOCKEY:** Minnesota, coached by John Mariucci

BOBBY BELL
Football, Minnesota

A high school quarterback who starred at defensive tackle for Minnesota from 1960-62, Bobby Bell enjoyed a spectacular career as a linebacker in the NFL, where he was an all-pro eight times in an 11-year career with the Kansas City Chiefs that spanned 1963-74. At Minnesota, he anchored a dominating defense that powered the Gophers to consecutive Rose Bowl appearances and a 22-6-1 record between 1960-62. In 1961, the Gophers led the nation in rushing defense after allowing only 52 yards a game. He also played basketball and was the first African-American to play in a varsity game for the Gophers. In football, Bell was a two-time all-American and the recipient of the 1962 Outland Trophy, awarded to college football's top interior lineman. In 1983, he became the first Kansas City Chiefs' player ever inducted into the pro football hall of fame. He was a key member of the 1969 AFL Chiefs' team that shocked the NFL's heavily favored Minnesota Vikings in the Super Bowl.

CLARK GRAEBNER
Tennis, Northwestern

Clark Graebner's tennis career grew beyond his collegiate accomplishments, but that was a good foundation. He teamed with Marty Riessen as a sophomore in 1963 to win the Big Ten doubles championship and helped Northwestern win the Conference team title. He repeated his doubles title with Riessen the following year, and won the No. 2 singles title as well. He won the league's No. 1 singles title as a senior in 1965. He and Riessen received All-America honors as a doubles team in 1964, and Graebner earned the same recognition for his singles play in '65, thus becoming the only two-time tennis All-American in school history. Graebner, a tennis hall of fame member, went on to enjoy a productive professional career and, along with Arthur Ashe, was the subject of a highly regarded book, "Levels of the Game."

JIMMY RAYL
Basketball, Indiana

Nicknamed "The Splendid Splinter" because of his willowy frame, Jimmy Rayl, all 6-foot-1, 145 pounds of him, was one of the greatest shooters ever to play in the Big Ten. He scored 56 points—still IU's all-time single-game scoring record—twice his senior season, against Minnesota and Michigan State, and he did it without the benefit of a three-point line. Rayl shot from just about anywhere once he crossed the midcourt line; 30-footers were almost routine, and some were nearly 40 feet out. Rayl averaged just 4.0 points as a sophomore, but scored 29.8 points per game as a junior and 25.3 as a senior. He earned All-America recognition in 1962 and '63, and later played one full season and part of another for the Indiana Pacers in the American Basketball Association.

PAT RICHTER
Football, Wisconsin

An exceptional all-round athlete who went to Wisconsin on a basketball scholarship, Pat Richter ultimately became one of the Badgers' greatest football players. He won a total of nine varsity letters between 1960 and '63 in football, basketball and baseball. But his greatest exploits were on the gridiron, where he was a two-time All-America wide receiver (1961, '62) and a nine-year player for the NFL's Washington Redskins. In his junior season, he won major "W" awards again in all three sports and was a first team all-conference pick after leading the Big Ten in receiving with 36 catches for 656 yards and seven touchdowns. He was also a first team All-American. His senior year, Richter was co-captain of the Badgers' Big Ten champion football team. He again led the Conference in receiving and punting. He was first team All-Conference, All-America and set a Rose Bowl receiving record with 11 catches for 163 yards. After a successful career in business, Richter currently serves as the athletic director for his alma mater.

LEADING THE WAY

RICHARD LARKINS
Ohio State

He served as athletic director at Ohio State from July, 1946, until his retirement in the fall of 1970, and Richard Larkins guided an athletic program that expanded to a total of 18 varsity sports. The total was the largest of any state university in the nation. The athletic plant was greatly improved with the building of St. John Arena, one of the finest college basketball arenas, a building that seats 13,300 fans with marvelous sight lines. Also built was the French Field House, used for indoor track teams and practice sessions for other sports, and an enclosed baseball field. New athletic department offices were constructed and a facility to house medical, dental and equipment offices, plus locker room spaces and coaches headquarters. Larkins was a firm believer in the value of intercollegiate athletics, adroitly administered and kept in its proper perspective to the college curriculum. He was a guiding for athletic administration in the Conference and NCAA, serving on Conference, NCAA and Rose Bowl committees. Larkin graduated from Ohio State in 1931, and he earned three letters apiece in football and basketball.

ALL-AROUND CHAMPIONS

Big Ten gymnasts have won 12 all-around titles at the NCAA Championships:

1938— Joe Giallombardo, Illinois
1939— Joe Giallombardo, Illinois
1940— Joe Giallombardo, Illinois, and
Paul Fina, Illinois (tie)
1941— Courtney Shanken, Chicago
1942— Newton Loken, Minnesota
1956— Don Tonry, Illinois
1958— Abie Grossfeld, Illinois
1963— Gil Larose, Michigan
1990— Mike Racanelli, Ohio State
1991— John Roethlisberger, Minnesota
1992— John Roethlisberger, Minnesota
1993— John Roethlisberger, Minnesota

Academic Achievements

The University of Illinois campus was the first in the country to provide comprehensive services for those with severe disabilities. The services, facilities and special programs offered make it the most accessible university campus in the nation today.

1962-63
Conference MEDAL OF HONOR
Winners

ILLINOIS	David J. Downey
INDIANA	Chester A. Jastremski
IOWA	Ralph W. Trimble
MICHIGAN	Charles F. Aquino
MICHIGAN STATE	Richard Schloemer
MINNESOTA	Robert J. Bateman
NORTHWESTERN	Paul Flatley
OHIO STATE	Jerry R. Lucas
PURDUE	Ronald S. Meyer
WISCONSIN	Hugh V. (Pat) Richter

THE BIG EVENT

Siebert's Golden Gophers win NCAA title

The 1964 Gophers weren't among legendary coach Dick Siebert's best hitting teams. But they hit well enough to complement a brilliant pitching staff and a stellar defense to propel Minnesota to its third — and final — NCAA championship under Siebert in a victory against Missouri. The Gophers won the Big Ten championship en route to the national title with an 11-3 Conference record. Minnesota ranked seventh in league hitting but was at the top in pitching and fielding. Starting pitchers Joe Pollack and Frank Brosseau sported identical 4-1 Conference records and respective ERAs of 1.50 and 1.56. They were supported by a defensive unit that ranked second in the Conference. Dave Huffman and Al Druskin were regarded as two of college baseball's finest outfielders. Likewise, All-Big Ten catcher Ron Wojciak was renowned as one of the nation's best at his position. But the Gophers weren't devoid of potent hitters. First baseman Bill Davis led the way with his .377 average, while standout second baseman Duane Marcus batted .333.

OTHER MEMORABLE EVENTS

- Ohio State's Gary Bradds was named the national basketball player of the year.

- Wisconsin's Rick Reichardt won his second straight Conference batting crown.

- Michigan won the NCAA hockey championship, led by Tom Polonik, Gordon Wilkie and Bob Gray.

- Illinois' Craig Bell won the NCAA sabre fencing title.

- Illinois' Allen Carius won his second straight Conference cross country championship.

Illini beat Spartans, win Big Ten title

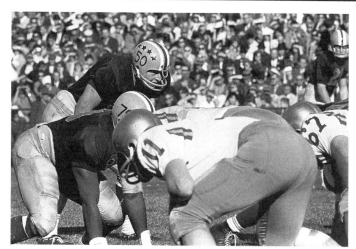

Dick Butkus (50) was a two-time All-American.

It's easy for some people to remember November, 1963. President John F. Kennedy was killed by an assassin's bullet on Nov. 22 that year. His death forced the postponement of the Big Ten showdown between Illinois and Michigan State. Five days later, Illinois made a second trip to Michigan State under coach Pete Elliott to face the fourth-ranked Spartans on Thanksgiving Day. Michigan State featured All-America halfback Sherman Lewis, but Illinois countered with a stifling defense led by linebacker Dick Butkus. The Illinois defense was the difference, causing the Spartans to cough up three fumbles and throw four interceptions in the Illini's 13-0 victory. The Illinois offense was led by fullback Jim Grabowski, who gained 85 yards against Michigan State's respected defense. The triumph gave Illinois its 12th Big Ten title and third trip to the Rose Bowl, where Illinois scored a 17-7 win over Washington for the Illini's third straight win in Rose Bowl appearances. Grabowski gained 125 yards to earn Rose Bowl MVP honors as Illinois rallied from a 7-0 deficit before former President Dwight D. Eisenhower.

OTHER BIG TEN CHAMPIONS

- **BASEBALL:** Minnesota, coached by Dick Siebert
- **GYMNASTICS:** Michigan, coached by Newton Loken
- **OUTDOOR TRACK:** Wisconsin, coached by Charles Walter
- **INDOOR TRACK:** Michigan, coached by Don Canham
- **BASKETBALL:** Michigan, coached by David Strack, and Ohio State, coached by Fred Taylor
- **CROSS COUNTRY:** Michigan State, coached by Fran Dittrich
- **TENNIS:** Indiana, coached by William Landin
- **SWIMMING:** Indiana, coached by James Counsilman
- **WRESTLING:** Michigan, coached by Clifford Keen
- **GOLF:** Purdue, coached by Sam Voinoff
- **FENCING:** Illinois, coached by Maxwell Garret
- **HOCKEY:** Michigan, coached by Al Renfrew

GARY BRADDS
Basketball, Ohio State

A spindly, raw-boned center was able to flex his muscles on the basketball court. Gary Bradds followed legendary Jerry Lucas as the Buckeyes' center, and the 6-foot-8 product of Jamestown, Ohio, made a name for himself at the position. Bradds was a two-time All-American and the national player of the year in his senior season in 1963-64, when he averaged 30.6 points and 13.4 rebounds. Bradds led the Buckeyes to Big Ten titles in his last two seasons, including his senior year when he put together a string of six consecutive games of 40 or more points that set a Big Ten record. A two-time Big Ten MVP, he was a top reserve as a sophomore on the 1961-62 Ohio State team that finished as the NCAA tournament runner-up. Bradds led the Big Ten in scoring in his last two seasons. He is deceased.

JIM GRABOWSKI
Illinois

He broke nearly all of Red Grange's school records at Illinois and played in the first two Super Bowls with the Green Bay Packers during his six-year NFL career, but two-time All-America running back Jim Grabowski was also a first-team Academic All-American in 1964 and '65. He was inducted into the GTE Academic All-America Hall of Fame. Grabowski was just as talented on the gridiron, rushing for 239 yards against Wisconsin to break the single-game school record set by Red Grange and establishing a single-game Big Ten mark. He ended his career with single-season (1,258 yards) and career (2,878) school rushing records. The Rose Bowl MVP in 1964 and the Big Ten's MVP in 1965, Grabowski was a unanimous selection on six All-America teams in 1965, and a first-round pick by the Packers. He owns Motivation Merchandise Company in Palatine, Ill.

RICK REICHARDT
Baseball, Wisconsin

Regarded as one of the greatest baseball players in Wisconsin history, Rick Reichardt was an outstanding hitter, a gifted base stealer, a top-notch centerfielder and a superior all-around player. A career .394 hitter during his two years with the Badgers (1963-64), Reichardt led his team in hitting, home runs and stolen bases each year before signing a Major League Baseball contract with the American League's Los Angeles Angels after his junior season. He was a first team All-American his junior year and was the first player since 1939 to win back-to-back Big Ten batting titles. He hit .343 overall as a sophomore with six home runs and batted .443 as junior. In Big Ten games his junior season, he hit .472 and stole a conference-best nine bases. In overall games, he stole a then-school record 20 bases. Reichardt, a right-hander, was also a star receiver on Wisconsin's football team in 1963, when he led the Big Ten in receiving with 26 catches for 383 yards and a touchdown.

MARTY RIESSEN
Tennis, Northwestern

Marty Riessen, who played for his father Clare at Northwestern, made a clean sweep of the Big Ten tennis titles during his collegiate career. He won the Conference singles and doubles titles from 1962-64, teaming with Jim Erickson for the first doubles title and with fellow All-American Clark Graebner for the next two. Riessen, like Graebner a member of the U.S. Davis Cup team and an International Tennis Association hall of fame member, became one of the country's top professional players following his collegiate career.

LEADING THE WAY

HOBIE BILLINGSLEY
Indiana

Although overshadowed by the success of his coaching partner Doc Counsilman, Hobie Billingsley built an impressive legacy as Indiana's diving coach. Like Counsilman, Billingsley was a Big Ten champion competitor at Ohio State. He arrived at Indiana in 1959, one year after Counsilman, and helped establish a dynasty that included 20 consecutive Big Ten championships and six straight NCAA titles. The two put together teams so talented and so deep some years that many believed their Indiana squads could have competed against an all-star team of collegians from around the country. Billingsley coached 115 national champions, 22 Big Ten champions, three Olympic gold medalists and five world champions. He coached Olympic teams from the U.S. and other countries in 1968, '72, '76 and '80, and was a nine-time diving coach of the year. Billingsley founded the World Diving Coaches Association in 1968 and founded a similar American organization in 1970. A Swimming Hall of Fame member, he also won the 1994 Sammy Lee Award, the highest honor awarded in amateur diving. A noted instructor and author, he ranks as one of the great diving coaches of all time.

· BIG TEN PIONEERS ·

Woodworth Award for SIDS

Robert C. Woodworth set a standard in the sports informational field that would set the tone for years to come. Purdue's athletic publicity director from 1928-64, Woodworth was one of the founders of the Football Writers Association, which twice honored him for outstanding service. He was Purdue's acting athletic director in 1937 and three times was the school's acting news service director. In December 1964, the Big Ten Sports Information Directors Association established the Robert C. Woodworth Award to honor a media member - who is no longer actively covering college sports - for outstanding contributions to the Big Ten and intercollegiate athletics. Woodworth, a Purdue graduate, was born in Chicago and was an Oak Park High School classmate of Ernest Hemingway. Woodworth died in 1964 at the age of 61.

Robert C. Woodworth

Academic Achievements

Did you ever think about how swimming judges used to decide who won a race? After all, with most of the bodies underwater and all the splashing, how did they do it? It was in the 1960s when Michigan physics professor Bill Parkinson addressed that problem and came up with an automatic timing device similar to what is used today. Now times can be measured in a hundredth of a second.

1963-64 Conference MEDAL OF HONOR Winners

ILLINOIS	Richard W. Deller
INDIANA	James L. Binkley
IOWA	Andrew J. Hankins, Jr.
MICHIGAN	Gordon J. Wilke
MICHIGAN STATE	George (Pete) Gent
MINNESOTA	Arthur (Bill) Davis
NORTHWESTERN	Martin C. Riessen
OHIO STATE	Donald H. Flatt
PURDUE	Melvyn J. Garland
WISCONSIN	William R. Smith

THE BIG EVENT

Michigan makes Final Four in second NCAA appearance

Michigan, making only its second appearance in the NCAA basketball tournament, advanced to the 1964 Final Four behind sophomore All-American Cazzie Russell and junior Bill Buntin. Russell paced the Wolverines with a 24.8 average while Buntin scored at a 23.2 clip, leading Michigan to an unbeaten home slate and its first Big Ten title in 16 years. Dave Strack's team defeated Loyola, 84-80, and Ohio, 69-57, to advance to Kansas City, where it ran up against an experienced Duke team in the semis and lost, 91-80. Michigan dropped Kansas State, 100-90, in the third place game. Russell and Buntin again led Michigan to a Conference title encore and NCAA berth in 1965. The Wolverines beat Princeton and two-time All-American Bill Bradley, 93-76, in the semis before losing 91-80, to John Wooden's UCLA Bruins in the national title game.

OTHER MEMORABLE EVENTS

- The Big Ten finally made it official after all the years: team trophies were awarded for football, basketball, baseball and hockey champions.
- The last tumbling championship was awarded at the Conference gymnastics meet.
- Indiana's Jon McGlocklin made 92.3 percent (36-39) of his free throws to set a Conference record that stood for 20 years.
- Michigan pulled down 1,521 rebounds in a single season, still the highest total in Conference basketball history.
- Northwestern's Lee Assenheimer won the first of two straight Conference cross country titles.
- Ohio State's Steve Arlin struck out a record 20 batters at the College World Series. He pitched all 15 innings of the game.

IT'S BEEN A LONG TIME

When Minnesota won the Big Ten cross country title in 1964, it marked the first cross country crown in 50 years for the Golden Gophers. Here are some of the other dry spells for schools in particular sports:

95 years— Northwestern and Purdue track (never have won)
94 years— Indiana and Northwestern gymnastics (never have won), Purdue (never has competed)
87 years— Purdue baseball, 1909-present
86 years— Purdue tennis (never has won)
85 years— Wisconsin and Purdue swimming (never have won)
83 years— Wisconsin and Northwestern wrestling (never have won)

Gopher harriers end 50-year drought

When Minnesota won its first men's Big Ten cross country championship in 1914, little did anyone associated with the Gophers' program know that it would be 50 years before they won another. But when the drought ended in 1964, Gopher harriers found the majesty of their achievement to be worth the wait. Minnesota, under the direction of coach Roy Griak, dominated the meet. The Gophers placed four runners in the top 10 and had three others in the top 20. The ease with which Minnesota won surprised some observers, since the Gophers were predominately underclassmen who didn't have much experience in big meets. But the win didn't surprise the Gophers themselves, who had enjoyed a remarkably successful regular-season campaign. Minnesota was 7-1 in dual meet competition, with its lone loss coming against Michigan State. Minnesota avenged the loss at the Big Ten meet, where the Spartans were a distant runner-up. Leading the way for the Gophers was senior captain Norris Peterson, who finished second in the individual standings. Sophomore Tom Heinonen was fourth, followed by freshmen Bob Weigel in eighth and Dave Wegner, 10th. Other Gophers in the top 20 were freshman John Valentine (11th), junior Mike Elwell (14th) and freshman Stan Gaffin (17th).

OTHER BIG TEN CHAMPIONS

- **FOOTBALL:** Michigan, coached by Chalmers Elliott
- **BASEBALL:** Ohio State, coached by Martin Karow
- **GYMNASTICS:** Michigan, coached by Newton Loken
- **OUTDOOR TRACK:** Michigan State, coached by Fran Dittrich
- **INDOOR TRACK:** Wisconsin, coached by Charles Walter
- **BASKETBALL:** Michigan, coached by David Strack
- **TENNIS:** Michigan, coached by William Murphy
- **SWIMMING:** Indiana, coached by James Counsilman
- **WRESTLING:** Michigan, coached by Clifford Keen
- **GOLF:** Purdue, coached by Sam Voinoff
- **FENCING:** Illinois, coached by Maxwell Garret
- **HOCKEY:** Minnesota, coached by John Mariucci

DICK BUTKUS
Football, Illinois

Just how good was Dick Butkus? Consider this. Butkus was a two-time All-Big Ten and All-America selection playing linebacker and center at Illinois. He was such an imtimidating player that an award in his name is given to the nation's top college linebacker. He was the Big Ten's most valuable player in 1963, and he finished third in voting for the Heisman Trophy, completing his three-year varsity career as the Illini's all-time leading tackler. The No. 50 that Butkus wore at Illinois was retired, one of only two football numbers (Red Grange's 77 the other) retired by the school. A first-ballot selection to the college and pro football halls of fame, Butkus was an eight-time Pro Bowl pick in his nine-year career with the Bears. The game's greatest linebacker, as chosen by a vote of NFL fans, Butkus has stayed busy as a broadcaster, actor and fundraiser.

DAVE SCHELLHASE
Basketball, Purdue

When he completed his career at Purdue, Dave Schellhase was the school's all-time scoring leader. Schellhase was a two-time All-American, three-time All-Big Ten and three-time Purdue MVP. He finished his career with 2,074 points, led the nation in scoring as a senior (32.5 ppg) and was fourth as a junior (29.3 ppg). He earned Academic All-Big Ten honors for three straight years. Schellhase tied a school record for a sophomore by scoring 43 points against Notre Dame, and he set a school record for a senior by scoring 781 points during his final season. Schellhase was picked in the first round of the NBA draft by the Chicago Bulls, with whom he played two years. He later coached at Indiana State and is currently at Moorhead State (Minn.).

GLENN GAILIS
Gymnastics, Iowa

Glenn Gailis had quite a run during his final two years of gymnastics competition at Iowa. Gailis was captain of the Hawkeyes as a senior and at the Big Ten Conference meet he took first place in the all-around competition, the high bar, pommel horse and still rings. He was NCAA champion in the still rings and was named All-America in still rings and all-around. Gailis also received the Big Ten Medal of Honor in '65. During his junior year, he was Big Ten pommel horse champion and a still rings All-American. Gailis was inducted into the National Iowa Letterman's Club Athletic Hall of Fame in 1993.

LOU HUDSON
Basketball, Minnesota

On the basketball court, Lou Hudson was called "Sweet Lou." His smooth shooting touch, rare leaping ability and propensity for scoring points and grabbing rebounds in bunches were the reasons why. During three standout varsity seasons at Minnesota, Hudson established himself as one of the nation's best players, as he averaged 20.4 points and 8.8 rebounds a game from 1964-66. His remarkable seasons with the Gophers, with whom he played for coach John Kundla, launched an even more remarkable career in the NBA, where he played 13 seasons and scored nearly 18,000 points, finishing 12th on the all-time scoring list. His best seasons were with the St. Louis/Atlanta Hawks, where he played nine years and was a six-time all-star. After retiring from the NBA in 1979, Hudson and his family moved to Park City, Utah, where he entered politics and became a city councilman.

LEADING THE WAY

GEORGE SZYPULA
Michigan State

As Michigan State's men's gymnastics coach from 1947-89, George Szypula made the Spartans a regular Conference and national contender and produced 47 Big Ten and 18 NCAA champions. The son of a father who was a circus performer, Szypula came by gymnastics naturally, beginning training as a tumbler at age five with the Turners in Philadelphia. A 1943 graduate of Temple University, Szypula won an NCAA tumbling championship, four straight AAU tumbling titles and five horizontal and parallel bars crowns while just missing the 1948 Olympic team. Starting a program from scratch as MSU's first coach in 1947, Szypula was quickly successful, guiding State to second in its first Big Ten meet as Mel Stout won the all-around title. Within seven years, Szypula's team tied for the NCAA championship and, in 1968, for the Big Ten crown, State's only Conference title. His teams finished second five times and third 11 times in the competitive Big Ten. One of his gymnasts, Jim Curzi, won the inaugural Nissen Award, the sport's highest honor, in 1966, and Olympian Dave Thor won it two years later. Szypula retired in 1989 from MSU and coached two state championship teams at East Lansing High School before retiring again. Szypula still lives in East Lansing.

· BIG TEN PIONEERS ·

Micki King, Michigan

For more than three decades, Micki King has been a force in U.S. and international diving as both an athlete and coach. Twice an Olympian and a 10-time AAU diving champ, King won the gold medal in the 1972 Munich Olympics to redeem herself after the 1968 Olympics, where she led the competition until a broken arm relegated her to fourth. A Pontiac, Mich., native who trained under esteemed coach Dick Kimball as a Michigan undergraduate, King spent 26 years in the Air Force, retiring as a colonel. At the Air Force Academy from 1973-77, she became the first woman to coach a male diver to a national championship. King is now special assistant to the athletics director at Kentucky.

Academic Achievements

No matter how you say it, in any of 26 languages, chances are good that you'll be understood on the Ohio State campus. OSU is the nation's leader in foreign language instruction, offering courses in 26 different languages or dialects.

The BIG TEN's First 100 Years
Big Ten Men's Gymnastics
In NCAA Competition
(Top Four Conference Schools)

SCHOOL	TEAM TITLES	INDIVIDUAL TITLES
PENN STATE	*9	*42
ILLINOIS	*9	40
MICHIGAN	2	21
OHIO STATE	2	13
MICHIGAN STATE	1	18

* MOST IN NCAA HISTORY

1964-65
Conference MEDAL OF HONOR
Winners

ILLINOIS	G. Bogie Redmon
INDIANA	Douglas A. Spicer
IOWA	Glenn Gailis
MICHIGAN	Robert W. Timberlake
MICHIGAN STATE	David Price
MINNESOTA	Walter P. Richardson
NORTHWESTERN	Thomas W. Myers
OHIO STATE	Arnold M. Chonko
PURDUE	William B. Howard
WISCONSIN	Gary V. Kirk

BIG TEN

SINCE
1896

CENTENNIAL ™

1965-1974

1965-66

THE BIG EVENT

Ohio State "Arlinizes" Oklahoma State to claim NCAA title

Steve Arlin, an ace right-hander, was the backbone of the Ohio State baseball team that advanced to the College World Series after winning the Big Ten championship. The Buckeyes had finished second at the CWS the previous season, and Ohio State rode the right arm of Arlin to the title game. The best pitcher in the colleges in the 1965-66 season, Arlin was 11-1 with a 1.72 ERA He earned two wins and pitched in three other games for Ohio State, including the 8-2 victory over Oklahoma State in the CWS title game. Ohio State scored an early run, and teammates rubbed Arlin's shoulder during a one-hour rain delay. The result was a two-hitter and an Ohio State 1-0 victory to avoid elimination. Arlin later pitched in the majors for five years and is now a dentist in San Diego. Coach Marty Karow won 478 games before retiring in 1975.

OTHER MEMORABLE EVENTS

- Michigan State won the NCAA hockey championship; goalie Gaye Cooley was named the tournament's most outstanding player.

- Minnesota's pitching staff recorded a 0.99 team earned run average during the Conference season.

- Michigan set a Conference basketball single-game scoring record with 128 points.

- Iowa's Bernhardt Hermann won the NCAA epee fencing title.

- Purdue's Dave Schellhase led the nation in basketball scoring with 32.5 points per game.

- Northwestern's Jim Pitts became the first Conference basketball player with 10 blocked shots in a game.

Northwestern cross country team wins lone Big Ten title

Lee Assenheimer with Coach Bob Ehrhart.

The 1965 squad will forever stand alone as the only cross country team in Northwestern's athletic history to win a Big Ten championship, unless the school reinstates it as a varsity sport. The Wildcats' title was something of a shock. No Northwestern team had finished higher than fourth dating back to 1910, nor would one finish higher than third (1985) afterward before the sport was dropped in 1987. But the Wildcats, coached by Robert Ehrhart, dominated the 1965 meet, finishing with 40 points—well ahead of second-place Michigan State (65). NU's Lee Assenheimer, who had won the 1964 individual title, repeated in 1965, finishing the four-mile course in Minneapolis in 20:05.2. John Duffield placed second in 20:08. Also scoring were Craig Boydston (5th), Pat Edmondson (9th) and Pete Davis (23rd).

OTHER BIG TEN CHAMPIONS

- **FOOTBALL:** Michigan State, coached by Hugh "Duffy" Daugherty
- **BASEBALL:** Ohio State, coached by Martin Karow
- **GYMNASTICS:** Michigan, coached by Newton Loken
- **OUTDOOR TRACK:** Michigan State, coached by Fran Dittrich
- **INDOOR TRACK:** Michigan State, coached by Fran Dittrich
- **BASKETBALL:** Michigan, coached by David Strack
- **TENNIS:** Michigan, coached by William Murphy
- **SWIMMING:** Indiana, coached by James Counsilman
- **WRESTLING:** Michigan State, coached by Grady Peninger
- **GOLF:** Ohio State, coached by Floyd Stahl
- **FENCING:** Illinois, coached by Maxwell Garret
- **HOCKEY:** Minnesota, coached by John Mariucci

STEVE ARLIN
Baseball, Ohio State

Considered the top pitcher in Ohio State history, Steve Arlin's performance in the College World Series over a two-year span was capped by a victory over Oklahoma State in the 1966 championship game. Ending his two-year career with a 24-3 record, Arlin set school records for victories and strikeouts (294). He was 13-2 as a sophomore, leading the nation in strikeouts when he led the Buckeyes to a runner-up finish in the College World Series, including a 1-0 win over Washington State when he pitched all 15 innings and struck out 20. A year later, he was 11-1 after he pitched the Buckeyes to two wins and relieved three more games in the CWS. In his two years at the baseball championships, he was 4-1 with an 0.96 ERA. A two-time All-American and two-time All-Big Ten pick, he was chosen as a member of the all-1960s CWS team.

CHARLES "BUBBA" SMITH
Football, Michigan State

One of the great performers in the annals of MSU and the Big Ten, Charles "Bubba" Smith was a mainstay of State's national championship 1965 team and highly-touted '66 club. Selected by UPI as its Lineman of the Year for 1966, the 6-foot-7, 283-pound Smith was an agile performer with amazing speed for his size, so feared by opponents that they would run away from his end position. Even so, the Orange, Tex., native in 1966 had 15 solo and 15 assisted tackles and dropped ball carriers 10 times for 59 yards in losses while playing at middle guard and end. The National Football League's top draft choice in 1967 after twice being named first team All-America and All-Big Ten, Smith went on to play for eight years in the pros. Smith lives in Los Angeles, where he pursues his acting career.

GENE WASHINGTON
Football and Track, Michigan State

Gene Washington was another of a number of two-sport athletes who excelled at Michigan State in the mid-1960s. A two-time All-American at end for Duffy Daugherty's Big Ten champion and national title-holding (or sharing) teams of 1965 and '66, Washington played in three post-season all-star games in 1967. He also was a national champ in track, winning the 60-yard high hurdles in the inaugural NCAA indoor track championships in 1965 to go with his five Big Ten hurdle titles. The LaPorte, Tex., native was State's Conference Medal of Honor winner in 1967 and in 1970 was named to all-time MSU and Big Ten football teams. Washington had a six-year career with the NFL's Minnesota Vikings as a wide receiver, earning all-pro honors in 1969 and '70. He currently is a staffing manager with 3M Company in St. Paul, Minn.

CAZZIE RUSSELL
Basketball, Michigan

It's "Cazzie," and you don't have to add the "Russell" to identify one of Big Ten basketball's all-time greats. Nor do you question that Crisler Arena is "the house that Cazzie built." A three-time All-American, the high-scoring Chicago guard paced Michigan from 1963-66, leading the two-time Big Ten champs to the 1964 NCAA semifinals and the championship game a year later. Twice the Conference MVP, Russell led the Big Ten in scoring in 1966 with a 33.2 average, still the fourth best mark in league annals. He's the only player in Michigan history to have his number retired. Drafted by the Knicks, he played 12 years in the NBA, averaging 15.1 points a game in stints with four teams. Russell then coached nine seasons in the Continental Basketball Association. An ordained Baptist minister, Russell works with his church and helps coach high school ball in Columbus, Ohio.

LEADING THE WAY

FOREST EVASHEVSKI
Iowa

His tenure as Iowa's football coach was too brief to place his name among the league's legends, but Forest Evashevski made quite an impact during his nine-year stint. His 1958 team was named national champion by the Football Writers Association of America after a 38-12 victory over California in the Rose Bowl. His teams in 1953, '56, '57 and '60 also were ranked in the top 10 at the end of the season. The 1956 team also went to the Rose Bowl, defeating Oregon State, 35-19. He was named national coach of the year four times, and his teams finished 52-27-4. The Hawkeyes were 25-49-5 in the nine years before Evashevski; and 29-53-3 in the nine years after him. Iowa won three Big Ten championships—sharing one—under "Evy." After the 1960 season, at age 42, Evashevski resigned as football coach and became Iowa's athletic director. He served as AD until he retired in 1970. Evy, considered an offensive innovator of his era, is credited with having refined the Wing-T formation, which combined single-wing blocking with T-formation deception. Evashevski was a blocking back at Michigan from 1938-40. He was also a catcher on the baseball team.

CWS OUTSTANDING PLAYERS

Five Big Ten players have been named the Most Outstanding Players at the College World Series:

1954— Tom Yewcic, C, Michigan State

1956— Jerry Thomas, P, Minnesota

1960— John Erickson, 2B, Minnesota

1966— Steve Arlin, P, Ohio State

1973— Dave Winfield, P-OF, Minnesota

Academic Achievements

The National Organization for Women (N.O.W.) was launched by Kathryn Clarenbach and Betty Friedan in 1966. It was first housed in Clarenbach's faculty office on the Wisconsin campus.

1965-66 Conference MEDAL OF HONOR Winners

ILLINOIS	James S. Grabowski
INDIANA	Wayne L. Witmer
IOWA	James M. Moses
MICHIGAN	John Hedrick
MICHIGAN STATE	Stephen A. Juday
MINNESOTA	Paul T. Faust
NORTHWESTERN	Richard T. Abrahams
OHIO STATE	Donald V. Unverferth
PURDUE	Dave G. Schellhase
WISCONSIN	David N. Fronek

BIG TEN LIST

THE BIG EVENT

Michigan State and Notre Dame tie 10-10

Even 30 years later, it's still a game for the ages. One that MSU and Notre Dame students who weren't within shouting distance of Spartan Stadium will swear they were at. One that attracted media hordes to the overflowing. One that still causes taunts by State alumni of "Tie one for the Gipper." One that, as few other games have, grows bigger over time. One that ended, unhappily except for those who like kissing their sisters, in a 10-10 tie that resolved nothing. MSU won the first half 10-7, Notre Dame the second 3-0, and mild controversy swirled when Notre Dame coach Ara Parseghian elected to run out the clock with five running plays rather than risk an interception, possible field goal and loss. Though Spartan coach Duffy Daugherty said both teams deserved the national title, that honor went to Notre Dame, which had one game remaining and used the opportunity to trounce Southern Cal.

OTHER MEMORABLE EVENTS

- Michigan State won the NCAA wrestling championship.

- Purdue halfback LeRoy Keyes led the nation in touchdowns (19) and scoring (114 points).

- Michigan's Jack Clancy set a Conference record (later broken) with 76 pass receptions in a single season.

- Iowa's Larry Wieczorek won the first of two straight Conference cross country titles.

- Michigan's Carl Robie scored a rare triple at the Conference swimming meet, winning the 500 and 1650 freestyles and the 200 butterfly.

- Michigan State's Al Brenner returned a punt 95 yards to set a Conference record.

Hoosier cagers ride rollercoaster to the top

All-Big Ten forward Butch Joyner

Those Indiana basketball fans prone to motion sickness must have been looking for something to hold on to during the team's roller coaster ride that peaked in 1967. The Hoosiers, coached by Lou Watson, tied for last in the Big Ten in 1966 with a 4-10 record, but rebounded the following season to share the league championship with Michigan State by finishing 18-8 overall and 14-4 in league play. Led by All-Big Ten forward Butch Joyner, the Hoosiers took a 6-3 record into Conference play and opened with a loss at Iowa, then proceeded to run off six consecutive victories and win eight of the next nine games. Although they lost twice to Iowa, which finished 9-5, they closed league play with homecourt wins over Michigan and Purdue to wrap up the league's lone berth in the NCAA touranament — where they lost to Virginia Tech. Indiana opened the following season with a six-game winning streak and began Conference play with victories over Minnesota and Illinois. But it lost 10 of its next 11 games and finished last again at 4-10. It finished last in 1969 and '70 as well, but in 1973 began a four-year run of first-place finishes.

OTHER BIG TEN CHAMPIONS

- **FOOTBALL:** Michigan State, coached by Hugh "Duffy" Daugherty
- **BASEBALL:** Ohio State, coached by Martin Karow
- **GYMNASTICS:** Iowa, coached by Sam Bailie
- **OUTDOOR TRACK:** Iowa, coached by Francis Cretzmeyer
- **INDOOR TRACK:** Wisconsin, coached by Charles Walter
- **CROSS COUNTRY:** Iowa, coached by Francis Cretzmeyer
- **TENNIS:** Michigan State, coached by Stan Drobac
- **SWIMMING:** Indiana, coached by James Counsilman
- **WRESTLING:** Michigan State, coached by Grady Peninger
- **GOLF:** Purdue, coached by Sam Voinoff
- **FENCING:** Wisconsin, coached by Archie Simonson
- **HOCKEY:** Michigan State, coached by Amo Bessone

BOB GRIESE
Football, Purdue

Hard to say when Bob Griese was most successful: During his college career? In the pros? After football? At Purdue, Griese was a two-time All-American who led the Boilermakers to the 1967 Rose Bowl. He threw for 4,829 yards during his three-year career and set eight Purdue career records, seven single-season records and five single-game marks. Griese was second in the Heisman Trophy voting in 1966 (to Steve Spurrier). He was chosen as the National Player of the Year by the Cleveland Touchdown Club. As a senior, he led the Big Ten in total offense (1,387 yards) and scoring (81). Purdue was 21-7-1 (16-5 Big Ten) in his three years. He was honored by the *Chicago Tribune* in 1985 as the greatest quarterback in the history of the Big Ten. In his 14-year Hall of Fame NFL career, he led the Miami Dolphins to two Super Bowl titles—including the 17-0 1972 season—and was 91-39-1. He was a six-time Pro Bowler. Griese went on to a successful career as a TV commentator. He was inducted into Purdue's Hall of Fame in 1994.

LARRY WIECZOREK
Cross Country, Iowa

Larry Wieczorek had an eventful junior year, winning the Big Ten cross country championship (four-mile course) in the fall — while leading Iowa to a first-place team finish—and winning the league one-mile title during the indoor track season. The Maywood, Ill., native was third in the NCAA cross country championships and third in the NCAA indoor one mile. He was runner-up in the Big Ten in the outdoor one mile, and fourth in the NCAA outdoor one mile. Wieczorek was also runner-up in the U.S. Track and Field Federation outdoor one-mile run. As a senior, Wieczorek won another Big Ten cross country title (this time on a five-mile course), and was fourth in the NCAA championships. During the indoor track season, he won the Big Ten two-mile title and was seventh in the NCAA indoor two mile.

GEORGE WEBSTER
Football, Michigan State

Named "The Greatest Spartan of All-Time" in balloting by fans, George Webster single-handedly popularized the position of roverback, which in the form of the 6-foot-4, 222-pound Webster put fear into the hearts of mortal football players. That his No. 90 jersey was retired by MSU was a given, because no one could claim to be the next George Webster. "Part-safety, part-linebacker, all-destroyer" said one writer of Webster on the eve of his 1987 induction into the College Football Hall of Fame. A two-time consensus All-American from 1964-66, Webster was one of four Spartans among the first eight selections in the 1967 NFL draft; he spent 10 seasons in the pros with Houston, Pittsburgh and New England. He was an obvious choice as a charter inductee into State's Hall of Fame. Webster lives in Houston and is battling cancer.

KEN SITZBERGER
Diving, Indiana

Ken Sitzberger was the first of the great divers in the Hobie Billingsley regime at Indiana. A letterman from 1965-67, Sitzberger won the Big Ten one- and three-meter championships in 1966 and '67, the NCAA one-meter title in 1965, '66 and '67 and the NCAA three-meter title in '65 and '67. He also won national AAU titles in 1964 (one- and three-meter dives) and '65 (one-meter). Sitzberger preceded his collegiate career by winning a gold medal in springboard diving in the 1964 Olympics.

LEADING THE WAY

MARTY KAROW
Ohio State

When it comes to Ohio State baseball, the man who set school records for wins and league titles is Marty Karow, who coached the Buckeyes for 24 seasons. The rugged Karow posted an overall record of 478-343-16, a school record for wins that still stands. His teams also won 203 games in the Big Ten and registered five of the 12 Conference titles won in baseball by Ohio State. He led the Buckeyes to the NCAA College World Series title in 1966, the runner-up finish the previous season and three straight Big Ten titles, the last one in the 1967 season when the Buckeyes were 13-3 in the league, winning their third straight Big Ten title. Behind the pitching of Steve Arlin, who won two games and pitched in three others, the Buckeyes survived the consolation bracket to win the CWS title in 1966.

BIG TEN LIST

PURDUE FOOTBALL MVPS

Since 1930, the *Chicago Tribune* has selected a Big Ten Conference football Most Valuable Player. There have been five players from Purdue win the award:

1966—Bob Griese, QB

1967—Leroy Keyes, HB

1969—Mike Phipps, QB

1972—Otis Armstrong, HB

1980—Mark Herrmann, QB

BIG TEN SINCE 1896 CENTENNIAL ™

Academic Achievements

Michigan State is one of the leading cancer research centers in the nation. Cisplatin and carboplatin, two platinum-based compounds, were discovered and developed in MSU labs. They lead all other anticancer drugs in sales and have saved tens of thousands of lives in treatment of cancer.

1966-67 Conference MEDAL OF HONOR Winners

ILLINOIS	Robert J. Bachman
INDIANA	Kenneth R. Sitzberger
IOWA	Kenneth Gordon
MICHIGAN	David R. Fisher
MICHIGAN STATE	Eugene Washington
MINNESOTA	Thomas G. Heinonen
NORTHWESTERN	Kenneth C. Ramsey
OHIO STATE	Willard F. Sander
PURDUE	Robert A. Griese
WISCONSIN	Dennis J. Sweeney

THE BIG EVENT

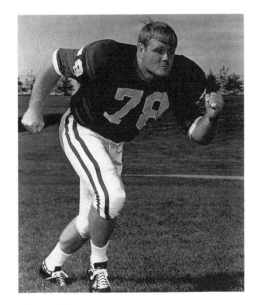

Doug Crusan

Indiana's "Cardiac Kids" surprise football champs

Indiana's 1967 football season came and went like a meteor, stunning the school's fans. The Hoosiers hadn't had a winning season since 1958, and were just 1-8-1 in 1966, but everything came together in '67. The "Cardiac Kids" won their first eight games, five of them by five points or less, lost at Minnesota, then beat third-ranked Purdue, 19-14, in Bloomington for a share of the Big Ten championship and the right to represent the Conference in the Rose Bowl — still the school's only appearance in Pasadena. Indiana lost to Southern Cal, 14-3, but that loss did little to sour a memorable season that made local legends of the likes of quarterback Harry Gonso, running backs John Isenbarger and Terry Cole and receiver Jade Butcher. The thrill was short-lived, however. The Hoosiers dropped to 6-4 the following year, and had to wait until 1979 before they managed another winning season.

OTHER MEMORABLE EVENTS

- Indiana won its first NCAA swimming championship; Charlie Hickcox won three national titles.

- Michigan won the first in a run of 16 consecutive Conference tennis team titles.

- Michigan State's Dave Thor won his third straight Conference all-around gymnastics championship.

- Michigan's Dave Porter won his second NCAA heavyweight wrestling crown.

- The Conference voted to use three basketball officials in each game.

BIG TEN LIST

SUPERVISORS OF OFFICIALS

Herm Rohrig was named the first full-time supervisor of officials in the Big Ten Conference in 1968. Here were the part-time supervisors prior to Rohrig's tenure:

1945-48	James C. Masker (football)
1950-67	A. William Haarlow (basketball)
1952-53	William A. Blake (football)
1953-60	Irish Krieger (football)
1961-67	Carlisle O. Dollings (football)
1963-67	Ike J. Armstrong (football)

Buckeyes beat Hawkeyes in basketball playoff game

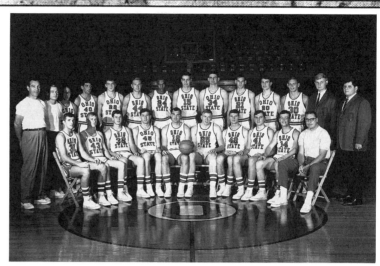

1967-68 Ohio State basketball team

The field for the NCAA tournament was already set following the regular season in 1967-68, although it lacked one thing — a Big Ten champion. The league needed a playoff for the first time ever to decide a league champ who would earn the automatic berth into the NCAA field. Ohio State and Iowa met on a neutral site at Purdue's Mackey Arena, a snowstorm keeping the crowd to 4,816. Iowa had scored an overtime win over Ohio State in a January showdown in Iowa City, but Bill Hosket tallied 24 points and 11 rebounds to lead the Buckeyes to an 85-81 win over Iowa, a victory that gave Ohio State Coach Fred Taylor his sixth Big Ten title in his first 10 years as Buckeyes coach. More importantly, Ohio State advanced to the NCAA Mideast Regional in Lexington, Ky. The Buckeyes defeated East Tennessee State, then edged host Kentucky 82-81 for the regional championship and the school's first berth in the Final Four since the last of three straight trips to the title game in 1961-62. Ohio State finished third, and Hosket averaged 20.1 points and 11.1 rebounds to become a two-time All-Big Ten selection.

OTHER BIG TEN CHAMPIONS

- **FOOTBALL:** Indiana, coached by John Pont, Minnesota, coached by Murray Warmath, and Purdue, coached by Jack Mollenkopf
- **BASEBALL:** Minnesota, coached by Dick Siebert
- **GYMNASTICS:** Iowa, coached by Sam Bailie, Michigan, coached by Newton Loken, and Michigan State, coached by George Szypula
- **OUTDOOR TRACK:** Minnesota, coached by Roy Griak
- **INDOOR TRACK:** Wisconsin, coached by Charles Walter
- **CROSS COUNTRY:** Indiana, coached by Jim Lavery
- **TENNIS:** Michigan, coached by William Murphy
- **SWIMMING:** Indiana, coached by James Counsilman
- **WRESTLING:** Michigan State, coached by Grady Peninger
- **GOLF:** Indiana, coached by Robert Fitch
- **FENCING:** Illinois, coached by Maxwell Garret
- **HOCKEY:** Michigan, coached by Allen Renfrew

CHARLIE HICKCOX
Swimming, Indiana

Charlie Hickcox's success ran the gamut. He won eight NCAA titles in the backstroke, individual medley and relays. He also won eight Big Ten titles, two Pan-American titles, four AAU indoor titles, and two AAU outdoor titles for a total of 12 national championships. Hickcox won three gold medals in the 1968 Olympics, setting Olympic records in the 200 individual medley, the 400 individual medley and the 400 medley relay. He also won a silver medal in the 100 backstroke. At one time he held the Big Ten records in the backstroke and medley, at all the distances, as well as four national records. An All-American all three of his years at IU, Hickcox swam on teams that won three Big Ten titles and two NCAA championships.

DAVE THOR
Gymnastics, Michigan State

Dave Thor is one of only six Big Ten gymnasts to win the all-around title three times since the meet's inception in 1902. He led the Spartans to a share of the Conference championship in 1968 with his 106.10 effort, a mark that would not be bettered in the Big Ten meet until 1977. Thor also had won the AA crown in 1966 and 1967 as well as Conference titles in the floor exercise and long horse as a sophomore and on the side horse as a senior. A native of Reseda, Calif., Thor won the 1968 Nissen Award, the sport's highest honor, and was a member of that year's U.S. Olympic team. He now operates a gymnastics school in Rohnert Park, Calif.

STEVE GARVEY
Baseball, Michigan State

Steve Garvey's lone baseball season in 1968 at Michigan State was spectacular, to say the least. His .376 batting average, 29 runs scored, 9 homers and 38 RBIs earned the Tampa, Fla., sophomore All-America honors. MSU Coach Danny Litwhiler called Garvey the best pure hitter he ever had and a long, dramatic big league career proved him right. The 1974 National League MVP, Garvey played in 1,207 consecutive games, the third longest streak ever, and had six seasons with 200 or more hits. Three times the National League Championship Series MVP and a 10-time All-Star, Garvey hit a dramatic 9th inning game-winning home run that helped propel the Padres to the 1984 National League pennant. A four-time Gold Glove winner, he played an NL record 193 straight errorless games at first base. Chairman of Garvey Communications and a frequent TV host, Garvey lives in Los Angeles.

DAVE PORTER
Wrestling, Michigan

Heavyweight Dave Porter won pairs of Big Ten and NCAA titles in a stellar three-year wrestling career that first germinated in seventh grade up the road in Lansing, where he eventually won three prep titles and 78 straight matches without defeat. Porter won Big Ten titles for legendary coach Cliff Keen in 1966 and 1967 and NCAA titles in 1966 and 1968. From 1965-67, he had 32 straight victories. Porter still shares the Michigan record for most falls in dual meets in a season, getting eight in both 1966-67 and 1967-68. He had 14 overall in the former season. Porter also has the two quickest falls in U-M history, pinning two Purdue opponents in 23 seconds, first in 1967 and then repeating the feat in 1968.

LEADING THE WAY

JOHN PONT
Indiana/Northwestern

John Pont had just two winning seasons in his eight years at Indiana, but the accomplishments of his 1967 team that finished 9-2 and represented the Big Ten in the Rose Bowl have made him one of the school's most popular coaches. A kind, unassuming man, Pont led his first two teams at IU to a combined 3-16-1 record. But his next team won more games than any team in school history as it won a share of the league title. He was named college football's Coach of the Year for 1967 by the Football Writers Association, The Sporting News, the Walter Camp Foundation and the Football Coaches Association. Pont's IU teams finished 31-51-1 overall. He took over at Northwestern in 1973, coaching the Wildcats for five seasons. His teams there finished with a combined record of 12-43, but his first one finished 4-4 in Conference play — the most recent non-losing season for the school until 1995. He also defeated Indiana his first three seasons in Evanston. He was voted into Indiana's athletic hall of fame in 1992.

· BIG TEN PIONEERS ·

Herm Rohrig

The Big Ten took one giant step forward when it hired Herman F. Rohrig to be its first full-time supervisor of officials on Jan. 1, 1968. In addition to being a football official in the Big Eight Conference for six years and in the National Football League for 11 years, Rohrig also was a basketball official for 13 years at the high school and small-college level. Rohrig is a 1941 Nebraska graduate who was an all-Big Six halfback in '39 and threw a 33-yard TD pass in a 21-13 loss to Stanford in the 1941 Rose Bowl. He played for the Green Bay Packers in 1941, '46 and '47. From 1942-46, he was an Air Force captain in Biloxi, Miss. Rohrig retired from the Big Ten in July 1983.

Academic Achievements

Minnesota's University Hospital ranks first in the world in the amount of organ transplant activity yearly. It was the site of the first pancreas transplant in 1967 and the first bone marrow transplant in 1968.

The BIG TEN's First 100 Years
Latest Big Ten Football Championships

Here are the latest Big Ten football championships for each school

		UNCONTESTED
Chicago	1924	1924
Illinois	1990*	1983
Indiana	1967*	1945
Michigan	1992	1992
Michigan State	1990*	1987
Minnesota	1967*	1941
Northwestern	1995	1995
Ohio State	1993*	1984
Penn State	1994	1994
Purdue	1967*	1929

*cochampionship

1967-68 Conference MEDAL OF HONOR Winners

ILLINOIS	Paul Gary Shapin
INDIANA	Stanley Eugene Denisar
IOWA	Anthony Williams
MICHIGAN	Richard V. Vidmer
MICHIGAN STATE	Dale Anderson
MINNESOTA	Gary A. Gambucci
NORTHWESTERN	Thomas A. Garretson
OHIO STATE	Wilmer F. Hosket
PURDUE	James P. Beirne
WISCONSIN	Michael Gluck

1968-69

THE BIG EVENT

Ohio State football team wins national title

The Rose Bowl in 1969 between Ohio State and Southern California was played before a crowd that included President-elect Richard Nixon. The game featured two other legends, Ohio State coach Woody Hayes and Southern Cal running back O.J. Simpson, that season's winner of the Heisman Trophy. Simpson broke free on a spectacular 80-yard touchdown run to spot the Trojans a 10-0 lead in the first half, but Ohio State scored 27 unanswered points to lead the Buckeyes to a 27-16 victory, a win that left the Buckeyes with a 10-0 record and the third national championship under Hayes. Jim Otis led Ohio State with 101 yards rushing and quarterback Jim Kern earned Rose Bowl MVP honors, passing for 101 yards and two touchdowns. Hayes left soon after the game for a trip to Vietnam to show Rose Bowl films to the GIs.

OTHER MEMORABLE EVENTS

- Iowa won the NCAA gymnastics championship; Michigan took the NCAA trampoline crown.

- Indiana won its second NCAA swimming championship, led by Mark Spitz's three national titles.

- Wisconsin's Ray Arrington won his third consecutive NCAA 1,000-yard indoor track title.

- Minnesota's Mike Walseth led the Conference in both home runs and RBI for the second straight year.

- Michigan's Ron Johnson ran for a single-game Conference-record 347 yards.

Michigan wins Big Ten tennis title

Bill Murphy

In a display of dominance rarely seen in the Big Ten in any sport, Coach William Murphy's 1969 Michigan tennis team romped to the second of 16 straight Conference championships. The Wolverines put on a clinic at Michigan State, winning all six singles titles and two of the three doubles crowns in the 60th annual meet. Their 161 points easily outdistanced runner-up Indiana (86) in the combined dual meet and tournament scoring that determined the Conference title. Dick Dell led Michigan at No. 1 singles and teamed with Mark Conti for a win at No. 2 doubles. Also winning were Pete Fishbach at No. 2 singles, Brian Marcus at No. 3, Conti at No. 4, Jon Hainline at No. 5 and Dan McLaughlin at No. 6. The latter two also won at No. 3 doubles. Only the Northwestern pair of Don Lutz and Tom Rice at No. 1 doubles denied Michigan the sweep.

OTHER BIG TEN CHAMPIONS

- **FOOTBALL:** Ohio State, coached by Woody Hayes
- **BASEBALL:** Minnesota, coached by Dick Siebert
- **GYMNASTICS:** Michigan, coached by Newton Loken
- **OUTDOOR TRACK:** Wisconsin, coached by Charles Walter
- **INDOOR TRACK:** Wisconsin, coached by Charles Walter
- **BASKETBALL:** Purdue, coached by George King
- **CROSS COUNTRY:** Michigan State, coached by James Gibbard
- **SWIMMING:** Indiana, coached by James Counsilman
- **WRESTLING:** Michigan State, coached by Grady Peninger
- **GOLF:** Michigan State, coached by Bruce Fossum
- **FENCING:** Ohio State, coached by Charles Simonian
- **HOCKEY:** Michigan, coached by Allen Renfrew

LEROY KEYES
Football, Purdue

Perhaps this says it all: Leroy Keyes was voted by fans in 1987 as the best player in the first 100 years of Purdue football. The tailback and defensive back holds Boilermaker records for points (222), rushing TDs (29) and rushing average (5.97). He is Purdue's No. 5 all-time rusher (2,090 yards). Keyes rushed for 1,003 yards in 1968, one of only five Purdue players to surpass the 1,000-yard mark in a season. The Newport News, Va., native finished second in the 1968 Heisman Trophy voting (to O.J. Simpson) and third in the 1967 voting. The two-time All-American, Big Ten and Purdue MVP was picked second overall in the NFL draft by the Philadelphia Eagles behind—you guessed it—Simpson. He played eight years in the NFL. Keyes was inducted into the College Football Hall of Fame in 1990 and was among the first class inducted to Purdue's Hall of Fame in 1994. He returned to Purdue as an assistant football coach in 1995.

JACK TATUM
Football, Ohio State

There was no greater fear than crossing the middle of the field when Jack Tatum was playing defense. A three-year letterman who played on three Big Ten championship teams, Tatum was a two-time All-America pick at defensive back, the second time as a senior in 1970. He was a member of the 1968 team that finished the season 10-0 and won the national championship for coach Woody Hayes. An unusually gifted athlete, Tatum had the speed of a top halfback and the strength of a linebacker. When he arrived at Ohio State from his home in Patterson, N.J., Tatum was a fullback who was moved to defense. A first-round draft pick by the Oakland Raiders, Tatum played for nine years in Oakland, winning one Super Bowl championship before moving to the Houston Oilers.

DON McKENZIE
Swimming, Indiana

Indiana's Don McKenzie won Big Ten, NCAA and Olympic championships during his college career. A letterman at Indiana in 1968 and '69, he won gold medals in the 1968 Mexico City Olympics in the 100-meter breaststroke and the 400 medley relay. He came back in 1969 to win the NCAA championship in the 100-meter breaststroke in 58.36 seconds, an American record at the time, and participated on the winning medley relay team with Charlie Hickcox, Steve Borowski and Bryan Bateman that set an American record of 3:25.8. He also swam on two Big Ten championship medley relay teams, and at one time held league records in both the 100- and 200-meter breaststrokes.

RUDY TOMJANOVICH
Basketball, Michigan

When fans of the Houston Rockets yell "Rudy T!" at their coach, the younger among them may not realize that Michigan fans were yelling the same thing for Hamtramck's Rudy Tomjanovich, the player, in the late 1960s. Twice an All-Big Ten and All-America pick, Tomjanovich has the best rebounding average in U-M history (14.4 per game) and is the fifth leading scorer. He still holds the Wolverines' single game rebounding mark of 30. Selected by the Rockets in the 1970 NBA draft, Tomjanovich was a five-time all-star, averaging 17 points and 9 rebounds in 11 seasons. His No. 45 jersey was retired by the Rockets in 1982. After serving as a scout and assistant coach, Tomjanovich was named Houston's head coach in 1992 and within three years had guided the Rockets to two NBA titles.

LEADING THE WAY

DON CANHAM
Michigan

Don Canham, it can be argued with little fear of contradiction, changed the face of intercollegiate athletics when he became Michigan's fifth athletic director in 1968. A highly successful track coach who won the 1940 NCAA high jump title for the Wolverines, the Oak Park, Ill., native applied the same formula for success in athletic administration as he had in building a track team that won 12 Big Ten titles in 19 seasons. As AD, Canham became college athletics' ultimate promoter, marketing Michigan football and other sports throughout the state via direct mail and advertising, and changing the face of sports promotion. As a result of his efforts, Michigan consistently led the nation in football ticket sales and attendance. Revenue skyrocketed from $3 million in Canham's first year to more than $18 million in 1988, his last year as director. Under his direction, Michigan's program won 73 Big Ten titles and, more importantly, expanded to 21 varsity sports while remaining self-sufficient, never using state, federal or university funds for athletics. Honors he has received are legion and even today he continues to be recognized for his contributions. Still active in the athletic supply company he founded, Canham lives in Ann Arbor.

· BIG TEN PIONEERS ·

Judith Sweet, Wisconsin

When Judith Sweet was a student/athlete at Wisconsin in the 1960s, organized women's athletics were virtually non-existent at the school. By the mid-1970s, she was one of the first women in the nation to head a combined men's and women's collegiate athletic program when she became athletic director at the University of California-San Diego. Sixteen years later, she made history by becoming the first woman to serve as president of the NCAA when she began her two-year term in 1991. Her presidency followed a two-year term as secretary-treasurer of the NCAA. As president, she helped negotiate a $1 billion television contract with CBS. In 1991, she was voted by the *Los Angeles Times* as the Top College Sports Executive of the Eighties.

Academic Achievements

Wisconsin's Space Astronomy Laboratory constructed the world's first true observatory in space in 1968, the Orbital Astronomical Observatory. It was designed to measure ultraviolet light.

The BIG TEN's First 100 Years
Facts About Big Ten Universities

Big Ten universities were the first to offer classes in...

Journalism, Pharmacy and Data Processing (Michigan)

The Practice of Law (Minnesota)

1968-69 Conference MEDAL OF HONOR Winners

ILLINOIS	Dennis A. Rott
INDIANA	Richard A. Fuhs
IOWA	Scott Miller
MICHIGAN	Ronald A. Johnson
MICHIGAN STATE	Allen Brenner
MINNESOTA	Noel C. Jenke
NORTHWESTERN	Ralph Schultz
OHIO STATE	David Foley
PURDUE	Charles Kyle
WISCONSIN	Karl Rudat

1969-70

THE BIG EVENT

Bo takes Michigan to Rose Bowl in first year

Bo Schembechler (at left with Ohio State's Woody Hayes) quickly showed athletic director Don Canham he'd made the right move in naming him head football coach in 1969. The Wolverines outrushed Vanderbilt 367-55 and swamped the Commodores 42-14 in Bo's debut at a packed Michigan Stadium. Michigan was led by All-Americans Jim Mandich at end, who caught 119 passes for almost 1,500 yards in his career, and Tom Curtis at safety, who had eight interceptions and 45 unassisted tackles as a senior. Heading into the final game against top-ranked and unbeaten Ohio State, the 7-2 Wolverines mixed their attack with 266 yards on the ground and 108 in the air to beat the Bucks, 24-12, for the Big Ten title and Rose Bowl berth. Southern Cal's third quarter touchdown gave the Trojans a 10-3 win in the 1970 Rose Bowl, which Schembechler missed after suffering a heart attack on New Year's Eve.

OTHER MEMORABLE EVENTS

- Indiana's Jim Henry won his third straight NCAA diving title to lead the Hoosiers to their third swimming and diving national championship.

- Ohio State set a national record (later broken) by connecting on 80.9 percent of its free throws during the season.

- Wisconsin's Alan "A-Train" Thompson set an NCAA record with 220 rushing yards, the most in the first game of a player's career.

- Michigan won the NCAA gymnastics and trampoline titles.

- Iowa scored 102.9 points per Big Ten game, the only time in league history a team has exceeded the century mark.

- Michigan State's Herb Washington set an NCAA indoor track meet record in the 60-yard dash in 5.9 seconds. The record still stands.

- Purdue's Rick Mount scored a record 61 points in a Conference basketball game.

Michigan gymnasts win Big Ten, two NCAA titles

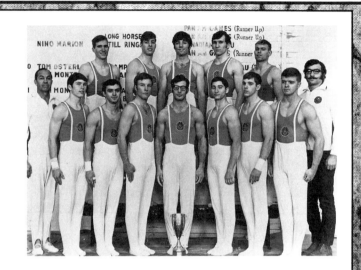

Michigan became the only school ever to win two NCAA team titles in the same competition in 1970, taking its second gymnastics championship and winning the NCAA trampoline title to boot. In one of the closest NCAA gymnastics meets ever, Michigan scored 164.150 points to second place Iowa State's 164.050—one-tenth of a point difference. In the Big Ten, Rick McCurdy won his second of three straight Big Ten all-around championships to pace the Wolverines to their second consecutive win. The only apparatus winner for Coach Newt Loken was Ron Rapper on the parallel bars, but Michigan's depth held off Iowa State. In the NCAA, Rapper took the parallel bars. In the same meet, Michigan's second trampoline title, this time over New Mexico State, also was the NCAA's second—and last. Giving Michigan the win in the discontinued championship were George Huntzicker, who took first, and teammates Dave Jacobs and Wayne Miller, who shared runner-up honors.

OTHER BIG TEN CHAMPIONS

- **FOOTBALL:** Michigan, coached by Glenn "Bo" Schembechler, and Ohio State, coached by Woody Hayes
- **BASEBALL:** Minnesota, coached by Dick Siebert
- **OUTDOOR TRACK:** Indiana, coached by Sam Bell
- **INDOOR TRACK:** Wisconsin, coached by Robert Brennan
- **BASKETBALL:** Iowa, coached by Ralph Miller
- **CROSS COUNTRY:** Minnesota, coached by Roy Griak
- **TENNIS:** Michigan, coached by Brian Eisner
- **SWIMMING:** Indiana, coached by James Counsilman
- **WRESTLING:** Michigan State, coached by Grady Peninger
- **GOLF:** Indiana, coached by Robert Fitch
- **FENCING:** Ohio State, coached by Charles Simonian
- **HOCKEY:** Minnesota, coached by Glen Sonmor

MIKE ADAMLE
Football, Northwestern

Many college football scouts told Mike Adamle he would never make it at the major college level. Too small and too slow, they said. But the 5-foot-9, 190-pound running back proved them wrong in a big way, setting 11 school records and six Big Ten marks during his career from 1968-70. He earned Big Ten most valuable player and All-America honors following his senior season, when he led the Wildcats to a 6-4 record. He rushed for 316 yards against Wisconsin as a junior, setting a school single-game rushing record that still stands, and rushed for 192 yards on 48 carries (another surviving record) and rushed for four touchdowns (also a record) in a 28-14 victory over Minnesota as a senior. He played seven years in the NFL before a knee injury cut short his career, and then became a television commentator.

TOM MILKOVICH
Wrestling, Michigan State

One of only nine four-time champions in Big Ten wrestling history, Tom Milkovich paced State to the final three of its then-record seven straight Conference titles in his four seasons. Milkovich, a member of a prominent Maple Heights, Ohio, wrestling family—brother Pat was an NCAA titlist and three-time Conference champ for State—won Big Ten crowns at 134 lbs. in 1970 and '71 before moving up to 142 as a junior and winning another pair at that weight. He also won two Midlands titles and in his junior season won the NCAA championship at 142. Heavily favored to repeat in 1973, Milkovich suffered a shoulder separation in the national collegiate semi-finals and finished sixth. He had a career record of 93-9-1, including a 29-3 record with five pins as a freshman.

RICK MOUNT
Basketball, Purdue

There were no three-point field goals when Rick Mount played, and most of his shots were launched from beyond where the arc would have been. Still, the former Indiana Mr. Basketball from Lebanon, Ind., averaged 28.4, 33.3 and 35.4 points per game during his three seasons at Purdue, finishing with an incredible 32.3 career average and school-record 2,323 points. He is acknowledged by some as perhaps the greatest pure shooter ever. Mount, nicknamed "The Rocket," was an All-American all three years, and was twice team MVP and first-team All-Big Ten. He was drafted in the first round by the Indiana Pacers of ABA. During his junior season, Mount helped lead Purdue to the NCAA championship game, which it lost to UCLA, 92-72. In 1972, he was inducted into the Indiana Basketball Hall of Fame, and in 1994, he was elected to Purdue's Athletic Hall of Fame. In August 1995, Mount was named one of the guards (the other was Magic Johnson) on the Chicago Tribune's All-Time Big Ten Basketball First Team.

DAN DIERDORF
Football, Michigan

One of the best offensive tackles in Michigan history, Canton, Ohio, native Dan Dierdorf bucked Buckeye tradition to come to Ann Arbor. It was a wise recruiting move for Michigan coach Bump Elliott, since Dierdorf would twice earn All-Big Ten honors and would be a consensus All-American after his senior season of 1970. He combined speed and strength to become a key blocker as the Wolverines set a series of rushing records. Dierdorf went on to become an all-pro with the St. Louis Cardinals and was twice named best offensive lineman in the NFL. He was named to the Street & Smith's and College and Pro-Football magazine's team of the decade for the 1970s. His 13-year career ended in 1983 and Dierdorf then pursued a career in broadcasting. He currently is a color commentator on ABC's "Monday Night Football."

LEADING THE WAY

BOB JOHNSON
Wisconsin

At every stop, on every level, Bob Johnson was a winner on the hockey rink. At Wisconsin, where he coached 15 years between 1966 and 1981, he guided the Badgers to unprecedented success within the Big Ten and nationwide. He guided Wisconsin to three NCAA championships and helped build the hockey program into the school's second-highest money-making sport. Johnson's teams routinely led the Conference — and the nation — in hockey attendance in the early and mid-1970s, including a then-all-time collegiate record 167,902 in 1973. He led the Badgers to NCAA titles in 1973, 1977 and 1981. He was named NCAA Coach of the Year in 1977 and posted a career 367-175-23 record at Wisconsin. He also coached the 1976 U.S. Olympic Team and Team USA in 1981, 1984 and 1987. He departed for the NHL after the 1981 college campaign. Johnson coached the Calgary Flames between 1982 and 1987 and led them to their first Campbell Conference Championship and Stanley Cup Finals berth. He coached the Pittsburgh Penguins to the 1990 Stanley Cup championship in 1990 and remained with the Penguins until his death Nov. 26, 1991 of a brain tumor.

· BIG TEN PIONEERS ·

Ralph Simpson, Michigan State

Unlike today, when players routinely enter the NBA draft before their collegiate eligibility expires, Ralph Simpson's "hardship" signing by the American Basketball Association's Denver Rockets in 1974 was big news in basketball, and bad news for Michigan State. Simpson, an All-Big Ten first-team pick as well as a member of the Helms Foundation's 36-man All-America squad, was the first Conference player to go "hardship" and bypass his remaining eligibility. Simpson, who had broken the Spartans' single-season scoring record in his lone season, signed a deal with the Rockets for an estimated $1 million package, then big money. Simpson was a second team ABA all-star in 1972-73.

Academic Achievements

I t was Purdue alumnus Neil Armstrong who said, "That's one small step for man, one giant leap for mankind," when he became the first man to walk on the surface of the moon. He is the most famous, but certainly not the only astronaut from Purdue. The West Lafayette campus is known as the Mother of Astronauts. More than 20 Purdue alumni have been selected for the space program at NASA.

The BIG TEN's First 100 Years
Big Ten Men's Basketball
Per Game Average Season Records
(Conference games only)

Points	39.4	Rick Mount, PUR, 1970
Rebounds	18.3	Horace Walker, MSU, 1960
Assists	7.7	Cal Wulfsberg, IOWA, 1976
Steals	3.4	Melvin Newbern, MINN, 1991
Blocked Shots	3.9	Acie Earl, IOWA, 1992

1969-70 Conference MEDAL OF HONOR Winners

ILLINOIS	Lawrence B. Schwartz
INDIANA	William H. Wolfe
IOWA	Dick Jensen
MICHIGAN	Mark W. Henry
MICHIGAN STATE	Richard R. Saul
MINNESOTA	David A. Cosgrove
NORTHWESTERN	Bruce Hubbard
OHIO STATE	Bruce T. Trott
PURDUE	Michael E. Phipps
WISCONSIN	Douglas R. McFadyen

THE BIG EVENT

Indiana wins NCAA swim title

1970-71 Indiana swimming team

Indiana's swimming and diving program won six consecutive NCAA championships from 1968-73, and the '71 team was typical of the dominance of that period. They won all 14 of their dual meets with ease, running their streak to 62 in a row, then captured the Big Ten title at Ohio State with 601 points — well ahead of second-place Michigan's 325. That was just a warm-up for the NCAA meet, which the Hoosiers won with 351 points. USC was second with 260, leading a parade of four California colleges that had the advantage of recruiting where most of the outstanding high school prospects lived. IU's outstanding individual performances included future Olympic hero Mark Spitz, who won the 100- and 200-meter butterfly; Gary Hall, who won the 200 and 400 individual medleys in American and NCAA records; and John Kinsella, who won the 500 freestyle in an NCAA record and the 1,650 freestyle in American and NCAA records.

OTHER MEMORABLE EVENTS

- Ohio State's Jim Stillwagon won the Outland Trophy as the nation's most outstanding lineman and the Lombardi Award.
- Purdue's George Faerber set a Conference basketball record by making all 12 of his field goal attempts in one game.
- Ohio State's Ray Hupp won the NCAA decathlon championship; Wisconsin's Mark Winzenried won his second straight NCAA indoor 880 crown; and Minnesota's Garry Bjorklund set an NCAA outdoor record in the six miles that still stands.
- Purdue's Terry Wedgewood recorded a triple crown in baseball, leading the Conference in home runs, RBI and batting average.
- Michigan's Rick McCurdy won his third straight Conference all-around gymnastics title.
- Purdue's Stan Brown set an NCAA record with three kickoff returns for touchdowns in one season.

Purdue wins 11th Conference golf title

Coach Sam Voinoff

Coach Sam Voinoff saw the Purdue golf team win his 11th and final Big Ten championship. The Boilermakers, who finished 16th at the NCAA meet, went 106-10-1 in invitationals and finished first at the Illinois Invitational (12 teams), Miami Invitational (17 teams), Indiana Invitational (9 teams) and Purdue Invitational (8 teams). Team captain Bill Hoffer was All-Big Ten and named Purdue's most valuable golfer. Don Denger also was an All-Conference selection. Gary Gant and Jeff Radder tied for fourth at the Big Ten meet. Other members of the team: Ross Biddenger, Fred Clark, John Gilliam, Larry Nicolet and Bill Shulha. Gant was All-Big Ten and team MVP in 1972. In 1984, Hoffer won the first USGA Mid-Amateur championship - a tournament for golfers over age 25. Voinoff would retire after the 1974 season - his 23rd - with a record of 229-58-6 in dual meets and 748-236-4 in invitationals. His 1961 team won the national championship.

OTHER BIG TEN CHAMPIONS

- **FOOTBALL:** Ohio State, coached by Woody Hayes
- **BASEBALL:** Michigan State, coached by Dan Litwhiler
- **GYMNASTICS:** Michigan, coached by Newton Loken
- **OUTDOOR TRACK:** Indiana, coached by Sam Bell
- **INDOOR TRACK:** Wisconsin, coached by Robert Brennan
- **BASKETBALL:** Ohio State, coached by Fred Taylor
- **CROSS COUNTRY:** Michigan State, coached by James Gibbard
- **TENNIS:** Michigan, coached by Brian Eisner
- **SWIMMING:** Indiana, coached by James Counsilman
- **WRESTLING:** Michigan State, coached by Grady Peninger
- **FENCING:** Michigan State, coached by Charles Schmitter
- **HOCKEY:** Michigan State, coached by Amo Bessone

TERRY WEDGEWOOD
Baseball, Purdue

Purdue's most valuable baseball player, Terry Wedgewood pulled off a triple crown in the Big Ten Conference. The all-league third baseman led the Big Ten in hitting (.467), RBIs (19) and tied for the home run title (6). The senior set a Conference record with 54 total bases and tied another mark with 28 hits. The Evansville, Ind., product led the Boilermakers in hits (52), average (.406), runs scored (32), RBIs (26), doubles (10), homers (7) and total bases (85). He tied for the team lead in triples (2) and was second in plate appearances (128). During the off-seasons, Wedgewood had played on state championship teams in the Pony League World Series and American Legion tournaments.

JIM CLEAMONS
Basketball, Ohio State

Jim Cleamons was a three-year starter for Ohio State, leading the Buckeyes to the 1971 Big Ten basketball title as a senior. He was selected the Conference's MVP and earned a Conference Medal of Honor for academic and athletic proficiency. A forward his first two years and a guard the third, he scored 1,335 points in his college career. The Columbus, Ohio, native was a first-round draft choice of the Los Angeles Lakers and played nine years in the NBA (for the Lakers, Cleveland, Knicks and Washington). After stints as an assistant coach at Furman and Ohio State, Cleamons was named head coach at Youngstown State from 1987-89. He then joined the staff of the four-time NBA champion Chicago Bulls. Cleamons was named the head coach of the Dallas Mavericks in the summer of 1996.

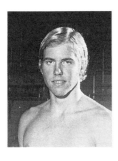

GARY HALL
Swimming, Indiana

One of the most versatile swimmers in the world, Gary Hall held world records in the 200 and 400 individual medleys, the 200 backstroke and the 200 butterfly. He won 13 Big Ten championships in all, swimming for a team that never lost a college meet. He won nine AAU indoor and six AAU outdoor championships and was selected World Swimmer of the Year in 1969 and '70. Hall competed in three Olympics. He placed second in the 400 individual medley in 1968, second in the 200 fly in 1972 and third in the 100 fly in 1976, when he was selected to carry the American flag in the opening ceremonies. Hall was famous for his work ethic, and it extended beyond the pool. He's now an eye surgeon in Phoenix. His son, Gary Jr., also is a world class swimmer and a member of the 1996 U.S. Olympic team in the 50 and 100 freestyles.

JIM STILLWAGON
Football, Ohio State

If there were three yards and a cloud of dust in the Ohio State offense under coach Woody Hayes, then there were men who cleared the way. Ohio State's Jim Stillwagon made college football history in his senior season in 1970, becoming the first player to win the Outland Trophy and Lombardi Award in the same year. A three-year starter at middle guard, Stillwagon was a unanimous All-America pick his final two years. In his three seasons, Ohio State compiled a 27-2 record, won three Big Ten championships, two Rose Bowls and one national championship. With Stillwagon clogging the middle, Ohio State's defense allowed just 93 points in 1969 and held five teams to under 10 points in his senior season. He played in the Canadian Football League and is a member of the College Football Hall of Fame.

319

LEADING THE WAY

BO SCHEMBECHLER
Michigan

For Bo Schembechler, everything always came down to "the team." In 27 years as a college coach, including his tenure at Ann Arbor from 1968-89, Bo kept his philosophy that simple, and it made him the winningest coach in Michigan gridiron history. Schembechler, who played his college football under Woody Hayes at Miami (Ohio), would later become his old coach's fiercest rival. Schembechler's ability to motivate his players to perform as a cohesive unit made his accomplishments possible. They include a 194-48-5 record at Michigan which, coupled with his six-year mark at Miami, ranks him fifth in all-time NCAA Division I-A coaching victories with 234. Thirteen of his 21 Michigan teams either won or tied for the Big Ten title while 17 of them, and each of his last 15 squads, went to bowl games. Under his tutelage, 39 different players earned all-America honors, 97 were first team all-Conference and 13 of his assistant coaches became head coaches. Schembechler served as Michigan's athletic director from 1988-91, leading the drive to build a $12 million football complex and sports services building that would eventually bear his name. He then became president of the Detroit Tigers, a position he held until 1995. He is now retired.

· BIG TEN PIONEERS ·

Lee LaBadie

Though he won only one Big Ten title during his three-year track career at Illinois, Lee LaBadie will be remembered for a breakthrough performance. In the 1970-71 season, LaBadie became the first Big Ten runner to break the four-minute barrier in the mile. LaBadie finished the final 440 yards of that race in 58.3 to clock a 3:58.8. He was a key member of the Illini's 1971-72 two-mile relay team that set a world record and won the NCAA indoor title. He served as a junior college coach for nine years, then accepted a position at Bowling Green. A former Ohio State assistant, LaBadie now is a real estate agent.

Academic Achievements

Michigan was the first and only school to provide the entire crew of a moon shot (Apollo 15 in 1971). During the same voyage, Michigan launched the first-ever school alumni chapter on the moon, established by astronauts Dave Scott, Al Worden and Jim Irwin.

The BIG TEN's First 100 Years
Best Big Ten Football Coaching Records

(by winning percentage; minimum 10 years at a school)

	Years	Won	Lost	Tied	PCT
Fielding "Hurry Up" Yost, MICH	1901-23, 1925-26	165	29	10	.833
Glenn "Bo" Schembechler, MICH	1969-89	194	48	5	.796
Joe Paterno, PSU	1966-	278	72	3	.792
Henry Williams, MINN	1900-21	140	33	11	.791
Herbert "Fritz" Crisler, MN-MI	1930-31, 1938-47	81	23	4	.796
W.W. "Woody" Hayes, OSU	1951-78	205	61	10	.761

1970-71 Conference MEDAL OF HONOR Winners

ILLINOIS	Ernest Clements
INDIANA	Mark Stevens
IOWA	Craig Sandvig
MICHIGAN	Richard A. Rydze
MICHIGAN STATE	Thomas Muir
MINNESOTA	Wally Olds
NORTHWESTERN	John Rodman
OHIO STATE	James Cleamons
PURDUE	George Faerber
WISCONSIN	Don Vandrey

THE BIG EVENT

Wayne Duke takes over as Big Ten's fourth commissioner

Wayne Duke, the Big Ten's fourth commissioner, apprenticed for the position in the Big Eight Conference, where he served 10 years as its commissioner prior to his Big Ten appointment in 1971, when he succeeded the late William R. Reed. During his tenure, which lasted until his retirement in 1989, Duke created an image for the Big Ten as arguably the most recognizable—and respected—conference in the nation. Duke's tenure with the Big Ten was marked by his theme of gaining "competitive equality through legislative equality." Perhaps his crowning achievement was forging a historic television contract with ABC-TV to broadcast regular season football games and the Rose Bowl from 1988 to 1997, a deal that guaranteed the Conference the biggest and broadest exposure. Duke was also a pioneer in the area of expanding minority participation in administrative positions in athletics, having hired the first African-American (Dr. Charles Henry) and the first woman (Phyllis Howlett) to assistant commissioner positions for a major conference. He was also instrumental in the fruition of women's athletics as it evolved in the early 1980s to be integrated into the Conference. The first Conference championships in women's sports were offered in 1981-82. Duke was succeeded in 1989 by James E. Delany.

OTHER MEMORABLE EVENTS

- Indiana won the NCAA swimming championship, led by Mark Spitz's fourth straight title in the 100 butterfly.
- Michigan State's Mike Robinson led the Conference in basketball scoring the first of two straight seasons.
- Minnesota's Garry Bjorklund won his third straight Conference cross country championship.
- Michigan State's Greg Johnson won his third straight NCAA wrestling title.
- Purdue's Larry Burton tied Conference records that still stand for the 100- (9.2) and 200-yard (20.3) dashes.
- Michigan State's Eric Allen set an NCAA record (since broken) with 350 yards rushing vs. Purdue.

BIG TEN ADVISORY COMMISSION

In 1972 the Big Ten Advisory Commission was created to advise the Conference on matters of student-athlete welfare, and in particular the concerns of African-American student-athletes. Here are the nine members of the first Commission:

Claude "Buddy" Young (Illinois)
George Taliaferro (Indiana)
Thomas Goss (Michigan)
Horace L. Walker (Michigan State)
Ernie Cook (Minnesota)
Judge A. Dickson (Minnesota)
James Pitts (Northwestern)
Robert Dorsey (Ohio State)
Willie D. Jones (Purdue)

Garret's Illini fencers capture title

Alan Acker (left) and Nate Haywood helped the Illini fencing team win the 1972 Big Ten title.

Max Garret's run as Illini coach was nearing an end when he took his 1971-72 team into the season. The Illini had finished fourth in the Big Ten championships the previous season, so Illinois was hoping to build upon that and move up the Conference standings. Undefeated against league foes in the dual meet season, Illinois managed to win the Big Ten championship despite winning only one individual title. The Illini scored 36 points, enough to finish ahead of Wisconsin. The runner-up Badgers compiled 33 points while earning second place. Illinois received its lone championship from Nate Haywood, a freshman from Marshall High School in Chicago. Haywood won the individual championship in the epee. The team championship was the seventh in Big Ten history for Illinois under Garret, who later left the school to coach at Penn State.

OTHER BIG TEN CHAMPIONS

- FOOTBALL: Michigan, coached by Glenn "Bo" Schembechler
- BASEBALL: Iowa, coached by Duane Banks
- GYMNASTICS: Iowa, coached by Dick Holzaepfel
- OUTDOOR TRACK: Michigan State, coached by Fran Dittrich
- INDOOR TRACK: Michigan State, coached by Fran Dittrich
- BASKETBALL: Minnesota, coached by Bill Musselman
- CROSS COUNTRY: Michigan State, coached by James Gibbard
- TENNIS: Michigan, coached by Brian Eisner
- SWIMMING: Indiana, coached by James Counsilman
- WRESTLING: Michigan State, coached by Grady Peninger
- GOLF: Minnesota, coached by Les Bolstad
- HOCKEY: Wisconsin, coached by Robert Johnson

ERIC ALLEN
Football and Track, Michigan State

Fantastic manueverability was the hallmark of running back Eric Allen, who had one of the great days in college football history on Oct. 30, 1971, when he ran for an NCAA record 350 yards against Purdue. It was one of 13 times that "the Flea" would rush for 100 or more yards in a game. In 1971, Allen had an All-America season with the Spartans, racking up 1,494 rushing yards. He also ran for 18 touchdowns and scored 110 points, both then Big Ten marks for league games. Allen, a native of Georgetown, S.C., earned All-Big Ten honors three times, including the *Chicago Tribune's* Silver Football award as 1971 Conference MVP; he was the first Spartan so honored. He placed 10th in balloting for the Heisman Trophy. Allen also won two track letters and once held the Big Ten's triple jump record.

GREG JOHNSON
Wrestling, Michigan State

The first three-time NCAA champ from the Big Ten, Greg Johnson nearly left his native Lansing, Mich., to wrestle down the road in Ann Arbor. Turned off by some hotshot wrestlers on his recruiting visit to State, Johnson almost went to Michigan, but Coach Grady Peninger convinced him to remain at home. That he did was a boon for the Spartans during their halcyon mat years. Johnson compiled a 54-5-2 mark in his three seasons of varsity eligibilty, winning Conference and NCAA titles each time at 118 lbs. "He was absolutely the toughest wrestler I ever had," said Peninger. "Physically, nobody could stay with him." Johnson coached in the prep ranks and at Utah before taking the head job at Illinois in 1978, where he coached five years. He later helped Peninger at MSU and later coached two years in Australia.

MARK SPITZ
Swimming, Indiana

Mark Spitz was probably the most famous athlete in the world after the 1972 Olympics in Munich, West Germany. There, he won an unprecedented seven gold medals and set seven world records in the 100 and 200 butterfly, the 100 and 200 freestyle, the 400 and 800 freestyle relays and the 400 medley relay. Swimming for Indiana from 1970-72, he won 13 Big Ten championships and held virtually every Big Ten record at one time. He also won five indoor AAU and seven outdoor AAU titles, along with two gold medals, a silver and a bronze in the 1968 Olympics. Spitz won the Sullivan Award as the world's outstanding amateur athlete and was twice voted World Swimmer of the Year. Spitz's poster boy looks helped him transcend sports, making him one of the best-known people in America after the '72 Olympics.

GARRY BJORKLUND
Cross country, Minnesota

Garry Bjorklund is, according to long-time Minnesota men's track and cross country coach Roy Griak, "the finest distance runner of all time to wear a Minnesota uniform." Bjorklund's accomplishments as a member of the Gophers' track and cross country teams from 1970-72 support Griak's claim. A former collegiate record holder in the 6-mile run, Bjorklund broke 11 Minnesota cross country and track records and still holds school records in the 3,000 and 5,000 meters. He won the 1971 NCAA 6-mile run championship and the Big Ten cross country championship that same season, one of 10 league titles he collected in track and cross country. He was a five-time All-American and finished runner-up in the 3-mile run at the 1970 NCAA meet. Foot surgery sidelined him for the 1972-73 season. After lengthy rehabilitation, he returned to form to later earn a spot on the 1976 U.S. Olympic team. He also competed on two U.S. Pan American teams and 10 U.S. national teams.

LEADING THE WAY

BOB KNIGHT
Indiana

Bob Knight is one of those rare coaches who transcends his sport, a dominant figure who commands an audience on national television shows and in commercials. His career in the Big Ten began in the 1971-72 season when, after six seasons at Army, he took over Indiana's program. Since then, he has accumulated three NCAA championships (1976, '81 and '87), 11 Big Ten titles and more Conference victories (316) than any coach in league history. He also is the only coach to have won an NCAA championship, an NIT championship, an Olympic gold medal and a Pan American Games gold medal. Knight, a reserve player on the Ohio State teams that won Big Ten titles in 1960, '61 and '62 and the NCAA championship in '60, almost singlehandedly changed the face of Big Ten basketball when he took over at IU, emphasizing defense and shot selection. His 1975 team went undefeated during the regular season and his '76 team won the national championship without losing a game, the most recent team to do so. Those two teams were at the heart of a run of 37 consecutive Conference victories, a league record. He is a member of the Naismith Hall of Fame.

· BIG TEN PIONEERS ·

Herb Washington, Michigan State

Herb Washington made speed pay as the first "designated runner" in major league baseball history. While purists derided his 1974 signing by Oakland A's owner Charles O. Finley, the wily magnate knew that the man who was called the "World's Fastest Human" in 1970 would bring another element into a strategic game. Washington, a two-time NCAA sprint champ at MSU, offered his world records in the 50- and 60-yard dashes as credentials for base-stealing. He equated getting a jump on a pitcher with anticipating a starter's commands in the sprints. He appeared in 91 games for Oakland in 1974, stealing 30 bases and scoring 33 runs without ever going to bat. He's now a business owner in Rochester, N.Y.

Academic Achievements

Preserving food has been a challenge for humans since caveman days. Researchers at Illinois helped solve a lot of the problems when they developed the freeze-drying process. Research continued through the 1960s and '70s to reach the point where it is today—safe, easy and effective.

The BIG TEN's First 100 Years
Big Ten Men's Basketball
Winning Streaks

All Games

34	Indiana	1974-75
33	Indiana	1976-77
32	Ohio State	1960-61

Conference Games Only

37	Indiana	1974-76
27	Ohio State	1960-62
23	Wisconsin	1912-13

1971-72
Conference MEDAL OF HONOR
Winners

ILLINOIS	Robert Bucklin
INDIANA	Chuck Thomson
IOWA	Dave Triplett
MICHIGAN	Bruce N. Elliott
MICHIGAN STATE	Herb Washington
MINNESOTA	Craig Lincoln
NORTHWESTERN	Maurice Daigneau
OHIO STATE	Rich Simon
PURDUE	Bob Ford
WISCONSIN	Pat Matzdorf

THE BIG EVENT

Talafous leads Badgers to hockey crown

Powered by the heroics of tournament MVP Dean Talafous and the sensational play of goaltender Jim Makey, coupled by a stellar team effort, the Wisconsin ice hockey team won its first ever NCAA championship with a 4-2 victory against Denver University Mar. 17, 1973, at Boston Garden under the direction of coach Bob Johnson. The Badgers won the title the old fashioned way — they earned it. Wisconsin erased a 4-0 deficit to beat Cornell 6-5 in overtime the previous day — thanks to tying and game-winning goals by Talafous — to advance to the title match against Denver, which led 2-1 early in the second period. Wisconsin captain Tim Dool tied it at 2-2, setting the stage for what proved to be the game-winning goal by Talafous, tallying at the 8:30 mark of the second period. Jim Johnston, who scored the Badgers' first goal, tallied the insurance goal at 3:34 of the third period. Defensively, Makey made 32 stops. Talafous, Makey, John Taft and Stan Hinkley made the first team all-tournament team. Dave Arundel was named to the second team.

OTHER MEMORABLE EVENTS

- **Michigan State's Tom Milkovich won his fourth straight Conference wrestling title.**

- **Ohio State's Harold Henson set a Conference football scoring record (later broken) with 20 TDs and 120 points in one season.**

- **Minnesota's Dave Winfield was chosen the most outstanding player at the College World Series.**

- **Northwestern's Jim Nash set a Conference record (later broken) with 226 pass receiving yards in a game.**

- **Indiana won the NCAA swimming championship.**

- **Michigan wins its sixth consecutive tennis championship.**

- **Wolverines end MSU's seven-year domination of wrestling by winning team title.**

Indiana wins league golf title

Indiana's men's golf team placed second behind Minnesota in the 1972 Big Ten golf championship in Minneapolis, but that set up a run of three consecutive titles. The Hoosiers, coached by Bob Fitch, came back in 1973 to finish 86-12 and win the Kempler Invitational, the Purdue Invitational, the Mid-American Invitational and the Northern Intercollegiate championships before capturing the Big Ten meet at Purdue by eight strokes over Ohio State. Gary Biddinger, Kelley Roberts and Kevin Procter all received All-Conference recognition. Indiana finished 23rd in the NCAA meet that year. The Hoosiers won the 1974 Conference title at Iowa by 28 strokes over Ohio State and placed sixth in the NCAA's, and then won the '75 league title in Bloomington.

OTHER BIG TEN CHAMPIONS

- **FOOTBALL:** Michigan, coached by Glenn "Bo" Schembechler, and Ohio State, coached by Woody Hayes
- **BASEBALL:** Minnesota, coached by Dick Siebert
- **GYMNASTICS:** Michigan, coached by Newton Loken
- **OUTDOOR TRACK:** Indiana, coached by Sam Bell
- **INDOOR TRACK:** Indiana, coached by Sam Bell
- **BASKETBALL:** Indiana, coached by Bob Knight
- **CROSS COUNTRY:** Indiana, coached by Sam Bell
- **TENNIS:** Michigan, coached by Brian Eisner
- **SWIMMING:** Indiana, coached by James Counsilman
- **WRESTLING:** Michigan, coached by Rick Bay
- **FENCING:** Illinois, coached by Arthur Schankin
- **HOCKEY:** Michigan State, coached by Amo Bessone, and Wisconsin, coached by Robert Johnson

DAVE WINFIELD
Basketball and Baseball, Minnesota

Dave Winfield could have written his own professional ticket in any one of the two varsity sports he starred in at Minnesota — basketball and baseball — or in a third he never played in college, football. Winfield ultimately chose baseball after a brilliant career at Minnesota, where he was a three-time All-Big Ten pitcher with a career 19-4 record; a career .353 hitter; a first team All-American; and MVP of the 1973 College World Series. His 109 strikeouts in 1973 are the single-season Conference record. Winfield was an outfielder for most of his distinguished 23-year professional career, which ended with his retirement after the 1995 season with the Cleveland Indians. He ranks 11th on the career major league RBI list (1,833), 14th in hits (3,110) and 19th in home runs (465). He is one of only three players in big league history to collect 3,000-plus hits, 450-plus home runs and 200 stolen bases.

BRAD VAN PELT
Football, Michigan State

One of the great multi-sport stars in Big Ten history was Brad Van Pelt, a seven-letter man and the 1972 Maxwell Award winner as the outstanding college football player. Twice a first-team All-America and All-Big Ten safety for Duffy Daugherty's Spartans from 1970-72, Van Pelt also excelled in baseball and earned two basketball letters. Football, though, is where the Owosso, Mich., native made his mark, with his 14 career interceptions among the leaders on State's all-time list. He's still the only Spartan to be honored by the Columbus Touchdown Club as the college defensive back of the year. The strong-throwing righthander also had 2.25 and 2.06 ERAs while earning second team All-Conference baseball honors. Five times an all-pro outside linebacker with the New York Giants, Van Pelt today operates Duffy's Gridiron Grill in Santa Barbara, Calif.

JOHN KINSELLA
Swimming, Indiana

John Kinsella won 11 Big Ten individual championships, in the 200, 500 and 1,650 freestyles and swam on five Big Ten relay champions. He also won six NCAA individual titles and swam on two NCAA championship relay teams, and added nine AAU titles. Perhaps his greatest moment came in the 1972 Olympics, when he won a gold medal as a member of the 800 freestyle relay team. He also won a silver medal in the 1,650 freestyle in the 1968 Olympics. Kinsella variously held American records in the 500 and 1,650 freestyle and NCAA records in the 500, 1000 and 1,650 freestyle. He won the Sullivan Award as the nation's outstanding amateur athlete in 1970. He later became a top-ranked marathon swimmer, winning $25,000 in a 32-mile race across Lake Ontario at the age of 25.

LARRY BURTON
Track and Football, Purdue

Having world-class speed certainly contributed to Larry Burton becoming a standout receiver at Purdue. In his final game, a 38-17 victory over rival Indiana, Burton caught three passes for 100 yards and two TDs (46 and 34 yards). By that time, however, Burton already had made his mark in another sport. Six months after going out for track at Purdue as a sophomore - and winning his first-ever 100-yard dash - Burton earned a spot on the 1972 U.S. Olympic team. He finished fourth in the 200-meter dash at the Games in Munich. By the end of his senior season, Burton was All-Big Ten, Big Ten All-Academic first team, Purdue MVP and *Sporting News* All-America. He was a first-round draft choice of the New Orleans Saints in 1975. He had tied the 300-yard dash world record in 1972, was the 1972 NCAA 200-meter dash champion, set numerous Purdue indoor and outdoor records and was a track All-American.

LEADING THE WAY

WOODY HAYES
Ohio State

For 28 years, the Ohio State football team could be described in two words: Woody Hayes. His toughness was as much a legend as his Buckeyes, whose grind-it-out style was described as three yards and a cloud of dust. In the years that Hayes stalked the sidelines, Ohio State won five national championships and narrowly missed out on two others, while capturing 13 Big Ten crowns. The Buckeyes were 205-61-10 under Hayes, winning a Big Ten record 17 straight games twice during his tenure. Four of his teams were undefeated and five others notched just one loss. From 1968-70, the Buckeyes were 27-2 with two Big Ten titles and one national championship. In a six-year period that began with the 1972 season, Ohio State reeled off six consecutive league championships and a 49-8 record, led by the only two-time Heisman Trophy winner, Archie Griffin. The Buckeyes won national championships from the wire service polls in 1954, '57 and '69. A noted historian, he held the rank of associate professor at Ohio State and took great pride in teaching in the off season. He died in 1987.

BIG TEN LIST

NCAA HOCKEY CHAMPIONS

1948—	Michigan
1951—	Michigan
1952—	Michigan
1953—	Michigan
1955—	Michigan
1956—	Michigan
1964—	Michigan
1973—	Wisconsin
1974—	Minnesota
1976—	Minnesota
1977—	Wisconsin
1979—	Minnesota
1981—	Wisconsin
1983—	Wisconsin
1986—	Michigan State
1990—	Wisconsin
1996—	Michigan

BIG TEN
SINCE 1896
CENTENNIAL ™

Academic Achievements

Indiana's Lilly Library has one of the most outstanding rare-book collections in the country with nearly 400,000 books, six million manuscripts and 100,000 pieces of music. Meanwhile, at Michigan, the first book purchased for the library was a copy of J.J. Audubon's Birds of North America. In 1836, the Regents authorized $970 for its acquisition. The appraised value of the book is now $300,000.

1972-73 Conference MEDAL OF HONOR Winners

ILLINOIS	Robert J. Mango
INDIANA	Gary W. Hall
IOWA	Daniel Sherman
MICHIGAN	Godfrey E. Murray
MICHIGAN STATE	Ken Popejoy
MINNESOTA	James T. Brewer
NORTHWESTERN	Gregory J. Strunk
OHIO STATE	David A. Hoyles
PURDUE	James H. Pratt
WISCONSIN	Keith D. Nosbusch

THE BIG EVENT

Iowa pins hopes on wrestling

Dan Holm

The tradition. The proud history. It had to start somewhere, and the 1973-74 wrestling season was when Iowa first became a dominating presence at the Big Ten level. The Hawkeyes went 17-0-1, setting a school record for victories, winning the Big Ten title. They would go on to win their first NCAA title in 1974-75 and continue on to capture 11 national titles in 13 years. This Iowa team had five All-Americans (John Bowlsby, Chris Campbell, Dan Holm, Greg Stevens and Chuck Yagla) and two national champs (Yagla and Holm). Campbell and Stevens were runners-up at the NCAA meet, and Bowlsby took third place. Yagla, at 150 pounds, was the only Big Ten champion. Iowa's lone blemish was a tie against Iowa State in the sixth dual meet of the season. The Hawkeyes were so dominating that the only other team to even come close was Wisconsin, which lost 17-14. Gary Kurdelmeier, in his third season, would coach just one more season before turning the program over to the now legendary Dan Gable. Kurdelmeier's teams finished 51-7-5 with two NCAA titles and three Big Ten championships.

OTHER MEMORABLE EVENTS

- Minnesota won the NCAA hockey championship; goalie Brad Shelstad was chosen the tourney's most outstanding player.

- Ohio State averaged 365.1 rushing yards per game, the highest average in Conference history.

- Michigan's Victor Amaya won his second straight Conference tennis singles title.

- Illinois' Dan Beaver kicked five field goals to beat Purdue, 15-13; that was the first time in 68 years that any Conference kicker had booted that many in a single game.

- Northwestern's Mitch Anderson tied a Conference record (later broken) with five touchdown passes in one game.

- Purdue scored 111 points in a triple overtime basketball game, the most ever scored in a losing cause in a Conference game.

Gophers win NCAA hockey title with Americans

1973-74 Minnesota hockey team

Minnesota added another riveting chapter to its storied hockey tradition by capturing the 1974 NCAA championship — the first of three the Gophers would win between then and 1979 under former U.S. Olympic coach Herb Brooks. Minnesota, which has made more NCAA tournament appearances than any team in the country with 23, has also won the most national championships of any Big Ten team with seven. They also won a Conference-high 10 league titles. The 1974 Gophers were renowned for their hustle and desire, a reflection of Brooks' hard-driving motivation. They were runners-up in the Western Collegiate Hockey Association standings but proved their mettle at the NCAA tournament, where, by the time it was over, they had no peer. The Gophers became the first team in 25 years to win the title with a team comprised exclusively of American players. Among their stars was senior goalie and captain Brad Shelstad, who was regarded as one of college hockey's best that season. Defensemen Les Auge, Brad Morrow and Joe Micheletti were also standouts at their positions. Offensively, Mike Polich was the Gophers' top scorer. He got help from the likes of John Harris, Tim Carlson, John Matschke, Cal Cossalter, Mike Phippen, Tom Dahleim, and Warren Miller.

OTHER BIG TEN CHAMPIONS

- **FOOTBALL:** Michigan, coached by Glenn "Bo" Schembechler, and Ohio State, coached by Woody Hayes
- **BASEBALL:** Iowa, coached by Duane Banks, and Minnesota, coached by Dick Siebert
- **GYMNASTICS:** Iowa, coached by Dick Holzaepfel
- **OUTDOOR TRACK:** Indiana, coached by Sam Bell
- **INDOOR TRACK:** Indiana, coached by Sam Bell
- **BASKETBALL:** Indiana, coached by Bob Knight, and Michigan, coached by John Orr
- **CROSS COUNTRY:** Indiana, coached by Sam Bell
- **TENNIS:** Michigan, coached by Brian Eisner
- **SWIMMING:** Indiana, coached by James Counsilman
- **WRESTLING:** Iowa, coached by Gary Kurdelmeier
- **GOLF:** Indiana, coached by Robert Fitch
- **FENCING:** Illinois, coached by Arthur Schankin

CHARLTON EHIZUELEN
Track, Illinois

The first time Nigerian-born Charlton Ehizuelen jumped at an indoor track meet at Illinois in 1974, his coach said the school had a problem. The pit wasn't long enough to hold Ehizuelen, who set Illinois and Big Ten records in the long jump and triple jump in his debut indoor season. Before he completed his Illini career, Ehizuelen won 11 Big Ten titles and four NCAA championships, numbers kept lower because of a bout with malaria that kept him out of the Big Ten outdoor meet as a freshman and a suspension from the team as a junior. Ehizuelen's biggest jump may have come in 1975, when he won the triple jump title in the Big Ten outdoor championships. His victory handed Illinois its first team title in any Big Ten sport (other than fencing) for the first time in 12 years—or 130 straight Big Ten championship competitions.

JOHN HICKS
Football, Ohio State

The running backs always run for the Heisman Trophy. The linemen often play in anonymity, although John Hicks was a rare exception. A tackle who helped clear the way for future Heisman winner Archie Griffin, Hicks was a runner-up in balloting for the Heisman in 1973, when he swept both of the top awards for college linemen — the Outland Trophy and the Lombardi Award. An All-Big Ten pick in his junior and season seasons, he was also an All-American both years. A starter on three Big Ten championship teams, he was known for his dominant play and inspirational leadership. He entered the Ohio State Sports Hall of Fame in 1985. He was originally from Cleveland.

BILLY McKINNEY
Basketball, Northwestern

Billy McKinney is the most respected and recognized Northwestern basketball player of the modern era. No more than 6-feet and 170 pounds, the quick guard is the only Wildcat player to be named the team's MVP three consecutive years, and is the school's all-time leading scorer — a landmark he achieved during his junior season. McKinney averaged 15.8 points per game as a freshman, 18.2 points as a sophomore, 19.8 points as a junior and 20.6 points as a senior to lead the team in scoring all four seasons. He scored in double figures every game his senior season, and received an invitation to try out for the 1976 U.S. Olympic team. He went on to play in the NBA for eight seasons and later became a front office executive, first with Chicago, then with Detroit and now with Seattle.

VICTOR AMAYA
Tennis, Michigan

An awesome serve helped propel 6-foot-7, 225-lb. Victor Amaya to Big Ten singles titles in 1973 and 1974. The big lefthander narrowly missed a third straight title which would have tied him with Northwestern's Marty Riessen for most Big Ten championships. Amaya lost to Francisco Gonzales of Ohio State in the finals, a match he later described as the most important of his collegiate career. Amaya, from Holland, Mich., also won doubles titles those two years as Michigan won the sixth and seventh of 16 straight Conference team championships.

LEADING THE WAY

PAUL R. GIEL
Minnesota

It was only fitting that Paul Giel wound up serving as athletic director at Minnesota from 1971-89. After all, he was directly responsible for the Gophers' success in two varsity sports as a player there from 1950-54. So successful was Giel as a football and baseball player — and academically — that he was awarded the coveted Big Ten Medal of Honor in 1954. In football, he was a two-time All-America halfback, two-time Big Ten MVP and was runner-up for the Heisman Trophy in 1953, the same year he was named UPI Player of the Year and AP Back of the Year. He was the first player in Conference history to be named MVP two years in a row. In baseball, he was an All-America pitcher in 1952 and was signed in '54 by the New York Giants. He served in the U.S. Army for two years before joining the Giants. He pitched in the big leagues until 1961, including stints with the Pittsburgh Pirates and Minnesota Twins. He later worked as a business manager for the Minnesota Vikings football team and was sports director of a Minnesota radio station before becoming the Gophers' athletic director.

· BIG TEN PIONEERS ·

First Big Ten NIT Championship

When Purdue beat Utah 87-81 at Madison Square Garden, the Boilermakers became the first Big Ten team to win the National Invitation Tournament title. All-American Frank Kendrick, a first-team All-Big Ten pick and two-time Purdue MVP who would become an assistant men's basketball coach in 1990, was named to the all-tournament team. The Boilermakers had to defeat North Carolina, Hawaii and Jacksonville to get to the final game. Utah had defeated Purdue 87-85 in the regular season. The Boilermakers won the championship game without Jerry Nichols, who suffered a season-ending knee injury at the end of the victory over Hawaii. The Boilermakers finished 21-9 and No. 11 in the final Associated Press poll.

Academic Achievements

Among the most famous alumni from Wisconsin are: actor Daniel Travanti; MRI inventor, Raymond Damadian; diplomat Lawrence S. Eagleburger; two-time Nobel Prize winner, John Bardeen; novelist Joyce Carol Oates; jazz pianist Ben Sidran; ABC news analyst, Jeff Greenfield; N.Y. Times columnist, Jane E. Brody; A.C. Nielsen Co. chairman, Arthur C. Nielsen; and Radcliffe College president, Linda Smith Wilson.

The BIG TEN's First 100 Years
Big Ten Men's Basketball Championships

Total		Total Uncontested	
21 Purdue		11 Indiana	
19 Indiana		11 Purdue	
15 Ohio State		10 Ohio State	

Consecutive		Consecutive Uncontested	
5 Ohio State	(1960-64)	3 Ohio State	(1960-62)
4 Indiana	(1973-76)	3 Purdue	(1994-96)
4 Chicago	(1907-10)		

1973-74 Conference MEDAL OF HONOR Winners

ILLINOIS	Howard Beck
INDIANA	Dan Hayes
IOWA	Carl Walin
MICHIGAN	David D. Gallagher
MICHIGAN STATE	Robert Casselman
MINNESOTA	Garry Bjorklund
NORTHWESTERN	Steven A. Craig
OHIO STATE	Randolph C. Gradishar
PURDUE	Jeffrey T. Bolin
WISCONSIN	Gary D. Anderson

1974-75

THE BIG EVENT

Michigan State upsets No. 1 Ohio State, 16-13

It may have been one of the biggest miracles ever conjured up by any Big Ten football team. No one gave Denny Stolz's 4-3-1 Michigan State squad much of a chance on that early November day in 1974 against top-ranked Ohio State, which had stormed to eight straight wins and appeared headed for its annual showdown with unbeaten Michigan. But someone forgot to give that script to the Spartans, who scored two touchdowns in the final six minutes and then held on for a 16-13 win over Woody Hayes' Buckeyes in as wild and wooly a finish as the venerable Conference is ever likely to see. Ohio State was knocking at the Spartan end zone as time ran out when Brian Baschnagel took a fumble over the goal line. But officials ruled that time had expired, a decision reiterated, officially, one hour later after discussion with Commissioner Wayne Duke, who was at the game.

OTHER MEMORABLE EVENTS

- **Iowa won the NCAA wrestling championship.**

- **Purdue's Mike Pruitt ran 94 yards for a touchdown, the fourth-longest run from scrimmage in Conference history.**

- **Ohio State's Francis Gonzales won the first of two straight Conference tennis singles titles.**

- **Wisconsin's Billy Marek became just the fourth Conference back in history to rush for more than 300 yards in a game with 304 against Minnesota.**

- **Purdue's Bruce Parkinson set a Conference basketball record with 18 assists in a game.**

- **Ohio State's Archie Griffin won the first of his two Heisman Trophies, the only two-time winner in history.**

Indiana's nearly perfect basketball team

The Indiana basketball team that won the Big Ten championship in 1975 ranks as one of the greatest ever not to win the NCAA tournament. The Hoosiers swept through the regular season undefeated with only a few close calls—an overtime victory at Kansas, a six-point win at Ohio State and a one-point victory at Purdue. The win over the Boilermakers proved costly, however, as All-America forward Scott May fractured his left arm in the first half. The Hoosiers were so talented and well-drilled that they won the final three games of the regular season by more than 15 points on average, and captured the first two games of the NCAA tournament in similar fashion. But the next game would be against a powerful Kentucky team that Indiana had embarrassed in Bloomington earlier in the season, 98-74. Coach Bob Knight elected to start May for the first time since his injury, but he was far less than 100 percent. The Hoosiers went on to lose a 92-90 heartbreaker that soured one of the sweetest seasons in league history. They returned in 1976 to go undefeated again and win the championship. Many believe the '75 team was better — just not as fortunate.

OTHER BIG TEN CHAMPIONS

- **FOOTBALL:** Michigan, coached by Glenn "Bo" Schembechler, and Ohio State, coached by Woody Hayes
- **BASEBALL:** Michigan, coached by Milbry Benedict
- **GYMNASTICS:** Michigan, coached by Newton Loken
- **OUTDOOR TRACK:** Illinois, coached by Gary Wieneke
- **INDOOR TRACK:** Indiana, coached by Sam Bell
- **CROSS COUNTRY:** Michigan, coached by Ron Warhurst
- **TENNIS:** Michigan, coached by Brian Eisner
- **SWIMMING:** Indiana, coached by James Counsilman
- **WRESTLING:** Iowa, coached by Gary Kurdelmeier
- **GOLF:** Indiana, coached by Robert Fitch
- **FENCING:** Illinois, coached by Arthur Schankin
- **HOCKEY:** Minnesota, coached by Herb Brooks

LEROY P. "LEE" KEMP
Wrestling, Wisconsin

Regarded as one of America's top amateur wrestlers in the late 1970s and early '80s, Lee Kemp is also one of the greatest wrestlers in Wisconsin history. His career record, established from 1975-78, is a school record 143-6-1. He posted a remarkable 143-1 record during his final three seasons, going unbeaten his sophomore and senior years. Kemp was a three-time NCAA and Big Ten champion (1976, '77, '78) at 158 pounds and was a member of the 1980 U.S. Olympic wrestling team. He was voted the outstanding freshman in the nation by Amateur Wrestling News and was voted outstanding sophomore in the nation after being the only NCAA Division I wrestler to have an undefeated season en route to an NCAA championship. He was a three-time world freestyle gold medalist (1978, '79, '82) and was named the USWF "Man of the Year" in 1978. He was also a seven-time national freestyle wrestling champion. In 1978, he became only the seventh American to win a world wrestling championship and was the second African-American to do so.

SCOTT MAY
Basketball, Indiana

The best player on one of the best college basketball teams ever, Scott May distinguished himself throughout his career at Indiana. Although more highly recruited for football than basketball coming out of high school in Sandusky, Ohio, the 6-foot-7 forward was named the Big Ten MVP and a first-team All-American in 1975 and '76, and was the consensus national player of the year in '76 when he led IU to the NCAA title. His arm fracture in 1975 may have prevented the Hoosiers from winning the title that year, as well. May wasn't flashy, but he overwhelmed opponents with his solid fundamentals and outstanding shooting. He averaged 17.7 points for his three-year career, shooting 51 percent from the field. He was a first-round draft pick of the Chicago Bulls and played seven seasons in the NBA before completing his career overseas.

TIM MOORE
Diving, Ohio State

The most dominant name in college diving during the mid-1970s, Tim Moore was a four-time All-America selection who won 21 major titles during his career, including seven of the eight Big Ten spring board championships. Moore was equally impressive in NCAA competition, winning five NCAA diving titles and never finishing lower than fifth at the national collegiate championships. In the 1975 Pan American Games, Moore won the gold medal on the 3-meter board and the silver medal on the 10-meter platform, and he competed in the 1976 Montreal Olympics. Equally talented in the classroom, Moore graduated in pre-med with a 3.95 grade-point average and was a four-time scholar-athlete and was one of five scholar-athletes awarded nationally by the NCAA. A graduate of the OSU School of Medicine, he resides in Cincinnati.

ROB LYTLE
Football, Michigan

The Big Ten's most valuable player in 1976 and a consensus All-American, running back Rob Lytle gained 1,469 yards as a senior to set a U-M mark. The Ohio native's 3,317 yards broke the Wolverines' career rushing record and still ranks third. Third in the voting for the Heisman Trophy, Lytle played on teams that went 28-5-2 and won two Big Ten titles. Known for his great speed and toughness, Lytle set a Conference record by rushing for 180 yards in just 10 carries against Michigan State, an unprecedented 18-yard per carry average. He won honors as Michigan's top senior athlete and as Michigan's Amateur of the Year. Lytle was drafted by the Denver Broncos in the second round of the NFL draft and played professionally for eight years before retiring.

LEADING THE WAY

BRIAN EISNER
Michigan

Though he was an outstanding athlete at Michigan State, Brian Eisner has established himself as a legendary figure for his one-time arch-rival. Over a span of 27 years at the helm of Michigan's men's tennis program, the 1960s Spartan standout is much more comfortable wearing Maize and Blue. To say that Eisner has been successful at Michigan would be an understatement. His Wolverine squads have won 18 Big Ten titles, including 14 consecutive between 1970 and 1983. Eisner's dual meet career coaching record, which includes six seasons at Toledo, is a glowing 487 victories against only 202 losses. That ranks among the top dozen on the win list for active Division I coaches. Three of his most outstanding teams at Michigan were his 1974, 1975 and 1988 editions. Each placed among the top four during those respective seasons. Eisner's individual all-stars have included Victor Amaya, Mike Leach, Fred DeJesus, current UM assistant coach Dan Goldberg, and MaliVai Washington.

· BIG TEN PIONEERS ·

Bowl game expansion

From 1901-74, the Rose Bowl was the only postseason game in which the Big Ten was allowed to participate. But that changed in May 1975, when the Conference voted to permit teams to accept invitations to other bowl games. Commissioner Wayne Duke lobbied hard within the league, and with Pac-10, Rose Bowl and NBC-TV officials for the change. To maintain a competitive balance recruiting and on the field, Duke thought it essential that other schools have an opportunity at postseason play. On New Year's Day 1976, Michigan competed in the Orange Bowl, losing 14-6 to Oklahoma. The Big Ten would get as many as seven teams in bowl games (1993) and earn substantial revenue for their participation.

Academic Achievements

The Big Ten has the largest living alumni of any intercollegiate conference, close to three million. Of those alumni, more than one million are active members of their institutional alumni associations.

1974-75 Conference MEDAL OF HONOR Winners

ILLINOIS	Howard Beck
INDIANA	Orlando Fernandez
IOWA	Robert C. Fick
MICHIGAN	Jerry Karzan
MICHIGAN STATE	Dennis Olmstead
MINNESOTA	Michael T. Polich
NORTHWESTERN	David A. Froehlich
OHIO STATE	Patrick T. Moore
PURDUE	Lawrence G. Burton
WISCONSIN	James R. Dyreby, Jr.

BIG TEN
SINCE
1896
CENTENNIAL
™

1975-1984

THE BIG EVENT

Perfect Hoosiers win NCAA basketball title

Indiana had the nation's best basketball team in the 1974-75 season, completing the regular season undefeated and ranked No. 1. But star forward Scott May fractured his arm late in the year and the Hoosiers lost to Kentucky in the tournament. That disappointment set up the following season, when a team on a mission conducted a scorched-earth campaign that burned every opponent. Indiana's 32-0 season — no NCAA champion since has gone undefeated — ended with an 86-68 victory over Big Ten rival Michigan that provided final and thorough proof of their dominance. But the final-game win over the Wolverines didn't come without obstacles. Starting guard Bobby Wilkerson suffered a concussion early in the game and was hospitalized, but Indiana overcame a six-point halftime deficit by shooting 60 percent in the second half when it outscored Michigan, 57-33. May led the way with 26 points and Final Four MVP Kent Benson added 25.

OTHER MEMORABLE EVENTS

- Ohio State's Archie Griffin won his second Heisman Trophy.

- Minnesota won the NCAA hockey championship, led by Tom Vanelli's seven tourney goals.

- Iowa won the NCAA wrestling championship with Chuck Yagla named the tourney's most outstanding wrestler.

- Illinois' Craig Virgin won the NCAA cross country title.

- Indiana's Scott May was named the national basketball player of the year.

- Michigan State's Terry Furlow was the last player to score 50 or more points in a Conference basketball game.

Iowa wins NCAA wrestling title for Kurdelmeier

It was close for a while, but not at the end. Iowa's wrestling team convincingly captured its second consecutive NCAA title, setting a record with 123$\frac{1}{4}$ points while winning by almost 40 points over rival Iowa State. Brad Smith, Chuck Yagla and Chris Campbell each won individual national championships for the Hawkeyes; the three titles set a school record. Yagla, at 150 pounds, beat Iowa State's Pete Galea, 5-0, for his second straight title. Galea was the Big Eight Conference's first-ever four-time league champion. Yagla also was named the Outstanding Wrestler at the meet and was the first Hawkeye to win that honor. Smith won at 142 pounds, and Campbell at 177. The Hawkeyes had gone through the season with a 14-1 record in dual meets on their way to winning a third Big Ten Conference title in a row. The only loss was to Oklahoma. Campbell, Yagla and Bud Palmer won individual Big Ten championships. Campbell, Yagla, Smith, Palmer (third place, 190 pounds), Doug Benschoter (fifth, heavyweight), Tim Cysewski (third, 134) and Dan Wagermann (second, 167) were named All-America. This was the final season for coach Gary Kurdelmeier, a former Iowa All-American whose teams went 51-7-5 in four years with two NCAA titles and three league championships. He was succeeded by Dan Gable.

OTHER BIG TEN CHAMPIONS

- **FOOTBALL:** Ohio State, coached by Woody Hayes
- **BASEBALL:** Michigan, coached by Moby Benedict
- **GYMNASTICS:** Minnesota, coached by Fred Roethlisberger
- **OUTDOOR TRACK:** Michigan, coached by Jack Harvey
- **INDOOR TRACK:** Michigan, coached by Jack Harvey
- **BASKETBALL:** Indiana, coached by Bob Knight
- **CROSS COUNTRY:** Michigan, coached by Ron Warhurst
- **TENNIS:** Michigan, coached by Brian Eisner
- **SWIMMING:** Indiana, coached by James Counsilman
- **GOLF:** Ohio State, coached by Jim Brown
- **FENCING:** Wisconsin, coached by Anthony Gillham
- **HOCKEY:** Michigan State, coached by Amo Bessone

ARCHIE GRIFFIN
Football, Ohio State

He rushed for 239 yards in his second game as a college freshman, tipping Ohio State fans to something special by setting a single-game school record. By the time Archie Griffin ended his Buckeye career, the hometown hero from Columbus was the only player to win the Heisman Trophy during his junior and senior seasons and the only player to start in four Rose Bowl games. By rushing for 1,695 yards as a junior and 1,450 the following season, he became the first player to gain 5,000 yards rushing in college play, finishing with a school record of 5,589 yards and an NCAA record of 31 consecutive games of 100 yards or more. During his four-year career, Ohio State compiled a 40-5-1 record with four Big Ten championships. A first-round pick by the Cincinnati Bengals, Griffin now is an associate athletic director at Ohio State.

CHUCK YAGLA
Wrestling, Iowa

Chuck Yagla, like many Iowa wrestling stars before him and after him, finished his career in style. He won five straight matches—three by pins—to capture his second consecutive NCAA title at 150 pounds and earn most valuable wrestler honors at the meet. The Waterloo, Iowa, native was a two-time Big Ten champion who was named Iowa's most valuable wrestler as a senior after a 41-1 season. He also won the team award for most pins (15). Yagla was 34-2-1 as a junior. His last two years he helped lead the Hawkeyes to national championships as a co-captain. After his junior season, he received the Nile Kinnick Scholarship for outstanding achievements in academics, athletics and leadership. A three-time All-American, Yagla was second in the Big Ten and fourth at the NCAA meet as a sophomore, and finished with a career record of 129-17-2. His older brother, Steve, also wrestled for Iowa.

MYCHAL THOMPSON
Basketball, Minnesota

No player in Minnesota basketball history, with the possible exception of former NBA star Kevin McHale, could dominate a game the way center Mychal Thompson could. A prolific scorer, a tireless defender and a relentless rebounder, Thompson is the leading scorer in Gophers' history and is tied with McHale for highest career rebounding average (10.0 rpg). A native of Nassau, Bahamas, he was formerly the all-time Big Ten scoring leader with 1,477 points scored during a brilliant four-year career between 1974-78. He averaged a school-record 20.8 points for his career and grabbed a team record 956 rebounds. His best season was his sophomore year, when he averaged 25.9 points and 12.5 rebounds — the best single-season numbers of his career. He was a career 56.6 percent field goal shooter and shot just above 60 percent his junior and senior seasons. He was the first player selected in the NBA draft and enjoyed a successful pro career.

BRUCE DICKSON
Swimming, Indiana

Bruce Dickson was a member of four Big Ten championship teams at Indiana, and contributed five individual league titles and swam on two winning relay teams. He won the 500- and 1,650-meter freestyle events and the 400 individual medley in the 1975 Big Ten meet, and swam on the winning 800 frestyle relay team. He came back in 1976 to win the 500 freestyle and 400 individual medley events, and helped repeat the 800 freestyle relay title.

LEADING THE WAY

HERB BROOKS
Minnesota

Long before he coached the fabled 1980 U.S. hockey team to Olympic gold, Herb Brooks led Minnesota to the forefront of collegiate success. An ex-Gopher star, Olympic co-captain, and insurance salesman, Brooks became Minnesota's coach in 1972. He led the Gophers to the Western Collegiate Hockey Association championship that same year and to the NCAA national championship the next — the first of three national titles Minnesota would win under Brooks. The others came in 1976 and '79. Minnesota was NCAA runner-up in 1975. In 1980, he guided the U.S. Olympic team to its legendary upset of the heavily-favored Soviet Union. The shocking victory set the stage for the U.S. win against Finland in the gold medal game. The gold medal was the first for a U.S. hockey team since 1960, the same year, ironically, that Brooks tried out for the team as a player, but missed the final cut. Following the success of the 1980 squad, Brooks coached in the NHL after posting a 175-100-20 record at Minnesota, where he starred as a player in the late 1950s. He won three varsity letters and was considered one of the fastest college skaters of that era. As a player, he competed on five U.S. national teams in addition to playing on the 1964 and '68 U.S. Olympic teams.

· BIG TEN PIONEERS ·

Unofficial Big Ten women's championships

Prior to 1981, women's teams did not compete for Big Ten championships—officially. Unofficially, women's teams sparred for Conference titles, beginning in the middle 1970s. In 1975, for example, Illinois won its first unofficial Big Ten gymnastics championship and had several of its individuals win titles, along with several individuals in track and field. Michigan added five women's sports that same year, and the rest of the schools were on the cusp of hiring —or had hired—full-time administrators for women's athletics. Before 1981, women's teams competed under the auspices of the Association of Intercollegiate Athletics for Women, which sanctioned national championships, but had no authority to recognize official conference champions. By the fall of 1981, women's sports—and championships—were sanctioned by the Big Ten when the NCAA began offering national championships for women.

Academic Achievements

Michigan State is the only university in the nation with three medical schools: osteopathy, veterinary and human medicine.

The BIG TEN's First 100 Years
Big Ten Universities Were The First To...

Sponsor a Homecoming celebration (Illinois)

Admit women on an equal basis with men (Iowa)

Own and operate a hospital (Michigan)

Confirm the existence of planets outside our solar system (Penn State)

Serve beer at the student union of a public university (Wisconsin)

1975-76 Conference MEDAL OF HONOR Winners

ILLINOIS	Glenn Hummell
INDIANA	Bruce Dickson
IOWA	Bob Elliott
MICHIGAN	Richard Walterhouse
MICHIGAN STATE	Patrick Milkovich
MINNESOTA	Jeffrey N. LaFleur
NORTHWESTERN	Kim Girkins
OHIO STATE	Brian Baschnagel
PURDUE	Ken Novak
WISCONSIN	Patrick J. Christenson

THE BIG EVENT

Wisconsin captures NCAA hockey championship

Wisconsin beat arch-rival Michigan six times during the 1976-77 campaign—but the sixth time was definitely the sweetest. Wisconsin's Steve Alley scored a rebound goal 23 seconds into overtime to give the Badgers' a 6-5 win against the Wolverines in the NCAA championship game Mar. 26, 1977 at Olympia Stadium in Detroit. The victory gave coach Bob Johnson and his Badgers their second national title—their first coming in 1973—and avenged an overtime defeat against Michigan in the season-opener. The victory capped a dazzling 37-7-1 campaign in which the Badgers had three All-Americans and won the Western Collegiate Hockey Association championship. In the NCAA title match, Alley—a freshman along with teammate John Taft, of the 1973 championship team—scored the game's first and last goals respectively. Mark Johnson, Coach Johnson's son, also had two scores with goals in the first and third periods. Dave Herbst and Mike Meeker scored goals, respectively, in the first and third periods. The championship was the second of five NCAA titles for Wisconsin hockey teams. The Badgers last won an NCAA title in 1990.

OTHER MEMORABLE EVENTS

- Michigan's Mark Churella notched a pin in a record 29 seconds (later broken) at the Big Ten wrestling championship.

- Purdue's Paul Beery intercepted four passes in a single game, a Conference football record he shares with three other players.

- Illinois' Craig Virgin won his fourth straight Conference cross country title.

- Michigan's Rob Lytle averaged 18.0 yards per carry (10-180) versus Michigan State to set a Conference record.

- Ohio State's Pete Johnson set a Conference career scoring record (later broken) with 348 points (58 touchdowns).

- Illinois' Charlton Ehizuelen won his second straight NCAA indoor long jump championship.

- Michigan wins its 10th consecutive tennis title.

- Indiana claims 17th straight swimming crown.

Illinois sweeps track titles

The track season in 1976-77 concluded at Illinois when the Illini played host to the NCAA championships in June at Memorial Stadium. The Illini track fans had plenty of reason to buy a ticket, more than just a chance to see the nation's top track stars. Illinois won the Big Ten indoor and outdoor championships and placed fourth in the NCAA indoor championships heading into the outdoor meet, much of the success based upon the talent of distance runner Craig Virgin and jumping specialist Charlton Ehizuelen. In the six Big Ten meets in which he competed, Ehizuelen won 11 titles in the long jump and triple jump. As a senior in 1976-77, he won the long jump at the NCAA indoor meet and placed third in the triple jump. In the outdoor NCAA championship, Ehizuelen was second in the long jump and third in the triple jump. Meanwhile, Virgin completed a collegiate career in which he was a nine-time All-American by placing second in the 10,000 meters and fourth in the 5,000 meters at the NCAA outdoor championships as Illinois finished seventh in the NCAA outdoor meet.

OTHER BIG TEN CHAMPIONS

- **FOOTBALL:** Michigan, coached by Glenn "Bo" Schembechler, and Ohio State, coached by Woody Hayes
- **BASEBALL:** Minnesota, coached by Dick Siebert
- **GYMNASTICS:** Minnesota, coached by Fred Roethlisberger
- **BASKETBALL:** Michigan, coached by John Orr
- **CROSS COUNTRY:** Michigan, coached by Ron Warhurst
- **TENNIS:** Michigan, coached by Brian Eisner
- **SWIMMING:** Indiana, coached by James Counsilman
- **WRESTLING:** Iowa, coached by Dan Gable
- **GOLF:** Ohio State, coached by Jim Brown
- **FENCING:** Ohio State, coached by Charles Simonian
- **HOCKEY:** Wisconsin, coached by Robert Johnson

KENT BENSON
Basketball, Indiana

Kent Benson manned the middle for Indiana's greatest teams, the 1975 and '76 squads that won Big Ten basketball titles without losing a game during the regular season. Benson, 6-foot-11, was the perfect complement to a team filled with future NBA players, a powerful inside force with a sweeping hook shot. He averaged 15.3 points for his career, including 17.3 in 1976 when the Hoosiers won the NCAA title, and he was named MVP of the Final Four. He was named Big Ten MVP in 1977 when he averaged 19.8 points and was the first player selected in the NBA draft by Milwaukee. He went on to play for the Bucks, Detroit, Utah and Cleveland. He still ranks as IU's seventh all-time leading scorer (1,740 points) and third all-time leading rebounder (1,031).

PAUL MOLITOR
Baseball, Minnesota

By the time he signed with the Milwaukee Brewers after his junior season, Paul Molitor had established himself as one of the greatest all-around baseball players in Minnesota history. A starting second baseman his freshman season in 1975, he was moved to shortstop during a spectacular sophomore year in which he batted a career-best .376 with 10 home runs and 40 RBIs en route to earning first team All-America recognition. He was a two-time All-Big Ten pick, leading the Gophers to the league championship and the College World Series in 1977. When he departed for the Brewers, he was Minnesota's career leader in runs scored, hits, RBIs, triples, home runs, total bases and stolen bases. His 11 triples is the only record he still owns. Molitor played 15 brilliant seasons for the Brewers before joining the Toronto Blue Jays in 1993. He helped lead Toronto to the World Series championship and was named MVP of the series.

JIM MONTGOMERY
Swimming, Indiana

Jim Montgomery earned the unofficial title of "world's fastest swimmer" in 1976 after winning the 100-meter freestyle in the Montreal Olympics. He became the first person to break 50 seconds in that event. He also swam on the winning 400 medley and 800 freestyle relay teams, for three gold medals overall. That was the peak of a mountainous list of accomplishments that included an NCAA championship in the 200 freestyle in 1974 and the 100 and 200 freestyles in 1976, when he set American records. He also swam on four NCAA championship relay teams for seven NCAA titles overall. Montgomery won 14 Big Ten championships, six in individual events and eight in relays, before finishing his collegiate career in 1977. He also won a Pan American Games gold medal in the 200 freestyle that year.

CRAIG VIRGIN
Cross country, Illinois

The young farm boy from southwestern Illinois overcame a serious bladder and kidney ailment at age five to become one of the finest homegrown distance runners in NCAA history. Craig Virgin became the Big Ten's first four-time cross country champion during his Illini career from 1973-76, won the NCAA cross country title in 1975 and completed his career as a nine-time Big Ten champ and nine-time All-American in cross country, and indoor and outdoor track. Virgin finished as the NCAA runner-up in 1976 and '77 in the 10,000 meters, a three-time member of the U.S. Olympic team (1976, '80, '84) and American recordholder in the 10,000. His record time of 27:29.2 was the fastest in the world in 1980, but the United States boycott kept him from competing in the 1980 Olympics. Virgin now directs his own sports marketing company.

LEADING THE WAY

GEORGE KING
Purdue

By the time he retired as Purdue's athletic director in June 1992, George King had managed to be a success at every level of collegiate sports: as an athlete, coach and administrator. King came to Purdue in 1965 to become its basketball coach. His teams went on to a 109-64 record in seven years, winning the Big Ten championship in '69 —the first for the school in 29 years—and finishing second to UCLA in the NCAA Tournament that year. King succeeded Red Mackey as Purdue's seventh athletic director in 1971 (he coached one season as A.D. before resigning from that position) and he became nationally recognized, eventually receiving the prestigious James J. Corbett Memorial Award in 1990 from the National Association of Collegiate Directors of Athletics. During his time as A.D., King was president of the NACDA. King was a standout basketball player at Morris Harvey, leading the nation in scoring as a senior (31.2 ppg). He went on to play six years as a professional with the Syracuse Nationals and Cincinnati Royals. King was amateur athlete of the year in West Virginia in 1949 and '50 and was selected to the National Association of Intercollegiate Athletic Hall of Fame (1967), the West Virginia Sportswriters Hall of Fame and the University of Charleston Hall of Fame. King coached basketball one season at Morris Harvey, then coached three years at West Virginia, leading the Mountaineers to three league titles and three NCAA Tournament appearances.

IOWA'S TOP WRESTLERS

In winning 15 NCAA wrestling championships, Iowa has had seven athletes chosen as the meet's Most Outstanding Wrestler:

1976—Chuck Yagla

1979—Bruce Kinseth

1984—Jim Zalesky

1985—Barry Davis

1986—Marty Kistler

1992—Tom Brands

1993—Terry Steiner

B I G T E N L I S T

Academic Achievements

The historic Old Capitol building is the symbol of the University of Iowa. Construction began in 1839 on the structure, which was Iowa's last territorial capitol and its first state capitol until 1857. After extensive restoration, it was opened as a public museum in 1976 and continues to adorn the school seal.

1976-77
Conference MEDAL OF HONOR
Winners

ILLINOIS	Craig Virgin
INDIANA	James P. Montgomery
IOWA	Rich Zussman
MICHIGAN	Steve Grote
MICHIGAN STATE	Lionel (Ty) Willingham
MINNESOTA	Tony Dungy
NORTHWESTERN	Randy Dean
OHIO STATE	John Sandlund
PURDUE	Bruce Parkinson
WISCONSIN	Peter W. Brey

THE BIG EVENT

Hawkeye wrestlers dominate Big Ten

For nine years, starting in 1978, Iowa would be the only school to win the NCAA wrestling title. This was Dan Gable's second year as coach, and he led the Hawkeyes to a 15-1 record and their third national championship in four years. During Iowa's nine-year reign, it lost a total of six times and never was beaten more than once during a season. Iowa won the 1978 national championship by one-half point, and it became the first team to win the title without an individual national champion. There were, however, six All-Americans: Bruce Kinseth and Randy Lewis were NCAA runners-up; Dan Glenn and Scott Trizzino were third; John Bowlsby finished in fifth place; and Mike DeAnna was sixth. All but Kinseth won Big Ten titles, and Steve Hunte also won a league championship. DeAnna went on to become a four-time Big Ten champ and four-time All-American.

OTHER MEMORABLE EVENTS

- Michigan's Mark Churella was named the most outstanding wrestler at the NCAA championship, while Wisconsin's Lee Kemp won his third straight NCAA title.

- Purdue blocked 15 shots in a Conference basketball game, a record that remains unbroken.

- Minnesota's Kent Kitzmann rushed the football 57 times versus Illinois to set an NCAA record, a mark that remains the best in Conference play.

- Minnesota's Paul Rogind set a Conference football record (since broken) with 18 field goals in a season.

- Michigan's Jeff Etterbeek won his third straight Conference tennis doubles title.

- Minnesota's Tim LaFleur won his third straight Conference all-around gymnastics title.

Minnesota gymnasts win third consecutive Big Ten title

Powered by all-around sensation Tim LaFleur and a remarkably talented supporting cast, Minnesota secured its grip on the Big Ten men's gymnastics championship by claiming its third straight title. The Gophers, under the direction of coach Fred Roethlisberger, cruised to a 7-2 dual meet record and placed seventh at the NCAA meet. The Conference crown capped the dazzling careers of LaFleur, Jay Lowinske, Shawn Hayth, Bob Waldron and Bob McHattie. The quintet laid the foundation for a reign of Gopher dominance that would extend deep into the 1990s. Minnesota won five straight league titles from 1976-80 and would finish no lower than fourth in the Conference standings through 1995, when the Gophers won their 11th championship under Roethlisberger. As for the 1978 squad, LaFleur was the undisputed star. He won three straight Big Ten all-around championships and was awarded the Nissen Award —presented to the nation's top college gymnast—in 1978. But LaFleur wasn't the only standout. Lowinske and Hayth were also outstanding all-around competitors. And Waldron and McHattie were spectacular in their respective events. The group helped the Gophers repel annual challenges to their title from perennial league powers Michigan and Illinois.

OTHER BIG TEN CHAMPIONS

- **FOOTBALL:** Michigan, coached by Glenn "Bo" Schembechler, and Ohio State, coached by Woody Hayes
- **BASEBALL:** Michigan, coached by Milbry Benedict
- **OUTDOOR TRACK:** Michigan, coached by Jack Harvey
- **INDOOR TRACK:** Michigan, coached by Jack Harvey
- **BASKETBALL:** Michigan State, coached by Jud Heathcote
- **CROSS COUNTRY:** Wisconsin, coached by Dan McClimon
- **TENNIS:** Michigan, coached by Brian Eisner
- **SWIMMING:** Indiana, coached by James Counsilman
- **WRESTLING:** Iowa, coached by Dan Gable
- **GOLF:** Ohio State, coached by Jim Brown
- **FENCING:** Wisconsin, coached by Anthony Gillham
- **HOCKEY:** Wisconsin, coached by Robert Johnson

KIRK GIBSON
Football and Baseball, Michigan State

Kirk Gibson can be remembered for so many things that it's difficult to conjure up a single memory. There was the famous pinch-hit homer the limping Gibson hit for the Dodgers to win the first game of the 1988 World Series. There was his 1978 All-America football season, when the flanker caught 112 passes for 2,347 yards and 24 touchdowns, which won him the Downtown Athletic Club's (N.Y.) award as the nation's top offensive end. There was his 1978 baseball season at State, with a .390 batting average, 16 homers and 52 RBI in 48 games earning him All-America status. Drafted by the Detroit Tigers and the NFL's St. Louis Cardinals, the Waterford, Mich., native opted for baseball, where he starred for 17 years, winning playoff series MVP honors in both leagues, before retiring in 1995. Gibson now has a real estate business in Michigan.

MIKE BODDICKER
Baseball, Iowa

In 1975, Mike Boddicker, a senior at Norway (Iowa) High School, turned down $17,000 from the Montreal Expos (they drafted him in the eighth round) to accept a full scholarship to play baseball at Iowa. He won his first 10 games as a pitcher for the Hawkeyes and was 13-2 combined his first two seasons, despite being hampered by tendinitis in his right arm as a freshman when he went 5-0. Boddicker also played third base for Iowa. In three years, Boddicker was 19-6 with a 2.71 ERA at Iowa, striking out 149 batters in 166.2 innings pitched. He was drafted in the sixth round in 1978 by Baltimore, and spent most of five seasons in the minor leagues. He went 16-8 for the Orioles in his first full-time stint in 1983, helping lead them to the World Series while being named American League Rookie Pitcher of the Year by *The Sporting News*. He was an all-star in 1984 and later pitched in the playoffs with the Boston Red Sox in 1988 and '90. He also pitched for Kansas City and Milwaukee before retiring in 1993.

MARK JOHNSON
Hockey, Wisconsin

Regarded as one of the greatest hockey players in Wisconsin history, Mark Johnson hailed from a family drenched in winning hockey tradition, and his performances showed it. The leading scorer on the 1980 U.S. Olympic gold-medal hockey team, he played 10 years in the NHL after a spectacular three-year career with the Badgers. As a freshman center in 1977, he led the Badgers to a national championship and a share of the Big Ten title. He tallied 80 points that season, including 36 goals. Johnson, whose father was legendary college and professional coach Bob Johnson, set the all-time school record of 48 goals as a sophomore and registered 38 assists for a total of 86 points. He collected 41 goals and 90 points his junior season. In the 1980 Olympics, he scored two of the United States' four goals during its historic 4-3 win against the Soviet Union in Lake Placid. He also scored the insurance goal in the victory over Finland in the gold medal game.

TIM LAFLEUR
Gymnastics, Minnesota

When it came to dominating a gymnastics event, no Minnesota athlete did it any better in the modern era than three-year standout Tim LaFleur. A gifted athlete with rare talent and skills, he was the Gophers' first superstar gymnast. LaFleur was the marquee performer on the first of long-time coach Fred Roethlisberger's 11 Big Ten championship teams in 1976. LaFleur won three straight Conference all-around titles from 1976-78. He was also awarded the Nissen Award in 1978, which is presented to the nation's top college gymnast. John Roethlisberger is the only other gymnast in Minnesota history to have received the award (1993). LaFleur was once the seventh-ranked male gymnast in the country who competed at Minnesota with his older brother, Jeff LaFleur. Tim later joined the U.S. national team and competed at the U.S. Gymnastics Championships and at the National Sports Festival.

LEADING THE WAY

DR. CHARLES D. HENRY II
Big Ten Conference

Dr. Charles D. Henry brought many gifts when he joined the Big Ten Conference as assistant commissioner on June 1, 1974. Until his death in 1982, Henry was a committed man with foresight who helped usher in the era of women's athletics in the league. He motivated and inspired staff members with his enthusiasm and patience. Above all, he had high standards. Henry was the first African-American assistant commissioner of any league office. He had served as executive secretary for the National Athletic Steering Committee, which was an athletic policy-making board for all African-American colleges. As committed as he was to easing the transition for black athletes in college, Henry displayed the same zeal as the staff liaison for women's intercollegiate athletics. He was instrumental in preparing the Big Ten for officially instituting women's competition in 1981-82. Henry earned a master's degree and PhD from Iowa, then was head of Grambling (La.) College's Health, Physical Education and Recreation Department from 1958-74, before joining the Big Ten. After his death, the Big Ten created an internship in his name, which provides training for minorities interested in careers in intercollegiate athletics.

BIG TEN
ASSISTANT COMMISSIONERS

BIGTENLIST

Associate Commissioners
1984-89 John Dewey
1989- Kevin Weiberg

Assistant Commissioners
1951-61 William R. Reed
1974-82 Dr. Charles D. Henry II
1974-84 John Dewey
1982- Phyllis Howlett
1983-90 Dr. Clarence Underwood, Jr.
1989- Rich Falk
1990- Carol Iwaoka
1990- Mark Rudner
1990-94 Charles Waddell
1994-96 Robert C. Vowels, Jr.

Assistant to the Commissioner
1961-74 John Dewey
1990-96 Jo Ann Dial

Academic Achievements

Ohio State has the largest single campus enrollment in the U.S. with more than 54,000 students in Columbus. Despite that number, each graduate gets his or her own diploma at graduation ceremonies. It's believed to be the only university of comparable size where this occurs.

1977-78
Conference MEDAL OF HONOR
Winners

ILLINOIS	Steve Yasukawa
INDIANA	Richard R. Hofstetter
IOWA	Rod Sears
MICHIGAN	Derek Howard
MICHIGAN STATE	Larry Bethea
MINNESOTA	Timothy J. LaFleur
NORTHWESTERN	Alan E. Marzano
OHIO STATE	Frank D'Amico
PURDUE	Noel Ruebel
WISCONSIN	Michael Eaves

1978-79

THE BIG EVENT

Magical Spartans win
NCAA basketball title

Front row: (l to r): Randy Bishop, manager; Ed Belloli, equipment manager; Fred Paulsen, asst. coach; Bill Berry, asst. coach; Jud Heathcote, head coach; Dave Harshman asst. coach; Clint Thompson, trainer; Darwin Payton, manager. Back row: 11-Terry Donnelly; 10-Greg Lloyd; 43-Gerald Gilkie; 21-Don Brkovich; 42-Rick Kaye; 15-Ron Charles; 33-Earvin Johnson; 32-Gregory Kelser; 31-Jay Vincent; 35 Rob Gonzalez; 12-Mike Brkovich; 24-Jaimie Huffman; 23-Mike Longaker.

It was a "Magic" and "Special (K)" season for Michigan State, which climaxed a magnificent run to its first NCAA basketball title with a 75-64 win over top-rated and undefeated Indiana State in the most-watched championship game in history. Tourney MVP Earvin "Magic" Johnson scored 24 points, pulled down 10 rebounds and had five assists, while Gregory "Special K" Kelser totaled 19 points, eight rebounds and nine assists. Despite a 7-1 start and No. 1 national ranking, Coach Jud Heathcote's Spartans didn't even look like a Big Ten championship contender with a 4-4 mark after its first eight conference games, including a stunning 18-point loss at Northwestern. But a 10-game winning streak propelled State to a rare three-way tie for the Big Ten title and provided momentum for the NCAA tourney, where MSU coasted to the championship games, winning its first four contests by a combined 93 points.

OTHER MEMORABLE EVENTS

- Minnesota won the NCAA ice hockey championship behind Bill Baker, Steve Janaszak and Neal Broten.
- Iowa won the NCAA wrestling title with 150-pounder Bruce Kinseth named the Most Outstanding Wrestler.
- Ohio State linebacker Tom Cousineau was the No. 1 selection in the NFL draft.
- Indiana, led by Mike Woodson, won the men's basketball National Invitation Tournament.
- Ohio State won the NCAA golf championship.
- Wisconsin's Ira Matthews led the nation in punt returns after winning the national kickoff return crown in '76.
- Iowa's Lance Platz stole a Conference record five bases in one game.

NCAA BASKETBALL CHAMPS

1940—Indiana

1941—Wisconsin

1953—Indiana

1960—Ohio State

1976—Indiana

1979—Michigan State

1981—Indiana

1987—Indiana

1989—Michigan

Buckeye golfers earn NCAA title

Joey Sindelar

Behind the sweet swings of Joey Sindelar and John Cook, the Ohio State Buckeye men's golf team won its first NCAA title in 33 years, edging defending champion Oklahoma State by just two strokes. Called a "total team effort" by OSU coach Jim Brown, the Bucks charged to the championship from as far away as 13th place on Friday, later rising to fifth place as they entered the final 18 holes. Sindelar, a sophomore, led the way for Ohio State, tying for fifth place with a four-round total of 297 on the par-72, 7,023-yard Winston-Salem, N.C. Bermuda Run course. His season-best, third-round 68 helped get the Buckeyes back into contention for the team crown. Other OSU contributors were U.S. Amateur Champion John Cook, who tied for 13th place with 300 strokes; Rick Born and Rocky Miller, who tied for 28th place at 303; and Mark Balen, who tied for 48th at 307. Wake Forest's Gary Hallberg was the tournament medalist with a 287. The Buckeye golfers' performance gave Ohio State its first NCAA men's team title since 1966, when the OSU baseball team took the championship.

OTHER BIG TEN CHAMPIONS

- **FOOTBALL:** Michigan, coached by Glenn "Bo" Schembechler, and Michigan State, coached by Darryl Rogers
- **BASEBALL:** Michigan State, coached by Dan Litwhiler
- **GYMNASTICS:** Minnesota, coached by Fred Roethlisberger
- **OUTDOOR TRACK:** Indiana, coached by Sam Bell
- **INDOOR TRACK:** Indiana, coached by Sam Bell
- **BASKETBALL:** Iowa, coached by Lute Olson, Michigan State, coached by Jud Heathcote; and Purdue, coached by Lee Rose
- **CROSS COUNTRY:** Wisconsin, coached by Dan McClimon
- **TENNIS:** Michigan, coached by Brian Eisner
- **SWIMMING:** Indiana, coached by James Counsilman
- **WRESTLING:** Iowa, coached by Dan Gable
- **FENCING:** Wisconsin, coached by Anthony Gillham
- **HOCKEY:** Minnesota, coached by Herb Brooks

BRUCE KINSETH
Wrestling, Iowa

Iowa was the only school to offer a scholarship to Bruce Kinseth when he was in high school in Decorah, Iowa, and he rewarded the Hawkeyes by being named outstanding wrestling at the Big Ten and NCAA meets as a senior. He pinned nine consecutive opponents through the league and national tournaments on his way to the 150-pound title. Kinseth was a two-time All-American and two-time Iowa team MVP, compiling a 34-1 record as a senior with a team-high 23 falls. His only loss was in a dual meet to Dick Knorr of Oregon State, by a score a 9-8, and Kinseth avenged that by pinning Knorr in just 2:34 in the national championship final. Kinseth won NCAA and Big Ten awards for most pins in the least amount of time. He finished his Iowa career with a mark of 95-17-0 with 41 falls.

JOHN COOK
Golf, Ohio State

He first swung a golf club at age 4. By the time he was 7, he had won a tournament. At age 12, he began taking lessons from Ken Venturi. Yes, for a skinny, blond-haired kid from Palm Springs, John Cook's destiny seemed to be quite predictable. "With my growing up in Southern California," said Cook, "one might think that my decision to go to Ohio State was questionable at best. But I had played golf in California all my life and felt that, if I wanted to further develop my skills as a golfer, I had to learn to play in all kinds of conditions." As a Buckeye, Cook played in the legendary shadow of another OSU alumnus, Jack Nicklaus. But Cook's accomplishments as a collegian match anything the Golden Bear was able to achieve. Three times he was a first-team All-America and All-Big Ten selection, posting the Conference's lowest average (73 strokes) all three seasons. In 1978, his junior year, Cook equalled one of Nicklaus' proudest achievements, winning the U.S. Amateur Championship. Today, Cook is a consistent money-winner on the PGA tour.

RICK LEACH
Football and Baseball, Michigan

Versatility was the byword for two-time All-America quarterback Rick Leach, who could pass or run with equal efficiency as he led Michigan to a 38-4-3 regular-season mark and to three Big Ten co-championships and four bowl games in four years as a starter. The left-hander was the first in NCAA history to score 200 points and pass for 200. In his career, Leach passed for 4,284 yards and 48 touchdowns—then a Conference record—and rushed for 2,176 yards and 34 TDs. Though he was the Big Ten's Most Valuable Player and was named college football player of the year by six different groups, the strong-hitting centerfielder—one of just a few players to be All-America in football and baseball—opted for a baseball career. A first-round pick of the Detroit Tigers in 1979, he played 10 years in the majors for four different teams. Leach now is a business executive in Livonia, Mich.

EARVIN "MAGIC" JOHNSON
Basketball, Michigan State

Perhaps no Big Ten basketball player has ever had a greater impact on the game than Earvin "Magic" Johnson. After pacing State to the 1977-78 Conference title and NCAA regional final his freshman year, Johnson encored in spectacular fashion as a sophomore. A strong scorer and rebounder, he really made his mark with 269 assists, still the Big Ten record. His passing wizardry helped the Spartans to a 26-6 record and their first NCAA championship in 1978-79. Magic's tourney MVP effort in the epic 75-64 win over top-rated Indiana State and eventual NBA rival Larry Bird became the stuff of legend. That championship game was Johnson's last; he turned pro and won three league MVP awards while leading the Los Angeles Lakers to five NBA titles. After retiring in 1991 following an HIV-positive diagnosis, Johnson played on the 1992 Olympic "Dream Team".

LEADING THE WAY

DAN GABLE
Head wrestling coach, Iowa

There was no way to foresee the remarkable consistency with which Iowa and its coach, Dan Gable, would dominate collegiate wrestling for the next two decades. The 1979 championship was the second of nine consecutive NCAA titles for the Hawkeyes, and they would go on to win 14 national crowns in Gable's first 20 years as coach. During that span, Iowa won all 20 Big Ten championships and produced 104 individual Big Ten champs, 40 NCAA titlists, and 144 All-Americans. Seven times Gable's teams finished undefeated, and he was NCAA Coach of the Year in 1978 and 1983. Prior to becoming the nation's premier wrestling coach, Gable was an outstanding competitor. He was 64-0 and won three state titles at Waterloo (Iowa) West High School and was 118-1 at Iowa State, winning two NCAA championships. Gable was a three-time All-Big Eight and All-America selection. He won a gold medal at the 1972 Olympic Games and has been named one of the top 100 U.S. Olympians of all-time. In 1980, Gable was selected to the USA Wrestling Hall of Fame, and, in 1985, he was inducted into the U.S. Olympic Hall of Fame. He coached U.S. Olympic teams in 1980 and 1984, and was an assistant in 1988.

· BIG TEN PIONEERS ·

Gwen Norrell
Michigan State

Her precedent-setting 1979 appointment as the first female faculty representative in the Big Ten never bothered Michigan State's Gwen Norrell. She saw it as an opportunity to be a role model for future women athletic administrators. But Norrell still had to convince some skeptics than a woman could do the job. That she did it well paved the way for other women to move into leadership roles in both the Big Ten and NCAA—something now taken for granted. The esteem in which she was held was evident in her election in 1983 as the first Division I vice president. Now retired and a professor emeritus, Norrell lives in East Lansing, Mich.

Academic Achievements

Some of Hollywood's biggest names are Northwestern alumni. The "Wildcats of the Arts" include Ann-Margret, Warren Beatty, Richard Benjamin, Robert Conrad, Charleton Heston, Garry Marshall, Cloris Leachman, Shelly Long, Patricia Neal, Paula Prentiss, Tony Randall, McLean Stevenson and Julia Louis-Dreyfus.

The BIG TEN's First 100 Years

Four-Time Big Ten Wrestling Champions

Verne Gagne, MINN	1944 (175 lbs.), 1948 (191), 1947, '49 (heavyweight)
Arnold Plaza, PUR	1947, '49-50 (121), 1948 (114.5)
Joe Scarpello, IOWA	1947-50 (175)
Tom Milkovich, MSU	1970-71 (134), 1972-73 (142)
Mike DeAnna, IOWA	1977-79, '81 (167)
Ed Banach, IOWA	1980-82 (177), 1983 (190)
Barry Davis, IOWA	1981-82 (118), 1983, '85 (126)
Duane Goldman, IOWA	1983-84 (177), 1985-86 (190)
Jim Heffernan, IOWA	1983, 1985-87 (155)

1978-79 Conference MEDAL OF HONOR Winners

ILLINOIS	John Davis
INDIANA	David Abrams
IOWA	Tim Gutshall
MICHIGAN	Mark Churella
MICHIGAN STATE	Gregory Kelser
MINNESOTA	Bill Baker
NORTHWESTERN	Scott Stranski
OHIO STATE	Doug Dillie
PURDUE	Joe Menzyk
WISCONSIN	Steve Lacy

THE BIG EVENT

Women's athletics voted in

Female athletes had been competing on the intercollegiate level for decades and decades. They played in championship games. Set records. Took it quite seriously. It's just that it wasn't recognized by the National Collegiate Athletic Association nor the individual conferences. All that started to change, however. On July 7, 1980, the presidents of Big Ten universities adopted a resolution establishing a task force to incorporate women athletes in the league. The Big Ten was one of the first major conferences to take such steps to include women's athletics under the league's umbrella. The task force would include a faculty representative from each school, as well as another representative from the faculty to ensure balanced perspectives. The task force was charged with reporting to the Council of Ten, the league's presidents, that December to—among other things—recommend a timetable for the "absorption" process.

OTHER MEMORABLE EVENTS

- Iowa won the NCAA wrestling championship.

- Michigan State's Ron Charles made all 12 of his field goal attempts in a game to tie a Conference basketball record.

- Michigan State's Shawn Whitcomb recorded a pin in a record 25 seconds (later broken) at the Big Ten wrestling meet.

- Ohio State's Herb Williams led the Conference in rebounding for the second straight season.

- Michigan's Butch Woolfolk had a 92-yard run from scrimmage, the fifth longest rushing play in Conference history.

- Purdue's Joe Barry Carroll concluded his career with a Conference record (later broken) 349 blocked shots.

Michigan dominates Big Ten tennis

Mike Leach

Michigan won its 13th straight Big Ten tennis championship, and 11th consecutive under the direction of Coach Brian Eisner, in 1980, scoring 67 points to Northwestern's 33 in the Conference championship at Minnesota. The Wolverines won four of six singles matches and two of three in doubles. Heading their effort was Michael Leach, who defeated Ohio State's Ernie Fernandez 7-6, 4-6, 7-5. Leach also paired with No. 2 singles winner Matt Horwich to take the top doubles title. Other U-M winners included Mark Mees at No. 3 singles, Jack Neinken at No. 5 singles and the No. 3 doubles team of Neinken and Jack Haney.

OTHER BIG TEN CHAMPIONS

- FOOTBALL: Ohio State, coached by Earle Bruce
- BASEBALL: Michigan, coached by Bud Middaugh
- GYMNASTICS: Minnesota, coached by Fred Roethlisberger
- OUTDOOR TRACK: Michigan, coached by Jack Harvey
- INDOOR TRACK: Indiana, coached by Sam Bell
- BASKETBALL: Indiana, coached by Bob Knight
- CROSS COUNTRY: Wisconsin, coached by Dan McClimon
- SWIMMING: Indiana, coached by James Counsilman
- WRESTLING: Iowa, coached by Dan Gable
- GOLF: Ohio State, coached by Jim Brown
- FENCING: Illinois, coached by Arthur Schankin
- HOCKEY: Minnesota, coached by Brad Buetow

JOE BARRY CARROLL
Basketball, Purdue

Capping an incredible four-year career at Purdue, Joe Barry Carroll scored a school-record 158 points in six NCAA Tournament games while leading the Boilermakers to the Final Four as a senior. After being held to 17 points in a semifinal loss to UCLA, Carroll came back and totaled 35 points (14-of-17 from the field) and 12 rebounds in a 75-58 victory over Iowa in the third-place game. Carroll was a two-time All-American, twice the team MVP and twice first-team All-Big Ten. He was the No. 1 overall pick in the NBA draft, taken by the Golden State Warriors. Carroll is Purdue's No. 2 all-time scorer (2,175 points, behind Rick Mount) and No. 1 all-time rebounder (1,148). The Denver, Colo., native averaged 22.8 ppg as a junior and 22.3 ppg his senior season. The Boilermakers were a combined 50-18 in his last two years.

KEVIN McHALE
Basketball, Minnesota

Long before his legendary days as an unstoppable power forward for the Boston Celtics, Kevin McHale established a reputation at Minnesota as one of the greatest basketball players in school history. Certainly, he is its most well-known. A dominating player between 1976-80, McHale averaged 16.7 points and 10.0 rebounds for his college career. He is the Gophers' career leader in blocked shots (235) and is their second-leading rebounder (950) and fifth-leading scorer (1,704). He and former star Mychal Thompson led the Gophers to their best record in school history in 1976-77, when they finished 24-3. McHale was a first-round draft pick of the Celtics in 1980, when they tabbed him No. 3 overall. He averaged 17.9 points in a stellar 13-year career, helping Boston win NBA championships in 1981, '84 and '86. He was a member of the 1981 all-rookie team and is currently vice president of basketball operations for the Minnesota Timberwolves in the NBA.

ISIAH THOMAS
Basketball, Indiana

Isiah Thomas played just two basketball seasons at Indiana before turning professional, but that was enough time for him to lead the Hoosiers to the 1981 NCAA championship. The 6-foot-1 guard was never named the Big Ten's MVP or even IU's MVP, but he was the MVP of the Final Four when the Hoosiers defeated LSU and North Carolina, and earned All-American status. Thomas led Indiana in scoring, assists and steals both of his seasons there. He was the second player chosen in the 1981 NBA draft by Detroit. He retired in 1994 from a career that is certain to gain him admittance to the Naismith Hall of Fame, having led the Pistons to championships in 1989 and '90. He is now the General Manager of the NBA Toronto Raptors.

JIM PACIOREK
Baseball, Michigan

Jim Paciorek led Michigan to two Big Ten baseball championships, hitting a Conference-record .443 to claim All-America honors in 1982. Paciorek, a rightfielder from Detroit, led coach Bud Middaugh's Wolverines in hitting three consecutive years as UM placed fifth in the 1981 and seventh in the 1982 College World Series. The three-time all-Big Ten outfielder hit .375 for his career and set UM single-season marks for home runs, runs scored, total bases, slugging percentage and RBI. In 1981, Paciorek went 52 at-bats without striking out, one of only three players in Conference history to do so. Drafted by the Cleveland Indians after his junior season, Paciorek was then picked by the Milwaukee Brewers in 1982. He made their roster in 1987, joining brothers Tom and John as major leaguers. Jim Paciorek starred in Japanese baseball for eight years.

JIM BROWN
Ohio State

The Ohio State University golf program has prospered under the direction of long-time golf coach Jim Brown. In his first 23 years as OSU coach, Brown's teams have qualified for the NCAA tournament 22 times. The Buckeyes won the 1979 NCAA title, the first by a northern school in nearly two decades, and have finished fourth in that tourney in 1980, '83 and '87. Ohio State has dominated Big Ten play under Brown, capturing 14 Conference team championships and 140 tournament titles during his tenure. He has produced 45 All-American golfers, including 1986 NCAA individual champ Clark Burroughs. Brown's program has boasted 10 Big Ten medalists, 71 All-Big Ten selections and 11 first-team All-America picks. The 1966 OSU graduate, a Buckeye letter winner in golf and basketball, is a two-time Coach of the Year who already is enshrined in the Golf Coaches Association of America Hall of Fame.

NBA NO. 1 DRAFT PICKS

1994— Glenn Robinson, Purdue

1993— Chris Webber, Michigan

1980— Joe Barry Carroll, Purdue

1979— Earvin Johnson,
Michigan State

1978— Mychal Thompson,
Minnesota

1977— Kent Benson, Indiana

1966— Cazzie Russell, Michigan

1961— Walt Bellamy, Indiana

 Academic Achievements

Michigan State was the site of the world's first superconducting medical cyclotron, which was built at Michigan State's National Superconducting Cyclotron Laboratory. The cyclotron is now in use at Harper Hospital in Detroit, where it is used to treat cancer patients.

1979-80 Conference MEDAL OF HONOR Winners

ILLINOIS	Dave Stoldt
INDIANA	Marc Schlatter
IOWA	Dan Glenn
MICHIGAN	George Foussianes
MICHIGAN STATE	Mark Brammer
MINNESOTA	Dan Zilverberg
NORTHWESTERN	Mike Campbell
OHIO STATE	Steve Crane
PURDUE	Ken Loushin
WISCONSIN	Thomas G. Stauss

THE BIG EVENT

Youthful Isiah leads Indiana to NCAA basketball title

Ray Tolbert

The prophecy could be found in an appropriate Biblical verse, Isaiah 11, which read, "... and a child shall lead them..." Sophomore Isiah Thomas, wearing No. 11 for Indiana, led the Hoosiers to the NCAA championship in Philadelphia, where five years earlier another Indiana team had won the title. The 1981 team, which included future NBA players Randy Wittman, Ray Tolbert and reserve Jim Thomas, defeated a North Carolina team that included Al Wood, James Worthy and Sam Perkins. Thomas scored 19 of his game-high 23 points in the second half when the Hoosiers shot 63 percent from the field. Wittman's baseline jumper at the first-half buzzer gave the Hoosiers a 27-26 lead, then Thomas led an early second-half surge that enabled them to jump out to an 11-point lead seven minutes into the period. Thomas, who would enter the NBA draft after the season — Detroit made him the No. 2 overall choice — was named the Final Four MVP.

OTHER MEMORABLE EVENTS

- Iowa won the NCAA wrestling championship; Lou Banach won the first of two NCAA heavyweight titles and Mike DeAnna won a fourth straight Conference title.

- Wisconsin won the NCAA hockey championship with goalie Marc Behrend chosen the tourney's most outstanding player.

- Illinois' baseball team had a fielding percentage of .986, an all-time best.

- Purdue's Mark Herrmann set a Conference record (later broken) with 3,212 yards passing in a season.

- The baseball standings were broken into two divisions—East and West—for the first time.

- Illinois' Dave Wilson threw for an NCAA record 621 yards in a game.

Minnesota wins Big Ten, but loses NCAA to Badgers

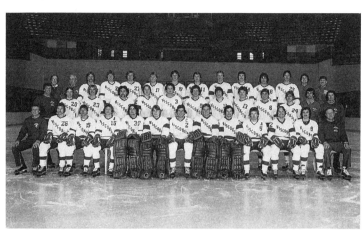

It was a case of Coach Brad Buetow's Minnesota Golden Gopher hockey team winning the battle, but losing the war during the 1980-81 season. Minnesota skated to victory in 11 of its 12 regular-season games against Big Ten competition, going 4-0 against Michigan, 2-0 versus Michigan State and Ohio State, and 3-1 against Wisconsin. The Gophers and the Badgers met once more in post-season play, the national championship game at Duluth, Minn., but Minnesota came up on the short end, losing 6-3. Centerman Aaron Broten was UM's Most Valuable Player, setting single-season scoring marks for assists (59) and total points (106), while brother Neal won first-team All-America laurels for the Gophers. Other key members of the Minnesota squad included defensemen Mike Knoke and Bob Bergloff, winger Steve Ulseth, and goaltender Paul Ostby. The Gophers finished the season with an overall mark of 33-12 and a Western Collegiate Hockey Association championship record of 20-8.

OTHER BIG TEN CHAMPIONS

- **FOOTBALL:** Michigan, coached by Glenn "Bo" Schembechler
- **BASEBALL:** Michigan, coached by Bud Middaugh
- **GYMNASTICS:** Illinois, coached by Yoshi Hayasaki
- **OUTDOOR TRACK:** Michigan, coached by Jack Harvey
- **INDOOR TRACK:** Illinois, coached by Gary Wieneke
- **BASKETBALL:** Indiana, coached by Bob Knight
- **CROSS COUNTRY:** Indiana, coached by Sam Bell, and Michigan, coached by Ron Warhurst
- **TENNIS:** Michigan, coached by Brian Eisner, and Minnesota, coached by Jerry Noyce
- **SWIMMING:** Iowa, coached by Glenn Patton
- **WRESTLING:** Iowa, coached by Dan Gable
- **GOLF:** Purdue, coached by Joe Campbell
- **FENCING:** Illinois, coached by Arthur Schankin

MARK HERRMANN
Football, Purdue

Nobody took Purdue to the promised land like Mark Herrmann. From 1977-80, Herrmann led the Boilermakers to three consecutive bowl appearances and was most valuable player in all three games. He threw for four touchdowns in a 28-25 upset victory over Missouri in the 1980 Liberty Bowl. Herrmann threw for 303 yards and three TDs in the 1979 Blue-Bonnet Bowl, which Purdue won 27-22 over Tennessee on Herrmann's 17-yard TD pass to Dave Young in the final minute. That capped the only 10-victory season in Purdue history. Herrmann threw for two touchdowns and ran for another in a 41-21 victory over Georgia Tech in the 1978 Peach Bowl. The Boilermakers were 28-7-1 during Herrmann's last three seasons. He is Purdue's all-time leader in career pass attempts (1,309), pass completions (722), and passing yards (9,946).

JOEY SINDELAR
Golf, Ohio State

Joey Sindelar was a second-team All-American and second-team all-Big Ten selection as a sophomore during the 1978-79 season, but he fired a four-round total of 297 to place fifth in the NCAA championships to lead Ohio State to its first title in golf in 34 years and the school's first NCAA team title in any sport since the Buckeyes' baseball team won the College World Series in 1966. A native of Horseheads, N.Y., Sindelar won 10 tournaments in his Buckeye career. A three-time All-American, Sindelar passed the PGA qualifying school in 1983, and he has won six PGA tour events, including two in 1985 and two in '88. He has seven second-place finishes and seven more thirds, earning $3,570,000. He recorded three top 10 finishes and seven top 25s in 1995.

ANTHONY CARTER
Football, Michigan

Anthony Carter came a long way from Riviera Beach, Fla., to play football in Ann Arbor. But it was well worth it, for him and the Wolverines. Carter in 1982 became the eighth three-time All-American in Big Ten history (and the first in 36 years). He also became the first receiver to surpass 3,000 yards in pass receptions. Just 5-foot-11 and 165 pounds, "A.C." had outstanding quickness. His 14 touchdown receptions set a single season UM record and his 33 receptions during regular season games is second best in NCAA history. Carter also compiled the highest yard average for all-purpose running in national collegiate annals (17.4). He capped his career with his selection in 1982 as the Big Ten's most valuable player and a fourth place ranking in the Heisman balloting.

NEIL BROTEN
Hockey, Minnesota

It only took one season for Neal Broten long to establish himself as one of Minnesota's greatest hockey players in school history. Billed as the nation's top freshman prior to the start of the 1979 campaign, Broten exceeded everyone's lofty expectations when he set the school assists record (50); and helped lead the Gophers to the NCAA championship. He scored the game-winning goal in a 4-3 win against North Dakota in the championship game. His dynamite debut landed him a spot on the celebrated 1980 U.S. Olympic team, which captured the gold medal and stunned the heavily-favored Soviet Union along the way. Broten, winner of the first Hobey Baker Award, was a consensus All-American at Minnesota, where he was a teammate of his brother, Aaron, prior to turning professional. He played his first 13 NHL seasons with the Minnesota North Stars and Dallas Stars before joining the New Jersey Devils in 1994, whom he helped lead to the Stanley Cup championship.

LEADING THE WAY

SAM BELL
Indiana

Sam Bell has become one of the most respected coaches in America while never losing sight of his primary obligation: helping student-athletes become better. "Satisfaction comes in a lot of ways, but as a coach it is more gratifying when you see your athletes striving for excellence and achieving it," he says. "Much of the general public can't relate to that because it's looking at just the 'big name.' It doesn't see the kid who works to just make the travel squad or the one who scores just one point in a meet." Bell has had success coaching both the premier and unknown athletes, leading Indiana's men's and women's track and cross country teams to 26 Big Ten championships. He has also coached 19 individual NCAA champions, more than 270 Conference titlists and more than 180 All-Americans. Indiana is the only school to win men's Big Ten championships in cross country and indoor and outdoor track in consecutive years, 1973 and '74. Bell coached the U.S. distance runners in the 1976 Olympic Games and served as chairman of the Men's Olympic Development Committee from 1976-80. He was elected to the National Track and Field Hall of Fame in 1992.

· BIG TEN PIONEERS ·

Mike McGee
Michigan

For Mike McGee, scoring was what came naturally, but he didn't shoot from just anywhere. "Never before he gets across the center line," said former Michigan coach Johnny Orr. "I've never seen that." Anywhere else was fair game, however, as McGee became the most prolific scorer in Big Ten history in 1980-81, scoring 2,439 points in his four seasons to eclipse Rick Mount's record. He was remarkably consistent, averaging 24.4 ppg as a senior after scoring 22.2 as a junior. Twice an all-Big Ten selection, McGee was an AP honorable mention All-America. He was a first round pick of the Los Angeles Lakers in 1981.

Mike McGee

Academic Achievements

Purdue has awarded more bachelor's degrees in engineering than any other university in the nation. One of every 17 engineers in America is a Purdue graduate. Also, the university ranks first in the nation in the number of women undergraduates studying engineering.

1980-81 Conference MEDAL OF HONOR *Winners*

ILLINOIS	John Kakacek
INDIANA	Kevin Speer
IOWA	Steve Waite
MICHIGAN	John Wangler
MICHIGAN STATE	Jay Vincent
MINNESOTA	Thomas Lehman
NORTHWESTERN	Jim Ford
OHIO STATE	Mike Wukelic
PURDUE	Brian Walker
WISCONSIN	David C. Goodspeed

THE BIG EVENT

First season of women's competition

Indiana's Denise Jackson

Finally, women got an opportunity to compete for Conference championships that would be recognized by the Big Ten. This was also the first academic year that female administrators and faculty representatives became part of the Big Ten's governing structure. It wasn't until 1982-83 that the women got their own Big Ten Athlete of the Year Award. Ellen O'Keefe, a Northwestern softball player, was the only female nominee by a Conference school in 1981-82. The first women's champion in any sport was Iowa's field hockey team, which won the Big Ten title on Oct. 17, 1981. Other first-year champions: Michigan (volleyball, gymnastics), Michigan State (cross country, outdoor track, golf), Ohio State (basketball, swimming), Wisconsin (indoor track), Indiana (tennis) and Northwestern (softball). On a national level, this was also the year that the National Collegiate Athletic Association began offering championshps in women's sports, effectively putting an end to the Association of Intercollegiate Athletics for Women (AIAW), which had been governing women's athletics.

OTHER MEMORABLE EVENTS

- **Iowa won the NCAA wrestling championship.**

- **Indiana's Jim Spivey was named the first Big Ten Athlete of the Year.**

- **Minnesota's Brian Meeker won his second straight Conference all-around gymnastics title.**

- **Illinois southpaw Rick Filippo pitched 21 innings without giving up a run during the Conference season.**

- **Michigan's Michael Leach won the NCAA tennis championship, but Ohio State's Ernie Fernandez won the Conference crown for the third time.**

- **Iowa's Reggie Roby set NCAA punting records for a season and career.**

Hawkeyes are surprise team of Big Ten football season

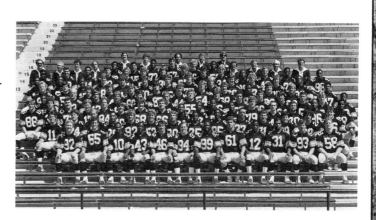

Few saw this coming. Picked to finish fourth by the Big Ten sports writers, Iowa - coming off a 4-7 season in 1980 - stunned the Conference by going 8-4 and sharing the league title with Ohio State. The Hawkeyes earned their first Rose Bowl berth in 23 years (they got to go since OSU had been to Pasadena more recently). The pieces needed to fall into place on the final day of the regular season for Iowa. And they did. The Hawkeyes defeated Michigan State 36-7, and Ohio State beat Michigan 14-9. Hayden Fry, in his third season, was named national coach of the year and Big Ten coach of the year by several organizations. DE Andre Tippett and P Reggie Roby were consensus All-Americans. Those two, DT Mark Bortz, LB Mel Cole, NG Pat Dean, G Ron Hallstrom and DB Lou King were first-team all-Big Ten. Washington defeated Iowa 28-0 in the Rose Bowl. The Hawkeyes' eight victories were their most in 21 years. They finished No. 18 in the Associated Press poll. Iowa had its first winning season since 1961 and was ranked in the top 20 for the first time since early in the 1964 season. During the year, the Hawkeyes upset No. 6 Nebraska—a 16-point favorite (10-7), No. 6 UCLA — a 10-point favorite (20-7) and No. 6 Michigan (9-7). It was Iowa's first victory at Ann Arbor since 1958. The Hawkeyes also ended a 20-game losing streak to Purdue (33-7).

OTHER BIG TEN CHAMPIONS

Men
- BASEBALL: Minnesota, coached by John Anderson
- GYMNASTICS: Minnesota, coached by Fred Roethlisberger
- OUTDOOR TRACK: Michigan, coached by Jack Harvey
- INDOOR TRACK: Michigan, coached by Jack Harvey
- BASKETBALL: Minnesota, coached by Jim Dutcher
- CROSS COUNTRY: Wisconsin, coached by Dan McClimon
- TENNIS: Michigan, coached by Brian Eisner
- SWIMMING/DIVING: Iowa, coached by Glenn Patton
- WRESTLING: Iowa, coached by Dan Gable
- GOLF: Ohio State, coached by Jim Brown
- FENCING: Wisconsin, coached by Anthony Gillham

Women
- BASKETBALL: Ohio State, coached by Tara Van Derveer
- CROSS COUNTRY: Michigan State, coached by John Goodridge
- FIELD HOCKEY: Iowa, coached by Judith Davidson
- GOLF: Michigan State, coached by Mary Fossum
- GYMNASTICS: Michigan, coached by Sheri Hyatt
- SOFTBALL: Northwestern, coached by Sharon Drysdale
- SWIMMING/DIVING: Ohio State, coached by Jim Montrella
- TENNIS: Indiana, coached by Lin Loring
- INDOOR TRACK: Wisconsin, coached by Peter Tegen
- OUTDOOR TRACK: Michigan State, coached by Karen Dennis
- VOLLEYBALL: Michigan, coached by Sandy Vong

ROBIN HUEBNER
Gymnastics, Minnesota

Prior to her arrival, no gymnast in Minnesota history accomplished as much in a four-year career as Robin Huebner, a standout from 1979-83. A gifted performer in every phase of the sport, Huebner's forte was all-around competition. She won Big Ten all-around championships in 1979 and '82, setting school records and earning All-America honors along the way. In 1979, she won the Conference uneven bars and floor exercise championships in addition to all-around. In 1982, she set school record scores in all-around (37.15), vault (9.40), bars (9.40) and floor exercise (9.60) en route to league championships in all-around and floor exercise. She was also an AIAW All-American. She captained the Gophers in 1983 and re-set the uneven bars record at 9.65. She was second in Conference all-around competition; set a Big Ten floor exercise record with a composite score of 18.50; and led the Gophers to a 7-0 dual meet record.

MICHAEL LEACH
Tennis, Michigan

You could say that four-time Big Ten champ and two-time all-American Michael Leach grew up with the sport. Leach and his father Robert were highly ranked in father-son tennis and Leach was a junior all-American at 17 and member of the Junior U.S. Davis Cup team at 18. Leach, who ended his Michigan career by taking the NCAA singles title in 1982 after losing the Big Ten singles crown, won four Big Ten championships during his career. He won singles as a freshman and sophomore and doubles titles those same seasons. Leach had a 99-18 overall singles record and 80-15 doubles mark, including 26-8 in his NCAA championship season. He was ranked as high as ninth nationally and was named to the National Davis Cup team.

JIM SPIVEY
Track, Indiana

Jim Spivey was one of the nation's best middle distance runners while running for Indiana. He earned four letters in both cross country and track. He won the Big Ten cross country championship in 1980 and '82 and was an All-American in 1978, '79 and '80. He won six Big Ten indoor titles in the mile and two-mile runs and five Big Ten outdoor championships in the 1,500 and 5,000 meters. Spivey won NCAA championships in the indoor mile in 1983 and the outdoor 1,500-meter run in '82. He was voted the Big Ten's Athlete of the Year in 1982. He was still running strong a decade later, earning a spot on the 1992 Olympic team in the 1,500-meter run and on the 1996 team in 5,000 meters. He still holds Indiana and Big Ten records in the indoor mile.

ELLEN O'KEEFE
Softball, Northwestern

Ellen O'Keefe grew up in Ann Arbor, Mich., so it was ironic that one of her greatest moments as a pitcher for Northwestern's softball team came in Ann Arbor. During the Wildcats' bid to win the Big Ten's first softball championship in 1982, O'Keefe pitched two-hit shutout victories over Indiana and Ohio State and then went the distance to defeat host Michigan, setting up the final victory in the double-elimination tournament. She finished the season with an 18-2 record, an ERA of 0.42, and was named Northwestern's athlete of the year. O'Keefe pitched in 24 of the team's 41 games that season, starting 21 and completing 13, with one save. She struck out 119 batters and walked just 19 while recording 10 shutouts. She also was a standout defensive player and a solid hitter.

LEADING THE WAY

SHARON DRYSDALE
Northwestern

Sharon Drysdale has enjoyed tremendous success during her 18-year career as Northwestern's softball coach, directing her teams to five Big Ten championships and a winning percentage of greater than 60 percent. Drysdale, a native of Syracuse, N.Y. and a 1966 graduate of Brockport (N.Y.) State College, began her coaching career as an assistant basketball coach at Eastern Kentucky. She completed her doctorate work in physical education at Iowa in 1972 and later took over the softball program at Kansas, where she compiled a 64-17 record. She also served as field hockey coach for two years, basketball coach for one year and athletic director for two years at Kansas. She was hired by Northwestern in 1978, serving initially as both softball and field hockey coach. The Wildcats won the first Big Ten softball title in 1982 with an 8-0 record, placed second in '83 and won the title the following four seasons. Her teams made three consecutive College World Series appearances from 1984-86 and reached the regional playoffs in 1987. She is the author of a softball instructional book, and is primarily responsible for writing the bylaws for the National Softball Coaches Association. She got her 500th victory at Northwestern during the 1996 season and has 571 wins overall.

· BIG TEN PIONEERS ·

Phyllis L. Howlett

Phyllis Howlett broke new ground when she was named assistant commissioner of the Big Ten in 1982, during the first season of women's competition in the league. The first female senior staff member of the Conference office, Howlett had experience as assistant director of athletics at Kansas (1979-82) and assistant to the men's director of athletics at Drake University (1974-79). She was a pioneer in the NCAA as well, where she served many groups, including the NCAA Football Television Committee, Chair of the Committee on Women's Athletics and co-Chair of the NCAA Gender Equity Task Force. She concluded her career as the second woman in the history of the NCAA to serve as its second ranking officer as secretary-treasurer.

The BIG TEN's First 100 Years
Big Ten - Suzy Favor Women's Athlete Of The Year Award Winners By School

4	WISCONSIN	W
2	MICHIGAN STATE	S
2	NORTHWESTERN	N
2	PURDUE	
1	IOWA	IOWA
1	MICHIGAN	M
1	OHIO STATE	
1	PENN STATE	

Academic Achievements

Business education is a strength at all Big Ten schools. Northwestern's graduate school of management twice in the last three years has been named the best graduate school of business in the country. And Michigan's executive education programs were ranked No. 1 in the nation by Business Week.

1981-82 Conference MEDAL OF HONOR Winners

ILLINOIS	Lisa Robinson, Randy Conte
INDIANA	Karen Marinsek, Bob Stephenson
IOWA	No women's award, Brad Webb
MICHIGAN	Diane Dietz, Jim Paciorek
MICHIGAN STATE	Lisa Speaker, Morten Andersen
MINNESOTA	Chris Curry-Gentz, Brian Meeker
NORTHWESTERN	Patience Vanderbush-Murphy, Bob Grady
OHIO STATE	Karen Callaghan, Greg Rake
PURDUE	Anne McMenamy, Tim Seneff
WISCONSIN	Ann French, David Mohapp

THE BIG EVENT

Badgers win cross country title before coach's tragic death

Led by the fleet, tireless feet of a bevy of standout underclassmen, Wisconsin raced to the 1982 NCAA men's cross country championship on a soggy 10,000-meter course at Indiana University. Under the direction of coach Dan McClimon, the Badgers out-distanced second-place Providence, 59-138. Wisconsin, winning its first NCAA title, became the first Big Ten team to do so since Michigan State in 1953. Tragically, McClimon died in a plane crash in April, 1983 after being named NCAA Coach of the Year a second time. His 1982 Badgers were Big Ten champions and placed five runners in the top 26 in the NCAA tournament field. Sophomores Tim Hacker and Scott Jenkins finished fourth and fifth, respectively. Junior teammate John Easker was 16th; sophomore Joe Stintzi was 23rd; and junior Jim Brice was 26th. Hacker, Jenkins and Stintzi returned in 1985 to lead the Badgers to another NCAA title.

OTHER MEMORABLE EVENTS

- Iowa won the NCAA wrestling championship, led by Ed Banach's third national title.

- Illinois' Kendra Gantt scored 49 points in a game to set the Conference women's basketball scoring record in a single game.

- Indiana's Kerry Zimmerman won the NCAA decathlon title, while Hoosier Jim Spivey won his second Conference cross country championship.

- Northwestern's Jon Harvey set an NCAA record for most pass receptions in a game by a tight end with 17.

- Michigan State's Ralf Mojsiejenko kicked a 61-yard field goal on the first attempt of his career.

Ohio State wins women's golf title with star-studded lineup

If there was ever a Dream Team in women's golf in the Big Ten, then it must have been at Ohio State when coach Steve Groves' Buckeyes won eight of the nine tournaments they entered. The season was capped by a five-tournament run when Cathy Kratzert won all five tournaments, defending the Big Ten title she won the previous season to finish the year as an All-America pick and Ohio State's athlete of the year. Susan Fromuth and Cheryl Stacy also won tournament titles that season as Ohio State won its third Big Ten title in four years. Kratzert, Stacy, Meg Mallon and Molly Baney all placed in the top six at the Big Ten championships. Mallon completed her college career as a two-time All-Big Ten pick who finished as the runner-up at the Big Ten championships in 1985. Kratzert (now Cathy Gerring) and Mallon later enjoyed long careers on the LPGA tour. Kratzert won all three of her LPGA career titles in 1990 when she amassed more than $487,000 in earnings. Her career has been slowed by an accident in 1992. Mallon has six LPGA tour victories, including major championships in the U.S. Open and LPGA Championship. She has $2.2 million in earnings.

OTHER BIG TEN CHAMPIONS

Men
- FOOTBALL: Michigan, coached by Glenn "Bo" Schembechler
- BASEBALL: Michigan, coached by Bud Middaugh
- GYMNASTICS: Illinois, coached by Yoshi Hayasaki, and Ohio State, coached by Michael Wilson
- INDOOR TRACK: Indiana, coached by Sam Bell
- OUTDOOR TRACK: Michigan, coached by Jack Harvey
- BASKETBALL: Indiana, coached by Bob Knight
- CROSS COUNTRY: Wisconsin, coached by Dan McClimon
- TENNIS: Michigan, coached by Brian Eisner
- SWIMMING/DIVING: Indiana, coached by James Counsilman
- WRESTLING: Iowa, coached by Dan Gable
- GOLF: Ohio State, coached by Jim Brown
- FENCING: Illinois, coached by Arthur Schankin

Women
- BASKETBALL: Indiana, coached by Maryalyce Jeremiah, and Ohio State, coached by Tara Van Derveer
- CROSS COUNTRY: Iowa, coached by Jerry Hassard
- FENCING: Ohio State, coached by Charlotte Remenyik
- FIELD HOCKEY: Iowa, coached by Judith Davidson
- GYMNASTICS: Ohio State, coached by Larry Cox
- SOFTBALL: Indiana, coached by Gayle Blevins
- SWIMMING/DIVING: Ohio State, coached by Jim Montrella
- TENNIS: Indiana, coached by Lin Loring
- OUTDOOR TRACK: Wisconsin, coached by Peter Tegen
- VOLLEYBALL: Purdue, coached by Carol Dewey

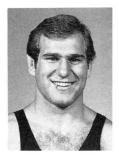

ED BANACH
Wrestling, Iowa

For four years, Ed Banach owned the Big Ten Conference. He won four consecutive Conference titles, setting Iowa records for victories (141) and pins (73) in the process. Banach won three national championships (1983, '81, '80) and was runner-up in '82. As a senior, the Port Jervis, N.J. native wrestled at 190 pounds for the first time and was 34-3 with a team-leading 22 pins. Iowa State's Mike Mann beat Banach three times during the regular-season, but Banach beat Mann in the NCAA final. Banach was Iowa's most valuable wrestler, most valuable wrestler at the Big Ten meet and Big Ten Athlete of the Year. He won a gold medal at 198 pounds at the 1984 Olympic Games. Banach's brother, Lou, was 90-14-2 at Iowa with two Big Ten and NCAA titles and also won a gold medal at the 1984 Olympics.

JUDI BROWN
Track, Michigan State

East Lansing native Judi Brown has come full circle in her track and field career, going from competitor to coach with barely a step lost. Brown became MSU's first female NCAA champion in 1983 when she won the collegiate 400-meter hurdles title in a then-meet record 56.44. She also captured five Big Ten titles that year and 12 in her career en route to becoming the first woman recipient of the Conference's Jesse Owens Athlete of the Year Award. Brown's track career reached its zenith in 1984 as she won a silver medal in the Los Angeles Olympics. She also won golds in the hurdles at the 1983 and 1987 Pan American Games. A 1995 inductee into MSU's athletics hall of fame, Brown has served as State's head women's track and field coach since 1993.

TIM GILLHAM
Fencing, Wisconsin

It didn't take long for Tim Gillham to establish himself among the elite fencing performers in Big Ten history. Gillham, son of Wisconsin coach Tony Gillham, won the Conference epee championship his freshman season in 1983. He successfully defended his title in 1984 and '85, becoming the only athlete in 61 years of Conference men's fencing to win more than two Big Ten championships. In 1983, Gillham earned All-America honors and placed third at the NCAA championships. He was voted the Badgers' Most Valuable Performer after leading them to a second-place Conference finish and a 10th-place showing at the NCAA team championships. Gillham was an All-American again in 1984 and '85, but was denied a chance for a fourth league title and All-America honors when men's and women's fencing was discontinued as a Big Ten sport in 1986.

CATHY KRATZERT
Golf, Ohio State

There may have been no more a dominant golfer at Ohio State than Cathy Kratzert-Gerring, the Big Ten individual champion in 1981-82 who was a two-time Indiana junior champion from Fort Wayne. Kratzert won five straight tournaments during the 1982-83 season when she finished as back-to-back Big Ten champ to earn all-America honors and the Ohio State Athlete of the Year award. She joined the LPGA tour in 1984 after passing the Qualifying School on the third attempt, and she earned more than $100,000 in her second and third seasons on the tour. Her best year came in 1990, when Kratzert-Gerring scored all three of her LPGA wins — the Lady Keystone Open, Stratton Mountain Classic and Trophee Urban World Championship — in a season when she earned $487,326. She returned to the tour in 1996 after an accident left her hands burned in 1992.

LEADING THE WAY

LIN LORING
Indiana

When discussing the career of Indiana's Lin Loring, start with this: he is the winningest women's tennis coach in NCAA Division I history. That just about says it all, particularly for a coach working outside the warm weather climates that usually attract the top players. Loring, who graduated from the University of California-Santa Barbara, took over at Indiana in 1977. His teams won nine straight Big Ten titles, and 14 over a 16-year period, up to 1996. His teams went undefeated in Conference play from the end of the 1977-78 season through most of the 1984-85 season, a string of 104 consecutive victories. Loring has coached one national team champion, two national singles champions and one national doubles champion. He was named the Big Ten coach of the year in 1989, '91, '92 and '95 and earned national coaching honors in 1982 and '92. Loring rarely attracts the most highly-ranked high school players; he's been able to recruit good athletes and make them better players. He also hasn't forgotten the higher purpose of collegiate athletics: all of the women who have played four years for him have earned their degrees. "Athletic ability is only temporary, but an education lasts a lifetime," he says.

· BIG TEN PIONEERS ·

Diane Dixon, Ohio State

A native of Brooklyn, N.Y., Diane Dixon was a sprinter on the Ohio State women's track team who would be the first individual to place first nationally among Big Ten Conference women. She won the 400-meter dash at the 1983 NCAA indoor track championships. She was also the Big Ten's indoor champ in the 300-yard dash the same season, and later that season she won the Big Ten title in the 200 at the Conference's outdoor track championships. Dixon later owned the American indoor record in the 400, an event in which she also held the outdoor record. She also notched the American records in the 300-meter and 300-yard dashes.

 ### The BIG TEN's First 100 Years

**Four-Time All-Big Ten
Women's Tennis Players**

Elaine Demetroulis, Wisconsin (1988-91)
Laura Dvorak, Iowa (1992-95)
Deb Edelman, Indiana (1990-93)
Reka Monoki, Indiana (1985-88)
Kelly Mulvihill, Indiana (1986-89)
Marija Neubauer, Wisconsin (1991-94)
Stephanie Reece, Indiana (1989-92)
Jody Yin, Indiana (1991-94)

Academic Achievements

Michigan State offers the largest number of for-credit study programs of any single U.S. college: 79 programs in 32 countries. MSU offerings include British literature courses in London, but also stretch to studies in social work in India, telecommunications in Paris, Geneva and Brussels and urban planning in Tokyo.

1982-83
Conference MEDAL OF HONOR
Winners

ILLINOIS	**Mary Ellen Murphy, Rich Baader**
INDIANA	**Trish Eiting, Tony Nelson**
IOWA	**Kerry Stewart, Ed Banach**
MICHIGAN	**Melanie Weaver, Brian Diemer**
MICHIGAN STATE	**Karen Wells, Mike Brown**
MINNESOTA	**Jill Halsted, Randy Breuer**
NORTHWESTERN	**Sue Hebson, Jeff Munn**
OHIO STATE	**Nancy Pearson, Sam Linzell, Joe Smith, Steve Hirsch**
PURDUE	**Jane Neff, Jack Farson**
WISCONSIN	**Rose Thomson, David Farley**

1983-84

THE BIG EVENT

Northwestern women capture softball title

"This is our strongest team ever at Northwestern," softball coach Sharon Drysdale said before the season. "We are better balanced, we have more speed and we have more consistent hitters throughout the lineup." She was right. The Wildcats went on to finish 41-17 overall and 17-4 in Big Ten play to capture the league championship, and placed third out of 16 teams in the NCAA finals. The Wildcats won with defense, allowing opponents a mere .136 batting average and 76 runs in 58 games. Freshman pitcher Lisa Ishikawa (left) set school records for wins (33) and strikeouts (469) and the team committed just 58 errors for a fielding percentage of .966. Shortstop Lisa Koser led the offense, hitting .266, driving in 24 runs and hitting five home runs — all team highs. The league championship was the second under Drysdale, and the first of four straight.

OTHER MEMORABLE EVENTS

- Iowa won the NCAA wrestling championship; Jim Zalesky won his third national title and was chosen the meet's most outstanding wrestler.

- Ohio State's Chris Perry won his third straight Bolstad Award, given to the Conference golfer with the lowest season scoring average.

- Michigan won the men's basketball National Invitation Tournament.

- Wisconsin's men's cross country team had the first, second and third place finishers in the Conference meet.

- Michigan State heavyweight Mike Potts recorded the fastest pin for a Conference championship match: 43 seconds.

- Indiana's Steve Alford led the nation in free throw percentage at .913.

Illini football team beats all nine Conference foes

Between 1896 and 1982, 50 of the first 87 Conference championship football teams wound up unbeaten or untied. In 1983, coach Mike White's Illinois football team became the first Big Ten club to post victories over all nine of the Conference foes. Victories over unbeaten Michigan State, fourth-ranked Iowa, Wisconsin, Purdue and sixth-ranked Ohio State left Illinois 5-0 heading into a showdown with Michigan, and Illinois' defense didn't allow a touchdown in the 16-6 victory. Illinois cruised to its last three wins over Minnesota, Indiana and Northwestern, the finale played in front of 30,000 Illinois fans who made the trip to Northwestern. Illinois had already clinched its first Rose Bowl trip in 20 years with the 49-21 victory at home over Indiana, and the Illini finished the perfect Big Ten season with a 32-point win over the Wildcats. Defensive tackle Don Thorp was named the Big Ten's most valuable player, and White was the consensus pick as national coach of the year. Illinois traveled to Pasadena to meet local favorite UCLA, and the perfect Conference season ended with a sour taste. The fourth-ranked Illini fell, 45-9.

OTHER BIG TEN CHAMPIONS

Men
- BASEBALL: Michigan, coached by Bud Middaugh
- GYMNASTICS: Minnesota, coached by Fred Roethlisberger
- OUTDOOR TRACK: Wisconsin, coached by Ed Nuttycombe
- INDOOR TRACK: Indiana, coached by Sam Bell
- BASKETBALL: Illinois, coached by Lou Henson, and Purdue, coached by Gene Keady
- CROSS COUNTRY: Wisconsin, coached by Martin Smith
- TENNIS: Minnesota, coached by Jerry Noyce
- SWIMMING/DIVING: Indiana, coached by James Counsilman
- WRESTLING: Iowa, coached by Dan Gable
- GOLF: Ohio State, coached by Jim Brown
- FENCING: Wisconsin, coached by Anthony Gillham

Women
- BASKETBALL: Ohio State, coached by Tara Van Derveer
- CROSS COUNTRY: Wisconsin, coached by Peter Tegen
- FENCING: Ohio State, coached by Charlotte Remenyik
- FIELD HOCKEY: Iowa, coached by Judith Davidson, and Northwestern, coached by Nancy Stevens
- GOLF: Ohio State, coached by Stephen Groves
- GYMNASTICS: Ohio State, coached by Larry Cox
- SOFTBALL: Northwestern, coached by Sharon Drysdale
- SWIMMING/DIVING: Ohio State, coached by Jim Montrella
- TENNIS: Indiana, coached by Lin Loring
- INDOOR TRACK: Wisconsin, coached by Peter Tegen
- OUTDOOR TRACK: Wisconsin, coached by Peter Tegen
- VOLLEYBALL: Northwestern, coached by Jerry Angle

LISA ISHIKAWA
Softball, Northwestern

Lisa Ishikawa was voted Northwestern's female athlete of the decade for her accomplishments as a softball pitcher. Ishikawa, who graduated with a degree in industrial engineering, was a two-time All-American who led the Wildcats to three College World Series appearances. As a freshman in 1984, she led the team to a Big Ten championship and a third-place national finish, setting an NCAA record by striking out 469 batters. She set another NCAA record as a junior when she struck out 20 batters in a 2-0 no-hit victory over Iowa. She finished her career with a 97-30 record and a 0.47 ERA and held 22 individual records for the Wildcats, including most wins in a season (33), career strikeouts (1,200), most consecutive batters retired (39) and consecutive scoreless innings (90).

SUNDER NIX
Track, Indiana

Sunder Nix won six Big Ten titles and one NCAA championship while running for Indiana. The Chicago native accounted for 43 points in the NCAA meet during his career, and made a worldwide impact as a quarter-miler. Nix won four straight Big Ten indoor titles, the first athlete ever to do so, and won six league championships overall. He became the first Conference runner to break 45 seconds in the 400 meters, and did it five times. He won the 1983 NCAA 400-meter title, then earned a gold medal in the 1984 Olympics as the leadoff runner on the 4x400 meter relay team, and placed fifth in the 400-meter run. He was the No. 1-ranked 400-meter runner in the world by *Track and Field News*, and was voted Big Ten Athlete of the Year in 1985.

JIM ZALESKY
Wrestling, Iowa

You wonder how Iowa's wrestling program has dominated so consistently over years, then you see records of athletes like Jim Zalesky. A three-time NCAA and Big Ten champion at 158 pounds, Zalesky finished his career with back-to-back perfect seasons and an 89-match winning streak surpassed in history only by Zalesky's coach, Dan Gable, who won 100 straight matches as an undergraduate at Iowa State. Zalesky, a Shueyville, Iowa, native, was a four-time All-American and as a senior was most valuable wrestler at the Big Ten and NCAA tournaments. He was Iowa's most valuable wrestler as a senior and shared the award as a junior. His final record was 131-7-1, and Iowa won national championships his last three seasons. His freshman year, Zalesky was second in the Big Ten and fifth at the NCAA meet.

DENISE JACKSON
Basketball, Indiana

Denise Jackson is one of the best basketball players to come out of Indiana's women's program. The 5-foot-11 native of Miami, Fla. is the Hoosiers' all-time leading scorer and rebounder, and was a first team All-Big Ten selection in 1983 and '84. Jackson finished her career with 1,917 points, a four-year average of 15.6. She scored a career-high 32 points against Michigan State in 1981 and also had games of 31 and 30. She averaged 10.3 rebounds over her career, far and away the best in IU's history. She holds the school record for rebounds in a season (12.2 per game in 1983) and in a game (22 against Purdue in 1981). Jackson also led the Hoosiers in blocked shots her final three seasons and ranks seventh all-time in steals.

LEADING THE WAY

MARTIN SMITH
Wisconsin

Dominate and win championships — Martin Smith's teams have done both during his remarkably successful tenure as head coach of the Wisconsin men's cross country team. He is renowned mostly for his work in cross country, although much of his success there carried over to track. His career with the cross country team began in 1983, when the Badgers won the first of 11 Big Ten championships under Smith. Regarded as one of the nation's premier distance running coaches, he guided Wisconsin to the 1985 and '88 NCAA championships. The Badgers have finished runner-up twice in the NCAA meet, third twice and have finished in the top 10 a total of 10 times. Wisconsin won eight straight Big Ten championships between 1985 and '92, the sixth-longest domination streak in league history for any sport. A five-time Big Ten Coach of the Year award recipient and a two-time NCAA Coach of the Year honoree, he has coached a combined 64 All-Americans in cross country and track and 30 Big Ten champions. Smith's athletes enjoy scholastic, as well as athletic, success as his teams boast an average GPA of 3.0. Smith was the men's and women's cross country coach at Virginia before going to Wisconsin. At Virginia, his women's cross country team won back-to-back NCAA cross country titles in 1981 and '82.

· BIG TEN PIONEERS ·
Illinois beats 'em all

Generally speaking, bragging rights aren't ever secured over the entire league. While a university's football and basketball teams may win league titles in the same school year, there is always one school that holds a key win to keep the talking minimal. Such was not the case in the 1983-84 school year at Illinois, when the Illini beat every other member school in both football and basketball. Under coach Mike White, Illinois defeated all nine of the other Conference schools, the only time in league history that a Conference team knocked off every other one in a season. Then during the basketball season, Illinois shared the league championship for coach Lou Henson's only Big Ten title, and the Illini managed to defeat all nine league opponents at least once on their way to a 15-3 Big Ten record.

Academic Achievements

Minnesota's *"College Bowl"* (the Super Bowl of the mind) team traditionally ranks among America's strongest, winning national championships in 1984, '87 and '89.

1983-84
Conference MEDAL OF HONOR
Winners

ILLINOIS	Karen Brems, Kerry Dickson
INDIANA	Lynne Beck,
	George Gianakopolous
IOWA	Lisa Anderson, David Ross
MICHIGAN	Alison Noble,
	Stefan Humphries
MICHIGAN STATE	Anne Pewe, Kelly Miller
MINNESOTA	Nancy Harris, Joe Ray
NORTHWESTERN	Lorie Miller, John Kidd
OHIO STATE	Kelly Robinson, John Frank
PURDUE	Jan Hoosline, Adam Abele
WISCONSIN	Janet Huff, John Johannson

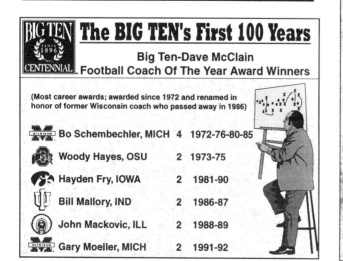

The BIG TEN's First 100 Years
Big Ten-Dave McClain
Football Coach Of The Year Award Winners

(Most career awards; awarded since 1972 and renamed in honor of former Wisconsin coach who passed away in 1986)

Bo Schembechler, MICH	4	1972-76-80-85
Woody Hayes, OSU	2	1973-75
Hayden Fry, IOWA	2	1981-90
Bill Mallory, IND	2	1986-87
John Mackovic, ILL	2	1988-89
Gary Moeller, MICH	2	1991-92

THE BIG EVENT

Twins lead Ohio State to NCAA gymnastics title

The twin brothers were identical on the parallel bars, and Ohio State managed to pull away slightly in the final event to win the NCAA championship, the school's first team title since the Buckeyes won the NCAA golf title in 1979. Senior Noah Riskin scored a 9.75 to win the parallel bars during team competition to help push Ohio State past host Nebraska by a 285.35-284.55 margin, the narrowest in NCAA men's gymnastics in 15 years. Later, Noah Riskin tied his brother, Seth, on the parallel bars during individual competition. Tim Muench finished second on the pommel horse to join the Riskins as All-Americans under coach Mike Wilson. Ohio State had earlier grabbed the Big Ten championship and finished the dual meet regular season with a 16-0 record. The Buckeyes finished third in the NCAA championships the previous season.

OTHER MEMORABLE EVENTS

- Illinois' Charles Lakes won his second straight Conference all-around gymnastics title.

- Iowa won the NCAA wrestling title; Barry Davis won his third national title and was chosen the meet's most outstanding wrestler.

- Wisconsin won the NCAA women's cross country championship; Cathy Branta was the individual NCAA winner after winning her third straight Conference crown.

- Iowa's Chuck Long completed an NCAA record 22 straight passes in one game; Illinois' David Williams led the nation with 101 pass receptions; Ohio State's Keith Byars led the nation in scoring, rushing and all-purpose running.

- Ohio State's Bill Cunningham had 17 strike outs in a Conference playoff game; Michigan's Ken Hayward led the Conference in RBI for the second straight year.

- Ohio State's Clark Burroughs won the NCAA golf title.

Wildcat women finally get over the top

The Northwestern women's tennis team knocked on the door for four consecutive years, placing second in the Big Ten meet from 1981-84. It finally broke through in 1985, winning the championship by capturing 26 of the 27 tournament matches. The Wildcats had lost to Indiana, 5-4, for the title in 1984, and had lost the services of Maeve Quinlan, who had earned All-America honors and gone on to compete in individual tournaments. Still, coach Sandy Stap Clifton, was optimistic heading into the season. "This team is different from any other I've coached in that we have fighters at every position who will do anything to win. This gives the team a lot of confidence." With just one senior, the Wildcats swept through Big Ten play with an 11-0 record and finished 22-7 overall. (It finished ninth out of 16 teams in the NCAA championships.) The Big Ten title came over Indiana, 8-1, with the the Hoosiers' only victory coming at No. 1 singles. Northwestern lost just two sets in winning the other eight matches. Team members included Kelly Boyse, Diane Donnelly, Kim Gandy, Jennifer Hilton, Kristin Laux, Stephanie Lightvoet, Eva Lucido and Tina Oechsle.

OTHER BIG TEN CHAMPIONS

Men
- FOOTBALL: Ohio State, coached by Earle Bruce
- BASEBALL: Minnesota, coached by John Anderson
- GYMNASTICS: Ohio State, coached by Michael Wilson
- OUTDOOR TRACK: Indiana, coached by Sam Bell
- INDOOR TRACK: Indiana, coached by Sam Bell
- BASKETBALL: Michigan, coached by Bill Frieder
- CROSS COUNTRY: Illinois, coached by Gary Wieneke
- TENNIS: Michigan, coached by Brian Eisner
- SWIMMING/DIVING: Indiana, coached by James Counsilman
- WRESTLING: Iowa, coached by Dan Gable
- GOLF: Ohio State, coached by Jim Brown
- FENCING: Wisconsin, coached by Anthony Gillham

Women
- BASKETBALL: Ohio State, coached by Tara Van Derveer
- CROSS COUNTRY: Wisconsin, coached by Peter Tegen
- FENCING: Ohio State, coached by Charlotte Remenyik
- FIELD HOCKEY: Northwestern, coached by Nancy Stevens
- GOLF: Ohio State, coached by Stephen Groves
- GYMNASTICS: Ohio State, coached by Larry Cox
- SOFTBALL: Northwestern, coached by Sharon Drysdale
- SWIMMING/DIVING: Ohio State, coached by Jim Montrella
- INDOOR TRACK: Wisconsin, coached by Peter Tegen
- OUTDOOR TRACK: Wisconsin, coached by Peter Tegen
- VOLLEYBALL: Northwestern, coached by Jerry Angle

BARRY DAVIS
Wrestling, Iowa

Barry Davis' collegiate wrestling career ended with fitting flair: 21 consecutive victories, his third national championship and the men's Big Ten Jesse Owens Athlete of the Year award. Davis won four Conference titles and finished his career as Iowa's all-time winningest wrestler with a 163-9-1 overall record. He was 43-1 as a senior and was most valuable wrestler at the Big Ten meet. His only loss during the season was to Michigan's John Fisher. Davis was ranked No. 1 in the country at 126 pounds all season. He won a silver medal at the 1984 Olympic Games at 125.5 pounds, losing in the final to Hideaki Tomiyama of Japan, 8-3. Davis redshirted the 1983-84 season at Iowa to prepare for the Olympics. As a sophomore in 1981-82, the Cedar Rapids, Iowa, native set an Iowa record with 46 victories.

CATHY BRANTA
Cross Country, Wisconsin

Cathy Branta was one of the most dominating collegiate distance runners of the early and mid-1980s. She was a four-time All-American in cross country and won Big Ten championships in 1982, '83 and '84. She won the NCAA championship and TAC national championship in 1984; in 1985 she finished second in a field of 200 at the IAAF World Cross Country Championships. In track, Branta was a seven-time All-American and won five NCAA championships and two TAC national championships. She also won eight Big Ten championships, including one in 1983, four in 1984 and three in 1985. She won the 1985 Broderick Award as the nation's top collegiate distance runner and also won the 1985 Jumbo Elliot Award, given to the nation's outstanding track athlete. She was Wisconsin's Female Athlete of the Year three times (1982-85) and won the prestigious Big Ten Medal of Honor for excellence in academics and athletics. In 1985, she also won the women's Big Ten-Jesse Owens Athlete of the Year Award.

ANUCHA BROWN
Basketball, Northwestern

Anucha Brown was perhaps the greatest women's basketball player in the history of the Big Ten when she completed her career at Northwestern in 1985. As a junior, the 6-foot-1 center became the first woman in league history to lead the Conference in scoring and rebounding in the same season. She led the nation in scoring as a senior with a 30.5 average, and her 855 points that season was the fifth-highest single-season total in NCAA history at the time. She completed her career as the Big Ten's all-time leading scorer with 2,307 points. She earned first-team All-Big Ten honors three times, was the league's most valuable player as a junior and senior — the first two-time winner of the award — and was a first-team All-American her final season.

BARRY LARKIN
Baseball, Michigan

It's not surprising that Barry Larkin has become a National League all-star shortstop for his hometown Cincinnati Reds. From his first days at Fisher Stadium, Larkin showed promise, hitting .352 and striking out only 10 times as a freshman en route to third-team all-Big Ten honors. He only got better after that, becoming the first man in Big Ten history to twice be named Conference MVP. An all-American in both 1984 and 1985, Larkin posted .363 and .368 averages those two seasons and left Michigan for the majors with a nifty .361 career mark. He made just seven errors as a junior to lift his career fielding mark to .947 after a 19-error freshman campaign. Larkin hit .311 for Team USA, which captured the silver medal in the 1984 Olympic Games in Los Angeles.

LEADING THE WAY

CHARLOTTE REMENYIK
Ohio State

Making history by becoming the first woman in the Midwest to coach both men's and women's fencing, Charlotte Remenyik had won six Big Ten championships with her women's program and has six second-place finishes in the last seven years at the Big Ten championship in men's fencing. Born and raised in Hungary, she became one of her home country's finest duelists, placing fifth in the World University Games in 1954. After immigrating to the United States in 1956, Remenyik continued to be a driving force in competitive fencing. She won the Illinois Divisional seven times, and she embarked on her college coaching career at Northwestern, where her women's program won the unofficial Big Ten championship in 1977 and 1978. She moved to Ohio State for the 1978-79 season, and her teams won the first of four Big Ten titles in 1980-81. Her Buckeyes women's programs also won Big Ten titles in 1989 and 1990, although the Big Ten discontinued fencing championships in 1987. As the only woman coaching a men's program east of the Mississippi River, she has produced three men's Big Ten champs.

TENNIS PLAYERS OF THE YEAR

In 1984 the Big Ten began awarding a Player of the Year award to the top women's tennis player. The winners:

1984— Claudia Brisk, Minnesota
1985— Molly McGrath, Purdue
1986— Lisa Fortman, Wisconsin
1987— none selected
1988— Tina Basle, Michigan, and Kelly Mulvihill, Indiana (tie)
1989— Kelly Mulvihill, Indiana
1990— Deb Edelman, Indiana
1991— Stephanie Reece, Indiana
1992— Stephanie Reece, Indiana, and Deb Edelman, Indiana (tie)
1993— Lindsey Nimmo, Illinois
1994— Jody Yin, Indiana
1995— Sarah Cyganiak, Michigan
1996— Melissa Zimpfer, Wisconsin

BIG TEN
SINCE 1896
CENTENNIAL

Academic Achievements

Garfield might have Ohio State University to thank for a continued run in the comic strips. The first successful feline leukemia vaccine was invented at OSU in 1985 by Richard G. Olsen, a professor of veterinary biosciences in the College of Veterinary Medicine. Olsen is now a professor emeritus.

1984-85 Conference MEDAL OF HONOR Winners

ILLINOIS	Sue Arildsen, Peter Bouton
INDIANA	Kelly Greenlee, Uwe Blab
IOWA	Dee Ann Davidson, Rob Moellering
MICHIGAN	Andrea Williams, Ken Hayward
MICHIGAN STATE	Kelly Belanger, Carlton Evans
MINNESOTA	Jocelyn Smith, Dave Morrisson
NORTHWESTERN	Anucha Browne, Jim Bobbitt
OHIO STATE	Sarah Josephson, Robert Playter
PURDUE	Annette Bauer, Steve Reid
WISCONSIN	Cathy Branta, John Easker

BIG TEN

SINCE 1896

CENTENNIAL ™

1985-1996

1985-86

THE BIG EVENT

Wisconsin wins NCAA men's and women's cross country championships

For Wisconsin's men's and women's cross country teams, it was greatness revisited—and an introduction to immortality. In 1985, the squads made Big Ten and NCAA history with an unprecedented sweep of the NCAA Men's and Women's Championships at Dretzka Park in Milwaukee. Both teams were ranked No. 1 and had one previous NCAA title each. The men, led by coach Martin Smith, won in 1982 under the late Dan McClimon. The women, coached by Peter Tegen, won in 1984. The Badger men out-distanced second-place Arkansas, 67-104, and were led by senior individual NCAA champion Tim Hacker. Seniors Joe Stintzi, Scott Jenkins and Kelly Delaney, who were also members of the 1982 team, placed 11th and 24th and 26th, respectively. In the women's race, the Badgers cruised past Iowa State, 58-98, and were paced by sophomore Stephanie Herbst, who finished seventh. Teammates Katie Ishmael (15th), Lori Wolter (22nd), Kelly McKillen (31st), Holly Hering (36th) and Brigit Christinsen (44th) finished in the top 50.

OTHER MEMORABLE EVENTS

- Iowa won the NCAA wrestling championship; Marty Kistler was chosen the most outstanding wrestler; Duane Goldman won his fourth straight Conference title.

- Michigan's Casey Close recorded baseball's triple crown, leading the Conference in home runs, RBI and batting average.

- Ohio State won the men's basketball National Invitation Tournament.

- Purdue's Bob Shoulder hit three home runs in a Conference playoff game.

- Indiana finished fourth at the NCAA softball world series.

- Iowa's Gary Kostrubala became the first Conference athlete to throw the discus more than 200 feet.

- Purdue quarterback Jim Everett led the nation in total offense with 326.3 yards per game.

No. 1 Hawkeyes and No. 2 Wolverines square off

When Chuck Long decided to return for a fifth year to quarterback Iowa, there were great expectations in Iowa City. The Hawkeyes were ranked No. 5 in the preseason and quickly climbed to No. 1 after trouncing Drake (58-0), Northern Illinois (48-20) and Iowa State (57-3). It marked the seventh time in history Iowa was No. 1 and the first time since Oct. 3, 1961. After two closer calls (35-31 over Michigan State and 23-13 over Wisconsin), Iowa got ready for the REALLY big game against No. 2-ranked Michigan. It was the 12th time ever the top two teams in the country met and the first time in five years. Both teams were 5-0, but the visiting Wolverines were three-point favorites. A record-crowd of 66,350 filled Kinnick Stadium. Iowa dominated statistically (422 total yards to Michigan's 182) but needed a last-second field goal by Rob Houghtlin to win 12-10. Thousands stormed the field. "There's no doubt this was my biggest win at Iowa," coach Hayden Fry said afterward. Iowa was unanimously voted the No. 1 team in the country the next week. They stayed on top until losing at Ohio State (22-13) to drop to 7-1 and No. 6 in the country. Iowa finished 10-1 in the regular season and earned a date with UCLA in the Rose Bowl. The Bruins won 45-28 when freshman Eric Ball rushed for 227 yards and four TDs.

OTHER BIG TEN CHAMPIONS

Men
- BASEBALL: Michigan, coached by Glenn "Bo" Schembechler
- GYMNASTICS: Iowa, coached by Tom Dunn
- OUTDOOR TRACK: Wisconsin, coached by Ed Nuttycombe
- INDOOR TRACK: Wisconsin, coached by Ed Nuttycombe
- BASKETBALL: Michigan, coached by Bill Frieder
- CROSS COUNTRY: Wisconsin, coached by Martin Smith
- TENNIS: Minnesota, coached by Jerry Noyce
- SWIMMING/DIVING: Michigan, coached by Jon Urbanchek
- WRESTLING: Iowa, coached by Dan Gable
- GOLF: Ohio State, coached by Jim Brown
- FENCING: Illinois, coached by Arthur Schankin

Women
- BASKETBALL: Ohio State, coached by Nancy Darsch
- CROSS COUNTRY: Wisconsin, coached by Peter Tegen
- FENCING: Wisconsin, coached by Tony Gillham
- FIELD HOCKEY: Northwestern, coached by Nancy Stevens
- GOLF: Indiana, coached by Sam Carmichael
- GYMNASTICS: Ohio State, coached by Larry Cox
- SOFTBALL: Indiana, coached by Gayle Blevins, Minnesota, coached by Linda Wells, and Northwestern, coached by Sharon Drysdale
- SWIMMING/DIVING: Ohio State, coached by Jim Montrella
- TENNIS: Northwestern, coached by Sandy Stap Clifton
- INDOOR TRACK: Wisconsin, coached by Peter Tegen
- OUTDOOR TRACK: Wisconsin, coached by Peter Tegen
- VOLLEYBALL: Purdue, coached by Carol Dewey

CHUCK LONG
Football, Iowa

He was the Big Ten MVP, a consensus All-American and runner-up to Bo Jackson in the closest Heisman Trophy voting ever. And Chuck Long showed why in the Freedom Bowl, when he threw a bowl-game record six touchdown passes in a 55-17 victory over Texas. The Wheaton, Ill., native was a first-team All-Big Ten pick three times. Long was the first quarterback in NCAA history to throw for more than 10,000 yards in his career and he set an NCAA record with 22 consecutive completions in 1984 at Indiana. Long won the Davey O'Brien award as the nation's top quarterback and the Maxwell Trophy as the top player. Long finished as Iowa's leader in career pass attempts (1,203), completions (782), yards (10,461) and touchdown passes (74). He was selected by the Detroit Lions in the first round of the NFL draft.

MARTY KISTLER
Wrestling, Iowa

When it ended, Marty Kistler was still on a roll. The senior from Riverside, Calif., won 30 matches in a row to close out his college career, winning his second straight national championship (at 158 pounds) and third consecutive Big Ten Conference title. He was 37-1 as a senior, after a junior year in which he went 39-1. Kistler defeated Mark Van Tine of Oklahoma State to win the NCAA championship as senior and beat Greg Elinsky of Penn State to win it his junior year. Kistler was NCAA runner-up as a sophomore and finished his Iowa career with a record of 118-25-0. In his freshman season (1981-82), he finished third at the Big Ten meet. Kistler's success with the Hawkeyes wasn't exactly a surprise: His brothers Lindley and Harlan were All-Americans at Iowa, as well.

KATRINA ADAMS
Tennis, Northwestern

Katrina Adams played just two years of collegiate tennis at Northwestern before turning pro, but left behind records that should stand for years to come. The two-time Illinois state high school champion earned first-team All-Big Ten and All-America honors as a freshman and sophomore in both singles and doubles. Adams was named the Intercollegiate Tennis Coaches Association Freshman of the Year in 1986. The following year she compiled a 23-3 record at No. 2 singles for the Wildcats and teamed with Diane Donnelly for a 21-0 doubles record. They went on to win the NCAA doubles championship, Northwestern's first individual national championship since 1973. Adams relinquished her final two years of college eligibililty to turn professional. Several of the school doubles records she and Donnelly set still stand.

STEPHANIE HERBST
Cross country, Wisconsin

Keeping in step with Wisconsin's celebrated distance running tradition, Stephanie Herbst established herself as a shining Badgers' star during her stellar cross country and track careers from 1984-87. A combined six-time All-American in both sports, she won three NCAA track titles and is a former world record holder in the 10,000 meters. In cross country, she was a two-time Big Ten champion who led the Badgers to a successful defense of their NCAA championship in 1985 as a sophomore, posting a team-best seventh-place finish. She was also a cross country All-American in 1985 and '86 and was an academic All-American in 1986 and '87. In track, she won seven Big Ten championships and won NCAA titles in the 10,000-, 5,000-, and 3,000-meter indoor races in 1986. In 1986 she was an All-American, was voted the Big Ten Jesse Owens Female Athlete of the Year, Wisconsin's Athlete of the Year and was nominated for the Broderick Award.

LEADING THE WAY

ART SCHANKIN
Illinois

The year was 1972. Illinois was in search of a coach, so what better than to hire former Illinois fencing champion Art Schankin, who stayed with the team as an assistant. The appointment was made on a one-year basis—until a full-time coach could be found. Twenty years later, it was hard to tell if Schankin performed better as a fencer or a coach. As an athlete, Schankin has a reason to claim himself as the best in NCAA history, tying for fifth nationally in sabre as a sophomore in 1955-56 before placing third in foil as a junior and winning the NCAA sabre title as a senior, when he became the first intercollegiate fencer to win a national championship with an undefeated record. His title also helped Illinois win the NCAA team championship. In 1964, just six weeks before his wedding day, Schankin's fencing career ended because of an automobile accident. So he turned to coaching, first as an assistant at Illinois. As a head coach, Schankin's Illini teams compiled a 391-51 record with seven Big Ten team championships. Schankin retired as coach in 1992 and works in private business in Champaign, Ill.

· BIG TEN PIONEERS ·

Spartan All-Americans

Excellence in football, basketball and hockey was personified by MSU during 1985-86 as all three squads advanced to post-season play. More noteworthy than even that was the appearance on All-America lists by Spartans in each sport. Lorenzo White led State to its second straight bowl appearance and set a regular season NCAA rushing mark for sophomores with 1,908 yards. All-America guard and Conference scoring leader Scott Skiles led State's surprising cagers to a berth in the NCAA basketball tourney, averaging 27.4 points a game to finish second in the national scoring derby. In hockey, senior Mike Donnelly had 59 goals in 44 games and was tourney MVP as the Spartans won the NCAA hockey championship.

MSU All-Americans Mike Donnelly, Lorenzo White and Scott Skiles.

Academic Achievements

The Opera Theater at Indiana University is renowned throughout the world for the excellence of its productions in a year-round season. In January, 1986, *Smithsonian* magazine featured the IU School of Music, calling it "not only the nation's largest, but one of its best."

1985-86 Conference MEDAL OF HONOR Winners

ILLINOIS	Christy Flesvig, Jim Juriga
INDIANA	Lynn Dennison, Terry Brahm
IOWA	Marcia Pankratz, Larry Station
MICHIGAN	Sue Schroeder, Casey Close
MICHIGAN STATE	Julie Polakowski, Don McSween
MINNESOTA	Jody Eder, Ron Backes
NORTHWESTERN	Amy Kekelsen, Joe Girardi
OHIO STATE	Adrian Lehman, Mike Lanese
PURDUE	Cheryl Flowers, Jim Everett
WISCONSIN	Lisa Fortman, Tim Hacker

THE BIG EVENT

Indiana's "Smart Bomb" brings fifth NCAA basketball title

Keith Smart

Indiana coach Bob Knight had been an outspoken critic of the three-point shot that was instituted for the 1986-87 season, but it played right into his team's collective hands. With sharpshooting senior guard Steve Alford taking aim, the Hoosiers gunned down 30 of the 34 teams they faced, including Syracuse in the NCAA championship game in New Orleans. Alford, the Big Ten's all-time leading scorer when he finished his career, hit 53 percent of his three-point shots that season, including 7 of 11 in the final game. But junior college transfer Keith Smart will be remembered as the hero of Indiana's 74-73 victory. He hit a 16-foot jumper from the left baseline with four seconds remaining, capping a personal storybook finish; just a few years earlier, he had been flipping hamburgers at McDonald's. Smart, who scored 12 of his team's final 15 points, and 21 overall, was named the tournament's MVP.

OTHER MEMORABLE EVENTS

- Northwestern's Katrina Adams and Diane Donnelly won the doubles title at the NCAA tennis championships.

- Iowa's Jim Heffeman won his fourth straight Conference wrestling crown.

- Fencing was dropped as a Conference sport.

- Minnesota's Mark McKiernan was the Conference's first four-time All-Big Ten gymnast.

- Ohio State women's swimmers had three national champs: Janelle Bosse, Karen LaFace and Kim Fuggett.

- Ohio State's Dennis Hopson finished second in the nation in basketball scoring with 29.0 points per game.

Hawkeyes win 1986 NCAA field hockey title

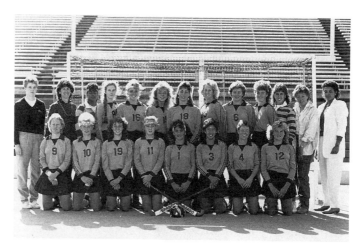

1986 Iowa field hockey team

A funny thing happened on the way to a rebuilding season: Iowa won the Big Ten field hockey title and went on to win the 1986 national championship. Coach Judith Davidson was counting on some growing pains. After all, she had eight freshmen, and no matter how good freshmen are, there usually is some adjustment period. Here's how the Hawkeyes "adjusted" to their youth invasion: They went 19-3 and won the Conference title outright; they totaled 13 shutouts and outscored their opponents 69-10. The postseason capped off an incredible year. Iowa defeated Northwestern (2-1) and Penn State (2-0) to earn a shot at defending champion New Hampshire in the title game in Norfolk, Va. Senior Patti Wanner scored both of the Hawkeyes' goals in a 2-1 double-overtime victory for the NCAA championship. Even Davidson conceded in the aftermath: "I'm certainly the first to say this was beyond my wildest expectations." Karen Napolitano, Deb Robertson, Liz Tchou and Wanner were first-team All-Big Ten. Napolitano and RosAnna Salcido were first-team All-America.

OTHER BIG TEN CHAMPIONS

Men
- FOOTBALL: Michigan, coached by Glenn "Bo" Schembechler, and Ohio State, coached by Earle Bruce
- BASEBALL: Michigan, coached by Bud Middaugh
- GYMNASTICS: Ohio State, coached by Michael Wilson
- OUTDOOR TRACK: Illinois, coached by Gary Wieneke
- INDOOR TRACK: Illinois, coached by Gary Wieneke
- BASKETBALL: Indiana, coached by Bob Knight, and Purdue, coached by Gene Keady
- CROSS COUNTRY: Wisconsin, coached by Martin Smith
- TENNIS: Michigan, coached by Brian Eisner
- SWIMMING/DIVING: Michigan, coached by Jon Urbanchek
- WRESTLING: Iowa, coached by Dan Gable
- GOLF: Ohio State, coached by Jim Brown

Women
- BASKETBALL: Iowa, coached by Vivian Stringer, and Ohio State, coached by Nancy Darsch
- CROSS COUNTRY: Wisconsin, coached by Peter Tegen
- FENCING: Wisconsin, coached by Tony Gillham
- GOLF: Indiana, coached by Sam Carmichael
- GYMNASTICS: Ohio State, coached by Larry Cox
- SOFTBALL: Northwestern, coached by Sharon Drysdale
- SWIMMING/DIVING: Michigan, coached by Jim Richardson
- TENNIS: Indiana, coached by Lin Loring
- INDOOR TRACK: Wisconsin, coached by Peter Tegen
- OUTDOOR TRACK: Purdue, coached by Fred Wilt
- VOLLEYBALL: Illinois, coached by Mike Hebert

STEVE ALFORD
Basketball, Indiana

Few players have wrung every ounce from their physical potential as well as Steve Alford, a not particularly athletic 6-foot-2 guard who led Indiana to the 1987 NCAA basketball championship. Alford started all four seasons for the Hoosiers and finished his career as the Big Ten's all-time leading scorer, a record since broken. He averaged 19.5 points for the Hoosiers, hitting .532 from the field and .898 from the foul line. In his only season of competition with a three-point line, he hit 53 percent of his bonus shots. More than just a shooter, he led IU in assists as a senior and in steals for three seasons. Alford played four seasons in the NBA, and has since enjoyed successful stints as a head coach at Manchester College and Southwest Missouri State.

JENNIFER AVERILL
Field Hockey, Northwestern

Jennifer Averill was named the Big Ten's Female Athlete of the Year for the 1986-87 school year because of her accomplishments in field hockey and lacrosse at Northwestern. Averill received All-America honors all four of her seasons with the Wildcats' field hockey team, earning first-team recognition as a freshman and senior and honorable mention status as a sophomore and junior. She was named to the NCAA's all-tournament team as a freshman. Averill was selected to the U.S. National Team in 1985 and '86, and received the Broderick Cup Award, symbolic of the national player of the year, in 1986. Northwestern finished among the top five teams in the NCAA's 12-team tournament each year of Averill's career, including a third-place finish in 1985. She has gone on to a career in coaching, currently serving as head coach at Wake Forest.

TRACEY HALL
Basketball, Ohio State

She finished a career with so many firsts, Tracey Hall must be considered Ohio State's first women's basketball star. A two-time Kodak All-American, Hall finished her career in 1986-87 as Ohio State's all-time leader in scoring (1,912) and rebounding (1,115), reaching double figures in 101 games and recording 39 double-doubles in scoring and rebounding. The Big Ten's leading rebounder during her junior and senior seasons, she also led the league in shooting percentage over her last three seasons, finishing with a 60-percent mark. Hall's ability led Ohio State to Big Ten titles in her sophomore, junior and senior seasons, and the Buckeyes compiled a 102-20 record and made four trips to the NCAA tourney during her four years. A two-time Big Ten player of the year and three-time All-Big Ten first-team pick, Hall resides in Cleveland Heights, Ohio.

ROD WOODSON
Football and Track, Purdue

The parting gift Rod Woodson gave to Purdue fans was his final game: In a 17-15 victory over rival Indiana in Ross-Ade Stadium, the defensive back (10 tackles, 1 forced fumble) also played running back (93 yards rushing), wide receiver (3 passes, 67 yards) and returned punts and kickoffs. He was named first-team All-America in 1986 and was first-team All-Big Ten three times. He was the team MVP as a senior and picked 10th overall in the first round of the NFL draft by the Pittsburgh Steelers. The Fort Wayne, Ind., native also was a track standout at Purdue. He won Big Ten indoor titles in the 55-meter hurdles and 55-meter dash, and was named the Big Ten Indoor Track Championships Athlete of the Meet. He was an All-American with a third-place finish in the 55 hurdles at the NCAA championships. Woodson was the NFL's Defensive Player of the Year in 1993 and was named to the NFL's 75th anniversary team.

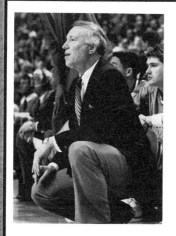

LEADING THE WAY

LOU HENSON
Illinois

In 1975, Illinois was searching for a basketball coach. The names thrown about included Kansas State's Jack Hartman, Virginia Tech's Don DeVoe and two Illini assistants. Nobody mentioned Lou Henson, a 43-year-old who had led New Mexico State to the the NCAA tournament's Final Four in 1969-70. But under Henson, within four years, Illinois started the season 15-0 and reached the NIT semifinals in the 1979-80 season, a prelude to an NCAA tournament team the following season—Illinois' first in 18 years. Henson coached Illinois to a record of 663-331, finishing 12th for wins among Division I coaches. His best teams at Illinois came during an eight-year run that began with an NCAA tournament berth in 1982-83, the first of eight straight appearances in the NCAAs. Illinois reached the regional finals in 1983-84, when Illinois shared a piece of the Big Ten title, and the team was nicknamed the Flying Illini in 1988-89, when an undersized squad reached the NCAA tournament's Final Four. Henson is one of 10 coaches who has led more than one school to the Final Four. He retired following the 1995-96 season.

· BIG TEN PIONEERS ·

Judith Davidson
Iowa

In Judith Davidson's 10 years as coach of Iowa's field hockey team, she never had a losing season. Her Hawkeyes won seven consecutive Big Ten championships, starting with the first year of league play in 1981, with a combined record of 52-4-3. They were 185-51-16 overall. Iowa won 18 consecutive Big Ten games and didn't lose in the Conference until the last regular-season game of 1983, the third season of Big Ten competition. The Hawkeyes were a force, nationally, as well, going to the NCAA tournament every year after its inception in '82. Iowa lost in the 1984 title game to Old Dominion, but in 1986 the Hawkeyes won the national championship with a 2-1 double-overtime victory over defending champion New Hampshire. At Iowa, Davidson coached more than 40 all-Big Ten selections and more than 35 All-Americans.

Academic Achievements

Wisconsin's Center for Dairy Research was the nation's first established at a university in 1986. The center is home to nearly 40 research projects investigating how to make new and better dairy products and find new uses for milk.

1986-87 Conference MEDAL OF HONOR Winners

ILLINOIS	**Jonelle Polk,**
	Graeme McGufficke
INDIANA	**Karleen Moore, Steve Alford**
IOWA	**Karen Napolitano,**
	Andy Wiese
MICHIGAN	**Heide Cohen, Ken Higgins**
MICHIGAN STATE	**Lisa Marino, Dean Altobelli**
MINNESOTA	**Sue Roell, Collin Godkin**
NORTHWESTERN	**Jennifer Averill, Bob Dirkes**
OHIO STATE	**Kathy Zittel, Mike Wantuck**
PURDUE	**Karen Moschetto,**
	Kevin Gregory
WISCONSIN	**Amy Justeson, J.J. Weber**

The BIG TEN's First 100 Years

Most Big Ten Women's Team Championships Won By School, All-Time

OHIO STATE 30
MICHIGAN 28
WISCONSIN 26
INDIANA 25
IOWA 18

THE BIG EVENT

Illinois dominates volleyball season

Two years earlier, Illinois swept through the Big Ten season to finish with an 18-0 record, an unprecedented sweep through the volleyball season. Illinois repeated the feat in 1987-88, as Illinois completed the season with a 30-4 record, an NCAA regional championship and the school's second trip to the Final Four. During the three-year span, Illinois was 55-1 in the Big Ten under coach Mike Hebert with three outright Big Ten titles and two trips to the Final Four. Illinois has just one other Big Ten championship, tying for the title with a 19-1 record overall in 1991-92. Mary Eggers was a major cog in Illinois' three titles, and she was honored in 1988 with the Honda Award that goes to the nation's top college volleyball player. A former Big Ten freshman of the year, she led the nation in hitting percentage her sophomore and senior seasons.

OTHER MEMORABLE EVENTS

- **Ohio State's Chris Spielman won the Lombardi Award.**

- **Indiana's Kimberly Beltz won the NCAA cross country title.**

- **Wisconsin's Tom Fischer had a record 19 strike outs in a Conference game.**

- **Minnesota's Darrell Thompson had a 98-yard touchdown run, tying the longest play in Conference history.**

- **Baseball went back to single-division play.**

- **Michigan's Mary Fischbach won both NCAA diving titles.**

Lorenzo White

Michigan State wins football crown and Rose Bowl

"An old Midwestern team like Duffy had" was also George Perles' kind of team, one that won eight of its last nine games en route to its first undisputed Big Ten championship since 1966. It was the kind of team that legendary Spartan coach Duffy Daugherty, who died just before State's third game, would have liked. Tough on both sides of the ball, with a great kicking game to boot, MSU started its 9-2-1 season with a 27-13 win over Southern Cal and ended it with a 20-17 triumph over those same Trojans in State's first Rose Bowl appearance in 22 years. After dropping its second and third games to Notre Dame and Florida State, MSU never had another "L" on its slate, with only a 14-14 tie with Illinois marring its otherwise perfect Conference mark (7-0-1). The run-oriented attack featured All-America back Lorenzo White rushing for 131 yards per game and QB Bobby McAllister throwing to targets like Andre Rison. Led by Percy Snow's 127 tackles, State topped the nation in rushing defense. Kicker John Langeloh was 17-24 on field goals while punter Greg Montgomery's 45-yard average was among the nation's best.

OTHER BIG TEN CHAMPIONS

Men
- BASEBALL: Minnesota, coached by John Anderson
- GYMNASTICS: Illinois, coached by Yoshi Hayasaki
- OUTDOOR TRACK: Illinois, coached by Gary Wieneke
- INDOOR TRACK: Illinois, coached by Gary Wieneke
- BASKETBALL: Purdue, coached by Gene Keady
- CROSS COUNTRY: Wisconsin, coached by Martin Smith
- TENNIS: Michigan, coached by Brian Eisner
- SWIMMING/DIVING: Michigan, coached by Jon Urbanchek
- WRESTLING: Iowa, coached by Dan Gable
- GOLF: Illinois, coached by Ed Beard

Women
- BASKETBALL: Iowa, coached by Vivian Stringer
- CROSS COUNTRY: Wisconsin, coached by Peter Tegen
- FIELD HOCKEY: Iowa, coached by Judith Davidson
- GOLF: Ohio State, coached by Jana Edwards Shipley
- GYMNASTICS: Minnesota, coached by Katalin Deli
- SOFTBALL: Minnesota, coached by Linda Wells
- SWIMMING/DIVING: Michigan, coached by Jim Richardson
- TENNIS: Indiana, coached by Lin Loring
- INDOOR TRACK: Indiana, coached by Carol Stevenson
- OUTDOOR TRACK: Illinois, coached by Gary Winckler
- VOLLEYBALL: Illinois, coached by Mike Hebert

SUZY FAVOR HAMILTON
Cross country, Wisconsin

Suzy Favor Hamilton, in honors and achievements, is the most decorated female athlete in Wisconsin history. Between 1987-91, the track star earned All-America recognition 14 times in track and cross country—the most All-America honors ever bestowed on any Badger athlete. She won nine NCAA individual track titles between 1987 and 1990, including an unprecedented four straight championships in the 1,500-meter run. She also won three TAC titles and is the winningest woman in collegiate track and field history. She won 23 Big Ten titles, the most ever by a Conference athlete. She won six straight Big Ten Indoor and Outdoor Triple Titles and seven triples in eight meets. She broke seven school indoor and outdoor records and had a string of 40 consecutive wins in finals races. In 1991, on the occasion of the 10th anniversary of women's athletics in the Conference, she was honored to be the namesake for the Big Ten Athlete of the Year. She was a three-time recipient of the Big Ten Jesse Owens Female Athlete of the Year in 1988, '89 and '90.

LORENZO WHITE
Football, Michigan State

Two-time All-American Lorenzo White ran to daylight often throughout his career. Twice fourth in the Heisman Trophy balloting, the Fort Lauderdale native rushed for 4,887 yards in his career, second best in Big Ten history, and had 23 100-yard rushing games. As a senior, White paced the Spartans to the 1988 Rose Bowl, their first in 22 years, running for two touchdowns and 113 yards in State's 20-17 win over Southern Cal. He was named the Big Ten's most valuable player for 1987, the third Spartan to be honored with the Silver Football. In 1985, White rushed for 1,908 yards for an NCAA single-season record for sophomores and took national rushing honors at 173.5 per game. After seven seasons with the Houston Oilers during which he became the team's No. 2 all-time rusher, White signed with the Cleveland Browns, now the Baltimore Ravens.

MICHELLE EDWARDS
Basketball, Iowa

Her career statistics indicate not just the ability to score, but comparable stellar defensive and passing skills. That's what made Michelle Edwards such a force in the Big Ten Conference, where she was three times first-team All-Big Ten. As a senior, she was the league's Player of the Year, an All-American and named Division I Player of the Year by Champion Products. Edwards was Iowa's team MVP, the school's athlete of the year, and she finished as the Hawkeyes' all-time leader in steals (235), assists (431) and No. 2 in scoring (1,821 career points). The Boston native led Iowa in scoring, steals, field goal and free throw percentage her junior year, and as a sophomore she led the team in scoring and assists. She had an immediate impact on the program, averaging 10.3 ppg as a freshman, was first on the team in steals and second in assists. You want consistency? Edwards scored in double figures in 70 of her 72 college games dating back to late in her sophomore season.

JIM ABBOTT
Baseball, Michigan

Jim Abbott never thought there was anything special about the way he played baseball. Only others did. Abbott, who was born without a right hand and so he throws from the port side, quickly puts his glove on his left hand and prepares to field a batted ball. Abbott, a native of Flint, posted a 26-8 career record for Michigan with a 3.03 ERA and six shutouts. Twice named to All-America teams, Abbott was the 1987 winner of the Sullivan Award, presented by the Amateur Athletic Union to the nation's top amateur athlete. He led Michigan to regular season Big Ten titles in each of his three campaigns, including a win over Minnesota in the 1986 Conference title game. Abbott has pitched in the majors since 1989 with the New York Yankees, Chicago White Sox and California Angels.

LEADING THE WAY

GENE KEADY
Purdue

As Purdue's men's basketball coach since 1980, Gene Keady built a reputation for getting the most out of his players. This was a special year for Keady and the Boilermakers. It marked the sixth straight season with 20 or more victories and a sixth straight NCAA Tournament appearance. With Troy Lewis, Todd Mitchell and Everette Stephens, Purdue advanced to the Sweet 16 of the NCAA before losing to Kansas State in the Midwest Regional semifinal. Keady's team would not advance that far again until 1994, the same season it matched the school record of 29 victories set in 1987-88. This was Keady's third Big Ten title in his first eight years at Purdue, and he would later win three more in a row (1994-96). The Boilermakers were ranked No. 3 in the final regular-season Associated Press poll. Keady, who competed in baseball, football and track as a student-athlete at Kansas State, brought his hard-nosed, defensive-minded teamwork approach to Purdue after two seasons as head coach at Western Kentucky. Before his Western Kentucky stint, Keady coached Hutchinson (Kan.) Junior College to six league championships and a second-place finish in the national junior college tournament (1973). He was an assistant coach at Arkansas from 1975-78, helping Eddie Sutton recruit the famous "triplets"—Ron Brewer, Sidney Moncrief and Marvin Delph—and earn a Final Four appearance in '78.

· BIG TEN PIONEERS ·

Bill Heinz—Four homers in one game

When Iowa and Minnesota squared off on the baseball diamond on April 20, 1988, Bill Heinz put on a show the likes of which the Big Ten Conference had never seen. The Hawkeye senior right fielder hit four home runs and finished with nine RBI and 17 total bases—all three Big Ten records. Heinz's performance began with a first-inning grand slam, and continued with a two-run homer in the third inning, another two-run shot in the fourth and a solo home run to lead off the seventh. He added a single and finished 5-for-5. Iowa won 17-3 in the second game of a doubleheader after winning the opener 4-1.

Academic Achievements

The Advanced Computing Center for the Arts and Design (ACCAD) was named in 1987, making Ohio State University one of the national leaders in the field. ACCAD had evolved from the Computer Graphics Research Group which was formed in Columbus by Chuck Csuri in 1971. ACCAD has produced computer graphics, animation and scientific visualization.

1987-88 Conference MEDAL OF HONOR Winners

ILLINOIS	Disa Johnson, Tim Simon
INDIANA	Karen Dunham, Sven Salumaa
IOWA	Liz Tchou, Mike Flagg
MICHIGAN	Tina Basle, Jonathan Morris
MICHIGAN STATE	Kim Hartwick, Mike Davidson
MINNESOTA	Rochele Goetz, Paul Gisselquist
NORTHWESTERN	Barb Harris, Shon Morris
OHIO STATE	Karen LaFace, Ron Gharbo
PURDUE	Sharon Versyp, Bob Stolz
WISCONSIN	Chris Gilles, Paul Gruber

The BIG TEN's First 100 Years
Big Ten Universities
Offered The First Programs In...

Aeronautical and nuclear engineering (Michigan)

Medical technology (Minnesota)

Computer graphics and animation (Ohio State)

Industrial and architectural engineering (Penn State)

Wildlife Management (Wisconsin)

1988-89

THE BIG EVENT

Jim Delany appointed Big Ten's fifth commissioner

Before he became the Big Ten's fifth commissioner, Jim Delany got his training for the Conference's chief executive position on the basketball courts of North Carolina, in the law offices of the NCAA and at the top of the administrative ladder of the Ohio Valley Conference. Delany was a former standout basketball player at the University of North Carolina, where he also earned a law degree that led to a position in 1975 as an enforcement representative for the NCAA. After four years there, he ascended to commissioner of the Ohio Valley Conference, where he served 10 years before being appointed to the same post for the Big Ten. Under Delany's leadership, the Conference has expanded to 11 institutions, relocated to its own office building that also serves as a meeting center for the Conference, increased its bowl tie-ins from one to five, negotiated unmatched football and basketball television agreements, enhanced the Conference championship experience for student-athletes, and added 700 additional participation opportunities. In 1992, the Conference was the nation's first to adopt a voluntary Conference-wide commitment to reach a goal of 60-40 male-female participation in athletics within five years.

OTHER MEMORABLE EVENTS

- Michigan won the NCAA men's basketball championship, with Glen Rice named the tourney's most outstanding player. Illinois also was among the Final Four.

- Wisconsin won the NCAA men's cross country title for the third time in seven years.

- Indiana freshman Bob Kennedy won the NCAA men's cross country championship, while Indiana's Michelle Dekkers won the women's title.

- Michigan's MalaVai Washington was the top ranked NCAA men's tennis player.

- Wisconsin's women's soccer team and Illinois' women's volleyball team both advanced to the NCAA semifinal competition.

- Iowa quarterback Chuck Hartlieb led the nation in interception avoidance by throwing just nine INTs out of 409 passes.

NCAA gymnastics crown returns to Illinois

After a three-decade waiting period, a national championship trophy returned to Illinois in gymnastics. Ending a 31-year journey, Illinois won the NCAA championship by defeating Nebraska on the Cornhuskers' home mat to win the national championship by 1.1 points. To cap off the near perfect weekend, Illinois' David Zeddies and Chris McKee earned All-America honors in leading the Illini to their ninth NCAA title overall in the sport. Zeddies was an All-American in the floor exercise, rings and high bar. McKee became a two-time All-American in the floor exercise and also received All-America honors in the vault. The team title meant that coach Yoshi Hayasaki earned the NCAA's Coach of the Year honors. As a collegian, Hayasaki won two all-around titles while attending the University of Washington. Earlier in the season, Illinois had already won the Big Ten title, a season when Conference schools were strong. The league placed four teams in the top 10 at the NCAA meet. Trailing Illinois were the Minnesota Gophers, who finished third ahead of seventh-place Ohio State and 10th-place Iowa.

OTHER BIG TEN CHAMPIONS

Men
- FOOTBALL: Michigan, coached by Glenn "Bo" Schembechler
- BASEBALL: Illinois, coached by Augie Garrido
- OUTDOOR TRACK: Illinois, coached by Gary Wieneke
- INDOOR TRACK: Illinois, coached by Gary Wieneke
- BASKETBALL: Indiana, coached by Bob Knight
- CROSS COUNTRY: Wisconsin, coached by Martin Smith
- TENNIS: Minnesota, coached by David Geatz
- SWIMMING: Michigan, coached by Jon Urbanchek
- WRESTLING: Iowa, coached by Dan Gable
- GOLF: Ohio State, coached by Jim Brown

Women
- BASKETBALL: Iowa, coached by Vivian Stringer, and Ohio State, coached by Nancy Darsch
- CROSS COUNTRY: Wisconsin, coached by Peter Tegen
- FIELD HOCKEY: Northwestern, coached by Nancy Stevens
- GOLF: Minnesota, coached by Nancy Harris
- GYMNASTICS: Minnesota, coached by Katalin Deli
- SOFTBALL: Iowa, coached by Gayle Blevins
- SWIMMING/DIVING: Michigan, coached by Jim Richardson
- TENNIS: Indiana, coached by Lin Loring
- INDOOR TRACK: Illinois, coached by Gary Winckler
- OUTDOOR TRACK: Illinois, coached by Gary Winckler
- VOLLEYBALL: Illinois, coached by Mike Hebert

GLEN RICE
Basketball, Michigan

The top scorer in Big Ten history and the Conference MVP in 1989, Flint native Glen Rice led interim coach Steve Fisher's surprising Wolverines to the '89 NCAA championship, scoring 184 points in six games. The 6-foot-7 forward was named the tournament's outstanding player and an All-American and national player of the year by United Press International. His career stats are filled with superlatives, including 2,442 points, an 18.2 average. Rice is also Michigan's all-time leader in field goals, field goal percentage and games played. He led the Big Ten in scoring as a junior and senior, averaging 22.1 and 25.6 points per game, respectively, and scored 20 or more points in 24 of U-M's 31 games in 1988-89. He's now in the National Basketball Association with the Charlotte Hornets.

MARY EGGERS
Volleyball, Illinois

Mary Eggers, wrote one journalist, "stalks onto the court with an icy look of controlled violence that combines the cool of Star Trek's Mr. Spock with the rage of a pit bull." Eggers was the biggest star in an Illinois volleyball program that has reached the NCAA tournament for 11 straight seasons. Eggers was named the Big Ten's freshman of the year following her first season in 1985-86. She led the nation in hitting percentage her sophomore and senior seasons, setting Illinois career records for aces, blocks, kills and attack percentage. The four Illinois teams during her career compiled a 136-17 record, including a perfect 18-0 mark during her junior year. Following her senior campaign, Eggers earned the Honda Broderick Award, given to the nation's top collegiate player. She currently is an assistant coach at Illinois State.

STEVE STRICKER
Golf, Illinois

It took something—or someone—a little special to end a 47-year championship drought in golf for Illinois. Steve Stricker won the second of his three Big Ten golf titles in 1988—winning the meet by 14 strokes—when Illinois won the team championship for the first time since 1941. A native of Wisconsin, Stricker was a four-time All-Big Ten pick, the individual champion in the Big Ten in 1986, '88 and '89, and a first-team All-America selection in 1988 and '89. Stricker earned his PGA Tour card in 1993, competing on the tour for his first full season in 1994. He finished 50th on the PGA money list with $334,409 in 1994 and 40th in 1995, earning $438,931. Stricker excelled during the 1996 season, winning two PGA tournaments, including the prestigious Western Open in suburban Chicago.

MICHELLE DEKKERS
Cross country, Indiana

Michelle Dekkers perhaps gained her greatest fame when she won the 1988 NCAA cross country championship as a sophomore while running barefoot in 28-degree weather. Dekkers, who won the race by 25 meters, said "you feel so much lighter, so much freer." She was much more than a novelty, however. The Capetown, South Africa native, who moved to the U.S. in 1986 (she enrolled first at Houston before transferring to IU), finished third in the 1989 NCAA cross country meet, but won the Big Ten meet in 1988 and '89. Dekkers also won two Big Ten indoor 5,000-meter titles and one outdoor title. She was unable to defend her outdoor title in 1990 because of a stress fracture. She was twice named IU's Female Athlete of the Year and a two-time All-Big Ten selection.

LEADING THE WAY

MIKE HEBERT
Illinois/Minnesota

A Californian who brought the game from the beaches to the Midwest, Mike Hebert transformed a struggling Illinois volleyball program into a big winner and a fan favorite. He began slowly, recording a 5-25 record in his first year at Illinois in 1983-84, but that turned out to be his only losing season in Champaign. By 1985-86, Illinois finished second in the Big Ten race. A year later, Illinois began an amazing run in Big Ten play, winning three straight league championships and losing just one Big Ten match over those three years. In 1987-88 and 1988-89, Illinois advanced to the NCAA tournament's semifinals. The Illini have reached the NCAA tournament 11 straight years, and the success has helped make Illini volleyball an attractive ticket. In 1992, the Illini set an NCAA attendance record, drawing 52,666 fans, an average of 3,098 per match. Not surprisingly, Hebert has been chosen national Coach of the Year once and Big Ten Coach of the Year three times. Following the 1995-96 season, Hebert carried a 323-127 mark at Illinois, when he resigned to accept the head coaching position at the University of Minnesota.

· BIG TEN PIONEERS ·

Steve Fisher
Michigan

Betting and sports are not words that should be used together, but it's a safe bet that Steve Fisher may go down in NCAA history as the only interim coach to win an NCAA title. A relatively unknown assistant to Bill Frieder on Michigan's 1988-89 team, Fisher was named by athletic director Bo Schembechler to the head job, temporarily, for the duration of the Wolverines' season, when Frieder left for Arizona State prior to the start of the NCAA tournament. Fisher didn't remain unknown long as the Cinderella Wolverines went on a tear, going 6-0 in the tourney and beating Seton Hall for the national collegiate title.

Academic Achievements

Wisconsin professor Arthur Robinson was asked by Rand McNally to make an uninterrupted world map projection with the fewest possible distortions of major continents. The new "Robinson" projection changed the very art of map-making, and was celebrated in the 100th anniversary issue of National Geographic in 1988. It now is the official world map in NG's world atlas.

1988-89 Conference MEDAL OF HONOR Winners

ILLINOIS	Chris Schwarz, Peter Freund
INDIANA	Ann Mooney, Simon Katner
IOWA	Deb Robertson, Paul Wozniak
MICHIGAN	Traci Babcock, John Scherer
MICHIGAN STATE	Mary Schoenle, Danton Cole
MINNESOTA	Kate Hughes, Mike Zechmeister
NORTHWESTERN	Lori Holmes, Mark Whitehead
OHIO STATE	Michelle Schulte, Ted Glavas, Scott Powell
PURDUE	Barbara Meeker, John Stein
WISCONSIN	Maureen Hartzheim, Dave Lee

The BIG TEN's First 100 Years
Big Ten Men's Basketball
NCAA Appearances

Most NCAA Appearances	25 Indiana
Most NCAA Wins	50 Indiana
Most championships	5 Indiana (1940, '53, '76, '81, '87)
Most second place	4 Michigan
Most third place*	4 Ohio State
	4 Illinois
Most fourth place*	2 Iowa

*Third and fourth place not contested after 1981

THE BIG EVENT

Penn State joins the Conference

It was an unexpected announcement that paved the way for other conferences to expand, merge or realign. The Big Ten announced on Dec. 19, 1989 that Penn State would become the league's 11th school. The Conference's name wouldn't change, but the quality of the league was enhanced. Penn State was the first new member since Michigan State joined the Big Ten in 1949. The Nittany Lions had been playing football as an independent and competed in the Atlantic 10 Conference in other sports, including basketball. Penn State was a perfect fit for the Big Ten—it was a respected academic and research institution that shared the same values and principles as current Conference members, both in terms of the value of broad-based academic and research programs, and the appropriate role for intercollegiate athletics within the context of higher education. Penn State began Conference championship play in 18 sports during the 1991-92 season; wrestling and men's and women's basketball were integrated in 1992-93; and football officially began competing for the Conference title in the fall of 1993. In 1994, Joe Paterno's Nittany Lions went 11-0 in the regular season, winning their first Big Ten championship, and defeated Oregon 38-20 in the Rose Bowl. A little trivia: Penn State's first Big Ten competition was a men's soccer game on Sept. 8, 1991, which it lost to Indiana, 5-3.

OTHER MEMORABLE EVENTS

- **Ohio State's Mike Racanelli won the NCAA all-around gymnastics title.**

- **A total of seven Conference teams participated in the NCAA men's basketball tournament.**

- **Minnesota's Marie Roethlisberger won the NCAA uneven bars title.**

- **Indiana's Michelle Dekkers won the second of three straight Conference cross country championships.**

- **Illinois' Jeff George was the No. 1 pick in the NFL draft.**

- **Ohio State overcame a 31-0 deficit to defeat Minnesota, 41-37, setting an NCAA football record for the most points overcome to win a game.**

Michigan men, women take Big Ten swim crowns

Five and four were lucky numbers for the Michigan men's and women's swimming teams in 1990. The Wolverine men, under coach Jon Urbanchek, won their fifth straight Big Ten championship before a home crowd at Matt Mann Pool and broke the 200-point victory margin for the first time, scoring 697 points to Minnesota's 433. The Wolverines were led by nine men who won seven individual and two relay events. Junior Mike Barrowman and senior Brent Lang paced UM to fourth in the NCAA, its fourth straight top six finish, with Barrowman winning the 200 breaststroke en route to swimmer of the meet honors and Lang winning the 50 and 100 freestyle. Sophomore Eric Wunderlich was a four-time All-American with thirds in the 100 and 200 breaststroke. Jim Richardson's women's team won its fourth Big Ten meet in a row, totaling 699 points to Northwestern's 502. Eight Michigan women won Big Ten titles and nine women were All-Big Ten performers and All-Americans. Ann Colloton won the 200 breaststroke to become UM's first NCAA champ as the team finished seventh. The team also extended its dual meet winning streak to 36 before losing to NCAA runner-up Stanford.

OTHER BIG TEN CHAMPIONS

Men
- FOOTBALL: Michigan, coached by Gary Moeller
- BASEBALL: Illinois, coached by Augie Garrido
- GYMNASTICS: Minnesota, coached by Fred Roethlisberger
- OUTDOOR TRACK: Indiana, coached by Sam Bell
- INDOOR TRACK: Indiana, coached by Sam Bell
- BASKETBALL: Michigan State, coached by Jud Heathcote
- CROSS COUNTRY: Wisconsin, coached by Martin Smith
- WRESTLING: Iowa, coached by Dan Gable
- GOLF: Ohio State, coached by Jim Brown
- TENNIS: Northwestern, coached by Paul Torricelli

Women
- BASKETBALL: Iowa, coached by Vivian Stringer, and Northwestern, coached by Don Perrelli
- CROSS COUNTRY: Indiana, coached by Sam Bell
- GOLF: Indiana, coached by Sam Carmichael
- GYMNASTICS: Illinois, coached by Bev Mackes
- SOFTBALL: Iowa, coached by Gayle Blevins, and Ohio State, coached by Gail Davenport
- TENNIS: Indiana, coached by Lin Loring
- INDOOR TRACK: Wisconsin, coached by Peter Tegen
- OUTDOOR TRACK: Wisconsin, coached by Peter Tegen
- VOLLEYBALL: Ohio State, coached by Jim Stone

TONJA BUFORD
Track, Illinois

Tonja Buford's magnificent career at Illinois is underlined by the fact that she not only won more individual Big Ten track titles than any other Illini athlete, but also more than any other men's or women's athlete in the history of the Conference. Her total of 25 championships broke the record of 23, set by Wisconsin track ace Suzy Favor, the namesake of the Big Ten's Female Athlete of the Year award. In her senior season of 1992-93, Buford won eight individual titles and two relay titles in Big Ten competition. A four-time Big Ten Track Athlete of the Year, Buford was the first women's track athlete from the Illinois program to compete in the Olympics when she qualified for the 400-meter hurdles in the 1992 Barcelona Games. Buford shared Illinois' Female Athlete of the Year award in 1991-92 and won it outright her senior year.

TODD MARTIN
Tennis, Northwestern

The challenges of collegiate tennis competition weren't great enough to contain Northwestern's Todd Martin, who turned professional after his sophomore season. Martin was the Big Ten freshman of the year in 1989 and the Conference player of the year in 1990. He posted a 79-9 overall singles record, including a 51-3 mark as a sophomore when he was 12-0 in Conference play and the Wildcats won the league title. He was the nation's top-ranked collegian the spring season of his sophomore year. Martin, an East Lansing, Mich. native, has enjoyed success on the professional circuit as well. He was a member of the U.S. Davis Cup team in 1994 and '95 and was a semifinalist at Wimbledon and the U.S. Open and a finalist in the Australian Open, in 1994.

MARIE ROETHLISBERGER
Gymnastics, Minnesota

The most decorated female athlete in Minnesota history, Marie Roethlisberger was the first Gopher gymnast to win an NCAA championship and be selected for the U.S. Olympic team. She overcame a partial hearing loss caused by spinal meningitis at age two to become a four-time All-American and a four-time NCAA champion. She capped her senior year in 1990 with an NCAA uneven bars title. She earned the NCAA's highest honor the same year when she was named an NCAA Top Six recipient, awarded to the nation's top six athletes. Roethlisberger, who also received a Big Ten Medal of Honor, was the first Minnesota athlete to receive the NCAA award. She was the Big Ten Gymnast of the Year in 1987, '88 and '89 and was a member of the 1984 Olympic team, although an injury prevented her from competing. She was a three-time Big Ten All-Academic selection and is the daughter of Fred Roethlisberger, coach of the Minnesota men's gymnastics team, and is the sister of former NCAA men's all-around champion and Gopher star John Roethlisberger.

ANTHONY THOMPSON
Football, Indiana

The only Indiana athlete to have his jersey number retired, Anthony Thompson is probably the most notable player in the school's football history. He set NCAA records for career touchdowns (65), points (394) and single-game rushing (377 yards) during his career. He was named the Big Ten's MVP as a junior and senior (one of only three two-time winners) and was runner-up for the Heisman Trophy as a senior in 1989. He is IU's all-time leading rusher with 5,299 yards. Thompson wasn't a natural. He lacked break-away speed, but excelled because of his durability and relentless work ethic. His lack of speed was partially responsible for his limited NFL career, as he played just four years with the Cardinals and Rams—further testament, in a sense, to the significance of his collegiate accomplishments.

LEADING THE WAY

JUD HEATHCOTE
Michigan State

The winningest basketball coach in Michigan State history, Jud Heathcote epitomized intensity as he roamed the sideline, arms flailing, railing with equal alacrity at players and officials. His two-fisted smack-himself-in-the-head emotions-bared manuever was a TV camera's and crowd's delight. A throwback to an era of discipline and adherence to a coach's wishes, Heathcote was the boss. Honest to a fault, Heathcote would say "We could be pretty good" or "We stink" with equal candor. Innovative and smart, Heathcote popularized the match-up zone defense that State used so effectively. In his 19 years there, Jud made State a Conference force, with seven 20 or more win seasons, including an MSU record 28 in 1989-90 and the 26 victories of the 1978-79 NCAA championship unit. It was the latter that made Heathcote a national figure, with Earvin "Magic" Johnson leading State to its epic NCAA victory over top-ranked Indiana State. But Heathcote was hardly a flash-in-the pan, as his 420-273 mark in 24 seasons at MSU and Montana attests. He produced seven All-Americans and 19 NBA draft picks and his three Big Ten titles are half of those earned by State. He was named 1994-95 coach of the year by *The Sporting News*. Jud and his wife, Beverly, now live in Spokane, Wash.

· BIG TEN PIONEERS ·

Percy Snow
Michigan State

Percy Snow, a ferocious defender who averaged 151 tackles per season during his final three years, in 1989 became the first Big Ten football player to win the Butkus Award, given annually to the best linebacker in college football. Snow, a 6-foot-3, 240-pounder from Canton, Ohio, showed career consistency and tenacity reminiscent of the legendary Dick Butkus. He had 464 tackles in his career despite playing only on special teams as a freshman. In his All-America senior year, Snow recorded seven tackles for loss, three interceptions, four passes broken up, one fumble caused, one fumble recovery and two blocked field goals.

Academic Achievements

The year 1989 was a very good year for Minnesota's academics. That year alone, 10 faculty members won Fulbright Senior Scholar awards and 41 patents were issued to the University's researchers.

1989-90
Conference MEDAL OF HONOR
Winners

ILLINOIS	Celena Mondie, John Murray
INDIANA	Julie Goedde, Scott Holman
IOWA	Erica Richards, Brian Wujcik
MICHIGAN	Jenny Allard, Brent Lang
MICHIGAN STATE	Eileen Shea, Walter Bartels
MINNESOTA	Marie Roethlisberger, Chuck Heise
NORTHWESTERN	Kim Metcalf, Jack Griffin
OHIO STATE	Joan Pero, Joe Staysniak, Mike Racanelli
PURDUE	Lori Overturf, Stephen Scheffler
WISCONSIN	Susan Temple, John Byce

The BIG TEN's First 100 Years
LONGEST PLAYS IN
BIG TEN FOOTBALL HISTORY

RUN	98 YARDS	MICKEY EREHART, IND AT IOWA, 1912	
RUN	98 YARDS	DARRELL THOMPSON, MINN VS. MICH. 1987	
PASS	99 YARDS	JOHN PACI TO THOMAS LEWIS, IND AT PS, 1993	
FIELD GOAL	63 YARDS	MORTON ANDERSEN, MSU AT NU, 1981	
PUNT	110* YARDS	PAT O'DEA, WIS AT IOWA, 1897	
PUNT	96** YARDS	GEORGE O'BRIEN, WIS AT IOWA, 1952	
PUNT RETURN	95 YARDS	AL BRENNER, MSU AT ILL, 1966	
PUNT RETURN	95 YARDS	BILL HAPPEL, IOWA AT MINN, 1984	
KICKOFF RETURN	100 YARDS	15 TIMES	
KICKOFF RETURN	100 YARDS	13 TIMES	

*110 - YARD FIELD   **100 - YARD FIELD

BIG TEN

SINCE 1896

CENTENNIAL ™

1985-1996

THE BIG EVENT

Four-way tie for football championship

***Illinois head football coach
John Mackovic***

The 1990-91 season was one truly like no other in the storied 100-year tradition of Big Ten football. Four teams—Iowa, Michigan, Illinois, and Michigan State—all grabbed a share of the league championship. The occasion marked the first time in history that more than three teams wore the crown. All four squads sported identical 6-2 Conference records. By virtue of winning the head-to-head tie-breaking criteria, Iowa was the league's Rose Bowl representative, having beaten each of the three co-champions on the road. Iowa, led offensively by powerful running back Nick Bell and quarterback Matt Rogers, was defeated, 46-34, by Washington in the highest-scoring Rose Bowl in history. Michigan, led by future Heisman Trophy winner Desmond Howard, had better luck in the Gator Bowl, where it rolled over Mississippi, 35-3. Michigan State, led by running back Hyland Hickson, triumphed against USC, 17-16, in the John Hancock Bowl. Illinois was stymied, 30-0, by Clemson in the Hall of Fame Bowl.

OTHER MEMORABLE EVENTS

- **Iowa won the NCAA wrestling championship.**

- **Iowa's Artur Wojdat won three NCAA swimming titles on the way to nine in his career.**

- **Michigan State's Julie Farrell-Ovenhouse won her second NCAA diving title.**

- **Illinois' Howard Griffith scored an NCAA record eight touchdowns in a game.**

- **Illinois' Jon Llewellyn won the NCAA heavyweight wrestling title.**

- **Northwestern's Todd Leslie made an NCAA record 15 consecutive three-point shots during the season.**

First volleyball championship for Wisconsin

The year 1990 marked a year of remarkable "firsts" for Wisconsin's women's volleyball team. First, the Badgers enjoyed their best campaign in school history, posting a 29-8 season record. Second, they won their first-ever Big Ten championship in volleyball and peaked at No. 10 in the national poll. As a result of all of the aforementioned, the Badgers made their NCAA tournament debut and enjoyed one of the biggest fan followings of any team in the country. They ranked third overall in the nation in overall attendance, averaging 2,199 spectators per match. They set a league record for attendance by drawing an average of 2,452 per match. And, they set the NCAA single match record with a single crowd of 10,935. Then again, fans had good reason to watch the Badgers as they featured many dazzling attractions—not the least of which was Lisa Boyd, who was named Big Ten Player of the Year. She was the first Badger ever to receive that honor, as she was also named a second-team All-American—the first Wisconsin player to earn All-America recognition. In addition, Wisconsin coach Steve Lowe was named Big Ten coach of the year and Mideast Region coach of the year.

OTHER BIG TEN CHAMPIONS

Men
- FOOTBALL: Illinois, coached by John Mackovic, Iowa, coached by Hayden Fry, Michigan, coached by Gary Moeller, and Michigan State, coached by George Perles
- BASEBALL: Ohio State, coached by Bob Todd
- GYMNASTICS: Minnesota, coached by Fred Roethlisberger
- OUTDOOR TRACK: Indiana, coached by Sam Bell
- INDOOR TRACK: Indiana, coached by Sam Bell
- BASKETBALL: Indiana, coached by Bob Knight, and Ohio State, coached by Randy Ayers
- CROSS COUNTRY: Wisconsin, coached by Martin Smith
- SWIMMING
- TENNIS: Ohio State, coached by John Daly
- WRESTLING: Iowa, coached by Dan Gable
- GOLF: Indiana, coached by Sam Carmichael

Women
- BASKETBALL: Purdue, coached by Lin Dunn
- CROSS COUNTRY: Indiana, coached by Sam Bell
- GOLF: Iowa, coached by Diane Thomason
- GYMNASTICS: Minnesota, coached by Katalin Deli
- SOFTBALL: Minnesota, coached by Teresa Wilson
- TENNIS: Indiana, coached by Lin Loring
- INDOOR TRACK: Indiana, coached by Sam Bell
- OUTDOOR TRACK: Wisconsin, coached by Peter Tegen
- VOLLEYBALL: Wisconsin, coached by Steve Lowe

JOY HOLMES
Basketball, Purdue

After her senior year, the Mansfield, Ohio, native became Purdue's first Kodak All-American, Big Ten Player of the Year and league female athlete of the year. *USA Today* selected Holmes as one of the top 15 players in the country after she led the Boilermakers in scoring (21.5), rebounding (9.2), steals (99) and blocked shots (42). Holmes was considered a standout defensive player. She led the Big Ten in rebounds and steals, was second in blocks and third in scoring. Holmes finished as Purdue's all-time leader in games played, points, steals, field goals, free throws and free throw attempts. She set an NCAA Tournament record in a second-round game against Vanderbilt with eight steals.

JULIE FARRELL-OVENHOUSE
Diving, Michigan State

From a four-time prep all-stater to a three-time All-American to the U.S. Olympic team in six short years—the story of Julie Farrell-Ovenhouse is one of perseverance and continued excellence. A native of nearby Holt, Mich., she is the only Michigan State diver to win a national title, taking the one-meter title in 1990 and a win on the three-meter board a year later. She won four Big Ten titles during her career and was co-winner of the Big Ten's Jesse Owens Award as athlete of the year in 1991. Three times Farrell-Ovenhouse received the George Alderton Award as State's top athlete, the first male or female to do so. After a brief retirement following her collegiate career, the criminal justice major made the 1992 Olympic team. She currently is in the insurance business in Novi, Mich.

MIKE SMITH
Baseball, Indiana

Mike Smith did little to draw attention to himself his first two seasons at Indiana, compiling a .249 batting average after his first two seasons. Then something happened. He hit .476, with 10 home runs and 26 RBI in Big Ten play as a junior, and came back the following year to become the first player in major college baseball history to win the national Triple Crown — a .490 batting average, 27 home runs and 95 RBI in just 55 games. He had a slugging percentage of 1.000 that season, compiling 202 total bases in 202 at-bats. The shortstop from Picqua, Ohio, was named *The Sporting News* national Player of the Year in 1992 and was selected fifth by the Texas Rangers in the Major League Baseball draft following his senior season.

MIKE BARROWMAN
Swimming, Michigan

Mike Barrowman's swimming resumé is one of which any Olympian would be proud. The breaststroker, who won three NCAA titles at 200 meters for Michigan from 1989-91, achieved the ultimate in 1992 with a gold medal in his specialty at the Olympic Games in Barcelona. Records came in bunches too, with Barrowman holding world, American, NCAA and Big Ten marks in the event. A five-time U.S. Swimming champ, Barrowman, a native of Potomac, Md., has three times been named U.S. swimmer of the year. He won five Big Ten titles as Michigan won Conference titles each year he competed. He also made the 1988 U.S. Olympic team and won a gold in the 1990 Goodwill Games in Seattle. Barrowman, a four-time finalist for the Sullivan Award, also was a three-time all-academic Big Ten honoree and won a 1991 NCAA post-graduate scholarship.

LEADING THE WAY

PETER TEGEN
Wisconsin

No coach in Wisconsin history has fostered more All-America athletes than Peter Tegen. And no Big Ten women's track and field/cross country coach has boasted more Conference and NCAA champions than Tegen, who guided the Badgers' women's cross country team to back-to-back NCAA titles in 1984 and '85. In 21 years at Wisconsin, Tegen has coached a combined 40 national champions in track and cross country. A total of 188 All-Americans have raced through his programs, including former Olympic track stars Suzy Favor, Cindy Bremser and cross country standouts Cathy Branta and Stephanie Herbst. A native of Germany, he was voted national cross country coach of the year in 1984 and '85. He has been named Big Ten coach of the year in track and cross country a combined seven times and was the first women's coach to be inducted into the Drake Relays Hall of Fame.

· BIG TEN PIONEERS ·

Big Ten-SEC women's challenge

The Big Ten, the new kids on the block among women's basketball's elite, issued a challenge in 1989 to the Southeastern Conference, which was widely regarded as the pace-setter in the sport: our two best against your two best in a doubleheader. Every year. National TV. Let's do it. On Jan. 5, 1991, it happened. The doubleheader matched Purdue against Auburn, followed by Iowa and Georgia at Carver-Hawkeye Arena. These were the first regular-season women's basketball games to be televised live to a national audience by a major network (CBS). "This is another step in the right direction for the sport as a whole," then-Iowa coach Vivian Stringer said at the time. For the record, Georgia (62-51) and Auburn (75-65) won the games that day, but everyone associated with women's basketball came out a winner.

Academic Achievements

I f it rains on your nuclear-powered hospital bed, chances are good you can blame some one from Penn State. One in four meteorologists and one out of every four health planners and administrators are Penn State-trained, and one in 16 nuclear engineers attended PSU.

1990-91 Conference MEDAL OF HONOR Winners

ILLINOIS	Lynn Devers, Aaron Mobarek
INDIANA	Joy Jordan, Scott Boatman
IOWA	Janet Moylan, David Brown
MICHIGAN	Stacy Berg, Mike Barrowman
MICHIGAN STATE	Emily Coatney, Walter Bartels
MINNESOTA	Rachel Lewis, Marty Morgan
NORTHWESTERN	Marilyn Peck, Bob Christian
OHIO STATE	Cheryl Perozek, Donna Rupolo, Michael DiSabato
PURDUE	Joy Holmes, Dave Barrett
WISCONSIN	Elaine Demetroulis, Jack Waite

The BIG TEN's First 100 Years
Big Ten Women's Basketball Championships

Total			Total Uncontested	
8	Ohio State		4	Ohio State
7	Iowa		3	Iowa
3	Purdue			
2	Penn State		**Consecutive**	
1	Indiana		6	Ohio State (1982-87)
1	Northwestern		4	Iowa (1987-90)

Consecutive Uncontested
3 Ohio State (1984-86)

THE BIG EVENT

First men's soccer championship

The birth of Indiana's dominance in Big Ten men's soccer started with the berth of the first Conference championship in 1991 at Bloomington, Ind. Coach Jerry Yeagley's Hoosiers, national powers long before the inception of Conference-sanctioned championships with three NCAA titles and 10 national semifinal appearances, won the first league crown after booting Wisconsin, 2-0, in the championship match. The crown was the first of three for Indiana between then and 1994. The only interruption to the Hoosiers' title collection was in 1993, when Penn State claimed the championship with a 1-0 win against Wisconsin. Between 1991 and 1994, the Hoosiers posted a remarkable 17-2 record in Conference games. Ironically, when the Hoosiers won their first title in 1991, they brought a 4-1 league slate to the tournament. Wisconsin had the only perfect Conference record at 5-0. Penn State, however, featured the first league MVP in Steve Sergi. Indiana's Todd Yeagley, the coach's son, made his first of a record four-straight appearances on the first-team All-Big Ten team.

OTHER MEMORABLE EVENTS

- Iowa won the NCAA wrestling championship, behind Tom Brands who won his third straight national title and the most oustanding wrestler award.

- Ohio State's Mark Mesewicz set a Conference record with eight saves during the baseball season.

- Indiana's Mike Smith recorded baseball's triple crown, leading the nation in home runs, RBI and batting average.

- Wisconsin's women's soccer team finished second at the NCAA championship.

- Ohio State's women's volleyball team advanced to the national semifinals of the NCAA championship.

- Michigan's Erick Anderson won the Butkus Award given to the nation's top linebacker.

- Michigan's Desmond Howard won the Heisman Trophy.

Buckeye volleyball team rolls to 20-0 Big Ten mark

The media guide predicted that Ohio State planned to return to the top as Big Ten champs in the 1991-92 season after finishing within one match of repeating as Conference champs under coach Jim Stone. The bold statement proved to be correct, as the Buckeyes compiled a 20-0 mark to win the league championship on their way to a 30-4 season, an NCAA tournament regional championship and an appearance in the national semifinals. Ohio State showed its grit early in the Big Ten season at Penn State, the league's newcomer which had defeated Ohio State in eight straight matches. Ohio State lost the first two games, but won the next two to force a fifth game. The Buckeyes finally won the match, 18-16, after taking advantage of their third match point, ending the Nittany Lions' 42-match home win streak and 52-match regular-season win streak. The Buckeyes defeated Penn State and Nebraska to reach the NCAA semifinals, where they lost to eventual champ UCLA. Ohio State's Leisa Wissler was the Big Ten Player of the Year while teammate Laura Davis earned Freshman of the Year and Stone Coach of the Year.

OTHER BIG TEN CHAMPIONS

Men
- FOOTBALL: Michigan, coached by Gary Moeller
- BASEBALL: Minnesota, coached by John Anderson
- GYMNASTICS: Minnesota, coached by Fred Roethlisberger
- OUTDOOR TRACK: Ohio State, coached by Russ Rogers
- INDOOR TRACK: Indiana, coached by Sam Bell
- BASKETBALL: Ohio State, coached by Randy Ayers
- CROSS COUNTRY: Wisconsin, coached by Martin Smith
- TENNIS: Minnesota, coached by David Geatz
- SWIMMING: Michigan, coached by Jon Urbanchek
- WRESTLING: Iowa, coached by Dan Gable
- GOLF: Iowa, coached by Lynn Blevins
- SOCCER: Indiana, coached by Jerry Yeagley

Women
- BASKETBALL: Iowa, coached by Vivian Stringer
- CROSS COUNTRY: Wisconsin, coached by Peter Tegen
- GOLF: Indiana, coached by Sam Carmichael
- GYMNASTICS: Michigan, coached by Beverly Plocki
- SOFTBALL: Michigan, coached by Carol Hutchins
- SWIMMING/DIVING: Michigan, coached by Jim Richardson
- TENNIS: Indiana, coached by Lin Loring
- INDOOR TRACK: Illinois, coached by Gary Winckler
- OUTDOOR TRACK: Illinois, coached by Gary Winckler

MaCHELLE JOSEPH
Basketball, Purdue

The senior from Auburn, Ind., finished her career as Purdue's all-time scoring and assist leader, as well as the Big Ten's all-time scoring leader. After leading the Boilermakers in scoring (22.2 ppg), assists (167), 3-pointers (51) and free throw percentage (83.2), Joseph was named the league's women's basketball Player of the Year and overall Female Athlete of the Year. She was a Kodak All-American and fifth in the voting for the Naismith Player of the Year Award. Purdue was 96-27 (.780) during Joseph's four years after which she held 33 Purdue game, season, career and postseason records. A three-time first-team all-Conference selection, Joseph was named to the Big Ten's All-Decade team. After serving as a graduate assistant and interim assistant coach at Illinois in 1992-93, Joseph returned to Purdue for a brief stint as an assistant coach to Lin Dunn.

DESMOND HOWARD
Football, Michigan

The 1991 Heisman Trophy winner and the second man from Michigan to win that award, two-time All-American Desmond Howard's acrobatic catches made him one of the most exciting players in the college game. At 5-foot-9 and 176 pounds, Howard in 1991 became the first receiver to lead the Big Ten in scoring (90 points) as he set or tied five NCAA records and 12 single-season UM marks. Howard had the highest number of first place votes (640, or 85 percent of those cast) in the Heisman balloting and won it by the second largest margin in its long history. He scored at least two touchdowns in nine of Michigan's 11 games. He was recognized as Player of the Year by receiving the Walter Camp Trophy and the Maxwell Award. Howard was a first-round selection of the Washington Redskins.

ARTUR WOJDAT
Swimming, Iowa

By the time he left, he was the most decorated swimmer in Iowa history, and Artur Wojdat made his mark nationally and internationally, as well. The Poznan, Poland native was a nine-time NCAA champion, a 19-time All-American and Big Ten swimmer of the year in 1990 and '91. As a senior, he won NCAA titles in the 500-yard freestyle and 1,650 free. In 1991 as a junior, Wojdat was a triple-winner (200, 500, 1,650 frees). He won the 500 and 1,650 as a sophomore. Wojdat set an NCAA record in 1989, winning the 500 free in 4:12.24. He won that event four consecutive years, and also won the 200 in '89. He won a bronze medal in the 400-meter freestyle and finished fourth in the 200 free while swimming for Poland in the 1988 Olympic Games.

BETH WYMER
Gymnastics, Michigan

The most honored gymnast in Big Ten history, Beth Wymer won an unprecedented third straight NCAA uneven bars championship in 1995 to pace Michigan to second place in the meet, its best finish ever. A three-time Big Ten Gymnast of the Year, Wymer, was awarded the Big Ten Medal of Honor in 1995. A native of Toledo, Wymer was a 13-time All-American and 14-time Big Ten champion, earning scores of 10.0 in the vault in the 1994 and 1995 Conference championships. Michigan won the team title each of the four years Wymer competed. She was nominated in 1995 for the Sullivan Award, presented by the Amateur Athletic Union to the nation's top amateur athlete. The first Michigan woman to score a perfect 10.0, Wymer was named the team's MVP four times. She is now serving as an assistant coach while pursuing a graduate degree.

LEADING THE WAY

C. VIVIAN STRINGER
Iowa

What C. Vivian Stringer did for the Iowa women's basketball program can be summed up easily: she took a team at the bottom of the Big Ten standings and turned it into a national power. Within five years she set a new standard for women's basketball at Iowa, and possibly the Conference. Stringer, who had led Cheyney State to the first women's national championship game in 1982, guided the Hawkeyes there 11 years later, making her the only coach to take two different teams to the Women's Final Four. Before leaving Iowa to coach at Rutgers in 1995 — and becoming the highest-paid coach in women's basketball history. Stringer's Hawkeye teams went 269-84 in 12 years, with six Big Ten titles, a league-record 29 victories and the No. 1 ranking in the country in 1988. Stringer was Big Ten coach of the year in 1991 and '93 and won National Coach of the Year honors in 1988 and '93. Under Stringer, Iowa women's basketball developed such a following that the program set an NCAA attendance record with a crowd of 22,157 at Carver-Hawkeye Arena in 1984, and had the first women's pregame sell-out in NCAA history for a 1988 game with Ohio State. Stringer became the winningest coach in school history and led Iowa to nine consecutive NCAA Tournament berths and 10 winning seasons in a row.

· BIG TEN PIONEERS ·

Calbert Cheaney

Indiana's Calbert Cheaney finished his career as the Big Ten's all-time leading scorer and the consensus national player of the year. But lost among all his honors was this historical footnote: he is probably the best lefthanded basketball player ever to play in the Conference. Cheaney, who was named the Big Ten's MVP in 1993, was relatively unheralded coming out of high school, in Evansville, Ind., but he made an immediate impact with the Hoosiers. He averaged 17.1 points as a freshman, 21.6 as a sophomore, 17.6 as a junior and 22.4 as a senior. He hit 56 percent of his field goal attempts and 79 percent of his foul shots. A first-round draft pick of the NBA's Washington Bullets—now the Washington Wizards—in 1993, he still plays there.

Calbert Cheaney

Academic Achievements

TIME *magazine named Michigan State's introduction of a plant that can be used in the production of a biodegradable plastic as one of the top science stories of 1992. A plant that grows plastic? Yes, the potato-like substance can be used to make a number of products like containers and diapers.*

1991-92 Conference MEDAL OF HONOR Winners

ILLINOIS	Kate Riley, Mike Hopkins
INDIANA	Katrin Koch, Mark Hagen
IOWA	Jennifer Brower, Paul Bautell
MICHIGAN	Amy Bannister, Eric Bailey
MICHIGAN STATE	Misty Allison, Stuart Hirschman
MINNESOTA	Uta Herrmann, Scott Tripps
NORTHWESTERN	Michele Savage, Matt Case
OHIO STATE	Stacia Goff, Paul Huzyak
PENN STATE	Michele R. Robinson, Gregory B. Guarton
PURDUE	MaChelle Joseph, Craig Riley
WISCONSIN	Heather Taggart, Matt Demaray

1992-93

1992-93 Iowa wrestling team

THE BIG EVENT
Iowa reigns again in wrestling

Was there a chink in the typically indestructible Iowa armor? After two straight NCAA titles, Iowa's wrestling team was struggling through the 1992-93 season. Well, struggling by Iowa standards. It lost its No. 1 ranking in late January after a loss to Nebraska and stood 6-1-1 in dual meets. That kind of mark would only be cause for concern in Iowa City. The "slump" didn't last long. The Hawkeyes won eight straight matches, captured their 20th Big Ten title in a row and went on to win a third consecutive national championship. There were seven All-Americans, including NCAA champions Lincoln McIlravy (the Big Ten Freshman of the Year) and Terry Steiner. Joel Sharratt and Chad Zaputil were runners-up, with Ray Brinzer, John Oostendorp and Troy Steiner finishing third. Terry Steiner was named the most outstanding wrestler at the NCAA meet. Troy Steiner and Zaputil won Big Ten titles, with Steiner winning Wrestler of the Year honors. It also was the first time Dan Gable was named Big Ten Coach of the Year.

OTHER MEMORABLE EVENTS

- Michigan's football team had a record 19-game Conference win streak snapped.

- Minnesota's John Roethlisberger won his third straight NCAA all-around gymnastics title and fourth consecutive Big Ten crown.

- Indiana's Bob Kennedy won his second NCAA cross country championship and fourth straight Conference crown.

- Indiana's Calbert Cheaney was the national basketball player of the year.

- Minnesota won the men's basketball National Invitation Tournament.

- Ohio State (2nd) and Iowa (lost in semis) both advanced to the NCAA Women's basketball Final Four.

- Michigan's Elvis Grbac led the nation in passing efficiency for the second straight season.

Buckeye "9" capture Big Ten title

1992-93 Ohio State baseball team

A team of survivors, the Ohio State Buckeyes matched the school's three-year run in 1965-67 by reaching the NCAA tournament for the third straight season, capped by a regular-season Big Ten championship in the 1992-93 season. The Buckeyes trailed Minnesota by one game heading into the final day of the regular season, but Ohio State's sweep of Penn State—and a doubleheader loss by Minnesota to Illinois—allowed the Buckeyes to win the Big Ten title. In the Big Ten playoffs, Ohio State survived a 3-hour, 48-minute marathon to defeat Minnesota to force a deciding game. The final day was washed out, and Ohio State was determined to receive the automatic berth to the NCAA tournament by virtue of winning the regular-season championship. Both Minnesota and Ohio State reached the NCAAs. The title was one of four won by the Buckeyes under coach Bob Todd, who holds a 324-169-1 record. Matt Beaumont was a first-team All-Big Ten pick who was named the MVP of the Conference playoffs. Chris Granata and Brian Mannino were also first-team All-Big Ten picks for the Buckeyes.

OTHER BIG TEN CHAMPIONS

Men
- FOOTBALL: Michigan, coached by Gary Moeller
- GYMNASTICS: Ohio State, coached by Peter Kormann
- OUTDOOR TRACK: Ohio State, coached by Russ Rogers
- INDOOR TRACK: Ohio State, coached by Russ Rogers
- BASKETBALL: Indiana, coached by Bob Knight
- CROSS COUNTRY: Wisconsin, coached by Martin Smith
- TENNIS: Minnesota, coached by David Geatz
- SWIMMING: Michigan, coached by Jon Urbanchek
- WRESTLING: Iowa, coached by Dan Gable
- GOLF: Wisconsin, coached by Dennis Tiziani
- SOCCER: Indiana, coached by Jerry Yeagley

Women
- BASKETBALL: Iowa, coached by Vivian Stringer, and Ohio State, coached by Nancy Darsch
- CROSS COUNTRY: Michigan, coached by Mike McGuire
- FIELD HOCKEY: Iowa, coached by Beth Beglin
- GOLF: Ohio State, coached by Therese Hession
- GYMNASTICS: Michigan, coached by Beverly Plocki
- SOFTBALL: Michigan, coached by Carol Hutchins
- SWIMMING/DIVING: Michigan, coached by Jim Richardson
- TENNIS: Indiana, coached by Lin Loring
- INDOOR TRACK: Illinois, coached by Gary Winckler
- OUTDOOR TRACK: Michigan, coached by James Henry
- VOLLEYBALL: Illinois, coached by Mike Hebert, and Penn State, coached by Russ Rose

RENEE HEIKEN
Golf, Illinois

The greatest women's golfer ever at Illinois, Renee Heiken began playing the game at age six. In high school she played on the boys' team and was named the squad's MVP each season before heading to Illinois, where winning tournaments was ordinary. Heiken claimed a total of 15 tournament championships in her four years at Illinois, including eight in her senior season of 1992-93. Heiken won the Big Ten championship in 1991 and '93 and played three straight years in the NCAA tournament—placing in the top six all three years. She was named national college Player of the Year by the coaches association and a golf magazine in 1992-93. She was a two-time winner of the Female Athlete of the Year award at Illinois, then turned her attention to a pro career. Heiken competed in 27 tournaments on the LPGA tour in 1995.

BOB KENNEDY
Track, Indiana

Bob Kennedy could just about finish one of his distance races in the time it takes to run off his list of accomplishments, but here goes: He won 20 Big Ten titles during his career at Indiana, four in cross country, nine in indoor track and seven in outdoor track. He was named the Big Ten Athlete of the Year for both the indoor and outdoor track seasons. He also won four NCAA championships, in cross country in 1988 and '92, in the outdoor 1,500-meter run in '90 and the indoor mile in '91. The native of Westerville, Ohio, was a 10-time All-American, and was named the *Runner's World* co-American Runner of the Year in 1992. His father, Bob, ran for Indiana's 1967 Big Ten championship cross country team. Kennedy placed 12th in the 1992 Olympics in the 5,000-meter run. A member of the 1996 U.S. Olympic team, he recently broke the American record in the 5,000 meters.

LARA HOOIVELD
Swimming, Michigan

NCAA swimmer of the year in 1993, Lara Hooiveld had the kind of season that athletes can only dream about. The Brisbane, Australia, native won NCAA titles in the 100 and 200 yard breaststroke and successfully defended all her 1992 Big Ten individual titles, and, with her teammates, the medley relay, giving her eight Conference titles in two years. Michigan won the Conference title in each of those years. In 1993, Hooiveld was twice named Big Ten female swimmer of the month. An excellent student, she was twice named Academic All-Big Ten and twice received the U-M Athletic Academic Achievement award. Hooiveld was a member of the 1988 Australian Olympic team, finishing 15th in the 100 and 30th in the 200 breaststroke as a 17-year-old.

JOHN ROETHLISBERGER
Gymnastics, Minnesota

Keeping in step with family tradition, John Roethlisberger concluded his remarkable four-year career as the most successful men's gymnast in school history. Then again, his sister — Olympian Marie Roethlisberger —did likewise in women's gymnastics a few years earlier at Minnesota. Their father, Fred Roethlisberger, is the Gophers' men's gymnastics coach as well as a former Olympian himself. John, a four-time Big Ten Athlete of the Year (1990-93), is a five-time NCAA champion, a 10-time league champion and a 15-time All-American. He won NCAA titles in the all-around in 1991, '92, '93; in parallel bars in 1991; and in pommel horse in 1993. A two-time academic All-American, Roethlisberger is the first gymnast in Big Ten history to win four all-around championships. He was an all-around finalist at the 1992 Summer Games in Barcelona. In 1993, he won the Nissen Award, presented to the nation's most outstanding senior gymnast based on athletic and academic achievement.

413

LEADING THE WAY

FRED ROETHLISBERGER
Minnesota

Fred Roethlisberger is the literal patriarch of gymnastics success at Minnesota. During his 25 years of coaching the men's team, the Gophers have won 11 Big Ten team titles and produced 48 individual league champions. Gophers routinely pop up on the U.S. national team and some, like former star John Roethlisberger — Fred's son — wind up on the U.S. Olympic team. And Fred's daughter, Marie Roethlisberger, is the most celebrated female gymnast in Minnesota history. Fred became the Gophers' men's coach in 1972. Between then and 1995, his teams amassed a 164-60-1 regular season record and finished in the top 10 of the NCAA meet 16 times. The Gophers made 20 straight NCAA appearances from 1976-95. Their best showing was a runner-up finish in 1990. They finished third once, fourth twice and fifth three times. A former Olympic performer himself (1968), Fred was named Big Ten Coach of the Year three times (1990, '91, and '92) and named Mideast Region Coach of the Year five times. He was inducted into the U.S. Gymnastics Hall of Fame in 1990 as a gymnast, a coach and a contributor.

· BIG TEN PIONEERS ·

Janice Voss
Purdue

Purdue alumni have played a prominent role in the U.S. space program, producing such luminary astronauts as Neil Armstrong, Virgil "Gus" Grissom, Roger Chaffee and Eugene Cernan. But Janice Voss broke new ground. The former Boilermaker tennis player (1972-73) became the first female alum to go into space. The mission specialist became the 18th woman astronaut in space on June 21, 1993 when she flew aboard the space shuttle Endeavor. Voss and five other crew members returned to Earth on July 1. The South Bend, Ind., native graduated from Purdue in 1975 at age 18 with a degree in engineering science. She earned a master's from Purdue in electrical engineering and a doctorate in aeronautics and astronautics from MIT.

Academic Achievements

It's been estimated that by the turn of the century, nearly half of this nation's population will be receiving information via the Internet. That information super highway is being traveled easier today thanks to MOSIAC, the first World Wide Web browser, developed at the University of Illinois in 1993.

1992-93
Conference MEDAL OF HONOR
Winners

ILLINOIS	Lindsey Nimmo, Brad Lawton
INDIANA	Courtney Cox, Dave Held
IOWA	Andrea Wieland, Matt Whitaker
MICHIGAN	Mindy Gehrs, Robert Pelinka
MICHIGAN STATE	Ruth Aguayo, Dave Smith
MINNESOTA	Laura Herman, John Roethlisberger
NORTHWESTERN	Nancy Kennelly, Mark Loretta
OHIO STATE	Erika Cottrell, Jim Knopp
PENN STATE	Jenny Kretchmar, Vitali Nazlimov
PURDUE	Heidi Reynolds, Brian Daly
WISCONSIN	Kim Sherman, Donovan Bergstrom

The BIG TEN's First 100 Years
Big Ten Universities
Were The Birthplace To...

First "talking" motion pictures (Illinois)

Buffered aspirin (Iowa)

First open-heart surgery and first successful bone marrow transplant (Minnesota)

First application of computer analysis to weather prediction (Penn State)

Discovery of vitamins A and B (Wisconsin)

1993-94

THE BIG EVENT

70,000 fans follow Badgers to Pasadena

Darrell Bevell

Powered by the precision running of Big Ten MVP Brent Moss and a stubborn, sturdy defense, Wisconsin won its first Rose Bowl in a 21-16 defeat of UCLA on Jan. 1, 1994 in Pasadena. An estimated 70,000 Badger fans made the trip to watch the team win its first "Grand Daddy of Them All" after three previous tries, the last being in 1963. The victory capped an unprecedented campaign for Wisconsin (10-1-1), which won a school record 10 games and only its second bowl game in history, under the direction of fourth-year coach Barry Alvarez. The Badgers — projected in preseason polls to place in the middle of the Big Ten pack — finished the year ranked No. 6 in the AP poll and set a school home-game average attendance record of 75,507. Moss was Rose Bowl MVP after rushing 36 times for 158 yards and two touchdowns. The Badgers' defense, meanwhile, allowed 500 total yards, but didn't surrender a touchdown until the fourth quarter, when the Bruins scored twice.

OTHER MEMORABLE EVENTS

- Minnesota (59) and Purdue (56) combined for the highest scoring football game in Conference history.

- Ohio State hit a record .398 and had a record 52 home runs in the Conference baseball season.

- Penn State women's volleyball team finished second in the nation. (Its men's team won the NCAA championship to become the first school outside of California to do so.)

- Indiana's Todd Leary made a record 46 straight free throws, but took four years to do it.

- Purdue women's basketball team reached the NCAA Women's Final Four.

- Purdue's Glenn Robinson led the nation in scoring with 30.3 points per game and was named the national basketball player of the year.

Purdue captures men's and women's basketball titles

The Boilermakers' men's basketball team began the season 14-0 - the best start in school history—and went on to tie the Purdue single-season record with 29 victories. It was the first of three consecutive Big Ten titles for Gene Keady & Co. The feature attraction was Glenn Robinson, who would lead the nation in scoring and become national player of the year as a senior. Purdue clinched the league title outright when, in its final regular-season game, it defeated Illinois to finish 14-4, while Northwestern upset Michigan. Robinson, a sophomore, led the Big Ten in scoring (31 ppg) and rebounding (9.8 rpg). Keady was named Conference coach of the year for the fourth time (he later won the award in '95 and '96). The men finished No. 3 in the final Associated Press poll and No. 5 in the final *USA Today*/CNN poll. The Purdue women held their own, finishing 29-5, sharing the Big Ten title with Penn State (at 16-2) and advancing to the Women's Final Four before losing to eventual national champion North Carolina in the semifinals. The Boilermakers finished No. 8 in the Associated Press rankings and third in the *USA Today*/CNN poll. Jennifer Jacoby and freshman Leslie Johnson shared team MVP honors. Johnson was the top scorer (18.5 ppg) and rebounder (9.1), and Jacoby led the team in assists (159), 3-point baskets (46) and free throw shooting (78.1%). Johnson was first-team all-Big Ten and Freshman of the Year.

OTHER BIG TEN CHAMPIONS

Men
- **FOOTBALL:** Ohio State, coached by John Cooper, and Wisconsin, coached by Barry Alvarez
- **BASEBALL:** Ohio State, coached by Bob Todd
- **GYMNASTICS:** Ohio State, coached by Peter Kormann
- **OUTDOOR TRACK:** Illinois, coached by Gary Wieneke
- **INDOOR TRACK:** Michigan, coached by Jack Harvey
- **CROSS COUNTRY:** Michigan, coached by Ron Warhurst
- **TENNIS:** Minnesota, coached by David Geatz
- **SWIMMING:** Michigan, coached by Jon Urbanchek
- **WRESTLING:** Iowa, coached by Dan Gable
- **GOLF:** Wisconsin, coached by Dennis Tiziani
- **SOCCER:** Penn State, coached by Barry Gorman

Women
- **CROSS COUNTRY:** Michigan, coached by Mike McGuire
- **FIELD HOCKEY:** Penn State, coached by Charlene Morett
- **GOLF:** Wisconsin, coached by Dennis Tiziani
- **GYMNASTICS:** Michigan, coached by Beverly Plocki
- **SOFTBALL:** Indiana, coached by Diane Stephenson
- **SWIMMING/DIVING:** Michigan, coached by Jim Richardson
- **TENNIS:** Indiana, coached by Lin Loring
- **INDOOR TRACK:** Michigan, coached by James Henry
- **OUTDOOR TRACK:** Michigan, coached by James Henry
- **VOLLEYBALL:** Penn State, coached by Russ Rose

GLENN ROBINSON
Basketball, Purdue

"Big Dog" wore a Purdue uniform for only two seasons, but couldn't have made more of an impact before leaving after his junior year and becoming the top pick in the NBA draft. He was a two-time All-American and national player of the year in 1994. Robinson led the country in scoring (30.3 ppg)—Purdue's first scoring champion since Dave Schellhase in 1966—and set Purdue (1,030 points) and Big Ten (560) single-season scoring records. Purdue was 47-15 during Robinson's reign. He scored a career-high 49 points in his last regular-season game in Mackey Arena, and during the NCAA Tournament he scored a school tournament-record 44 against Kansas as the Boilermakers advanced to the Elite Eight. After just two seasons, Robinson left as Purdue's No. 8 all-time scorer (1,706) and No. 15 rebounder (602).

KRISTY GLEASON
Field Hockey, Iowa

Nobody else could lay claim to Kristy Gleason's feat: She was the first player in the nation to be named first-team All-America four years in field hockey, and she finished her career as Iowa's all-time leading goal scorer and No. 2 in NCAA history (132 career goals). She was the Big Ten's MVP as a junior and senior and was selected to the league's All-Decade first-team as a sophomore. She was first-team All-Big Ten in 1989, '90, '92 and '93 and led the Hawkeyes to the national semifinals all four years. Gleason led the nation in scoring in 1992 and was second in '93. She finished holding Iowa records for career points (285), most points in a game (11) and most goals in a game (5). She did not play for Iowa in 1991 because she was training for the U.S. National team. She also competed on the U.S. Olympic Sports Festival Team in 1990 and the U.S. Pan American Games team in '91.

BRENT MOSS
Football, Wisconsin

Regarded as one of the greatest running backs in Wisconsin history, Brent Moss led the Badgers to heights they hadn't reached in more than 30 years. His school record 1,637 rushing yards as a junior in 1993 powered Wisconsin to the 1994 Rose Bowl and a 21-16 win over UCLA. The Rose Bowl appearance was the Badgers' first since 1963. A three-year letterman from 1991-93, Moss ended his career as Wisconsin's second all-time leading rusher with 3,428 yards. He collected 34 touchdowns and averaged 4.9 yards per carry during his tenure. Moss ran for 219 yards as a freshman, 739 as a sophomore and 833 as a senior, a campaign shortened by injuries. In 1993, Moss and teammate Terrell Fletcher combined for 4,942 yards, the eighth most yardage gained by a tandem in NCAA history. That same year, he was voted Big Ten MVP and named to several All-America teams. He was MVP of the Rose Bowl after rushing for 158 yards and two touchdowns. His streak of 17 100-plus yard rushing games is the second longest streak in Big Ten history.

CAROL ANN SHUDLICK
Basketball, Minnesota

Carol Ann Shudlick is the student-athlete by which other Golden Gophers are measured. During her basketball career from 1991-94, she set a total of eight Minnesota records and was the all-time leading scorer in Gopher history with 2,097 points. During her final season in 1993-94, the forward from Apple Valley, Minn., became Minnesota's first-ever winner of the Wade Trophy, given to the nation's most outstanding senior basketball player. Shudlick also was named a first-team Kodak All-American, as well as being honored as the Big Ten's Player of the Year. A journalism student, she also excelled in the classroom, earning three Academic All-Big Ten honors and her university's Conference Medal of Honor. Following a brief professional basketball career in Spain, she returned to Minnesota and is currently employed in public relations by the Missabe Group.

LEADING THE WAY

JERRY YEAGLEY
Indiana

No other men's soccer program in the country has enjoyed as much success as Indiana's over the last 20 years, and there is but one reason for it: Coach Jerry Yeagley. IU's only soccer coach, Yeagley started a club team in 1963, then began a varsity program in 1973. His accomplishments since then are unmatched. He has led the Hoosiers to three NCAA championships (1982, '83 and '88), eight final game appearances, 10 Final Fours and 20 NCAA tournaments. Every player who has competed at IU for four seasons has participated in at least one national semifinal game, a claim no other program can make. Yeagley's overall record of 396-74-34 entering the 1996 season ranks him fifth in NCAA history for victories, third among Division I coaches. He is 97 wins away from leader Steve Negoesco of San Francisco. His accomplishments have not gone unnoticed. He is the only person to be named NCAA Coach of the Year three times and was inducted into the National Soccer Hall of Fame in 1989. A member of a state championship team at Myerstown (Pa.) High School and an NCAA Division I champion for West Chester State, he also has been inducted into the Pennsylvania Athletic Hall of Fame.

· BIG TEN PIONEERS ·

Penn State Success

Penn State was accepted as the 11th member of the Big Ten in June of 1990. It made its Conference debut in 18 of its sports in the 1991-92 school year, with the men's and women's basketball teams and the wrestling squad joining the following year. The Nittany Lions won the 1994 Conference football title while going undefeated and defeating Oregon in the Rose Bowl in their second year of league competition in football. During its previous affiliation with the Atlantic 10 Conference, which dated back to 1979, the Nittany Lions won more than 40 league titles despite the football team's independent status.

Academic Achievements

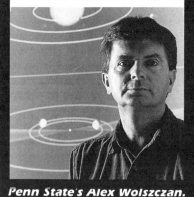

Penn State's Alex Wolszczan.

The first confirmation of the existence of planets outside our solar system occurred at Penn State in 1994.

1993-94
Conference MEDAL OF HONOR
Winners

ILLINOIS	Tonya Booker, Forry Wells
INDIANA	Anne Eastman, Vito Maurici
IOWA	Tina Stec, Kevin Herd
MICHIGAN	Molly McClimon, Tobin Van Pelt
MICHIGAN STATE	Laura Bell, Steve Wasylk
MINNESOTA	Carol Ann Shudlick, Martin Eriksson
NORTHWESTERN	Susan Donahoe, Kevin Rankin
OHIO STATE	Holly Humphrey, Mike Repasky
PENN STATE	Helen Holloway, Craig Fayak
PURDUE	Kim Fritsch, Ron Gabrisko
WISCONSIN	Susie Holt, Louis Hinshaw

The BIG TEN's First 100 Years

Big Ten Men's Soccer Top Goal Scorers

IN A SINGLE GAME

4-Sebastien Gouverneur 9/2/95 Penn State vs. Lafayette

4-Matt Schroeder 9/18/94 Ohio State vs. NU

4-Nick Scott 10/22/93 Penn State vs. Connecticut

IN A SINGLE SEASON

16-Harry Weiss Indiana 1993

16-Stuart Reid Penn State 1993

IN A CAREER

56-Stuart Reid
Penn State 1992-1995

1994-95

THE BIG EVENT

Penn State goes undefeated to win football title

Penn State's football team was not voted the national champion following the 1994 season—Nebraska was—but virtually everything else about that campaign was perfect. Starting with the record. The Nittany Lions, playing in just their second season as a Big Ten member, swept through the regular season without a loss, then defeated Oregon in the Rose Bowl, 38-20, to become the first league team to go undefeated since Ohio State in 1968. It was the fifth undefeated season for legendary coach Joe Paterno, who earned three national coach of the year awards. The foundation of Penn State's success was its offense, which featured running back Ki-Jana Carter and quarterback Kerry Collins. The Lions averaged 48.1 points per game, a Big Ten record, and led the nation in total offense at 520.2 yards per game, fourth-highest in NCAA history.

OTHER MEMORABLE EVENTS

- Illinois' Dana Howard won the Butkus Award as the nation's top linebacker, while Penn State's Bobby Engram won the Biletnikoff Award as the nation's top receiver.

- Michigan State's Shawn Respert concluded his basketball career with a record 1,544 points in Conference games.

- Michigan won the NCAA men's swimming and diving championship, and Iowa won the NCAA wrestling title.

- Michigan's Kevin Sullivan won his second straight Conference cross country title and set an NCAA indoor meet record in the mile.

- Michigan's Beth Wymer won her third straight NCAA uneven bars title, while Wolverine Alecia Humphrey won two individual titles and one relay at the NCAA swimming meet.

- The Conference awarded its first women's soccer championship.

- Two Conference teams—Iowa and Michigan—advanced to the NCAA softball world series.

Michigan's women gymnasts 1st in Big Ten, 2nd in nationals

Finishing second isn't bad when you're just hoping to break into the top three. That was the case for the 1994-95 Michigan women's gymnastics squad, which had hoped to move among the nation's elite collegiate teams and outdid themselves. Coach Bev Plocki's team rampaged through the season with an overall 24-2 mark and a 12-0 Big Ten slate before taking its fourth straight Big Ten title, beating Michigan State 196.500 to 193.025. At nationals, Michigan scored 196.425 points to tie with Alabama for second behind Utah (196.650). Pacing UM were All-Americans Beth Wymer, Wendy Marshall and Heather Kabnick, the Conference's top freshmen. Wymer scored 9.95 on the uneven parallel bars to capture her third straight NCAA title in the event and become one of only three women to accomplish that feat. She later won the Big Ten-Suzy Favor Athlete of the Year award as well as the Conference Medal of Honor. The team's second place finish was, at that time, the best ever in NCAA competition by a Michigan women's team, a performance equalled later that year by UM's cross country team and the next spring by the swimmers.

OTHER BIG TEN CHAMPIONS

Men
- FOOTBALL: Penn State, coached by Joe Paterno
- BASEBALL: Ohio State, coached by Bob Todd
- GYMNASTICS: Minnesota, coached by Fred Roethlisberger
- OUTDOOR TRACK: Wisconsin, coached by Ed Nuttycombe
- INDOOR TRACK: Wisconsin, coached by Ed Nuttycombe
- BASKETBALL: Purdue, coached by Gene Keady
- CROSS COUNTRY: Wisconsin, coached by Martin Smith
- TENNIS: Minnesota, coached by David Geatz
- SWIMMING/DIVING: Michigan, coached by Jon Urbanchek
- WRESTLING: Iowa, coached by Dan Gable
- GOLF: Ohio State, coached by Jim Brown
- SOCCER: Indiana, coached by Jerry Yeagley

Women
- BASKETBALL: Penn State, coached by Rene Portland, and Purdue, coached by Lin Dunn
- CROSS COUNTRY: Michigan, coached by Mike McGuire
- FIELD HOCKEY: Northwestern, coached by Marisa Didio
- GOLF: Indiana, coached by Sam Carmichael
- SOFTBALL: Michigan, coached by Carol Hutchins
- SWIMMING/DIVING: Michigan, coached by Jim Richardson
- TENNIS: Indiana, coached by Lin Loring
- INDOOR TRACK: Illinois, coached by Gary Winckler
- OUTDOOR TRACK: Illinois, coached by Gary Winckler
- VOLLEYBALL: Ohio State, coached by Jim Stone
- SOCCER: Wisconsin, coached by Dean Duerst

KERRY COLLINS
Football, Penn State

Kerry Collins quarterbacked the most explosive offense in Big Ten history with cool efficiency, setting Penn State records for total offense (2,660 yards), completions (176), passing yardage (2,679), completion percentage (66.7), yards per attempt (10.15) and passing efficiency (172.86). He finished his career with 5,304 passing yards, third in school history. The West Lawn, Pa. native didn't go unnoticed, as he received All-America honors from several organizations and was the recipient of the Maxwell Award, one group's choice as the nation's outstanding player. He also received the Davey O'Brien Award, given annually to the No. 1 quarterback, and was voted the Big Ten Player of the Year. The NFL noticed too, as the Carolina Panthers made him the fifth overall selection in the 1995 draft.

LAURA DAVIS
Volleyball, Ohio State

A native of Wheaton, Ill., Laura Davis chose Ohio State because its volleyball team's "uptempo offense was suited to me." It must have been the right decision, since Davis finished her career with school records of 12.87 assists per game and a total of 5,483 assists in her career. In her senior season in 1994, Davis was chosen as the league's player of the year and later earned the Honda Award given to the game's top college player. During that season, she led the nation by averaging 14.64 assists per game and finished as the Suzy Favor Award winner, signifying her as the Conference's top female athlete. The elementary education major was also a whiz in the classroom, where her prowess led to her selection as a four-time Ohio State scholar-athlete and a two-time academic all-Big Ten pick.

SALIMA DAVIDSON
Volleyball, Penn State

Salima Davidson is one of the best women's volleyball players in Big Ten history, earning first-team All-Conference honors her final three seasons of competition. The 5-foot-9 setter from Verona, Pa. was named the league's Most Valuable Player as a junior in 1993 while leading the Lions to a league co-championship. She also earned second-team All-America honors that year as the Lions reached the final game of the NCAA tournament. As a senior, Davidson led Penn State to an NCAA semifinal finish. She was named to the all-tournament team, as she had been the previous year, and received first-team All-America honors by the American Volleyball Coaches Association. She also received Mideast all-region recognition from 1991-94 and was named to the touring U.S. national team in 1993 and '94.

GUSTAVO BORGES
Swimming, Michigan

Eleven-time NCAA champion Gustavo Borges paved the way to Michigan's record-tying 11th national collegiate championship in 1995 with his three individual championships in the 50, 100 and 200 freestyle. Coach Jon Urbanchek's team thus won the team title for the first time since 1961, a year after Urbanchek last competed for Gus Stager. Borges, a native of Brazil, captured eight NCAA titles, and swam on three winning relays, during his four-year career at U-M. Silver medalist in the 1992 Barcelona Olympics, Borges was nominated twice for the Amateur Athletic Foundation World Trophy Award, emblematic of the world's top amateur athlete. A 24-time All-American and 20-time Conference champ, Borges was the 1994 Michigan athlete of the year and the 1992 Big Ten freshman swimmer of the year.

LEADING THE WAY

JOE PATERNO
Penn State

The fourth-winningest coach of all time ... the winningest bowl game coach of all time ... the only coach to win all four of the traditional New Year's Day bowl games ... winner of nearly 80 percent of his games. The accomplishments of Penn State's Joe Paterno are of enormous quality and quantity. He ranks as one of the true legends of the game, and not just for the success of his teams. His reputation as an educator and gentleman is impeccable as well, and his teams boast a 92 percent graduation rate. "We have the same obligations as all teachers at our institutions, except we probably have more influence over our young people than anyone other than their families," he once said. Paterno, born on Dec. 21, 1926 in Brooklyn, arrived at Penn State as an assistant coach in 1950 and took over as head coach in 1966. His 277 victories trail only Paul "Bear" Bryant (323), Glenn "Pop" Warner (319), and Amos Alonzo Stagg (314). Paterno's fundamental, team-oriented approach is best symbolized by his team's uniforms: plain white helmets, high-top black shoes, plain jerseys with no individual names on the back. "I think they say something to kids about team-oriented play and an austere approach to life," he says.

· BIG TEN PIONEERS ·

First women's soccer championship

The Wisconsin women's soccer team entered the inaugural Big Ten Championship a heavy favorite to win the title. The powerful Badgers proved the projections to be accurate, as they blanked the Minnesota Gophers, 3-0, to capture the first league crown in Madison on Nov. 7, 1994. Wisconsin advanced to its sixth straight NCAA tournament, where it was beaten, 3-1, by Washington State in the first round. Coach Dean Duerst's Badgers ended the season with a Conference-best 16-6 overall record and a 5-2 Big Ten slate. The Badgers landed four players on the first team All-Big Ten team. Those players were goalkeeper Ursula McKnight, defender Jill Stewart, and midfielders Jackie Billet and Marci Miller. Defender Heather Maier and midfielder Cheri Skibski made the second team.

1994-95 Wisconsin Women's Soccer Team

Academic Achievements

When the U.S. submitted a bid to host the 1994 World Cup soccer tournament, it knew that some of the country's best venues were indoor facilities. But each game must be played on grass, not artificial turf. That's when researchers at Michigan State came up with a turf grass that can survive indoors. It was used for the games at the nearby Pontiac Silverdome.

1994-95 Conference MEDAL OF HONOR Winners

ILLINOIS	Carmel Corbett, Steve Marianetti
INDIANA	Michelle Venturella, Erik Barrett
IOWA	Laura Dvorak, Bryan Crowley
MICHIGAN	Beth Wymer, Todd Collins
MICHIGAN STATE	Laura Bell, Emilio Collins
MINNESOTA	Kara Martin, Brian Yee
NORTHWESTERN	Gretchen Scheumann, Ron Rojas
OHIO STATE	Katie Hedman, Joey Galloway
PENN STATE	Jill Pearsall, John Amaechi
PURDUE	Cindy Lamping, Katy Koonz, Jon Pergande
WISCONSIN	Dana Tzakis, Jeff Gold

1995-96

The Gala Dinner

THE BIG EVENT

Big Ten celebrates its centennial anniversary

They returned to the scene of the birth, so to speak, to celebrate the 100th birthday of the Big Ten Conference. The league's Centennial Gala Dinner was held Aug. 1, 1995 at The Palmer House Hilton in Chicago—the very place seven presidents from Midwest universities met on Jan. 11, 1895 to decide to form the allegiance that would become the Big Ten. Each Conference school celebrated the 100-year anniversary in its own way, with some kind of recognition during an athletic contest on campus. The Gala Dinner, open to the public and attended by a crowd of about 700, kicked off a season-long celebration. Mayor Richard M. Daley declared July 30-Aug. 5, 1995 to be Big Ten Centennial Week in Chicago.

OTHER MEMORABLE EVENTS

- **Five Conference teams won NCAA championships: Iowa (wrestling), Michigan (ice hockey), Ohio State (men's gymnastics), Penn State (fencing) and Wisconsin (men's soccer).**

- **Ohio State's Eddie George won the Heisman Trophy.**

- **Wisconsin broke Indiana's streak of nine consecutive Conference women's tennis titles; Minnesota broke Michigan's streak of 10 straight men's swimming championships; and Michigan snapped Minnesota's string of four consecutive men's tennis crowns.**

- **Indiana's Erika Wicoff won an unprecedented third straight Conference women's golf championship.**

- **Penn State won its first Big Ten baseball title, but Indiana won the post-season tourney and made its first appearance in the NCAA tournament.**

- **Wisconsin's Kathy Butler won the NCAA women's cross country title.**

Northwestern's football season comes up roses

1995 Northwestern Wildcats

When Gary Barnett was introduced to Northwestern fans in the winter of 1992, at half-time of a men's basketball game, he announced he would "take the Purple to Pasadena." Even the most diehard followers probably greeted that promise with skepticism, but in 1995 Barnett made good on his promise. He coached the Wildcats to a Big Ten championship and a berth in the Rose Bowl in Pasadena, Calif., producing one of the most stunning success stories in league history. Northwestern's football teams had not had a winning season since 1971, and had managed four victories in a season just twice since then, so the entire nation took notice when the Wildcats swept through the 1995 season with a 10-1 record. After opening the season with a 17-15 victory at Notre Dame, they suffered their only loss of the season to Miami of Ohio. With Northwestern leading 28-7 late in the third quarter, Miami ran off the final 23 points for the victory. Undeterred, Barnett's team rolled through the rest of the season without a loss, highlighted by wins at Michigan and against Penn State in Evanston. Northwestern lost to Southern Cal in the Rose Bowl, but that did little to douse the fire of an unforgettable season.

OTHER BIG TEN CHAMPIONS

Men
- BASEBALL: Penn State, coached by Joe Hindelang
- BASKETBALL: Purdue, coached by Gene Keady
- CROSS COUNTRY: Wisconsin, coached by Martin Smith
- GOLF: Ohio State, coached by Jim Brown
- GYMNASTICS: Ohio State, coached by Peter Kormann
- INDOOR TRACK: Wisconsin, coached by Ed Nuttycombe
- OUTDOOR TRACK: Wisconsin, coached by Ed Nuttycombe
- SOCCER: Indiana, coached by Jerry Yeagley, and Wisconsin, coached by Jim Launder
- SWIMMING/DIVING: Minnesota, coached by Dennis Dale
- TENNIS: Michigan, coached by Brian Eisner
- WRESTLING: Iowa, coached by Dan Gable

Women
- BASKETBALL: Iowa, coached by Angie Lee
- CROSS COUNTRY: Wisconsin, coached by Peter Tegen
- FIELD HOCKEY: Iowa, coached by Beth Beglin
- GOLF: Indiana, coached by Sam Carmichael
- GYMNASTICS: Michigan, coached by Beverly Plocki
- INDOOR TRACK: Illinois, coached by Gary Winckler
- OUTDOOR TRACK: Wisconsin, coached by Peter Tegen
- SOCCER: Minnesota, coached by Sue Montagne
- SOFTBALL: Michigan, coached by Carol Hutchins
- SWIMMING/DIVING: Michigan, coached by Jim Richardson
- TENNIS: Wisconsin, coached by Patti Henderson
- VOLLEYBALL: Michigan State, coached by Chuck Erbe

EDDIE GEORGE
Football, Ohio State

When he was 8-years-old, Eddie George told his mother, Donna, he would someday win the Heisman Trophy. Years later, he figured he would finish second or third in balloting, but the Ohio State tailback scored a decisive victory in voting to become the school's sixth winner all-time and the first since the 1975 season. His early promise and a work ethic derived from one year at a military school gave George the edge he needed at Ohio State, where he rushed for a school record 1,927 yards and scored 25 touchdowns during his final season, leading the nation in scoring and finishing fifth with 152.1 yards a game. George reeled off 12 straight games of 100 yards or more, capped by a school-record 314 yards against Illinois, earning the Big Ten's Silver Football and the Doak Walker Award for the top running back. He was named the Big Ten Jesse Owens Athlete of the Year for 1995-96.

KATIE SMITH
Basketball, Ohio State

It's not hard to see why Katie Smith was a starter in a school-record 124 games during her basketball career at Ohio State. The Big Ten player of the year during her senior season in 1995-96, she finished her Buckeye career as the school's all-time leading scorer — men or women — with 2,578 points, the Big Ten's record for women which also ranks her second all-time for either men or women. In fact, she shattered the old mark for Big Ten women by 173 points and the school's mark by 493. Her total ranks her 16th all-time among the NCAA's Division I players. A unanimous all-Big Ten selection as a senior, she was named to five All-America teams. She was also the GTE Academic All-American of the Year. A veteran of internatonal competition, she served as an alternate on the 1996 U.S. Olympic Team.

SCOTT LAMPHEAR
Soccer, Wisconsin

The Badgers' choice of Scott Lamphear as the school's male athlete of the year was an easy one. Not only was the senior sweeper from Livonia, Mich. a first-team All-American on the soccer field, he was also named to the GTE Academic All-America first squad and to the Academic all-Big Ten team for the third year in a row. Lamphear started every Badger game for four consecutive seasons, setting school records for games played and starts. He anchored a defense which finished the season on a seven-game shutout streak, denying five ranked opponents during the NCAA tournament, including a 2-0 victory in the title game against Duke. Wisconsin set an NCAA record by posting 17 shutouts in 25 games. Following the season, Lamphear was drafted by the MetroStars in the second round of the Major League Soccer draft.

OLGA KALINOVSKAYA
Fencing, Penn State

One of the Big Ten's greatest athletes of 1995-96 made the long trek to State College, Pa. all the way from St. Petersburg, Russia. Senior fencer Olga Kalinovskaya got the most out of her mileage, becoming the first woman ever to win four individual NCAA fencing championships and only the second collegiate competitor to accomplish that feat. In addition, the Penn State fencing team won the national title in 1995 and '96. Like many other Big Ten athletes before her, Kalinovskaya not only excelled in the athletic arenas, but also in the classroom. Her cumulative grade-point average of 3.89 in Electrical Engineering and her two-time selection as a first-team Academic All-American outshone even her magnificent career dual meet record of 181-5. She was chosen the Big Ten Suzy Favor Athlete of the Year in 1995-96, even though fencing is no longer competed in the Conference.

Jim Richardson

JIM RICHARDSON, JON URBANCHEK, DICK KIMBALL
Michigan

John Urbanchek

Michigan swimming teams have set a standard of excellence since the days of Matt Mann, so it's no surprise that the current swimming and diving coaches have continued that winning tradition. Since taking over as men's coach in 1983, Jon Urbanchek has guided Michigan to 10 Conference titles and four straight top three NCAA finishes, including the 1995 national crown, Michigan's 11th. Urbanchek through 1996 has posted a phenomenal 115-13 dual meet record while producing 94 individual or relay Big Ten champs and 24 NCAA titlists. Since taking fifth in the 1985 Big Ten meet in Jim Richardson's first year as women's coach, the Wolverines haven't looked up at anybody, taking 10 straight Conference championships. Richardson has his teams peak at the right time, as evidenced by the Big Ten titles and five straight top eight NCAA finishes. He has produced seven NCAA winners and 31 All-Americans. Their partner on the deck, men's and women's diving coach Dick Kimball, has been synonomous with Michigan diving for 37 years, producing three Big Ten women's divers of the year and seven Conference diving titlists. Four Olympic gold medalists have learned under him and Kimball himself has served as U.S. diving coach for the 1964, 1980, 1984, 1988 and 1992 Olympic diving teams.

Dick Kimball

· BIG TEN PIONEERS ·

Tara VanDerveer
Olympic coach

Tara VanDerveer was ahead of her time as a basketball player at Indiana between 1973-75, as the sport had not yet been granted varsity status. She stood out enough to be invited to the tryouts for the 1972 World Games and the 1974 Olympics, however, and then embarked on a successful coaching career. VanDerveer was named the Big Ten coach of the year for the 1984-85 season while at Ohio State, and then moved on to Stanford, where she has been named national coach of the year three times and won NCAA titles in 1990 and '92. Her success culminated in her selection as the 1996 U.S. Olympic women's team coach.

Academic Achievements

P enn State ranks second nationally in industry-sponsored research; third in Department of Defense research; and ninth in total research expenditures in science and engineering.

1995-96 *Conference MEDAL OF HONOR Winners*

ILLINOIS	Dawn Riley, Marko Koers
INDIANA	Gina Ugo, John Hammerstein
IOWA	Kim Baker, Jay Thornton
MICHIGAN	Monika Black, Jay Riemersma
MICHIGAN STATE	Patti Raduenz, Brian Picklo
MINNESOTA	Lori Townsend, Bernie Zeruhn
NORTHWESTERN	Betsy Vance, Rohan Gardner
OHIO STATE	Katie Smith, Andy Gerken & Adam Spitznagel
PENN STATE	Olga Kalinovskaya, Jeff Hartings
PURDUE	Corissa Yasen, Chris Kessick
WISCONSIN	Lauren Gavaris, Scott Lamphear

The BIG TEN's First 100 Years
Big Ten Women's Basketball
Per Game Average Season Records

(Conference games only)

Points	29.4	Anucha Browne, Northwestern, 1985
Rebounds	12.9	Denise Jackson, Indiana, 1983
Assists	8.6	Nancy Kennelly, Northwestern, 1993 Tina Nicholson, Penn State, 1996
Steals	4.8	Keisha Anderson, Wisconsin, 1996
Blocked Shots	5.3	Trish Andrew, Michigan, 1992

426

UNIVERSITY PROFILES

UNIVERSITY OF ILLINOIS
FOUNDED 1867

First Graduating Class: 1872, 20 Students
Location: Chicago and Urbana/Champaign, Illinois
Status: Land-Grant Institution
Sports Teams Nickname: Fighting Illini
Enrollment (1994): 36,191
Graduating Class (1994): 9,602
Total Number of Degrees Awarded (through 1994): 430,000
Full-time Faculty (1994): 2,047
International Students (Autumn 1994): 2,732
Number of Countries Represented in Student Body (1994): 93
Number of Library Volumes (1994): 8.5 million
Operating Budget (1994): $874.5 million
Research Funding (1994): $196 million
Endowment Market Value (1994): $75.2 million
John Simon Guggenheim Memorial Fellowships (1988-94): 11

National Endowment for the Humanities Fellowships (1988-92): 30
National Medal of Science Winners: 10
National Merit Scholars (Autumn 1994): 198
Nobel Prize Laureates (Faculty and Alumni):
John Bardeen, Physics, 1956, 1972
Edward Doisy, Physiology and Medicine, 1943
Vincent Du Vigneaud, Chemistry, 1955
Robert Holley, Physiology and Medicine, 1968
Edwin Krebs, Physics/Medicine, 1992
Polykarp Kusch, Physics, 1955
Robert Schrieffer, Physics, 1972
Phillip Sharp, Physics/Medicine, 1993
Hamilton Smith, Physics/Medicine, 1978
Wendell Stanley, Chemistry, 1946
Rosalyn Sussman Yallow, Medicine, 1977
National Science Foundation Young Investigators (1988-92): 32
Rhodes Scholars (cumulative): 1
Sloan Foundation Research Fellowships (1988-92): 11

INDIANA UNIVERSITY
FOUNDED 1820

Founded: 1820
First Graduating Class: 1830, 3 Students
Location: Bloomington, Indiana
Status: State University
Sports Teams Nickname: Hoosiers
Enrollment (1995, Multiple Campuses): 91,393
Graduating Class (1993-94, Multiple Campuses): 13,970
Total Number of Degrees Awarded (as of 1994): 450,006
Full-time Faculty (1994): 3,985
International Students (1994): 3,773
Number of Countries Represented in Student Body (1994): 151
Number of Library Volumes (1994): 7.7 million

Operating Budget (1994-95): $1.8 billion
Research Funding (1993-94): $170.1 million
Endowment Market Value (end of 1994): $376 million
John Simon Guggenheim Memorial Fellowships (1987-95): 18
National Endowment for the Humanities Fellowships (1987-95): 70
Nobel Prize Laureates (Faculty and Alumni):
Hermann J. Muller, Physiology and Medicine, 1946
James D. Watson, Physiology and Medicine, 1962
National Science Foundation Young Investigators (1987-95): 5
Rhodes Scholars (cumulative): 6
Sloan Foundation Research Fellowships (1987-94): 19

UNIVERSITY PROFILES

UNIVERSITY OF IOWA
FOUNDED 1847

First Graduating Class: 1858, 1 Student
Location: Iowa City, Iowa
Status: State University
Sports Teams Nickname: Hawkeyes
Enrollment (Autumn 1994): 26,932
Graduating Class (1994-95, Multiple Campuses): 5,526
Total Number of Degrees Awarded (as of 1995): 243,608
Full-time Faculty (1994-95): 1,803
International Students (1994-95): 1,739
Number of Countries Represented in Student Body (1994-95): 99
Number of Library Volumes (1994-95): 3.3 million

Operating Budget (1994-95): $1.12 billion
Research Funding (1994): $187.7 million
Endowment Market Value (1992-93):
University of Iowa—$25 million
UI Foundation—$200 million
John Simon Guggenheim Memorial Fellowships (1987-95): 31
National Endowment for the Humanities Fellowships (1987-95): 17
National Medal of Science Winners: 1
National Merit Scholars (Autumn 1992): 25
National Science Foundation Young Investigators (1987-95): 7
Rhodes Scholars (cumulative): 18

UNIVERSITY OF MICHIGAN
FOUNDED 1817

First Graduating Class: 1845, 11 students
Location: Ann Arbor, Michigan
Status: State University
Sports Teams Nickname: Wolverines
Enrollment (Autumn 1994): 36,543
Graduating Class (1993-94, Multiple Campuses): 9,753
Total Number of Degrees Awarded to Date (as of spring 1994): 520,594
Full-time Faculty (Autumn 1994): 2,717
International Students (Autumn 1994): 2,750
Number of Countries Represented in Student Body (1994): 107
Number of Library Volumes (1994): 6.7 million
Operating Budget (1994-95): $2.28 billion
Research Funding (1994-95): $386 million
Endowment Market Value (June 1994): $1.03 billion

John Simon Guggenheim Memorial Fellowships (1981-95): 52
National Endowment for the Humanities Fellowships (1996): 5
National Medal of Science Winners (1994): 5
National Merit Scholars (Autumn 1994): 48
Nobel Prize Laureates (Faculty and Alumni):
Stanley Cohen 1986, Medicine (alumnus)
Jerome Karle, 1985, Chemistry (alumnus)
Lawrence R. Klein, 1980, Economics (alumnus)
Marshall Nirenberg, 1968, Medicine (alumnus)
Samuel C.C. Ting, 1976, Physics (alumnus)
Thomas H. Weller, 1956, physiology and medicine (alumnus)
Rhodes Scholars (cumulative): 23
Sloan Foundation Research Fellowships (Autumn 1995): 53

UNIVERSITY PROFILES

MICHIGAN STATE UNIVERSITY
FOUNDED 1855

First Graduating Class: 1861, 7 Students
Location: East Lansing, Michigan
Status: Land-Grant Institution
Sports Teams Nickname: Spartans
Enrollment (Autumn 1994): 40,254
Graduating Class (1994): 8,260
Total Number of Degrees Awarded (as of 1995): 381,731
Full-time Faculty (Autumn 1994): 3,996
International Students (Autumn 1994): 2,444

Number of Countries Represented in Student Body (1994): 111
Number of Library Volumes (1994-95): 3.8 million
Operating Budget (1993-94): $866 million
Research Funding (1993-94): $143 million
Endowment Market Value (1993-94): $111 million
National Merit Scholars (Autumn 1994): 39
Nobel Prize Laureate (Alumni): Alfred D. Hershey, Physiology and Medicine, 1969
Rhodes Scholars (cumulative): 14

UNIVERSITY OF MINNESOTA
FOUNDED 1851

First Graduating Class: 1873, 2 Students
Location: Minneapolis-St. Paul, Minnesota
Status: Land-Grant Institution
Sports Teams Nickname: Golden Gophers
Enrollment (Autumn 1994, Multiple Campuses): 47,647
Graduating Class (1993-94, Multiple Campuses): 10,630
Total Number of Degrees Awarded (as of June 1994): 483,944
Full-time Faculty (November 1994): 5,579
International Students (1994): 3,118
Number of Countries Represented in Student Body (1994): 124
Number of Library Volumes (1993-94): 5.7 million
Operating Budget (1995-96): $1.7 billion

Research Funding (1993-94): $293 million
Endowment Market Value (June 1994): $359 million
National Merit Scholars (Autumn 1994): 52
Nobel Prize Laureates (Faculty and Alumni):
John Bardeen, Physics, 1956, 1972
Saul Bellow, Literature, 1976
Norman C. Borlaug, Peace, 1970
Walter H. Brattain, Physics, 1956
Melvin Calvin, Chemistry, 1961
Arthur Compton, Physics, 1927
Philip S. Hench, Medicine, 1950
Edward C. Kendall, Medicine, 1950
Ernest O. Lawrence, Physics, 1939
William N. Lipscomb, Chemistry, 1976
George Stigler, Economics, 1982
John H. Van Vleck, Physics, 1977

UNIVERSITY PROFILES

NORTHWESTERN UNIVERSITY
FOUNDED 1851

First Graduating Class: 1859, 5 students
Location: Evanston and Chicago, Illinois
Status: Private
Sports Teams Nickname: Wildcats
Enrollment (1994-95, Both Campuses): 17,688
Graduating Class (1995): 3,545
Full-time Faculty: 1,879
International Students: 1,501
Number of Library Volumes: 3.6 million
Operating Budget (1994—95): $685.1 million
Research Funding (1994): $168.9 million
Endowment Market Value (1995): $1.7 billion

John Simon Guggenheim Memorial Fellowships: NA
National Endowment for the Humanities Fellowships: NA
National Merit Scholars (1994-95): 368
Nobel Prize Laureates (Faculty and Alumni):
Saul Bellow, Liberal Arts, 1937
George J. Stigler, Graduate Management, 1932
National Science Foundation Young Investigators (1987-94): 36
Rhodes Scholars (cumulative): 5, 1984-94
Sloan Foundation Research Fellowships (cumulative): 75

OHIO STATE UNIVERSITY
FOUNDED 1870

First Graduating Class: 1878, 6 Students
Location: Columbus, Ohio
Status: Land-Grant Institution
Sports Teams Nickname: Buckeyes
Enrollment (1994, Multiple Campuses): 55,787
Graduating Class (1994-95, Multiple Campuses): 11,146
Total Number of Degrees Awarded (as of 1995): 450,592
Full-time Faculty (1994): 4,088
International Students (1994): 3,766
Number of Countries Represented in Student Body (1994): 124
Number of Library Volumes (1992-93): 4.7 million
Operating Budget (1993-94): $1.3 billion

Research Funding (1992-93): $188 million
Endowment Market Value (May 1993): $455.9 million
John Simon Guggenheim Memorial Fellowships: 1
National Endowment for the Humanities Fellowships: 5
National Merit Scholars (Autumn 1992): 100
Nobel Prize Laureates (Faculty and Alumni):
Paul J. Flory, Chemistry, 1974
William Alfred Fowler, Physics, 1983
Kevin G. Wilson, Physics, 1982
National Science Foundation Young Investigators (1995): 235
Sloan Foundation Research Fellowships (1995): 17

UNIVERSITY PROFILES

PENN STATE UNIVERSITY
FOUNDED 1855

First Graduating Class: 1861
Location: University Park, Pennsylvania
Status: Land-Grant Institution
Sports Teams Nickname: Nittany Lions
Enrollment (1995, Multiple Campuses): 68,826
Graduating Class (1995, Multiple Campuses): 12,897
Total Number of Degrees Awarded (as of 1995): 428,000
Full-time Faculty (1994-95): 4,296
International Students (1994-95, Multiple Campuses): 2,025
Number of Countries Represented in Student Body (1995): 112

Number of Library Volumes (1994-95): 3.6 million
Operating Budget (1995-96): $1.6 billion
Research Funding (1993-94): $268 million
Endowment Market Value (1995): $327 million
National Merit Scholars (1995-96): 80
Nobel Prize Laureate (Faculty and Alumni): Paul Berg, Chemistry, 1980
National Science Foundation Young Investigators (1994-95): 5
Sloan Foundation Research Fellowships (1994-95): 4

PURDUE UNIVERSITY
FOUNDED 1869

First Graduating Class: 1875, 1 student
Location: West Lafayette, Indiana
Status: Land-Grant Institution
Sports Teams Nickname: Boilermakers
Enrollment (1995, Multiple Campuses): 63,640
Graduating Class (1994-95, Multiple Campuses): 11,234
Total Number of Degrees Awarded (as of 1995): 368,315
Full-time Faculty (1994): 3,528
International Students (1995): 2,584
Number of Countries Represented in Student Body (1995): 112

Number of Library Volumes (1995-96): 2.3 million
Operating Budget (1995-96): $849 million
Research Funding (1994-95): $185 million
Endowment Market Value (1993-94): $493 million
John Simon Guggenheim Memorial Fellowships: 20
National Medal of Science Winners: 2
National Merit Scholars (1994): 22
Nobel Prize Laureates (Faculty and Alumni): Herbert C. Brown, Chemistry, 1979
Ben Mottelson, Physics, 1975
National Science Foundation Young Investigators (1987-95): 44
Sloan Foundation Research Fellowships (1987-94): 27

UNIVERSITY PROFILES

UNIVERSITY OF WISCONSIN
FOUNDED 1849

First Graduating Class: 1854, 2 Students
Location: Madison, Wisconsin
Status: Land-Grant Institution
Sports Teams Nickname: Badgers
Enrollment (1994-95): 40,305
Graduating Class (1994-95): 8,921
Total Number of Degrees Awarded (1994-95):
    258,190
Full-time Faculty (1994): 2,344
International Students (1994-95): 3,663
**Number of Countries Represented in Student
    Body (1994-95):** 122
Number of Library Volumes (1992-93): 5.4 million
Operating Budget (1993-94): $1.3 billion
Research Funding (1992-93): $372.4 million
Endowment Market Value (1992): $141.2 million
**John Simon Guggenheim Memorial Fellowships
    (1987-90):** 1
**National Endowment for the Humanities
    Fellowships (1987-90):** 53

National Medal of Science Winners: 10
National Merit Scholars (Autumn 1992): 21
Nobel Prize Laureates (Faculty and Alumni):
    John Bardeen, Physics, 1956, 1972
    Joseph Erlanger, Physiology and Medicine, 1944
    Herbert S. Gasser, Physiology and Medicine, 1944
    H. Gobind Khorana, Medicine and Physiology,
    1968
    Joshua Lederberg, Medicine and Physiology, 1958
    Stanford Moore, Chemistry, 1972
    Edwin Neher, Medicine and Physiology, 1991
    Theodore Schultz, Economics, 1979
    Edward L. Tatum, Physiology and Medicine, 1958
    Howard Temin, Medicine and Physiology, 1975
    Eugene P. Wigner, Physics, 1963
    John H. Van Vleck, Physics, 1977
**National Science Foundation Young
    Investigators (1993):** 7
Rhodes Scholars (cumulative): 26
**Sloan Foundation Research Fellowships
    (1988-90):** 6

UNIVERSITY OF ILLINOIS

| *James J. Stukel, President* | *Michael Aiken, Chancellor* | *David L. Chicoine, Faculty Representative* | *Mildred R. Griggs, Faculty Representative* | *Ron Guenther, Director of Athletics* | *Karol Kahrs, Associate Athletic Director* |

FACULTY REPRESENTATIVES

1896-1898	Henry H. Everett
1898-1899	Jacob K. Shell
1899-1906	Herbert J. Barton
1906-1929	George A. Goodenough
1929-1936	Alfred C. Callen
1936-1949	Frank E. Richart
1950-1959	Robert B. Browne
1959-1968	Leslie A. Bryan
1968-1976	Henry S. Stilwell
1976-1981	William A. Ferguson
1981-1989	John Nowak
1981-1987	Alyce T. Cheska
1988-	Mildred B. Griggs
1989-	David Chicoine

ATHLETIC DIRECTORS

1892-1894	Edward K. Hall
1894-1895	Fred H. Dodge
1895-1898	Henry H. Everett
1898-1901	Jacob K. Shell
1901-1936	George A. Huff
1936-1941	Wendell S. Wilson
1941-1966	Douglas R. Mills
1966-1967	Leslie Bryan (interim)
1967-1972	E.E. (Gene) Vance
1972	Charles E. Flynn (interim)
1972-1979	Cecil N. Coleman

1979	Ray Eliot (Interim)
1980-1988	Neale R. Stoner
1988	Ronald E. Guenther (interim)
1988	Karol A. Kahrs (interim)
1988-1991	John Mackovic
1991-1992	Robert Todd (interim)
1992-	Ronald E. Guenther

WOMEN'S ATHLETICS ADMINISTRATORS

| 1974- | Dr. Karol Kahrs |

SPORTS INFORMATION DIRECTORS

1922-1943	L.M. (Mike) Tobin
1943-1956	Charles E. Flynn
1956-1970	Charles M. Bellatti
1970-1974	Norman S. Sheya
1974-1989	Tab Bennett
1980-1985	Lani Jacobsen (women's)
1985-1987	Thomas Boeh (women's)
1987-1989	Mary Fowler (women's)
1989-1996	Mike Pearson
1996-	Dave Johnson

BASEBALL COACHES

| 1896-1919 | George A. Huff |
| 1920 | George Clark |

1921-1934	Carl Lundgren
1935-1951	Walter Roettger
1952-1978	Lee Eilbracht
1979-1987	Tom Dedin
1987-1990	Augie Garrido
1990-	Richard "Itch" Jones

BASKETBALL COACHES - MEN'S

1906	Elwood Brown
1907	F.L. Pinckney
1908	Fletcher Lane
1909-1910	H.V. Juul
1911-1912	T.E. Thompson
1913-1920	Ralph R. Jones
1921-1922	Frank J. Winters
1923-1936	J. Craig Ruby
1937-1947	Douglas R. Mills
1948-1967	Harry Combes
1967-1974	Harv Schmidt
1974-1975	Gene Bartow
1975-1996	Lou Henson
1996-	Lon Kruger

BASKETBALL COACHES - WOMEN'S

1974-1976	Steven Douglas
1976-1979	Carla Thompson
1979-1984	Jane Schroeder

1984-1990	Laura Golden
1990-1995	Kathy Lindsey
1995-	Theresa Grentz

CROSS COUNTRY COACHES - MEN'S
1938-1960	Leo T. Johnson
1961-	Edward Bernauer
1962-1963	Phillip Coleman
1965-1966	Robert C. Wright
1967-	Gary Wieneke

CROSS COUNTRY COACHES - WOMEN'S
1977-1981	Jessica Dragicevic
1981-1983	Mary Beth Spencer
1984-1985	Patty Bradley
1985-1991	Gary Winckler
1992-1994	Marybeth Spencer-Dyson
1994-	Gary Winckler

DIVING COACHES
| 1975-1993 | Fred Newport |

FOOTBALL COACHES
1890	Scott Williams
1891	Robert Lackey
1892-1893	Edward K. Hall
1894	Louis D. Vail
1895-1896	George A. Huff
1897-1898	Fred L. Smith
1899	Neilson Poe
1900	Fred L. Smith
1901-1902	Edgar G. Holt
1903	George Woodruff
1904	Arthur R. Hall, Justa M. Lindgren, Fred Lowenthal, Clyde Mathews
1905	Fred Lowenthal
1906	Justa Lindgren
1907-1912	Arthur R. Hall
1913-1941	Robert C. Zuppke
1942-1959	Ray Eliot
1960-1966	Pete Elliott
1967-1970	Jim Valek
1971-1976	Bob Blackman
1977-1979	Gary Moeller
1980-1987	Mike White
1988-1991	John Mackovic
1991-	Lou Tepper

GOLF COACHES - MEN'S
1922-1923	George Davis
1924	Ernest E. Bearg
1925-1928	D.L. Swank
1929-1932	J.H. Utley
1933	Robert Martin
1934	F.H. Renwick
1935-1938	J.H. Utley
1939-1943	W.W. Brown
1944-1966	Ralph Fletcher
1967-1971	Richard Youngberg

| 1972-1980 | Ladd Pash |
| 1981- | Ed Beard |

GOLF COACHES - WOMEN'S
| 1974-1978 | Betsy Kimpel |
| 1978- | Paula Smith |

GYMNASTICS COACHES - MEN'S
1898	Adolph Kreikenbaum
1902	Adolph Kreikenbaum
1905	Leo G. Hana
1910-1913	Leo G. Hana
1914-1917	R.N. Fargo
1921	A.J. Schuettner
1922	S.C. Staley
1924-1925	J.C. Wagner
1926-1929	R.C. Heidloff
1930-1942	H D. Price
1947-1948	H.D. Price
1949-1961	Charles Pond
1961-1962	Pat Bird (Acting)
1962-1973	Charles Pond
1973-1993	Yoshi Hayasaki
1994-1996	Don Osborn
1996-	Yoshi Hayasaki

GYMNASTICS COACHES - WOMEN'S
1974-1975	Kim Musgrave
1975-1977	Allison Milburn
1977-1993	Bev Mackes
1994-	Lynn Brueckman

SWIMMING COACHES - MEN'S
1906-1909	W.H. Hockmeister
1910-1911	George B. Norris
1912-1917	E.J. Manley
1920-1952	E.J. Manley
1953-1970	Allen B. Klingel
1971-1993	Don Sammons

SWIMMING COACHES - WOMEN'S
1974-1975	Jeanne Hultzen
1975-1980	Ann Pollack
1980-1993	Don Sammons
1993-	Jim Lutz

TENNIS COACHES - MEN'S
1908-1913	P.B. Hawk
1914	W.A. Oldfather
1920-1924	E.E. Bearg
1925	B.P. Hoover
1926-1929	A.R. Cohn
1930	E.A. Shoaff
1931-1934	C.W. Gelwick
1935	Gerald Huff
1936-1937	Caspar H. Nannes
1938-1942	Howard J. Braun
1943-1946	Ralph Johnson
1946-1964	Howard J. Braun
1965	Bob Lansford (Acting)

1966-1972	Dan Olson
1972-1973	William Wright
1973-1977	Bruce Shuman
1977	John Avallone, Jr. (Acting)
1978-1981	Jack Groppel
1981-1985	Brad Louderback
1986-1992	Neil Adams
1992-	Craig Tiley

TENNIS COACHES - WOMEN'S
1974-1975	Peggy Pruitt
1975-1978	Carla Thompson
1978-1981	Linda Pecore
1981-1987	Mary Tredennick
1987-	Jennifer Roberts

TRACK AND FIELD COACHES - MEN'S
1895	Harvey Cornish
1896-1898	H.H. Everett
1899-1900	Jacob K. Shell
1901-1903	H B. Conibear
1904-1929	Harry L. Gill
1930	C.D. Werner
1931-1933	Harry L. Gill
1934-1937	Don Cash Seaton
1938-1965	Leo T. Johnson
1965-1974	Robert C. Wright
1974-	Gary Wieneke

TRACK AND FIELD COACHES - WOMEN'S
1974-1975	Jerry Mahew
1975-1981	Jessica Dragicevic
1981-1984	Mike Shine
1984-1985	Patty Bradley
1985-	Gary Winckler

VOLLEYBALL COACHES
1974-1975	Kathleen Haywood
1975-1977	Terry Hite
1977-1980	Chris Accomero
1980-1983	John Blair
1983-1996	Mike Hebert
1996	Don Hardin

WRESTLING COACHES
1911	R.N. Fargo
1912-1913	Alexander Elston
1914	Theodore Paulsen
1915-1917	Walter Evans
1921-1928	Paul Prehn
1929-1943	H.E. Kenney
1944-1946	Glenn C. Law
1946-1947	H.E. Kenney
1948-1950	Glenn C. Law
1950-1968	B R. Patterson
1968-1973	Jack Robinson
1973-1978	Tom Porter
1978-1983	Greg Johnson
1983-1992	Ron Clinton
1992-	Mark Johnson

INDIANA UNIVERSITY

Myles Brand,
President

William Perkins,
Faculty
Representative

Clarence Doninger,
Director of Athletics

Mary Ann Rohleder,
Associate Athletic
Director

FACULTY REPRESENTATIVES

1900-1906	M.W. Smapson
1906-1907	U.G. Weatherly
1907-1908	E.O. Holland
1908-1912	H.W. Johnston
1912-1919	Charles W. Sembower
1919-1941	William J. Moenkhaus
1941-1942	Bernard C. Gavit
1942-1943	Lee Norvelle
1943-1951	William R. Breneman
1951-1962	John F. Mee
1962-1973	Edwin H. Cady
1973-1978	Daniel W. Miller
1978-1985	Jack Wentworth
1985-1993	Haydn Murray
1986-1993	Marianne Mitchell
1994-	William Perkins

ATHLETIC DIRECTORS

1894-1896	Edgar Syrett
1897-1898	Madison G. Gonterman
1899-1905	James H. Horne
1906	Zora G. Clevenger
1907-1910	James M. Sheldon
1911-1913	Dr. C.P. Hutchins
1914-1915	Clarence C. Childs
1916-1922	E.O. Stiehm
1923-1946	Zora G. Clevenger
1946-1947	A.N. McMillin
1948-1954	Paul J. Harrell
1954-1955	W.W. Patty (Acting)
1955-1961	Frank E. Allen
1961-1975	J.W. (Bill) Orwig
1975-1978	Paul Dietzel
1978-1990	Ralph Floyd
1990-1991	Ed Williams (Interim)
1991-	Clarence Doninger

WOMEN'S ATHLETICS ADMINISTRATORS

1973-1979	Leanne Grotke
1979-1980	Ann Lawver (Interim)
1980-1994	Isabella Hutchison
1995-	Mary Ann Rohleder

SPORTS INFORMATION DIRECTORS

1935-1939	George Gardner
1939-1944	Bob Cook
1944-1946	Jack Overmyer (Acting)
1946-1953	Bob Cook
1953-1983	Tom Miller
1983-	Kit Klingelhoffer

BASEBALL COACHES

1899-1900	James H. Horne
1901	Robert K. Wicker
1902	George W. Moore
1903-1904	Philip O'Neil
1905-1906	Zora.G. Clevenger
1907	Jake Stahl
1908	Robert K. Wicker
1909-1911	Ralph C. Roach
1912	John Corbett
1913-1915	Arthur H. Berndt
1916	Frederick L. Beebe
1917	Roy M. Whisman
1918	Guy L. Rathbun
1919-1920	Harry Scholler
1921-1922	George W. Levis
1923-1924	Roscoe Minton
1925-1938	Everett S. Dean
1938-1947	Paul J. Harrell
1948	Donald Danielson

1949-1973	Ernest Andres
1973-1980	Bob Lawrence
1981-1983	Larry Smith
1984-	Bob Morgan

BASKETBALL COACHES - MEN'S

1901	James H. Horne
1902	Phelps Darby
1903-1904	Willis N. Coval
1905	Zora G. Clevenger
1906-1907	James M. Sheldon
1908	Edward Cook
1909	Robert Harris
1910	John Georgen
1911	Oscar Rackle
1912	James Kase
1913	Arthur I. Powell
1914-1915	Arthur H. Berndt
1916	Allan Williford
1917	Guy S. Lowman
1918-1919	Dana M. Evans
1920-1921	Ewald O. Stiehm
1922-1923	George L. Levis
1924	Leslie Mann
1925-1938	Everett S. Dean
1938-1942	Branch McCracken
1943-1945	Harry C. Good
1946-1965	Branch McCracken
1965-1971	Lou Watson
1971-	Bob Knight

BASKETBALL COACHES - WOMEN'S

1975-1976	Bea Gorton
1976-1980	Joy Malchodi
1981-1985	Maryalyce Jeremiah

| 1985-1988 | Jorja Hoehn |
| 1988- | Jim Izard |

CROSS COUNTRY COACHES - MEN'S

1912-1914	C.V. Hutchins
1915-1916	W.A. Cogshall
1917	Harvey Cohn
1918-1919	Dana Evans
1920-1921	W.A. Cogshall
1922	Lester Null
1923-1924	Jesse Ferguson
1925-1943	Earle C. "Billy" Hayes
1943-1944	J.C. Watson
1945-1961	Gordon Fisher
1962-1968	Jim Lavery
1969-	Sam Bell

CROSS COUNTRY COACHES - WOMEN'S

1978-1980	Mark Witten
1980-1989	Carol Stevenson
1989-	Sam Bell

DIVING COACHES

| 1959-1989 | Hobie Billingsley |
| 1989- | Jeff Huber |

FOOTBALL COACHES

1887	A.B Woodford
1891	Billy Herod
1894	Ferbert and Huddleson
1895	Osgood and Wren
1896-1897	Madison G. Gonterman
1898-1904	James H. Horne
1905-1913	James M. Sheldon
1914-1915	Clarence C. Childs
1916-1921	Ewald O. Stiehm
1922	James P. Herron
1923-1925	William A. Ingram
1926-1930	Harlan O. (Pat) Page
1931-1933	Earle C. (Billy) Hayes
1934-1947	Alvin N. (Bo) McMillin
1948-1951	Clyde B. Smith
1952-1956	Bernie Crimmins
1957	Bob Hicks (Acting)
1958-1964	Phil Dickens
1965-1972	John Pont
1973-1982	Lee Corso
1983	Sam Wyche
1984-	Bill Mallory

GOLF COACHES - MEN'S

| 1929 | Harper Miller |
| 1930 | Gerald Redding |

1931	Joe Greenwood
1932	Phil Talbot
1933	No Coach
1934-1941	Hugh E. Willis
1942-1947	James Soutar
1948-1957	Owen L. Cochrane
1958-1989	Robert Fitch
1989-	Sam Carmichael

GOLF COACHES - WOMEN'S

1975-1979	Margaret Cummins
1979-1981	Bruce Cohen
1981-	Sam Carmichael

SOCCER COACHES - MEN'S

| 1973- | Jerry Yeagley |

SOCCER COACHES - WOMEN'S

| 1993- | Joe Kelley |

SOFTBALL COACHES

1975-1976	Louetta Bloecher
1976-1979	Ann Lawver
1979-1987	Gayle Blevins
1987-	Diane Stephenson

SWIMMING COACHES - MEN'S

1919-1920	Guy L. Rathbun
1921	Robert Shafer
1922	Lester Null
1923-1924	William S. Merriam
1925	Oscar Tharp
1926	William S. Merriam
1927-1930	Paul Thompson
1931	No Coach
1932-1944	Robert Royer
1944-1946	Robert Stumpner
1946-1957	Robert Royer
1958-1990	James Counsilman
1990-	Kris Kirchner

SWIMMING COACHES - WOMEN'S

1975-1979	Don Glass
1979-1981	Pat Barry
1981-1982	Terry Townsend (Interim)
1982-1986	Bob Bruce
1986-1991	Chet Jastremski
1991-1992	Jill Sterkel
1992-	Nancy Nitardy

TENNIS COACHES - MEN'S

1930	Harlan Logan
1931-1933	Ralph Esarey
1934-1940	Ralph Graham

1941-1943	Ralph Collins
1944	Emory Clark
1945-1946	Ralph Collins
1947	William Johnson
1948	Don Veller
1949-1957	Dale Lewis
1958-1972	William Landin
1972-1981	Scott Greer
1981-1985	Steve Greco
1986-	Ken Hydinger

TENNIS COACHES - WOMEN'S

| 1975-1976 | Dean Summers |
| 1976- | Lin Loring |

TRACK AND FIELD COACHES - MEN'S

1915-1916	Clarence C. Childs
1917	Harvey Cohn
1918-1919	Dana M. Evans
1920	Guy L. Rathbun
1921	John Millen
1922	Lester Null
1923-1924	Jesse Ferguson
1925-1943	Earle C. (Billy) Hayes
1944	Clifford Watson
1945-1962	Gordon R Fisher
1962-1969	James Lavery
1969-	Sam Bell

TRACK AND FIELD COACHES - WOMEN'S

1978-1980	Mark Witten
1980-1989	Carol Stevenson
1989-	Sam Bell

VOLLEYBALL COACHES

1975-1983	Ann Lawver
1983-1987	Doug West
1987-1992	Tom Shoji
1993-	Katie Weismiller

WRESTLING COACHES

1910-1914	Prof. Elmer E. Jones
1915-1916	Edgar Davis
1917-1921	James A. Kase
1922	Guy L. Rathbun
1923-1927	Jack Reynolds
1927-1945	W.H. Thorn
1945-1972	Charles McDaniel
1972-1984	Doug Blubaugh
1985-1989	Jim Humphrey
1989-1991	Joe McFarland
1992-	Duane Goldman

UNIVERSITY OF IOWA

Mary Sue Coleman,
President

Yvonne C. Slatton,
Faculty
Representative

Robert A. Bowlsby,
Director of
Men's Athletics

Christine H. B. Grant,
Director of
Women's Athletics

FACULTY REPRESENTATIVES
1900-1914 Arthur G. Smith
1914-1916 W.J. Teeters
1916-1917 B.J. Lambert
1917-1920 H.J. Prentiss
1920-1923 B.J. Lambert
1923-1929 Louis Pelzer
1929-1932 Clement C. Williams
1932-1938 Clarence M. Updegraff
1938-1947 Karl E. Leib
1947-1955 Paul J. Blommers
1955-1982 Robert Ray
1981- Yvonne Slatton
1982-1994 Sam Becker

MEN'S ATHLETIC DIRECTORS
1910-1917 Nelson Kellogg
1918-1923 Howard Jones
1924-1928 Paul Belting
1929-1934 Edward Lauer
1934-1936 Ossie Solem
1936-1947 Ernest G. Schroeder
1947-1960 Paul W. Brechler
1960-1970 Forest Evasheveski
1970-1991 Chalmers W. Elliott
1991- Robert A. Bowlsby

WOMEN'S ATHLETIC DIRECTORS
1973- Christine H.B. Grant

SPORTS INFORMATION DIRECTORS - MEN'S
1923-1968 Eric C. Wilson
1968-1993 George Wine
1993- Phil Haddy

SPORTS INFORMATION DIRECTORS - WOMEN'S
1977-1978 John Monahan
1977-1980 Liz Ullman
1980-1983 Lee-Ann Hughes
1983-1987 Rick Klatt
1987-1989 Tammy Frank
1989-1993 Beth Weber
1993-1995 Cathy Bongiovi
1995- Sherilyn Fiveash

BASEBALL COACHES
1900-1901 A.A. Knipe
1902-1903 S.C. Williams
1904-1905 J.G. Chalmers
1906 John G. Griffith
1907 L.J. Storey
1908 Maury Kent
1909 Charles Kirk
1910 Ted Green
1911-1912 Walter Stewart
1913-1918 Viva Lindeman
1914-1918 Maury Kent
1919 Howard Jones
1920-1922 James Ashmore
1923-1924 Sam Barry
1925-1942 Otto Vogel
1943-1945 J.E. Davis
1946-1962 Otto Vogel
1963-1970 Richard Schultz
1970- Duane Banks

BASKETBALL COACHES - MEN'S
1902 Ed Rule
1903 Fred Bailey
1904 Ed Rule
1905 John Chambers
1906 Ed Rule
1907 John G. Griffith
1908 Ed Rule
1909-1910 John G. Griffith
1911-1912 Walter Stewart
1913 Floyd Thomas
1914-1918 Maury Kent
1919 Ed Bannick
1920-1922 James Ashmore
1923-1929 Sam Barry
1930-1943 Rollie Williams
1944-1949 Lawrence Harrison
1950-1951 Rollie Williams
1952-1958 Frank O'Connor
1959-1964 Milton Scheuerman
1965-1970 Ralph Miller
1970-1974 Richard Schultz
1974-1983 Lute Olson
1983-1986 George Raveling
1986- Tom Davis

BASKETBALL COACHES - WOMEN'S
1974-1979 Lark Birdsong
1979-1983 Judy McMullen
1983-1995 C. Vivian Stringer
1995- Angie Lee

CROSS COUNTRY COACHES - MEN'S
1898 Dad Moulton
1899-1902 A.A. Knipe
1903-1904 no coach
1905 Jerry Delaney
1906-1908 Mark Catlin
1909-1910 Jerry Delaney
1911-1913 Nelson Kellogg

1914-1920	Jack Watson
1921-1948	George Bresnahan
1949-1978	Francis Cretzmeyer
1978-1987	Ted Wheeler
1988-	Larry Wieczorek

CROSS COUNTRY COACHES - WOMEN'S

1974-1976	Shirley Finnegan
1976-1996	Jerry Hassard
1996-	TBA

DIVING COACH

1977-	Bob Rydze

FIELD HOCKEY COACHES

1974-1975	Christine Grant
1975-1978	Majorie Greenberg
1978-1987	Judith Davidson
1988-	Beth Beglin

FOOTBALL COACHES

1892	E.A. Dalton
1893	Benjamin Donnelly
1894	Roger Sherman
1896	A E. Bull
1897	Otto F. Wagonhurst
1898-1902	Alden A. Knipe
1903-1905	John G. Chalmers
1906-1908	Mark Callin
1909	J.G. Griffith
1910-1915	Jesse Hawley
1916-1923	Howard Jones
1924-1931	Burt Ingwersen
1932-1936	Ossie Solem
1937-1938	Irl Tubbs
1939-1942	Eddie Anderson
1943-1944	Slip Madigan
1945	Clem Crowe
1946-1949	Eddie Anderson
1950-1951	Leonard Raffensperger
1952-1960	Forest Evashevski
1961-1965	Jerry Burns
1966-1970	Ray Nagel
1971-1973	Frank X. Lauterbur
1974-1978	Bob Commings
1979-	Hayden Fry

GOLF COACHES - MEN'S

1924-1948	Charles Kennett
1949-1956	Frank O'Connor

1957	Glenn Devine
1958-1990	Charles Zwiener
1990-1993	Lynn Blevins
1994-	Terry Anderson

GOLF COACHES - WOMEN'S

1974-1975	Mary Foster
1975-	Diane Thomason

GYMNASTICS COACHES - MEN'S

1923	Harold Briceland
1924-1942	Albert Baumgartner
1943-1947	No Team
1948-1966	N.R. Holzaepfel
1967-1968	Sam Bailie
1968-1969	Michael Jacobson
1970-1980	Dick Holzaepfel
1980-	Tom Dunn

GYMNASTICS COACHES - WOMEN'S

1974-1975	Darlene Schmidt
1975-1979	Tera Haronoja
1980-	Diane DeMarco

ROWING COACHES - WOMEN'S

1994-	Mandi Kowal

SOFTBALL COACHES

1974-1980	Jane Hagedorn
1980-1987	Ginny Parrish
1988-	Gayle Blevins

SWIMMING COACHES - MEN'S

1917-1958	David Armbruster
1959-1975	Robert Allen
1976-	Glenn Patton

SWIMMING COACHES - WOMEN'S

1974-1981	Deborah Woodside
1981-1995	Peter Kennedy
1995-1996	Trish Myers
1996-	Mary Bolich

TENNIS COACHES - MEN'S

1923-1937	E.G. Schroeder
1938-1947	Arthur Wendler

1948-1968	Donald Klotz
1969-1981	John Winnie
1982-	Steve Houghton

TENNIS COACHES - WOMEN'S

1974-1977	Joyce Moore
1977-1984	Cathy Ballard
1984-1987	Charles Darley
1988-1995	Micki Schillig
1995-	Jennifer Mainz

TRACK AND FIELD COACHES - MEN'S

1898	Dad Moulton
1899-1902	A.A. Knipe
1903-1904	No Coach
1905	Jerry Delaney
1906-1908	Mark Catlin
1909-1910	Jerry Delaney
1911-1913	Nelson Kellogg
1914-1920	Jack Watson
1921-1948	George Bresnahan
1949-1978	Francis Cretzmeyer
1978-1996	Ted Wheeler
1996-	TBA

TRACK AND FIELD COACHES - WOMEN'S

1974-1976	Shirley Finnegan
1976-1996	Jerry Hassard
1996-	TBA

VOLLEYBALL COACHES

1974-1975	Peggy Heuser
1975-1977	Shirley Finnegan
1977-1980	Georgeanne Greene
1980-1982	Mary Phyl Dwight
1982-1989	Sandy Stewart
1989-1991	Ruth Nelson
1991-	Linda Schoenstedt

WRESTLING COACHES

1911-1915	E.G. Schroeder
1916-1920	Pat Wright
1921	E.G Schroeder
1922-1952	Harold Howard
1953-1972	David McCuskey
1972-1976	Gary Kurdelmeier
1976-	Dan Gable

UNIVERSITY OF MICHIGAN

Homer Neal,
President

Percy Bates,
Faculty
Representative

Joe Roberson,
Director
of Athletics

Peggy Bradley-Doppes,
Senior Associate
Athletic Director

FACULTY REPRESENTATIVES
1896	Dr. Joseph Nancrede
1896-1897	J.C. Knowlton
1898-1905	A.H. Pattengill
1906-1907	V.H. Lane
1907	H.M. Bates
1908	G W. Patterson
1917-1955	Ralph W. Aigler
1955-1979	Marcus Plant
1979-1982	Tom Anton
1981-1990	Gwen Cruzat
1983-1989	Paul W. Gikas
1989-1991	Douglas Kahn
1990-	Percy Bates

ATHLETIC DIRECTORS
1898-1908	Charles Baird
1908-1921	Philip Bartelme
1921-1940	Fielding H. Yost
1941-1968	H.O. Crisler
1968-1988	Donald B. Canham
1988-1990	Glenn E. Schembechler
1990-1994	Jack Weidenbach
1994-	Joe Roberson

WOMEN'S ATHLETICS ADMINISTRATORS
1973-1976	Marie Hartwig
1976-1977	Virginia Hunt
1977-1991	Phyllis Ocker
1991-	Peggy Bradley-Doppes

SPORTS INFORMATION DIRECTORS
1925-1938	Phil Pack
1938-1939	William R. Reed
1940-1944	Fred DeLano
1944-1968	Les Etter
1968-1980	Will Perry
1980-1982	John Humenik
1982-	Bruce Madej

BASEBALL COACHES
1891-1892	Peter Conway
1893	H G. Cleveland
1894	George Cadwell
1895	E.C. Weeks
1896	Frank Sexton
1897-1901	C.F. Watkins
1902	Frank Sexton
1903 S.	Roach
1904	Jerome Utley
1905-1906	L.W. McAllister
1907	R.L. Lowe
1908-1909	L.W. McAllister
1910-1913	Branch Rickey
1914-1920	Carl Lundgren
1921-1958	Ray Fisher
1959-1962	Don Lund
1963-1979	Milbry E. Benedict
1979-1989	Bud Middaugh
1989-1995	Bill Freehan
1995-	Geoff Zahn

BASKETBALL COACHES - MEN'S
1909	G.D. Corneal
1917-1918	Elmer Mitchell
1919-1928	E.J. Mather
1929-1930	George Veenker
1931-1937	Franklin Cappon
1938-1946	Bennie Oosterbaan
1946-1948	Osborne Cowles
1948-1952	Ernest B. McCoy
1953-1960	William Perigo
1960-1968	David Strack
1968-1980	John Orr
1980-1989	Bill Frieder
1989-	Steve Fisher

BASKETBALL COACHES - WOMEN'S
1973-1974	Vic Katch
1974-1977	Carmel Borders
1977-1984	Gloria Soluk
1984-1992	Bud Van De Wege, Jr.
1992- 1996	Trish Roberts
1996-	Sue Guevara

CREW COACHES- WOMEN'S
1996-	Mark Rothstein

CROSS COUNTRY COACHES - MEN'S
1911-1912	A.C. Kraenzlein
1913-1929	Stephen Farrell
1930-1939	Charles Hoyt
1940-1948	Kenneth Doherty
1948-1968	Donald Canham
1968-1971	David Martin
1971-1973	Dixon Farmer
1974-	Ron Warhurst

CROSS COUNTRY COACHES - WOMEN'S
1979-1981	Ken "Red" Simmons
1981-1983	Francie Goodridge
1984-1986	Sue Parks
1987-1991	Sue Foster
1992-	Mike McGuire

DIVING COACH
1973- Dick Kimball

FIELD HOCKEY COACHES
1973 Phyllis Weikart
1974-1978 Phyllis Ocker
1979-1983 Candy Zientek
1984-1988 Karen Collins
1988- Patti Smith

FOOTBALL COACHES
1891 Frank Crawford
1892-1893 F.E. Barbour
1894-1896 William McCauley
1897-1899 G.H. Ferbert
1900 Biff Lea
1901-1923 Fielding Yost
1924 George Little
1925-1926 Fielding Yost
1927-1928 E.E. (Tad) Wieman
1929-1937 Harry Kipke
1938-1947 H.O. Crisler
1948-1958 Bennie Oosterbaan
1959-1968 Chalmers W. Elliott
1969-1989 Glenn E. Schembechler
1989-1995 Gary Moeller
1995- Lloyd Carr

GOLF COACHES - MEN'S
1921-1935 Thomas Trueblood
1936-1944 Ray Courtright
1945-1947 William Barclay
1947-1968 Bert Katzenmeyer
1968-1978 William Newcomb
1979-1982 Tom Simon
1983- Jim Carras

GOLF COACHES - WOMEN'S
1977-1982 Tom Simon
1982-1993 Sue LeClair
1993- Kathleen Teichert

GYMNASTICS COACHES - MEN'S
1930-1932 Wilbur West
1947-1983 Newton C. Loken

1983-1996 Bob Darden
1996- Kurt Golder

GYMNASTICS COACHES - WOMEN'S
1975 Newt Loken
1976-1978 Ann Cornell
1978-1979 Scott Ponto
1979-1984 Sheri Hyatt
1984-1989 Dana Kempthorn
1989- Bev Plocki

SOCCER COACHES- WOMEN'S
1995- Debra Belkin

SOFTBALL COACHES
1977-1980 Gloria Soluk
1980-1984 Bob DeCarolis
1984- Carol Hutchins

SWIMMING COACHES- MEN'S
1922 J. Jerome
1923-1924 W.S. Brown
1925 Gerald Barnes
1926-1954 Matt Mann
1954-1979 Augustus P. Stager, Jr.
1979-1981 Bill Farley
1982 Augustus P. Stager, Jr.
1982- Jon Urbanchek

SWIMMING COACHES- WOMEN'S
1973-1974 Johanna High
1974-1983 Stu Isaac
1983-1985 Peter Lindsay
1985- Jim Richardson

TENNIS COACHES - MEN'S
1913-1915 A.O. Lee
1918 Chris Mack
1921 Walter Westbrook
1922 Thomas Trueblood
1923 Paul Leidy
1924 Robert Angell
1925 Henry Hutchins

1929-1936 John Johnstone
1937-1947 LeRoy Weir
1948 W. Robert Dixon
1949-1969 William Murphy
1970- Brian Eisner

TENNIS COACHES - WOMEN'S
1973 Janet Hooper
1974-1945 Carmen Brummet
1976-1977 John Atwood
1978 Theo Shepard
1979-1984 Oliver Owens
1984- Elizabeth "Bitsy" Ritt

TRACK AND FIELD COACHES - MEN'S
1911-1912 Dr. A.C. Kraenzlein
1913-1929 Stephen J. Farrell
1930-1939 Charles B. Hoyt
1940-1948 J. Kenneth Doherty
1948-1968 Donald B. Canham
1968-1971 David M. Martin
1972-1974 Dixon Farmer
1974- Jack R. Harvey

TRACK AND FIELD COACHES - WOMEN'S
1977-1981 Ken "Red" Simmons
1981-1984 Francie Goodridge
1984- James Henry

VOLLEYBALL COACHES
1973-1983 Sandy Vong
1984-1985 Barb Canning
1986-1990 Joyce Davis
1990-1991 Peggy Bradley-Doppes
1991- Gregory Giovanazzi

WRESTLING COACHES
1922 Thorn
1923-1924 Richard Barker
1925-1970 Clifford Keen
1970-1974 Rick Bay
1974-1978 Bill Johannesen
1978- Dale Bahr

MICHIGAN STATE UNIVERSITY

Peter McPherson,
President

Michael Kasavana,
Faculty
Representative

Merritt J. Norvell,
Director of
Athletics

Kathy Lindahl,
Associate Athletic
Director

FACULTY REPRESENTATIVES
1949-1953	Lloyd C. Emmons
1953-1955	Edgar L. Harden
1955-1956	Leslie W. Scott
1956-1959	Harold B. Tukey
1959-1979	John A. Fuzak
1979-1988	Gwen Norrell
1988-	Michael Kasavana

ATHLETIC DIRECTORS
1899-1900	Charles O. Bemies
1901-1902	George E. Denham
1903-1910	Chester L. Brewer
1911-1915	John F. Macklin
1916	George E. Gauthier (Acting)
1917	Chester L. Brewer
1918	George E. Gauthier (Acting)
1919-1921	Chester L. Brewer
1922	Albert M. Barron
1923-1954	Ralph Young
1954-1971	Clarence L. (Biggie) Munn
1971-1975	J. Burt Smith
1976-1980	Joe Kearney
1980-1990	Doug Weaver
1990-1992	George Perles
1992-1995	Merrily Baker
1995-	Merritt Norvell

WOMEN'S ATHLETIC ADMINISTRATOR
1981-	Kathy Lindahl

SPORTS INFORMATION DIRECTORS
1917-1924	Jim Hasselman
1924-1930	Student Directors: incl.: Keith Himebaugh, Ted Smits, Dale Stafford, Will Muller
1930-1944	George Alderton
1944-1948	Nick Kerbawy
1948-1980	Fred Stabley
1980-1988	Nick Vista
1988-	Ken Hoffman

BASEBALL COACHES
1887-1888	Professor Carpenter
1896-1898	Robert T. Gale
1899	Ferguson
1900-1901	Charles O. Bemies
1902-1903	George E. Denham
1904-1910	Chester L. Brewer
1911-1915	John F. Macklin
1916-1917	John Morrissey
1918-1920	Chester L. Brewer
1921	George (Potsy) Clark
1922	John Morrissey
1923-1924	Fred M. Walker
1925-1963	John H. Kobs
1964-1982	Dan Litwhiler
1983-1995	Tom Smith
1995-	Ted Mahan

BASKETBALL COACHES - MEN'S
1900-1901	Charles O. Bemies
1902-1903	George E. Denham
1904-1910	Chester L. Brewer
1911-1916	John F. Macklin
1917-1920	George E. Gauthier
1921-1922	Lyman F. Frimodig
1923-1924	Fred M. Walker
1925-1926	John H. Kobs
1927-1949	Benjamin F. Van Alstyne
1950-1951	Alton S. Kircher
1951-1954	Peter F. Newell
1954-1964	Forrest Anderson
1965-1969	John Benington
1969-1976	Gus Ganakas
1976-1995	Jud Heathcote
1995-	Tom Izzo

BASKETBALL COACHES - WOMEN'S
1973-1975	Mikki Bailey
1976	Dominic Marino
1977-	Karen Langeland

CROSS COUNTRY COACHES - MEN'S
1922	Albert M. Barron
1923	Jack Heppinstall
1924	Ralph H. Young
1925-1930	Morton F. Mason
1931-1946	Lauren P. Brown
1947-1957	Karl A. Schlademan
1958-1967	Fran Dittrich
1968-1983	James Gibbard
1984-	Jim Stintzi

CROSS COUNTRY COACHES - WOMEN'S
1974	Nell Jackson
1975-1977	Mark Pittman
1978	Eric Zemper
1979-1981	John Goodridge
1982-1986	Karen Dennis
1987-1988	Jim Stinzi

1988-1990 Sue Parks
1990-   Karen Lutzke

DIVING COACH
1966-   John Narcy

FIELD HOCKEY COACHES
1972-1974 Mikki Bailey
1975-1976 Diane Ulibarri
1977-1979 Samnao Kajornson
1980-1981 Nancy Reed
1982-1989 Rich Kimball
1989-1992 Martha Ludwig
1993-   Michele Madison

FOOTBALL COACHES
1897-1898 Henry Keep
1899-1900 Charles O. Bemies
1901-1902 George Denham
1903-1910 Chester L. Brewer
1911-1915 John F. Macklin
1916   Frank Sommers
1917   Chester L. Brewer
1918   George E. Gauthier
1919   Chester L. Brewer
1920   George (Potsy) Clark
1921-1922 Albert M. Barron
1923-1927 Ralph H. Young
1928   Harry G. Kipke
1929-1932 James H. Crowley
1933-1946 Charles W. Bachman
1947-1953 Clarence L. (Biggie) Munn
1954-1972 Hugh Duffy Daugherty
1973-1976 Dennis E. Stolz
1976-1980 Darryl Rogers
1980-1982 Frank "Muddy" Waters
1983-1994 George Perles
1995-   Nick Saban

GOLF COACHES - MEN'S
1929   Harry G. Kipke
1930-1931 James H. Crowley
1932-1961 Benjamin F. Van Alstyne
1962-1965 John Brotzmann
1966-1989 Bruce Fossum
1989-   Ken Horvath

GOLF COACH - WOMEN'S
1972-   Mary Fossum

GYMNASTICS COACHES - MEN'S
1948-1988 George Szypula
1988-   Rick Atkinson

GYMNASTICS COACHES - WOMEN'S
1974-1976 Barb Peacock
1977-1988 Michael Kasavana
1988-1990 Jill Hough
1990-   Kathie Klages

SOCCER COACHES - MEN'S
1956-1969 Gene Kenney
1970-1973 Payton Fuller
1974-1976 Ed Rutherford
1977-   Joe Baum

SOCCER COACHES - WOMEN'S
1986-1990 Joe Baum
1991-   Tom Saxton

SOFTBALL COACHES
1972-1973 Ann Irwin
1974-1975 Margo Snivley
1976-1979 Diane Ulibarri
1980-1992 Gloria Becksford
1993-   Jacquie Joseph

SWIMMING COACHES - MEN'S
1922   S.S. Flynn
1923   Richard H. Rauch
1924-1925 W.B. Jones
1926   R.D. Keifaber
1927-1928 W. Sterry Brown
1929   F.R. Hoercher
1930-1941 Russell B. Daubert
1942-1969 Charles McCaffree, Jr.
1970-1987 Richard B. Fetters
1988-1989 Bill Wadley
1989-   Richard Bader

SWIMMING COACHES - WOMEN'S
1974-1977 Jennifer Parks
1978   Joel Feldman
1979-1988 Jennifer Parks
1988   Bill Wadley
1989-1992 Corrin Convis
1993-   Richard Bader

TENNIS COACHES - MEN'S
1921-1922 H.C. Young
1923-1946 Charles D. Ball, Jr.
1947   Gordon A. Dahlgren
1948-1951 Harris F. Beeman
1952   John Friedrich
1953-1958 Harris F. Beeman
1959-1989 Stan Drobac

1989-1991 Jim Frederick
1992-   Gene Orlando

TENNIS COACHES - WOMEN'S
1973-1977 Elaine Hatton
1978-1985 Earl Rutz, Jr.
1985-   Heather Mactaggart

TRACK AND FIELD COACHES - MEN'S
1897-1898 Henry Keep
1899   Max Beutner
1900-1901 Charles O. Bemies
1902-1903 George E. Denham
1904-1910 Chester L Brewer
1911-1913 John F. Macklin
1914   Ion J. Cartright
1915-1916 George E. Gauthier
1917   Howard E. Beatty
1918-1919 George E. Gauthier
1920-1921 Arthur Smith
1922-1923 Albert M. Barron
1924-1940 Ralph H. Young
1941-1958 Karl A. Schlademan
1959-1975 Fran Dittrich
1976-1977 Jim Bibbs (Acting)
1977-1995 Jim Bibbs
1995-   Darroll Gatson

TRACK AND FIELD COACHES - WOMEN'S
1973-1977 Nell Jackson
1978   Cheryl Flanagan
1979-1981 Nell Jackson
1982-1992 Karen Dennis
1993-   Judi Brown

VOLLEYBALL COACHES
1972-1973 Karen Peterson
1974-1984 Annelies Knoppers
1985-1992 Ginger Mayson
1993-   Chuck Erbe

WRESTLING COACHES
1922-1923 James H. Devers
1924-1926 Leon D. Burhans
1927-1928 Ralph G. Leonard
1929   Glenn L. Rickes
1930-1962 Fendley A. Collins
1963-1986 Grady J. Peninger
1986-1991 Phil Parker
1991-   Tom Minkel

UNIVERSITY OF MINNESOTA

Nils Hasselmo, *President*

Norman Chervany, *Faculty Representative*

Mariah Snyder, *Faculty Representative*

Mark Dienhart, *Director of Men's Athletics*

Chris Voelz, *Director of Women's Athletics*

FACULTY REPRESENTATIVES
1896	Conway McMillan
1896	F.W. Denton
1897	Prof. Woodbridge
1897-1906	F.S. Jones
1906-1934	James Paige
1934-1957	Henry Rottschaefer
1957-1962	Stanley V. Kinyon
1962-1974	Max O. Schultze
1974-1981	Merle K. Loken
1981-1994	Robert A. Stein
1981-1993	Jo-Ida Hansen
1993-	Mariah Snyder
1994-	Norman L. Chervany

MEN'S ATHLETIC DIRECTORS
1922-1930	Fred Leuhring
1930-1932	H.O. Crisler
1932-1941	Frank G. McCormick
1941-1946	Lou Keller (Acting)
1945-1950	Frank G. McCormick
1950-1963	Ike J. Armstrong
1963-1971	Marshall J. Ryman
1971-1988	Paul Giel
1988-1989	Holger Christiansen (Interim)
1989-1991	Rick Bay
1991-1992	Dan Meinert (Interim)
1992-1995	McKinley Boston
1995-	Mark Dienhart

WOMEN'S ATHLETIC DIRECTORS
1974-1976	Belmar Gunderson
1976-1981	Vivian M. Barfield
1981-1982	M. Catherine Mathison (Interim)
1982-1988	Merrily Dean Baker
1988-	Chris Voelz

SPORTS INFORMATION DIRECTORS - MEN'S
1930-1935	Les Etter
1935-1944	Various people in News Service
1944-1975	Otis J. Dypwick
1975-1993	Bob Peterson
1993-	Marc Ryan

SPORTS INFORMATION DIRECTORS -WOMEN'S
1975-1977	Dru Ann Hancock
1977-1981	Carol Van Dyke
1981-1982	Marty Duda (Interim)
1982-1991	Karen Smith
1991-1996	Dianne Boyer
1996-	Lisa Nelson

BASEBALL COACHES
1923-1926	Lee R. Watrous, Jr.
1927	George (Potsy) Clark
1928-1930	A.J. Bergman
1931-1941	Frank G. McCormick
1942-1947	Dave MacMillan
1948-1978	Dick Siebert
1979-1981	George Thomas
1982-	John Anderson

BASKETBALL COACHES - MEN'S
1897-1924	L.J. Cooke
1924-1927	Harold Taylor
1927-1942	Dave MacMillan
1942-1944	Carl L. Nordly
1944-1945	Weston Mitchell
1945-1948	Dave MacMillan
1948-1959	Osborne B. Cowles
1959-1968	John Kundla
1968-1970	William Fitch
1970-1971	George Hanson
1971-1975	Bill Musselman
1975-1986	Jim Dutcher
1986-	Clem Haskins

BASKETBALL COACHES - WOMEN'S
1974-1977	Virginia Johnson
1977-1987	Ellen Hanson
1988-1990	LaRue Fields
1990-	Linda Hill-MacDonald

CROSS COUNTRY COACHES - MEN'S
1908-1911	no coach
1912-1914	Dick Grant
1915-1920	Leonard Frank
1921-1923	Nelson Metcalf
1924	Sherman Finger
1925-1926	E.W. Iverson
1927-1932	Sherman Finger
1933-1937	no coach
1938-1962	Jim Kelly
1963-1995	Roy Griak
1996-	Steve Plasencia

CROSS COUNTRY COACHES - WOMEN'S
1974-1985	Mike Lawless
1985-	Gary Wilson

DIVING COACHES
1974-1976	Craig Lincoln

1976-1982	Frank Oman
1982-1985	Craig Lincoln
1985-1989	Chris Gentz
1989-1996	Doug Shaffer
1996-	Kongzheng Li

FOOTBALL COACHES

1883	Thomas Peebles
1886-1889	Fred S. Jones
1890	Tom Eck
1891	Edward Moulton
1892	No Coach
1893	Wallie Winter
1894	Thomas Cochrane, Jr.
1895	W.W. Heffelfinger
1896-1897	Alexander N. Jerrems
1898	Jack Minds
1899	Wm. C. Leary, John Harrison
1900-1921	Dr. Henry L. Williams
1922-1924	William Spaulding
1925-1929	Dr. C.W. Spears
1930-1931	H.O. Crisler
1932-1941	Bernie Bierman
1942-1944	Dr. George W. Hauser
1945-1950	Bernie Bierman
1951-1953	Wesley E. Fesler
1954-1971	Murray Warmath
1972-1978	Cal Stoll
1979-1983	Joe Salem
1984-1985	Lou Holtz
1985-1991	John Gutekunst
1992-	Jim Wacker

GOLF COACHES - MEN'S

1930-1945	W.R. Smith
1946-1976	Les Bolstad
1976-1978	Rick Ehrmanntraut
1978-1990	Greg Harvey
1990-	John Means

GOLF COACHES - WOMEN'S

1974-1979	Carol Issacs Davy
1979-1982	Robert J. Kiebar
1982-1987	Anne Zahn
1988-1991	Nancy Harris
1991-	Kathy Williams

GYMNASTICS COACHES - MEN'S

1902-1906	Dr. L.J. Cooke
1907-1929	Dr. W.K. Foster
1930-1962	Dr. Ralph A. Piper
1962-1963	Pat Bird (Acting)
1963-1965	Dr. Ralph A. Piper
1965-1966	Pat Bird (Acting)
1966-1968	Dr. Ralph A. Piper
1968-1971	Pat Bird
1971-	Fred Roethlisberger

GYMNASTICS COACH - WOMEN'S

1974-1992	Katalin Deli
1992-	Jim Stephenson

SOCCER COACHES - WOMEN'S

1993-	Sue Montagne

SOFTBALL COACHES

1974-1975	Linda Wells
1975-1976	Virginia Johnson
1976-1989	Linda Wells
1989-1991	Teresa Wilson
1992-	Lisa Bernstein

SWIMMING COACHES - MEN'S

1920-1957	Niels Thorpe
1958-1962	William Heusner
1962-1975	G. Robert Mowerson
1975-1980	Alfred (Bud) Ericksen
1980-1985	Paul Stearns
1985-	Dennis Dale

SWIMMING COACH - WOMEN'S

1974-	Jean Freeman

TENNIS COACHES - MEN'S

1928-1956	Phil Brain
1957-1959	Chet Murphy
1960-1965	Donald R. Lewis
1966-1971	Joseph A. Walsh
1972-1973	John Santrock

1974-1988	Jerry Noyce
1988-	David Geatz

TENNIS COACHES - WOMEN'S

1974-1975	Belmar Gunderson
1975-1983	Ellie Peden
1983-1987	Jack Roach
1988-1990	David Creighton
1990-	Martin Novak

TRACK AND FIELD COACHES - MEN'S

1920-1921	Leonard Frank
1922-1923	T. Nelson Metcalf
1924	Leonard Frank
1925-1933	Sherman Finger
1934-1935	Clarence Munn
1936	George Otterness
1937-1963	James Kelly
1964-1995	Roy Griak
1995-	Phil Lundin

TRACK AND FIELD COACHES - WOMEN'S

1974-1985	Mike Lawless
1985-	Gary Wilson

VOLLEYBALL COACHES

1974-1975	Linda Wells
1975-1977	Rosie Wegrich
1977-1982	Linda Wells
1982-1995	Stephanie Schleuder
1995	Pam Miller-Dombeck
1996-	Mike Hebert

WRESTLING COACHES

1932-1935	Blain McKusick
1936-1942	Dave Bartelma
1943-1944	Stanley Hanson
1945	Clarence R. Osell
1946	Dave Bartelma
1947	Stanley Hanson
1948-1952	Dave Bartelma
1953-1986	Wallace Johnson
1986-	J. Robinson

NORTHWESTERN UNIVERSITY

Henry S. Bienen,
President

Fred Hemke,
Faculty
Representative

Rick Taylor,
Director of
Athletics

Betsy Mosher,
Associate Athletic
Director

FACULTY REPRESENTATIVES
1896-1898	J. Scott Clark
1898-1900	H.S. White
1900-1901	W.A. Locy
1901-1906	O F. Long
1906-1914	R.E. Wilson
1914-1918	G.V. Pooley
1918-1919	R.E. Wilson
1919-1940	O.F. Long
1940-1943	Walter K. Smart
1943-1945	Ward V. Evans
1945-1948	G.R. Lundquist
1949-1956	F. George Seulberger
1956-1970	T. Leroy Martin
1970-1975	Leon A. Bosch
1975-1981	Larry Nobles
1981-	Frederick Hemke

ATHLETIC DIRECTORS
1895-1896	Otto Miller
1897-1898	W.J. Bryan
1898-1902	Dr. C.M. Hollister
1903-1904	Horace Butterworth
1905-1906	F.O. Smith
1906-1910	Louis Gillesby
1910-1913	Charles Hammett
1913-1918	Fred Murphy
1919-1920	Charles W. Bachman
1921-1924	Dana Evans
1925-1945	Kennth L. Wilson
1945-1956	Thodore B. Payseur
1956-1966	Stuart K. Holcomb
1967-1974	W H.H. (Tippy) Dye
1975-1980	John Pont
1981-1987	Doug Single
1987-1993	Bruce Corrie

1993-1994	Bill Foster
1994-	Rick Taylor

WOMEN'S ATHLETICS ADMINISTRATORS
1975-1979	JoAnne Fortunato
1980-1984	Sandra McCullough
1985-1989	Sandy Barbour
1989-	Betsy Mosher

SPORTS INFORMATION DIRECTORS
1926-1969	Walt Paulison
1969-1973	George Beres
1973-1977	Jerry Ashby
1977-1978	Susie Prichard
1979-1982	Jim Vruggink
1982-1985	Mike Nemeth
1985-1989	Sharon Miller
1989-1992	Tim Clodjeaux

DIRECTOR OF MEDIA SERVICES
1992-1993	Rob Grady
1993-1995	Greg Shea
1995-	Brad Hurlbut

BASEBALL COACHES
1894-1897	John Kedzie
1898-1902	W.J. Bryan
1903	Horace Butterworth
1904	Harry Fleager
1905	Harley Parker
1906	Charles Hollister
1907-1908	A.B. Cunningham
1909-1911	A.G. Rundle
1912	L.C. Holsinger

1913	Dennis Grady
1914-1916	Fred Murphy
1917-1920	William McGill
1921	Jack Sawtelle
1922	Henry Szymanski
1923-1928	Maury Kent
1929-1935	Paul Steart
1936-1939	Burt Ingwersen
1940-1941	Stanley Klores
1942-1943	Maury Kent
1944-1946	Wesley Fry
1947-1948	Don Heap
1948-1961	Freddie Lindstrom
1961-1981	George McKinnon
1981-1986	Ron Wellman
1986-1987	Larry Cochell
1987-	Paul Stevens

BASKETBALL COACHES - MEN'S
1905-1906	Tom Holland
1907-1910	Louis Gillesby
1911	Stuart Templeton
1912	Charles Hammett
1913-1914	Dennis Grady
1915-1917	Fred Murphy
1918	Norman Elliott
1919	Tom Robinson
1920	Norman Elliott
1921	Ray Edler
1922	Dana Evans
1923-1927	Maury Kent
1928-1950	Arthur Lonborg
1950-1952	Harold G. Olsen
1953-1957	Waldo Fisher
1957-1963	William Rohr
1963-1969	Larry Glass

1969-1973	Brad Snyder
1973-1978	Tex Winter
1978-1986	Rich Falk
1986-1993	Bill Foster
1993-	Ricky Byrdsong

BASKETBALL COACHES - WOMEN'S
1975-1980	Mary DiStanislao
1980-1984	Annette Lynch
1984-	Don Perrelli

DIVING COACH
1989-1992	Kim DeCloux-Stuck
1992-	Dan Walter

FENCING COACHES
1975-1977	Charlotte Remenyik
1978-	Laurence Schiller

FIELD HOCKEY COACHES
1975	Mary Ann Kelling
1976	Mary DiStanislao
1978-1980	Sharon Drysdale
1981-1990	Nancy Stevens
1990-1995	Marisa Didio
1995-	Deb Brickey

FOOTBALL COACHES
1893	Paul Noyes
1894	A.A. Ewing
1895-1896	Alvin H Culver
1897	Jesse Van Doozer
1898	W.H. Bannard
1899-1902	Dr. C.M. Hollister
1903-1905	Walter McCormack
1908	Alton Johnson
1909	William Horr
1910-1912	C.E. Hammett
1913	Dennis Grady
1914-1918	Fred Murphy
1919	Charles Bachman
1920-1921	Elmer McDevitt
1922-1926	Glenn Thistlethwaite
1927-1934	Dick Hanley

1935-1946	Lynn Waldorf
1947-1954	Bob Voigts
1955	Lou Saban
1956-1963	Ara Parseghian
1964-1972	Alex Agase
1973-1977	John Pont
1978-1980	Rick Venturi
1981-1985	Dennis Green
1986-1991	Francis Peay
1991-	Gary Barnett

GOLF COACHES - MEN'S
1920	Arthur Sweet
1923-1932	Leon Kranz
1933-1945	Ted Payseur
1946-1976	Sid Richardson
1977-1978	Mickey Louis
1979-1981	Don MacLachlan
1982-1988	Wally Goodwin
1988-1990	Jim Suttie
1991-	Jeff Mory

GOLF COACHES - WOMEN'S
1992-	Chris Regenberg

LACROSSE COACHES
1981-1990	Cindy Timchal
1991-1992	Robin Cummings

SOCCER COACHES - MEN'S
1980-1981	Bob Krohn
1982-	Michael Kunert

SOCCER COACHES - WOMEN'S
1994-	Marcia McDermott

SOFTBALL COACHES
1975-1978	Mary Conway
1979-	Sharon Drysdale

SWIMMING COACHES - MEN'S
1910-1943	Tom Robinson
1944-1970	William Peterson
1970-1973	Bob Steele

1973-1981	Jack Bolger
1982-1988	Pat Barry
1988-	Bob Groseth

SWIMMING COACHES - WOMEN'S
1975-1981	Sally Marshall
1981-1987	Pat Barry
1988-1994	Kathie Wickstrand
1994-	Jimmy Tierney

TENNIS COACHES - MEN'S
1921-1922	Henry Raeder
1923-1930	Arthur Nethercot
1931-1958	Paul Bennett
1959-1975	Clare Riessen
1976-1983	Vandy Christie
1984-	Paul Torricelli

TENNIS COACHES - WOMEN'S
1976-1979	June Booth
1979-1989	Sandy Stap Clifton
1989-	Lisa Fortman

VOLLEYBALL COACHES
1975-1978	Mary Convey
1978-1993	Jerry Angle
1994-	Margie Fitzpatrick

WRESTLING COACHES
1917	Elmer Jones
1918-1919	Tom Robinson
1920-1921	Jack Sawtelle
1922-1923	Henry Szymanski
1924-1925	Eugene Maynor
1926	Bryan Hines
1927-1936	Orion Stuteville
1937-1942	Wesley Brown
1943-1945	Roy Greening
1946-1947	Wesley Brown
1948-1957	Jack Riley
1958-1980	Kenneth Kraft
1980-1989	Thomas Jarman
1989-	Tim Cyzewski

OHIO STATE UNIVERSITY

E. Gordon Gee,
President

Susan Hartmann,
Faculty
Representative

Andy Geiger,
Director of
Athletics

Miechelle Willis,
Associate Athletic
Director

FACULTY REPRESENTATIVES
1912-1944	Thomas E. French
1944-1946	James E. Pollard
1947-1961	Wendell Postle
1961-1971	James R. McCoy
1971-1977	Roy A. Laramee
1977-1983	Harold Schecter
1981-1985	JoAnne Stevenson
1983-1989	C. J. Slanica
1985	Laura Blomquist
1989-1995	Carol Kennedy
1995-	Susan Hartmann

ATHLETIC DIRECTORS
1912-1947	L.W. St. John
1947-1971	R. C. Larkins
1971-1977	J. Edward Weaver
1977-1984	Hugh Hindman
1984-1987	Richard Bay
1988-1994	James Jones
1994-	Andy Geiger

WOMEN'S ATHLETICS ADMINISTRATOR
1965-1994	Phyllis Bailey
1994-	Miechelle Willis

SPORTS INFORMATION DIRECTORS
1923-1933	William Griffith
1934-1935	James B. Reston
1936-1943	James L. Renick
1944-1973	Wilbur E. Snypp
1973-1987	Marv Homan
1988-	Steve Snapp

BASEBALL COACHES
1901-1902	Jack Reed
1903	C.W. Dickerson
1913-1928	L.W. St. John
1929-1932	Wayne Wright
1932-1938	Floyd Stahl
1939-1944	Fred Mackey
1945-1946	Lowell Wrigley
1947-1950	Floyd Stahl
1950-1975	Martin G. Karow
1976-1987	Richard D. Finn
1988-	Bob Todd

BASKETBALL COACHES - MEN'S
1902-1903	D.C. Huddleson
1909-1910	Thomas Kibler
1912-1919	L.W. St. John
1920-1921	George M. Trautman
1922-1946	Harold G. Olsen
1946-1950	W.H.H. (Tippy) Dye
1950-1958	Floyd S. Stahl
1958-1976	Fred Taylor
1976-1986	Eldon Miller
1986-1989	Gary Williams
1989-	Randy Ayers

BASKETBALL COACHES - WOMEN'S
1965-1970	Phyllis J. Bailey
1970-1972	Mary Combs
1972-1980	Debbie Wilson
1980-1985	Tara Van Derveer
1985-	Nancy Darsch

CROSS COUNTRY COACHES - MEN'S
1955-1964	Charles Beetham
1965-1976	Robert Epskamp

1976-1983	Jim McDonough
1984-1988	Roger Bowen
1989-1992	Russ Rogers
1993-1994	Mark Croghan
1995-	Jack Warner

CROSS COUNTRY COACHES - WOMEN'S
1975	Kit Boesch
1976-1994	Mamie Rallins
1994	Mark Croghan
1995-	Jack Warner

DIVING COACHES
1965-1978	Ron O'Brien
1978-	Vince Panzano

FENCING COACHES
1965-1967	
1967-1970	Natalie Goodhartz
1970-1972	
1972-1978	Kit Boesch
1974-1986	Charles Simonian (men's)
1978-	Charlotte Remenyik

FIELD HOCKEY COACHES
1965-1966	Louise Owens
1967-1969	Barbara Nelson
1970-1972	Mary Raysa
1973-1986	Harriet Reynolds
1987- 1996	Karen Weaver
1996-	Anne Wilkinson

FOOTBALL COACHES
1890	Jack Ryder
1890-1891	Alexander S. Lilley
1892-1895	Jack Ryder
1896	Charles A. Hickey
1897	David F. Edwards

1898	Jack Ryder
1899-1901	John B. Eckstrom
1902-1903	Perry Hale
1904-1905	E.R. Sweetland
1906-1909	A.E. Herrnstein
1910	Howard Jones
1911	Harry Vaughn
1912	John R. Richards
1913-1928	Dr. J.W. Wilce
1929-1933	Sam S. Willaman
1934-1940	Francis A. Schmidt
1941-1943	Paul E. Brown
1944-1945	Carroll C. Widdoes
1946	Paul O. Bixler
1947-1950	Wesley E. Fesler
1951-1978	W.W. Hayes
1979-1987	Earle Bruce
1988-	John Cooper

GOLF COACHES - MEN'S

1921-1923	Mike Godman
1924-1925	George Eckelberry
1926-1931	George Sargent
1932	Francis Marzolf
1933-1937	Harold G. Olsen
1938-1965	Robert Kepler
1966	Floyd S. Stahl
1967-1973	Roderick W. Myers
1974-	Jim Brown

GOLF COACHES - WOMEN'S

1965-1967	Ann Roberts Fox
1967-1968	
1968-1971	Ann Roberts Fox
1971-1973	Mary Jo Campbell
1973-1975	Sue Collins
1975-1980	J.R. Ables
1980-1986	Stephen E. Groves
1987-1991	Jana Edwards Shipley
1991-	Therese Hession

GYMNASTICS COACHES - MEN'S

1923	Glenn Alexander
1924-1932	Leo G. Staley
1947-1966	Joseph M. Hewlett
1967-1977	James Sweeney
1977-1988	Michael Willson
1988-	Peter Kormann

GYMNASTICS COACHES - WOMEN'S

1965-1967	Carolyn Osborne Bowers
1967-1970	Sharon Weber
1970-1975	Catherine O'Brien
1975-1979	Nancy Krattiger-Ziltener
1979-	Larry Cox

SOCCER COACHES - MEN'S

1953-1954	Bruce Bennett
1954-1958	Howard Knuttgen
1958-1969	Walter Ersing
1969-1971	Forest Tyson
1971-1976	Bill Servedio
1976-1978	Jerry Bell
1979-1987	Al Bianco
1987-	Gary Avedikian

SOCCER COACHES - WOMEN'S

1993-	Lori Henry

SOFTBALL COACHES

1967	Jan Felshin
1971-1973	Catherine O'Brien
1974-1977	Harriet Reynolds
1978	Don Dungee
1979-1985	Dianne Thompson
1986-1987	Barb Dearing
1987-1996	Gail Davenport
1996-	Linda Kalafatis

SWIMMING COACHES - MEN'S

1930-1963	Michael Peppe
1963-1967	Robert Bartels
1968-1975	John Bruce
1976-1989	Dick Sloan
1989-	Bill Wadley

SWIMMING COACHES - WOMEN'S

1965-1968	Peggy Richardson
1968-1971	Janet Walter
1971-1972	Peggy Richter
1972-1977	Linda Hall
1977-1980	Susie Atwood
1980-	Jim Montrella

TENNIS COACHES - MEN'S

1921	T.H. Connnell
1922-1924	R.L. Grismer
1925-1957	Herman Wirthwein
1958-1970	John W. Hendrix
1971-1972	Dave Robertson
1972-	John Daly

TENNIS COACHES - WOMEN'S

1965-1966	Fran Smith Olsen
1968-1969	Dorothy Allen
1971-1978	Mary Raysa
1978-1985	Barbara Mueller
1986-1996	Lee Ann Massucci
1996-	TBA

TRACK AND FIELD COACHES - MEN'S

1902-1903	D.C. Huddleson
1908	W.T. McCarty
1910-1912	Steve Farrell
1913-1931	Frank R. Castleman
1932-1942	Larry Snyder
1943-1945	George Haney
1946-1965	Larry Snyder
1965-1976	Robert Epskamp
1976-1988	Frank Zubovich
1988-	Russ Rogers

TRACK AND FIELD COACHES - WOMEN'S

1971	Janet Walter
1973	Annie Tolle
1974-1976	Kit Boesch
1977-1994	Mamie Rallins
1994-	Russ Rogers

VOLLEYBALL COACHES

1971-1972	Mary Jo Campbell
1973-1979	Sue Collins
1980-1981	Lisa Richards
1982-	Jim Stone

WRESTLING COACHES

1921-1925	Al Haft
1926-1942	Bernard Mooney
1943-1944	Lawrence Hicks
1945-1947	Bernard Mooney
1948-1976	Casey Fredericks
1976-1986	Chris Ford
1986-	Russ Hellickson

Graham Spanier,
President

John Coyle,
Faculty
Representative

Tim Curley,
Director of
Athletics

Ellen Perry,
Associate Athletic
Director

FACULTY REPRESENTATIVES
1953-1958	Norman R. Sparks
1958-1966	M. Nelson McGeary
1960-1969	R.H. "Sam" Wherry
1970	Edward Mattil
1970 -	John J. Coyle

ATHLETIC DIRECTORS
1918-1936	Hugo Bezdek
1937-1953	Dr. Carl P. Schott
1953-1968	Ernest B. McCoy
1968-1980	Edward M. Czekaj
1980-1982	Joe Paterno
1982-1993	James I. Tarman
1994-	Tim Curley

WOMEN'S ATHLETICS ADMINISTRATORS
1964-1989	Della Durant
1989-	Ellen Perry

SPORTS INFORMATION DIRECTORS
1922-1926	George W. (Pat) Sullivan
1926-1935	Wes W. Dunlap
1935-1943	Hugh R. "Ridge" Riley
1943-1958	James H. Coogan
1958-1970	James I. Tarman
1970-1979	John Morris
1979-1986	Dave Baker
1986-1993	L. Budd Thalman
1993-	Jeff Nelson

BASEBALL COACHES
1900	W.B. Burns
1903-1906	Pop Golden
1907-1910	Irish McIlveen
1911	Bull McCleary
1912-1914	Walter Manning
1915-1917	R.H. Harley
1919	George Wheeling
1920-1930	Hugo Bezdek
1931-1962	Joe Bedenk
1963-1981	Chuck Medlar
1982-1990	Shorty Stoner
1991-	Joe Hindelang

BASKETBALL COACHES - MEN'S
1916-1917	Burke Hermann
1919	Hugo Bezdek
1920-1932	Burke Hermann
1933-1936	Earl Leslie
1937-1949	John Lawther
1950-1954	Elmer Gross
1955-1968	John Egli
1968-1978	John Bach
1979-1983	Dick Harter
1984-1995	Bruce Parkhill
1996-	Jerry Dunn

BASKETBALL COACHES - WOMEN'S
1965-1970	Marie Litner
1971-1974	Mary Ann Domitrovitz
1975-1980	Pat Meiser
1981-	Rene Portland

CROSS COUNTRY COACHES - MEN'S
1912	W.N. Golden
1913-1916	C.W. Martin
1919	W.E. Lewis
1920-1921	C.W. Martin
1922-1932	Nate Cartmell
1932-1942	Chick Werner
1943	Ray Conger
1946-1961	Chick Werner
1962-1967	John A. Lucas
1968-	Harry Groves

CROSS COUNTRY COACHES - WOMEN'S
1974-1978	Chris Brooks
1979-1983	Gary Schwartz
1984-	Teri Jordan

DIVING COACH
1985-	Craig Brown

FIELD HOCKEY COACHES
1964-1968	Pat Seni
1969	Nancy Bailey
1970-1973	Tonya Toole
1974-1986	Gillian Rattray
1987-	Charlene Morett

FOOTBALL COACHES
1892-1895	George Hoskins
1896-1898	Samuel Newton
1899	Sam Boyle
1900-1902	Pop Golden
1903	Dan Reed
1904-1908	Tom Fennell
1909	Bill Hollenback
1910	Jack Hollenback
1911-1914	Bill Hollenback
1915-1917	Dick Harlow
1918-1929	Hugo Bezdek
1930-1948	Bob Higgins

1949	Joe Bedenk
1950-1965	Charles A. "Rip" Engle
1966-	Joe Paterno

GOLF COACHES - MEN'S
1922-1949	R.B. Rutherford, Sr.
1950-1956	R.R. Rutherford, Jr.
1957-1983	Joe Boyle
1983-1992	Mary Kennedy-Zierke
1992-	Greg Nye

GOLF COACHES - WOMEN'S
1965-1969	Mimi Ryan
1970-1971	Barbara Sanford
1971-1980	Annette Thompson
1980-1992	Mary Kennedy-Zierke
1992-	Denise St. Pierre

GYMNASTICS COACHES - MEN'S
1931-1932	J.H. Rammacher
1933-1936	Nels Walke
1937-1938	Julian Glasser
1939-1976	Gene Wettstone
1977-1991	Karl Schier
1992-	Randy Jepson

GYMNASTICS COACHES - WOMEN'S
1965-1967	Lu Magnusson
	Della Durant
	Tuovi Sappinem
1968	Kathy Corrigan
1969-1972	Betz Hanley
1973-1974	Barb Block
1975-1992	Judi Avener
1992-	Steve Shephard

SOCCER COACHES - MEN'S
1916-1917	Jim Crowell
1919-1920	Jim Crowell
1921	Compton Packenham
1922	Hugh Keenleyside
1923	Larry Longhurst
1924-1925	Ralph Leonard
1926-1952	Bill Jeffrey

1953-1967	Ken Hosterman
1968-1973	Herb Schmidt
1974-1987	Walter Bahr
1988-	Barry Gorman

SOCCER COACHES - WOMEN'S
| 1994- | Patrick Farmer |

SOFTBALL COACHES
1965-1972	Pat McTarsney
1973	Jackie Hudson
1974-1980	Pat McTarsney
1981	Dennis Helsel
1982-1995	Sue Rankin
1996	Laura Fillipp (interim)
1996-	Robin Petrini

SWIMMING COACHES - MEN'S
1936-1944	R.E. Galbraith
1947	Leonard Diehl
1948-1951	William Gutteron
1968-1984	Lou MacNeill
1984-	Peter Brown

SWIMMING COACHES - WOMEN'S
| 1970-1980 | Ellen Perry |
| 1981- | Bob Krimmel |

TENNIS COACHES - MEN'S
1923-1927	William R. Ham
1928-1931	Harvey W. Stover
1932	Leon Schios
1933-1935	Harvey W. Stover
1936	Robert B. Oxreider
1937	Robert E. Lake
1938	Harvey W. Stover
1939-1943	Ted Roethke
1944	Ray Dickinson
1947-1964	Sherman Fogg
1965-1990	Holmes Cathrall
1990-	Jan Bortner

TENNIS COACHES - WOMEN'S
| 1965 | Ann Valentine |
| 1966-1968 | Pat Seni |

1969-1977	Joan Nessler
1977-1981	Candy Royer
1981-1982	Kim Muller
1982-1990	Jan Bortner
1990-	Sue Whiteside

TRACK AND FIELD COACHES - MEN'S
1902-1912	W.N. Golden
1913-1917	C.W. Martin
1919	W.E. Lewis
1920-1922	C.W. Martin
1923-1933	Nate Cartmell
1934-1942	Chick Werner
1943	Ray Conger
1944-1945	G.W. Harvey
1946-1962	Chick Werner
1963-1968	John A. Lucas
1969-	Harry Groves

TRACK AND FIELD COACHES - WOMEN'S
1974-1979	Chris Brooks
1980-1984	Gary Schwartz
1985-	Teri Jordan

VOLLEYBALL COACHES - WOMEN'S
| 1976-1978 | Tom Tait |
| 1979- | Russ Rose |

WRESTLING COACHES
1909-1913	William E. Lewis
1914	J.H. Shollenberger
1915-1917	William E. Lewis
1918-1919	H.C. Yerger
1920-1921	William E. Lewis
1922-1924	D.D. Detar
1925-1926	Ralph G. Leonard
1927-1942	Charlie Speidel
1943-1946	Paul Campbell
1947-1964	Charlie Speidel
1965-1978	Bill Koll
1979-1992	Rich Lorenzo
1992-	John Fritz

PURDUE UNIVERSITY

Steven C. Beering,
President

Martha Chiscon,
Faculty
Representative

Phillip Nelson,
Faculty
Representative

Morgan Burke,
Director of
Athletics

Joni Comstock,
Associate Athletic
Director

FACULTY REPRESENTATIVES
1896-1897 W.E. Stone
1897-1900 C.A. Waldo
1900-1901 H.A. Huston
1901-1928 Thomas F. Moran
1928-1939 William Marshall
1939-1941 G.A. Young
1941-1945 J.A. Estey
1945-1969 Verne C. Freeman
1969-1980 Roy L. Whistler
1980-1985 Gilbert S. Banker
1985-1986 Jane Kahle
1985- Philip E. Nelson
1986- Martha Chiscon

ATHLETIC DIRECTORS
1904-1905 O.F. Cutts
1906-1914 Hugh Nichols
1915-1918 O.F. Cutts
1919-1930 N.A. Kellogg
1931-1936 Noble E. Kizer
1937 R.C. Woodworth (Acting)
1938-1939 Nobel E. Kizer
1940 E.C. Elliott (Acting)
1941 A.H. Elward
1942-1971 Guy J. Mackey
1971-1992 George King. Jr.
1992 John W. Hicks (Interim)
1992- Morgan J. Burke

WOMEN'S ATHLETICS ADMINISTRATORS
1975-1988 Carol Mertler
1989- Joni Comstock

SPORTS INFORMATION DIRECTORS
1925-1928 Robert A. McMahon
1928-1964 Robert C. Woodworth
1964-1970 Karl W. Klages
1970-1975 Ted Haracz
1975-1977 Gregg Knipping
1977-1982 Tom Shupe
1982-1990 Jim Vruggink
1990- Mark Adams

BASEBALL COACHES
1892-1893 W.M. Phillips
1901 W.H. Fox
1902 Friel
1903-1904 J.C. Kelsey
1905 P. O'Neil
1906-1914 H. Nicol
1915-1916 B.P. Pattison
1917 W.L. Lambert
1918 J. Pierce
1919-1935 W.L. Lambert
1936-1942 W.P. Fehring
1943 W.P. Fehring, C.S. Doan
1944 C.S. Doan
1945-1946 W L. Lambert
1947-1950 Mel Taube
1950-1955 Henry Stram
1956-1959 Paul Hoffman
1960-1977 Joe Sexson
1977-1991 Dave Alexander
1991- Steve Green

BASKETBALL COACHES - MEN'S
1901-1902 W.C. Curd
1903 C.L. Freeman
1905 J.J. Nufer
1906-1908 C.B. Jamison
1909 E.J. Stewart
1910-1912 R.R.Jones
1913-1916 R.E. Vaughan
1917 Ward L. Lambert
1918 J.J. Molony
1919-1946 Ward L. Lambert
1946-1950 Mel Taube
1950-1965 Ray Eddy
1965-1972 George King
1972-1978 Fred Schaus
1978-1980 Lee Rose
1980- Gene Keady

BASKETBALL COACHES - WOMEN'S
1975-1976 Deborah Gebhardt
1976-1986 Dr. Ruth Jones
1986-1987 Marsha Reall
1987-1996 Lin Dunn
1996- Nell Fortner

CROSS COUNTRY COACHES - MEN'S
1908 C.H. Wilson
1909-1911 Ralph Jones
1912-1913 Arbor Clow
1914-1915 James Temple
1916-1928 Eddie O'Connor
1929-1930 Earl Martineau
1931-1935 Orval Martin
1936-1942 Herman Phillips
1943-1945 Homer Allen
1946-1951 Dave Rankin
1952-1966 no team

1967-1972 Roger Kerr
1973-   Mike Poehlein

CROSS COUNTRY COACHES - WOMEN'S
1978-1989 Fred Wilt
1989-1992 Carol Stevenson
1993-   Ben Paolillo

FOOTBALL COACHES
1887   A. Berg
1889   G.A. Reisner
1890   C.L. Hare
1891-1892 K. Ames, B. Donnelly
1893   Balliet, Seixes, Randolph
1894-1895 D.W. Balliet
1896   S.M. Hammond
1897   W.S. Church
1898-1899 A.P. Jamison
1900-1901 D.W. Balliet, A.P. Jamison
1902   C.M. Best
1903-1904 O.F. Cutts
1905   A.E. Hernstein
1906   M.E. Witham
1907   L.C. Turner
1908-1909 Frederick Speik
1910-1911 M.H. Horr
1912   M.H. Horr, J.E. Moll
1913-1915 A.L. Smith
1916-1917 C.O. O'Donnell
1918-1920 A.G. (Butch) Scanlon
1921   W.H. Dietz
1922-1929 James Phelan
1930-1936 Noble Kizer
1937-1941 A.H. Elward
1942-1943 Elmer H. Burnham
1944-1946 Cecil Isbell
1947-1955 Stu Holcomb
1956-1969 Jack Mollenkopf
1970-1972 Bob DeMoss
1973-1976 Alex Agase
1977-1981 Jim Young
1982-1986 Leon Burnett
1987-1990 Fred Akers
1991-   Jim Colletto

GOLF COACHES - MEN'S
1922   G.A. Young
1923-1927 B.S. Swezey

1929-1937 J.E. Bixler
1938-1944 Harry Allspaw
1945   Sam Voinoff
1945-1950 Loomis Heston
1951-1974 Sam Voinoff
1974-1993 Joe Campbell
1993-   Bob Prange

GOLF COACHES - WOMEN'S
1975-1990 Paul Snider
1990-1993 Susan Stump
1993-   Bob Prange

SOFTBALL COACHES
1993-   Carol Bruggeman

SWIMMING COACHES - MEN'S
1920-1921 M.L. Clevett
1922   Barr
1923   C.J. Merriam
1924   G.H. Aylesworth
1925-1938 L.W. LaBree
1939-1970 R.O. Papenguth
1970-1985 Fred Kahms
1985-   Dan Ross

SWIMMING COACHES - WOMEN'S
1975-1976 Laura Pfohl
1976-1979 Tim Kurtz
1979-1981 Sherry Weeks
1981-1985 Fred Kahms
1985-1987 Dan Ross
1987-   Cathy Wright-Eger

TENNIS COACHES - MEN'S
1915-1916 C M. James
1920-1923 E.R. Sidwell
1924   G.H. Aylesworth
1925-1964 L.W. LaBree
1965-1979 Edward C. Eicholtz
1979-1983 Ron MacVittie
1984-1994 Ed Dickson
1994-   Tim Madden

TENNIS COACHES - WOMEN'S
1975-1977 Jocelyn "Cissy" Monroe
1977-1980 Ann Wilson
1980-1982 Nancy Janco

1982-1984 Carrie Meyer
1984-1987 Ed Dickson
1988-1991 Helyn Edwards
1991-   Mat Iandolo

TRACK AND FIELD COACHES - MEN'S
1900   Curtiss
1901   W.J. Hyland
1902-1903 C.I. Freeman
1904   E.L. Wheeler
1905   J.J. Nuler
1906-1907 C.B. Jamison
1908-1909 C.H. Wilson
1910-1912 R.R. Jones
1913   Arbor W. Clow
1914   J. Mahan
1915-1916 J. Temple
1917-1929 E.J. O'Connor
1930-1931 Earl T. Martineau
1932-1936 O.J. Martin
1937-1943 H.E. Phillips
1944 H E   Phillips, Homer Allen
1945-1946 Homer Allen
1945-1981 David Rankin
1981-   Mike Poehlein

TRACK AND FIELD COACHES - WOMEN'S
1976-1977 JoAnn Terry Grissom
1977-1978 Jim McMillan
1978-1989 Fred Wilt
1989-1993 Carol Stevenson
1993-   Ben Paolillo

VOLLEYBALL COACHES
1975- 1995 Carol Dewey
1995-   Joey Vrazel

WRESTLING COACHES
1914   N. Embleton
1915-1922 Frederick Paulsen
1923-1924 W.S Von Bermuth
1925-1929 H.A. Miller
1930-1932 L.B. Beers
1933-1936 G J. Mackey
1937-1970 C.C. Reeck
1970-1975 Don Corrigan
1976-1980 Mark Sothmann
1980-1988 Bill Trujillo
1988-1992 Mitch Hull
1992-   Jessie Reyes

UNIVERSITY OF WISCONSIN

David Ward,
Chancellor

James L. Hoyt,
Faculty
Representative

Pat Richter,
Director of
Athletics

Cheryl Marra
Associate
Athletic Director

FACULTY REPRESENTATIVES

1896	C.R. Barnes
1896-1899	E.A. Birge
1899-1905	C.S.Slichter
1905-1906	T.S.Adams
1906-1909	C.P. Hutchins
1910-1912	G.W. Ehler
1912-1931	J.F.A. Pyre
1932-1935	A.T. Weaver
1936-1947	William F. Lorenz
1947-1951	Kenneth Little
1951-1954	Kurt F. Wendt
1954-1959	George Young
1959-1970	Frank Remington
1970-1971	George Young
1971-1986	Frank Remington
1981-1987	Diane Lindstrom
1986-1987	David Tarr
1987-1989	Jane Voichick
1987-1991	Ted Finman
1989-1992	Cyrena Pondrom
1991-	James Hoyt
1992-1994	Jane Robbins
1994-1996	Barbara L. Wolfe

ATHLETIC DIRECTORS

1920-1924	Tom E. Jones (Acting)
1925-1932	George Little
1933-1935	Walter Meanwell
1936-1950	Harry Stuhldreher
1950-1955	Guy Sundt
1955-1969	Ivan Williamson
1969-1987	Elroy L. Hirsch
1987-1989	Ade Sponberg
1989-	Pat Richter

WOMEN'S ATHLETICS ADMINISTRATORS

1974-1990	Kit Saunders-Nordeen
1990-	Cheryl Marra

SPORTS INFORMATION DIRECTORS

1923-1929	Les Gage
1929-1941	George Downer
1941-1946	Bob Foss
1946-1956	Arthur G. Lentz
1956-1957	James A. Mott (Acting)
1957-1966	George L. Lanphear
1966-1990	James A. Mott (men's)
1975-1977	Phyllis Krutsch (women's)
1977-	Tamara J. Flarup (women's)
1990-	Steve Malchow (men's)

BASEBALL COACHES

1900-1901	Phil King
1902-1903	Oscar Bandelin
1904-1905	Bemis Pierce
1907	C.P. Hutchins
1908-1911	Tom Barry
1912	Gordon (Slim) Lewis
1913	William Juneau
1914-1917	Gordon (Slim) Lewis
1918	Guy Lowman
1919-1920	Maurice A. Kent
1921-1932	Guy Lowman
1933-1934	Irvin Uteritz
1935-1936	Robert Poser
1937-1939	Lowell Douglas
1940-1970	Arthur Mansfield
1971-1984	Tom Meyer
1984-1991	Steve Land

BASKETBALL COACHES - MEN'S

1899-1905	James Elsom
1905-1908	Emmett Angell
1909-1911	Haskell Noyes
1912-1917	Dr. Walter Meanwell
1918-1920	Guy Lowman
1921-1934	Dr. Walter Meanwell
1935-1959	Harold Foster
1960-1968	John E. Erickson
1969-1976	John Powless
1977-1982	Bill Cofield
1983-1992	Steve Yoder
1993-1994	Stu Jackson
1994-1995	Stan Van Gundy
1995-	Dick Bennett

BASKETBALL COACHES - WOMEN'S

1974-1976	Marilyn Harris
1976-1986	Edwina Qualls
1986-1994	Mary Murphy
1994-	Jane Albright-Dieterle

ROWING COACHES - MEN'S

1961-1969	Norm Sonju
1969-	Randy Jablonic

ROWING COACHES - WOMEN'S

1974-1979	Jay Mimier
1979-	Sue Ela

CROSS COUNTRY COACHES - MEN'S

1910-1911	Charles Wilson
1912	Clarence Cleveland

1913-1914	Thomas E. Jones
1915	Fred G. Lee
1916	Irvin A. White
1917	Thomas E. Jones
1918-1920	George T. Bresnahan
1921-1925	Meade Burke
1926-1947	Thomas E. Jones
1948-1949	Guy Sundt
1950-1959	J. Riley Best
1960	Tom Bennett
1961-1963	Charles Walter
1964	Tom Bennett
1965-1967	Charles Walter
1968-1970	Robert Brennan
1971-1982	Dan McClimon
1983-	Martin Smith

CROSS COUNTRY COACH - WOMEN'S
1974-	Peter Tegen

DIVING COACHES
1951-1964	Art Krueger (men's)
1964-1994	Jerry Darda
1994-	Jim Fischer

FENCING COACHES
1911	Walter Meanwell
1912-1914	H.D. MacChesney
1915	George Breen
1916-1917	H.D. MacChesney
1918-1919	No Team
1920-1926	Fred Schlatter
1927-1951	Arpad L. Masley
1952-1972	Archie Simonson
1972-1990	Tony Gillham
1990-1991	Jerzy Radz

FOOTBALL COACHES
1889	Alvin Kletsch
1890	Ted Mestre
1891	Herb Alward
1892	Frank Crawford
1893	Parke Davis
1894-1895	H.O. Stockney
1896-1902	Phil King
1903-1904	Art Curtis
1905	Phil King
1906-1907	C.P. Hutchins
1908-1910	J.A. Barry
1911	J.R. Richards
1912-1915	W.J. Juneau
1916	Paul Withington
1917	J.R. Richards
1918	Guy Lowman
1919-1922	J.R. Richards
1923-1924	Jack Ryan
1925-1926	George Little
1927-1931	Glenn Thistlewaite
1932-1935	Dr. C.W. Spears
1936-1948	Harry Stuhldreher
1949-1955	Ivan B. Williamson

1956-1966	Milt Bruhn
1967-1969	John Coatta
1970-1977	John Jardine
1978-1985	Dave McClain
1986	Jim Hilles
1987-1989	Don Morton
1990-	Barry Alvarez

GOLF COACHES - MEN'S
1926	Joe Steinauer
1927-1931	George Levis
1932-1951	Joe Steinauer
1952-1969	John Jamieson
1970-1977	Tom Bennett
1977-	Dennis Tiziani

GOLF COACHES - WOMEN'S
1975-1976	Jane Eastham
1976-1984	Jackie Hayes
1985-1989	Chris Regenberg
1989-	Dennis Tiziani

GYMNASTICS COACHES - MEN'S
1902-1905	J.C. Elsom
1906-1907	Emett Angell
1908-1909	J.C. Elsom
1910	Felix Zeidelhack
1911-1917	H.D. MacChesney
1918	Joe Steinauer
1919-1922	Fred Schlatter
1923	Frank Leitz
1924-1926	Fred Schlatter
1927-1935	A.L. Masley
1936-1947	No Team
1948-1959	Dean Mory
1960-1961	George Bauer, Gordon Johnson
1962-1971	George Bauer
1972-1978	Raymond Bauer
1978-1991	Mark Pflughoeft

GYMNASTICS COACHES - WOMEN'S
1974-1978	Marian Snowdon
1978-1984	Jenny Hoffman-Convisor
1984-1991	Terry Bryson

ICE HOCKEY COACHES
1916-1919	Joe Steinauer
1922-1923	Dr. A.K. Viner
1924-	Robert Blodgett
1925-1926	Kay Iverson
1927-	W.R. Brandow
1928-1930	John Farquhar
1931-	Spike Carlson
1932-1935	Art Thomsen
1936-1963	No Team
1963-1964	Art Thomsen, John Riley
1965-1966	John Riley
1967-1975	Bob Johnson
1975-1976	Bill Rothwell (Acting)

1977-1982	Bob Johnson
1983-	Jeff Sauer

SOCCER COACHES - MEN'S
1977-1981	Bill Reddan
1982-	Jim Launder

SOCCER COACHES - WOMEN'S
1981-1986	Craig Webb
1986-1994	Greg Ryan
1994-	Dean Duerst

SOFTBALL COACHES
1996-	Karen Gallagher

SWIMMING COACHES - MEN'S
1912-1913	Chauncey Hyatt
1914-1919	Harry H. Hindman
1932-1951	Joe Steinauer
1951-1969	John Hickman
1970-1994	Jack Pettinger
1994	John Davey (Acting)
1994-	Nick Hansen

SWIMMING COACHES - WOMEN'S
1973-1974	Jack Pettinger
1974-1977	Roger Ridenour
1977-1992	Carl Johansson
1992-	Nick Hansen

TENNIS COACHES - MEN'S
1919-1922	George E. Linden
1923-1925	Arpad Masley
1926-1930	William Winterble
1931	Loren Cockrell
1932-1935	Arpad Masley
1936-1937	William Kaeser
1938-1939	Roy Black
1941-1943	Carl Sanger
1944-1945	Harold A. Taylor
1946-1947	Carl Sanger
1947-1951	Al Hildebrandt
1952-1962	Carl Sanger
1963	David G. Clark
1964-1968	John Powless
1969-1972	John Desmond
1973-1981	Denny Lee Schackter
1982-1983	Dave Pelisek
1983-	Pat Klingelhoets

TENNIS COACHES - WOMEN'S
1974-1976	Pam McKinney
1976-1977	Laurel Holgerson
1977-1978	Katie Munns (Acting)
1978-1981	Laurel Holgerson
1981-1994	Kelly Ferguson
1994-	Patti Henderson

TRACK AND FIELD COACHES - MEN'S
1893	R.G. Booth
1894	M.J. Gillen

1895	W.B. Overson
1896	Charles Craigie
1897	E.W. Moulton
1898	James Temple & Charles Craigie
1899	John T. Moakley
1900-1904	C.H. Kilpatrick
1905	James Temple
1906	George Downer & Emmett Angell
1907-1908	Emmett Angell
1909	E.W. Moulton
1910	Charles Hutchins & James Lathrop
1911-1912	Charles Wilson
1913-1948	Thomas E. Jones
1949-1950	Guy Sundt
1951-1960	Riley Best
1961-1969	Charles Walter
1970-1971	Robert Brennan
1972-1977	Bill Perrin
1978-1983	Dan McClimon
1983-	Ed Nuttycombe

TRACK AND FIELD COACH - WOMEN'S

1974- Peter Tegen

VOLLEYBALL COACHES

1973-1975	Kay Von Guten
1975-1978	Pat Hielscher
1978-1981	Kristi Conklin
1981-1982	Niels Pedersen
1982-1985	Russ Carney
1986-1991	Steve Lowe
1991	Margie Fitzpatrick
1992-	John Cook

WRESTLING COACHES

1914-1916	Fred Schlatter
1917-1918	Arthur Knott
1919-1920	Joe Steinauer
1921-1933	George Hitchcock
1934-1935	Paul Gerlin
1936-1942	George Martin
1943	John Roberts
1944	Jim Dailey, Frank Jordan
1945	Frank Jordan
1946-1970	George Martin
1971-1982	Duane Kleven
1983-1986	Russ Hellickson
1986-1992	Andy Rein
1993-	Barry Davis

BIG TEN OFFICE

James Delany,
Commissioner

COMMISSIONERS
1922-1944	Major John L. Griffith
1945-1961	Kenneth L. (Tug) Wilson
1961-1971	William R. Reed
1971-1989	Wayne Duke
1989-	James E. Delany

ASSOCIATE COMMISSIONERS
1984-1989	John D. Dewey
1989-	Kevin Weiberg

ASSISTANT COMMISSIONERS
1951-1961	William R. Reed
1974-1982	Dr. Charles D. Henry II
1974-1984	John D. Dewey
1982-	Phyllis L. Howlett
1983-1990	Dr. Clarence Underwood, Jr.
1989-	Rich Falk
1990-	Carol Iwaoka
1990-	Mark Rudner
1990-1994	Charles D. Waddell
1994-	Robert C. Vowels, Jr.

EXAMINER
1957-1974	John D.Dewey

ASSISTANT TO THE COMMISSIONERS
1961-1974	John D. Dewey
1990-1996	Jo Ann Dial

COMPUTER SYSTEMS &SPORT MANAGEMENT DIRECTOR
1996-	Ryan McElrath

EXTERNAL RELATIONS DIRECTOR
1996-	JoAnn Dial

INFORMATION SERVICES DIRECTOR
1992-	Dennis LaBissoniere

MANAGING EDITOR & SPECIAL PROJECTS DIRECTOR
1990-	Mary Masters

MANAGING EDITOR & SPORT MANAGEMENT DIRECTOR
1996-	Mary Masters

ASSISTANT *SERVICE BUREAU DIRECTORS
1939-1942	William R. Reed
1942-1943	James T. Maher
1946-1947	William R. Reed
1947-1951	Walter Byers
1951-1961	William R. Reed
1961-1970	Kay Fred Schultz
1970-1973	Michael D. McClure
1974-1986	Jeff Elliott
1986-1990	Mark D. Rudner

ASSISTANT *SERVICE BUREAU DIRECTORS
1971-1974	Jeff Elliott
1975-1976	John Rosenthal
1977-1978	Gil Swalls
1979-1986	Mark D. Rudner
1987-1992	Dennis LaBissoniere
1987-1993	Jan Miller Martin

SUPERVISORS OF OFFICIALS
1945-1948	James C. Masker
1950-1967	A. William Haarlow (Basketball)
1952-1953	William A. Blake (Football)
1953-1954	William A. Blake (Tech. Adv. Football)
1953-1960	E.C. (Irish) Krieger (Tech. Adv. Football)
1961-1967	Carlisle O. Dollings (Tech. Adv. Football)
1963-1967	Ike J. Armstrong (Football)
1968-1983	Herman F. Rohrig
1983-1990	Gene S. Calhoun (Football)
1983-1985	Bob Burson (Men's Basketball)
1984-1996	Peter Dunn (Volleyball)
1984-1987	Marcy Weston (Women's Basketball)
1985-1989	Bob Wortman (Men's Basketball)
1987-	Patty Broderick (Women's Basketball)
1990-	David Parry (Football)
1996-	Marcia Alterman (Volley-ball)

* Renamed Communications Department, January 1, 1990